Ultimate Qlik Cloud Data Analytics and Data Integration

Master Data Integration and Analytics with Qlik Cloud to Drive Real-Time, Insightful, and Impactful Business Decisions Across Your Organization

Orange Editorial Board

www.orangeava.com

First Published: July 2025

Published By: Orange Education Pvt Ltd, AVA®

Address: 9, Daryaganj, Delhi, 110002, India

275 New North Road Islington Suite 1314 London,
N1 7AA, United Kingdom

ISBN (PBK): 978-81-97651-28-1

ISBN (E-BOOK): 978-81-97651-24-3

Scan the QR code to explore our entire catalogue

www.orangeava.com

About the Technical Reviewers

Bhargav Bachina is a seasoned IT professional, boasting a remarkable 12-year journey marked by innovation and leadership in software architecture. His career is a testament to his profound expertise across technological stacks, from front-end and back-end development to the complexities of cloud computing. He is highly proficient in languages such as Java, JavaScript, Python, and Node.js, making him a versatile and adept navigator in the world of software development.

As a visionary software architect, Bhargav is widely recognized for his skill in architecting and implementing comprehensive end-to-end solutions. His commitment to excellence and a deep-seated passion for technology have been instrumental in developing innovative web and mobile platforms. His approach, consistently driven by a quest for excellence, has not only led to the success of numerous projects but also established him as a thought leader in the field.

In his current role as the CTO of a startup in the educational domain, Bhargav is leading the launch of an innovative project, adding yet another milestone to his illustrious career. In addition to his full-time role, he serves as a fractional CTO, making him a sought-after mentor within the startup community. His insights and guidance are highly valued by emerging startups, many of which connect with him on LinkedIn to benefit from his expertise.

Beyond his technical and leadership roles, Bhargav is a prolific writer. His journey as a writer began five years ago on Medium, where he has penned over 700 articles. These writings have reached an audience of over 8 million globally, resonating deeply within the tech community. His articles have been pivotal in guiding and enlightening many, earning him a significant following of 22k on Medium. His influence extends to LinkedIn, where his contributions are frequently lauded for their impact.

Bhargav's commitment to sharing knowledge is further evidenced by his active presence on GitHub. With around 431 repositories, he has become a resource for many in the tech community, evidenced by the regular stars and forks his repositories receive. Bhargav Bachina's journey is more than a career narrative; it's a source of inspiration and a roadmap for aspiring IT professionals worldwide.

To learn more about Bhargav, please visit the following sites:

- **Medium:** https://medium.com/@bhargavbachina
- **GitHub**: https://github.com/bbachi
- **YouTube**: https://www.youtube.com/@bachinalabs

Guilherme Leite has 14 years of experience in analytics and data integration. As a consultant, he developed projects in Qlik Sense for major companies in Brazil across different verticals such as supply chain, retail, telecommunications, and more. He also worked on a project in Belgium where he applied tuning to Qlik Sense applications to optimize performance.

Currently, Guilherme works as a Technical Partner Enablement with Qlik Cloud at Qlik, where he is responsible for technically and commercially training resellers throughout Latin America. He is passionate about teaching and achieving results with Analytics, particularly seeing how data can help companies achieve results.

Nilson de Moraes Filho holds a PhD in Software Engineering from the Federal University of São Carlos (UFSCar), an MBA from the University of Texas at Dallas (UTD), and a degree in Computer Engineering from the University of Campinas (Unicamp). With over 30 years of experience, Nilson has helped companies transform their businesses through data, improving the way analysts adopt AI and machine learning together with Business Intelligence solutions.

Currently, Nilson works as Principal Solutions Architect for Qlik, where he assists customers in becoming AI and data literate through analytics, focusing on using Machine Learning for predictive analytics and GenAI for gaining insights from data. Nilson has been an evangelist of this technology, speaking at several conferences and events. Prior to joining Qlik, he worked at companies such as Itautec, Intervoice, and Convergys.

Preface

Welcome to *Ultimate Qlik Cloud Data Analytics and Data Integration*, your definitive guide to unlocking the full potential of data in the cloud. This book is not just a manual; it is a journey into the world of data-driven strategy. Hence, whether you are a seasoned data professional, seeking to refine your skills, or a newcomer eager to explore the power of analytics, this comprehensive resource will serve as your essential companion.

Moreover, in this book, you will discover how to master the core functionalities of **Qlik Cloud**, delving deep into advanced data analysis, and seamless integration techniques. We shall also equip you with the knowledge to navigate complex data landscapes, transforming raw information into actionable insights. So, by the time you reach the final chapter, you will be a confident data expert, ready to empower your organization with strategic, data-informed decisions. Thus, this book is your gateway to becoming a true architect of data-driven success in the cloud.

Now, let us go through a quick Summary of the Chapters in the Book:

- **Chapter 1:** "*Getting Started With Qlik Cloud*" provides a comprehensive high-level overview of the Qlik Cloud platform, exploring its diverse features, specific functions, and its intended purposes. This chapter lays the foundational understanding necessary for navigating and utilizing Qlik Cloud effectively in subsequent chapters.

- **Chapter 2:** "*Building Your First Application*" guides readers through the process of creating their first Qlik Cloud application. It also covers loading data from flat files, and building dimensional models effortlessly with Qlik Data Manager (without coding), and creating applications, using both simple and advanced editing modes, including intelligent chart suggestions.

- **Chapter 3:** "*Using Scripts*" delves into advanced scripting techniques, focusing on the Script asset for creating and executing scripts. Readers learn to write joins, limit data loads, utilize debugging tools, and efficiently store data using QVDs, a high-performance data storage format.

- **Chapter 4:** "*Set Analysis*" explores the Set Analysis, enabling users to craft complex, but easily understandable and maintainable calculations. This chapter covers the fundamentals, applications, and practical implementation of Set Analysis, including the use of Master Items.
- **Chapter 5:** "*Embedding and Extending*" teaches readers how to enhance Qlik Cloud's capabilities by creating mashups and extensions. It also covers embedding Qlik Cloud into various applications, expanding its integration and accessibility.
- **Chapter 6:** "*Navigating the Data Landscape*" explains how to trace data flow with lineage and impact analysis, and how to use a glossary to understand KPI and dimension definitions. This chapter focuses on the practical applications of these tools for data governance and clarity.
- **Chapter 7:** "*Advanced Analytics - AutoML*" introduces AutoML, an automated machine learning process for identifying data patterns and forecasting future outcomes. Readers learn how to experiment with AutoML as well as deploy predictive models, within Qlik Cloud.
- **Chapter 8:** "*Application Automation*" guides users through Qlik Application Automation, a no-code visual interface for creating automated analytics and data workflows. The chapter focuses on streamlining processes, and enhancing efficiency.
- **Chapter 9:** "*Insight Advisor*" explores the features of Insight Advisor which assists in data modeling, visualization creation, and data analysis, using natural language interaction. Readers learn to ask questions, and uncover insights more efficiently.
- **Chapter 10:** "*Reporting Service*" covers tabular reporting functionality, empowering users to create and distribute formatted XLS reports, directly from Qlik Cloud. This chapter focuses on fulfilling regulated reporting needs, and enhancing operational decision-making.
- **Chapter 11:** "*Direct Access Gateway*" explains how the Direct Access Gateway allows secure access to on-premises data sources from Qlik Cloud. This chapter details the setup and security aspects of connecting to data, behind firewalls.

- **Chapter 12:** "*Getting to Know Qlik Talend Data Integration*" provides a comprehensive overview of Qlik Talend Data Integration, a robust data integration framework for delivering, transforming, and consolidating enterprise data in real-time through automated, governed, and reusable pipelines.
- **Chapter 13:** "*CDC and Landing Data in Real Time*" guides readers through installing data movement gateways, and using Change Data Capture (CDC) to efficiently transfer data from on-premises systems to Qlik Cloud in real-time, without compromising on security.
- **Chapter 14:** "*Transforming Data*" delves into advanced data transformation techniques, using push-down SQL to apply complex business logic to data within Qlik Talend Cloud, improving data quality, and preparing it for analysis.
- **Chapter 15:** "*Data Marts*" explores the advanced capabilities of Qlik Talend Cloud for building data marts, associating facts with dimensions, and managing type 2 dimensions with minimal coding, facilitating efficient data architecture, and supporting sophisticated analytics.

Get a Free eBook

We hope you are enjoying your recently purchased book! Your feedback is incredibly valuable to us, and to all other readers looking for great books.

If you found this book helpful or enjoyable, we would truly appreciate it, if you could take a moment to leave a short review with a 5 star rating on Amazon. It helps us grow, and lets other readers discover our books.

As a thank you, we would love to send you a free digital copy of this book, and a **30%** discount code on your next cart value on our official websites:

www.orangeava.com

www.orangeava.in (For Indian Subcontinent)

☑ **Here's how:**

Leave a review for the book on Amazon.

Take a screenshot of your review, and send an email to **info@orangeava.com** (it can be just the confirmation screen).

Once, we receive your screenshot, we will send you the digital file, within 24 hours.

Thank you so much for your support – it means a lot to us!

Downloading the code bundles and colored images

Please follow the links or scan the QR codes to download the
Code Bundles and Images of the book:

https://github.com/ava-orange-education/Ultimate-Qlik-Cloud-Data-Analytics-and-Data-Integration

The code bundles and images of the book are also hosted on
https://rebrand.ly/01cea1

In case there's an update to the code, it will be updated on the existing GitHub repository.

Errata

We take immense pride in our work at **Orange Education Pvt Ltd,** and follow best practices to ensure the accuracy of our content to provide an indulging reading experience to our subscribers. Our readers are our mirrors, and we use their inputs to reflect and improve upon human errors, if any, that may have occurred during the publishing processes involved. To let us maintain the quality and help us reach out to any readers who might be having difficulties due to any unforeseen errors, please write to us at :

errata@orangeava.com

Your support, suggestions, and feedback are highly appreciated.

DID YOU KNOW

Did you know that Orange Education Pvt Ltd offers eBook versions of every book published, with PDF and ePub files available? You can upgrade to the eBook version at **www.orangeava.com** and as a print book customer, you are entitled to a discount on the eBook copy. Get in touch with us at: **info@orangeava.com** for more details.

At **www.orangeava.com**, you can also read a collection of free technical articles, sign up for a range of free newsletters, and receive exclusive discounts and offers on Print Books and eBooks.

PIRACY

If you come across any illegal copies of our works in any form on the internet, we would be grateful if you would provide us with the location address or website name. Please contact us at **info@orangeava.com** with a link to the material.

ARE YOU INTERESTED IN AUTHORING WITH US?

If there is a topic that you have expertise in, and you are interested in either writing or contributing to a book, please write to us at **business@orangeava.com**. We are on a journey to help developers and tech professionals to gain insights on the present technological advancements and innovations happening across the globe and build a community that believes Knowledge is best acquired by sharing and learning with others. Please reach out to us to learn what our audience demands and how you can be part of this educational reform. We also welcome ideas from tech experts and help them build learning and development content for their domains.

REVIEWS

Please leave a review. Once you have read and used this book, why not leave a review on the site that you purchased it from? Potential readers can then see and use your unbiased opinion to make purchase decisions. We at Orange Education would love to know what you think about our products, and our authors can learn from your feedback. Thank you!

For more information about Orange Education, please visit **www.orangeava.com**.

Table of Contents

Chapter 1
Getting Started With Qlik Cloud

Introduction

Qlik Cloud Analytics and Qlik Talend Data Integration is a single solution for data analysis, data integration, application automation, and machine learning. It allows organizations to create well-managed data pipelines, apply transformations and add context to them, and finally create interactive dashboards and reports that can help organizations gain insights from their data. In this book, you will learn how to use Qlik Cloud to create your own data applications, from data ingestions to data storytelling. You will also learn how to leverage the Qlik Cloud capabilities such as Machine Learning, Application Automation and Data Integration

Structure

In this chapter, we will discuss the following topics:

- Evolution of Data Analytics
- Understanding Qlik Cloud/Qlik Sense
- Qlik Associative Model
- Qlik Cloud/Qlik Sense Offerings
- Qlik Cloud Main Components
    - Analytics
    - Data Integration
    - Machine Learning
    - Catalog
    - Application Automation
- Qlik Academic Program

Evolution of Data Analytics

In the realm of data-driven decision-making, the evolution of data analytics has been a fascinating journey, marked by significant milestones and transformative shifts. This section explores the key phases in this evolution, highlighting the progression from conventional approaches to the sophisticated analytics landscape we navigate today.

- **Early Data Processing** (Pre-1950s): In the early days, data processing was a manual and labor-intensive task. Rudimentary methods were employed for data manipulation and analysis, setting the stage for the technological advancements to come. The IBM punched card is the icon of this era, where a pile of cards used to be inserted into a system and users needed to wait for the result.
- **The Emergence of Business Intelligence** (1960s-1970s): As computers gained prominence, Decision Support Systems (DSS) emerged as pioneers in aiding decision-making. This segment details the evolution of early business intelligence tools and their role in structuring decision-making processes. Example: The first experimental study using a computer-aided decision system was a production scheduling application running on an IBM 7094 (1).
- **Rise of Data Warehousing** (1980s-1990s): The era of data warehousing started with structured storage solutions, facilitating more efficient data organization. This development laid the groundwork for scalable and organized data analytics. A Data Warehouse is a system used for reporting and data analysis and is considered a core component of business intelligence. The most important writers who defined the rules of data warehouses were Bill Inom with his book "*Building the Data Warehouse*" and Ralph Kimball with "*The Data Warehouse Toolkit*."
- **The Big Data Revolution** (2000s): The 21st century witnessed the explosive growth of data, giving rise to the Big Data revolution. Organizations had to cope with and harness massive volumes of data, fundamentally reshaping analytics approaches and adding analysis for both structured and unstructured data. New platforms and frameworks were designed to support high volumes and multi-computer processing. The icon of this era is the Hadoop open-source ecosystem, which provides tools to process massive volumes using sparse clusters.
- **Introduction to Data Mining** (1990s-2000s): Organizations began leveraging advanced algorithms of machine learning and statistics to unearth hidden patterns and trends within expansive datasets. As an example, those techniques in data mining are heavily utilized to scrutinize social media content, including tweets, posts, and comments, for insights into consumer sentiments, feedback on products, and evolving trends. Through sentiment analysis, companies can grasp the public's views and perceptions of their brand.

- **The Era of Predictive Analytics** (2010s): The intelligence built with data mining leveraged the ability to make predictions about future trends and behaviors based on historical data. A very common use case is churn prediction, where algorithms based on trained datasets can predict if a customer is willing to leave the customer base.
- **Interactive Data Visualization** (2010s): Static reports became interactive data visualization platforms, allowing users to explore data dynamically. Qlik provided their solutions (QlikView and Qlik Sense) with these capabilities, allowing users to make any selection and see the results without any predefined scope.
- **Machine Learning and Artificial Intelligence** (2010s-2020s): Advanced machine learning and other artificial intelligence platforms and algorithms started revolutionizing analytics with automated insights and predictive modeling.
- **Real-Time Analytics** (2010s-2020s): Modern platforms now enable users to analyze data and make predictions based on data that is available in real-time and processed by smart algorithms to predict outcomes.

Understanding Qlik Cloud/Qlik Sense

Let us get back to some history before describing what Qlik Cloud/Qlik Sense is. Qlik (formerly known as Qliktech) was founded as a company in 1993 in Lund, Sweden, by Björn Berg and Staffan Gestrelius. The first product (QlikView, initially named QuikView, where the initial letters stand for Quality, Understanding, Interaction, and Knowledge) was built to enable users to consume and analyze data from several origins using a revolutionary patented data model engine based on associations, usually called the Qlik Associative Engine.

The company moved its headquarters to the United States in 2004 while keeping the R&D department in Sweden.

In 2014, Qlik launched a new product called Qlik Sense (codename Qlik.Next), a modern analytics tool that added self-service capabilities, was web and mobile-ready, and used the same engine as QlikView, reusing all the syntax of scripts and expressions. This product became the company's flagship, adding more and more capabilities based on internal development and acquisitions (see *Table* 1.1).

In 2016, Qlik became a company owned by a private equity firm called Thoma Bravo.

In 2019, Qlik launched Qlik Cloud, delivering all Qlik Sense and other solution capabilities as a Software as a Service (SaaS) platform, integrating all those features.

Qlik, as a company, acquired several other companies that brought more solutions to its portfolio. The most important acquisitions (for the scope of this book) were:

Company	Year	Solutions/Use Cases
Podium Data	2017	Data Catalog
Crunch Data	2019	Insight Advisor
Attunity	2019	Data Integration/Transformation
Big Squid	2021	Machine Learning
Talend	2023	Data Transformation/Data Catalog

Table 1.1: *Qlik Acquisitions*

Comparing Qlik Cloud and Qlik Sense, Qlik Sense is a product that can be deployed on-premises or as part of the Qlik Cloud platform, which has more capabilities.

Qlik Sense, as a powerful Business Intelligence (BI) and data visualization platform, boasts several capabilities. These capabilities collectively empower users to explore, visualize, and derive meaningful insights from their data dynamically and interactively. Here are some of the main Qlik Sense capabilities:

- **Associative Data Modeling:** Qlik Sense's patented feature is its associative data model, allowing users to dynamically explore and analyze data relationships. Unlike traditional BI tools that rely on predefined hierarchies, Qlik Sense enables users to make on-the-fly associations between data points, uncovering hidden insights.
- **Intuitive Data Visualization:** Qlik Sense provides a rich array of visualization options, including charts, graphs, and maps, to represent data in a visually compelling manner. The platform's intuitive drag-and-drop interface allows users to effortlessly create interactive dashboards and reports.
- **Self-Service Analytics:** With Qlik Sense, users can engage in self-service analytics, empowering them to independently explore and analyze data without the need for extensive technical expertise. This capability promotes a culture of data-driven decision-making throughout an organization.
- **Collaboration and Sharing:** Qlik Sense supports collaborative analytics by facilitating the sharing of insights and visualizations. Users can create and distribute interactive dashboards, reports, and data stories, fostering a collaborative environment where teams can work together to gain insights.
- **Dynamic Data Discovery:** The platform's associative search functionality allows for dynamic data discovery. Users can ask ad-hoc questions, and Qlik Sense responds by instantly updating visualizations to reflect relevant data, enabling a fluid and responsive exploration process.
- **Augmented Intelligence:** Qlik Sense incorporates augmented intelligence features, leveraging machine learning algorithms to provide smart suggestions and automated insights. This enhances the user experience by guiding users towards valuable discoveries and patterns within the data.

- **Mobile Accessibility:** Qlik Sense is designed with mobile accessibility in mind. Users can access and interact with their dashboards and reports seamlessly on various devices, ensuring that critical insights are available anytime, anywhere, using mobile-dedicated apps or mobile browsers.
- **Scalability and Enterprise Deployment:** Qlik Sense is scalable to meet the needs of both individual users (Qlik Sense Desktop) and large enterprises (Qlik Sense Enterprise Client Managed, or SaaS). The enterprise version supports centralized management, security protocols, and collaboration features for widespread adoption.
- **Storytelling with Data:** Qlik Cloud/Qlik Sense allows users to create compelling data stories by combining visualizations, text, and images. This storytelling capability enhances the communication of insights, making it easier for users to convey the narrative behind the data and publish the results to a broader audience.
- **Real-Time Data Integration:** Qlik Sense supports real-time data integration, enabling users to connect to various data sources, including live streaming data. This capability ensures that analyses and visualizations reflect the most up-to-date information for informed decision-making.

These capabilities collectively make Qlik Sense a versatile and comprehensive tool for organizations seeking to harness the full potential of their data for strategic decision-making and business success.

Qlik Associative Model

The associative model is a foundational concept that distinguishes Qlik Sense from traditional business intelligence tools. It is a unique and powerful approach to data modeling that allows users to explore and understand the relationships within their data dynamically and intuitively. Here is an overview of the associative model of Qlik Sense:

- **Dynamic Data Relationships:** In a traditional data model, relationships between different data tables are predefined. In contrast, the associative model of Qlik Sense allows for dynamic and on-the-fly associations between data points. This means that users can explore and analyze data without relying on predetermined paths or predefined joins.
- **Data Combination:** The Qlik Associative Engine can load and combine data from countless sources, converting it to a simple data model that will be served from memory. During the loading process, the Qlik Associative Engine seamlessly integrates those data sources, accomplishing a many-to-many full outer join. This means every value from every source is included in the combined data model, regardless of whether there are matching records between sources. This is achieved without any compromise in data integrity

or accuracy, avoiding the pitfalls associated with executing SQL joins during the load time.

- **In-Memory Data Indexing**: The Associative Model utilizes in-memory data indexing, where the entire dataset is loaded into memory. This allows for faster response times when users interact with the data, as associations are already established in memory. Users can navigate through vast amounts of data without experiencing delays typically associated with SQL queries executed by databases due to compression and other optimizations.
- **Associative Engine:** At the core of the associative model is Qlik Sense's associative engine. This engine is responsible for maintaining and optimizing associations between data values. When a user selects a data point or field, the associative engine dynamically identifies and highlights all related data points, creating a visually connected experience without any additional coding effort.
- **Flexibility in Data Exploration:** The associative model empowers users to explore data flexibly and iteratively. Users can start with a particular data point and explore its associations, leading to a deeper understanding of the relationships and connections within the dataset. This flexibility enhances the user's ability to discover insights organically.
- **Implicit and Explicit Associations:** Associations in Qlik Sense can be both implicit and explicit. Implicit associations are automatically identified by the system based on the data structure and data point values, while explicit associations can be defined by users to create custom relationships between data points.
- **Uncovering Hidden Insights:** The associative model is designed to uncover hidden insights and patterns within the data. As users explore and select different data points, the system dynamically adjusts visualizations to highlight relevant information, facilitating a more holistic and contextual understanding of the data.
- **Understand Related and Unrelated Data:** The engine enables users to instantly pivot the analysis based on what they observe. Qlik provides an intuitive color-coding scheme to make the user aware of what data points are related to each other and which data points are not related.
- **User-Driven Data Discovery:** Qlik Sense's associative model emphasizes user-driven data discovery. This means that users, regardless of their technical expertise, can actively engage in exploring and making sense of data without relying on preconceived queries or fixed data pathways.

As one example of Qlik´s associative model, let us use the Qlik Sense app and make some selections to identify the insights that this technology provides. As an example, after you register for a Qlik Cloud tenant (please refer to the later section in this chapter on how to create one), you can open the app **"Demo App - SAP Procurement"**, available at the **Getting Started** menu option.

***Figure 1.1:** Look for the SAP Procurement app*

Once the application is open, you will see this sheet:

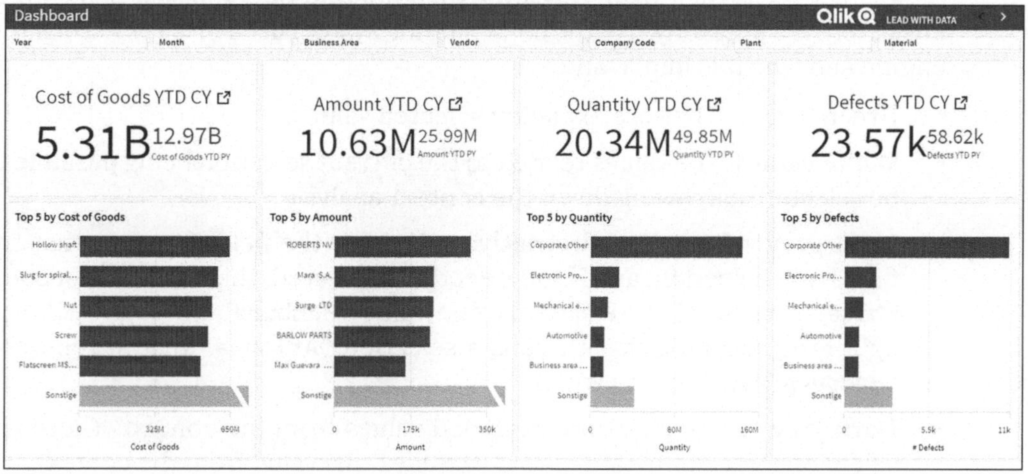

***Figure 1.2:** Dashboard*

If you make a selection on the filters at the top of the screen (using a mouse, click), some actions will be immediately executed:

- All objects on the screen will be automatically updated to reflect the selection.
- The selected values will be displayed at the top, making it evident to the user what selections were made. In the following figure, the user selected **Year = 2020** and **Plant = "Atlanta."**

- Selected values will remain selected until the user makes another selection or clears them. Even if the user navigates to other sheets, the context analysis will remain the same.
- Additional selections are added to the context analysis; for example, if the user makes a selection on the filter **`Business Area`,** this restriction will be added to the current context.
- A user can clear or modify any selection using the top context bar.
- Some data values will be greyed out; in *Figure* 1.3, **`"Business area 0001"`** in the filter **`Business Area`** and **`"Hamburg"`** in the filter **`Plant`** became grey while other values are white. Greyed values indicate that the value is unrelated to the selection. The data exists in the data model but has no relationship with **`Year = 2020`** and **`Plant = "Atlanta."`** This enables the concept of **Uncovering Hidden Insights**, which we discussed a few pages ago.

  Qlik's Associative Engine is a powerful analytics engine that differs significantly from traditional SQL-based query tools. It allows users to freely search and explore across all their data, **revealing insights that query-based tools might miss**. Here is a breakdown of the color-coding system used in Qlik's Associative Engine and why it is important:

  - **Green values**: They are explicitly **selected** values.
  - **White values**: The values related to the current selection being **possible** to be selected, narrowing down the context analysis.
  - **Light grey values**: The **alternative** values for the field. It means that the field has a selection, and if the selection is cleared, this value will become **`white. (possible).`** Please see the value **`"Hamburg"`** in *Figure* 1.3. It is light grey, meaning that there is a selection **`"Atlanta"`** that, if removed, **`"Hamburg"`** will become white.
  - **Dark grey values**: They are **excluded** values from the context. There is a selection (or a combination) that excludes this value from the context.

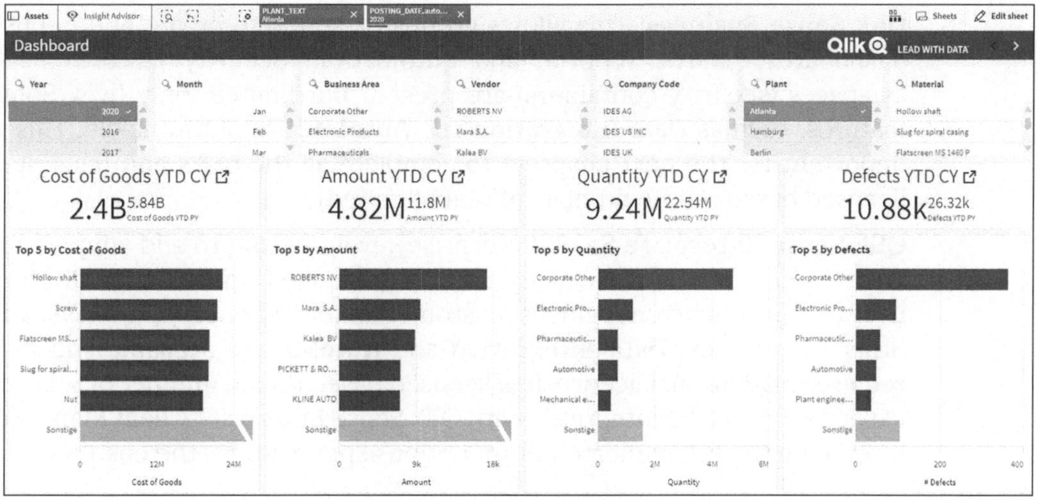

Figure 1.3: *Filtered Dashboard*

The engine's speed allows for "**speed of thought**" responses, updating all analytics instantly and revealing data relationships to help you make discoveries with each click or search.

This approach to data analysis is designed to support non-linear, free-form exploration, enabling users of all skill levels to ask questions and follow-up questions, prompting further exploration until the right insight is discovered. It is a powerful ally in a data-driven world, allowing for a more intuitive and insightful exploration of data.

Qlik Cloud/Qlik Sense Offerings

As this book is written, there are several options for customers to use or subscribe to the platform, including:

- **Client Managed**: The customer or user is responsible for downloading, installing, and configuring the solution:
    - **Qlik Sense Desktop**: Microsoft Windows application that provides the ability to create visualizations and dashboards. It can be used for developing, testing, or offline access. Lacks any security or sharing capabilities and requires authentication through a Qlik Sense Enterprise.
    - **Qlik Sense Enterprise**: It can be deployed in a mix of local and cloud Microsoft Windows environments, creating a controlled, self-service environment that offers scalability and security standards compliance. It is licensed based on seats or capability (the number of cores allocated to the platform).
- **Software as a Service**: The customer uses the solution that is hosted and managed by Qlik:

 - **Qlik Sense Business**: This allows groups or teams to create and publish dashboards, charts, reports, and automation. Security features such as spaces (security containers) are present but limited (only five). Some features, such as **Data Integration** and **AutoML**, are not available. This is important for the next chapters to complete all the tasks and tests. It is licensed based on the number of seats (limited).
 - **Qlik Sense Enterprise SaaS**: Enterprise-level offering to add support for larger apps, increased security control (managed spaces and different user roles), concurrent reloads, customer-managed encryption keys, and other capabilities. **Data Integration** and **AutoML** are available and may require an additional license. It is licensed based on the number of seats or capacity and can be integrated with Qlik Sense Enterprise Client Managed, leveraging the full implementation options spectrum for the customers.

Qlik Cloud Main Components

Qlik Cloud platform offers several features that can be used apart or together to address several use cases. Let us describe the main features and the use cases they address.

Analytics

Qlik Cloud Analytics is a Qlik Associative Engine provided as a service inside Qlik Cloud. It offers a cloud-based analytics platform that enables users to explore and visualize data from various sources. With Qlik Cloud Analytics, users can create and share interactive dashboards and applications, use natural language to ask questions and get insights, leverage mobile analytics to access data anytime and anywhere, and generate reports and alerts to stay informed of changes and trends.

Qlik Cloud Analytics is a sophisticated platform designed to foster data literacy and human intuition across all user skill levels. It enables individuals to effortlessly explore data and swiftly derive reliable insights to address problems, ranging from the simplest to the most complex.

- The platform serves as a collaborative environment for the development and sharing of content. It offers shared and managed spaces that provide intuitive and straightforward control over application content.
- The user interface is equipped with straightforward authoring tools that empower users at all levels to create advanced charts and visualizations.
- Insight Advisor, a fully conversational analytics experience native to Qlik Cloud, employs natural language processing to comprehend user intent. It learns from each interaction to reveal associations, correlations, and trends within the user´s data.

- The platform facilitates the swift detection of outliers and anomalies in the user's data through data-driven alerts, setting thresholds that, once reached, will trigger a message to the user (mobile or site).
- Users can subscribe to relevant content and receive a periodic copy of chosen visualizations.
- Users can prepare tabular reports to be distributed by e-mail to a group of users in a spreadsheet format.

All those features are consolidated in a **Hub,** which is the central access point for users where they create, share, and analyze analytic apps. Other content types, such as data sources, scripts, charts, notes, and links, are also managed and accessed through the **Hub.** It can be accessed through a web link usually in the format *<aliasname>.<region>.qlikcloud.com*, that points to a **tenant** provided by Qlik. Every customer has a completely isolated environment from other customers, there is no data movement or integration between two or more tenants. Tenants can have customer encryption keys to make sure that, eventually, Qlik has no access to the data or logs. When the user accesses the link and gives the correct credentials, it will automatically redirect them to the **Hub**.

Figure 1.4: *The Hub*

We will cover the aspects of creating apps, alerts, reports, and more later in this book. But the reader has access to several videos and tutorials by accessing the links from the hub, which is divided into the following sections (left menu):

- `Home`
- `+ Create`
- `Favorites`

- **Collections**
- **Automation**
- **Catalog**
- **Alerts**
- **Subscriptions**
- **Getting Started**

There are other options available at the top menu:

- **Search:** Search across all assets the user has access to.
- **Ask Insight Advisor:** Conversational analytics chatbot.
- **Notifications:** View your notifications.
- **Launcher menu:** Navigate to other parts of Qlik Cloud (**Data Integration**, **Application Automation**, **Admin Console**)
- **Profile:** Manage your profile.

Talend Data Integration

The **Talend Data Integration** capability of Qlik Cloud offers a comprehensive solution for the creation of data pipelines, facilitating the execution of diverse data integration tasks that, aligned with modern data stack architecture, capture data in real time from several relational sources or other SaaS-based solutions, making the data available to be consumed by Qlik Cloud Analytics or other BI Tools. The data is updated without manual intervention or scheduled extractions.

The processed data output derived from Qlik Cloud Data Integration serves several purposes and use cases, including:

- **Loading and Ingesting Data to a Centralized Data Warehouse**: The platform facilitates the seamless transfer and incorporation of data into a centralized data warehouse, ensuring a unified and structured repository for efficient data management.
- **Data Mining:** Leveraging the refined data, users can engage in data mining activities, extracting valuable insights and patterns that contribute to informed decision-making and strategic initiatives.
- **Automated Creation of Data for Analytics in the Cloud:** Qlik Talend Data Integration supports the automated generation of data tailored for cloud-based analytics, enhancing the agility and responsiveness of analytical processes in cloud environments.
- **Modernization of Data Repository to Support Machine Learning:** The data ingested and transformed by Qlik Talend Data Integration can support initiatives such as Machine Learning and other advanced analytics projects.

In the following image, we can see a data pipeline extracting data from an SAP system and adding several transformation layers to enrich the data, making it ready to be consumed by analytics apps.

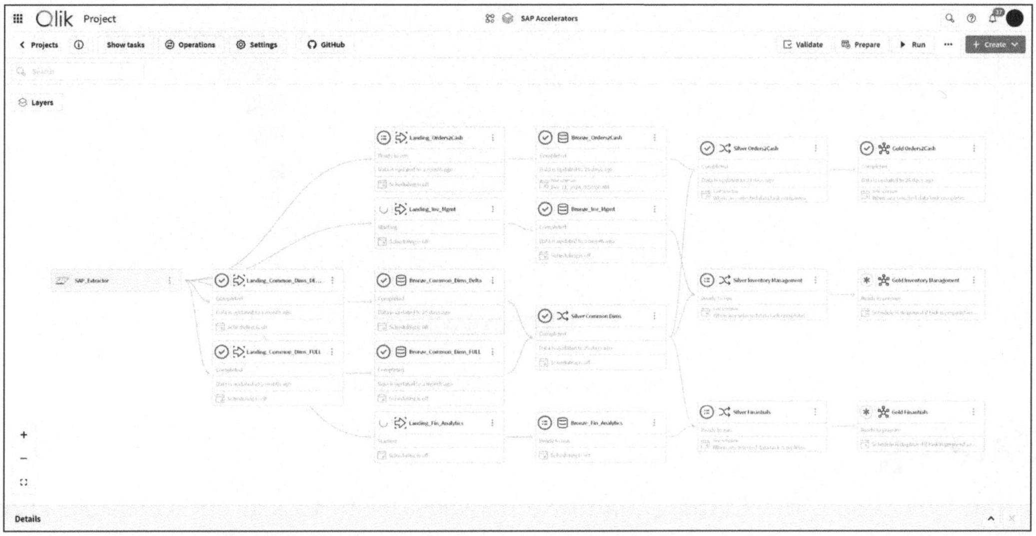

Figure 1.5: *Data Project*

Machine Learning

Automated machine learning within Qlik Cloud Analytics identifies patterns in loaded data and utilizes them for predicting future trends. Through machine learning experiments and deployments in the Qlik Cloud Analytics hub, users can collaborate with peers and seamlessly integrate predictive analytics into Qlik Sense applications. This functionality not only enables predictions but also supports detailed analyses of the key features influencing the anticipated outcomes.

Accordingly, "*Machine Learning is a branch of the broader field of artificial intelligence that makes use of statistical models to develop predictions*(2)," In Qlik Cloud, AutoML provides a zero-code experience and several prebuilt algorithms to learn from the data the customer has available, create a model, and make predictions or classifications on that data, bringing the Machine Learning capabilities to regular analytics users.

In the following image, we can see an AutoML experiment where the user is configuring which parameters should be included in the analysis.

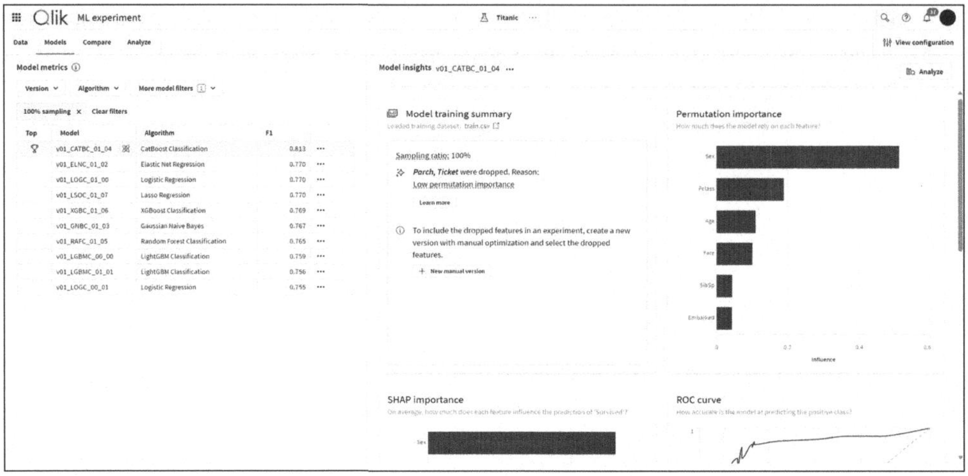

Figure 1.6: AutoML Experiment

Catalog

Within Qlik Cloud, the **Catalog** feature empowers users to search accessible apps, spaces, and additional content. It is equipped with a robust filtering system, offering users the capability to refine searches based on various parameters such as spaces, terms, charts, apps, automation, data, scripts, notes, owners, creators, and tags. This functionality streamlines the process of locating and accessing specific content tailored to individual requirements.

The ability to select individual spaces from the spaces drop-down menu further enhances user efficiency, particularly when focusing on content within a designated space. This feature proves invaluable for users working within specific contexts who seek a targeted exploration of content.

Figure 1.7: Catalog

Opting for the **`All-filters`** feature activates the filter pane, providing users with a comprehensive view of all active filters. Notably, when the filter pane is in use, the **`All-filters`** box adopts a grayed-out appearance, signaling its utilization. The box provides a clear indication of the number of active filters, furnishing users with a rapid overview of their applied filters.

This sophisticated functionality within Qlik Cloud's Catalog contributes to efficient content management and navigation, enabling users to harness the real-time, AI-driven, collaborative, and actionable data and analytics that define the essence of Qlik Cloud.

Application Automation

Qlik Application Automation is a special feature available in Qlik Cloud that enables users to create dynamic processes that automatically respond to business events and trigger informed actions in your most popular SaaS applications.

Qlik Application Automation uses a no-code approach based on connectors and blocks, allowing the users to implement any logic assembling blocks to create simple to elaborate workflows integrating SaaS applications (Qlik or other).

Automation can be triggered by several means. The user can schedule the automation to be executed every time or the automation can be triggered automatically based on events on Qlik Cloud (for example, an application reloads). The automation can be executed even by external tools using a REST endpoint.

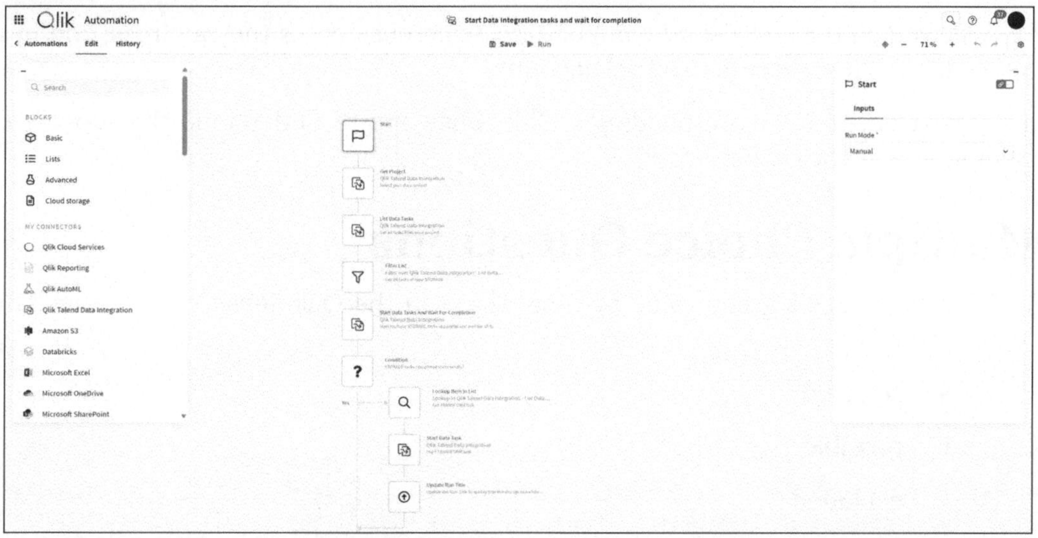

Figure 1.8: *Qlik Application Automation*

Qlik Academic Program

Qlik provides free licenses and learning resources to selected university students, educators, and researchers. They receive all the resources to leverage analytics and data literacy skills, getting ready to ask the right questions about the data and understand it completely. Please check this website for more information about this program: https://www.qlik.com/us/company/academic-program.

Conclusion

The collaboration between Qlik Cloud and Qlik Sense significantly influences the landscape of data analytics and business intelligence. Qlik Cloud, an integral component of the Qlik platform, extends Qlik Sense's reach by providing a cloud-based environment conducive to accessibility and collaborative analytics. It serves as a versatile and scalable platform suitable for both individual analysts and entire enterprises, facilitating a seamless transition from data ingestion and transformation to advanced analytics and machine learning.

Qlik Sense, as the core analytics engine, plays a central role in facilitating data exploration. With its associative data model, intuitive scripting capabilities, and user-friendly interface, Qlik Sense empowers users to navigate through their data landscape effortlessly. Collectively, Qlik Cloud and Qlik Sense redefine the narrative of data analytics, fostering a culture of collaboration and dynamic exploration that enables individuals and organizations to derive actionable insights from their data resources.

We reviewed all the Qlik Cloud components, which use cases they address, and how the reader can have access to a trial account.

In the next chapter, we are building a Qlik Sense app to understand the process of building an analytics experience.

Multiple Choice Questions

1. A user sees a green value of `"Americas"` in the Qlik Sense context bar. This value is:

    a. selected

    b. possible

    c. excluded

    d. alternative

2. A user sees a white value of `"Americas"` in a filter pane. This value is:
    a. selected
    b. possible
    c. excluded
    d. alternative
3. Choose the alternative that represents Qlik's current products:
    a. QlikView
    b. Qlik Sense Enterprise Manager
    c. Qlik Cloud Analytics
    d. Qlik Sense Desktop
    e. All of above
4. Which object type **cannot** be accessed from the Hub?
    a. Charts
    b. Scripts
    c. Automation
    d. Notes
    e. Reports
5. Which use cases are **not** covered by Qlik Talend Data Integration?
    a. Data ingestion
    b. Automated creation of data marts
    c. Data mining
    d. Scheduled reports
6. Where can a customer get support relative to an issue when opening a ticket?
    a. YouTube
    b. Google
    c. Qlik Help
    d. Qlik Community

Answers

1. a
2. b
3. e
4. e
5. d
6. d

Questions

1. What are the key components of Qlik Cloud?
2. Which use cases are not listed in this chapter that customers could solve using the solutions described?

Key Terms

- **Analytics**: The process of using data to improve business decisions. It involves collecting, sorting, transforming, processing, and studying business data to gain insights that can solve problems and improve efficiency, productivity, and revenue.
- **Data Integration:** Process of extracting data from source systems (databases, files, or applications) and transforming it to become consumable for users.
- **Self-service**: Process of allowing regular users to add or modify the content of an application without the assistance of an IT professional.
- **Space**: A logical security container that can contain apps, scripts, data sources, and other assets. Users and groups can have full or limited access to the space.

References

1. Decision Support Systems Resources [Online]: https://dssresources.com/history/dsshistory.html
2. Certificate in Quantitative Finance (CQF). What Is Machine Learning? Definition, Types, and Examples. *CQF Blog*. [Online]: https://www.cqf.com/blog/what-machine-learning-definition-types-and-examples.

Additional Resources

The following links are complimentary to this book, bringing more resources to the reader with up-to-date resources and information:

- **Qlik Help** (https://help.qlik.com/): A centralized documentation for all Qlik solutions and products. It is open and publicly available.
- **Qlik Community** (https://community.qlik.com/): It serves as a hub for members to search, discuss topics, and learn from one another. Features may include boards for Q and A, blogs for articles and comments, and idea exchanges for product suggestions and voting. It contains links to a support channel where customers can open tickets to engage Qlik Support to handle fixes for issues. It is open and publicly available for reading. For posting, free registration is required.
- **Qlik YouTube Channel** (https://www.youtube.com/qliktech): YouTube channel with demos, recorded webinars, and educational series.

CHAPTER 2
Building Your First Application

Introduction

Building a Qlik Sense app is a dynamic and empowering process that transforms raw data into actionable insights. At the intersection of intuitive design and powerful analytics, creating a Qlik Sense app involves seamlessly connecting to diverse data sources, unleashing the potential of associative data modeling, and crafting visually compelling dashboards. Assembling a Qlik Sense app is not just about visualizations; it is a journey of discovery, where data storytellers craft narratives that empower users to explore, analyze, and derive meaningful conclusions from their data. In this realm of interactive analytics, users embark on a journey that transcends traditional data processing, unlocking the true potential of their data for informed decision-making.

Structure

In this chapter, we will discuss the following topics:

- Qlik Sense Applications Concepts
- Loading and Associating the Data
- Transforming the Data
- Creating Analysis

Qlik Sense Applications Concepts

Some concepts are important to clarify before starting this chapter discussion:

- **Qlik Sense App**: A Qlik Sense app is a dynamic and interactive container that houses the entire analytical experience. At its core, the app is a repository where users seamlessly blend and model their data, allowing for a comprehensive exploration of information. The heart of a Qlik Sense app lies in its associative data model (refer to *Chapter 1: Getting Started with Qlik Cloud* for a full discussion about it), where relationships between data elements are dynamically created, fostering a fluid and intuitive environment for users to navigate through their data landscape.

- **Data Scripting and Loading:** The scripting phase of a Qlik Sense app is the first step in the data journey. Through Qlik's scripting language, users can connect to diverse data sources, transform raw data, and load it into the app's associative memory. This scripting process enables users to mold their data into a format that supports meaningful associations, laying the foundation for robust visualizations and analyses. As users modify scripts, they witness real-time updates in the app, fostering an iterative and responsive data modeling experience.
- **Data Manager:** To accelerate the scripting phase, Qlik Sense provides a guided GUI interface that allows inexperienced users to add sources, select tables, and add transformations. The Data Manager based on the user requirements will generate the script.
- **Designing Sheets and Visualizations:** Sheets in a Qlik Sense app serve as the canvas for data visualization and analysis. Within sheets, users can create a diverse range of visualizations, from simple charts to complex dashboards. The drag-and-drop interface empowers users to effortlessly design and arrange objects on sheets, fostering a user-centric approach to data representation. Each sheet becomes a canvas where users craft compelling data stories, providing a visually engaging means to convey insights and trends.
- **Interactive Objects and User Experience:** Objects within a Qlik Sense app represent the building blocks of visualization, ranging from simple tables to complex charts and filters. These objects are not static; they respond dynamically to user interactions. Users can click, select, and explore, prompting instant updates across the entire app. This interactivity forms the essence of a Qlik Sense app, transforming data analysis from a passive experience into an engaging and collaborative journey where users actively contribute to the discovery of insights. Overall, a Qlik Sense app is a manifestation of user-driven analytics, seamlessly blending data modeling, visualization design, and associative exploration to empower individuals across diverse roles within an organization.

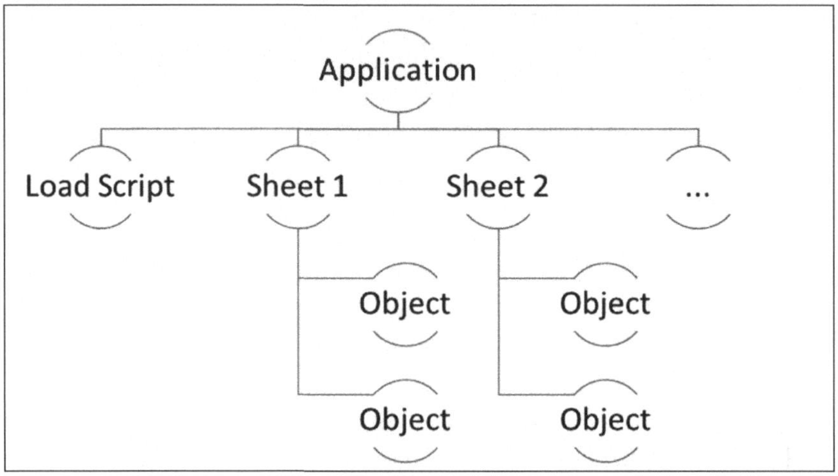

Figure 2.1: *App Structure*

Loading and Associating the Data

Let us get started with creating our first Qlik Sense app and downloading the dataset that will be used in this process. For this chapter, we are using the ubiquitous public-domain NorthWind database. The Northwind database serves as a demonstration database employed by Microsoft to showcase the functionalities of certain products. It includes fictitious sales data for Northwind Traders, a company specializing in the export and import of specialty foods. It was converted to be used by several platforms, such as MySQL and PostgreSQL. It is available on the Internet in several websites and formats, including this book repository: https://github.com/ava-orange-education/Ultimate-Qlik-Cloud-Data-Analytics-and-Data-Integration

Once you have downloaded, saved, and uncompressed the dataset to the local computer, you can start connecting to your Qlik Cloud Analytics.

In the hub, you will see the green button **+ `Create`** at the left, which will start our journey.

Figure 2.2: *+ Create button*

The first option is the one we will be using to create our **`Analytics app`** and give it a meaningful name.

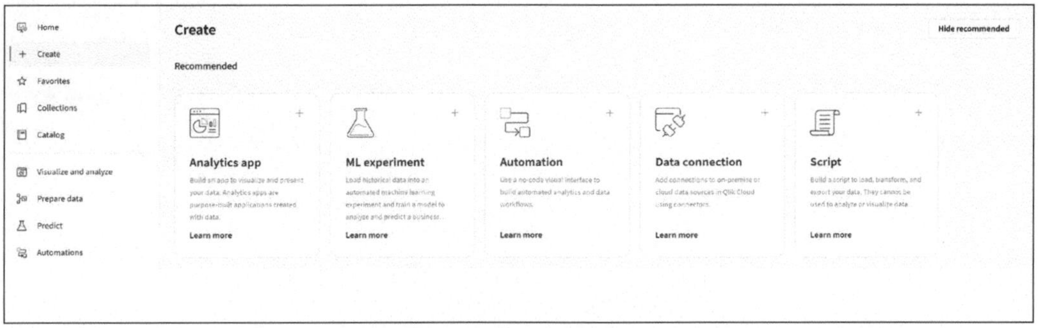

Figure 2.3: *New content*

You will be prompted to load data into your application because we need a data model to create our analytics objects. There are several ways to load data; let us start with the easiest process of dragging the files and dropping them on the screen. Please select the following files and drag them to the Qlik Sense screen.

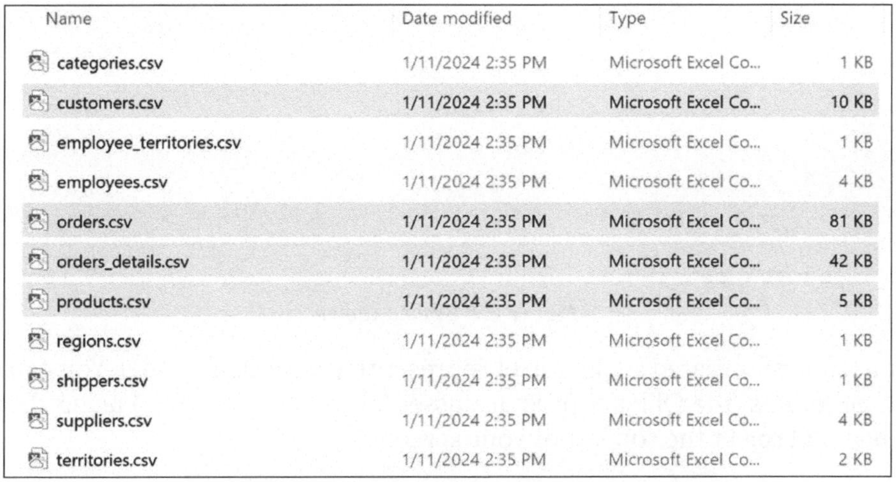

Figure 2.4: *File list*

Figure 2.5: *Dropping files*

Qlik Cloud will automatically upload the files and open the **`Data Manager`**, showing four circles representing tables, as in *Figure 2.6*.

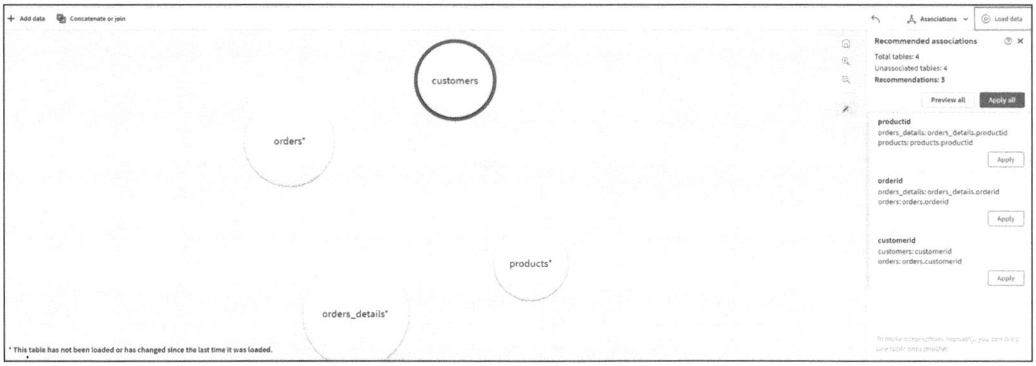

***Figure 2.6**: Tables Loaded*

You can manually configure the relationship between the tables, or let Qlik apply the recommended association using the button **`Apply all`**.

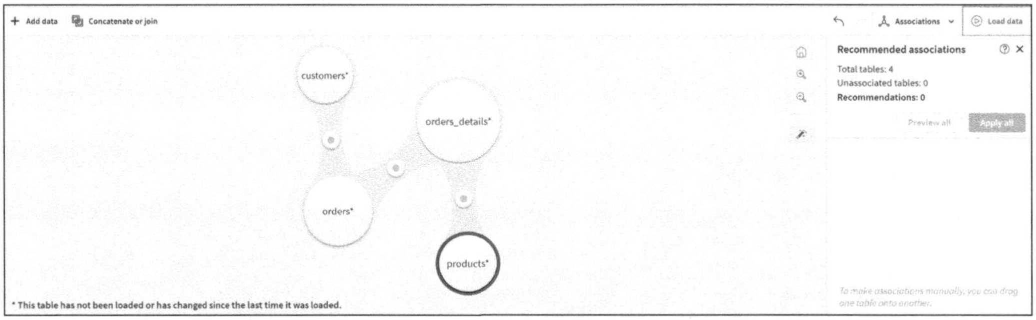

***Figure 2.7**: Linked tables*

The Data Manager created a Qlik script representing your data model. You can see the script it generates (the Qlik script is discussed in the next chapter) using the button **`Data Load Editor`** at the top left of your screen.

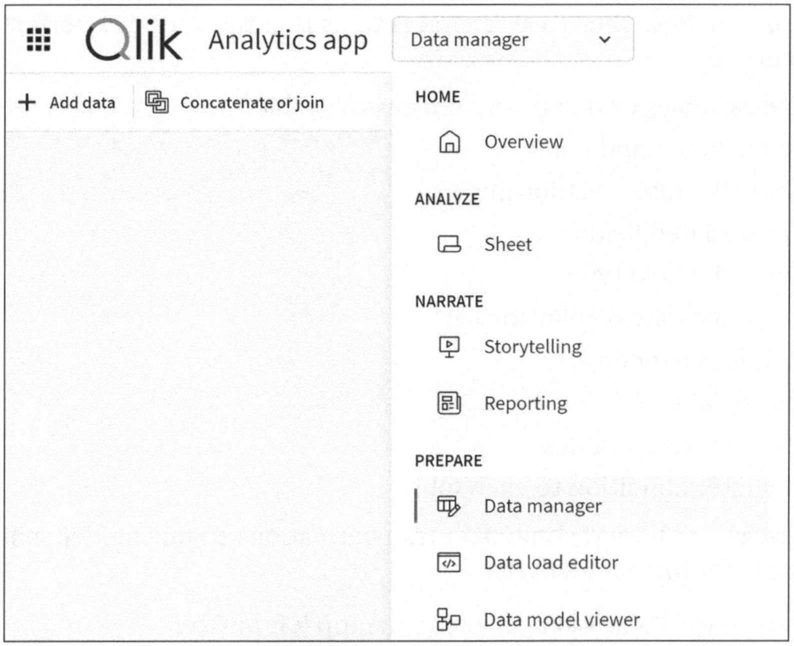

Figure 2.8: *Data load editor*

You will be redirected to the **`Data Load editor`** and will notice that there is a section named **`Auto-generated section`**. The Data Manager keeps this section locked and will update it for any future data model changes.

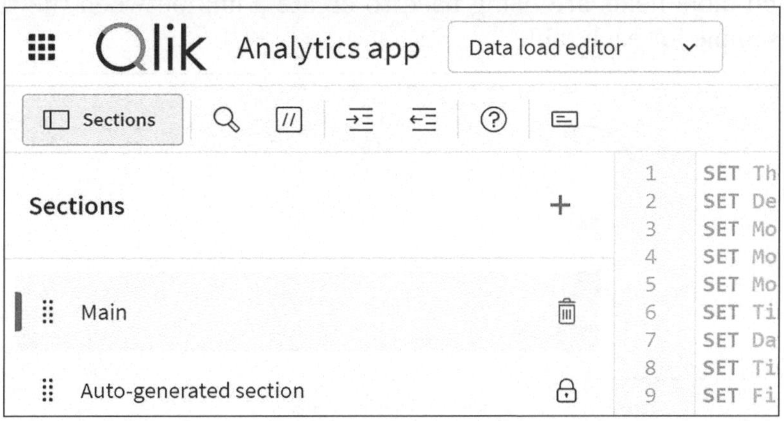

Figure 2.9: *First Script*

Transforming the Data

The Data Manager provides a full set of data transformation capabilities. With its user-friendly interface and drag-and-drop functionality, users can effortlessly manipulate data structures, ensuring that information is transformed into a meaningful format for insightful analytics. There are several actions that the user can perform using the Data Manager:

- Add new tables or delete an unnecessary table
- Rename tables and fields
- Change the table relationships
- Add calculated fields
- Change the field type
- Change the date display format
- Null values handling
- Replace data values
- Create bucketed values
- Add a filter condition to each table

For this exercise, let us add some data transformations to our model, making it even more complete for further analysis.

Navigate back to the **`Data manager`** using the top left button.

- **Reviewing the keys**

Let us start reviewing the keys between our tables, making sure they are correctly linked and able to deliver proper answers. Do that and press the small circle that connects every table pair. You will notice that the Data Manager will show at the bottom which table fields are being used to create a link between the tables, along with a data sample for each table.

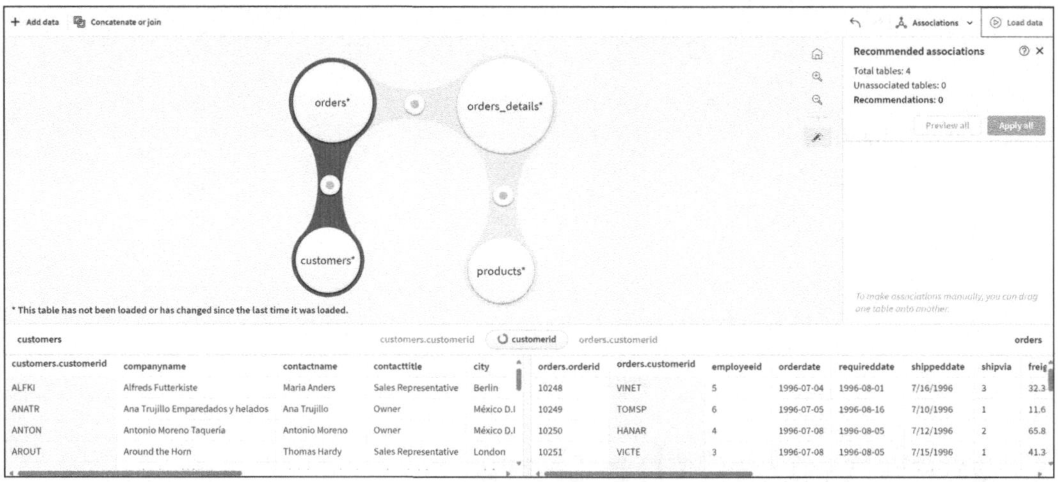

Figure 2.10: Keys

In the screen example, the fields **`customerid`** from both tables are used to create the link, and there is a small green gauge indicating almost all values are shared between both tables, creating a good key. Press the small circle between the **order_details** and **products.** Notice that an orange gauge will indicate that the correlation between the values is not perfect.

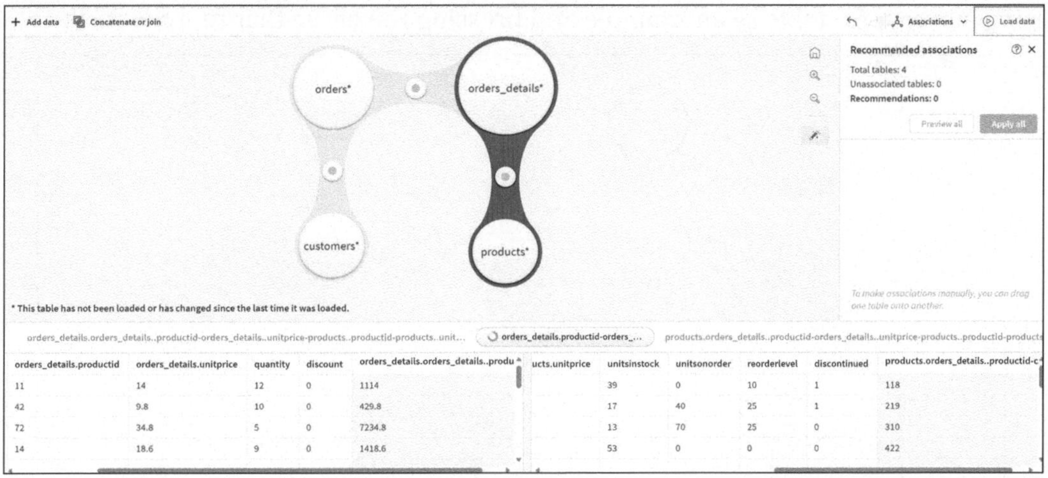

***Figure 2.11**: Keys*

Data Manager is trying to use a compound key, called the *Synthetic key* in the Qlik Associative Engine. It is compounded by two fields: **productid** and **unitprice.** In this dataset, the field **unitprice** in the **products** table refers to the listing price, the price at which a product should be sold. In the table **order_details,** the **unitprice** refers to the actual value. They may be the same or not. In this dataset, the correct key is only based on the **productid** field. Let us fix this by clicking the orange gauge. The interface will show you all the other key candidates. You will notice that there is a green proposal that is exactly what we need. Press this option to instruct the Data Manager to use this as the key.

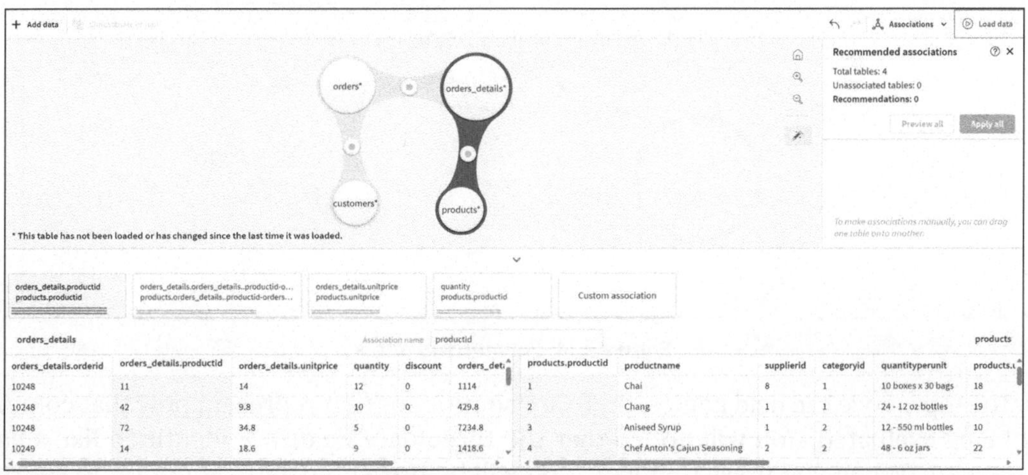

***Figure 2.12**: Editing the key*

- **Adjust values formatting**

It is important for analytics users to have a properly formatted field when they are using the app. Incorrect formatting may lead to incorrect analysis. Let us exercise this using our **`orders`** table as an example and pressing the circle that represents it.

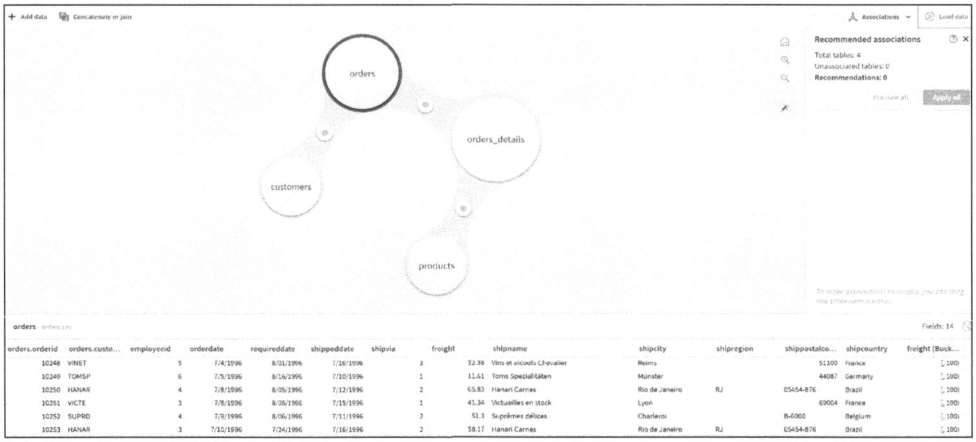

Figure 2.13: *Formatting*

Notice that there are three different dates (**`orderdate`, `requireddate`,** and **`shippeddate`**) and they are not consistent in formats. To fix it, press the small pencil icon at the bottom of your screen, and you will be prompted with a screen where you can edit a table.

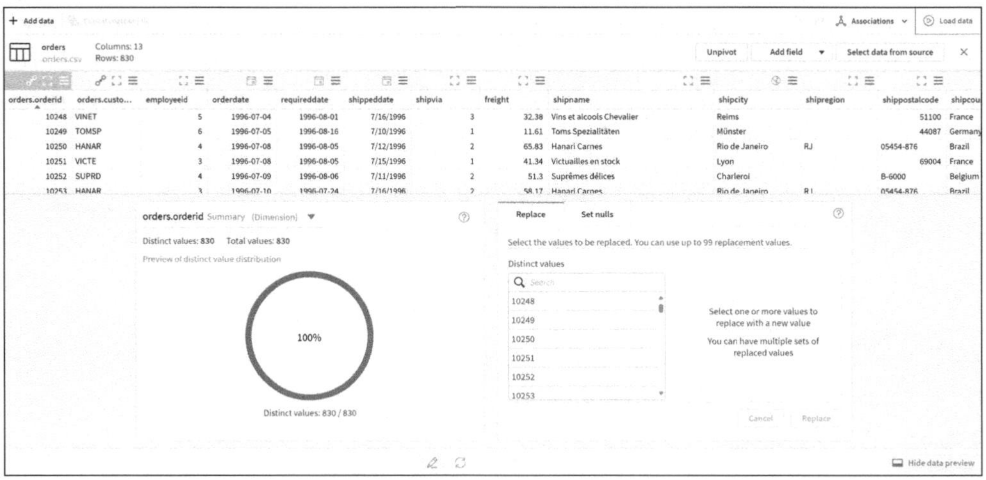

Figure 2.14: *Formatting dates*

At the top, above the field names, there are some icons that represent how that column is being evaluated. You will notice that the three date fields are identified like small calendars. When you press that icon, you will be presented with an option to set the format. In our example, let us use the US format (MM/DD/YYYY).

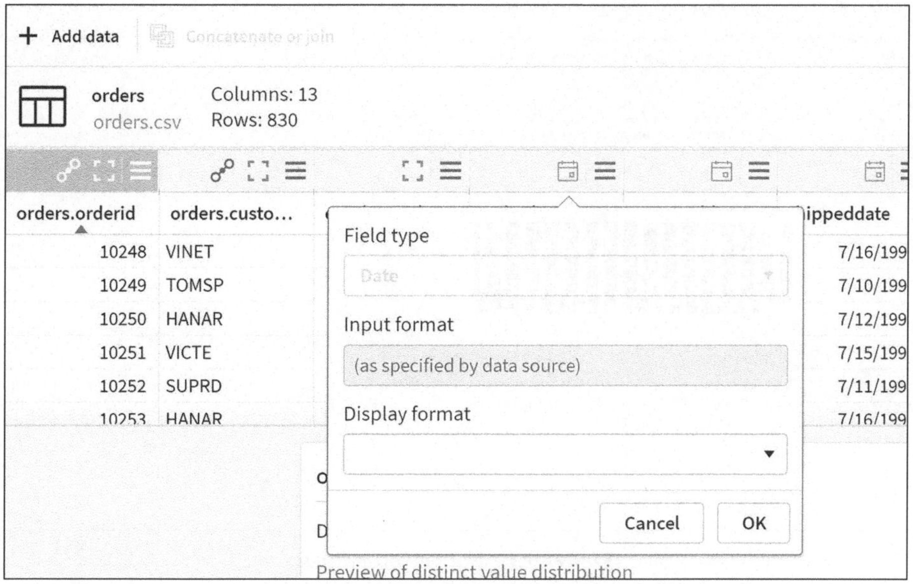

***Figure 2.15**: Display format*

Once you finish adjusting the three columns, you will notice that they have the same format.

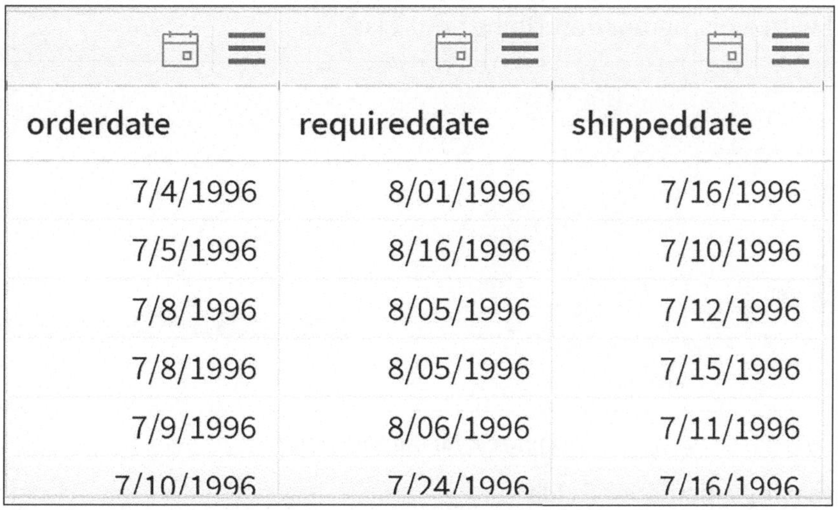

***Figure 2.16**: Formatted dates*

- **Bucketing values**

Sometimes, during an analysis, it is more important to have a value classification instead of an exact value. In our example, we have 799 (out of 830) distinct values for `freight`.

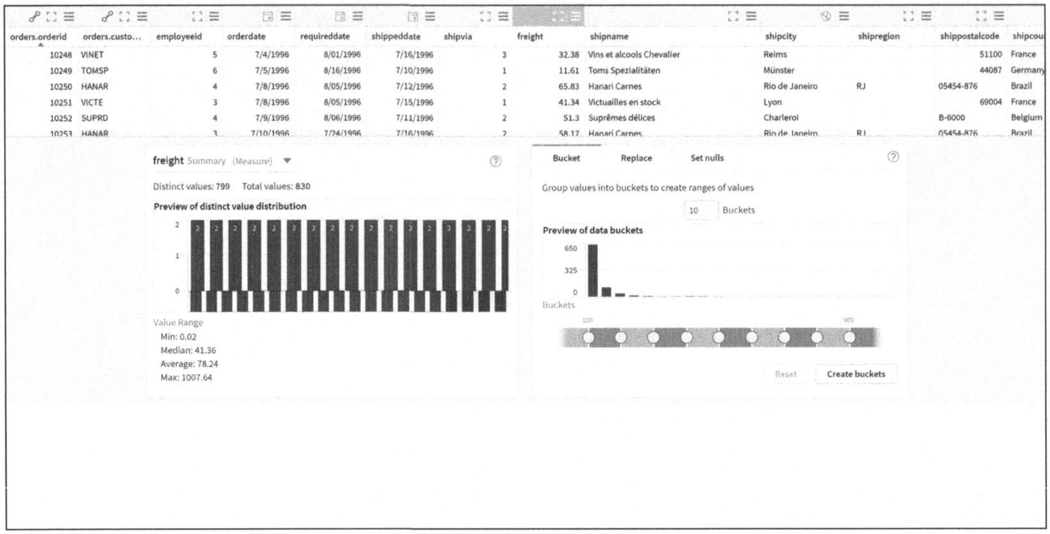

Figure 2.17: *Bucketing values*

Upon choosing the specified field, you will observe that the Data Manager will suggest a method for creating a class to aggregate the data into distinct categories. You can define how many classes and how "*wide*" they are. By pressing **`Create buckets`**, you will instruct the Data Manager to persist in your choice. By doing that, you will be presented with a histogram describing your classes.

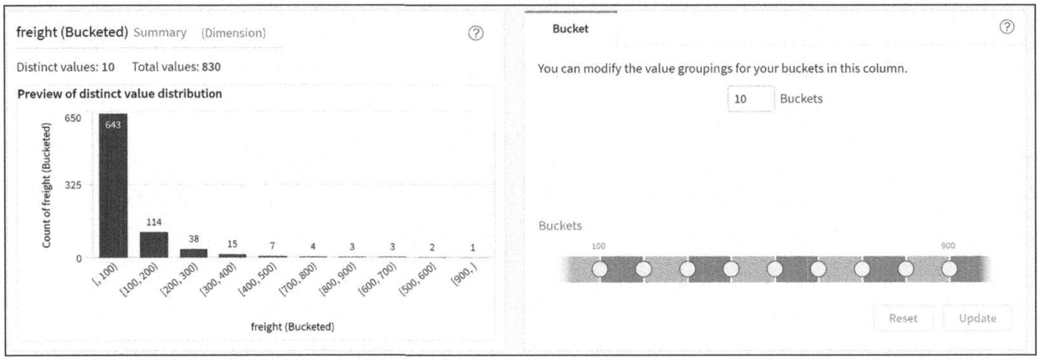

Figure 2.18: *Bucket values*

- **Creating calculated fields**

To facilitate more efficient and expedited analysis, it is advisable to establish fields within the model for consolidating frequently used calculations. In our example, there is a calculation that will frequently be executed, which is the net value for a specific row in the **`order_details`** table:

```
(quantity * [orders_details.unitprice])*(1-discount)
```

To create this field, press the **Add field** button on the top right of the screen and type the aforementioned code. You can use the field selector button as well to auto-populate the field names. It is necessary to add a **Name** to your field. Once you finish, you can press the **Create** button.

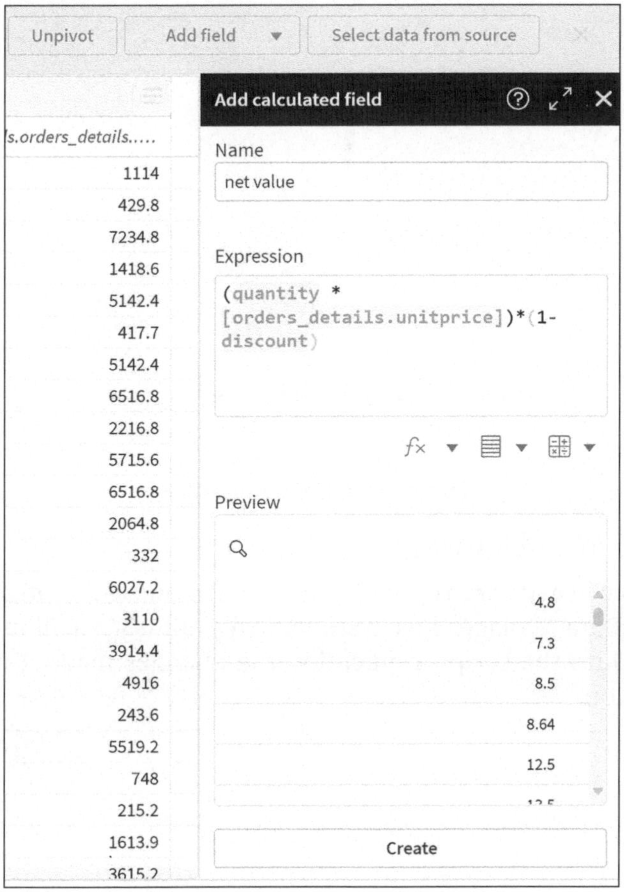

***Figure 2.19**: Custom field editor*

- **Replacing data values**

Occasionally, data cleaning involves transforming values into more comprehensible ones. For instance, assigning meaningful replacements for blank entries can enhance data readability by consolidating various representations of the United States (US, U.S., USA, and so on) into a uniform value. As an example, let us fix the field **shipregion** in the table **orders.** As previously, use the pencil icon at the bottom to edit the table and select that field. Upon accessing the **Replace** tab, you will observe the option to modify empty values, such as transforming them into a designated term such as **"<no region>".** Multiple replacements can be added to a field as required. After adjusting all necessary values, press the **Replace** button to persist in the replacements you made.

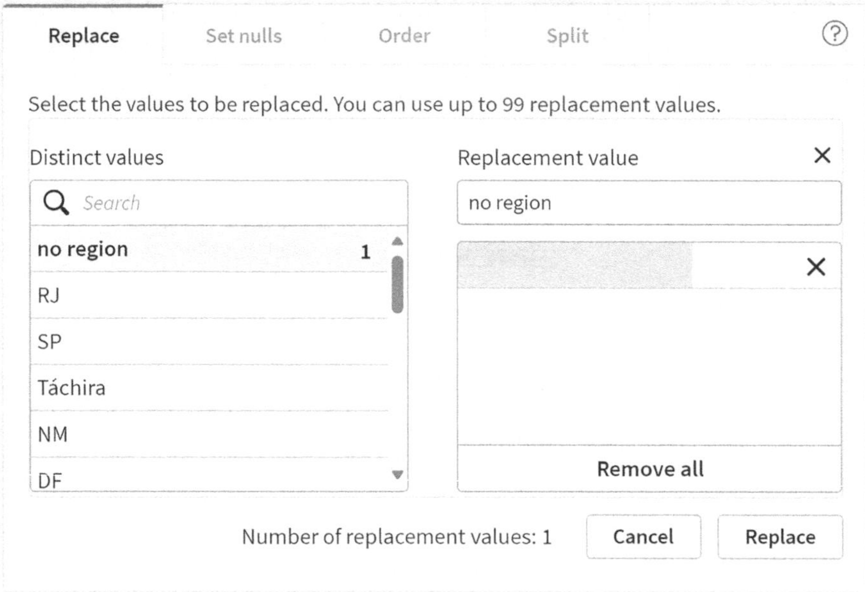

Figure 2.20: *Changing values*

- **Checking the script changes**

Return to the `Data Load Editor` and examine the autogenerated section. You will observe that the Data Manager has systematically translated all modifications made through the GUI into the script, replicating the changes made during the graphical interface interaction.

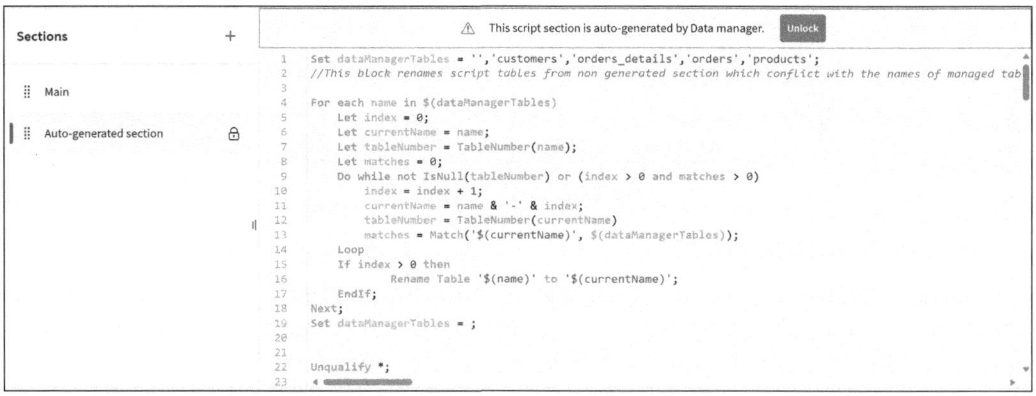

Figure 2.21: *Script with transformations*

- **Executing and applying the changes**

To incorporate the alterations into your data model, it is necessary to execute a script reload. This reload process will implement all changes, rendering the data model conducive to the subsequent step, which involves the creation of the analysis. To reload your script, press the **Load data** button at the far right of your screen. Some feedback will be provided to you while the script is being executed.

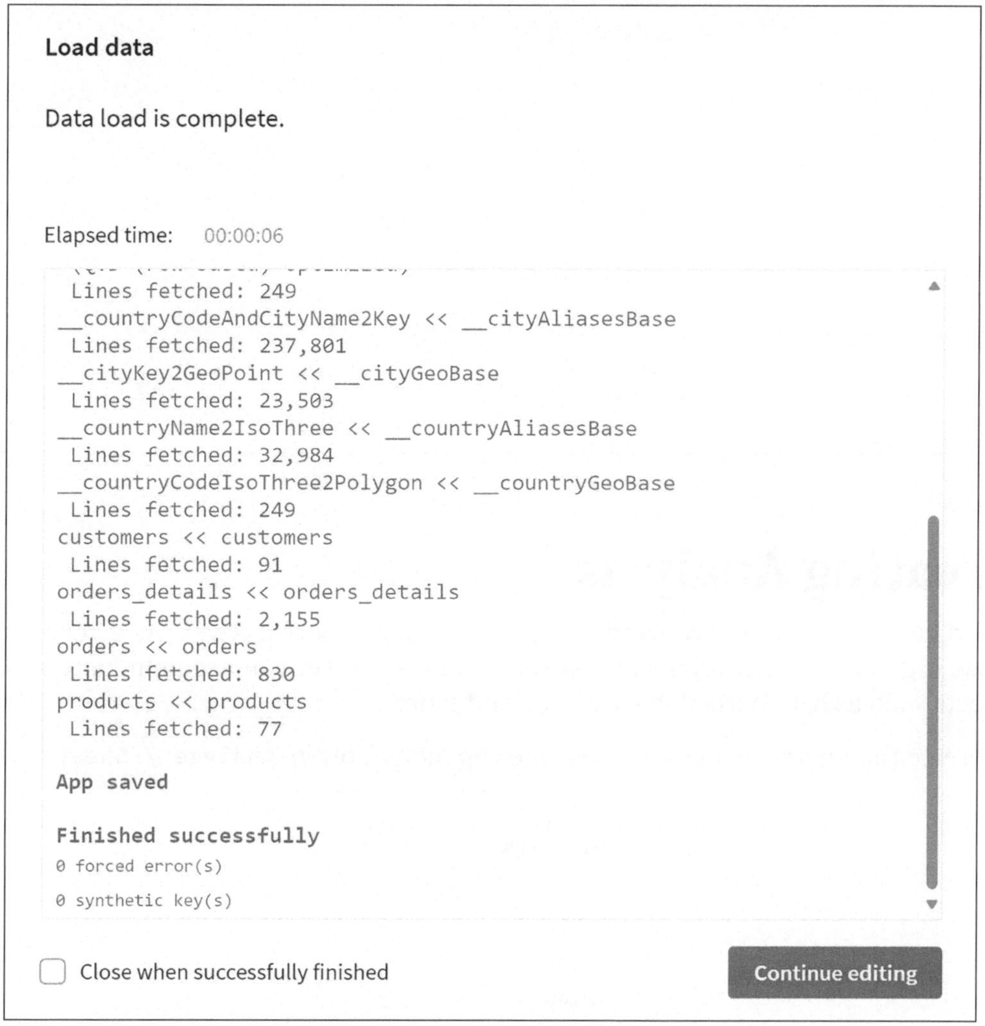

***Figure 2.22**: Script execution*

- **Reviewing the Data Model**

Utilize the **Data model viewer** button located at the top left of your screen to visually inspect the data model you have recently constructed.

Within this model, each block symbolizes a table, and the arrows denote the relationships between them. At the bottom, a data sample is provided along with additional metadata for your tables. As an illustration, the **customers** table comprises 91 rows, 12 fields, and a singular key.

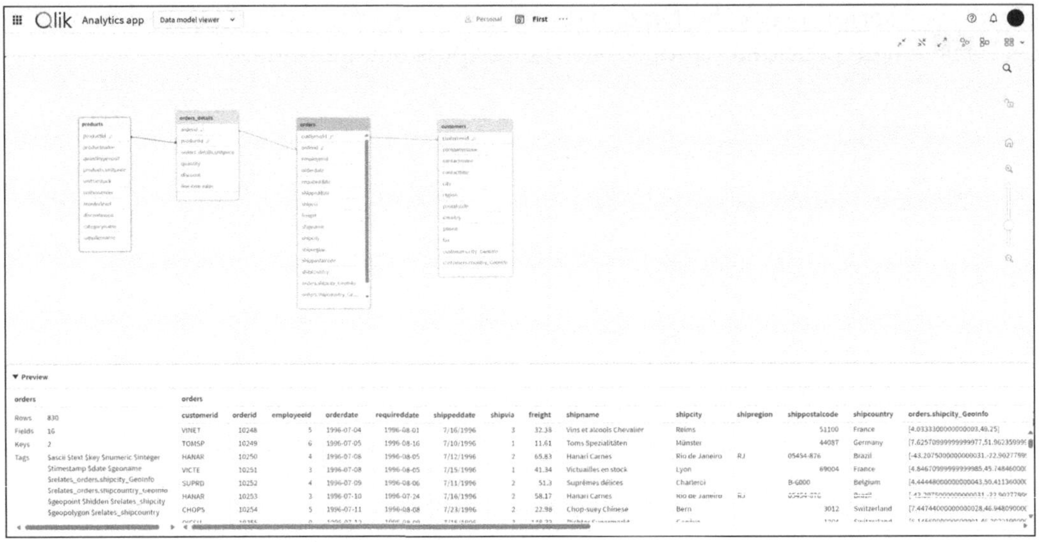

Figure 2.23: *Complete data model*

Creating Analysis

Our data model is now prepared to fulfill our analytics objectives. As a recap, Qlik Sense organizes visualizations into sheets, and each sheet can accommodate various objects such as bar charts, tables, filters, and more.

To create the first sheet, let us access the top menu option, **`Analyze / Sheet`**.

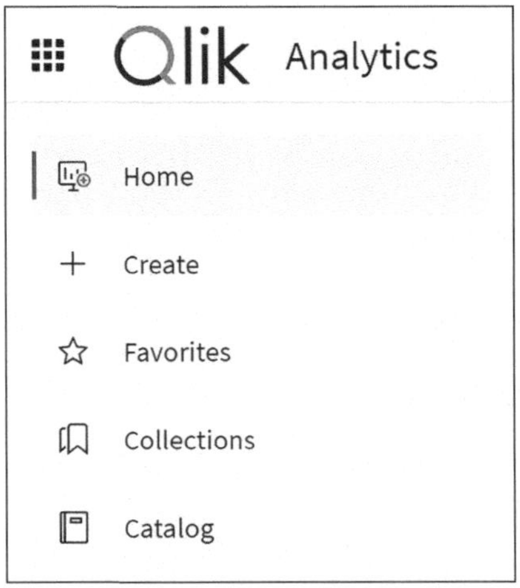

Figure 2.24: *Sheet menu*

This will open a blank sheet and give you assistance in creating your visualizations on that sheet. Qlik Sense will provide you with assistance in this process, making recommendations about what visualizations are more useful to show the information you want. If you are not familiar with data literacy and data visualization objects, we recommend you read this topic, "*Best practices for choosing visualization types*" (1), before continuing. A commendable approach is to commence with the **Dashboard, Analysis, and Reporting (DAR) methodology** (2), where the initial focus is on a Dashboard featuring Key Performance Indicators (KPIs) and consolidated information. This provides users with a quick overview to identify critical information at a glance. Subsequently, Analysis sheets can be developed to delve into more detailed insights, followed by another sheet dedicated to tabular reports. This phased strategy enhances the user experience and facilitates a comprehensive analysis.

To add KPIs to your dashboard sheet, you can use the drag-and-drop capabilities. Let us get started by selecting the **`order_details`** table and dragging the **`net value`** (the custom field created in the transformation step) to the canvas. Drop it over the **`Drop field for a suggestion`** and see the result.

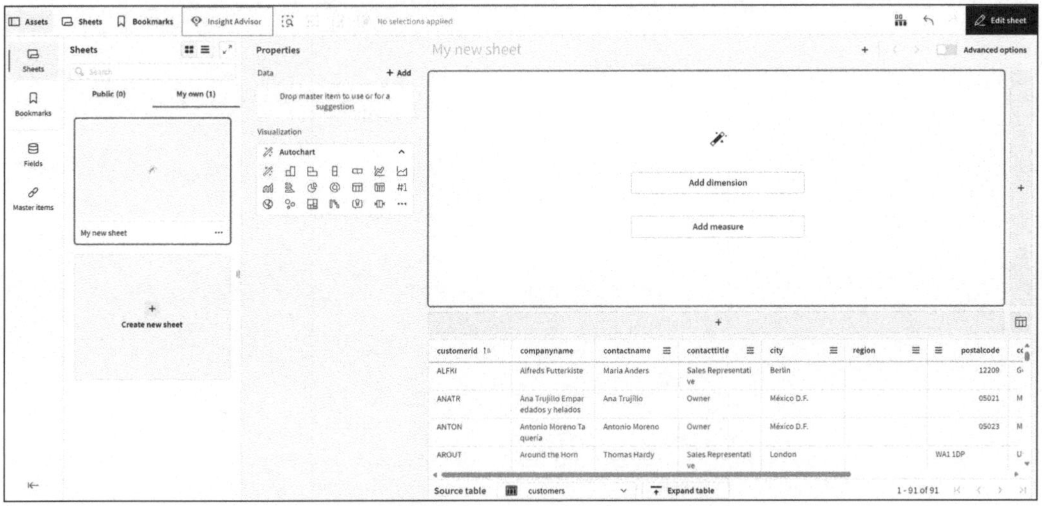

Figure 2.25: *Sheet editor*

In Qlik Assistant, you convert this action into an expression **`sum([net value])`** and add it to the sheet as a KPI that shows the expression value.

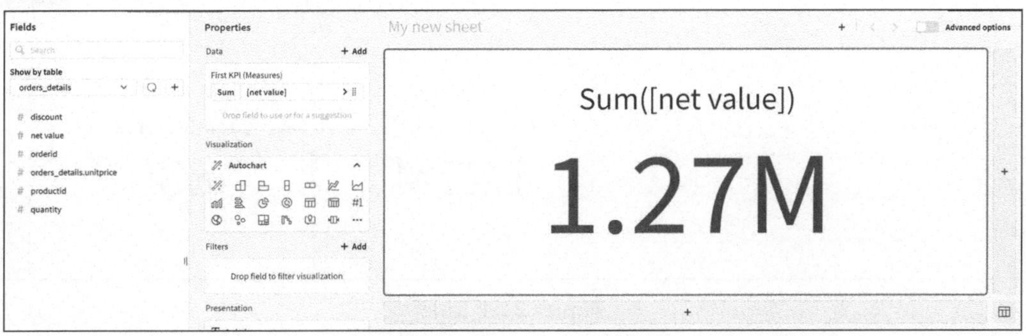

Figure 2.26: *First KPI Added*

Use the **+** button on the far right to add space for our second KPI, indicating how many orders we have. Let us do this by selecting the table **`orders`**, dragging the **`orderdate`** field, and dropping it over the **`Drop field to use as a measure`**.

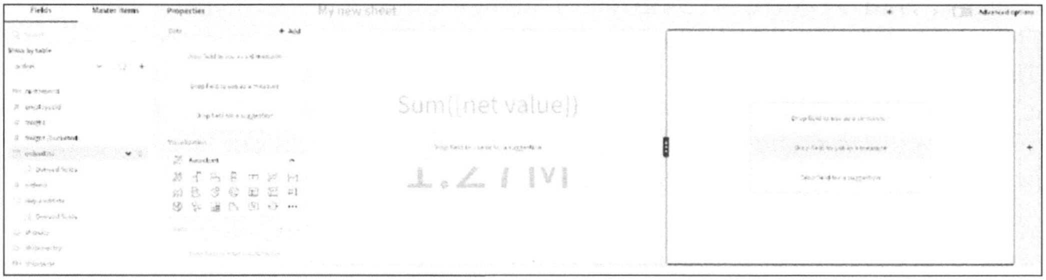

***Figure 2.27**: Adding another KPI*

Now in the **`Properties`** panel, change the expression to **`Count`**.

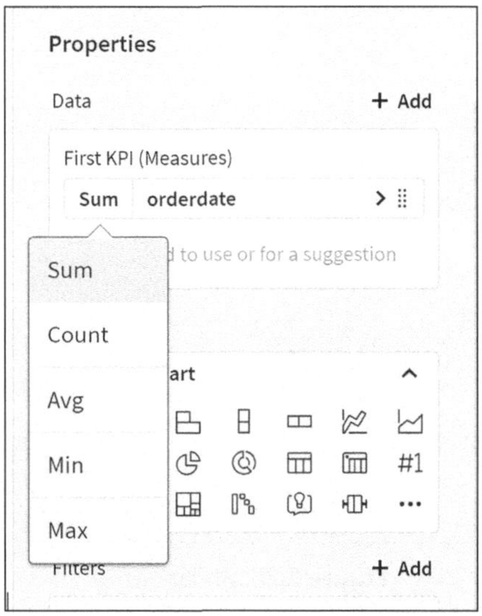

***Figure 2.28**: Adding a measure*

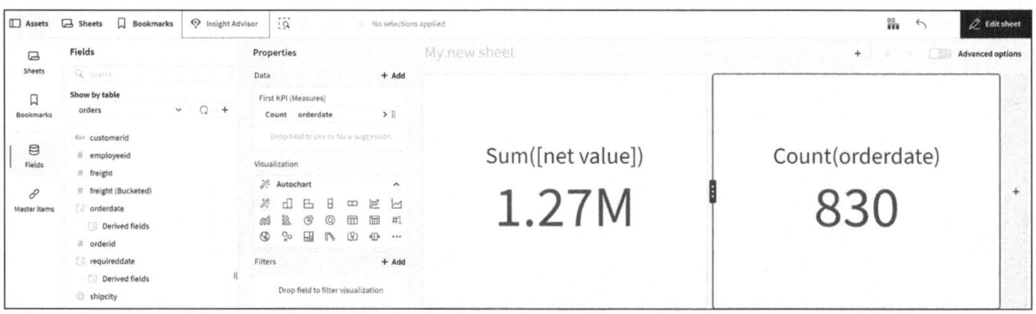

***Figure 2.29**: KPIs*

Now use the **+** button below both KPI's. Instead of drag-and-drop, let us use the assistant in the object. Press the **`Add measure`** button, select the **`net value`** field, and choose to **`sum`** the values.

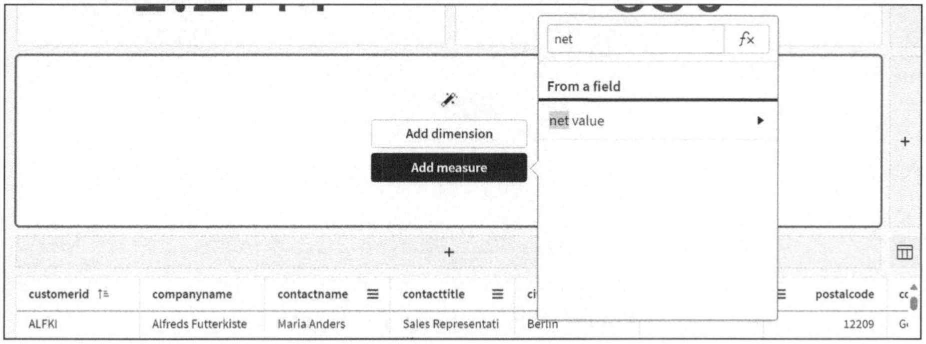

Figure 2.30: *Adding a measure*

Now, using the **`Properties`** panel again and using the **+Add** button, select the **`country`** field.

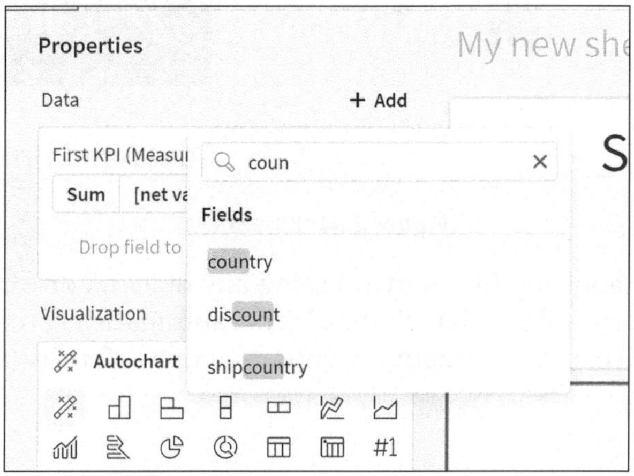

Figure 2.31: *Adding a dimension*

Since this information makes geographical sense, Qlik Assistant will convert your object into a map colored based on measure.

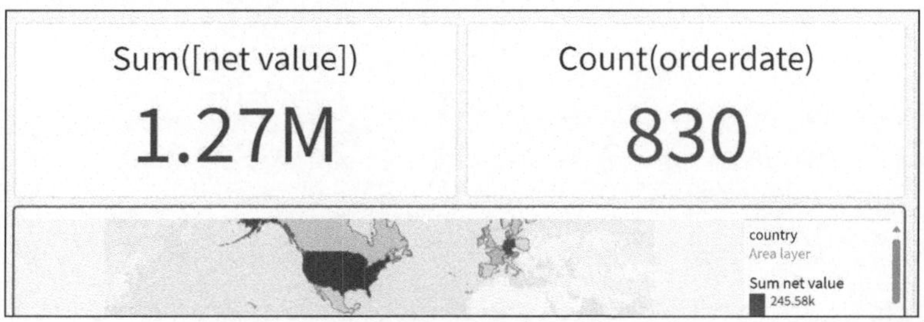

Figure 2.32: *Adding a map*

Repeat the same process, but instead of **country** use the **orderdate** field.

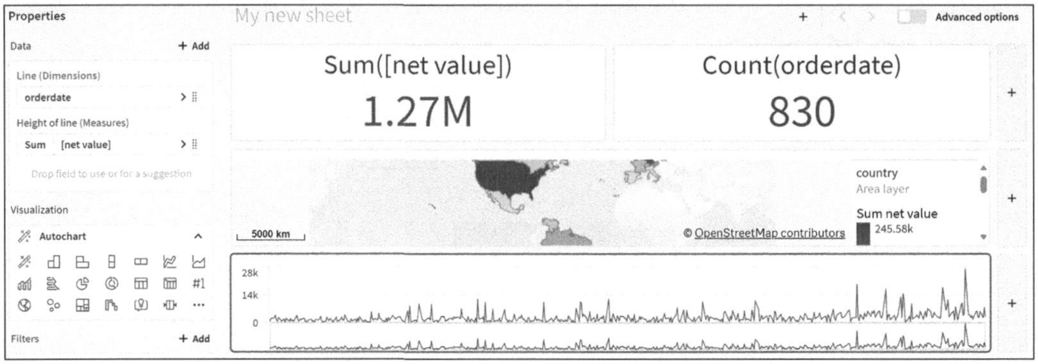

Figure 2.33: *Adding a line chart*

Our very simple first dashboard is ready. Let us switch to the view mode by clicking **Edit sheet** on the far top right.

Figure 2.34: *Edit Sheet*

Now, you can start applying filters by pressing any object. For example, if you select the United States, you will see that all the objects automatically reflect your selection. Even the map performs an auto-zoom to show you only US territory.

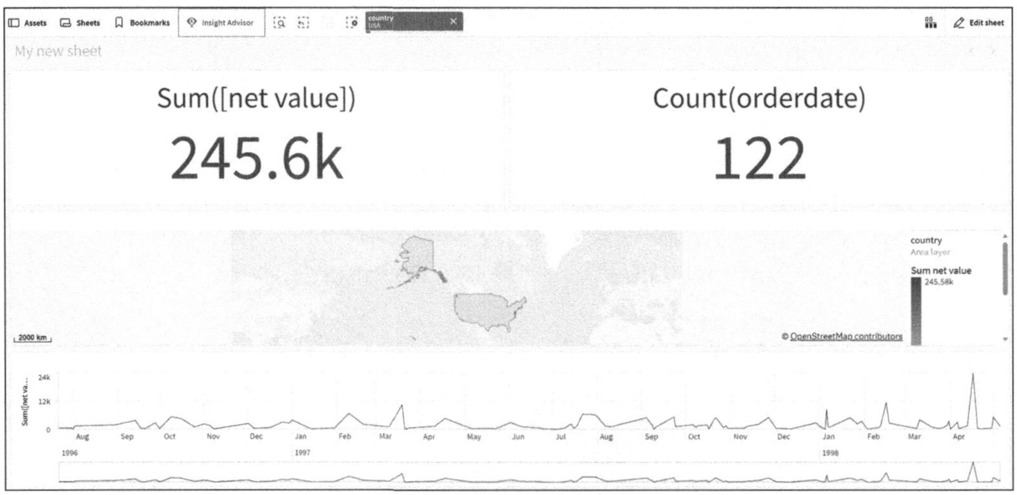

Figure 2.35: *Dashboard*

To enhance the visual aspects, adjusting object sizes and incorporating filters for user convenience, revisit the **Edit Sheet** option. This time, select the **Advanced Options** radio button. This action will present the sheet in edit mode with three primary columns. On the left, the Assets panel provides access to elements that can be dragged and dropped onto your sheet. On the right, the Properties panel facilitates the fine-tuning of objects with an extensive array of options. The canvas between them represents your sheet.

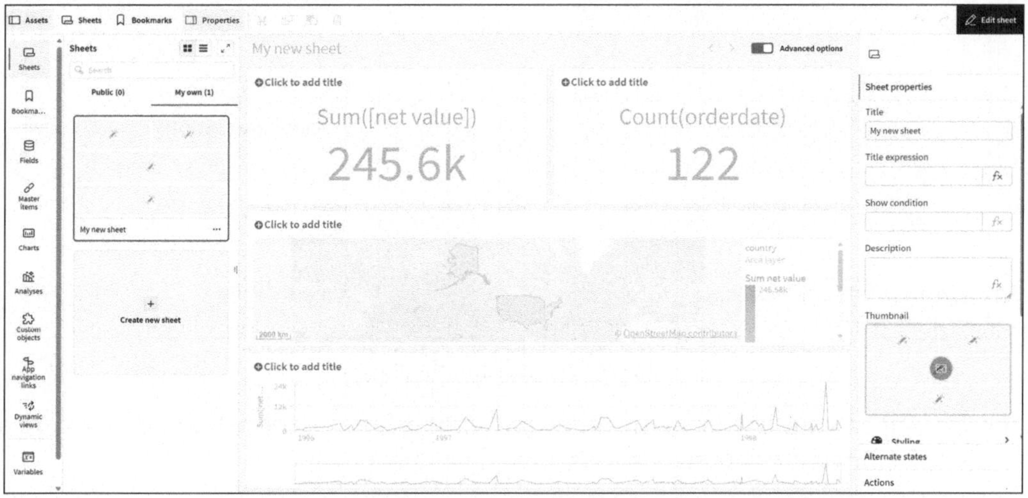

Figure 2.36: *Advanced mode*

When you select any object, you can move or resize it using the box corners of it.

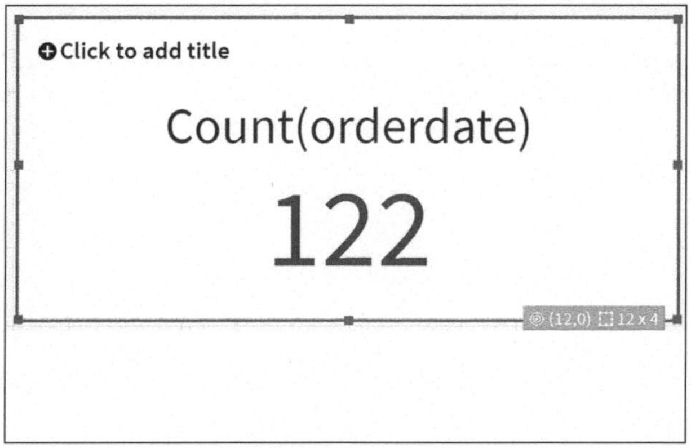

Figure 2.37: KPI

When one object is selected, the **Properties** panel can be used to configure all the options available for that object type. For example, when you select the map, you can hide the title using the **Show titles** option from the **General** tab.

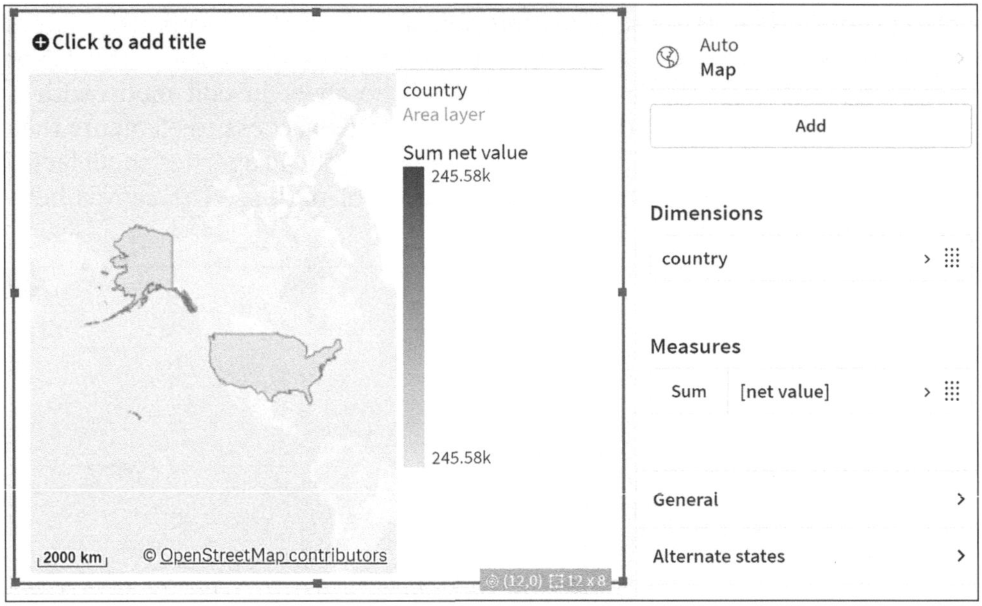

Figure 2.38: *Editing the map*

Exercise: Adjust your layout to the following screen, leaving room for adding filters on the top left side of the screen.

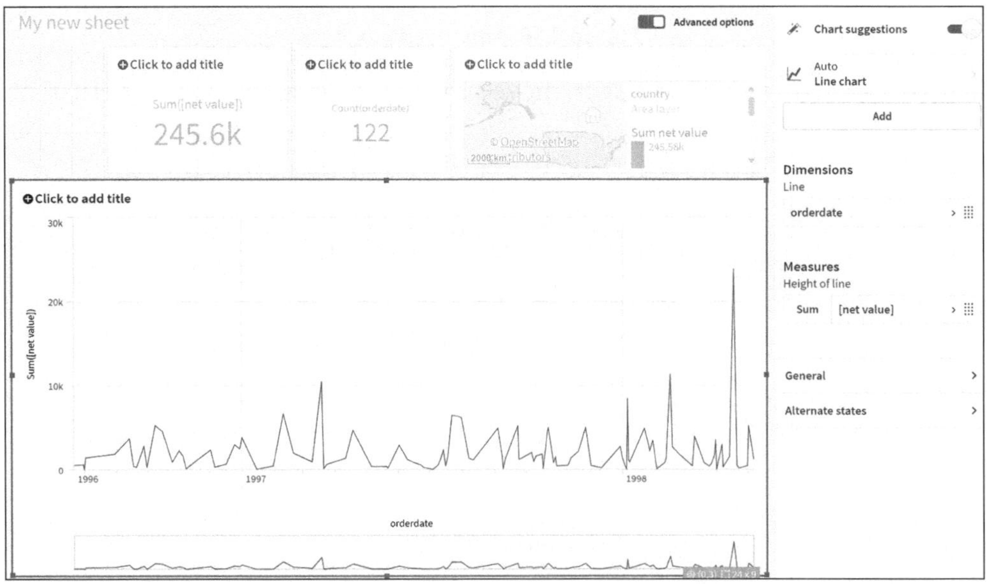

Figure 2.39: *Edited Dashboard*

Our final step will be to add some filtering capabilities to this sheet. To do that, select the **`Charts`** section of the Assets panel and drag a **`Filter pane`** to the empty space you left in your canvas.

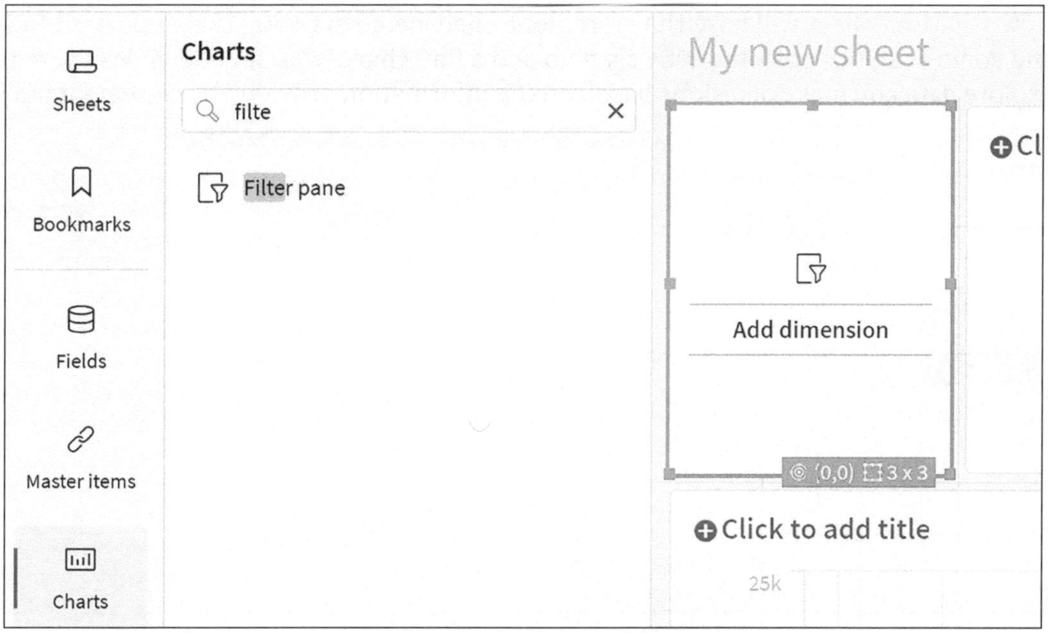

Figure 2.40: *Adding a filter pane*

Now using the properties panel, add **`country, city, companyname`**, and **`productname`** to the filter pane.

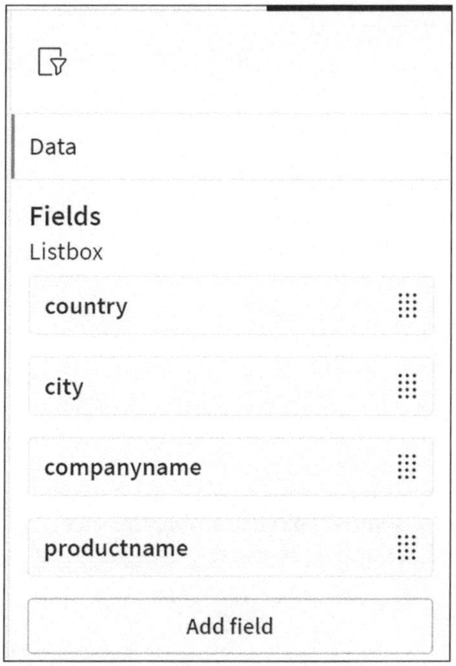

Figure 2.41: *Filter pane fields*

Now your first sheet will have the aforementioned layout showing two important KPIs and some analytics objects such as a map and a line chart. This sheet enables users to explore data and make decisions based on the information provided by the data model.

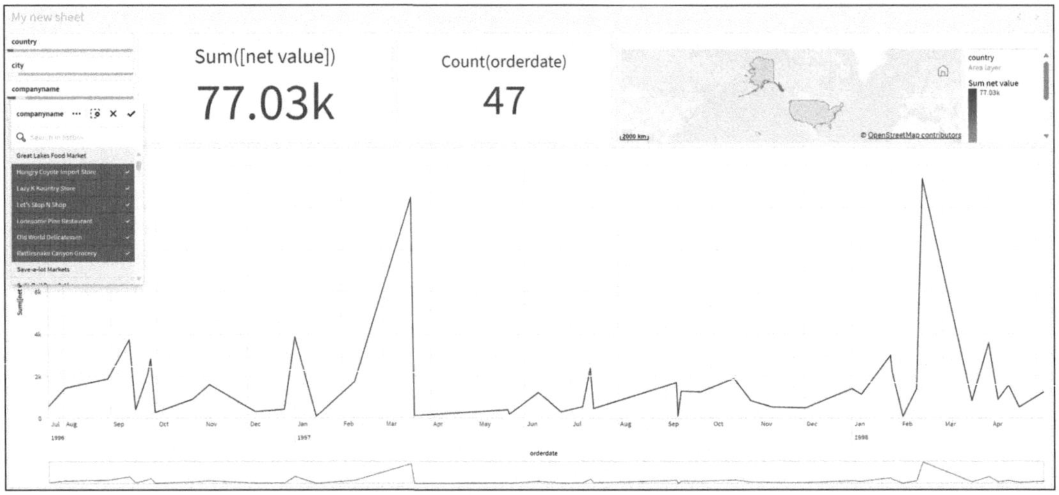

Figure 2.42: *Using the dashboard*

Finally, let us rename our sheet from **`"My new sheet"`** to something that relates to its content. To rename the sheet, click **`Edit sheet`** and change the **`Title`** using the **`Sheet properties`**.

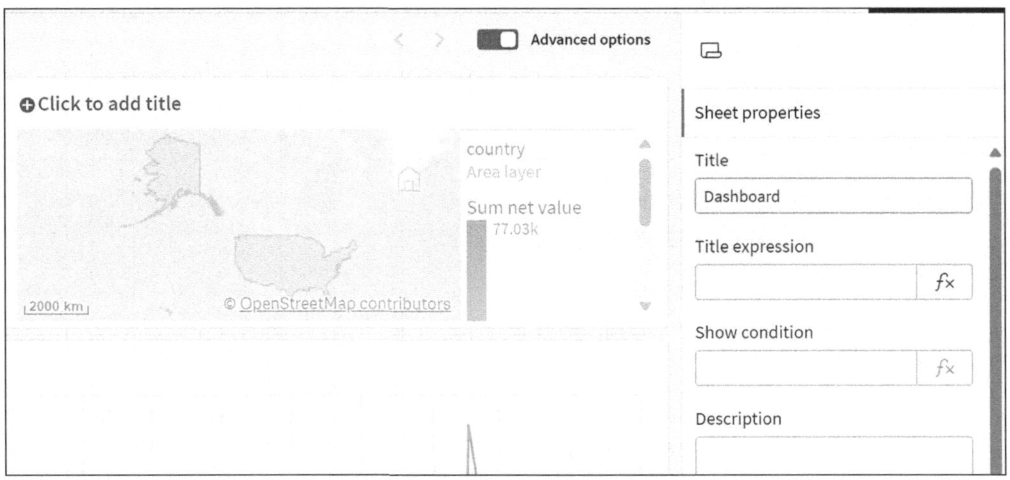

Figure 2.43: *Renaming the sheet*

Conclusion

This marks the conclusion of our chapter, where we explored various facets of data modeling. Throughout this journey, we focused on the building aspects of a comprehensive data model, which involved combining tables and applying transformative processes. With this refined data model in place, we successfully crafted our first sheet, now well-prepared for consumption by end-users.

We encourage the reader to go through all the assets in the *Additional Resources* for a more comprehensive view of all the aspects discussed in this chapter.

In the upcoming chapter, our attention will shift towards the scripting resources offered by Qlik Sense. We will **explore the process** of writing joins, implementing data load constraints, and leveraging debugging options for script optimization. Furthermore, our exploration will extend to QVDs, an exceptionally efficient data storage format that enhances Qlik's ability to store and manage data with efficacy.

Multiple Choice Questions

1. Creates and maintains scripts based on a graphical interface where the user configures the actions that need to be executed by the script.
    a. Data Manager
    b. Data Model Viewer
    c. Assets Panel
    d. Data Script Editor
2. Creates and maintains scripts based on a text editor where the user types commands.
    a. Data Manager
    b. Data Model Viewer
    c. Assets Panel
    d. Data Script Editor
3. Give the user the ability to drag and drop components onto the canvas.
    a. Data Manager
    b. Data Model Viewer
    c. Assets Panel
    d. Data Script Editor

4. Give the user the ability to inspect the Data Model.
    a. Data Manager
    b. Data Model Viewer
    c. Assets Panel
    d. Data Script Editor

Answers

1. a
2. d
3. c
4. b

References

1. Qliktech. Best practices for choosing visualization types. *Qlik.com Help*. [Online]: https://help.qlik.com/en-US/sense/November2023/Subsystems/Hub/Content/Sense_Hub/Visualizations/when-to-use-visualizations.htm.
2. Qlik Help. [Online]: https://help.qlik.com/#anchor-1.
3. Dashboard, Analysis, Reporting (DAR) . *Qlik Community* . [Online]: https://community.qlik.com/t5/Design/DAR-methodology/ba-p/1466733.

Additional Resources

The following links are complimentary to this book, bringing more resources to the reader with more examples and details.

- **Beginning with the Basics** (https://help.qlik.com/en-US/cloud-services/Subsystems/Hub/Content/Sense_Hub/Tutorials/introduction-beginning-with-basics.htm): A centralized documentation for all Qlik solutions and products. It is open and publicly available.
- **Navigating the User Interface** (https://help.qlik.com/en-US/cloud-services/Subsystems/Hub/Content/Sense_Hub/UserInterface/navigate-user-interface.htm): Reviewing all the options in the user interface.
- **Data Manager** (https://help.qlik.com/en-US/cloud-services/Subsystems/Hub/Content/Sense_Hub/LoadData/data-management.htm): Reviewing all the options available in the Data Manager

CHAPTER 3
Using Scripts

Introduction

This chapter serves as an exploration of Qlik Sense scripting, emphasizing the fundamental aspects of loading external files, orchestrating joins, and optimizing data storage through QVDs. The objective is to provide readers with an understanding of scripting principles essential for proficient data transformation and integration within the Qlik Sense environment.

Structure

In this chapter, we will discuss the following topics:

- Qlik Sense Script Concepts
- Data Load Editor
- Loading Data
- Joins
- Aggregations
- Loops
- QVD's

Qlik Sense Script Concepts

In the context of Qlik Sense, a script functions as a fundamental element that provides instructions for data processing, integration, and structuring within the Qlik Sense framework. It utilizes a scripting language proprietary to Qlik, enabling users to specify operations for data loading, transformation, and association. The Qlik Sense script serves as a procedural guide, outlining the steps necessary to convert raw data into a structured and analytically accessible format.

Qlik Sense scripts are integral to the implementation of an associative data model, a distinctive feature within Qlik's business intelligence tools. Through scripts, users define the rules governing data associations, fostering dynamic connections between various data elements. This associative model facilitates an interactive exploration of data, allowing insights to emerge through a natural process. Qlik Sense scripts play a central role in tasks such as loading external files, executing joins, and optimizing data storage through the creation of Qlik's proprietary data format, known as QVDs. Essentially, a Qlik Sense script functions as a guiding mechanism, shaping the procedural sequence that transforms data into a coherent structure for analytical purposes.

Data Refresh

In the previous chapter, we discussed the data model concepts. The data model is the final representation of the script statements. Every time the script is executed in scheduled or *ad hoc* mode, the original data model is rebuilt using the script logic. If the data sources the script uses do not contain historical values, the user needs to implement a logic to save the history and reload it again in the next refresh, usually using the QVD files described in the last section.

Data Load Editor

Even though it is possible to use any text editor to develop a Qlik Script, Qlik Cloud Analytics provides an integrated editor with all the important features needed, such as integrated version control integration, undo and redo, search and replace, and so on. You can access the **`Data load editor`** using the top menu in the **`Prepare`** section.

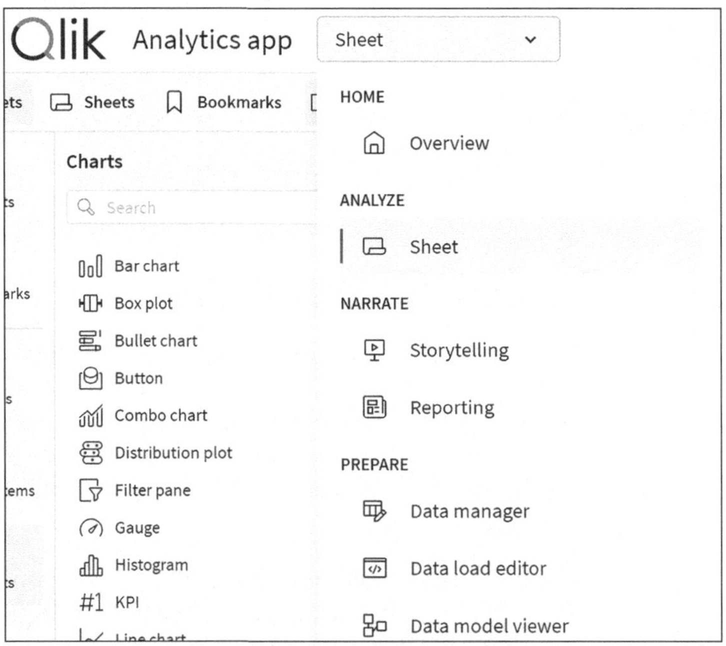

Figure 3.1: *Accessing the editor*

Once you click the option, the editor will open.

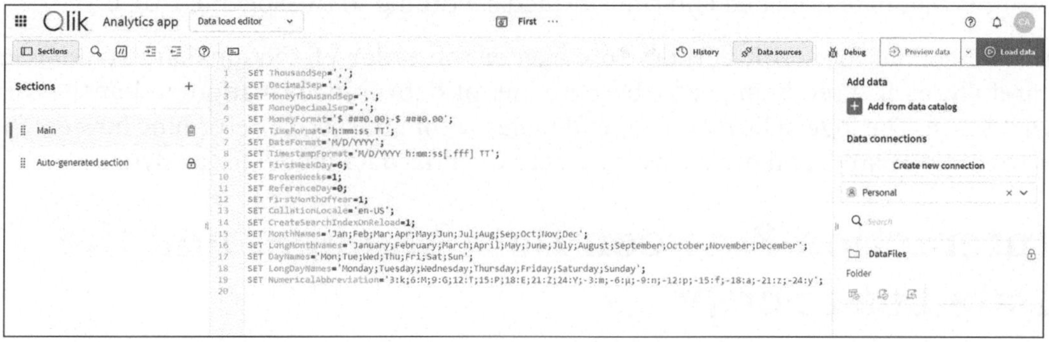

Figure 3.2: *The Editor*

From the aforementioned image, you can see four sections.

1. Top toolbar gives the user access to functions such as search and replace, comment code, indentation, version history, debug, and load data (reload script).

2. The **Sections**, located at the left side of the editor, is a panel that gives the user the ability to split the script into several sections, making the code easier to maintain. Providing meaningful names for these sections reduces the development effort. Using the **+** button will add more sections, and using the trash bin icon will delete the selected section.

3. **Add data** panel on the right side of the screen enables the user to ingest any data from supported sources.

4. At the center is the editor itself, which enables the user to work directly in the app load script, utilizing Qlik scripting functions. The load script specifies fields and tables for loading. The script will manipulate the data model with statements, performing operations such as loading new data sources, calculating new values, translating coded values, aggregating values, and joining or concatenating tables. The script editor features line numbering and color-coded syntax components for enhanced readability and comprehension.

Script Flow

In Qlik Sense, scripts are executed sequentially based on the order of sections and statements within the script. The execution process follows the linear flow of the script, moving from the beginning to the end. Each section, such as the **LOAD** or **SELECT** statement, is processed in the order it appears in the script.

The order of statements within a section is also significant. For instance, in the **LOAD** statement, fields and tables are specified, and subsequent operations within that statement are performed in the order they are written. This sequential execution ensures that data is loaded and transformed according to the specified logic.

It is essential for script authors to consider the order of sections and statements carefully, as it directly impacts the outcome of data transformation and analysis in Qlik Sense. The logical flow and dependencies within the script determine how data is loaded, associated, and processed to create the final data model for analytics.

Interaction Between Data Manager and the Data Load Script

When users add data tables in the Data Manager, the Data load script code is automatically generated. The script code can be viewed in the Auto-generated section of the data load editor. Users have the option to unlock and edit the generated script code; however, doing so results in the data tables no longer being managed in the Data Manager.

By default, data tables defined in the load script are not managed in the Data Manager. This means that while the tables are visible in the data overview, users cannot delete or edit them in the Data Manager, and association recommendations are not provided for tables loaded with the script. Synchronizing scripted tables with the Data Manager, however, adds the scripted tables as managed tables in the Data Manager.

The Main Section

By default, all scripts in Qlik Sense have a section named **`Main`**. It is automatically added to every new application and contains number interpretation variables that are automatically generated based on the regional settings of the user profile.

These variables are introduced at the beginning of the script and act as placeholders, replacing default number formatting settings from the operating system during script execution. Users have the flexibility to manage these variables, allowing for deletion, editing, or duplication as needed. This customization ensures that number formatting aligns with the specific requirements of the target application.

A typical **`Main`** section appears like the following image, where you can see the variables that will control the number and date display, month names, and more.

Figure 3.3: *Variables*

The Main section is usually the first script section, but this is not mandatory. Some users may add a section before the main section with documentation and versioning information, for example.

Debugging

You can utilize the debugging utilities within the Data Load Editor to methodically navigate through your script execution using breakpoints. Breakpoints provide the capability to examine variable values and observe the output generated during script execution. Within the debugging environment, you have the flexibility to select which aspects to monitor, whether they be Output, Variables, or Breakpoints. This comprehensive debugging functionality enhances your ability to troubleshoot and optimize your script effectively.

You can enable the **Debug** mode using the option on the top right of the screen.

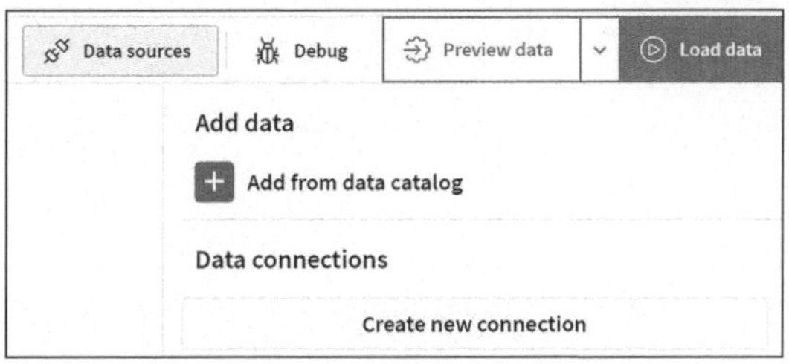

Figure 3.4: *Enabling Debug mode*

Pressing the **Debug** button will switch the interface into debug mode, displaying at the bottom a panel like this.

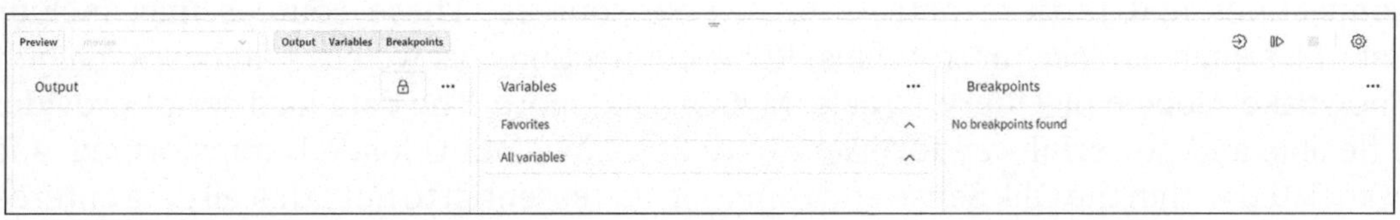

Figure 3.5: *Debug panel*

The options at the top facilitate step-by-step execution or execution until a breakpoint is encountered. Adding breakpoints is straightforward; simply click the row number in your script. This action will insert an orange mark, signifying the addition of a breakpoint to that particular row.

```
left join (products)
LOAD
    categoryid,
    categoryname
FROM [lib://DataFiles/categories.csv]
(txt, codepage is 28591, embedded labels, delimiter is ',', msq);
drop Field categoryid;

left join (products)
LOAD
    supplierid,
    companyname as suppliername
FROM [lib://DataFiles/suppliers.csv]
(txt, utf8, embedded labels, delimiter is ',', msq);
drop Field supplierid;
```

***Figure 3.6**: Adding a breakpoint*

Using the debug option provides the necessary information for troubleshooting your script. The editor displays the upcoming script step to be executed alongside the script's output. If needed, you can incorporate TRACE statements to showcase specific information in the output. Additionally, you can inspect the current values of variables at that particular point in the script.

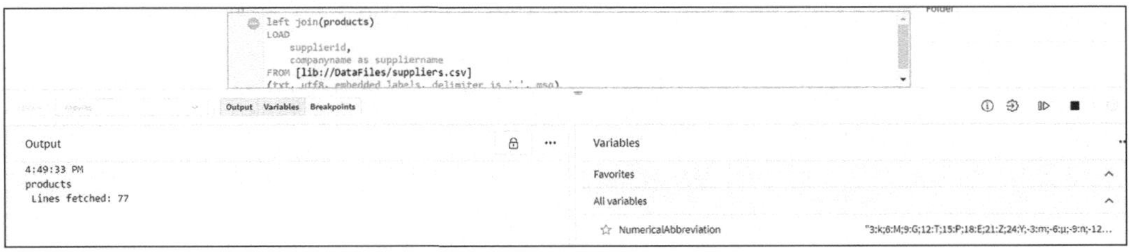

***Figure 3.7**: Debugging the script*

Loading Data

Qlik Sense employs a data load script managed in the Data Load Editor to establish connections and retrieve data from diverse sources. These sources may include data files such as Excel or .csv files, REST connections, as well as databases, namely Snowflake, Google BigQuery, Oracle, MySQL, and more. The data load script provides a flexible and powerful way for users to define how data is loaded, transformed, and associated within the Qlik Sense environment. It is essential to note that all data entered or stored by a Qlik Sense application must be managed through a data connection.

Extract, Transform and Load

The data loading process in Qlik Sense follows the Extract, Transform, and Load (ETL) paradigm, usually named by its acronym ETL:

1. **Extract**: In the extraction stage, data is sourced from the data system. In Qlik Sense scripts, **SELECT** or **LOAD** statements are employed for this purpose. **SELECT** is used for extracting data from a database, with the SQL statement being evaluated by the data provider. On the other hand, **LOAD** is versatile, allowing data extraction from files, script-defined data, previously loaded tables, web pages, subsequent **SELECT** statements, or automatic data generation.
2. **Transform**: The transformation phase involves manipulating the data using script functions and rules to shape it into the desired data model structure. Operations in this stage include calculating new values, translating coded values, renaming fields, joining tables, aggregating values, pivoting, and data validation.
3. **Load or Export**: In the final step, the script is executed to load the defined data model into the app or to export the loaded data. The goal is to create an efficient data model in Qlik Sense, typically a reasonably normalized star schema or snowflake schema without circular references. This involves having a central fact table containing keys to dimensions and numeric values for measure calculations, surrounded by tables containing dimensions with all their attributes (example, products, customers, categories, calendar, and suppliers).

Depending on how complex the application and the data model are, the script can have dedicated sections for data extraction, data transforming, storing intermediate results, and final loading. Sometimes you may see some scripts that perform the three steps in only one statement per table. Just as an example, let us understand what the following statement represents:

```
[orders_details]:
LOAD
       [orderid],
       [productid],
       [unitprice] AS [orders_details.unitprice],
       [quantity],
       [discount],
       ([quantity] * [unitprice])*(1-[discount]) AS [net value]
 FROM [lib://DataFiles/orders_details.csv] (txt, codepage is
28591, embedded labels, delimiter is ',', msq)
```

- The **[order_details]** tag instructs Qlik Sense to name the table that is being loaded.
- The **FROM [lib://DataFiles/orders_details.csv]** describes where Qlik Sense should extract the data from with some parameters (file type, file codepage encoding, how the header should be treated, and what the delimiter is).
- **[unitprice] AS [orders_details.unitprice]** instructs Qlik Sense to rename the fieldname.
- **([quantity] * [unitprice])*(1-[discount]) AS [net value]** instructs Qlik Sense to add a new column named **net value** to this table with that expression. A transformation rule like this can use any value or logic to create new fields.
- In summary, this statement extracts data from a csv file, adds a field, renames another, and loads the result data in memory.

Data Connections

In Qlik Sense, data connections serve as the bridges that facilitate the flow of data into and out of the application. A data connection is essentially a configuration that defines how Qlik Sense establishes a link to various data sources, allowing the application to retrieve, transform, store, and associate data. These connections enable Qlik Sense to seamlessly integrate with diverse data repositories, such as databases, cloud services, or files.

In this chapter, we are using a special data connection named **DataFiles** that links to the user's personal space storage. For the sake of simplicity, we are using this approach. In future chapters, we will discuss additional features for storing data to be reused by other users.

LOAD Statement

The LOAD statement in Qlik Sense is a versatile command that facilitates the extraction of fields from multiple origins. It can pull data from files, script-defined datasets, previously loaded tables, web pages, and the outcomes of subsequent SELECT statements. Additionally, the LOAD statement empowers users to automatically generate data. Notably, Qlik Sense extends this capability further by enabling the loading of data from analytic connections, providing users with a comprehensive suite of options for integrating diverse data sources into their analytics workflows. It has a specific syntax described by the following definition :

```
LOAD [ distinct ] fieldlist
 [(   from file [ format-spec ] |
from_field fieldassource [format-spec]|
```

```
          inline data [ format-spec ] |
          resident table-label |
          autogenerate size ) |
        extension pluginname.functionname([script] tabledescription
)]
 [where criterion | while criterion]
 [group by groupbyfieldlist]
 [order by orderbyfieldlist]
```

The LOAD statement in Qlik Sense offers a rich set of variations and capabilities. Thankfully, Qlik provides wizards to assist users in effectively leveraging this statement. These wizards serve as helpful tools, guiding users through the proper usage and configuration of the LOAD statement, enhancing the overall ease and accuracy of data loading and transformation processes within the Qlik Sense environment.

Adding a New Table

Using the Data Load editor, let us add more data to the data model we already loaded in *Chapter 2, Building Your First Application*. Accessing the **Data load editor** using the top menu in the **Prepare** section, let us add a new section to our script. This section will be added after the auto-generated section the Data Manager is managing. To add a section, press the **+** button, renaming the section to something meaningful and dragging it to the lower position.

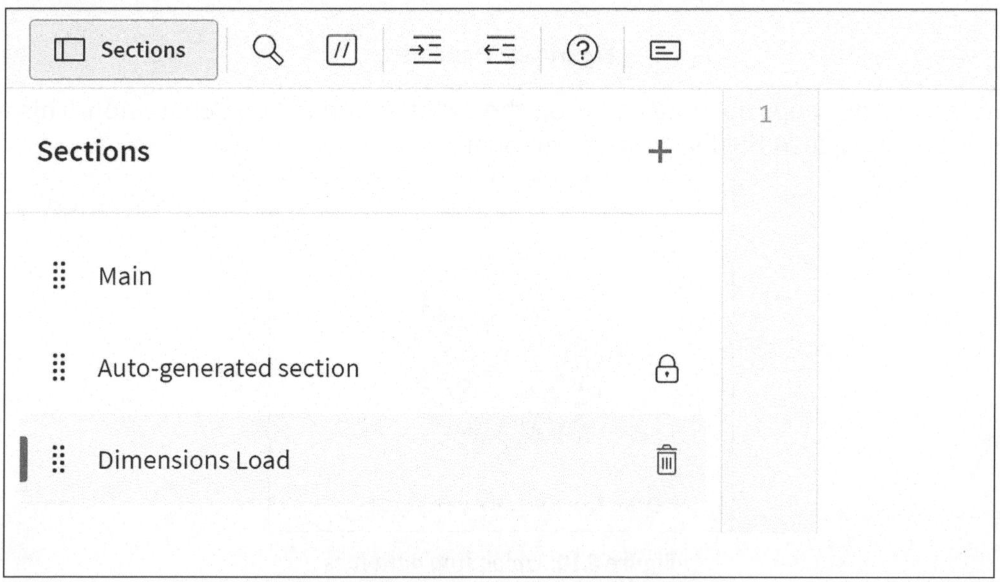

***Figure 3.8**: Adding a section to the script*

With the available space, we can now proceed to implement our code for loading additional tables into the data model. To begin, let us incorporate the **"categories"** table by extracting data from the **"categories.csv"** file within the same dataset discussed in the previous chapter. To do that, press the small table icon near **DataFiles** in the right panel.

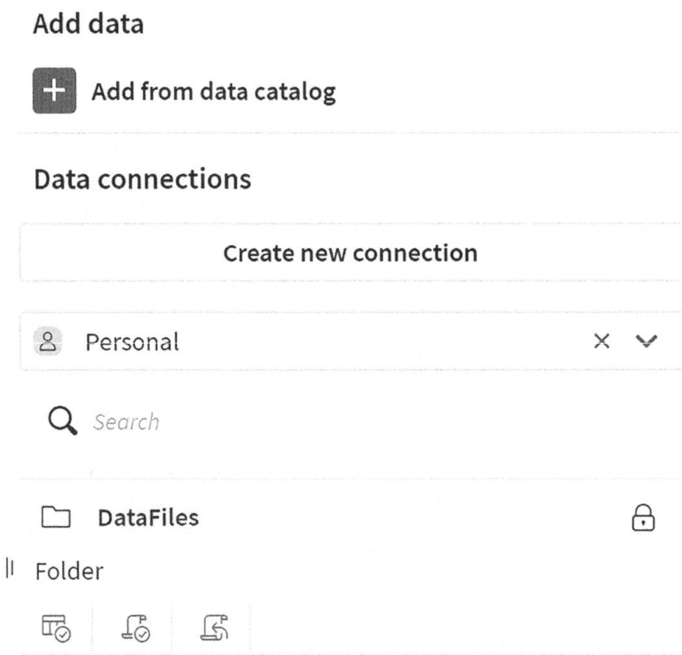

Figure 3.9: *DataFiles*

Once the wizard pops up, drag and drop the CSV file into the correct region. This will automatically upload the file to your personal space.

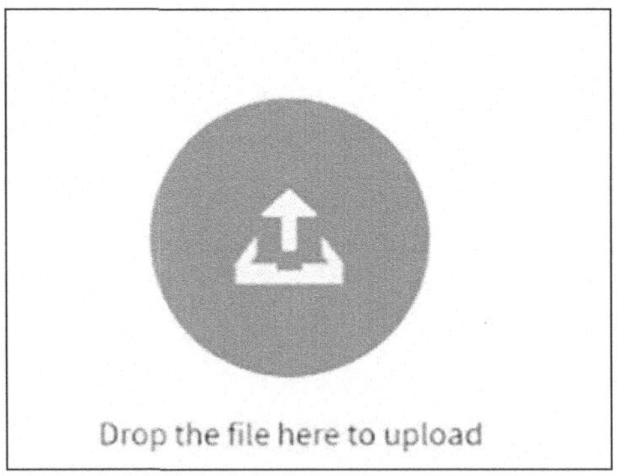

Figure 3.10: *Uploading data files*

Then select the CSV file from the list, opening the load wizard, and deselect the last two columns. For this exercise, we are only interested in the code and **categoryname**. The wizard will show you a preview of the code that will be generated by it.

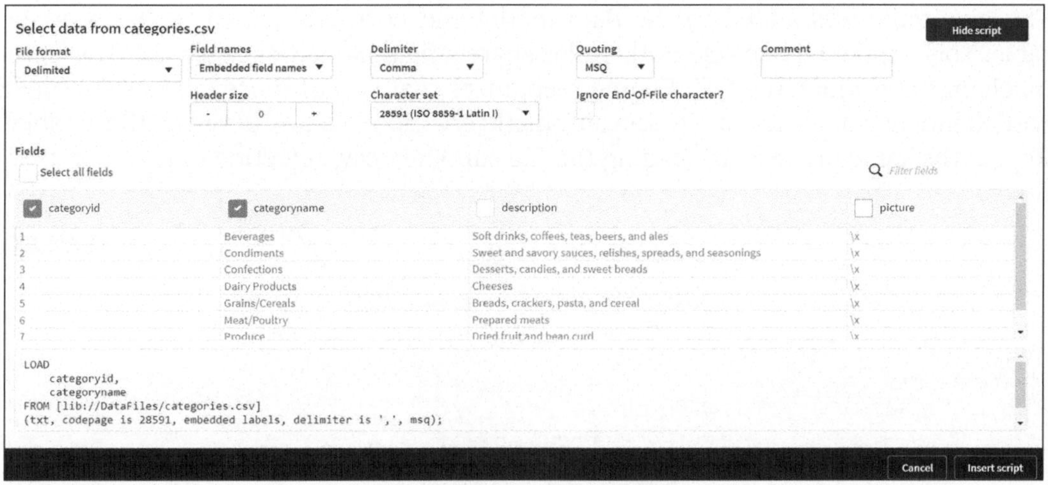

Figure 3.11: *Data file wizard*

By pressing **`Insert script`**, the load editor will add the command to your script.

```
LOAD
    categoryid,
    categoryname
FROM [lib://DataFiles/categories.csv]
(txt, codepage is 28591, embedded labels, delimiter is ',', msq);
```

Figure 3.12: *Load script added to the script*

Reload your script by pressing the **`Load data`** button, and inspect the new data model using the **`Data model viewer`** from the **`Prepare`** menu.

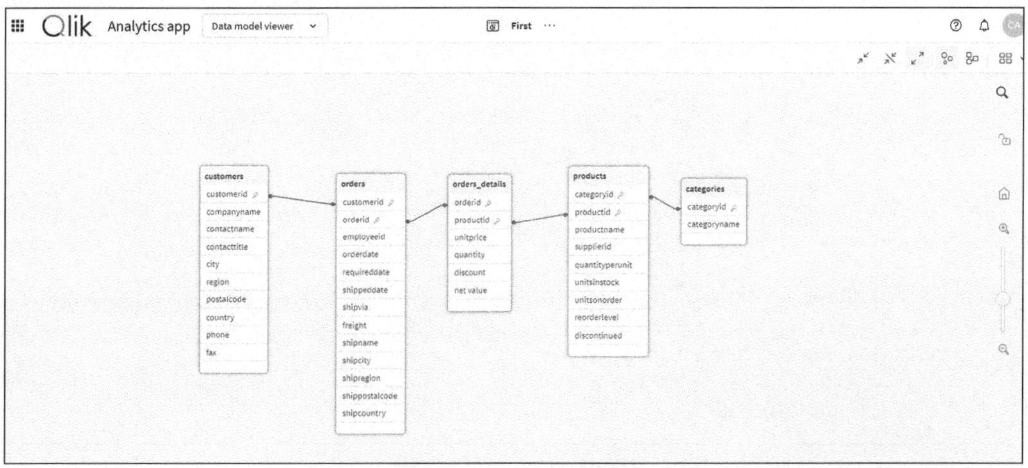

Figure 3.13: *Data Model*

The new table was added to the data model and correctly linked to the products table. This happened because both tables share a field named **`categoryid`**. This is the mechanism by which the Qlik Engine recognizes that two or more tables share fields with identical names, leading to the automatic creation of a link between these tables. Repeat the same process for loading the file suppliers.csv, selecting only the first two fields.

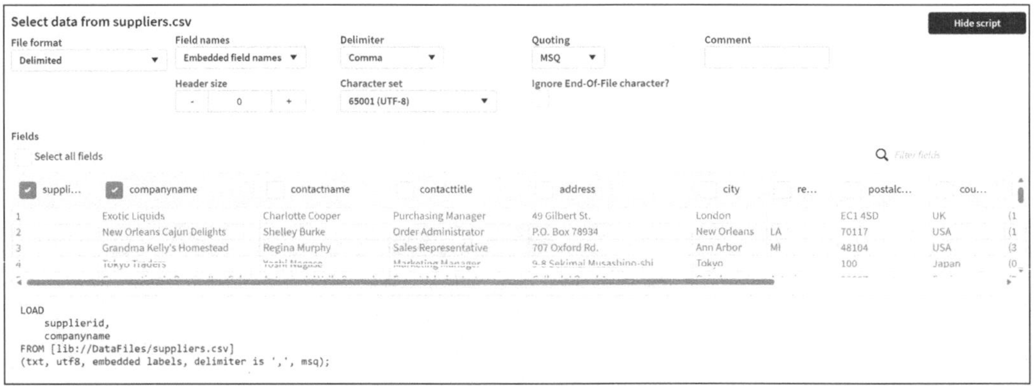

Figure 3.14: *Data Load wizard*

By reloading the script, a warning message will be displayed:

`Circular reference: One or more loops have been detected in your data-base structure. Loops may cause ambiguous results and should therefore be avoided. Loop(s) will be cut by setting one or more tables as loose-ly coupled.`

Inspecting the new data model, we can see that the field **`companyname`** is already present in the **`customers`** table. The Qlik Engine created a link between both tables. This leads to the creation of a closed loop in the data model.

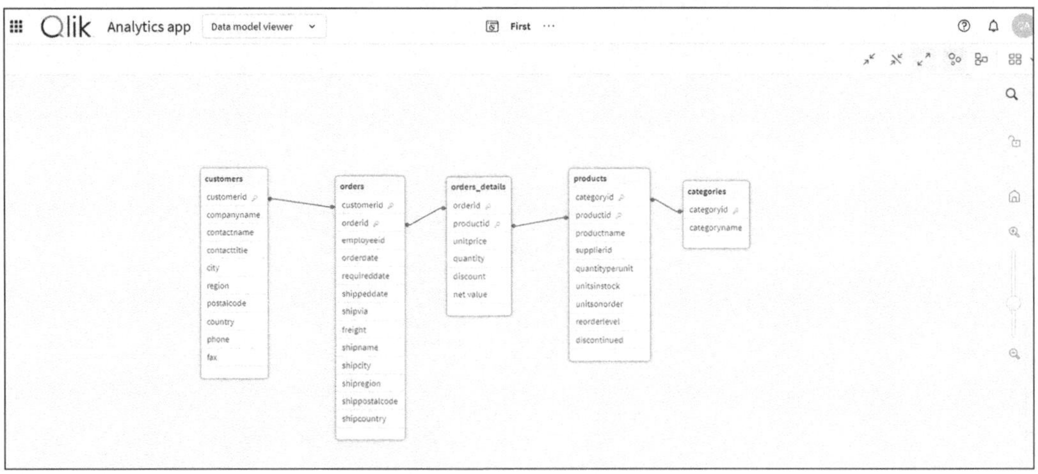

Figure 3.15: *Data model with loops*

If there are circular references (loops) in a data structure, the tables are associated in such a way that there is more than one path of association between two fields. Such circular references can lead to unexpected outcomes and often indicate a misunderstanding of what is represented in a particular field. In your example, the **"companyname"** field in both tables may embody different concepts; in the **"customer"** table, it represents the customer's name, while in the **"suppliers"** table, it represents the supplier's name. To address this, breaking the link is crucial, and one straightforward method is to rename the field in one or all the tables involved. Edit the script to look like the following code:

```
LOAD
    supplierid,
    companyname as suppliername
FROM [lib://DataFiles/suppliers.csv]
(txt, utf8, embedded labels, delimiter is ',', msq);
```

Reloading the script again, the circular reference is fixed, and you inspect the data model to check how the tables are linked.

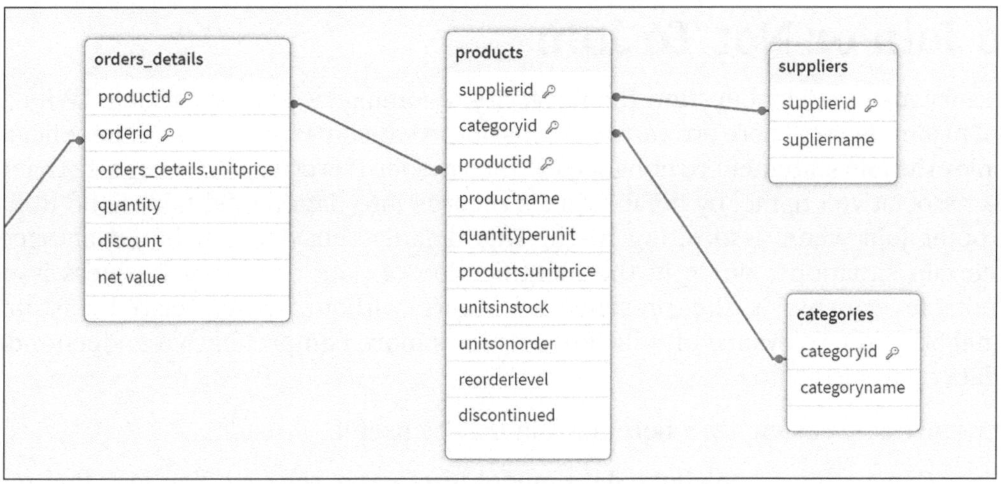

Figure 3.16: *Data Model with dimensions*

Joins

In the context of a Qlik Sense script, a join constitutes an operation that involves the junction of data from two tables based on shared fields. This step is used to create a consolidated dataset, harmonizing pertinent information across distinct tables. Qlik Sense offers support for various types of joins, encompassing inner joins, outer joins, and concatenations, thereby providing users with a flexible approach to structuring data connections tailored to specific analytical requirements. This capability empowers users with the proficiency to effectively leverage their data, seamlessly integrating and correlating information from diverse sources within the Qlik Sense environment.

Datasets

Original Table		
CustID	Name	Country
0001	Customer 0001	US
0002	Customer 0002	UK
0003	Customer 0003	US
0004	Customer 0004	CA

Added Table		
CustID	Address	Phone
0001	1456, Drive RD	(555) 123-4567
0002	456, Smith driveway	+44 20 7946 0958
0005	789, Whashington RD	(555) 156-9567

Operation	Result				
Left Join	CustID	Name	Country	Address	Phone
	0001	Customer 0001	US	1456, Drive RD	(555) 123-4567
	0002	Customer 0002	UK	456, Smith driveway	+44 20 7946 0958
	0003	Customer 0003	US		
	0004	Customer 0004	CA		
Inner Join	CustID	Name	Country	Address	Phone
	0001	Customer 0001	US	1456, Drive RD	(555) 123-4567
	0002	Customer 0002	UK	456, Smith driveway	+44 20 7946 0958
Outer Join	CustID	Name	Country	Address	Phone
	0001	Customer 0001	US	1456, Drive RD	(555) 123-4567
	0002	Customer 0002	UK	456, Smith driveway	+44 20 7946 0958
	0003	Customer 0003	US		
	0004	Customer 0004	CA		
	0005			789, Whashington RD	(555) 156-9567
Right Join	CustID	Name	Country	Address	Phone
	0001	Customer 0001	US	1456, Drive RD	(555) 123-4567
	0002	Customer 0002	UK	456, Smith driveway	+44 20 7946 0958
	0005			789, Whashington RD	(555) 156-9567

***Figure 3.17**: Joins Types*

To Join or Not To Join

A reader may initially question the necessity of joining two tables, asking, "*Why do I need to join them?*" There are various scenarios in which users may find it beneficial to employ the join statement to enhance the data model. It is crucial to recognize that the Qlik Associative Engine, by default, loads records into data model tables and utilizes an outer join when associating them. This default behavior can be advantageous in certain situations, aiding in the identification of data quality or business issues. A notable example is the presence of orders without an associated customer, highlighting the relevance of utilizing joins for a more comprehensive understanding of data relationships.

Let us give some examples where the join may be useful.

- **Converting a snowflake data model into a star schema:** You may find more information about why data models in a star schema perform better than snowflake models. Let us consider the following example from our last load, where the table suppliers and the table categories only exist to give a textual representation of the category and the supplier's name. Every selection made in those two fields will force the Qlik Associative Engine to go across one additional hop to apply the selections to the entire data model.

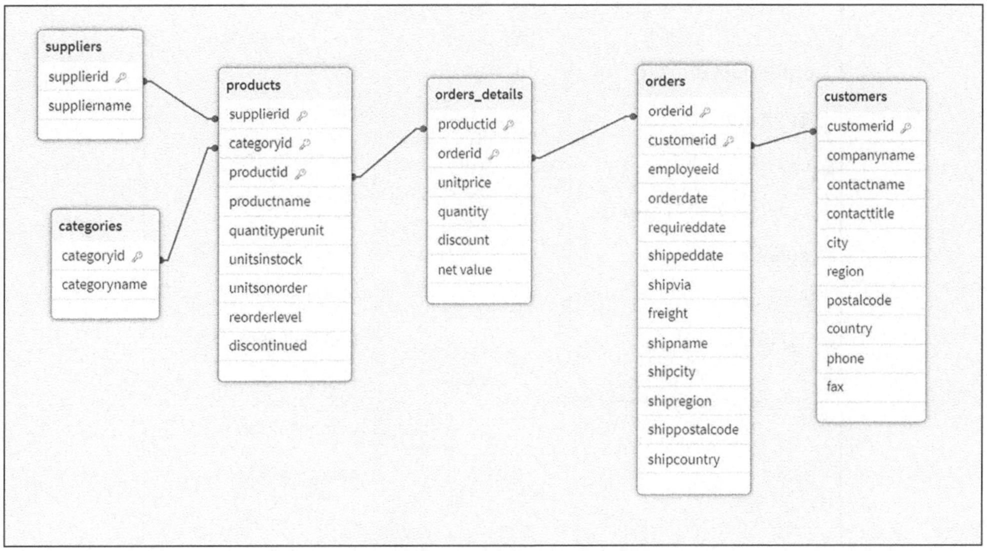

Figure 3.18: *Snowflake model*

Applying a JOIN to this segment of the data model can be achieved in the following manner:

```
left join(products)
LOAD
    categoryid,
    categoryname
FROM [lib://DataFiles/categories.csv]
(txt, codepage is 28591, embedded labels, delimiter is ',', msq);
drop Field categoryid;

left join(products)
LOAD
    supplierid,
    companyname as supliername
FROM [lib://DataFiles/suppliers.csv]
(txt, utf8, embedded labels, delimiter is ',', msq);
drop Field supplierid;
```

Figure 3.19: *Joins in the script*

Upon the execution of the script, the outcome will be the creation of a more compact data model, eliminating the need for **supplierid** and **categoryid**.

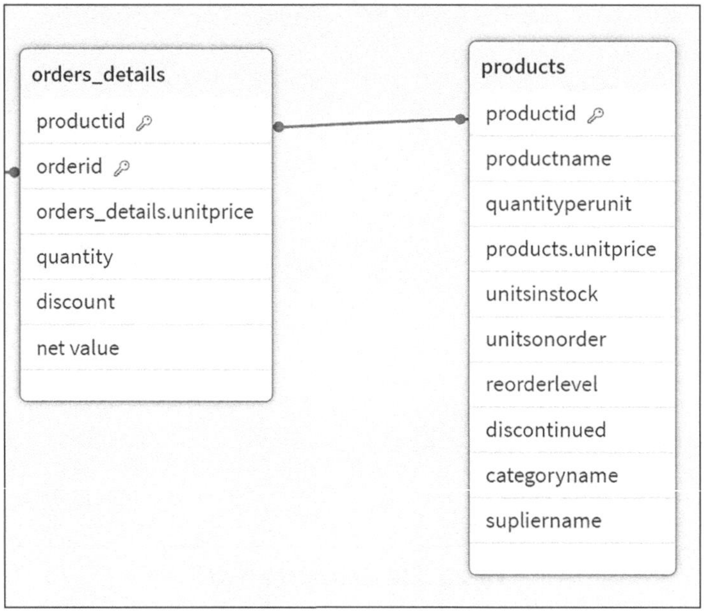

***Figure 3.20**: Dimensions flatted*

- **Reducing a target table based on a secondary master dataset:** You can use this approach, for example, to trim an orders table based on the customers dataset, only keeping orders that have a customer associated.

```
orders:
LOAD
    orderid,
    customerid,
    employeeid,
    orderdate,
    requireddate,
    shippeddate,
    shipvia,
    freight,
    shipname,
    shipcity,
    shipregion,
    shippostalcode,
    shipcountry
FROM [lib://DataFiles/orders.csv]
(txt, utf8, embedded labels, delimiter is ',', msq);
Right Join(orders)
LOAD
    customerid
FROM [lib://DataFiles/customers.csv]
(txt, utf8, embedded labels, delimiter is ',', msq);
```

***Figure 3.21**: Join in the script*

Aggregations

In Qlik Sense, aggregations refer to the process of summarizing or combining data to derive meaningful insights from large datasets. Aggregations are essential for performing calculations and analyses on grouped or summarized data rather than individual records. Qlik Sense supports various aggregation functions that can be applied to fields in the data model. Common aggregation functions include sum, average, count, min, and max, among others. These functions help users perform calculations on data dimensions, such as grouping sales data by product category or calculating the total revenue for each region.

Aggregations in Qlik Sense are dynamic and interactive, allowing users to explore data at different levels of granularity. The associative model in Qlik Sense enables users to aggregate data on the fly, making it easy to pivot and analyze information from multiple perspectives. Aggregations play a crucial role in creating visualizations and generating meaningful insights, empowering users to make data-driven decisions based on summarized data patterns and trends.

In certain scenarios where the data model in Qlik Sense is extensive, with millions or billions of rows, optimizing performance becomes crucial. Pre-aggregating data at the script level is an effective strategy to address this challenge. By pre-aggregating, you essentially perform summarization and consolidation of data during the script execution, storing only the essential information needed for analysis in memory.

This optimization technique ensures that the data model remains efficient and responsive, especially when dealing with large datasets. It allows users to strike a balance between retaining necessary insights and conserving system resources, making data analysis in Qlik Sense more streamlined and expedited. Pre-aggregation at the script level is a proactive measure to enhance the overall performance and responsiveness of the application, ensuring a more seamless experience for users interacting with extensive datasets.

At script level, you can use the **GROUP BY** clause of the **LOAD** statement to perform the aggregations. This clause is used to group rows based on specified fields, and it is often paired with aggregation functions to summarize data within each group. Here is an example:

```
SalesData:
LOAD
    Product,
    SUM(Sales) as TotalSales,
    AVG(Quantity) as AvgQuantity
RESIDENT RawSalesData
GROUP BY Product;
```

In this example, the script loads data from the `RawSalesData` table, grouping it by the "Product" field. The result is a new table (SalesData) where each unique product has total sales and average quantity calculated based on the grouped data. The GROUP BY clause is crucial for aggregating data at different levels in the Qlik Sense data model.

Loops

In Qlik Sense, loop structures are integral components of the script syntax designed to automate and iterate through specific tasks, providing enhanced control and efficiency in data transformations. These loop structures enable developers to repeat a set of script statements or actions based on predefined conditions or iterations, streamlining complex data processing tasks.

1. **For Each Loop:** The "for each" loop in Qlik Sense allows developers to iterate through a collection, such as fields or values, executing a set of script statements for each element in the collection. This loop structure is particularly useful when applying uniform operations to multiple entities within the data model.

```
For Each [FieldName] In FieldList
// Script statements to be executed for each field
Next
```

2. **For Loop:** The "for" loop facilitates iterative execution of script statements for a specified number of times or until a certain condition is met. This loop structure is beneficial when a repetitive action needs to be performed within a known range or condition.

```
For counter = start To end
// Script statements to be executed for each iteration
Next
```

3. **Do Loop:** The "do" loop, also known as a "do while" or "do until" loop, allows script statements to be repeated while or until a specific condition is true. This loop structure is valuable for scenarios where the number of iterations is not predetermined and the loop should continue until a certain criterion is satisfied.

```
   Do While condition
   // Script statements to be executed while the condition is
true
   Loop

   Do Until condition
   // Script statements to be executed until the condition is
true
   Loop
```

4. **Autogenerate/while:** This is an of a Load script that allows you to generate records based on the source table. In conjunction with Recno, Iterno, and Rowno they facilitate the creation of datasets according to specific rules. The following are examples illustrating these functionalities:

```
// Generate random data
MockData:
Load
        RecNo() as ID,
     'Customer ' &  RecNo() as Customer
AutoGenerate 100; // Generates 100 records


vStartDate=Num(MakeDate(2023,1,1));
vEndDate=Num(Today());
/// Generate a calendar between vStartDate and vEndDate
Calendar:
Load
     Date($(vStartDate)+RowNo()-1) as Date,
     MonthStart($(vStartDate)+RowNo()-1) as Month,
     WeekStart($(vStartDate)+RowNo()-1) as Week,
     Year($(vStartDate)+RowNo()-1) as Year
AutoGenerate 1                                  // generates one
record
While ($(vStartDate)+RowNo()-1) <= $(vEndDate);  // while vStart
< vDate
```

These loop structures enhance the scripting capabilities of Qlik Sense, providing developers with the tools to create dynamic, efficient, and flexible data transformations within the platform. By incorporating loops into scripts, developers can automate repetitive tasks, handle diverse data scenarios, and optimize the processing of complex datasets.

QVD

Qlik QlikView Data (QVD) is a proprietary file format used by Qlik applications to store and manage structured, compressed data efficiently. The QVD file format serves as a container for data tables, providing a means to optimize data storage, retrieval, and processing within the Qlik environment.

Key characteristics of Qlik QVD:

- **Optimized Storage:** QVD files are designed for efficient storage, utilizing compression techniques to minimize file size. This optimization enhances the performance of data loading and analysis within Qlik applications.
- **Incremental Data Loading:** QVD files support incremental data loading,

allowing users to add new or updated records to an existing QVD file by loading the historical data from the QVD and the fresh data from the source (database, files, and more) and then overwriting the QD file with the result. This incremental approach is valuable for managing large datasets without reloading the entire dataset each time.

- **Scripting Flexibility:** The Qlik scripting language provides flexibility in defining how data is loaded, transformed, and stored in QVD files. Developers can implement various scripting techniques to shape the data according to specific business requirements.
- **Security and Encryption**: QVD files can be encrypted to ensure data security and privacy. This is particularly important when handling sensitive or confidential information within Qlik applications.
- **Interoperability**: QVD files are compatible with both QlikView and Qlik Sense applications, promoting interoperability between these two Qlik platforms. This allows users to share and reuse QVD files across different Qlik applications seamlessly.
- **Reload Efficiency**: Due to the optimized storage and indexing, QVD files facilitate faster data reloads, contributing to improved application performance. This efficiency is crucial for delivering real-time or near-real-time insights. Just as an example, in the following screenshot, we can see that one Qlik Sense application can read 10 million records in half a minute.

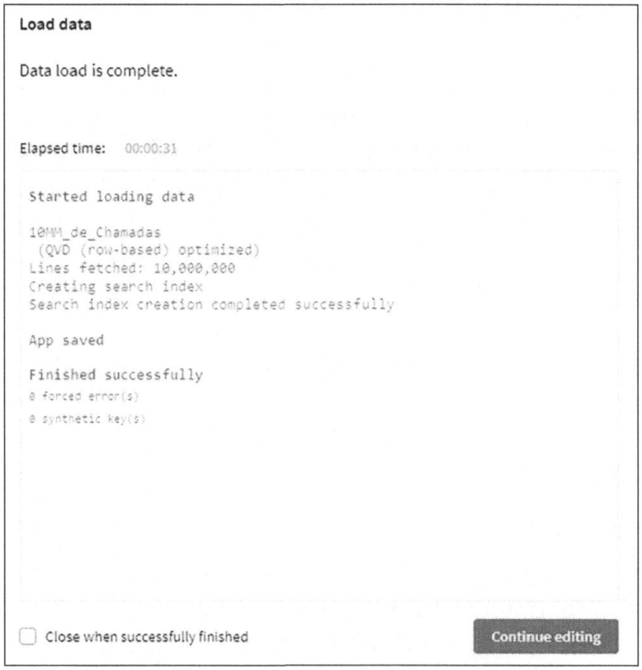

***Figure 3.22**: Script loading 10 million records*

In summary, Qlik QVD files play a vital role in the Qlik data ecosystem by providing a standardized, optimized, and secure format for storing and managing data.

Creating/Reading QVDs

Qlik scripts offer straightforward methods for generating and reading QVDs. The `STORE` command facilitates the saving of a table, previously in memory, to a QVD file on disk via a data connection. In our previous join example, incorporating the `STORE` command results in a file containing the **"products"** table, which becomes accessible for use by any application.

```
left join(products)
LOAD
    categoryid,
    categoryname
FROM [lib://DataFiles/categories.csv]
(txt, codepage is 28591, embedded labels, delimiter is ',', msq);
drop Field categoryid;

left join(products)
LOAD
    supplierid,
    companyname as supliername
FROM [lib://DataFiles/suppliers.csv]
(txt, utf8, embedded labels, delimiter is ',', msq);
drop Field supplierid;

STORE [products] INTO [lib://DataFiles/products_enriched.qvd](qvd);
```

***Figure 3.23**: Storing a QVD*

If another application requires the same data, users can simply load it using the standard process outlined in the **"Loading Data"** section.

```
LOAD
    productid,
    productname,
    quantityperunit,
    products.unitprice,
    unitsinstock,
    unitsonorder,
    reorderlevel,
    discontinued,
    categoryname,
    suppliername
FROM [lib://DataFiles/products_enriched.qvd]
(qvd);
```

***Figure 3.24**: Enriched table*

Script Structure for Larger Projects

When Qlik applications become more complex than reading the files that we described in this section, some governance and structure need to be added to the scripts. The decision to split Qlik Sense apps into extract and load phases depends on various factors, such as data volume, complexity, and performance considerations. Here are some situations where it may be beneficial to separate the extract and load phases:

- **Large Datasets:** When dealing with large datasets, splitting into extract and load phases allows for more efficient data handling. Extracting data from the source first and then loading it into Qlik Sense can enhance performance.
- **Complex Transformations**: If the data requires complex transformations or calculations before loading into Qlik Sense, separating the extract and load phases makes the scripting process more manageable and modular.
- **Incremental Loading**: For scenarios where incremental loading is necessary (loading only new or updated records), having distinct extract and load phases can simplify the implementation of incremental data loading strategies.
- **Parallel Execution**: Separating extract and load activities enables parallel execution. Extracting data from multiple sources simultaneously and then loading it concurrently can reduce overall processing time.
- **Data Source Dependencies**: When data is sourced from different systems or databases with varying update schedules, splitting into extract and load phases allows for better management of dependencies between data sources.
- **Performance Optimization**: In cases where the extraction process is resource-intensive, decoupling it from the loading phase can help optimize system resources and improve overall performance.
- **Data Source Constraints**: If data sources have limitations or restrictions on extraction operations, a phased approach allows adhering to those constraints during the extraction phase without affecting the loading process.
- **Modular Scripting**: Adopting a modular scripting approach, where the extract and load phases are separated, promotes script organization and facilitates easier maintenance.

It is essential to evaluate the specific requirements and characteristics of each Qlik Sense app to determine the most suitable approach for the extract and load phases. Considerations should include data complexity, update frequency, system resources, and overall performance objectives.

One architecture that can be implemented in large projects is very similar to the medallion architecture on data lakes. The Medallion Architecture in data lakes refers to a layered approach for organizing and managing data within the data lake environment. The architecture typically consists of three layers: Bronze, Silver, and

Gold. Each layer represents a stage of data refinement and serves specific purposes in terms of data quality, processing, and accessibility. Here's an overview of each layer:

- **Bronze Layer: Raw and Ingested Data**: This is the initial layer where raw and ingested data is stored without significant processing. It includes data in its original form as it enters the QVD layers. The script basically performs the extraction from the sources and stores the data as it is in a QVD. The primary goal of the Bronze layer is to preserve all incoming data, providing a historical record of the original data sources.
- **Silver Layer: Cleaned and Structured Data**: It involves processing and cleaning data to make it more structured and standardized. It includes data cleansing and transformation operations. Data quality checks and validation are performed in the Silver layer to identify and address any issues before the data progresses to the next layer. Usually makes intensive use of the resources described in this section, such as joins, loops, and so on.
- **Gold Layer: High-Quality and Business-Ready Data**: It represents the highest level of refinement, where data is optimized for specific business use cases. It includes aggregated, enriched, and business-ready datasets. Data in the Gold layer is optimized for performance and may be denormalized to support efficient querying and analytics.

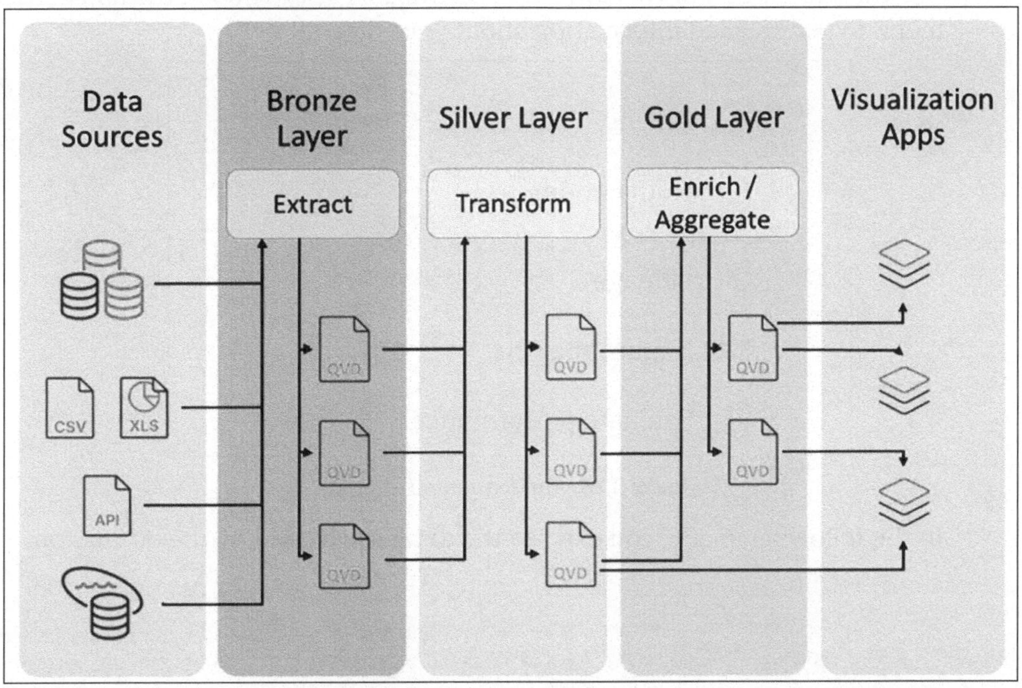

Figure 3.25: *Medallion Architecture*

Modeling Data

This section is not meant to be a final guide to best practices in the Qlik Data Model. Please check the Additional Resources section to have access to awesome blog posts and content.

There are several recommendations when loading data into the Qlik Associative Engine that will help your model be consistent, easy to maintain, and efficient.

- The preferred data model for Qlik is a **normalized star schema** due to its efficiency and clarity. While there are cases where a snowflake schema may be necessary to manage table widths, it can introduce inefficiency as associations traverse intermediary tables. On the other hand, flat tables (a single concatenated table) are inefficient, lack developer discipline, and exhibit scalability challenges when reusing data subsets across multiple apps. In contrast, a star schema typically includes a central fact table with dimensional keys and numerical fields used for calculations (example, Quantity, Sales amount). Surrounding the fact table are dimensional tables containing corresponding attributes, such as a product table with details like product number, product group, and product description.
- Use the **`Evaluate Performance`** option available at the hub in the app context menu to get detailed information about your data model.

Figure 3.26: *Application evaluation*

- In the following image, you can see the details provided by the evaluation.

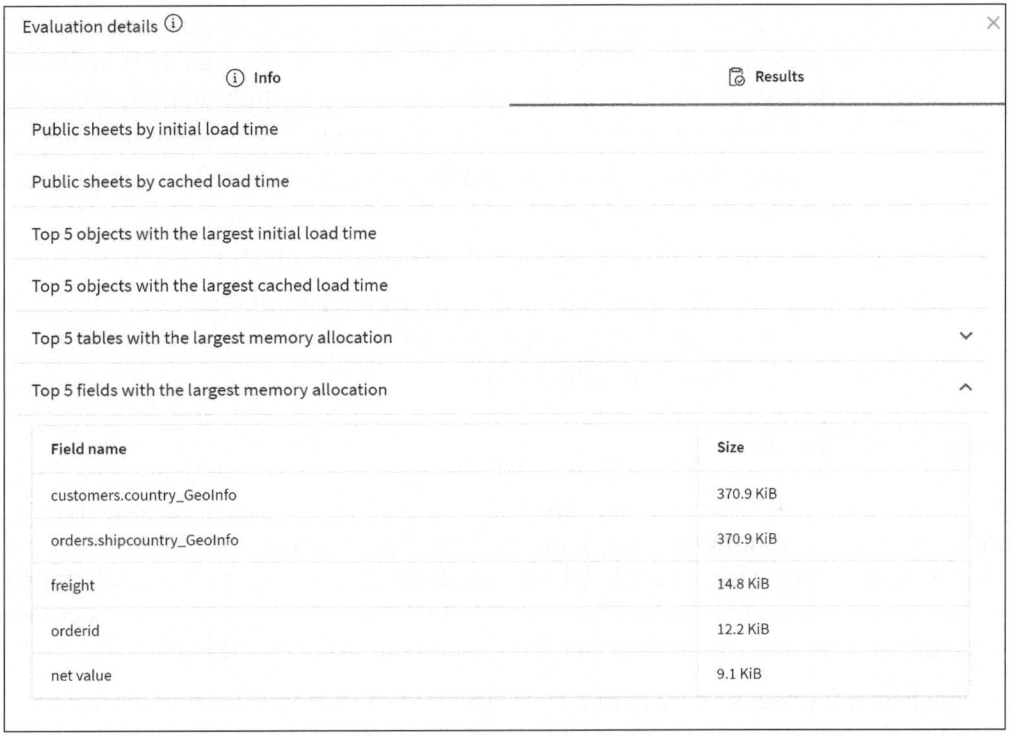

Figure 3.27: *Application evaluation*

- Avoid **data islands;** data islands are tables that are not linked to the model and are disconnected from it. Except for those tiny ones used for additional functionality, such as a list of currencies or languages, they should be avoided.
- **Drop** all tables and fields that are **not used** in any expression, measure, or key. Loading data that is not used will degrade the platform.
- Resolve **synthetic keys** to enhance efficiency using the **`autonumber`** function family, leading to numerical and optimized keys.
- **Eliminate circular references** in the data model.
- Apply **data formatting** directly to the data model to eliminate the necessity of applying it within the measures. Examples: apply the correct date format (MM/DD/YYYY) or money to the currency values during the script.
- **Truncate** or **round** numerical values to their meaningful precision to maintain a compact dataset. For instance, datetimes where only the date part is relevant can be converted to **`date(trunc(d_field))`** in the script. Similarly, currency values with excessive decimal precision can be safely rounded without significant loss of precision.
- **Intuitively name fields** for clarity and hide unused or compound fields. Tables should have intuitive names for easy filtering.

- Conduct **aggregations** on data that does not require detailed analysis. For instance, consider a contact center application built to analyze millions of daily calls. Instead of loading detailed call records, apply aggregation at the script level to retain in memory only the data essential for meaningful analysis.
- Avoid reloading data for previous-period calculations; instead, implement a robust calendar.
- For multiple dates, consider canonical dates with a master calendar.
- Ensure dimensional tables have a record for every value, appending missing link values and populating with arbitrary values such as a hyphen or 'Unknown' for insights in Qlik Sense.

Conclusion

This marks the conclusion of our chapter, where we explored various facets of data modeling. Throughout this journey, we focused on the building aspects of a comprehensive data model, which involved combining tables and applying transformative processes. With this refined data model in place, we successfully crafted our first sheet, now well-prepared for consumption by end-users.

We explored the process of writing joins, implementing data load constraints, and leveraging debugging options for script optimization. Furthermore, our exploration extends to QVDs, an exceptionally efficient data storage format that enhances Qlik's ability to store and manage data with efficacy.

We encourage the reader to go through all the assets in the **Additional Resources** for a more comprehensive view of all the aspects discussed in this chapter.

In the upcoming chapter, our attention will shift towards the scripting resources offered by Qlik Sense.

Multiple Choice Questions

1. What is the purpose of the Qlik Sense Data Load Editor?
   a. Visualization of data
   b. Scripting and loading data
   c. User interface customization
   d. Security configuration
2. Which file format can be used for external data sources in Qlik Sense Data Load Editor?
   a. .txt
   b. .csv

   c. .xlsx
   d. All of the above
3. What role does the LOAD statement play in Qlik Sense scripting?
   a. Data visualization
   b. Data extraction
   c. Data encryption
   d. Data security
4. How can you create a new table in Qlik Sense using the Data Load Editor?
   a. Use the CREATE TABLE statement
   b. Execute a LOAD statement
   c. Use the ADD TABLE button
   d. Tables are automatically created
5. What is the purpose of the GROUP BY clause in Qlik Sense scripting?
   a. Filtering data
   b. Sorting data
   c. Grouping and aggregating data
   d. Joins between tables
6. Which option is used for debugging scripts in Qlik Sense Data Load Editor?
   a. Breakpoints
   b. Debugging console
   c. Error logs
   d. All of the above
7. What is the significance of the STORE command in Qlik Sense scripting?
   a. Loading data from a file
   b. Creating synthetic keys
   c. Saving a table to a QVD file
   d. Data encryption
8. How can you add a breakpoint to a specific line in the script for debugging?
   a. Click the line
   b. Use the DEBUG button

   c. Type "`Breakpoint`" in the script
   d. Breakpoints are added automatically
9. Which function is used for aggregation in Qlik Sense scripting?
   a. `TRANSFORM`
   b. `AGGREGATE`
   c. `GROUP BY`
   d. `RESIDENT`
10. What does the `GROUP BY` clause do when used in combination with the LOAD statement?
    a. Sorts the data
    b. Groups data based on specified fields
    c. Filters the data
    d. Joins tables based on common fields

Answers

1. b
2. d
3. b
4. b
5. c
6. d
7. c
8. a
9. c
10. b

References

1. Best Practices for Data Modeling. *Qlik Help*. [Online] https://help.qlik.com/en-US/sense/November2023/Subsystems/Hub/Content/Sense_Hub/DataModeling/best-practices-data-modeling.htm.
2. Qliktech. Qlik Help. [Online]: https://help.qlik.com/#anchor-1.

3. Qliktech. Best practices for choosing visualization types. *Qlik.com Help.* [Online]: https://help.qlik.com/en-US/sense/November2023/Subsystems/Hub/Content/Sense_Hub/Visualizations/when-to-use-visualizations.htm.

4. Dashboard, Analysis, Reporting (DAR) . *Qlik Community* . [Online]: https://community.qlik.com/t5/Design/DAR-methodology/ba-p/1466733.

Additional Resources

The following links are complimentary to this book, bringing more resources to the reader, with more examples and details.

- **Beginning with the Basics** (https://help.qlik.com/en-US/cloud-services/Subsystems/Hub/Content/Sense_Hub/Tutorials/introduction-beginning-with-basics.htm): A centralized documentation for all Qlik solutions and products. It is open and publicly available.
- **Navigating the User Interface** (https://help.qlik.com/en-US/cloud-services/Subsystems/Hub/Content/Sense_Hub/UserInterface/navigate-user-interface.htm): Reviewing all the options in the user interface
- **Data Manager** (https://help.qlik.com/en-US/cloud-services/Subsystems/Hub/Content/Sense_Hub/LoadData/data-management.htm): Reviewing all the options available in the Data Manager
- **Qlik Best Practice – Data Modelling in Qlik Sense** https://ometis.co.uk/blog-news/qlik-best-practice-data-modelling-in-qlik-sense
- **Best practices for data modeling** https://help.qlik.com/en-US/qlikview/May2023/Subsystems/Client/Content/QV_QlikView/LoadData/best-practices-data-modeling.htm
- **Optimizing app performance** https://help.qlik.com/en-US/sense/May2023/Subsystems/Hub/Content/Sense_Hub/Apps/app-performance.htm

Chapter 4
Set Analysis

Introduction

In the context of Qlik Analytics solutions, Set Analysis stands out as a robust feature that offers users a powerful means to manipulate data analysis. It allows Qlik developers to define custom data sets based on specific conditions, providing precise control over the scope of analysis. This chapter aims to unravel the complexities of Set Analysis, shedding light on its syntax, application, and the significant impact it can have on data visualization and interpretation within Qlik Sense.

Set Analysis brings a dynamic approach to data selection and aggregation, offering a flexible method for representing data. By enabling users to create virtual sets based on customized criteria, Qlik Analytics solutions becomes a versatile tool for tailoring data views to meet specific business needs. As we navigate through this chapter, we will explore Set Analysis expressions, understand how to construct complex conditions, utilize modifiers, and master the various functions that Set Analysis offers. This chapter serves as a user-friendly guide to unlocking the potential of Set Analysis within the Qlik Analytics solutions environment, allowing users to enhance their analytical capabilities and gain deeper insights from their data.

Structure

In this chapter, we will discuss the following topics:

- Introduction to Set Analysis in Qlik Analytics Solutions
- Syntax and Structure
- Modifiers, Identifiers and Operators
- Advanced Techniques in Set Analysis
- Troubleshooting and Debugging

Introduction to Set Analysis

Set analysis in Qlik Sense provides a method for specifying a distinct set or grouping of data values that are different from the regular set determined by the existing selections. In the typical scenario, selections automatically shape the dataset for aggregation functions such as Sum, Count, Max, and Avg. However, with set analysis, you can create an independent group, allowing you to showcase specific values, such as the market share of a product across all regions, regardless of the ongoing selections. The strength of set analysis shines in diverse comparisons, such as identifying the top-selling products versus the underperforming ones or conducting year-over-year analyses.

Let's simplify this by using the following example, considering this dataset:

customerid	companyname	city	country
ALFKI	Alfreds Futterkiste	Berlin	Germany
ANATR	Ana Trujillo Emparedados y helados	México D.F.	Mexico
ANTON	Antonio Moreno Taquería	México D.F.	Mexico
AROUT	Around the Horn	London	UK
BERGS	Berglunds snabbköp	Luleå	Sweden
BLAUS	Blauer See Delikatessen	Mannheim	Germany
BLONP	Blondesddsl père et fils	Strasbourg	France
BOLID	Bólido Comidas preparadas	Madrid	Spain
BONAP	Bon app'	Marseille	France
BOTTM	Bottom-Dollar Markets	Tsawassen	Canada
BSBEV	B's Beverages	London	UK
CACTU	Cactus Comidas para llevar	Buenos Aires	Argentina
CENTC	Centro comercial Moctezuma	México D.F.	Mexico
CHOPS	Chop-suey Chinese	Bern	Switzerland
COMMI	Comércio Mineiro	Sao Paulo	Brazil
CONSH	Consolidated Holdings	London	UK
DRACD	Drachenblut Delikatessen	Aachen	Germany

Table 4.1: *Data Sample that will be used in the examples*

If we use the expression `Count(customerid)` and the user makes selections:

- "*Germany*" in the **`country`** field, the result will be 3 because only 3 records match that selection.
- "*Germany*" in the **`country`** field, and **`"Berlin"`** in the **`city`** field the result will be 1 because only 1 record satisfies both selections at same time (customer **`ALFKI`**).

By adding set analysis to the expression, we can override the user's current selection. One example could be **`Count({<country={'Brazil'}>}customerid)`** returning 1 for any possible selection in the field **`country`.** The count without Set Analysis depends on the current selection. For example, **`Count(customerid)`** would return 1 if only Brazil is selected, 3 if Germany is selected, or 4 if both Brazil and Germany are selected.

Syntax and Structure

To use set analysis, we need to define *set expressions* that represent the field list that will overwrite the current selection set.

There are some rules to create a set expression:

- Must be enclosed by braces {}
- Can have multiple **sets** delimited by `<>`
- Operators such as intersection and union combine different sets
- Can be used:
  - Inside a Qlik expression like **`Count({<country={'Brazil'}>}customerid)`**
  - Outside a Qlik expression like **`{<country={'Brazil'}>} Count(customerid)`**

A set can be created using:

- Delimited by **`<>`**, like **`< country={'Brazil'} >`**
- Containing a field list and the search expressions such as **`< country={'Brazil'}, city={ 'Sao Paulo'} >`**

Modifiers, Identifiers, and Operators

Qlik Set Analysis provides a powerful syntax for users to define and analyze subsets of data consisting of various elements such as modifiers, operators, and identifiers.

- **Identifiers**: It establishes the connection between the set expression and the field values or expression under evaluation. It is placed just after the opening curly brace **`"{''`** and identifies the set expression evaluation scope. Some examples: **`$, 1, BookMarkSales, State`.** The most common identifiers are listed:

Identifier	Description
$	Represents the records of the current selection. It is the default identifier. If nothing is included as identifier, it means this will be used. Example: **`Count({$<country={'Brazil'}>}customerid)`** is exactly equals to **`Count({<country={'Brazil'}>}customerid)`** and represents Count all customers where country is Brazil and keep other selections.

1	Instructs Qlik Engine to ignore all selections. Example: **Count({1<country={'Brazil'}>}customerid)** represents Count all customers where country is Brazil and ignoring all selections.
$1	Represents the previous selection. $2 represents the previous selection-but-one, and so on. Example: **Count({$1<country={'Brazil'}>}customerid)** represents Count all customers where country is Brazil, considering the previous selection.
BM	Represents the selections made in the Bookmark BM. Example: **Count({BMLY<country={'Brazil'}>}customerid)** represents Count all customers where country is Brazil and considering the bookmark **BMLY** selections.

***Table 4.2:** Identifiers*

- **Modifiers**: A set modifier, enclosed in angle brackets, can alter the default selection. It consists of field names followed by selections, modifying the set expression using a fixed list or a search expression:
    - **Fixed list**: The values are used as they are. We can use singlequotes or no quotes at all. Example **<Year={2023,2024}>** represents the sales from the years 2023/2024.
    - **Search Expression**: It is delimited by double quotes and allows any search capability. Please refer to the Cheat Sheet (1) to see all the search capabilities. Just one example: **<Customer={"=Sum(Sales)>100000"}>** represents customer selection based on sales performance.

Example	Meaning
<country={'Brazil'}>	matches the selection *Brazil* in the field **country**
<country=country+{'Brazil'}>	matches the selection *Brazil* in the field **country** added to the current selection in the same field
<country={Brazil,Germany}>	matches the selection *Brazil and* Germany in the field **country**
<country={Brazil|Germany}>	matches the selection *Brazil or Germany* in the field **country**
<country={"Bra*"}>	field **country** starts with *Bra*
<country={"*Bra*"}>	field **country** contains *Bra*
<salesyear={2024}>	that field **salesyear** = 2024

<Customer={"=Sum(Sales)>100000"}>	All records where the customer has more than 100K in sales
<salesyear={">2020<=2023"}>	All records that field **salesyear** is between 2021 and 2023
<Customer={"^A"}>	All records where the customer has a word starting with A. Examples: Acme Co, The Awesome Co

***Table 4.3:** Modifiers*

- **Operators**: They are symbols or keywords used to perform specific operations on sets of data. They allow you to include, exclude, or intersect parts of or whole data sets within the set analysis syntax. Some common set analysis operators include:
    - **Intersection Operator ("*"):** Represents the intersection of two sets. For example, **<Customer={"=Sum(Sales)>100000"}>*<Country={USA}>** the sets that attend both selections at the same time.
    - **Union Operator "+":** Represents the union of two sets. For example, **<Customer={"=Sum(Sales)>100000"}>+<Country={USA}>** the sets that attend the sales condition or the country selection.
    - **Exclusion Operator ("-"):** Excludes one set from another. For example, **<Customer={"=Sum(Sales)>100000"}>-<Country={USA}>** excludes the US companies from the customer list that had the sales over 100k.

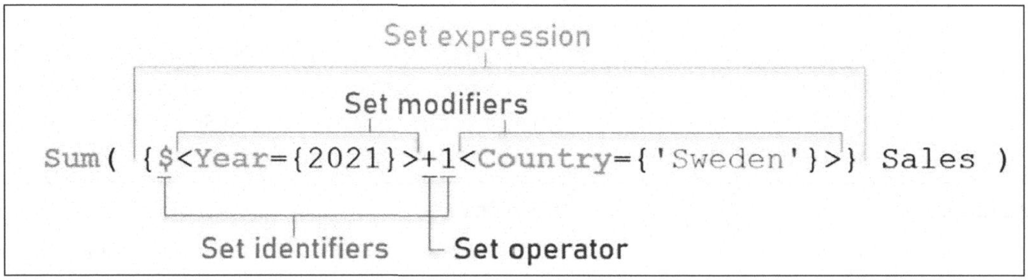

***Figure 4.1**: Set Expression structure*

Advanced Techniques in Set Analysis

In the advanced section of Qlik Set Analysis, users can explore nuanced techniques for crafting intricate expressions. These advanced methods offer increased flexibility and precision in data analysis. Topics include combining multiple conditions, handling nested expressions, and addressing complexities in various scenarios. This section aims to provide users with the expertise to extract detailed insights and maximize the analytical capabilities of Qlik Sense.

Inner and Outer Set Expressions

Set expressions are typically used within an aggregation function, yet they can also be applied outside of any function. This means that the selection defined by the expression will affect all subsequent expressions. Using outer set expressions in Qlik Set Analysis is advisable in scenarios where you need to apply a consistent selection or filter across multiple measures or calculations within your analysis. This approach ensures that the specified set expression criteria are uniformly applied, providing a coherent and unified view of the data.

Example:

```
Sum({<Year={2024}>}Sales)
```

Can be converted to

```
{<Year={2024}>}Sum(Sales)
```

In the aforementioned situation, the reading effort and the final result is the same, no improvement was added.

Now, let us consider the following example:

```
Sum({<Year={2024}>}Sales)/Count({<Year={2024}>}Customer)
```

Can be converted to the following expression, making it shorter and easier to read:

```
{<Year={2024}>}Sum(Sales)/Count(Customer)
```

When a set expression is utilized outside of aggregation functions, it impacts the whole expression. However, if it is contained within parenthesis, these parenthesis then specify its scope. In the following example of lexical scoping, the set expression is applied exclusively to the aggregation within the parenthesis, allowing us to make a comparison between two years.

```
({<Year={2024}>}Sum(Sales)/Count(Customer)) /  ({<Year={2023}>}
Sum(Sales)/Count(Customer))
```

Element Set Assignment

The way two selections merge depends on the element set assignment. A standard equals sign prioritizes the inner set expression's selection, while without it, an implicit set operator is applied.

{<Field={value}>}: This syntax overrides any existing selection in "Field" with the inner selection.

{<Field+={value}>}: This syntax combines the inner selection with any existing selection in "Field" through a union operation.

`{<Field-={value}>}`:- This syntax combines the inner selection with any existing selection in "Field," deselecting the value from the selection

`{<Field*={value}>}`: This syntax merges the inner selection with any existing selection in "Field" via an intersection operation.

Element Functions `P()` and `E()`

In Qlik Set Analysis, **`P()`** and **`E()`** are powerful functions used to dynamically define sets based on the current selections in the application.

- **`P()`** stands for Possible values. It returns the set of all possible values for a field based on the current selections. This function is particularly useful when you want to include only the values in a field that are possible within the current selection context, effectively allowing your expressions to dynamically adapt based on user interactions. Example: **`sum({<Month=P(Month)>}Sales).`**
- **`E()`** stands for Excluded values. It returns the set of values that are currently excluded based on the current selections. This can be useful for highlighting or analyzing data that is not currently selected, providing insights into what data is being filtered out by the current selection state. Example: **`sum({<Month=E(Month)>}Sales).`**

These functions can be combined to form dynamic analysis expressions. Consider an example where we aim to analyze the sales ratio between a user-defined customer list (selections may be made based on criteria such as region, customer category, salesperson, and so on) and those customers not selected. Essentially, this involves calculating what percentage the selected customer sales represent in comparison to those of the unselected customers.

A very simple expression can return this value:

```
sum({<Customer=P(Customer)>}Sales) / sum({<Customer=E(Customer)>}Sales)
```

The aforementioned expression represents the sum of sales of the possible customers (affected by any selection in any field) divided by sum of sales of the excluded customers (affected by the same selection).

Combining Multiple Conditions

In Set Analysis, the ability to combine multiple conditions is a powerful feature. This feature allows users to craft intricate criteria using logical operators, such as AND, OR, and NOT, enabling precise data filtering. This flexibility is crucial for tailored analysis, providing granular control for complex business scenarios. Combining multiple conditions offers users the capability to define nuanced rules for data selection, facilitating a detailed exploration of relationships and dependencies within complex datasets. This technique enhances the ability to extract valuable insights, contributing to informed decision-making.

Here are a few examples of Set Analysis with multiple conditions:

Use Case	Example	Meaning
AND	Sum({ <Category={'Electronics'}, Year={2022}> } Sales)	Sums the sales for the Electronics category in the year 2022.
OR	Sum({ <Category={'Electronics'}> +<Category={'Clothing'}> } Sales)	This sums the sales for either the Electronics or Clothing category
AND OR	Sum({ <Category={'Electronics'}, Year={2022}> + <Category={'Clothing'}> } Sales)	This sums the sales for Electronics in 2022 and Clothing for all years
NOT	Sum({ <Category={'Electronics'}, Year-={'2021'}> } Sales)	Sums the sales for Electronics but excludes the year 2021
Multiple AND	Sum({<Category={'Electronics'}, Year={2022}, ProductType={"*Mobiles*"}>} Sales)	Sums the sales for Electronics for the year 2022 and only products that contains the word mobiles
Exclusion	Sum({ <Category={'Electronics'}, Year={"*"}>- <Year={'2023,2024'}> } Sales)	Sums sales for Electronics for all years except 2023/2024

Table 4.4: *Multiple conditions examples*

These examples showcase the flexibility of Qlik Sense Set Analysis in constructing intricate conditions for data selection.

Dynamic Calculations

Set Analysis enables users to perform dynamic calculations, offering flexibility and context-aware data analysis. A key feature is its ability to establish dynamic conditions based on variables or functions, allowing users to adjust calculations in real-time, ensuring effortless navigation and analysis as requirements change.

When Set Analysis expressions incorporate expressions enclosed in dollar signs (example, **`$(variable)`**), the dollar expansion ensures that the expression's value is substituted into the expression during evaluation. This dynamic substitution enables real-time adjustments based on user selections, timeframes, or other dynamic factors, resulting in context-sensitive evaluations that respond to user interactions.

The evaluation process involves replacing the variable with its current value at the moment of execution. As users interact with the data, altering selections or variable values, Set Analysis adapts accordingly, delivering a tailored and responsive analysis experience. Dollar sign evaluation empowers users to dynamically calculate expressions, combining available Qlik Sense engine functions for set modifiers, allowing the creation of dynamic expressions.

Let us explore examples that showcase the use of variables and set analysis expansion for dynamic calculations based on the following table:

Date	Sales	Year	Month	YearMonth	categoryname
4/18/2022	$2861.10	2022	4	202204	Beverages
8/19/2023	$4011.58	2023	8	202308	Beverages
4/26/2022	$2937.83	2022	4	202204	Beverages
11/9/2021	$3478.97	2021	11	202111	Beverages
4/10/2022	$4890.66	2022	4	202204	Beverages
3/25/2022	$637.36	2022	3	202203	Beverages
3/17/2022	$735.04	2022	3	202203	Beverages
5/4/2022	$1695.73	2022	5	202205	Beverages

Figure 4.2: *Data Sample to be used in this example*

Based on the aforementioned table, let us inspect some examples and the meaning:

Example	Meaning
Sum({<Category={'$(vSelectedCategory)'}>} Sales)	Here, the variable **vSelectedCategory** holds the dynamically chosen category or categories, enabling the sum of sales to adjust based on the user's selection.
Avg({<Date={">=$(=(AddMonths(Today(), -$(vMonthsBack))))<=$(=Today()))"}>} Sales)	In this example, the variable **vMonthsBack** dictates the time range for average sales calculation, dynamically adjusting the analysis window.
Sum({<Year={$(=Max(Year))}, Month={"$(=Max({<Year={$(=Max(Year))}>} Month))"}>} Sales)	**Year={$(=Max(Year))}**: It filters data for the latest year, dynamically determined by the maximum year in the dataset. **Month={"$(=Only({<Year={$(=Max(Year))}>} Month))"}**: It filters data for the max month in the latest year, ensuring a dynamic selection based on the latest year.
Sum({<YearMonth={">=$(=Max(YearMonth,11)) <=$(=Max(YearMonth))"}>} Sales)	This expression computes the rolling 12 months total sales based on the latest selected month Please note the the function Max has an optional parameter to return the nth max value.

`Sum({<categoryname={"=Sum({<Year=$(=Max(Year,2))>}Sales)>$(vLimitAnalysis)"}>}Sales)`	This expression yields the total Sales sum for categories that, in the year before the current selection, exceeded the variable **vLimitAnalysis**.

Table 4.5: *Dynamic Calculations example*

Flags

In the previous sections, we considered the dynamic evaluation of the set modifiers, leveraging very powerful analysis, but "*with great power comes great responsibility,*" according to a famous cartoon character. There are two main concerns when building complex expressions. They can hinder readability and maintenance, which is especially problematic for those needing to alter them. Additionally, in large datasets (such as hundreds of millions of rows or dozens of tables), performance can suffer from intensive set analysis calculations. Enhancing both readability and performance in these situations is crucial.

In Qlik Set Analysis, flags are commonly used within a data model to simplify expressions by pre-defining certain conditions or characteristics of the data. These flags serve as Boolean indicators (usually 0 or 1, for false or true, respectively) or integer numerical values that categorize records for easy aggregation or filtering based on specific criteria. Here are some examples of how flags can be used in Qlik Set Analysis to streamline expressions:

Example	Meaning
`Sum({$<ActiveCustomerFlag={1}>} Sales)`	A flag that indicates whether a customer is considered active (example, has made a purchase in the last 12 months). During the script, a logic to retrieve the total sales of last year for each customer is calculated and included in the customer table
`Sum({$<CurrentYearFlag={1}>} Sales)`	A flag that marks records belonging to the current year
`Count({$<HighValueProductFlag={1}>} ProductID)`	A flag to identify products that are classified as high value based on complex business rules evaluated during the script
`Sum({$<RegionFlag_East={1}>} Sales)`	Flags for specific regions to facilitate regional analysis.
`Sum({$<RollingMnths={"<=12"}>} Sales)`	Rolling months in a simplified way

Table 4.6: *Flag expressions examples*

Using flags in your data model can dramatically simplify your Qlik Set Analysis expressions by allowing you to filter and aggregate data based on pre-computed conditions, improving readability, and potentially enhancing performance by reducing the complexity of calculations performed at runtime.

In Qlik Set Analysis, a notable application of flags involves *Point-in-Time Reporting*. This technique simplifies analytical tasks by integrating flags into the date calendar of the data model. These flags are so important that when the Qlik Data Manager loads a date field, it automatically appends these flags to the data model to streamline analysis. To observe these enhancements, one can inspect the Assets Panel on a sheet by switching to edit mode.

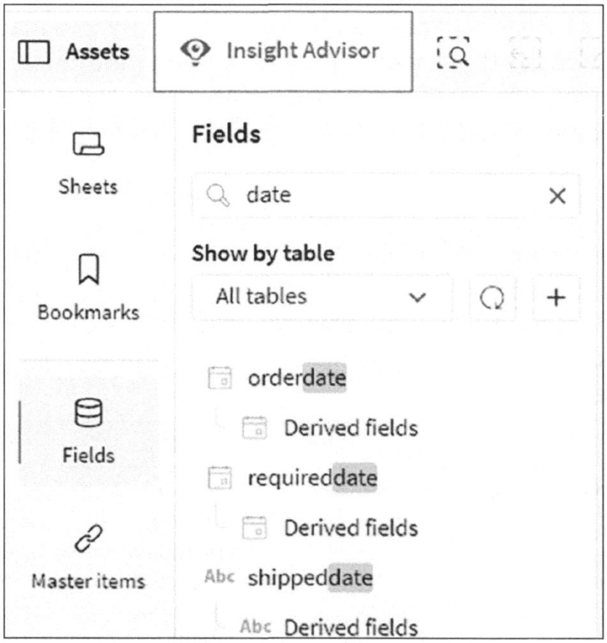

Figure 4.3: *Derived fields*

You can use the script editor as well to create those calendar flags in your data model as exemplified in *Figure 4.4*:

```
LOAD
    orderid,
    customerid,
    employeeid,
    orderdate,
    // Adding flags to the order date to simplify PIT analysis
    Year(orderdate) as Year,
    Year(orderdate)*100+Month(orderdate) as YearMonth,
    Month(orderdate) as Month,
    requireddate,
    shippeddate,
    shipvia,
    freight,
    shipname,
    shipcity,
    shipregion,
    shippostalcode,
    shipcountry
FROM [lib://DataFiles/orders.csv]
(txt, utf8, embedded labels, delimiter is ',', msq);
```

Figure 4.4: *Creating date fields using the script*

Troubleshooting and Debugging

Troubleshooting Qlik's Set Analysis may be challenging, with small errors leading to significant issues in data analysis outcomes. This section focuses on debugging, offering insights into identifying and resolving common problems. Mastering the troubleshooting of set analysis expressions is crucial for maximizing data insights and making the analysis correct and performant.

Qlik Analysis Expression Editor provides a syntax checker and expression evaluation to simplify this process. The expression editor is available in the Properties Panel and is identified by an orange ***fx*** button.

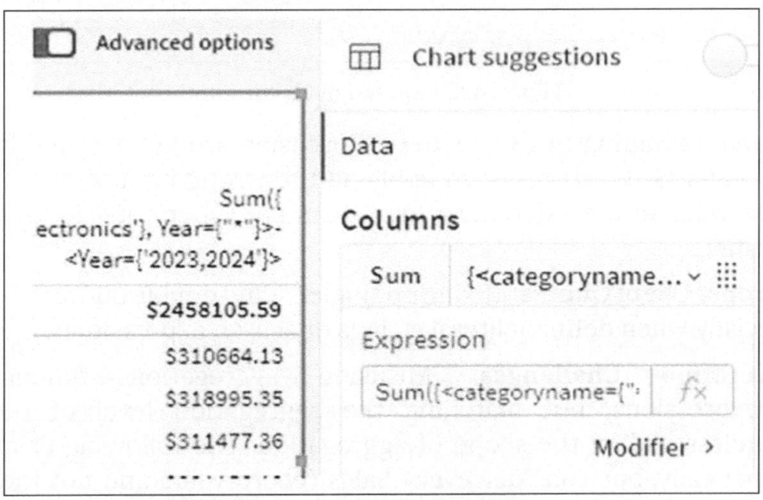

Figure 4.5: *How to access the Expression Editor*

When you press that button, the Expression Editor will be displayed with the expression, and at the bottom, it will display how that expression will be evaluated.

```
Edit expression

Sum({<categoryname={"=Sum({<Year=$(=Max(Year,2))>}Sales)>$(vLimitAnalysis)"}>}Sales)

OK
Sum({<categoryname={"=Sum({<Year=2023>}Sales)>300000"}>}Sales)
```

Figure 4.6: *Expression expansion, the editor indicates how the expression is being evaluated*

Here are some frequently encountered challenges when troubleshooting set analysis expressions.

- **Syntax Errors:** Minor typos or incorrect use of syntax can cause expressions to fail, such as missing brackets, quotation marks, or misplacing semicolons.

```
Error in expression
Error in set modifier expression
Sum({<categoryname="=Sum({<Year=2023>}Sales)>300000"}>}Sales)
```

Figure 4.7: *Error example*

- **Incorrect Field References**: Using field names that do not exactly match those in the data model, including case sensitivity issues, can lead to unexpected results. The syntax is valid, but the field selector does not match with a field that exists in the data model. In the following example, the field is **`categoryname`**, not **`categoryName`**.

```
OK
Sum({<categoryName={"=Sum({<Year=2023>}Sales)>300000"}>}Sales)
```

Figure 4.8: *Expression expansion*

- **Misunderstanding Set Identifiers**: Confusion around set identifiers such as `$`, `1`, and `$_1` can result in applying the wrong context to an expression. Please refer to the "Modifiers, Identifiers and Operators" for a review about identifiers.
- **Improper Use of Quotes**: Mixing up single (' ') and double quotes (" ") incorrectly, especially when defining literal strings or search expressions.
- **Aggregation Challenges**: Misusing aggregation functions within set expressions, not matching the aggregation level of the chart, or misunderstanding the scope of aggregation. The following example is valid synthetically, but consider every Sales record value and not the aggregated sum.

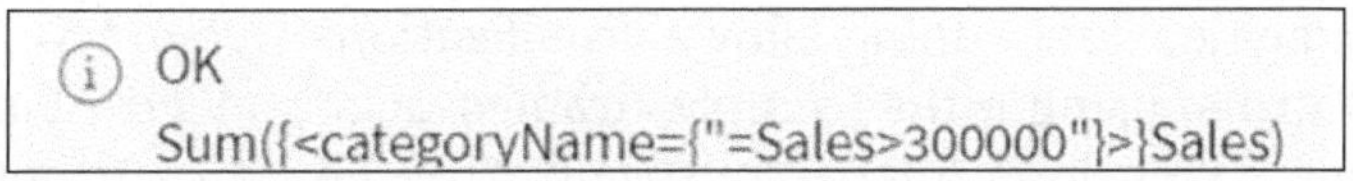

***Figure 4.9**: This expression is syntactically correct but refers to a row-by-row evaluation*

- **Date and Time Formatting**: Issues with date and time formatting lead to mismatches between the expression and the data model's date and time fields. In the following example, the date field is stored as MM/DD/YYYY, and the expression uses a different format.

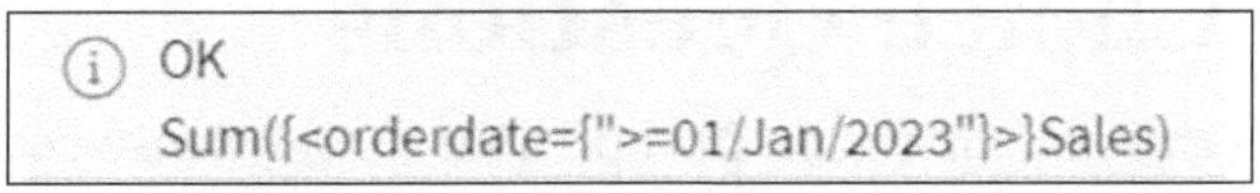

***Figure 4.10**: Date incorrectly formatted*

- **Overlooking Data Model Changes**: Failing to update set analysis expressions to reflect changes in the data model, such as renamed or dropped fields or altered table structures.
- **Set Modifier Complexity**: Creating overly complex set modifiers that are difficult to interpret and debug, especially when using advanced set analysis syntax.
- **Ignoring Selections**: Not accounting for current selections properly, which can significantly affect the outcome of set analysis expressions.

Conclusion

Mastering Set Analysis is an essential skill for any data analyst aiming to leverage the full power of Qlik Analytics solutions for dynamic and complex data analysis. Through this chapter, we have explored the intricacies of set analysis, from its syntax and operators to the practical application of advanced techniques. We have also addressed common pitfalls and provided strategies for effective troubleshooting and debugging, ensuring that you can navigate challenges with confidence. The ability to craft precise set expressions not only enhances the accuracy of your data insights but also significantly expands your analytical capabilities.

As we wrap up this chapter, it is important to remember that proficiency in set analysis comes with practice and experimentation. The examples and techniques discussed serve as a foundation upon which to build more complex analyses, tailored to your specific data needs. By applying the principles covered, you will be better equipped to unlock the potential of your data, driving more informed decision-making processes. Whether you are analyzing sales trends, customer behavior, or operational efficiency, the power of Analysis is a key tool in your data analysis arsenal, enabling you to deliver deeper insights and more impactful results.

In the next chapter, let us go through Qlik Analytics solutions to enhance web applications with their embedding and extension features, enabling seamless integration of analytics. Embedding allows visualizations to be incorporated directly into digital platforms, using either simple iframes or advanced APIs for interactive data engagement. Extensions further customize the analytics experience, allowing developers to create unique visualizations or functionalities with JavaScript, HTML, and CSS and to integrate third-party libraries. These features together provide robust tools for embedding sophisticated data analysis and personalized visualizations into various applications, supporting enhanced decision-making and user engagement.

Multiple Choice Questions

1. What does the set expression {1} represent in Qlik Sense set analysis?
   a. All records in the application
   b. No records (empty set)
   c. Default set expression
   d. Current selection
2. Which set analysis operator is used to represent the union of two sets?
   a. “+”
   b. “,”
   c. “-”
   d. “*”
3. What does Set Analysis in Qlik allow users to do?
   a. Connect to multiple data sources
   b. Perform dynamic data calculations within a specific set of data
   c. Create visualizations without any data
   d. Export data to external databases
4. How can you ignore all selections made in the app except for the Year field in a set expression?
   a. Use the expression `=Sum({$<Year=>} Sales)`
   b. Use the expression `=Sum({1<Year=P(Year)>}Sales)`
   c. Use the expression `=Sum({1<Year=*>} Sales)`
   d. Use the expression `=Sum({$<Year>} Sales)`

5. What is the purpose of using the P() function in a set expression?
    a. To return possible values of a field based on current selections
    b. To calculate the percentile of a given set
    c. To add a field to the current selection
    d. To perform a mathematical power operation

Answers

1. a
2. a
3. b
4. b
5. a

References

1. Qlik Sense Cheat Sheet. *Qlik Community*. [Online]: https://community.qlik.com/t5/Design/Qlik-Sense-Cheat-Sheet-version-2-0/ba-p/1667455.

Additional Resources

The following links are complimentary to this book, bringing more resources to the reader, with more examples and details.

- **Set analysis and set expressions** (https://help.qlik.com/en-us/sense/2.0/Subsystems/Hub/Content/ChartFunctions/SetAnalysis/set-analysis-expressions.htm)
- **Advanced Set Analysis in Qlik:** https://community.qlik.com/t5/Member-Articles/Advanced-Set-Analysis-in-Qlik/ta-p/2025831

CHAPTER 5
Embedding and Extending

Introduction

In today's data-driven world, the integration of analytics into existing platforms is a game-changer for organizations aiming to harness insights across their operations. Qlik Analytics Solutions, renowned for its powerful analytics engine and flexible integration capabilities, offers a pathway to embedding analytics and creating mashups within web applications and interfaces. This chapter provides a concise guide to leveraging Qlik Analytics for embedding visualizations and developing custom mashups, which are essential for enhancing data interaction and accessibility.

We will cover the basics of embedding and mashup creation with Qlik Analytics, from understanding the technical requirements to practical implementation strategies. Aimed at developers and analysts alike, this guide will navigate through the process of integrating interactive Qlik Sense analytics into your applications, ensuring a seamless user experience. With a focus on practical examples, optimization tips, and troubleshooting advice, this chapter is designed to equip you with the knowledge to create integrated BI solutions that foster informed decision-making and innovation in your organization.

Structure

In this chapter, we will discuss the following topics:

- Benefits and Use Cases
- Technical Foundations
- Embedding Qlik Objects
- Developing Mashups
- Developing Qlik Sense Extensions

Benefits and Use Cases

Embedding Qlik Analytics into web applications and enterprise solutions offers numerous benefits that can significantly enhance data accessibility, decision-making processes, and overall business intelligence capabilities. Here are some key advantages:

- **Enhanced Data Visualization and Interactivity:** Qlik Analytics solutions provide powerful data visualization objects that can be embedded into applications, making complex data more understandable and actionable through interactive dashboards and reports.
- **Seamless Integration:** Embedding Qlik Analytics solutions into existing systems or applications allows for a seamless user experience, enabling users to access advanced analytics without leaving their workflow or needing to switch between applications.
- **Customized Analytics Solutions:** With Qlik Analytics solutions, organizations can create tailored analytics solutions that meet specific business needs, enhancing the relevance and impact of insights derived from data.
- **Real-time Decision Making:** The ability to embed real-time analytics into applications supports immediate decision-making, allowing businesses to respond swiftly to market changes, customer behavior, and internal performance metrics.
- **Increased User Adoption:** By integrating analytics directly into the daily tools and applications employees use, organizations can boost the adoption of data-driven decision-making practices across all levels.
- **Data Democratization:** Integrating Qlik Analytics into systems allows for wider access to analytics among users, effectively democratizing data and fostering a culture where insights inform decisions throughout the entire organization. A prevalent application is seen in public sector entities that manage analytics portals with anonymous access, providing citizens with transparency into expenses and salaries within the organization.
- **Scalability and Flexibility:** Qlik Analytics solutions′ architecture supports scalable solutions that can grow with your business, and its flexible nature allows for customization and expansion to meet evolving analytics needs.
- **Cost Efficiency:** By integrating analytics directly into existing platforms, businesses can reduce the need for separate analytics tools and platforms, streamlining operations and reducing costs associated with maintaining multiple systems.
- **Security and Compliance:** Embedding Qlik Analytics solutions within applications can leverage existing security frameworks, ensuring that data access and analytics are governed by the same protocols and compliance standards as the host application.

- **Enhanced Collaboration and Sharing:** Integrated analytics facilitate easier sharing of insights and collaborative decision-making within teams, enhancing communication and alignment on strategic objectives.

By leveraging these benefits, organizations can create a more integrated, insightful, and responsive business environment, driving efficiency, innovation, and competitive advantage.

Extending Qlik Sense objects allows developers to customize analytics and data visualization beyond the platform's standard offerings, using APIs to create or modify visualizations and integrate with external data sources. This customization meets specific business needs, enhancing the analytics experience and enabling integration with enterprise applications for seamless data access within existing workflows. Such extensions improve decision-making and efficiency, fostering a data-driven culture.

Beyond the technical capabilities, the advantages of extending Qlik Sense are significant. By addressing unique analysis needs, developers can solve specific challenges with custom visualizations tailored to their data and industry. This capability enhances user engagement through interactive and immersive experiences that truly resonate with the audience and allow for differentiation in analysis, enabling organizations to stand out with innovative data exploration tools. Visualization extensions are built using the same technologies as standard Qlik Sense visualizations, and when developed correctly, their management is indistinguishable from that of standard visualizations. It relies on the Extension API to correctly communicate with the backend services to get the up-to-date data that needs to be plotted by the extension. As an example, the following extension captures the value input and displays it dynamically.

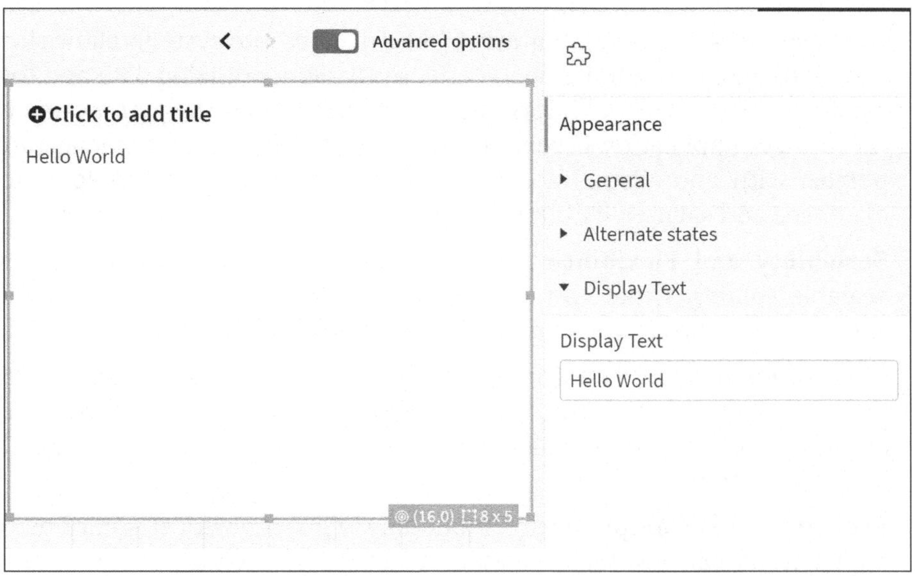

***Figure 5.1**: Visualization Extension with a parameter*

The following code shows a way to capture the input value and display it:

```
    },
    paint: function ($element, layout) {
        $element.empty();
        $element.append('<div class="hw-content">' + layout.displayText + '</div>');
    }
```

***Figure 5.2**: Paint function*

Technical Foundations

Embedding Qlik Analytics within applications requires the use of several strategies, ranging from the simplest to the most complex. It is crucial to utilize the most effective approach to ensure optimal results.

Integration Options

At the time of writing this book, the suggested methods for integrating Qlik Analytics into portals or applications depend on the specific needs and the degree of control desired by the developer over the outcome. Following is a list of options along with recommendations on when to employ each:

- **App Integration API or Single Integration API:** These simplified APIs are your go-to choice for embedding specific apps, sheets, or objects within your app without worrying about technical complexities. You just create a URL pointing to the object you want to display and use it in the HTML code of the third-party application. This is generally the most used when integrating into CRM/ERP solutions that provide ways to add custom HTML to the page.
- **Capability APIs:** For a more robust embedding experience, including the ability to embed Qlik Sense visualizations, generate visualizations dynamically, interact with data fields, make selections, and create objects within your web application. The Capability APIs offer a streamlined approach to interface with the Qlik Engine JSON API.
- **`enigma.js`:** Developers seeking direct interaction with the Qlik Sense Engine JSON API, with minimal abstraction, should utilize enigma.js. It can be utilized to develop custom clients or Node.js services. Potential applications include the creation of browser-based analytics tools, backend services, or command-line scripts utilizing the enigma.js library. This option is ideal for those not needing to embed Qlik Sense visualizations and who possess a higher level of technical proficiency than what is required for using the Integration APIs or the Capability APIs. This library can be downloaded from the Qlik GitHub repository (https://github.com/qlik-oss/enigma.js/).
- **`nebula.js`:** Developer kit for building data visualizations. It offers pre-made charts and tools to easily integrate visuals into web apps or build entirely

custom ones. Whether you need standard charts or unique designs, nebula.js simplifies the process for Qlik developers. This library can be downloaded from the Qlik GitHub repository (https://github.com/qlik-oss/nebula.js/).

- **`qlik-embed`:** The library that simplifies embedding Qlik visualizations in various web apps, from basic HTML to React and Svelte. It offers consistent configuration and secure authentication (OAuth2) over iframes. Plus, Qlik-embed's API access allows deeper integration with the surrounding web page. This makes it a more flexible and secure choice for embedding Qlik content than the App Integration API or Single Integration API.

Please refer to the Additional Resources section to get the full documentation list.

Authentication Methods

Authentication in Qlik Analytics solutions is designed to ensure secure access to data and analytics resources. At its core, the authentication process involves verifying the identity of users before granting them access to the system, leveraging industry-standard protocols and methodologies. Qlik Analytics solutions support a range of authentication methods, discussed later in this section, for integration with enterprise identity providers. This enables organizations to implement single sign-on (SSO) capabilities, allowing users to access the embedded analytics using their existing organizational credentials, thus enhancing security while simplifying the user experience. By incorporating these high-level authentication concepts, Qlik Cloud ensures that data and analytics are securely managed, aligning with the organization's security policies and compliance requirements, thereby safeguarding sensitive information and maintaining trust among users.

In **Qlik Sense Enterprise on Windows** (often referred to as Qlik Sense Client-Managed), there is support for a variety of authentication methods meeting different security requirements and infrastructure setups. Here is a list of supported authentication methods:

- **Anonymous access**: This enables users to consume embedded analytics dashboards without authenticating, making it ideal for sharing insights broadly without requiring a login. This feature requires capacity or token-based licensing to allow access to anonymous viewers, helping organizations manage public access.
- **Windows Authentication**: Utilizes the built-in Windows authentication mechanism, ideal for organizations using Active Directory for user management.
- **Ticket Authentication:** Allows for the generation of tickets for users to authenticate against the Qlik Sense repository. This is useful for SSO scenarios where users are authenticated through an external system.
- **Header Authentication:** Uses HTTP headers for authenticating users. This

method is commonly used with reverse proxy servers that handle user authentication and then pass the user information to Qlik Sense through headers.

- **Security Assertion Markup Language (SAML) Authentication:** Enables SSO using SAML to authenticate users against an external identity provider (IdP). This method is widely used for cloud-based identity providers.
- **JSON Web Token (JWT) Authentication:** Allows for secure, token-based user authentication. JWT is particularly useful for mobile apps or web services where embedding authentication information in a JSON web token is required.
- **OpenID Connect (OIDC):** An open and decentralized authentication protocol that enables users to log into multiple websites using a single identity, managed by a third-party OpenID provider. By utilizing a URL-based identity verified by their OpenID provider, users can authenticate once and gain access to all participating sites without needing separate usernames and passwords for each.

In **Qlik Cloud Analytics**, there are authentication options to meet different security requirements and integration needs. Here are the primary authentication methods available in Qlik Cloud:

- **Qlik Account:** An authentication mechanism managed by Qlik to access content within the qlik.com and qlikcloud.com domains.
- **JWT:** Supports authentication with JSON objects, enabling secure transmission of information between parties, useful for server-to-server authentication and authorization scenarios.
- **OAuth 2.0:** A widely used, open standard for access delegation, allowing users to authenticate and authorize applications to use Qlik Cloud without exposing their passwords directly.
- **OIDC:** A simple identity layer on top of the OAuth 2.0 protocol, allowing for authentication with an external OIDC provider, facilitating SSO, and modern authentication practices.

Embedding Qlik Objects

Embedding Qlik Sense objects into web pages and applications allows for the seamless integration of powerful, interactive data visualizations directly within your digital environment. This process transforms how users interact with data, offering them insightful analytics without leaving the application or website they are using. For instance, embedding a Qlik Sense dashboard into a company's intranet site enables employees to access real-time sales data, inventory levels, or performance metrics at a glance. Similarly, integrating Qlik Sense charts into a customer-facing portal can provide clients with personalized insights, such as their spending patterns or service usage trends. These practical examples illustrate how embedding Qlik Sense objects can enhance decision-making processes, improve user engagement, and deliver tailored analytics experiences directly within the context where they are most needed.

In this example, you will be using Qlik-embed to embed some objects from Qlik Cloud using interactive login. The user will be redirected to the Qlik Account login page to get access to the page.

To use this example, you will need:

- Access to a Qlik Cloud tenant with admin privileges to create a web integration
- A text editor (such as Visual Studio Code)
- Some HTTP hosting service
- Basic understanding of HTML and JavaScript

Creating the WebIntegration

Navigate to your Qlik Cloud Management (usually accessible on this URL https://<tenant>.<region>.qlikcloud.com/console/web-integrations). You will be prompted with a screen just like the following image:

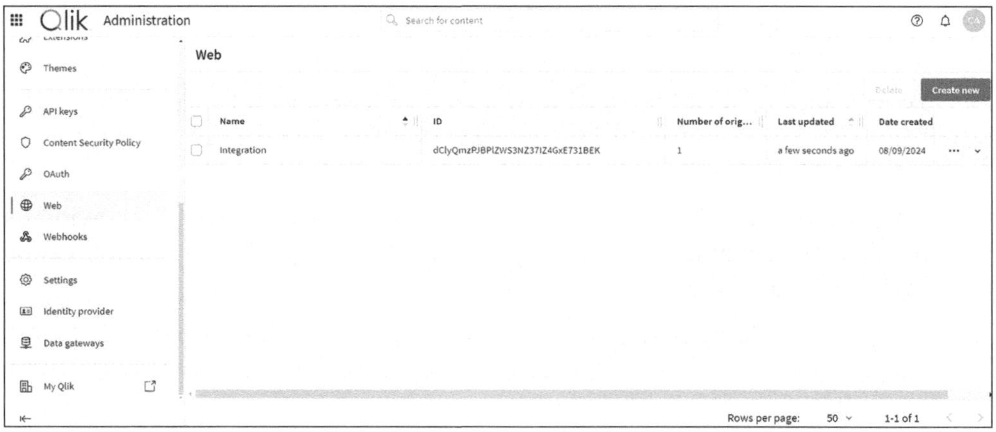

***Figure 5.3**: Console web integrations list*

1. Click `Create new` to get access to add a new WebIntegration.

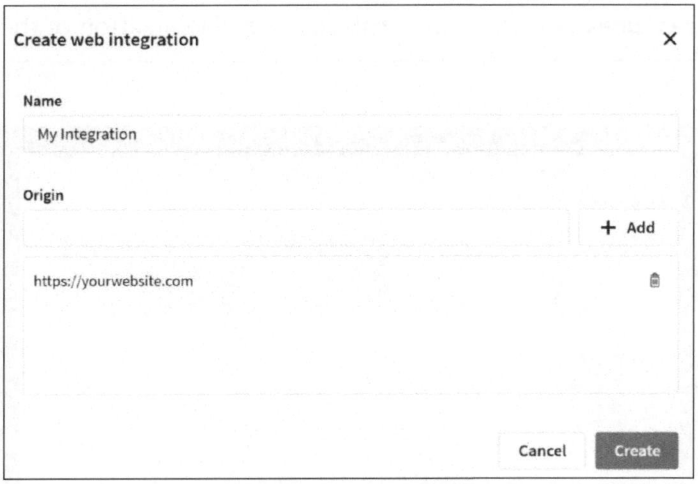

***Figure 5.4**: Web integration creation*

2. Enter a meaningful **`Name`** and provide an **`Origin https URL`** from your secure https server, then copy the ID from your WebIntegration for later usage in this chapter.

Collecting the Object Parameters

In this example, we need two object IDs to embed those objects in our project. To get the information we need, please open any Qlik Sense app that you have access to on your tenant:

1. Press the right button over the object, then press **`Share`**, and option **`Embed`**.

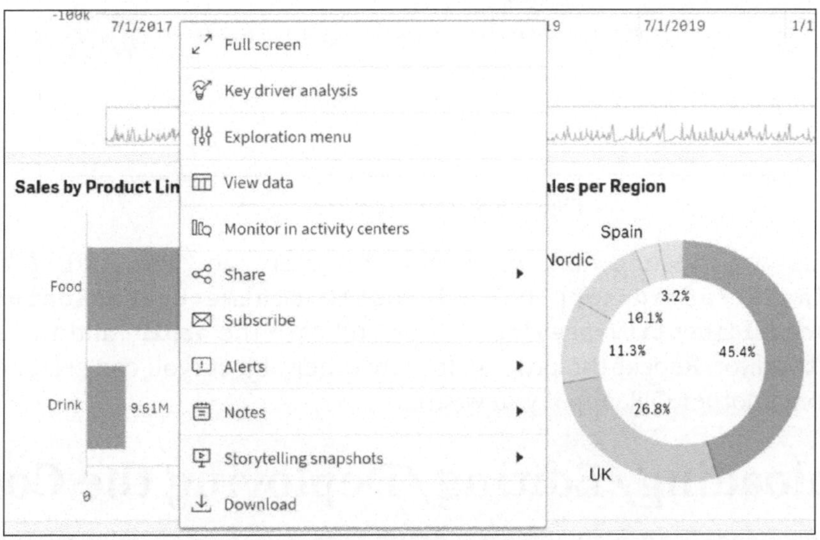

***Figure 5.5**: Object context menu*

2. Click `Open preview in a new tab` to see a visualization of the object.

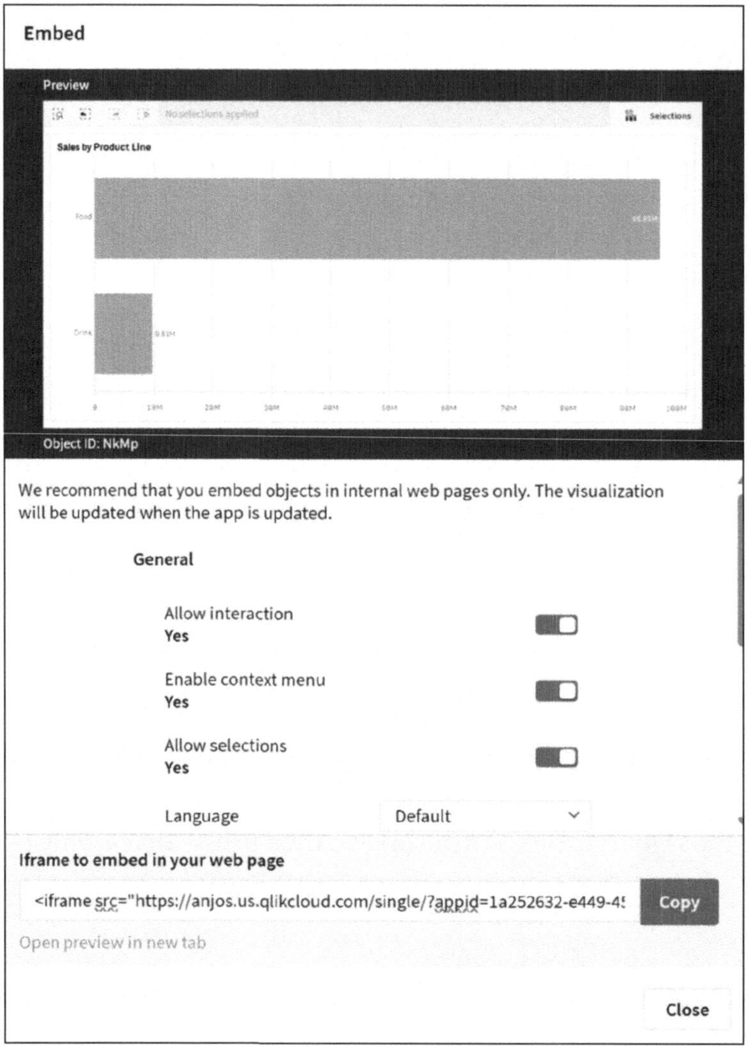

Figure 5.6: *Embedding interface*

3. This will open a link in a new browser tab. The URL format is `/single/?appid=<appID>&obj=<objID>&theme=breeze&opt=ctxmenu,currsel&identity=preview`. Copy and save the `appID` and the `objID` in a text editor. Repeat the process for any other object (you can select one object from another Qlik app if you wish).

Downloading/Editing/Deploying the Code

You can download this project, https://github.com/ava-orange-education/Ultimate-

Qlik-Cloud-Data-Analytics-and-Data-Integration, to your workstation using git (or by downloading a zip file and unpacking it).

```
git clone https://github.com/ava-orange-education/Ulti-
mate-Qlik-Cloud-Data-Analytics-and-Data-Integration.git
```

After the code is stored on your workstation, check the Chapter 5 folder and make some parameters:

- **`index.html`**
  - Change line 6, parameter **`data-host`** to match your tenant address.
  - Change line 7, parameter **`data-web-integration-id`** to match your **`WebIntegrationID.`**
  - Change lines 26 and 30, parameters **`app-id`** and **`object-id`** to match your objects parameters..
- **`oauth-callback.html`**, adjust the **`data-host`** parameter to match your tenant address.

Upload all files to your HTTP server with public access. A server is required because the authorization flow will make a call to oauth-callback.html to enable the communication.

Testing Our Project

Navigate to the address of your HTTP server using your browser. You will encounter an **`Authorize`** button. Upon clicking this button, you will be redirected to the Qlik Cloud instance. After entering your credentials there, you will be automatically sent back to your HTTP server, where two objects will then be displayed.

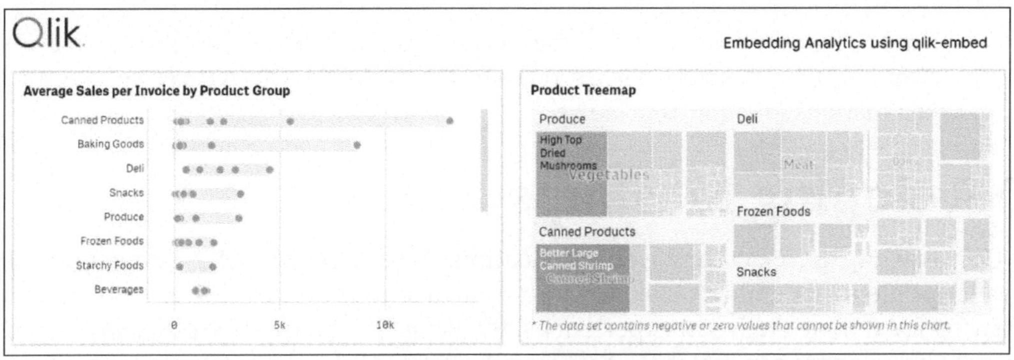

Figure 5.7: *Web page display*

Explaining the Project

Let us now review all the aspects of the project.

1. Importing **qlik-embed**: The following code will load all the libraries needed for our project using the **src** attribute. All other parameters are self-explanatory.

```
        <script crossorigin="anonymous" type="application/
javascript"
         src="https://cdn.jsdelivr.net/npm/@qlik/embed-web-
components"
 data-host="https://tenant.us.qlikcloud.com"
         data-web-integration-id=»_BJZ6XoVXRlMAW3pbYfbDSE-
UR65d9k3»
         data-cross-site-cookies="true">
         </script>
```

2. Embedding objects: Using the tag **<qlik-embed ui="analytics/chart" object-id="<objID>" app-id="<appId>"></qlik-embed>** will instruct the browser to connect to your tenant, open the app, and embed the referred object. You can embed as many objects from any application into a single HTML page. You are free to use any web technology, such as CSS and Javascript, to add formatting to your page, making it appealing to users. The tag **<qlik-embed>** will handle all the complexity of embedding the objects.

3. Authorization flow: When embedding an object with **<qlik-embed>,** the initial step involves verifying the user's authentication status. If the user is unauthenticated, they will be redirected to an **oauth-callback.html** page located in the same repository as your pages. After the user enters their credentials, a cookie will be stored in the session to authenticate the user.

   Note: *This happens in this case because we are using the interactive login flow and Qlik Account. Please refer to the Additional Resources section to get instructions on other topologies.*

Developing Mashups

A Qlik mashup is a custom web application (HTML pages, CSS documents, and JavaScript files) that embeds Qlik Analytics visualizations into a tailored web interface, allowing for unique analytics experiences. By using Qlik Sense's APIs discussed in this chapter, developers can integrate data visualizations with other web content, creating seamless and interactive user experiences. Mashups enable the customization of analytics solutions to meet specific business needs, incorporating unique designs and brand elements. This approach enhances user engagement and decision-making by presenting data in innovative ways, leveraging the flexibility of web technologies to fully exploit data's potential within custom web environments.

Visiting the website https://demos.qlik.com/qliksense?tags=Mashup will display a variety of mashup examples for you to explore. The following examples showcase how the synergy between a skilled web UI developer and Qlik Analytics can become a formidable asset in crafting compelling analytics applications:

Oscar:

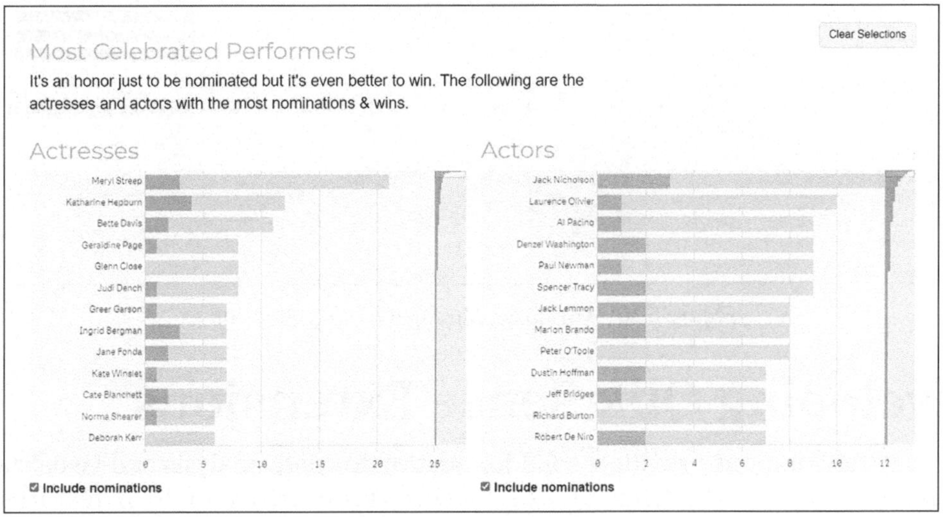

Figure 5.8: *Oscar nominees' application*

Football Fantasy:

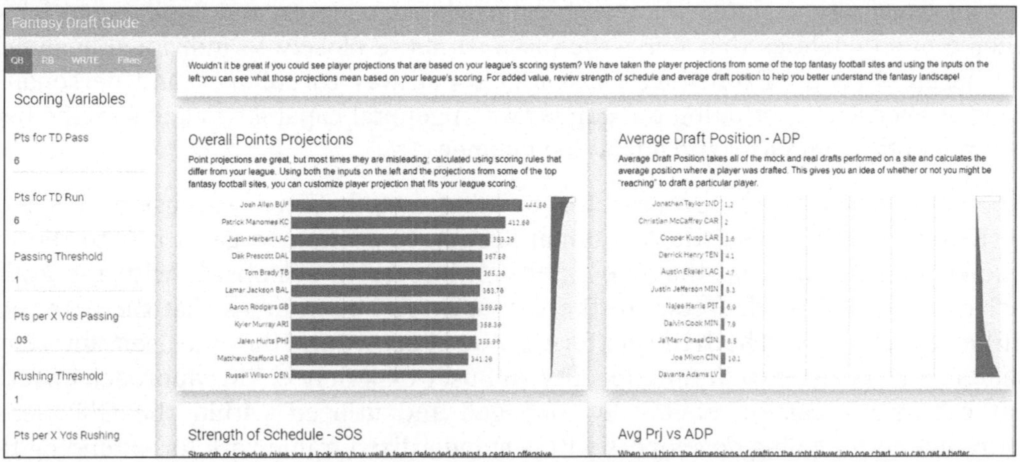

Figure 5.9: *Football Fantasy application*

Workforce Management:

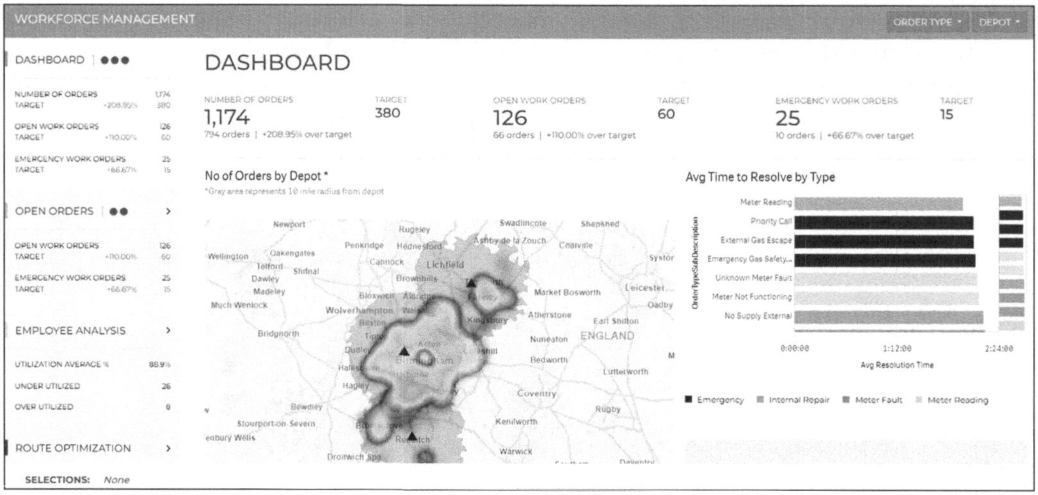

Figure 5.10: *Workforce Management application*

Developing Qlik Sense Extensions

Qlik Analytics solutions provide a solid foundation for data analysis and visualization, catering to a broad spectrum of user needs. However, its built-in features and visualizations may not always fully meet the specialized requirements of every project or business case. This is where Qlik extensions play a crucial role. They offer the flexibility to extend the platform's core capabilities, enabling the creation of custom visualizations, integration with external data sources, and implementation of specific functionalities that tailor the platform more closely to individual analytical and business needs. Extensions thus offer a pathway to enhance and personalize the user experience, bridging the gap between general capabilities and specific user requirements in a neutral and adaptable manner.

The entire development process for building a Qlik Sense extension relies on the Extension API (check the Additional Resources section to get a link to the full documentation), ensuring that the extension integrates seamlessly with the entire analytics stack. This adherence to the Extension API guarantees that the extension will be compatible with both the platform's infrastructure and the end-user's interface, maintaining consistency in functionality and user experience. This approach ensures that extensions can be effectively managed and utilized within the Qlik Sense environment, providing developers with a standardized framework for extending the platform's capabilities.

Developers have the flexibility to employ any JavaScript library or framework, such as jQuery, in their extension development, provided they adhere to the Extensions API interface. This approach offers developers creative freedom in implementation while ensuring consistency with other objects within a Qlik application. By respecting the Extensions API, extensions can seamlessly integrate into the Qlik ecosystem, maintaining a uniform user experience and compatibility across the platform.

Anatomy of a Qlik Extension

An extension is composed of several key components that work together to integrate custom visualizations and functionalities into the Qlik Sense platform. Understanding these components is essential for developers looking to create extensions that enhance data analysis and visualization capabilities. Here are the primary components of a Qlik Sense extension:

- **JavaScript File:** The core of the extension, containing the logic and functionality. This file defines how the extension interacts with data, how it renders visualizations, and how it responds to user inputs. It leverages the Qlik Sense APIs to access and manipulate data within the Qlik engine.
- **QEXT (Extension) File**: A JSON file that serves as the manifest for the extension. It includes metadata such as the extension's name, description, version, type, and author. This file is crucial for Qlik Sense to recognize and properly load the extension.
- **HTML File**: Optional but commonly used for defining the user interface of the extension. It specifies the structure of the extension's visual elements and can include placeholders for dynamic content that will be rendered through JavaScript.
- **CSS File:** Used to style the extension's visual components. Through CSS, developers can customize the appearance of their extensions to match specific branding requirements or to ensure consistency with the overall design of the Qlik application.
- **Properties Panel Definition**: Defines the configuration options available to users in the Qlik Sense interface. This can include settings for customizing the appearance, data handling, or any other aspect of the extension that should be configurable by the end user.
- **Assets**: This category includes images, icons, libraries, or any other resources that the extension requires to function properly or to enhance its appearance. These assets are referenced within the extension's code and are essential for creating a visually appealing and functionally rich user experience.
- **Documentation**: While not technically part of the extension's code, comprehensive documentation is vital for supporting users and developers who will work with the extension. It should explain how to install, configure, and use the extension, along with any dependencies or prerequisites.

The first four components, encompassing the JavaScript, QEXT, HTML, and CSS files, are bundled into a .zip file for deployment on either the Qlik Sense Client Managed or

Qlik Cloud Analytics platforms. During deployment, this .zip file is unpacked, making the extension accessible to users via the **Custom objects** section of the Assets panel. Once deployed, the extension can be utilized in the same manner as any built-in visualization tool.

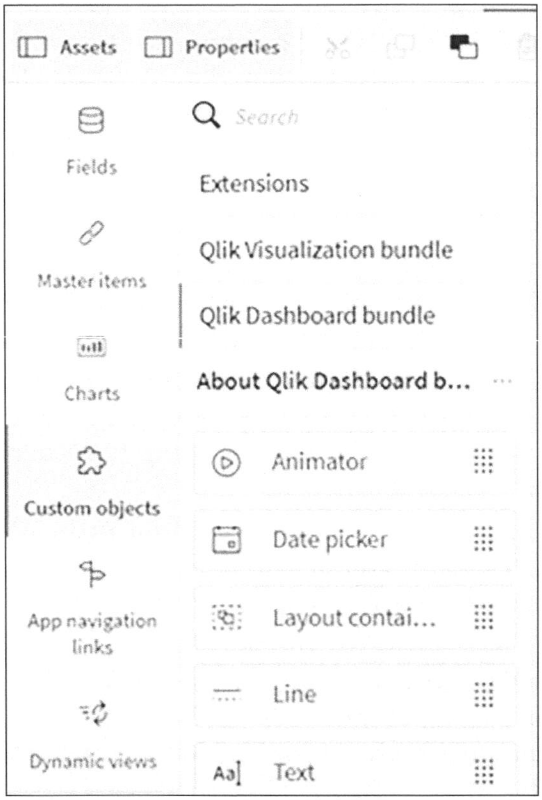

Figure 5.11: *Custom objects panel*

Qlik Extension Example

Let us analyze a very simple extension by downloading it from the link (https://github.com/ava-orange-education/Ultimate-Qlik-Cloud-Data-Analytics-and-Data-Integration/tree/main/Chapter%205/Extension) using the **Download as a zip** option.

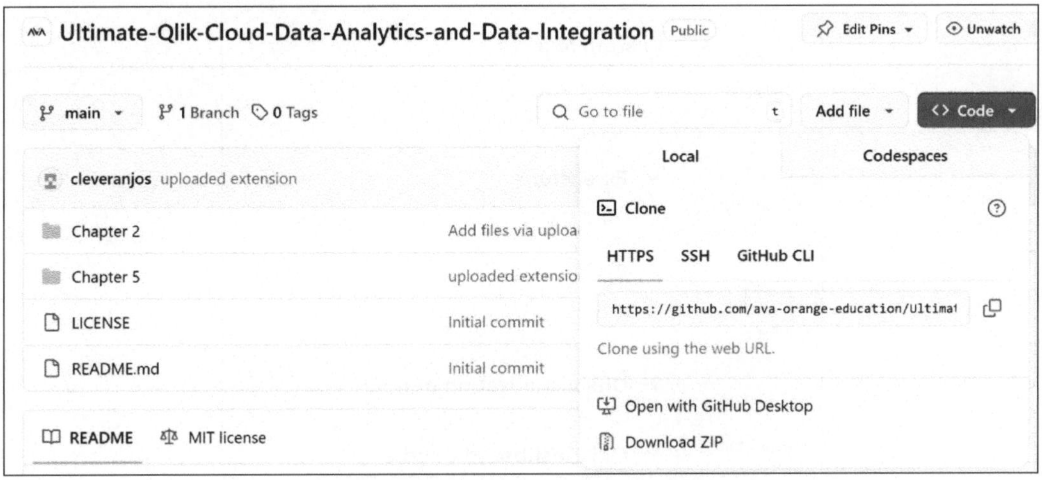

***Figure 5.12**: Downloading the extension*

Store the zip file on your workstation. Navigate to the `Extensions` section of your Qlik Cloud Management Console and press the **Add** button to upload and deploy your extension.

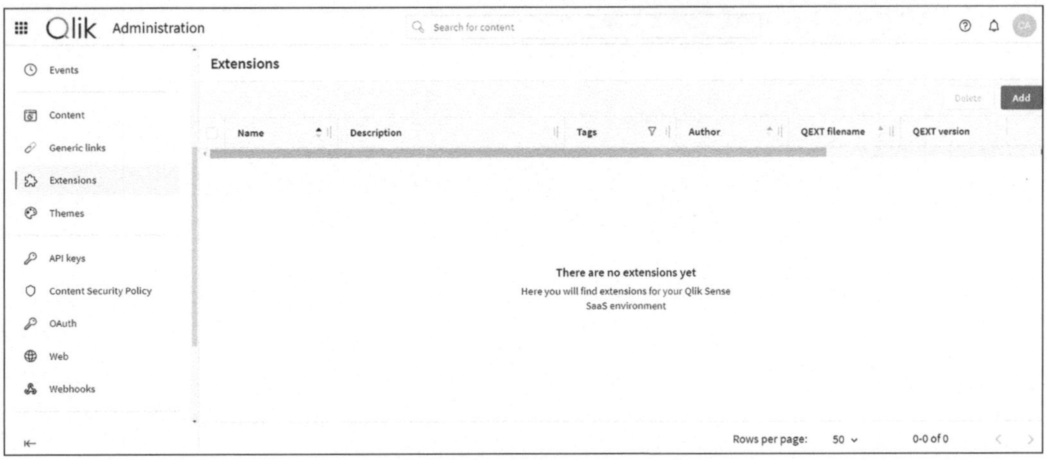

***Figure 5.13:** Deploying the extension*

Now, navigate to a Qlik Analytics application and go to edit mode. Under the `Custom Objects` section of the Assets panel, locate the Hello World extension and drag it into the sheet.

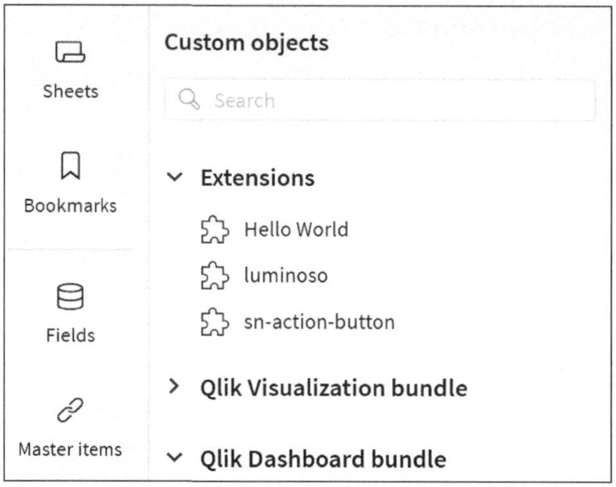

Figure 5.14: *Custom objects panel*

Using the properties panel, change the display text.

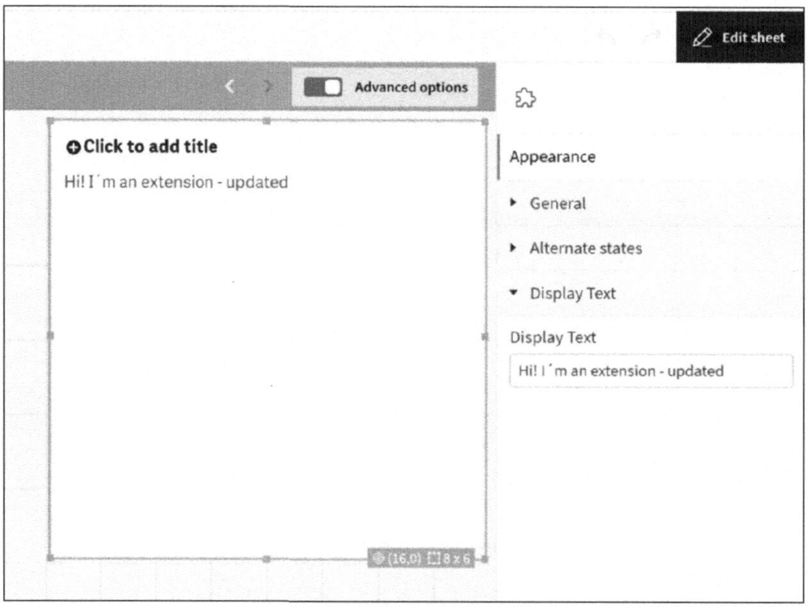

Figure 5.15: *Properties panel*

Now, let us understand how the extension works based on the file **helloworld.js**.

```
define(['jquery', 'text!./style.css'],
    function ($) {
        'use strict';
        return {
            definition: {
                type: "items",
```

```
                    component: "accordion",
                    items: {
                        appearancePanel: {
                            uses: "settings",
                            items: {
                                DisplayText: {
                                    ref: "displayText",
                                    type: "string",
                                    label: "Display Text",
                                    defaultValue: "Hi! I´m an
extension"
                                }
                            }
                        }
                    }
                },
                paint: function ($element, layout) {
                    $element.empty();
                    $element.append('<div class="hw-content">' +
layout.displayText + '</div>');
                }
            };
        });
```

Following is an explanation of the aforementioned code:

1. **`define(['jquery', 'text!./style.css'],`** This part instructs which libs (jquery) or content (CSS file) need to be imported into the extension.
2. The Extension API mandates that each extension must return a single object containing, at a minimum, a **`paint`** function. This function is called whenever the extension requires rendering. Our function starts cleaning the extension canvas using the **`$element.empty();`** statement and then adds text (with a hw-content CSS class). We are using a property to define which text needs to be rendered. This property is configured by the property **`definition.items`**, which we defined as a string and a default value.
3. The paint function plays a critical role in rendering all content within the extension canvas. The Qlik Extension API triggers this function in response to any interaction leading to a change in context, such as user actions, data refreshes, selections, sheet navigation, or variable assignments. This process ensures that the extension can update its content accordingly.

Extensions often incorporate existing libraries to simplify tasks, such as using jQuery for easier DOM manipulation in our example. Developers are free to incorporate those third-party libraries, like D3 or nebula.js, to create and integrate visualizations, enhancing the extension's functionality.

Conclusion

Concluding our discussion on Qlik Sense embedding, it becomes clear that embedding Qlik Sense into web pages and applications is a strategic method for incorporating analytics into various digital environments. This chapter has illustrated the significant benefits of embedding, such as improved user interaction and broader data accessibility, through the utilization of both basic and advanced embedding techniques. The versatility provided by these embedding options enables organizations to tailor data presentation to specific requirements, ensuring that insights are both accessible and relevant. Embedding Qlik Analytics objects streamlines the integration of analytics with existing digital platforms, facilitating a more cohesive and efficient approach to data visualization. As the demand for integrated analytics solutions grows, the utility of Qlik Sense embedding in enhancing data-driven decision-making processes and enriching digital experiences is underscored.

Qlik Sense extensions represent a powerful means for enhancing and customizing the analytics and visualization capabilities of the Qlik Sense platform. Through the strategic use of JavaScript, CSS, HTML, and the Qlik Extension API, developers can create bespoke visualizations, integrate additional functionalities, and tailor the analytics experience to meet specific business needs. The process of developing, deploying, and managing these extensions is streamlined, allowing for seamless integration within both Qlik Sense Client Managed and Qlik Cloud Analytics environments. With the ability to respond dynamically to user interactions and data changes, extensions ensure that analytics content remains relevant and engaging. As we have explored the fundamentals, components, and operational mechanics of Qlik Sense extensions, it is clear that they offer a valuable avenue for businesses to leverage their data more effectively, fostering a more insightful and interactive data exploration environment. The potential for innovation and customization with Qlik Sense extensions is vast, opening up new possibilities for data-driven decision-making and analytics presentation.

In the following chapter, lineage and impact analysis will enable us to trace the origins of data flow and comprehend the transformations applied to it. By utilizing a glossary, we will be able to readily grasp the functional definition of a KPI or a dimension observed in a report. This chapter will delve into understanding these concepts and their practical applications.

Multiple Choice Questions

1. What is the primary purpose of embedding Qlik Sense objects into web applications?

    a. To increase the website's loading speed

    b. To enhance data visualization and interactivity within the application

   c. To replace all web content with Qlik Sense dashboards
   d. To secure web applications with Qlik Sense's authentication methods
2. Which of the following methods can be used for embedding Qlik Sense visualizations into web pages?
   a. Using direct database queries
   b. Employing iframe tags
   c. Utilizing CSS styling only
   d. Applying PHP scripts
3. What advantage does using the Qlik Sense APIs for embedding offer over simpler methods such as iframes?
   a. It requires less coding knowledge
   b. It allows for the embedding of external websites into Qlik Sense
   c. It provides greater control and customization of the embedded content
   d. It eliminates the need for Qlik Sense licensing
4. Which component is essential for a Qlik Sense extension to function properly?
   a. A Python script
   b. A paint function in the JavaScript file
   c. An external SQL database
   d. A dedicated web server
5. What is the purpose of the QEXT (Extension) file in a Qlik Sense extension?
   a. To store the extension's compressed data
   b. To serve as the manifest detailing the extension's properties
   c. To encrypt the extension's code
   d. To provide a backup of the extension's settings

Answers

1. b
2. b
3. c

4. b
5. b

Additional Resources

The following links complement this book, bringing more resources to the reader with more examples and details. Please be aware that as Qlik introduces new product versions, the documentation might be found under a different link. Always refer to the latest versions. For instance, what is labeled as November 2023 documentation could be updated to May 2024, and so on.

- **Embedded analytics:** (https://qlik.dev/embed)
- **Qlik Cloud Code Examples:** (https://qlik.dev/examples/)
- **Overview of Qlik APIs:** (https://qlik.dev/apis/)
- **Qlik OSS Repositories:** (https://github.com/qlik-oss)
- **enigma.js:** (https://help.qlik.com/en-US/sense-developer/November2023/Subsystems/APIs/Content/Sense_ClientAPIs/enigmajs/enigmajs-introduction.htm)
- **nebula.js:** (https://help.qlik.com/en-US/sense-developer/November2023/Subsystems/APIs/Content/Sense_ClientAPIs/nebulajs/nebulajs-introduction.htm)
- **qlik-embed:** (https://qlik.dev/embed/qlik-embed/why-qlik-embed)
- **Extension API:** (https://help.qlik.com/en-US/sense-developer/November2023/Subsystems/APIs/Content/Sense_ClientAPIs/extensions-api-reference.htm)
- **Qlik Sense Extension Tutorial:** (https://github.com/stefanwalther/qliksense-extension-tutorial)

CHAPTER 6

Navigating The Data Landscape

Introduction

In this chapter, we will delve into foundational services. We will gain a comprehensive understanding of Lineage and Impact Analysis, which are functionalities aiding in comprehending the origin, transformation, and destination of data across various systems. Lineage illustrates the historical journey of a data field or dataset, tracing from its inception to its utilization in end-user applications.

Impact Analysis reveals the downstream dependencies associated with a data field or dataset, elucidating how alterations would affect other data tasks, datasets, or applications. These features instill confidence in and optimize the data pipeline, furnishing complete audit trails and visual representations of data flows. Access to lineage and impact analysis graphs and views is available through different entry points within the data pipeline, including data tasks, datasets, or columns.

The Glossary feature furnishes a compilation of common terms and definitions employed in Qlik Cloud. It serves as a resource to enhance understanding of Qlik Cloud concepts and features, with links to pertinent help pages. Regular updates to the glossary ensure alignment with the latest modifications and additions to Qlik Cloud.

Vocabulary functionality facilitates the creation and management of custom terms and definitions for data fields and datasets. Standardizing nomenclature and semantics of data elements, Vocabulary enhances clarity and context for data consumers. It promotes data literacy and collaboration within the organization while ensuring the consistency and accuracy of data assets.

These features are pivotal as they facilitate deeper insights and value extraction from data, enabling informed, data-driven decision-making. They also facilitate adherence to data governance and quality standards, nurturing a culture of data excellence.

Structure

In this chapter, we will discuss the following topics:

- Business Glossary
- Lineage
- Impact Analysis

Business Glossary

Let us begin with the Business Glossary feature. A business glossary serves as a tool for standardizing terms and definitions within the Qlik Cloud platform. Establishing a common vocabulary is vital for promoting data discovery and fostering collaboration across various departments. Within Qlik Cloud, business glossaries are categorized as a specific resource type. These glossaries encompass logical groupings populated with clearly defined terms, articulated in language accessible to all members of an organization.

The benefits of a business glossary include aiding app designers in locating standardized definitions and associated datasets, assisting business analysts in comprehending and addressing business inquiries, imbuing confidence in linked datasets and applications through contextual information, and promoting enhanced communication and collaboration across different business units.

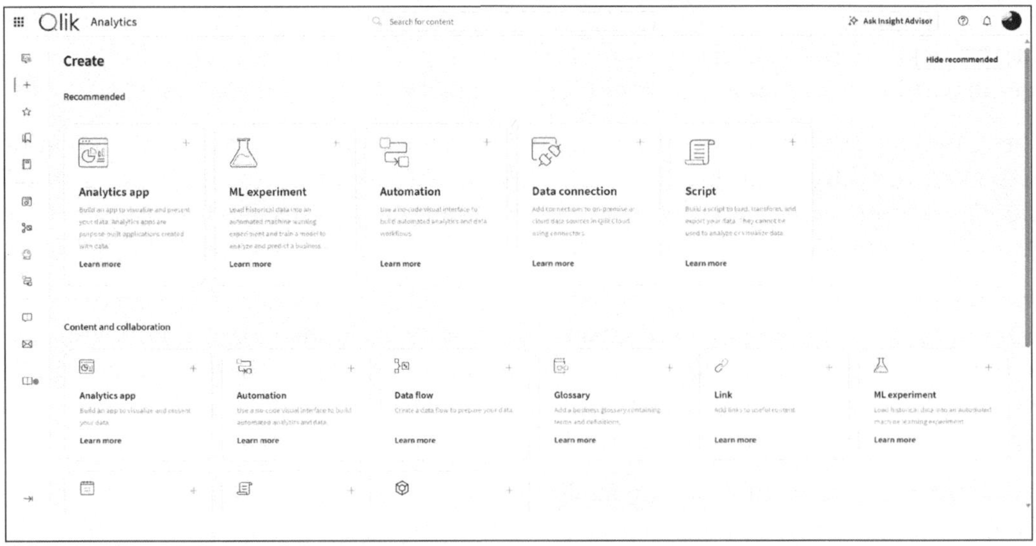

Figure 6.1: *Creating Glossary*

To begin using the business glossary, we need to assign the right role. Not everyone is a data steward. To be one, we simply assign the role called **`"Steward".`** In Qlik Sense, this role is responsible for creating and managing business glossaries. A steward can make, change, or delete glossaries, as well as edit or remove terms that are verified. Their job is to ensure the glossaries are correct and useful for the people who use them. To give someone the steward role, we use the Management Console in Qlik Cloud.

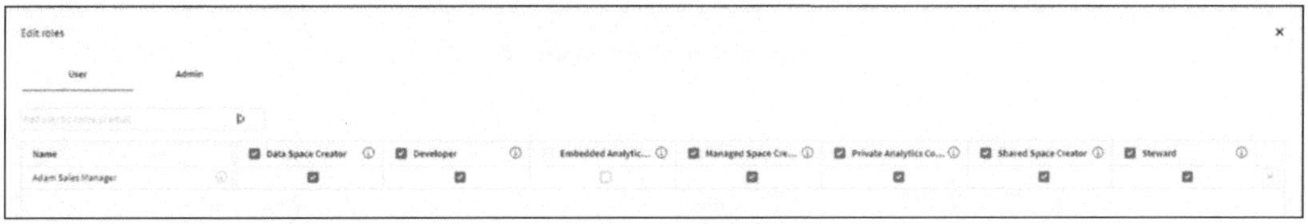

***Figure 6.2**: Steward Role*

Once the correct role is assigned, we can proceed to create new glossaries. When we navigate to "`Create Glossary`," we begin by providing the name and associated description. Then, we select the space where we want the glossary to be located. Choosing a glossary within a space allows us to manage who can access it. Additionally, we have the option to add tags to facilitate easier searching.

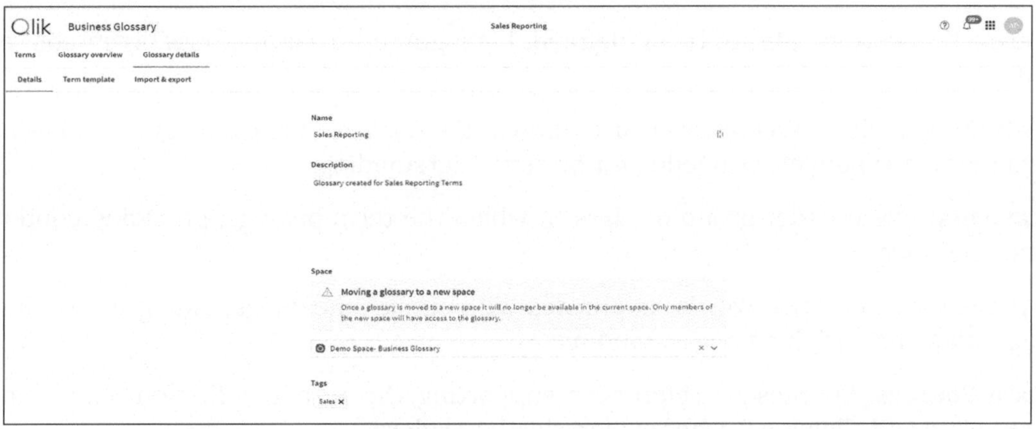

***Figure 6.3**: Configuring the Glossary*

Once we have set up the basic details of the glossary, we will move on to defining the **term template**. This feature in Qlik's business glossary enables us to outline the attributes and metadata for each term within the glossary.

With the term template, we can tailor the information we want to gather and showcase for every term, including definitions, synonyms, data sources, related terms, and more. By utilizing the term template, we ensure a standardized format and content for all terms, while also enriching them with additional details that enhance understanding and usage. Accessible through the Glossary Details tab, the steward of the glossary can both access and modify the term template. The primary purpose of the term template is to establish and uphold consistent and thorough business terms, facilitating easy search, navigation, and connection to other resources within Qlik Cloud. Once we define the term template, we select the **Save** option.

Figure 6.4: *Term Template in a business glossary*

A well-structured term glossary should include these components:

Term: The word or phrase being defined, highlighted for clarity, possibly in bold or italic font.

Definition: A clear and concise explanation of the term, avoiding ambiguity and using examples or synonyms as needed for better understanding.

Category: The broader group or class to which the term belongs, providing context and relevance.

Synonyms: Alternative words or phrases with similar meanings, aiding in avoiding repetition and enriching understanding.

Data Sources: Sources or references supporting the term's definition, enhancing credibility and allowing further exploration by readers.

After creating a business glossary, we will proceed to check the Import and Export option. Next, we will navigate to the **`Glossary Overview`** tab. This tab in Qlik's business glossary features a rich text editor that allows us to craft an overview for the glossary. Here, we can describe the objectives, operational methods, contacts, and other pertinent information related to the glossary. Additionally, we have the flexibility to incorporate hyperlinks, mission statements, and any other type of content that fosters engagement and collaboration among users of the glossary.

The purpose of the Glossary overview tab is to furnish a clear and comprehensive introduction to the glossary, delineating its purpose, scope, and context.

It is important to note that while the glossary overview tab provides a general description of the glossary as a whole, the term template tab offers a specific structure for individual terms within the glossary.

Figure 6.5: *Defining business glossary overview*

A helpful business glossary overview should cover these key points:

Overview: A short summary explaining what the business glossary is, what it includes, and why it matters.

Objectives: A list of goals and benefits for the organization and its users.

Ways of Working: A description of the roles and responsibilities of those involved in creating and maintaining the glossary, along with the processes for updating it.

Contacts: A list of names and contact details for important people involved with the glossary, such as the steward and contributors.

Having defined both the Glossary verview and term template, which will serve as our reference for structuring the glossary going forward, we will now proceed to define the terms and categories.

- **Terms**: These are the fundamental elements comprising the business glossary, encompassing business concepts, words, or phrases. They are characterized by clear definitions, abbreviations, relationships, and links to supporting resources.
- **Categories**: These are the logical classifications used to organize and group terms within the glossary. Categories follow a hierarchical structure, mirroring how users typically search for information. They may include sub-categories and relate terms across various domains.

To begin creating a category, we navigate to the **`"Create"`** option and then select **`"Category"`**.

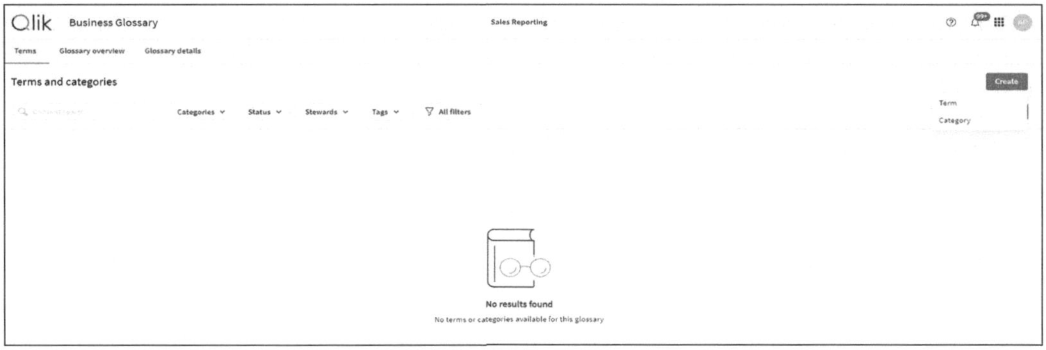

Figure 6.6: *Create a Category*

First, we will create a category named **`"Transactional KPI".`** Then, we will repeat the process to create another category to store dimensional definitions, labeled **`"Legal Definitions."`**

Figure 6.7: *Configuring a category*

Now, we have two categories defined: one for storing KPI definitions and another for legal terms. The choice between these categories typically depends on the specific report and business definitions required.

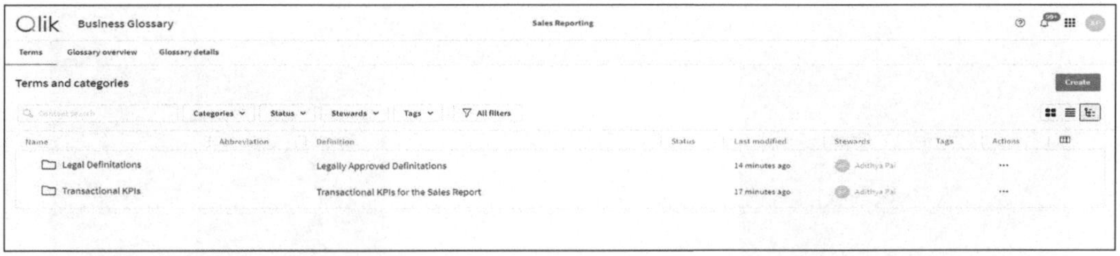

Figure 6.8: *Categories defined*

We have two methods for defining terms:

1. Within the business glossary itself: Here, we navigate to the glossary and create terms directly.
2. Utilizing an analytics application: We can open an analytics application and select the master items already set up. From there, we create a term and add it to the business glossary.

For instance, if we have a pre-built report with the sales amount displayed as a master item in the top left corner, we can select this item within the analytics application and proceed to create a corresponding term, subsequently adding it to the business glossary.

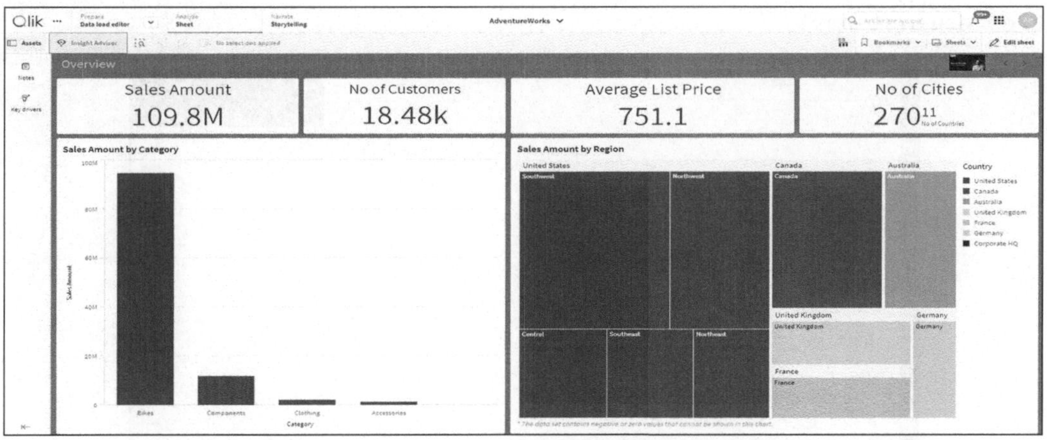

Figure 6.9: *Adding Terms from a pre-built report to a business glossary*

We will begin by opening the report in edit mode. Then, we navigate to the measures section, located under master items. Here, we will find the relevant master item named **"`Sales Amount`."**

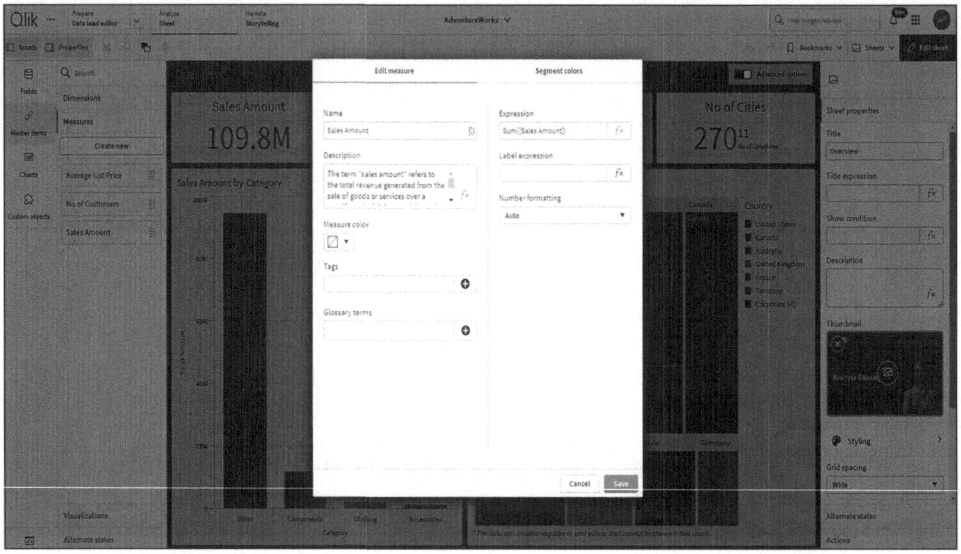

Figure 6.10: *Setting up master items to Business Glossary*

In the master item for sales amount, we will choose the "+" symbol to incorporate glossary terms. Here, we have the option to either associate this master item with an existing glossary term or to generate a new glossary term by selecting the "+" for "`Create new terms`".

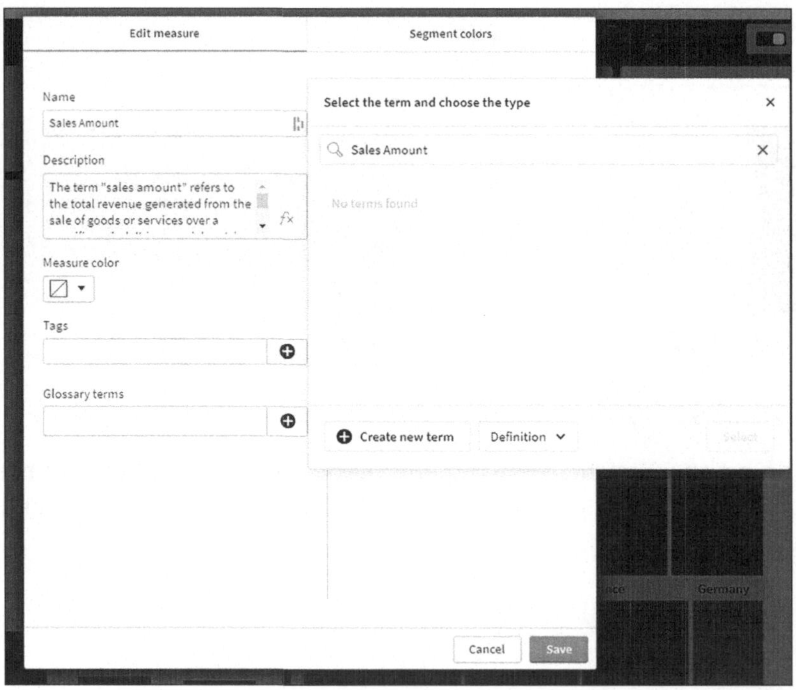

Figure 6.11: *Selecting the (+)* ***`Create new term`*** *option*

Once we input a definition for the glossary term, we offer pertinent context about the term we are defining. Following this, we designate the glossary to which we wish this term to belong by choosing the desired glossary from the drop-down menu labeled **`"Select glossary."`**

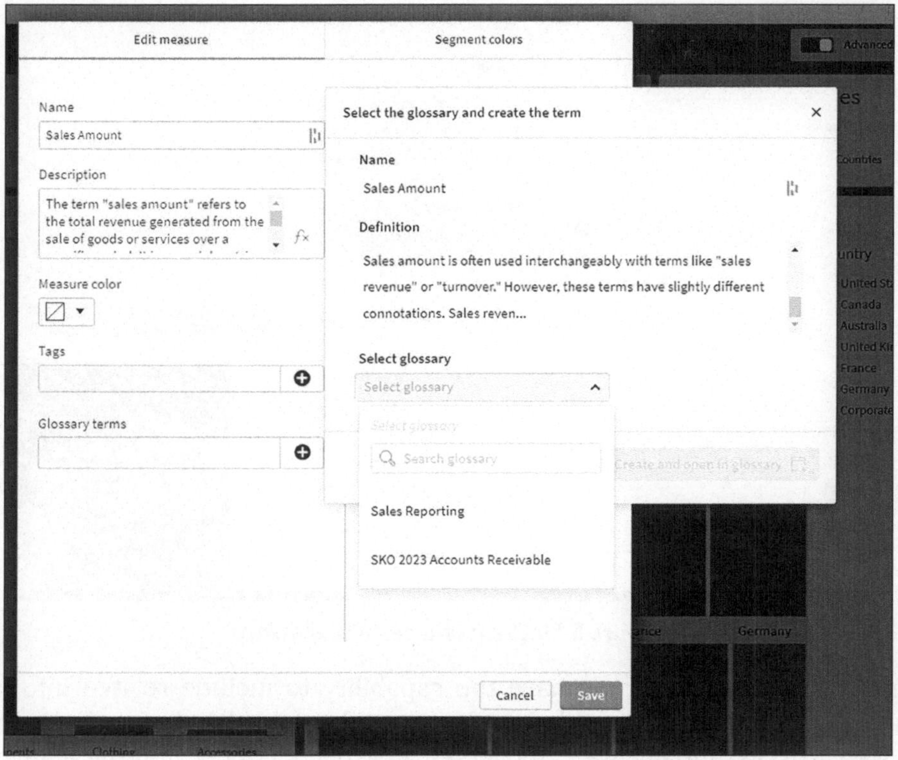

Figure 6.12: *Providing glossary definition*

Now that we have established the glossary, we can choose the "**`Create and open in glossary`**" option. This action will generate the term and seamlessly transition us from the current pop-up window within the application for building the glossary to the interface of the actual glossary.

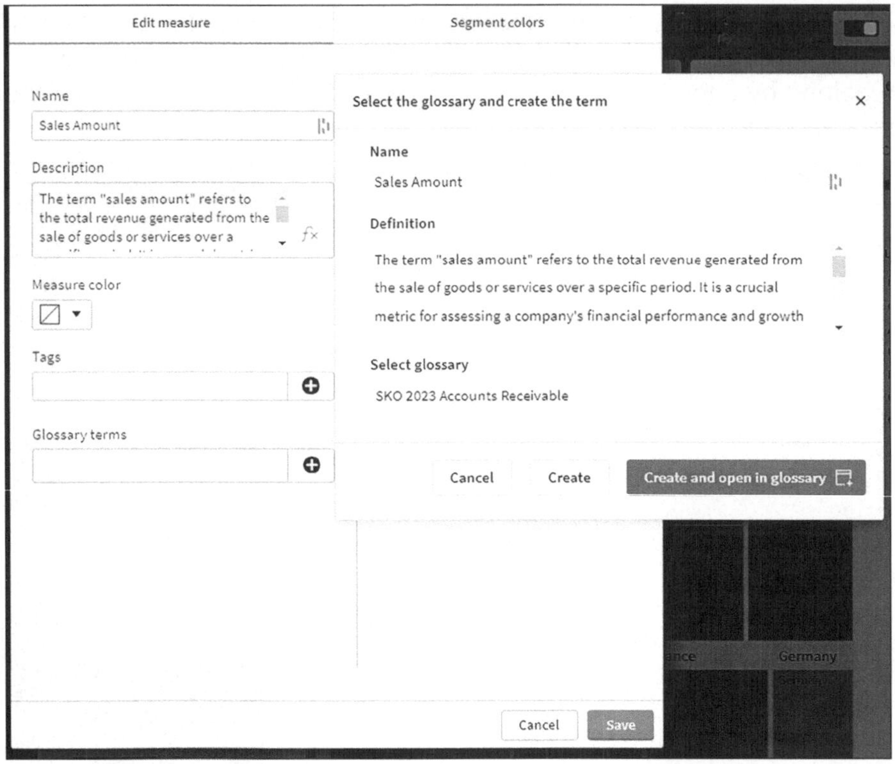

Figure 6.13: *Create the term in glossary*

Within the glossary screen, we have the capability to include related information, designate the status as draft, verified, or deprecated, establish links to other terms, and assign stewards. Essentially, we can oversee all aspects concerning the management of the glossary.

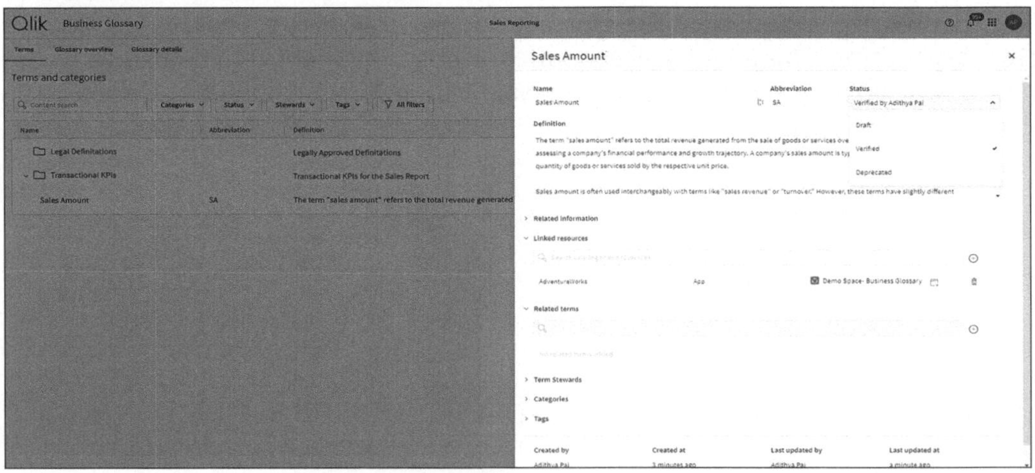

Figure 6.14: *Opening the newly defined glossary in the glossary screen*

In addition, we can observe that the recently included term "**`Sales Amount`**" is categorized under Transactional KPIs.

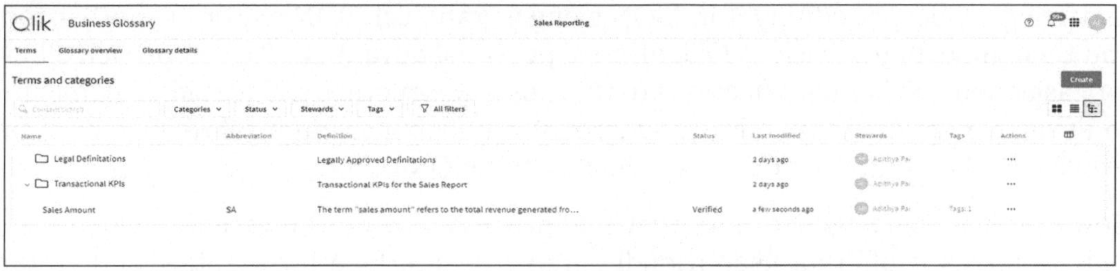

Figure 6.15: *Glossary Terms and Categories*

Importing and Exporting Glossaries

Now, let us delve into the process of importing and exporting glossaries. This functionality serves several purposes:

- Facilitating the creation and updating of your glossary from external sources, such as Atlan or Apache Atlas.
- Enabling the backup of your glossary or its importation into a different environment, such as a distinct space or tenant.
- Allowing the archiving of different versions of your glossary for reference or comparison purposes.

The file formats supported for importing and exporting glossaries are JSON files. Qlik Cloud accommodates the Qlik glossary format as well as the Atlan and Apache Atlas glossary formats. Moreover, we have the flexibility to customize the attributes and metadata of terms within the glossary file.

We first navigate to the Glossary details and then click **`Import & export`**. If we intend to reimport a glossary, select "**`Download glossary`**" to export a backup of the glossary.

Figure 6.16: *Exporting a business glossary in JSON Format*

Importing a Business Glossary

Exporting a glossary, editing it in JSON using a graphical JSON editor in another tool, and then importing it back to Qlik offers a potential advantage. This approach allows for easier and quicker modifications to the glossary structure and metadata compared to using a traditional text editor. Additionally, utilizing a graphical JSON editor can help in avoiding syntax errors and validating the JSON schema.

However, it is important to note that this process may not be essential when using Qlik Cloud, as it offers a user-friendly graphical interface for creating and editing glossaries.

Furthermore, Qlik provides glossary APIs for managing and accessing glossaries in the Qlik Cloud. These APIs enable users to perform various operations on glossaries, including creating, updating, deleting, importing, exporting, and searching glossaries. Additionally, users can utilize the APIs to establish links between glossary terms and datasets or apps, as well as to obtain term suggestions and definitions.

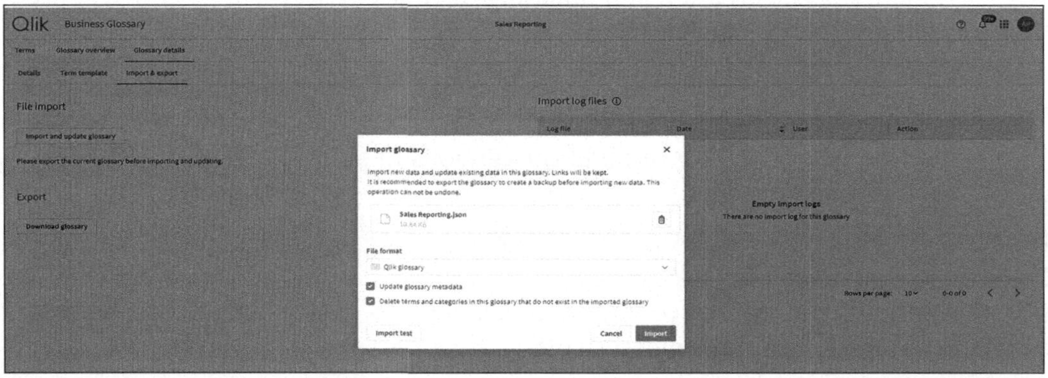

Figure 6.17: *Importing a business glossary*

We proceed by clicking **`Import and update glossary`**. If necessary, choose **`Update glossary metadata`** to update the glossary overview and details. Optionally, to remove all terms and categories not present in the import file, tick the box for **`Delete terms and categories in this glossary that do not exist in the imported glossary`**. You may also optionally click **`Import test`** to test the import and review the log, which can be downloaded as a TXT file. Finally, click **`Import`** to complete the process, and once done, we can see the detailed status of the process, as in *Figure* 6.18.

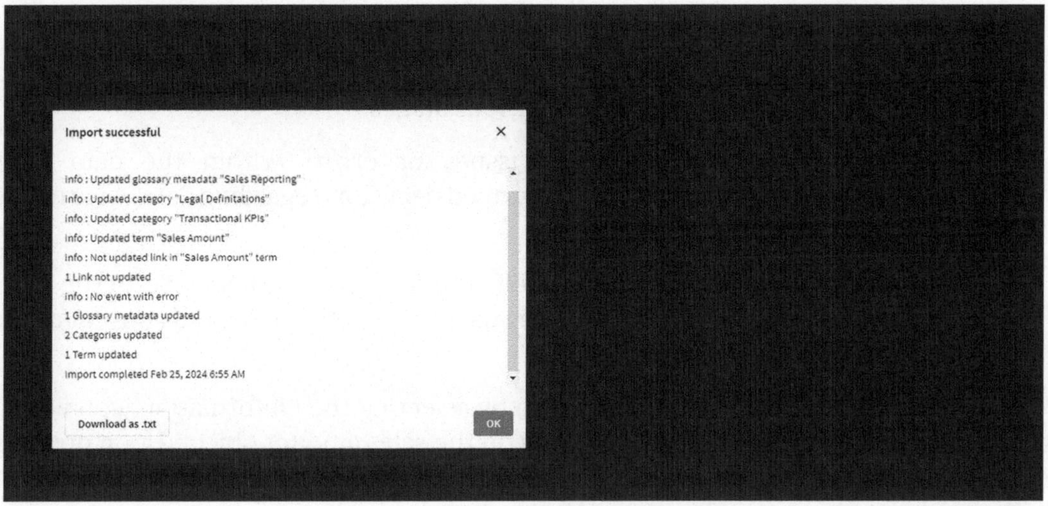

***Figure 6.18**: Successful import log*

Business glossary users have the option to subscribe to glossary notifications, ensuring they are promptly informed of any new glossary term creations, deletions, or updates. Notification recipients vary based on their roles: the owner of the glossary receives notifications regarding added terms, while the stewards of a term receive notifications regarding any changes to those terms. This feature facilitates efficient communication and ensures relevant stakeholders stay updated on glossary modifications in a timely manner.

Now that we have seen Business glossary, let us now go ahead and understand what lineage and impact analysis are. Illustrating the relationship between a business glossary and lineage and impact analysis is akin to comparing them to a map and a GPS navigation system for your data journey. In this analogy, **a business glossary functions as a map**, providing visual guidance by depicting the landmarks and destinations of your data, including terms, definitions, categories, and datasets. Conversely, **lineage + impact analysis acts as a GPS navigation system**, offering real-time guidance by indicating the direction and distance of your data journey, such as its origins, destinations, and associated impacts. Together, these tools serve to navigate the complex data landscape, aiding users in understanding and reaching their desired outcomes effectively.

Lineage

In Qlik Cloud, Lineage is a feature designed to facilitate tracking data and its transformations from its original source to the final output. It furnishes users with a visual representation delineating the historical trajectory and dependencies of their data, applications, scripts, and fields. Lineage serves as a valuable tool for understanding, trusting, and optimizing the data pipeline.

Among the benefits of utilizing Lineage in Qlik Cloud are:

1. Visualization of the data's source and quality, along with its calculation and transformation processes across various stages.
2. Identification and resolution of issues or errors within the data flow, empowering users to make well-informed decisions regarding data governance and compliance.
3. Exploration and analysis of the ramifications of alterations made to the data, applications, or scripts, thus enabling users to prevent undesired consequences or disruptions.

We can access detailed lineage information by selecting the i information icon within the object. In this instance, we are focusing on the sales amount object. Upon opening it, a pop-up window will appear. Initially, we will encounter the glossary associated with the object, as previously defined.

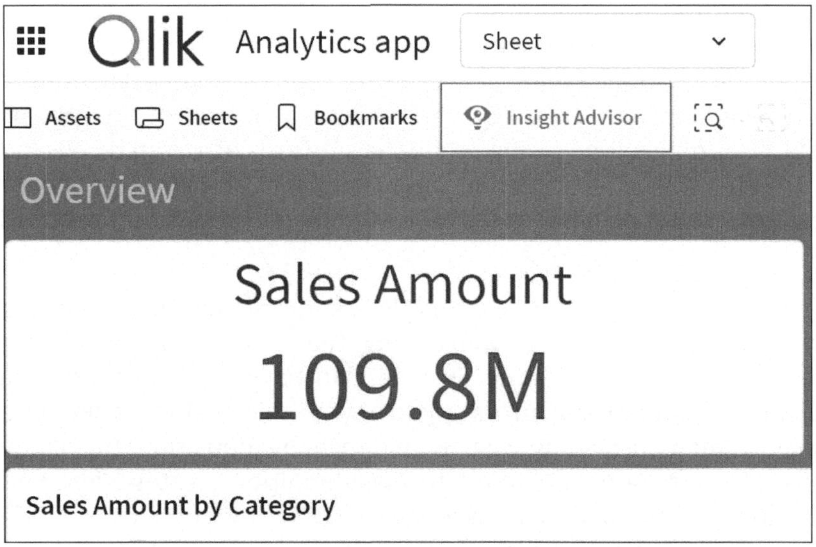

Figure 6.19: *Linking lineage for an already created master item*

Within the pop-up view, we can observe a summary of the measure.

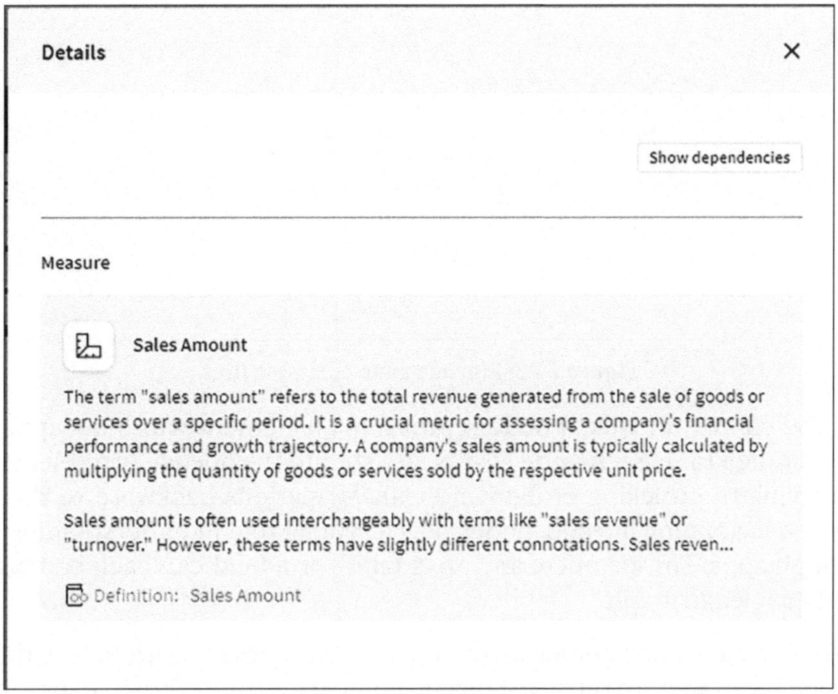

Figure 6.20: *Master Item shows link to the Glossary*

In the initial popup window, we choose **`Show Dependencies`**, which directs us to a screen displaying the measures, fields, and sources. In this scenario, the KPI is solely derived from the Sales Amount. Therefore, we observe only one value listed under **`"Fields": Sales Amount`**. If there were multiple sources, they would all be listed here. We can then trace the lineage at the field level for each of these sources.

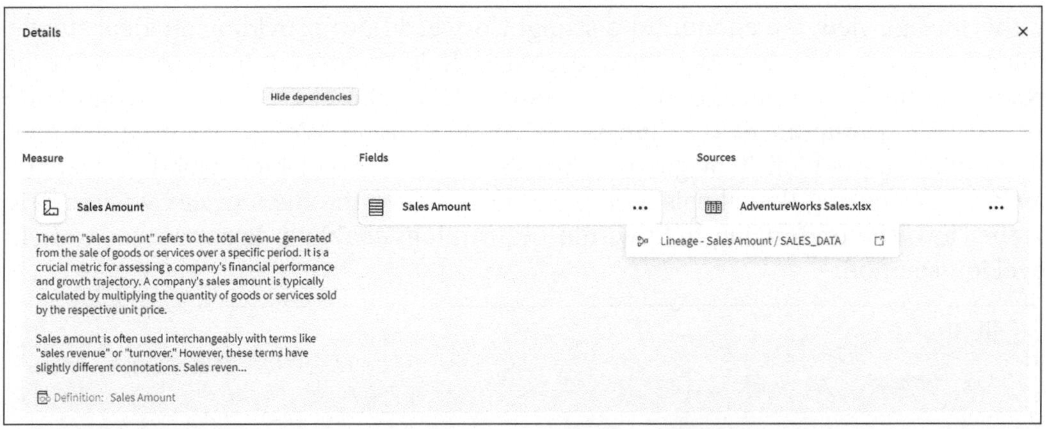

Figure 6.21: *Dependency screen showing the underlying fields, measures, and sources*

We select the ellipsis icon next to the Sales Amount field and then proceed to select **`Lineage`**. This action directs us to a detailed lineage view.

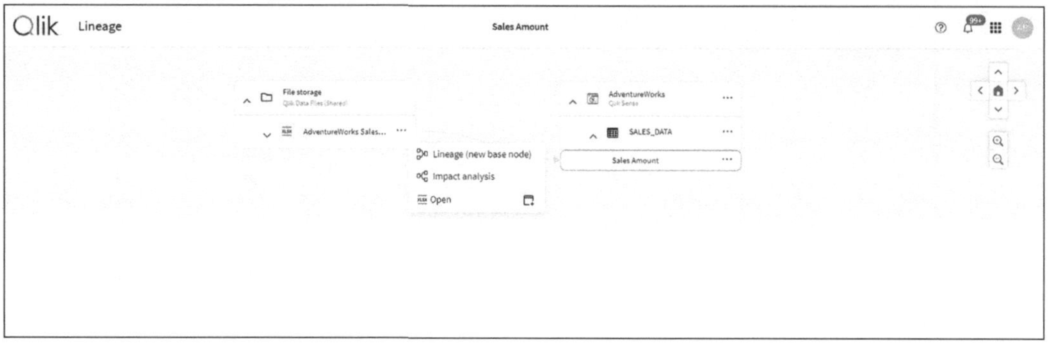

***Figure 6.22**: Lineage view of simple flow*

Nodes: In the context of Qlik, a node represents an element within an app, such as a table, field, or data task. Each node serves as a step in the lineage of a selected dataset or app, enabling the tracking of data and transformations backward to their original source. When examining lineage, nodes play a crucial role in understanding how data flows through apps. For instance, an app, a table, or a field can each be considered a node within a lineage graph.

Base Node: The base node serves as the focal point of investigation. It is the singular node for which you want to retrieve lineage or impact analysis. When exploring lineage or impact, the base node is typically the right-most node on your screen, outlined in blue. Only inputs to this base node are presented during the analysis.

Selecting an Object as a New Base Node: When you choose an object, such as a field or dataset, and designate it as a new base node, the selected object becomes the focus of your investigation. You can explore its upstream lineage (how it is sourced) or downstream impact (which objects depend on it).

In this lineage view, we encounter a straightforward flow, providing an ideal starting point for comprehending the lineage charts. It is important to note that we are examining field-level lineage in this instance. Thus, the chart essentially illustrates that our Sales Amount field originates from file storage. We can observe the name of the file from which it originates–in this case, an Excel file named **"`Adventure Works.`"** By clicking the ellipsis icon once more under the file storage, we can delve deeper into the underlying field within the catalog, enabling direct access to field-level information.

***Figure 6.23:** Lineage view of a flow that has data from a MySQL Server*

In the second example depicted in *Figures* 6.24(*a*) and 6.24(*b*), we observe the field-level lineage view of another use case. Please refer to the provided screenshots. In this instance, we are examining a single lineage flow presented across two screenshots. *Figure* 6.24(*a*) displays the Presentation layer and the underlying transformation layer. We are specifically tracking the lineage for a field called **`"Full_Name"`**. It is evident that this field is generated by the transformation application. The name of the application is visible, and of course, we can seamlessly navigate to the application from the lineage view to analyze the underlying code.

Figure 6.24 (a): *Lineage view of the Presentation and underlying transformation layer*

In the next stage of our lineage exploration, we navigate to the left to track and trace the source, where the underlying transformations occur, and discern the actual source fields. In this case, we observe that the extraction application directly retrieves the underlying fields from the MySQL source. Neither in the source nor in the source extraction do we encounter any business logic for this field; rather, we obtain directly what exists in the source.

Moving on to the next step, the Transformation application, this is where the real magic unfolds. We can meticulously track all of this directly in the lineage. Here, we see that the transformation application selects two fields—**`first_name`** and **`last_name`**—and combines them to generate a new field called **`"Full_Name"`**. This level of transparency is truly remarkable. We gain a comprehensive understanding of the entire process, from its origins to each subsequent step, without the need to navigate through numerous applications or sift through extensive code. This is precisely what makes the lineage view incredibly valuable and efficient.

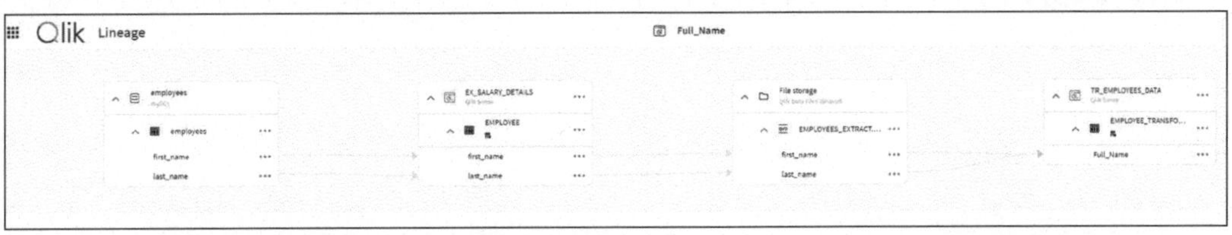

Figure 6.24 (b): *Extraction and transformation part of the lineage view*

Field-level lineage serves to enhance understanding and confidence in data integrity by meticulously tracing the calculation process of fields and pinpointing their precise origins throughout various transformations and applications. The lineage graph provides a visual depiction of the data flow across applications. Each node within the graph symbolizes a stage in the lineage of a chosen dataset or application. At their most granular level, field-level lineage graphs delineate the data sources and transformations from which a node (field or dataset) originates or upon which it relies.

Lineage View at Application Level

Similar to field-level lineage, application-level lineage provides comprehensive tracking of data and its transformations but operates at the macro level of the entire Qlik Sense application. It offers an intricate visual representation of the data flow history within the app, tracing it back to its original source. The lineage graph at the application level illustrates how data progresses from its initial sources, such as data connectors or files, through various transformations like data modeling, calculations, and joins, until it reaches the final state within the app. It encompasses all aspects of the application, including fields, tables, and transformations.

Application-level lineage covers the entirety of the Qlik Sense app, while field-level lineage focuses on individual fields.

Application-level lineage aids in comprehending the overall data flow and establishing trust in the data.

Field-level lineage is indispensable for understanding the specifics of field calculations and dependencies.

In essence, application-level lineage provides the overarching perspective, while field-level lineage delves into the finer details. Both forms of lineage are integral components of effective data governance and analysis within Qlik Sense.

To access the field-level lineage of an application, we initiate the process by selecting the application from the hub. Following this, we right-click the application and opt for the "`Lineage`" option. This action directs us to the lineage view, akin to what we have encountered previously. However, this flow encompasses the lineage for the entire application, providing a comprehensive overview of the data flow and transformations within the app.

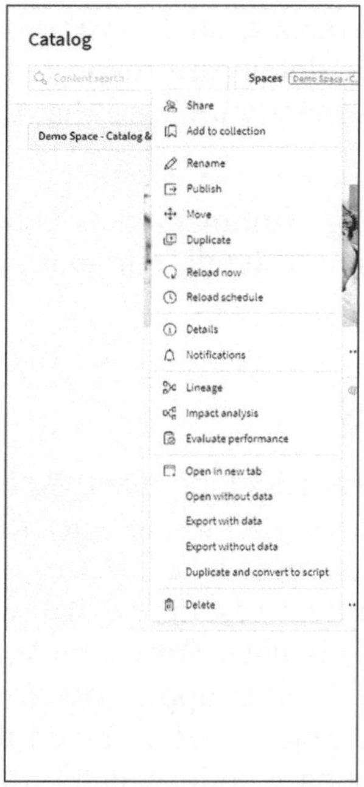

Figure 6.25: *Opening the field level linage of an application*

In the application view, we observe the involvement of multiple extractor apps and transformation apps within the application's ETL (Extract, Transform, Load) process. These components can be summarized collectively in a single view, providing an overview of the entire ETL workflow within the application.

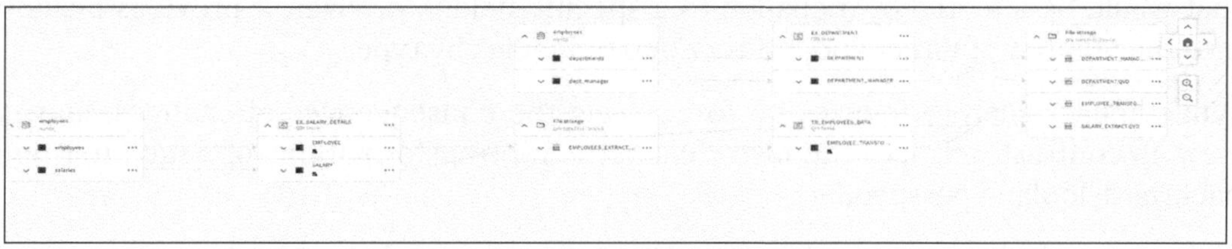

Figure 6.26: *Application level lineage*

To view the lineage for an app or dataset from the hub, it is necessary to have viewing access to that particular item. If you have access to view the lineage graph for a base node, you will also be able to see basic details and metadata for the upstream lineage objects. This ensures that users can understand the flow of data and access relevant information about the data sources and transformations involved in the lineage.

Apps that have not undergone a reload subsequent to the introduction of lineage in Qlik Cloud may not have comprehensive lineage information available until they are reloaded. In such cases, details for some nodes may be limited. This limitation applies particularly to nodes that have not been loaded after lineage was enabled for your tenant.

For datasets external to your tenant, such as those sourced from SQL Server or Google Drive connections, node details are restricted to the dataset type and name. Additionally, REST connections merely indicate that the data originates from a REST source.

It is worth noting that the lineage summary view is not compatible with Button and Map charts. Furthermore, the chart details summary view is presently unavailable in mobile mode.

Impact Analysis

Impact analysis offers a forward-looking perspective on dependencies within a database, application, or field, revealing the potential ramifications of alterations to data or application components. It addresses inquiries regarding databases, applications, files, links, and other resources that would be directly or indirectly influenced if the value of a field changes. For example, when modifying a field, impact analysis illuminates the objects, such as applications, datasets, or reports, that would be impacted. These influenced objects are referred to as dependents, representing the downstream nodes from the base node, which is the field or object under analysis. Impact analysis answers questions such as: Where else is this used? How much is this utilized? What is the impact if we make a change to this?

In Qlik Cloud, users benefit from an aggregated summary of downstream impact, enabling interactive exploration of both direct and indirect dependencies. This summary showcases the types of objects, including databases, applications, and files, that would be affected by a change to a specific field. Moreover, it provides insights into the number of direct and indirect dependencies by type.

While impact analysis focuses on forecasting the consequences of changes, lineage view, in contrast, retraces the historical path and transformations of data, offering a backward-looking perspective.

In this scenario, let us proceed with conducting impact analysis at both the dataset and field levels. To initiate the process, we navigate to the catalog and locate the dataset for which we intend to perform the impact analysis. We aim to understand where this dataset is utilized throughout the system.

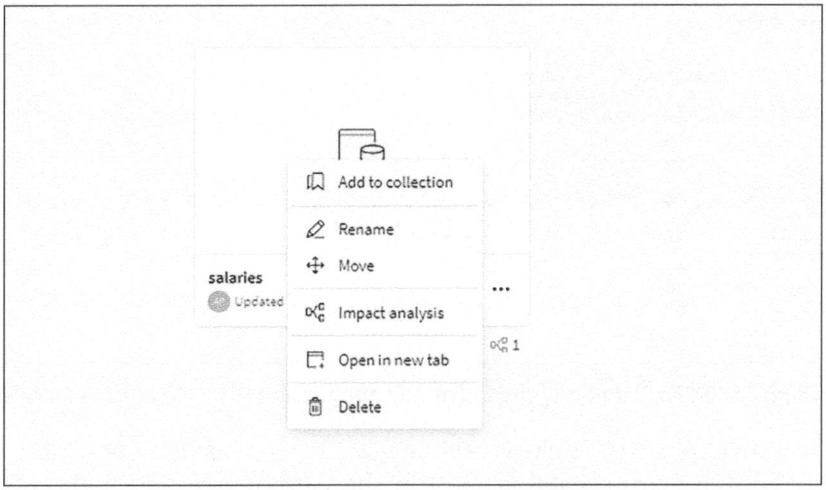

Figure 6.27: *Impact analysis of the Data Set starting from the catalog*

In the impact analysis view for the "**Salaries**" dataset, we observe that the dataset is utilized within the "**Extractor**" application. While the extractor naturally generates a new file, the impact analysis tool efficiently tracks the data flow through subsequent transformations. Following extraction, the data flow proceeds to the “Salary Analysis” application, which serves as the presentation layer.

Additionally, on the left side of the view, we can identify the applications and file storage locations that contain the "**Salary**" dataset. By toggling the option to show only direct dependencies, we streamline the view to display solely the first-level dependents of the selected field or object. These direct dependencies encompass objects directly linked to the dataset or field under analysis.

For instance, when examining a specific field within the dataset, the direct dependencies would encompass other fields, charts, reports, or applications that directly rely on the value of that field. This simplifies the view by excluding secondary or cascading impacts, providing a clearer understanding of the immediate dependencies.

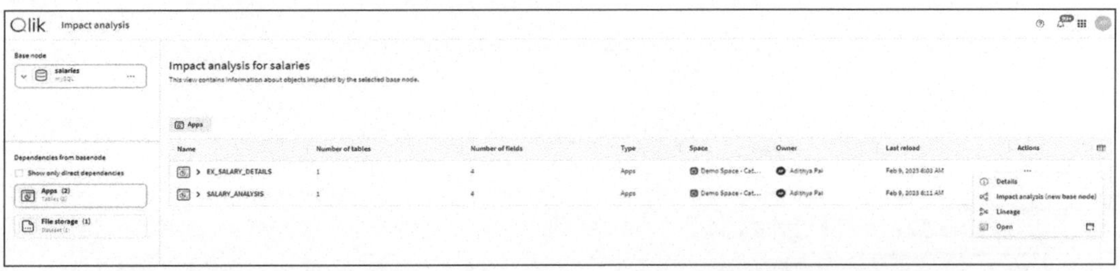

Figure 6.28: *Impact analysis of the Data Set showing the related applications*

We have the capability to drill down to various levels, commencing from the app, then proceeding to drill down to the table, and subsequently examining individual fields.

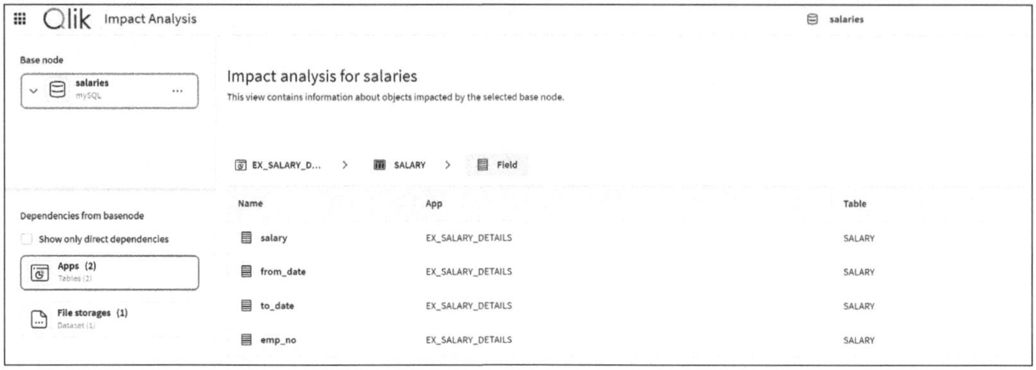

***Figure 6.29**: Drill down of the Extractor application to see field level details*

Likewise, we can explore the field-level lineage. Let us consider a new example where we open a CSV file via the catalog. Within the catalog, we locate the CSV file and then proceed to select the ellipsis (**...**) icon to access additional options, including the option to navigate to the impact analysis. This allows us to analyze the impact of changes at the field level within the CSV file.

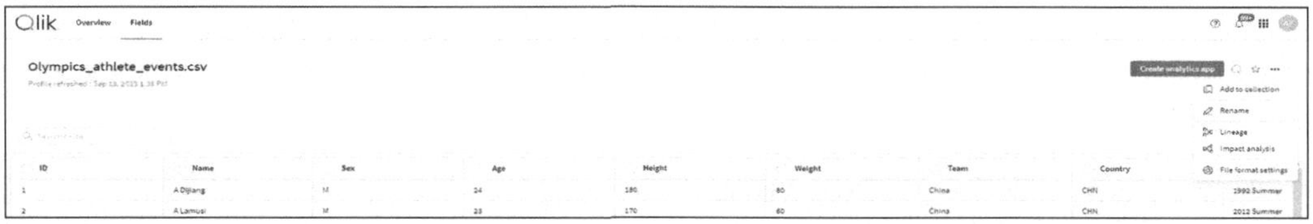

***Figure 6.30**: Navigation to the field level–impact analysis view from the catalog*

In the subsequent step, we gain insight into the entirety of applications utilizing the CSV file as a dataset. An intriguing feature is the **"number of fields"** column, which provides valuable information indicating how many fields from the CSV file are being loaded into each of the applications. This feature allows us to understand the extent of utilization of the CSV file across different applications.

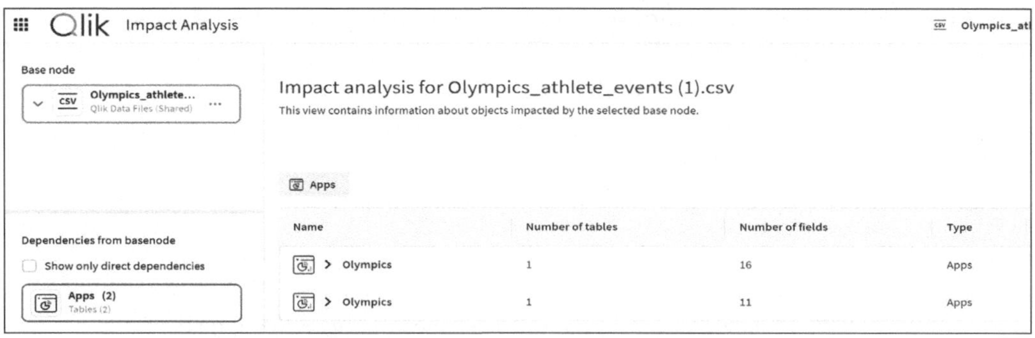

***Figure 6.31:** Field level impact analysis*

Number of Tables:

This column indicates the count of distinct tables that are directly or indirectly impacted by changes to a specific field. It answers questions like: "*If the value of a particular field changes, how many different tables would be affected?*" For example, if you modify a field in one table, the impact analysis will reveal how many other tables rely on that field, either directly or indirectly.

Number of Fields:

This column represents the total number of fields (also known as columns or attributes) that are impacted by changes to the selected field. It provides insight into the breadth of the impact caused by altering a specific field. For instance, if you change the value of a field, this column will show how many other fields across various tables are influenced by that change.

From the CSV file, we have the capability to filter fields. Let us take an example where we filter the field named **"NOC"**. Once this filter is applied, we observe that the number of applications is reduced to 1. Consequently, the application that does not utilize the "NOC" field is no longer displayed in the impact analysis. This filtering mechanism enables a focused analysis tailored to specific fields of interest.

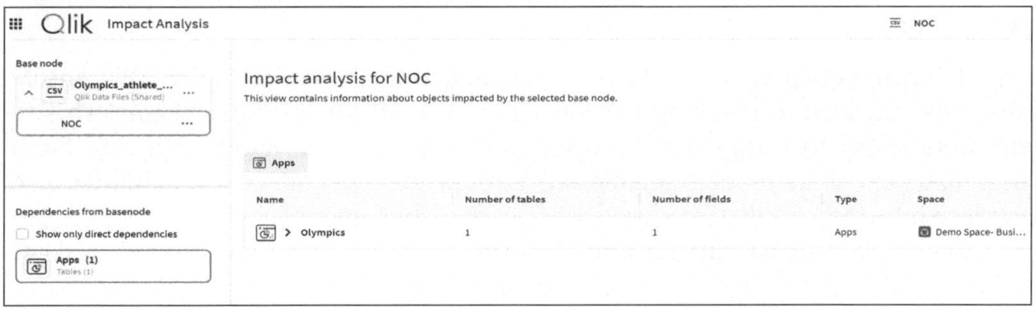

***Figure 6.32**: Selecting a field to see the impact analysis*

Users without view permissions will have restricted access to certain information and functionalities within the Qlik platform. Specifically, they will not be able to view dependent resource names or access details such as the Last reload column for dependent apps or the Last modified column for other resource types. Additionally, these users will be unable to access the context menu or drill-in options for the resource. This limitation ensures that users without view permissions cannot view or interact with sensitive information beyond their authorized access level.

Conclusion

A business glossary serves as a valuable asset within the Qlik Cloud platform, aiming to standardize terms and definitions across the organization. Its key features include standardization, data discovery, and collaboration. Standardization ensures consistent terminology usage across departments, while data discovery assists users in discovering and comprehending data through clear definitions. Collaboration is facilitated by the glossary, enabling communication across various lines of business.

Components of a business glossary typically include the name, description, terms, categories, and additional details. The name represents the title of the glossary, while the description provides an overview of its purpose. Terms are logical categories populated with standardized terms, organized within the glossary's categories. Additional details may include abbreviations, relations, and links to supporting assets. Glossaries can be linked to datasets and apps to provide deeper context and validation.

Impact analysis aids in understanding how changes to one element affect others. Key aspects of impact analysis include choosing a focal point (for example, a field or dataset) as the base node, exploring how the base node is sourced in upstream lineage, and identifying objects dependent on the base node in downstream impact. This analysis provides confidence in linked datasets and apps.

Lineage illustrates the flow of data within an app. Its components include nodes representing elements such as tables, fields, and tasks. Lineage helps in understanding the movement of data from source to destination, with the base node determining the lineage path.

In the following chapter, we will explore advanced analytics, including Qlik AutoML, a no-code, automated machine learning tool tailored for analytics teams. This tool empowers users to design machine learning experiments, identify pivotal factors within data, and train models seamlessly. With predictive analytics capabilities, users can make informed predictions and assess various business scenarios. Integrated into Qlik Cloud, Qlik AutoML further amplifies the potency of Qlik's distinctive analytics engine.

Multiple Choice Questions

1. What is the primary purpose of a business glossary in Qlik?
    a. To standardize terms and definitions across the organization
    b. To create complex data visualizations
    c. To automate data loading processes
    d. To track user activity within apps
2. What does impact analysis in Qlik help you understand?
    a. The history of a field or dataset
    b. The ultimate source of data

   c. How changes to a specific field affect other elements
   d. The number of apps in your environment
3. What does lineage represent in Qlik?
   a. The flow of data from end-user applications to original data sources
   b. The dependencies of a specific field
   c. The history of a field or dataset
   d. The number of transformations applied to data
4. Which component of a business glossary organizes terms into logical groups?
   a. Abbreviations
   b. Categories
   c. Additional Details
   d. Terms
5. What is the role of the base node in impact analysis?
   a. It represents the most critical field in the app
   b. It determines the lineage path
   c. It identifies the ultimate source of data
   d. It is the focal point for investigation

Answers

1. a
2. c
3. c
4. b
5. d

References

1. *Qlik Help*: https://help.qlik.com/
2. What Is a Business Glossary? - DATAVERSITY

CHAPTER 7
Advanced Analytics - AutoML

Introduction

In this chapter, we will explore the utilization of AutoML, an automated machine-learning process that identifies patterns within our data to forecast future outcomes. While AutoML is a vast topic deserving of its dedicated book, here we will begin by laying the groundwork. We will focus on understanding the basics, serving as a stepping stone for embarking on your AutoML journey.

Structure

In this chapter, we will cover the following topics:

- Why AutoML
- Experiment
- Models

Introduction to AutoML

In Analytics, we have been transitioning from analytics being solely IT-driven to recognizing the value of democratizing data. This involves enabling self-service capabilities, whether for the end user or within specific business areas, by equipping them with the necessary tools for analytics.

Self-service business intelligence (BI) tools streamline the data analysis process, allowing users to interact directly with their data and generate tailored reports. This approach empowers users by providing them with the means to address their inquiries, explore data autonomously, and make informed decisions, all without necessitating specialized training.

Similarly, AutoML introduces advanced analytics opportunities by automating the intricate processes inherent in machine learning. This technology empowers data analysts to construct and implement machine learning models without requiring extensive technical expertise, thus democratizing access to advanced analytics capabilities.

Qlik AutoML streamlines the process of leveraging machine learning insights, making them accessible to analytics teams across diverse domains.

One might question the relevance: ***Shouldn't we delegate advanced tasks to data scientists and focus solely on analytics?*** However, this perspective overlooks the significance of democratizing data. Democratizing machine learning (ML) holds pivotal importance for various reasons:

- **Lowering Entry Barriers**: Historically, accessing the extensive data and computational capabilities essential for machine learning (ML) was primarily within the reach of large corporations with substantial resources. Democratization breaks down these barriers, granting access to individuals and startups, thereby facilitating the exploration of ideas and validation of concepts without significant initial investments.
- **Encouraging Wider Adoption and Innovation**: By disseminating ML tools and knowledge to a broader audience, we stimulate widespread adoption, fostering innovation across various domains. Enhanced accessibility empowers more individuals to experiment, innovate, and refine ML techniques.
- **Increased Efficiency**: AutoML streamlines numerous time-consuming tasks associated with machine learning, such as algorithm selection and hyperparameter tuning. This enhanced efficiency translates into expedited insights and accelerates decision-making processes.
- **Cost-Effectiveness**: By empowering non-experts to undertake tasks traditionally reserved for data scientists, organizations can optimize their workforce and diminish the necessity for a large team of highly specialized individuals.
- **Innovation and Competitive Edge**: Democratizing access to machine learning tools can spur innovative solutions and confer a competitive advantage in the marketplace. Diverse teams leveraging AutoML capabilities can unearth distinctive insights and propel innovation forward.

While the democratization of machine learning (ML) indeed promotes inclusivity, spurs innovation, and unlocks transformative applications across diverse fields, there are valid reasons why not every organization opts to hire a data scientist.

- **Difficulty in Finding Qualified Data Scientists**: The demand for data scientists has surpassed the available talent pool, posing challenges for companies seeking qualified individuals. The field of data science is continually evolving, requiring increasingly specialized skill sets, which contributes to the scarcity of suitable candidates.

- **Cost Implications of Hiring Data Scientists**: Data scientists command substantial salaries due to their specialized expertise and the high demand for their skills. This can lead to significant operational costs for companies, particularly for startups and small to medium-sized businesses.
- **Advantages of Leveraging Data Analysts with AutoML**: Existing data analysts within a company possess a deep understanding of the organization's data, its structure, and its business context. They are familiar with specific company challenges and objectives, which is essential for effective data analysis.

AutoML operates as a complementary tool for data scientists, enriching their capabilities rather than replacing them. Through automating routine tasks within machine learning, it empowers data scientists to dedicate their efforts to solving complex problems and fostering innovation. This approach facilitates resource optimization, particularly given the scarcity and cost associated with data science expertise. By streamlining mundane tasks, AutoML allows organizations to allocate their resources efficiently, enabling data science teams to focus on high-value activities and thereby maximize their impact.

Here is a breakdown of typical use cases managed by a data scientist compared to those handled by automated machine learning (AutoML):

Handled by Data Scientist	**Handled by AutoML**
Complex data preprocessing	Standard data preprocessing
Custom model development	Pre-built model selection
Advanced feature engineering	Basic feature engineering
Domain-specific model tuning	General hyperparameter optimization
Interpretation of model results	Automated model evaluation
Deployment of custom models	Deployment of standard models
Ethical considerations in modeling	Routine data predictions
Research and development of new algorithms	Application of established algorithms

Table 7.1: *Comparison of Data Scientist Use Case versus AutoML*

Data scientists primarily tackle intricate, customized, and research-oriented tasks demanding profound expertise in data, domain knowledge, and modeling techniques. Conversely, AutoML is tailored for automating routine, standardized tasks, making it beneficial for swift deployment and accessible to users with less proficiency in machine learning.

Qlik AutoML

In 2021, Qlik acquired Big Squid, a leading provider of no-code automated machine learning (AutoML). By integrating Big Squid's AutoML into Qlik's platform, data and analytics teams gain access to AI-driven models for on-demand predictions directly within Qlik.

Qlik AutoML, now seamlessly integrated into Qlik Cloud, offers a user-friendly, no-code interface that empowers analytics teams to effortlessly create machine learning experiments and identify key drivers in their data. With this platform, users can generate future predictions on current data, complete with prediction influencer data (Shapley values) at the record level, facilitating a deeper understanding of prediction rationale.

Qlik AutoML complements existing analytics within Qlik:

- **Model Generation**: It automates the generation of predictive models by discerning key drivers in historical data and employing optimal algorithms for model creation.
- **Predictive Insights**: Users can load data and automatically generate likely outcomes based on predictive models, enhancing decision-making with data-driven predictions.
- **What-If Scenarios**: Leveraging Qlik's Associative Engine, users can explore predictive data and test what-if scenarios in real-time, obtaining instant calculations and evaluations of potential outcomes.
- **Integration with Qlik Sense**: Qlik AutoML seamlessly integrates with Qlik Sense for interactive exploration, enabling users to harness Qlik's powerful analytics engine for enhanced insights.

Qlik AutoML enriches Qlik's analytics capabilities by introducing predictive analytics, transitioning business analytics from retrospective to predictive and prescriptive. This integration empowers users to not only comprehend past data but also forecast future events and outcomes, thereby facilitating more informed decision-making processes.

Model Types

In Qlik AutoML, we primarily work with three types of models, each serving distinct purposes:

- **Binary Classification**: This machine learning problem entails predicting whether something belongs to one of two possible categories, such as **Yes or No**.

  For instance, one might aim to predict whether an email is spam or not, or whether a customer will purchase a product. In binary classification, the output is represented by either 0 or 1, signifying the two classes.

- **Regression**: In this machine learning problem, the objective is to predict a **continuous value**, such as a number.

  For example, one might seek to predict the price of a house, the weight of a person, or the revenue of a company. In regression, the output comprises a real number capable of taking any value within a specified range.

- **Multiclass Classification**: This machine learning problem involves predicting which of **more than two possible categories something belongs to**.

  For instance, one might endeavor to predict the type of animal in a picture, the genre of a book, or the sentiment of a review. In multiclass classification, the output consists of one of several potential labels, representing the classes.

Experiments

In the realm of AutoML, we begin by delving into two primary types of assets: the first being an experiment.

By referencing the dictionary definition of "experiment," we understand it as "**a procedure carried out to support or refute a hypothesis, or to determine the efficacy or likelihood of something previously untried.**"

In the context of Qlik AutoML, an experiment entails training machine learning algorithms using a specific dataset and a designated target. This process yields machine learning models suitable for predictive analysis. The majority of this procedure is automated, streamlining the workflow for data analysts and scientists. Upon creating an experiment and loading a dataset, the data undergoes automatic analysis and preprocessing to prepare it for machine learning tasks. Through conducting experiments in Qlik AutoML, users gain insights into various crucial aspects associated with machine learning and predictive analytics.

- **Model Performance and Accuracy**:
  - Through experiments, we obtain insights into the performance of our machine-learning model.
  - Metrics such as accuracy, precision, recall, and F1-score offer a quantitative evaluation of the model's effectiveness.
  - Understanding these metrics aids in assessing whether the model achieves the desired accuracy level for prediction.
- **Feature Importance**:
  - Experiments reveal the features (variables) that exert the most significant influence on the model's predictions.

    - Identifying influential features enables us to prioritize optimizing or enhancing them to enhance overall model performance.
- **Algorithm Comparison**:
    - Qlik AutoML facilitates experimenting with various machine-learning algorithms.
    - By comparing different algorithms (for example, random forests, gradient boosting, or neural networks), we can determine the most suitable one for our specific use case.
- **Hyperparameter Tuning:**
    - Experiments involve adjusting hyperparameters, which are settings governing the model's behavior.
    - We explore different hyperparameter values to discover the optimal configuration.
    - This process assists in fine-tuning the model for improved prediction accuracy.
- **Overfitting and Generalization:**
    - Experiments aid in identifying overfitting, which occurs when a model performs well on training data but poorly on unseen data.
    - Understanding overfitting ensures that the model generalizes effectively to new, real-world examples.

Having **unlimited experiments** in Qlik AutoML is significant because it allows us to explore diverse combinations of targets, features, and settings, aiding in finding the optimal model for our data and business objectives.

With this capability, we can compare the performance and accuracy of various models and versions, gaining insights into the key drivers and predictions of our model. Unlimited experiments empower us to delve into different types of data and models, including binary classification, multiclass classification, and regression. This exploration enables us to uncover new patterns, trends, and opportunities within our data, thereby enhancing our analytics capabilities.

To commence our work with experiments, we will initially create a space wherein we intend to save this asset. We have the option to utilize our personal space or a shared space. Once the space is established, **we can proceed to create a new experiment**.

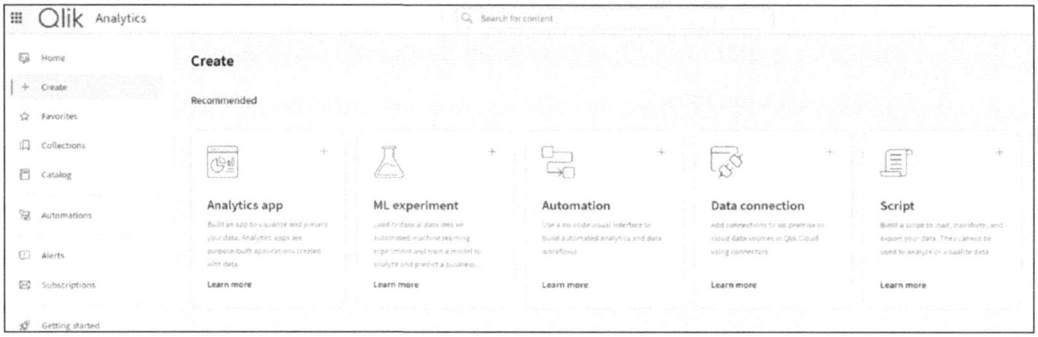

Figure 7.1: *Creating an AutoML Experiment*

We navigate to "**`+ Create`**", and then select "**`ML Experiment`**". Following this, we provide the necessary details such as the name, and description, and add tags as required. Additionally, there is a checkbox that determines whether this experiment should open immediately after creation or if we should remain on the same screen.

Figure 7.2: *Configuring an experiment*

To view and work with Qlik AutoML, we need to meet some requirements:

1. **User Type**: We must be a Professional or Full User within the tenant.
2. **Permissions**: The tenant admin or service account owner must give us access as either an **AutoML Deployment Contributor or AutoML Experiment Contributor**.

The AutoML Experiment Contributor assumes the role of designing and experimenting with machine learning models, essentially serving as the "innovators." Conversely, the

AutoML Deployment Contributor is designated for those who deploy these models into real-world applications, functioning as the "implementers." Together, these roles encompass the full lifecycle of machine learning models, from creation to deployment.

3. **Access to Space**: We need permission to access the space where AutoML resources are stored. It could be our own space, a shared one, or a managed space, depending on how we want to collaborate with others.

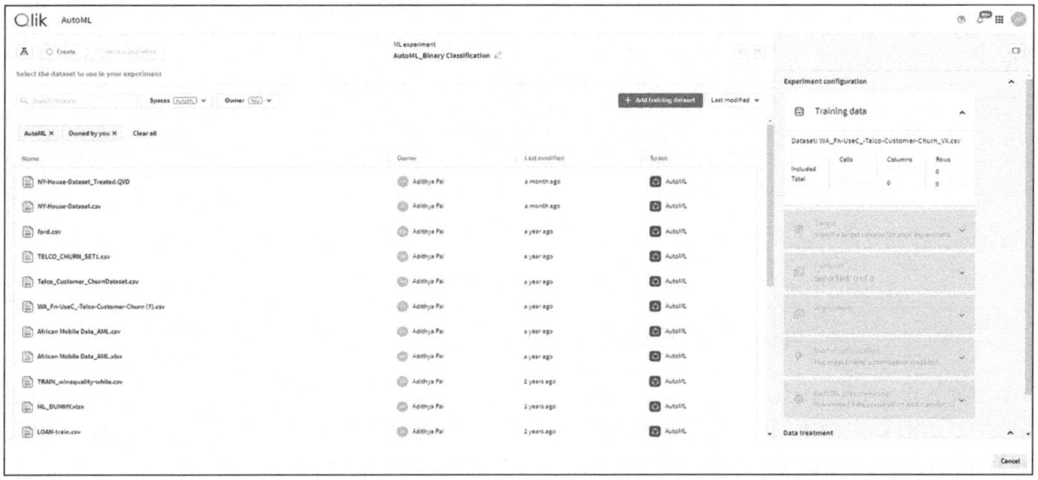

Figure 7.3: *Selecting the training data set*

In the subsequent section, we will proceed to choose the training dataset, which may be in any format supported by Qlik. Initially, we will designate the location where the training dataset is stored, followed by selecting the specific file intended for training the model. As an example, we downloaded this file (https://www.kaggle.com/datasets/blastchar/telco-customer-churn) and uploaded it to the Qlik Cloud tenant.

The training dataset and the testing dataset are two essential components utilized in the development of machine learning models, each fulfilling a distinct purpose:

Training Dataset:

Purpose: We use this dataset to train the machine learning model.

Content: It comprises input data (features) along with the corresponding output data (target variable).

Usage: Through this data, the model learns to formulate predictions or decisions.

Testing Dataset:

Purpose: We employ this dataset to assess the performance of the trained model.

Content: It contains input data that the model hasn't encountered previously, while withholding the expected outcomes.

Usage: This dataset aids in evaluating how effectively the model generalizes to new, unseen data.

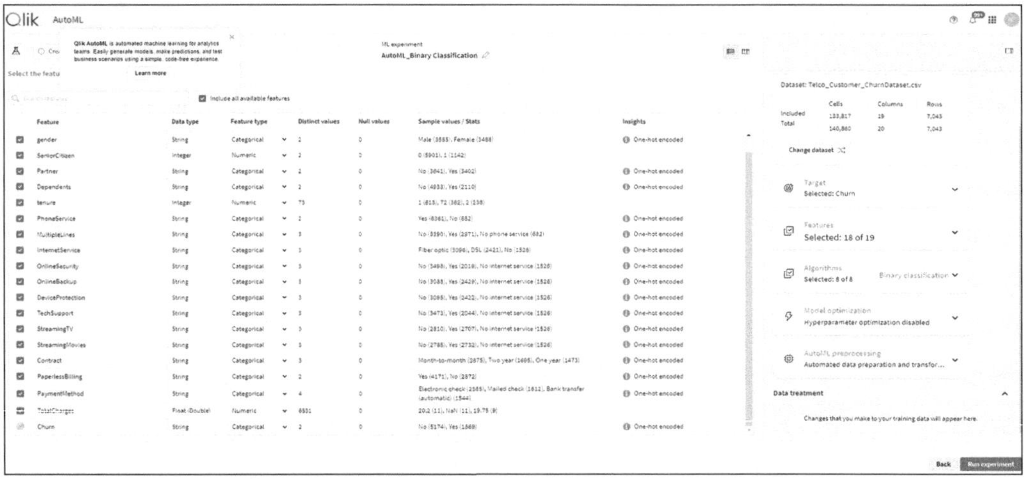

Figure 7.4: *Selecting the fields in the training dataset*

In this phase, our primary task involves designating the **"Churn"** field as our target variable and defining the parameter the model will learn to predict. When selecting a target dataset, several critical considerations must be taken into account.

Firstly, the chosen target should exhibit strong relevance to the business context and align closely with the specific problem we aim to solve using machine learning. Secondly, the target column must demonstrate high data quality, minimizing instances of missing values to ensure the reliability of predictions.

Additionally, the nature of the target field determines the type of model—be it binary classification, multiclass classification, or regression—thus influencing the choice of appropriate algorithms. Furthermore, the availability of sufficient historical data about the target variable is crucial for effective model training.

Lastly, it is essential to contemplate the actionable outputs derived from predicted values and ensure alignment between the target field and the actions to be undertaken based on these predictions.

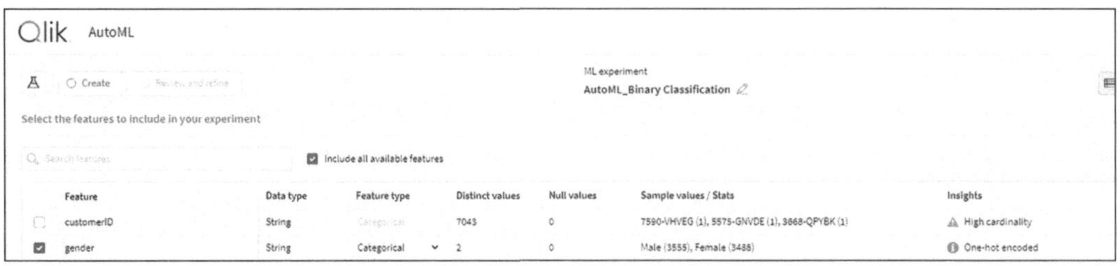

Figure 7.5: *Observe the insights, we can see that the gender field is "one-hot encoded"*

One of the advantages of utilizing AutoML is that it handles complex machine learning tasks, such as pre-processing, on our behalf.

After the target column is selected, AutoML segregates rows where the target value is missing, forming a training set with known targets. Only data from this training set is utilized for subsequent steps. The procedures and data information are saved and applied to any new data for accurate predictions.

When initiating a new experiment, AutoML prepares the data by computing the average (mean) for numerical values and the most common value (mode) for categories. It fills in missing values, converts categories into numbers, and automatically generates new features from existing ones. AutoML also examines if certain columns may contain sentences, checking the average word length. If it exceeds five words, it treats it as a special text feature; otherwise, a warning is issued. If a column doesn't perform well as text, especially with numerous different values, it is excluded. AutoML calculates basic statistics for each column to facilitate feature standardization, ensuring uniform scaling across all columns. Lastly, AutoML reserves a portion of the data for model testing and utilizes cross-validation to evaluate its performance.

In this case, we can see that the `CustomerID` shows "high cardinality." High cardinality refers to a feature in a dataset having many different values. For instance, a column like "customer ID" or "product ID" with numerous unique identifiers would demonstrate high cardinality.

High cardinality can pose challenges in AutoML predictions for various reasons:

Complexity: It can increase the complexity of the model, making it harder to train effectively.

Overfitting: There is a risk of overfitting, where the model learns from noise rather than the actual patterns in the data.

Performance: High cardinality features may slow down the training process and require more computational resources.

Generalization: Models might struggle to generalize well to new data if they focus too much on high-cardinality features.

For the `"gender"` field, we observe the insight termed `"one hot encoded"`. This technique is employed to convert categorical variables into a numerical format suitable for machine learning algorithms. Here is how it operates:

Categorical Variable: This variable comprises two or more categories without any inherent order among them. For instance, a feature like `"color"` may include categories such as red, green, and blue.

Encoding Process: For each category, a vector is generated where:

- The element corresponding to that category is assigned the value 1.
- All other elements in the vector are assigned the value 0.

For instance, if we consider a **"color"** feature with three possible values (red, green, and blue), one-hot encoding will produce three new features, each representing one color. If the color is red, the resulting binary vector would be [1, 0, 0]; for green, it would be [0, 1, 0]; and for blue, it would be [0, 0, 1].

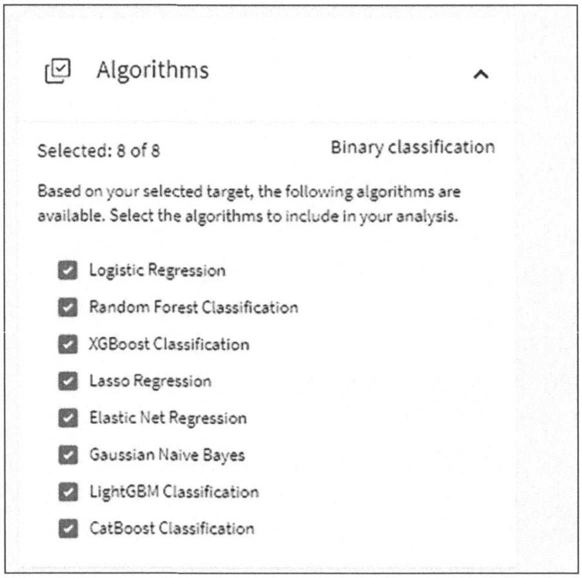

***Figure 7.6**: Algorithms that will be applied to the training dataset are displayed*

Understanding Algorithms in Everyday Life

Traditionally, the application of ML algorithms necessitates a profound comprehension of their mathematical foundations and practical implications. Data analysts would be required to grasp the intricacies of algorithms such as Random Forest or XGBoost to effectively employ them. However, with AutoML, this prerequisite is no longer necessary. The Qlik AutoML platform is engineered to enable analysts to concentrate on the data and the problem at hand, while the system manages the selection, tuning, and deployment of the most suitable algorithms. Manually applying a single ML algorithm to a dataset can take anywhere from a few hours to several days, contingent upon the complexity of the task and the analyst's proficiency. Conversely, an AutoML platform such as Qlik can accomplish the same task in a fraction of the time.

Leveraging a Range of Algorithms for Optimal Results

Utilizing various algorithms on a training dataset is imperative as each algorithm possesses its own set of strengths and weaknesses. This diversity facilitates a more comprehensive analysis of the data. For instance, certain algorithms may exhibit superior performance with specific types of data distributions or relationships within the dataset. By employing multiple algorithms, we can assess their performance and select the most suitable model for our specific problem.

Furthermore, different algorithms offer distinct perspectives on the data, thereby enhancing our insights. For instance, one algorithm may adeptly capture linear relationships, while another may excel at identifying complex, non-linear interactions. This multifaceted approach contributes to a more thorough comprehension of the underlying patterns and trends within the data.

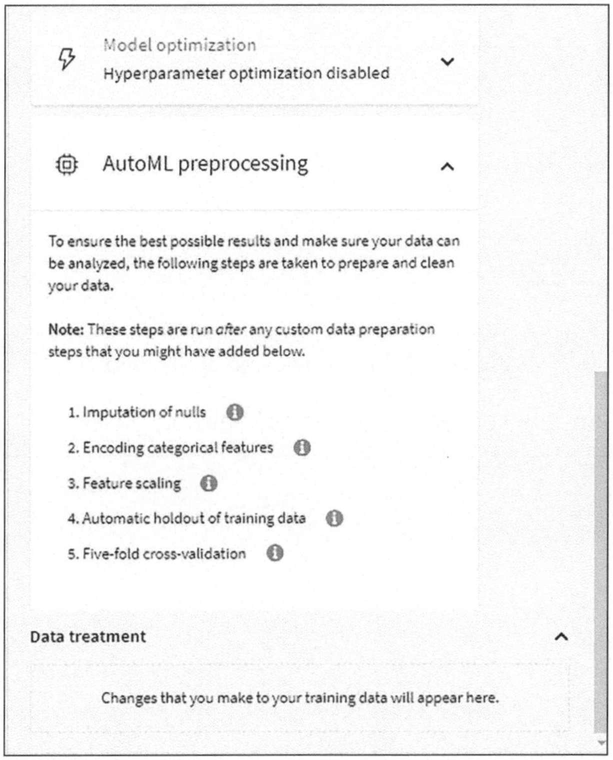

***Figure** 7.7: Pre-processing steps detailed that will be applied by Qlik*

Hyper Parameter Optimization

Qlik AutoML incorporates built-in hyperparameter optimization capabilities to enhance the performance of your models. The process involves two main components:

Firstly, Qlik AutoML employs pre-defined, optimized hyperparameter values for each algorithm used during model training. These values serve as a reliable starting point, widely recognized within the data science community.

Secondly, Hyperparameter Optimization (HPO) is available as an optional feature during experiment configuration. However, enabling HPO comes with some crucial considerations. Notably, it significantly extends the training time for experiments.

While the base training process may take minutes, HPO can prolong it to hours or even days, depending on the complexity of the model and data.

It is advisable to utilize HPO when the initial model performance with default hyperparameters is below expectations and further optimization avenues need exploration. However, it is essential to note that HPO should not be employed for the initial training run of a new model. Instead, it is recommended to evaluate the baseline performance with default settings before delving into hyperparameter tuning.

Once the run is initiated, we observe that Qlik automatically executes the initial "Pre-Processing" steps.

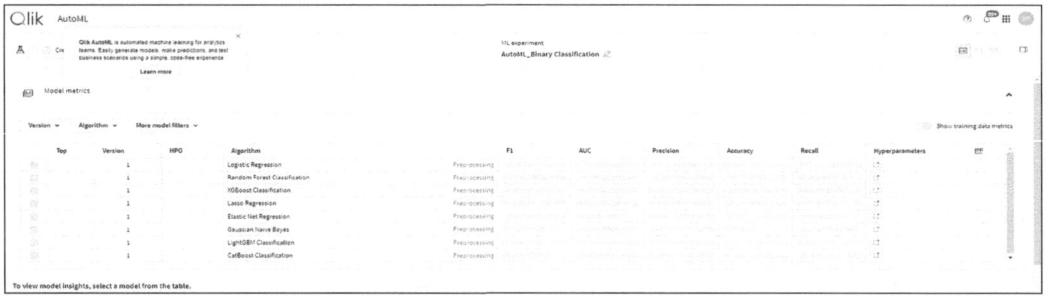

Figure 7.8: *Pre-processing of the data.*

After the preparation, the screen shifts to the Training Phase.

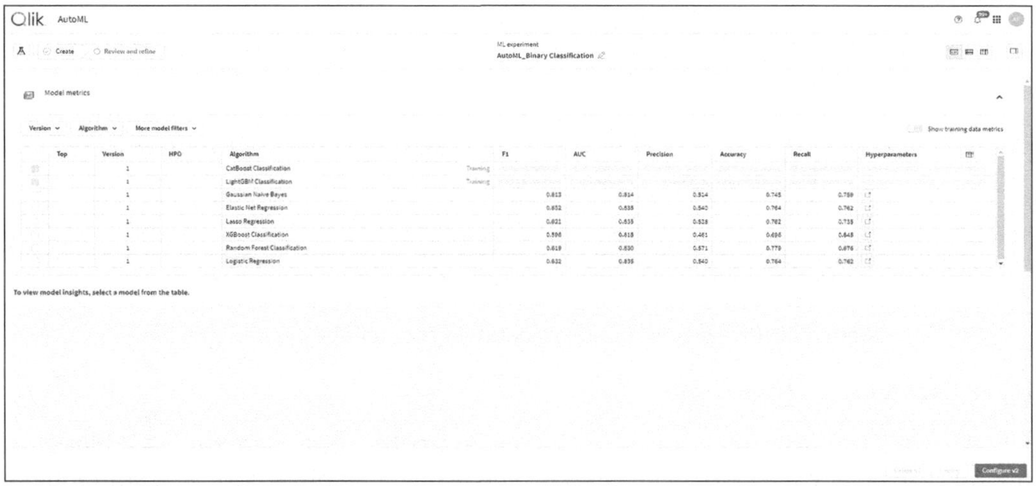

Figure 7.9: *Upon pre-processing the experiment enters into the Training Phase*

Let us now delve into these terminologies: F1 Score, AUC, Precision, Accuracy, and Recall.

- **Accuracy**: This metric represents the overall effectiveness of predictions. For instance, if you correctly predict the outcome of a coin flip 8 out of 10 times, your accuracy stands at 80%.

- **Precision**: It measures the accuracy of positive predictions made by the model. Using the coin flip analogy, if you correctly guess heads 8 out of 10 times when predicting heads, your precision would be 80%.
- **Recall**: This metric evaluates the model's ability to correctly identify all actual positives. For example, if there were 10 instances of heads and the model correctly identified 8 of them out of the 10 times it predicted heads, the recall rate would be 80%.
- **F1 Score**: It represents the harmonic mean of precision and recall. Balancing the importance of being correct (precision) and covering all actual positives (recall), an F1 Score of 80% implies both precision and recall are at that level.
- **AUC**: The Area Under the ROC Curve quantifies the model's ability to distinguish between positive and negative classes across different thresholds. A higher AUC value, closer to 1 (or 100%), indicates better predictive performance, portraying the model's effectiveness in making correct predictions. Machine learning models use **hyperparameters**, such as constraints, weights, and learning rates, to control the learning process. AutoML defaults to standard, optimized hyperparameter values, automatically selecting the best combination. For optimal predictive results, fine-tuning can be done using hyperparameter optimization (HPO).

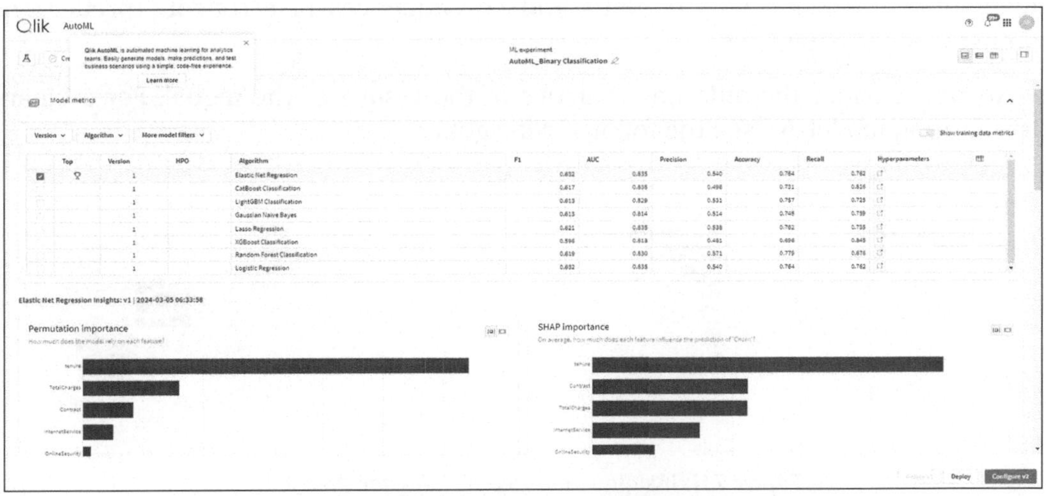

Figure 7.10: *Top performing model selected (based on F1 Score) upon completion of application of algorithms.*

In this scenario, Elastic Net regression emerges as the top-performing model based on the F1 score. Now, the pivotal decision lies in determining which model to employ, whether it aligns with Qlik's recommendation or not. The optimal model choice varies depending on the specific use case and objectives at hand.

High Recall: This is pertinent in medical diagnostics, where missing a true case (false negative) could pose life-threatening consequences. Emphasizing high recall ensures capturing as many true cases as possible, even if it results in some false positives.

High Precision: Ideal for applications like email spam filters, where it's preferable to allow some spam through (false negatives) rather than misclassify important emails as spam (false positives). Prioritizing high precision minimizes the occurrence of false positives.

High Accuracy: Crucial for general classification tasks such as recognition, where both false positives and false negatives are equally undesirable. High accuracy ensures overall effectiveness in classification.

High AUC: Essential in ranking or scoring models, such as credit scoring, where clear differentiation between classes (example, good versus bad credit) is imperative. Maximizing the AUC aids in achieving a distinct margin between classes.

High F1 Score: Necessary in situations where false negatives and false positives carry equal costs, as seen in legal document retrieval or precision engineering. A high F1 score ensures balanced performance by minimizing both types of errors.

Each metric serves a distinct purpose, and the selection of the appropriate metric hinges on the specific requirements and consequences of erroneous predictions within the given application.

Let us now explore the different analytics of the results of the model. For a binary classification model, we see the following insights:

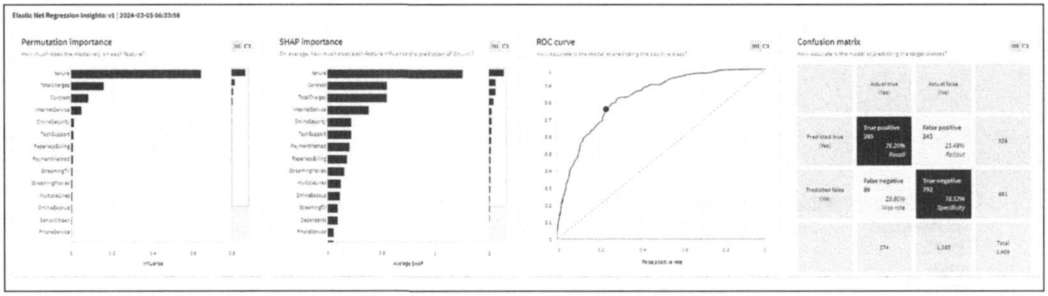

***Figure 7.11:** Insights analyzed visually for the model*

Permutation Importance

Permutation importance in Qlik AutoML serves as a valuable metric for understanding the significance of features within your machine learning model. Permutation importance gauges the importance of a feature in determining the overall prediction of a model.

In essence, it addresses the question: **How would the model's predictive capability be affected if we were to eliminate the ability to learn from a specific feature?**

By analyzing permutation importance, valuable insights are garnered regarding the features that exert a substantial influence on the model's predictions.

Qlik AutoML computes permutation importance using the sci-kit-learn permutation importance method, where the process unfolds in the following steps:

Initially, the model's performance score (such as accuracy or mean squared error) is determined. Subsequently, the values of a particular feature are randomly shuffled (permuted) throughout the dataset, and then the model's performance score is recalculated. If the shuffling of feature values leads to a decline in the model's score, the feature is identified as "important," indicating the model's reliance on it for predictions. Conversely, if the shuffling maintains the model's performance unchanged, the feature is labeled "unimportant."

SHAP Importance

SHAP importance in Qlik AutoML offers crucial insights into feature importance within machine learning models. Let's delve into its significance and how it shapes decision-making. Shapley Additive exPlanations (SHAP) importance measures how a single feature impacts the prediction for a particular data point. It assesses the contribution of that feature relative to the average outcome across the entire dataset. In essence, SHAP importance addresses the question: **How does a feature influence the prediction for a specific instance compared to other features?**

- SHAP values are calculated at the individual row level.
- Each SHAP value reflects the direction and magnitude of a feature's influence on a specific prediction.
- Positive SHAP values indicate that the feature contributes to a higher prediction, while negative values signify the opposite.

  Through the analysis of SHAP values, valuable insights are gained into the features driving specific predictions.

SHAP values derive from Shapley values in cooperative game theory, pioneered by Lloyd Shapley in 1953. They operationalize the abstract notion of "fair distribution" into a pragmatic tool for interpreting models, likening each feature within a model to a "player" in a game.

The concept of Shapley values initially emerged to ensure equitable distribution of payouts among players based on their individual contributions to the collective reward in a game. SHAP values extend this concept to the domain of machine learning, enabling quantification of each feature's influence on a model's predictions.

The advancement of SHAP values is driven by the imperative for transparency and interpretability in artificial intelligence, notably in sensitive sectors such as finance and healthcare, where understanding model decisions is of paramount significance.

Permutation Importance VS SHAP

Permutation importance looks at how much model performance drops when you shuffle feature values randomly. SHAP importance shows how each feature affects individual predictions. SHAP importance focuses on the magnitude of feature attributions, whereas permutation importance is based on the decrease in model performance.

Here is how we can use them together to improve the model:

- **Start with Permutation Importance**: This helps you pick out the most important features overall.
- **Dig Deeper with SHAP Importance**: Use SHAP to see how each feature affects specific predictions.
- **Keep Refining**: Use both techniques to keep improving your model. You can use what you learn to make new features or split your data into groups for better results.

For example, if we are predicting who might stop using a telecom service, permutation importance helps us choose which features to focus on. Then, SHAP importance helps you understand why certain customers might leave.

SHAP also helps you see how features work together, so you can make your model even better. Visualizing SHAP values can make all of this easier to understand.

By using both permutation and SHAP importance, we have a clearer picture of your model and can make better decisions.

ROC Curve

Originating during World War II, the ROC curve emerged through the efforts of electrical and radar engineers in 1941. Initially devised for detecting adversary objects on battlefields, its application extended to psychology for discerning perceptual stimuli. Subsequently, it found widespread adoption in diverse domains such as medicine, radiology, and machine learning.

The **Receiver Operating Characteristic (ROC)** curve serves as a visual tool for assessing the efficacy of binary classification models across various threshold settings. It juxtaposes the True Positive Rate (TPR) against the False Positive Rate

(FPR), facilitating the examination of trade-offs between accurate identifications and erroneous alarms.

Within machine learning, ROC curves play a pivotal role in model selection, aiding in the rejection of subpar models irrespective of cost considerations or class distributions. Particularly in medical diagnostics, they ascertain the sensitivity and specificity of tests, and in machine learning, they facilitate comparative analysis of various classifiers.

An ideal ROC curve closely adheres to the top-left corner of the plot, indicating heightened sensitivity (minimal false negatives) and specificity (negligible false positives).

The Area Under the Curve (AUC) quantifies the overall discriminatory capacity of the test between positive and negative classes. An AUC of 1 signifies perfection, while an AUC of 0.5 suggests random guessing.

Decision-making guided by the ROC curve involves selecting a threshold that strikes a balance between TPR and FPR, tailored to the specific requirements of the application. For instance, in medical diagnostics for a treatable yet severe ailment, prioritizing sensitivity (TPR) over specificity ensures comprehensive case identification.

A favorable ROC curve is characterized by a high TPR and low FPR, resulting in rapid ascent towards the upper-left corner of the plot. Conversely, an unfavorable ROC curve closely aligns with the diagonal line (45 degrees), indicative of performance akin to random chance.

In the realm of Qlik AutoML, the ROC curve emerges as a valuable tool for gauging the efficacy of predictive models, facilitating the selection of models aligning with data and business objectives.

Confusion Matrix

Although the term "**confusion matrix**" is relatively modern, its conceptual roots trace back to the early 20th century, notably with Karl Pearson's work on contingency tables in 1904. Its significance is buried in the field of machine learning, becoming an integral part of pattern recognition tools and gaining wider recognition with the emergence of AutoML platforms, which streamline the application of machine learning models to datasets. Think of it as akin to a report card for your model, delineating areas of proficiency and identifying potential areas for improvement. Contrary to its name, the primary objective of a confusion matrix is to enhance the clarity of a model's performance, thereby mitigating confusion.

The confusion matrix utilized in Qlik AutoML serves as a diagnostic tool, offering insight into the performance of binary classification models. It delineates the counts of True Positives, True Negatives, False Positives, and False Negatives. This matrix is derived from the holdout set during data training, wherein data partitioning occurs on an **80/20** basis.

- **True Positives (TP)**: Instances where actual true values are correctly predicted as true.
- **True Negatives (TN):** Cases where actual false values are correctly predicted as false.
- **False Positives (FP):** Instances where actual false values are erroneously predicted as true.
- **False Negatives (FN):** Cases where actual true values are erroneously predicted as false.

The confusion matrix offers a comprehensive assessment of model performance, encompassing various metrics such as recall, accuracy, precision, and overall effectiveness in-class differentiation. Particularly beneficial in scenarios featuring imbalanced class distributions, providing insights beyond rudimentary accuracy measurements. The confusion matrix Facilitates the evaluation of prediction accuracy and the equilibrium between distinct error types. Aids in decision-making regarding model adjustments, predicated on specific performance indicators like recall and precision.

An imbalanced class distribution within a dataset denotes a scenario where the instances among various classes are not evenly distributed. This typically results in one or more classes, known as the majority classes, having significantly more instances than others, termed the minority classes.

Qlik AutoML tackles imbalanced class distribution by stipulating that every unique value within the target column must appear at least 10 times, thereby mitigating errors during experimentation. This prerequisite is instrumental in guaranteeing adequate representation of data across all classes. Moreover, Qlik AutoML may autonomously apply weights to achieve class balance if it enhances performance on a specific subset of the user's data. Additionally, it is advisable to address imbalanced datasets prior to feeding the training data into an AutoML experiment, potentially through techniques such as undersampling the majority class or employing other appropriate methods.

Following the initial model iteration, our next step involves selecting the top-performing model and subsequently reducing the number of features. Although permutation importance was not available during the first run, we can now utilize it to identify and remove less important features conveniently from the interface. However, it is essential to consider various factors alongside permutation importance:

- **Redundancy**: Features exhibiting high correlation with each other may be redundant and thus eligible for removal.
- **Domain Knowledge:** Domain experts can provide valuable insights into the

significance of features for interpretability or future data scenarios. Their input is crucial in assessing the impact of removing specific features.

- **Model Complexity**: While simplifying the model enhances interpretability, it is imperative to balance this with maintaining accuracy.
- **Data Quality**: Poor-quality or noisy data can distort feature-important metrics. Ensuring data quality is paramount before making decisions regarding feature removal.

Relying solely on permutation importance within the AutoML context might lead to the exclusion of valuable features. Therefore, a comprehensive approach that integrates automated techniques with domain expertise, generalizability assessment, and strategic feature engineering is essential for effective feature selection within AutoML workflows.

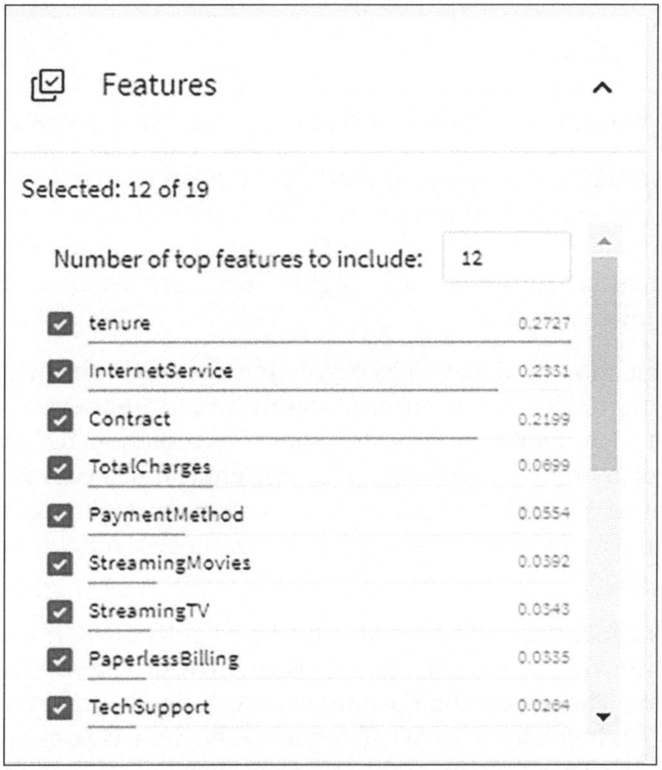

***Figure 7.12**: Selecting 12 features*

When we decide to remove features based on their permutation scores and what we know about the subject, it is important to remember that simply taking out features does not always make the F1 score better. The F1 score, which looks at both precision and recall, tells us how accurate our model is overall. Sometimes, cutting down on features can make the model too simple, leading to it not understanding the data well enough. Also, while some features might seem less important on their own, they could be really important when you look at them together with other features. And remember, the importance of features can change if the data changes, too.

On the other hand, reducing the number of features can help in a few ways. It might stop the model from fitting too closely to the noise in the data, which is called overfitting. Having fewer features can also mean the model trains and makes predictions faster. And simpler models with fewer features are usually easier to understand. So, it is about finding the right balance between having enough complexity to predict well and being simple enough to understand easily. Sometimes, accepting a slightly lower F1 score can be worth it if it makes the model stronger overall.

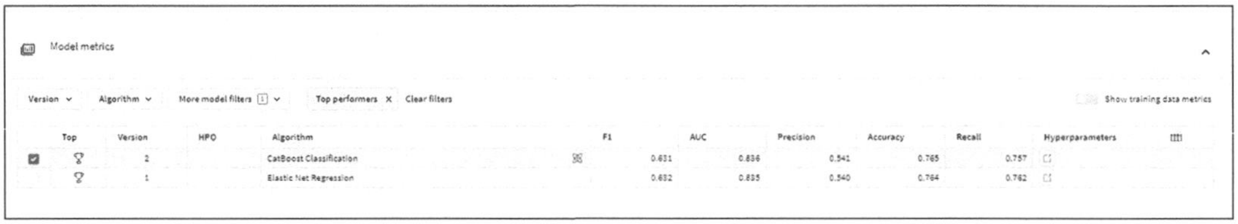

***Figure 7.13**: Evaluation of the 2 models based on the scores*

Now that we have the scores for both models, we need to decide whether to deploy the first version, the second one or opt for a third round of refinement. It is important to closely examine all values, not just the F1 score. The second model shows a lower feature importance score but slightly higher AUC, precision, and accuracy while having a slightly lower recall.

In a binary classification model such as predicting customer churn, selecting a model with a slightly higher AUC, precision, and accuracy indicates several positive aspects. Firstly, it suggests stronger overall performance, as a higher AUC indicates a better ability to distinguish between churners and non-churners across various thresholds. Secondly, improved precision reduces false positives, meaning the model more accurately identifies true churners, minimizing unnecessary interventions with on loyal customers.

However, there is a potential caveat to consider: the slightly lower recall suggests a small possibility of overlooking actual churners. This could be crucial, depending on the cost of missing a churn. **Therefore, the optimal choice depends on prioritizing based on business needs.** If minimizing misclassifying non-churners is paramount and the cost of unnecessary interventions outweighs missing a small portion of churners, then the model with high precision might be preferable. Conversely, if catching most churners, even at the risk of some false positives, is critical, especially for high-value customers, then a different model with a higher recall might be necessary. This consideration is particularly relevant in situations where churners represent significant lost revenue or have a detrimental impact on brand reputation.

Deployment

Now that we have chosen version 2, we are ready to put the model into action. In Qlik AutoML, a deployment asset is like a finished product of a machine learning model. It is trained and good to go for making predictions on new data, like in apps or for decision-making.

On the other hand, an experiment is more like the process of creating, training, and checking how well a machine-learning model works. It involves picking features, choosing ways to train the model, and seeing how well it does. Experiments are where we tweak the model until it is ready to be used for real. **So, the main difference is that an experiment is when we are still working on the model, while a deployment asset is the model ready to make predictions.**

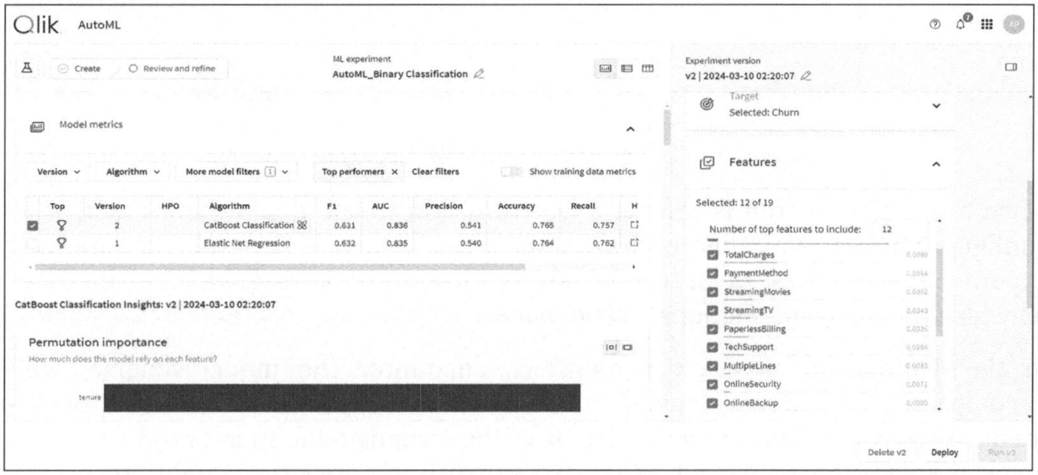

Figure 7.14: *Selecting the model to be deployed and select the "deploy" option*

We navigate to the **`deployment configuration`** pop-up window, where we define the deployment parameters. Here, we select names, designate the space where they reside, and have the option to add tags. Within this configuration, there's a feature known as the "**Enable real-time API access"** checkbox. When activated during the model deployment process, it allows us to access the deployed model for real-time predictions via an API. This capability enables us to programmatically send data to the model and promptly receive predictions. This functionality is crucial for applications that necessitate immediate decision-making based on the model's insights.

Enabling this option generates an endpoint URL and mandates an API key for authentication. Subsequently, we can utilize this endpoint within our applications to obtain real-time predictions. This aspect proves particularly beneficial for incorporating machine learning capabilities into production environments where decisions need to be made swiftly, such as in personalizing customer experiences, detecting fraud, or optimizing operational processes.

Figure 7.15: *Configuring the AutoML Deployment Asset*

Once the deploy button is selected, we transition to the deployment asset, where configurations are set. This process is similar to selecting the training data in the experiment asset. Now, we proceed to select the applied dataset, which is the dataset on which the actual predictions will be made.

In the deployment overview screen, we encounter the model schema, which encompasses the features retained in the model after filtering out irrelevant ones for predictions. Within this overview, details of the training data, such as the experiment name, the algorithm employed, and the version utilized, are visible. Additionally, direct navigation to the experiment underlying the model is facilitated.

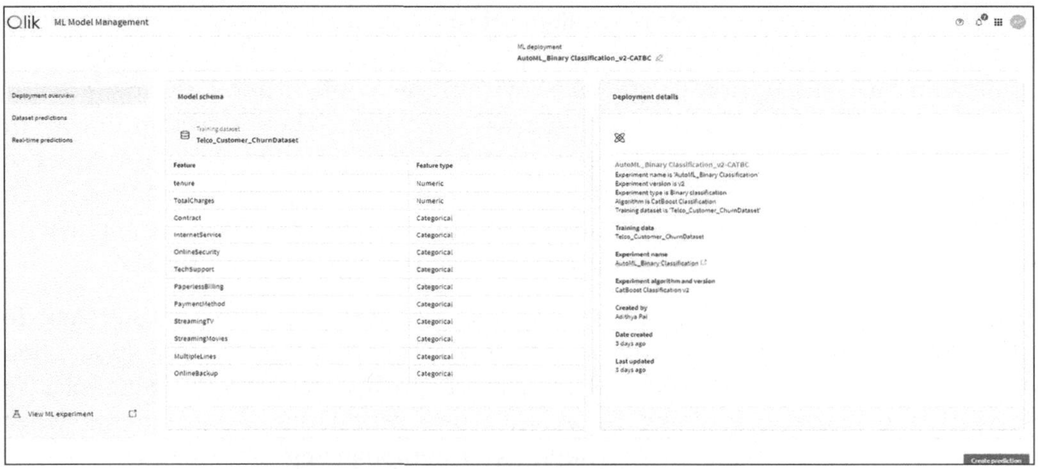

Figure 7.16: *Deployment Overview Screen*

On the dataset prediction screen, as this is a new model, we currently observe the absence of predictions. To change this, let us proceed with generating predictions. Navigating to the bottom right, we encounter a button labeled "`Create Predictions`". Clicking this button will allow us to add our applied dataset.

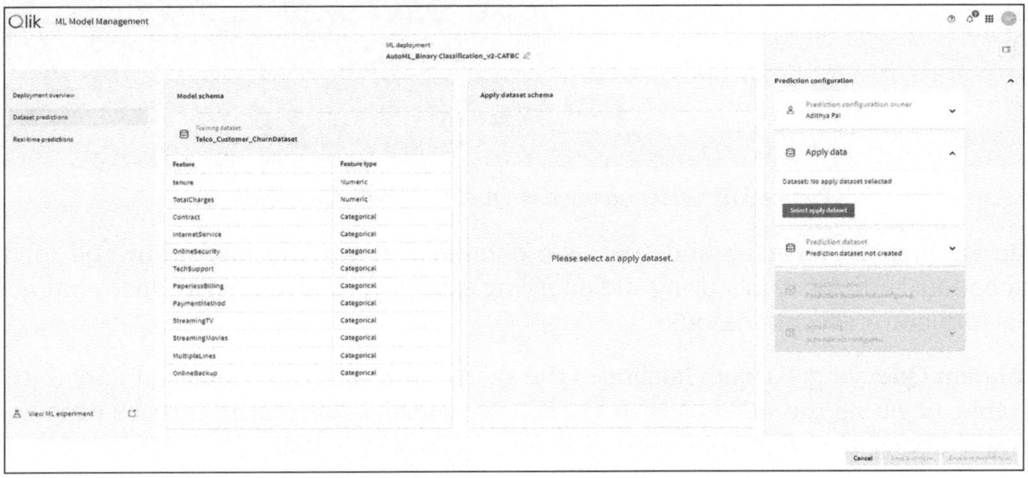

Figure 7.17: *Data Set Prediction screen.*

On the apply dataset screen, our next step involves navigating to select the dataset on which we intend to apply the predictions.

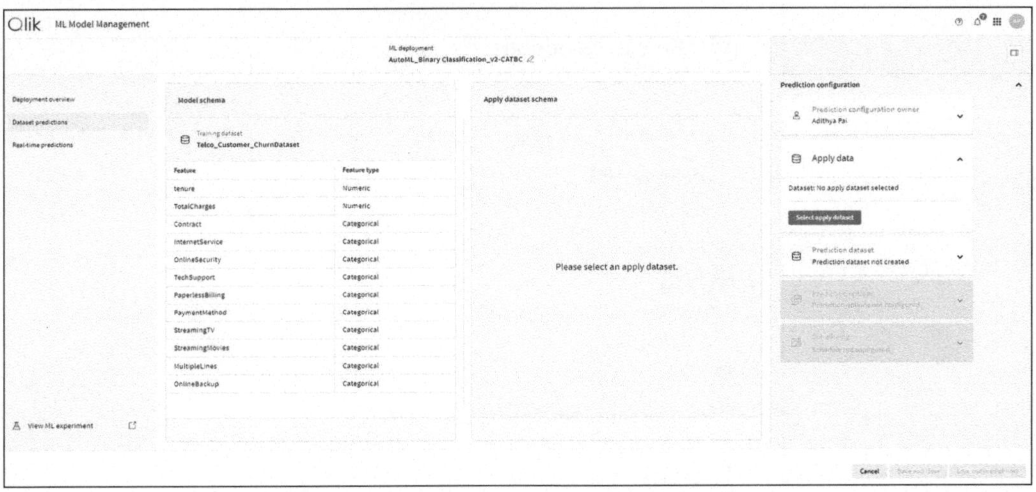

Figure 7.18: *Selecting the applied dataset.*

We will now select the prediction data set, which can be generated in different formats– we can either select CSV, QVD, or even parquet.

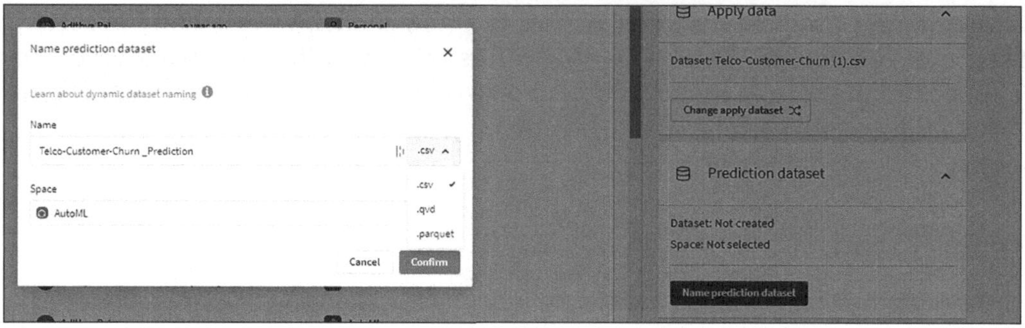

Figure 7.19: *Selecting the format of the predictions data set*

The Parquet file format stands out as a columnar storage format renowned for its exceptional efficiency in storing and querying extensive datasets. Qlik Sense embraces this format for several reasons:

Efficient Querying: Parquet facilitates the swift querying of individual columns within a table, negating the need to scan the entire dataset. This feature proves especially advantageous in scenarios involving substantial data processing.

Compression and Encoding: Parquet supports advanced compression and encoding techniques, effectively minimizing storage requirements while enhancing query performance.

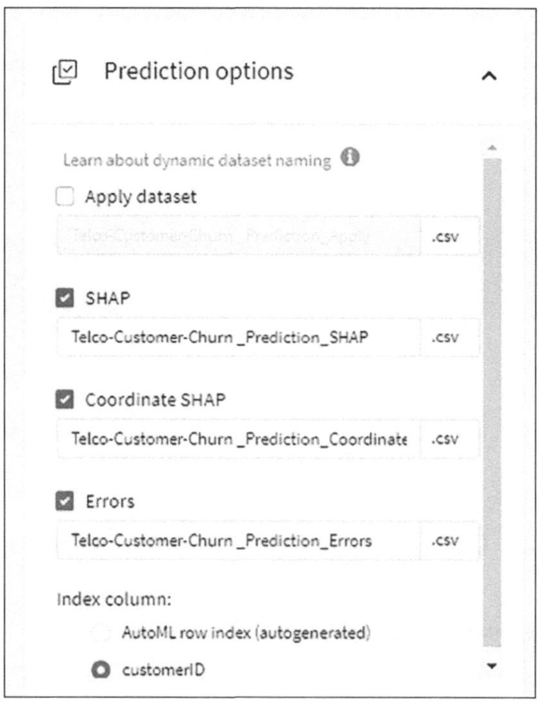

Figure 7.20: *Selecting the format of the SHAP, coordinate SHAP, and Errors data set*

The SHAP, Coordinate SHAP, and Errors datasets are optional features that we can choose to generate. The Coordinate SHAP feature includes a table that transforms feature importance values (SHAP values) into record-level measures, making analysis and visualization more detailed. It helps us understand how each feature influences predictions for individual records, providing insights into individual feature contributions to model predictions.

This feature has two main columns: **`"Feature",`** which shows the name of the input feature used in the model, and **`"Value",`** representing SHapley Additive explanations (SHAP) value indicating a feature's influence on the predicted outcome for a specific data point.

When interpreting Coordinate SHAP values, positive values suggest that the feature's presence increases the predicted value (for example, a higher probability in classification), while negative values indicate the opposite. The magnitude of the SHAP value reflects the strength of the feature's influence.

The Errors dataset captures information about prediction errors made by the model, typically including the differences between predicted values and actual values. This dataset is essential for evaluating the model's performance and identifying patterns in predictions that may need further investigation.

Index Column

We must establish a connection between the predictions we generate and the original data model when visualizing them. The **`AutoML_row`** index column in Qlik AutoML serves as an autogenerated field, providing a unique identifier for each row in your dataset during machine learning experiments. This feature becomes particularly valuable when there is not an existing unique identifier in your dataset or when you prefer not to utilize any of the dataset fields as an index.

When setting up a machine learning deployment, if an index column is not specified, Qlik AutoML automatically employs **`AutoML_row`** as the default. This ensures that every prediction can be accurately traced back to the corresponding row in your dataset. Such traceability is essential for analyzing the outcomes of your model. In our case, we have the **`customerID`** field that can act as an index, so we will go ahead and keep the index as the customer ID.

Once all parameters have been selected and configured, we proceed by selecting the deploy option. This action initiates the deployment process by activating the data model and commencing the generation of predictions based on our configuration settings.

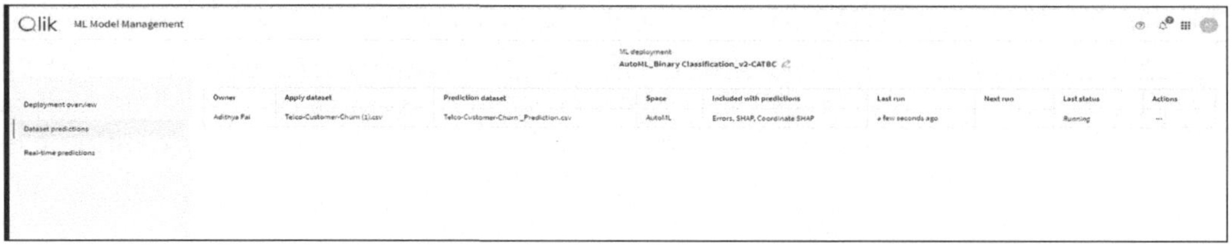

Figure 7.21: *The deployment running and generation of predictions*

Upon successful creation of predictions, we can see that the status changes, as shown in *Figure* 7.22.

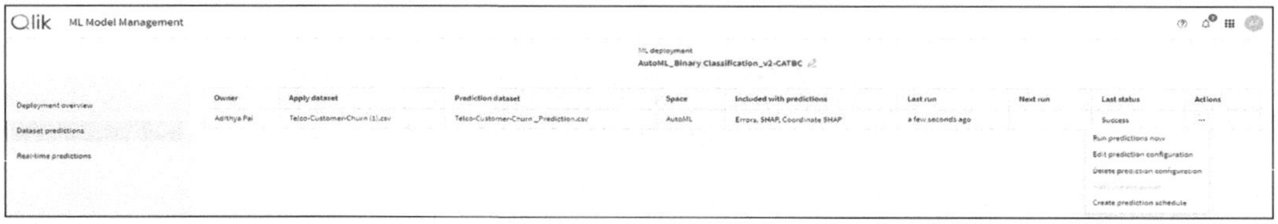

Figure 7.22: *Successful creation of the predictions*

In this scheduled deployment, the results have been stored in the chosen file format according to our previous configuration. We can then load these results into an application for detailed dataset analysis. Additionally, we have the option to perform this analysis in real-time, as indicated in the next tab labeled `"Realtime Predictions"`.

The real-time prediction feature within Qlik AutoML enables the utilization of our ML deployment to predict future outcomes on new data. This can be achieved programmatically through the prediction API, facilitating bi-directional communication between AutoML and various capabilities within Qlik Cloud, such as Qlik Sense and Automation, as well as external applications.

The Real-time Prediction feature in Qlik AutoML's deployment asset offers several advantages:

- **Instant Predictions**: Receive immediate outcomes for different scenarios by sending data to the deployed machine learning model.
- **API Integration**: Seamlessly integrate the prediction API into applications to enable dynamic, on-the-fly predictions.
- **What-If Analysis**: Experiment with different input values to observe their effects on the predicted results.

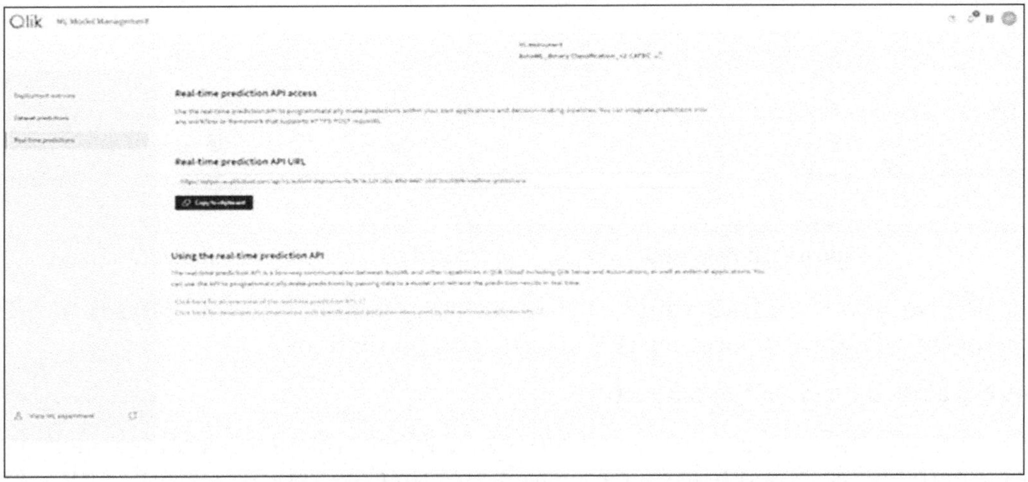

Figure 7.23: *Real-Time Prediction Options*

Real-time predictions facilitated by Qlik AutoML empower us to swiftly make data-driven decisions as new data becomes available. Let us look at some key considerations regarding its utilization, applications, and advantages. We can seamlessly integrate real-time predictions into web applications, fostering immediate insights, and incorporate predictive insights into Qlik Sense applications for visualization and interactive exploration. Utilizing Qlik Cloud Automation alongside Qlik AutoML optimizes workflows for enhanced efficiency. Qlik AutoML furnishes instant predictions, enabling prompt responses to evolving circumstances, and seamlessly integrates with various Qlik capabilities and external applications, ensuring smooth operation within our ecosystem. Accessible via an API, it simplifies incorporation into existing systems, facilitating seamless integration. By enhancing data quality, Qlik AutoML contributes to better business decisions and fosters increased trust in data. Employing real-time predictions through Qlik AutoML significantly elevates our business's responsiveness and agility, enabling us to make more informed and timely decisions.

Analyzing the Resulting Data Set of the Deployments

Now, let us review and analyze the files that were generated. We will understand what each file contains and explore how we can use them to create value in analytics.

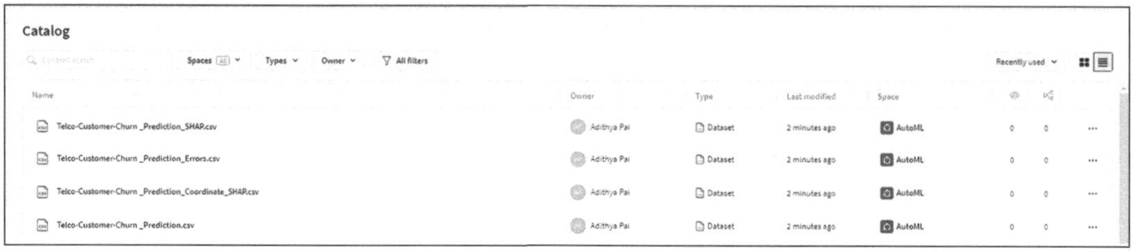

Figure 7.24: *Resulting Data Sets generated by deploying the model*

Let us dive into the **SHAP values**. Qlik AutoML generates a SHAP dataset to offer insights into feature importance and its effect on predictions.

Here is a breakdown of the dataset:

It includes fields such as the record identifier, which uniquely identifies each data point in the dataset, and feature names representing the various features utilized by the model for predictions.

The SHAP values column contains crucial information, with each value indicating how much a specific feature in a data point contributes to the overall model prediction.

When interpreting these values, positive ones signify that the feature value increases the predicted outcome, such as a high income positively contributing to predicting loan approval. Conversely, negative values suggest a decrease in the predicted outcome, such as a low credit score negatively impacting loan approval predictions.

The magnitude of the value reflects the strength of the feature's influence, with higher values indicating a stronger impact on the prediction, whether positive or negative.

For example, in a dataset with features such as age, sex, BMI, and smoker status used to predict medical costs, the SHAP dataset shows how each feature influenced the predicted cost for each individual. A high SHAP value for smoker status might indicate a significant increase in predicted medical costs due to smoking.

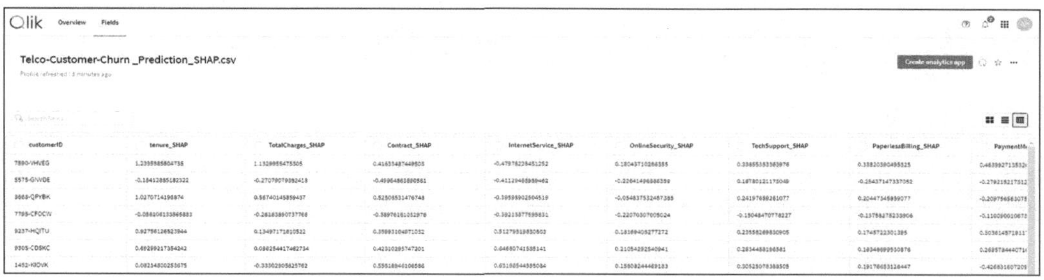

Figure 7.25: *Sample SHAP Values*

Of course, being in QlikSense, we enjoy making visualizations. Let us talk about the types of visuals we can make with these SHAP values and how they benefit our business. Here are some key ways:

- **Feature Importance Ranking**: We can make a list of ranking features based on their impact on predictions using SHAP values.
- **Direction and Distribution Analysis**: We can see if features have a positive or negative impact and how they spread out across predictions.
- **Cohort Analysis**: We compare feature importance across different groups in our data to see how they're influenced by different features.
- **Row-Level Importance**: We can see which features matter most for individual predictions.
- **Feature Variation Analysis**: We can see how different values of a feature affect predictions.
- **Trend Analysis with Continuous Variables**: Using scatter plots, we can see how changes in continuous variables affect predictions over time.

These visuals help us understand our model better and make better business decisions.

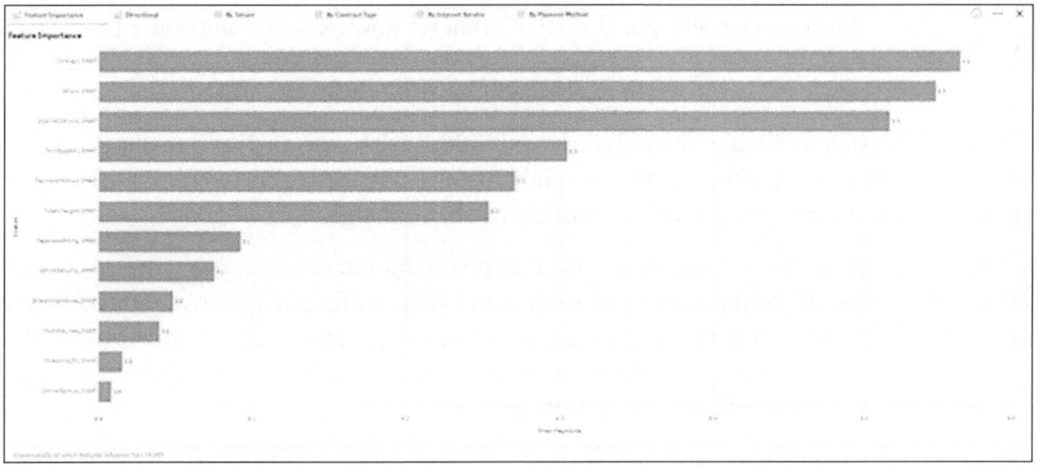

Figure 7.26: *Feature importance ranking based on SHAP Values*

Coordinate SHAP Data Set

After examining the SHAP dataset, the next step is to explore the **coordinate SHAP dataset**. Here are the key differences:

Structure: Unlike the SHAP dataset, where each feature has its column, the coordinate SHAP dataset stores all SHAP values in two columns: `"automl_feature"` and `"SHAP_value"`. This structure simplifies visualization by allowing all feature influences to be represented in a single chart.

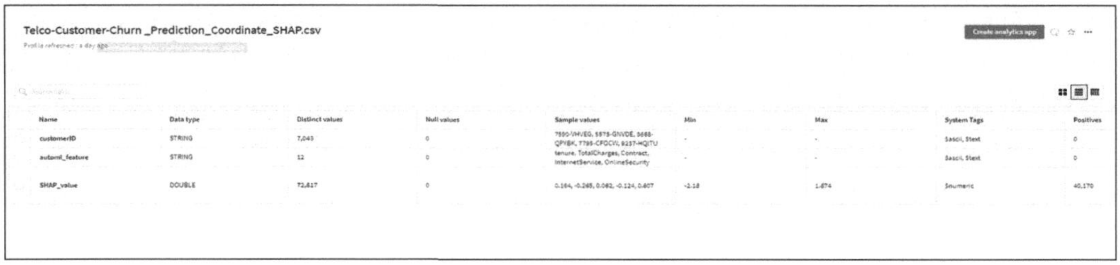

Figure 7.27: *Co-ordinate SHAP Dataset*

Here is a comparison between the visualization approaches for the SHAP Dataset and the Coordinate SHAP Dataset:

Visualization	**SHAP Dataset**	**Coordinate SHAP Dataset**
Focus	Individual feature analysis	Comparative analysis of multiple features
Suitable visualizations	Bar charts, Violin plots, Scatter plots	Heatmaps, Parallel coordinates plots
Strengths	Reveals overall feature importance	Shows how features contribute to individual predictions

Table 7.2: *Comparison of SHAP vs Co-Ordinate SHAP Data Set*

The SHAP Dataset is ideal for analyzing individual features and understanding their overall importance in predictions. Visualizations like bar charts, violin plots, and scatter plots are commonly used to represent these insights.

On the other hand, the Coordinate SHAP Dataset facilitates comparative analysis of multiple features, allowing users to understand how different features contribute to individual predictions. Visualizations such as heatmaps and parallel coordinate plots are well-suited for depicting these relationships, providing deeper insights into feature contributions at the individual prediction level.

Prediction Data Set

The resulting Prediction dataset in Qlik AutoML contains information regarding the predictions made by the trained model on a new set of data (apply dataset). Here is a breakdown of the fields and their meanings:

Fields:

- **Original data fields**: These fields are directly copied from the applied dataset and represent the features or attributes used by the model for predictions.
- **Predicted target value**: This field holds the predicted value for the target variable specified during model training. The interpretation of this value varies based on the type of model:
    - **For classification models**: It represents the predicted class label.

- o **For regression models**: It denotes a numerical value indicating the predicted outcome.
- **Confidence Score**: This is a numerical value ranging from 0 to 1, indicating the probability assigned by the model to a particular prediction. A score closer to 1 suggests high confidence in the prediction, while a score closer to 0 indicates low confidence.

For binary classification models, such as our use case of predicting customer churn, confidence scores are particularly useful. They aid in understanding the likelihood of an event occurring, such as whether a customer will churn or not. These scores in Qlik AutoML are derived from the underlying statistical models trained on your data.

When conducting a model experiment, Qlik AutoML generates a confusion matrix for binary classification models, which includes True Positives, True Negatives, False Positives, and False Negatives. The confidence score influences these values, reflecting the model's certainty in classifying each instance correctly.

In practical applications, confidence scores can be utilized to:

- **Set thresholds**: Establish a cutoff point above which predictions are deemed 'positive' or 'negative'.
- **Evaluate risk:** Higher confidence levels may signify lower risk, enabling prioritization of actions based on confidence levels.
- **Enhance decision-making**: Integrate confidence scores with other business rules or criteria to make more informed decisions.

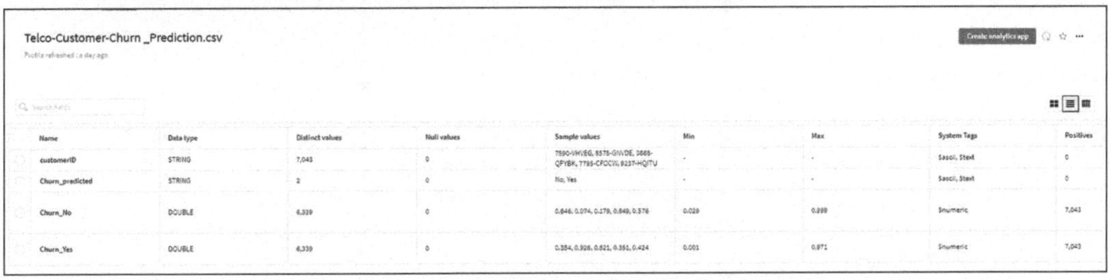

Figure 7.28: *Prediction Data Set Generated in AutoML*

Creating clear visualizations to show data is very important for getting the most out of AutoML. This is where Explainable AI (XAI) in Qlik AutoML comes in. XAI means using techniques and processes to make the reasons behind machine learning results easy to understand. This is especially important in business, where people need to trust and understand why AI makes its predictions.

Deployment Methods

There are several deployment methods available to operationalize machine learning models. One such method is a scheduled deployment, as we have utilized thus far, where we manually select the dataset. This approach proves useful for scenarios necessitating consistent, periodic predictions, such as daily sales forecasts or weekly inventory levels. Additionally, it is beneficial when dealing with large volumes of data that do not require immediate action.

When there is a need to update and generate predictions based on fresh training data daily, we rely on the AutoML connector. This method is best suited for integrating predictive analytics within Qlik Sense applications, particularly when visualizing predictions in dashboards or reports. With this approach, users can continually refresh the prediction dataset. The Qlik AutoML connector serves as a bridge between deployed Qlik AutoML models and Qlik Sense applications. It essentially enables us to leverage the power of trained models for making predictions directly within the familiar Qlik Sense environment. This connector facilitates the utilization of deployed models within Qlik Sense apps, allowing configuration for real-time predictions as part of the data load script or in chart expressions.

Let us see a step-by-step guide on how to create a connection. We create a new connection -- > select **Qlik AutoML**.

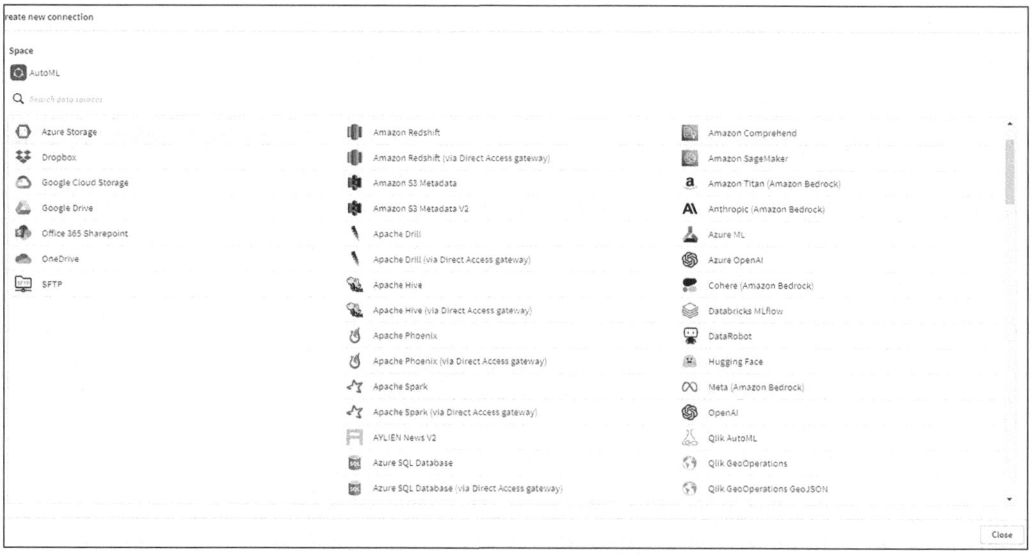

Figure 7.29: *Creating a AutoML Connection*

In the connection configuration, we select the deployment model, which includes specifying the name of the returned table and whether to include SHAP, Apply DataSet, and Error. Additionally, we choose the **Association** field, which serves as the key between the predictions and the actual dataset.

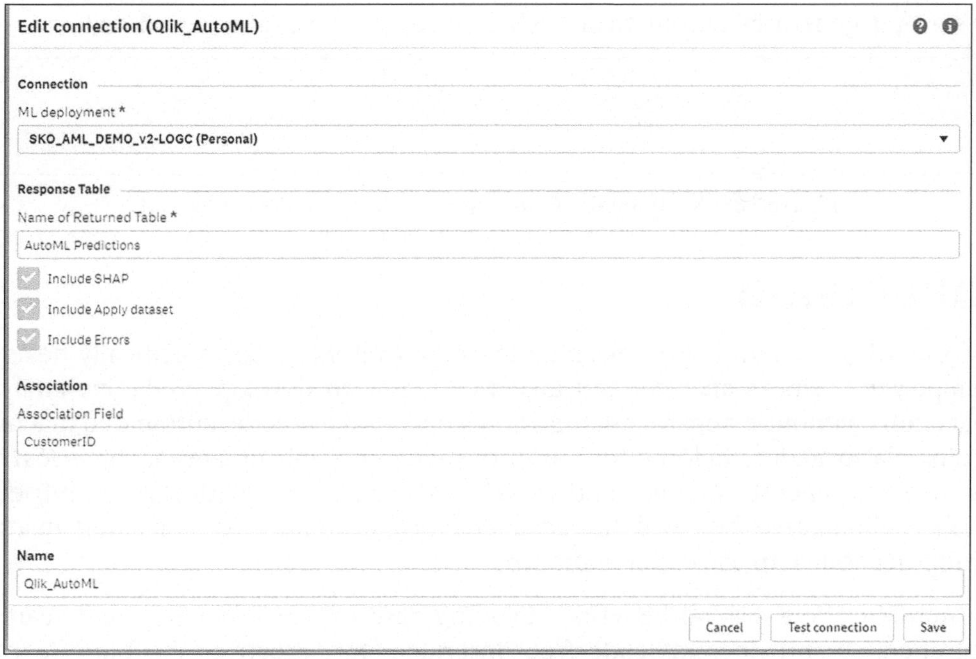

***Figure 7.30**: Creating an AutoML Connection*

We will select the **RESIDENT TABLE**. This is the table that will be passed to the deployment for it to run the algorithms we selected in the experiment step and return the results to us.

***Figure 7.31**: Selecting the Dataset to pass to the AutoML Deployment*

The script is generated automatically, which includes the connection details.

```

[AutoML Predictions]:
LOAD * EXTENSION endpoints.ScriptEval('{"RequestType":"endpoint", "endpoint":{"connectionname":"AutoML:Qlik_AutoML"}}', RESIDENT);
```

Figure 7.32: *Applying the AutoGenerated script to the load script*

Conclusion

Qlik AutoML is an automated machine learning (AutoML) tool specifically designed to empower business analysts and analytics teams to develop predictive analytics applications without extensive coding knowledge. As a no-code, automated machine-learning platform, it is tailored for analytics teams to easily create machine-learning experiments, generate models, and make predictions. The platform's user-friendly interface eliminates the need for advanced programming skills, making machine learning accessible to a broader audience.

Qlik AutoML offers several benefits, including ease of use, efficiency, and seamless integration. It provides a code-free interface for creating machine learning experiments and generating predictions, simplifying the process for users without advanced programming skills. The platform efficiently identifies key drivers in data, generates predictive models, and refines them for optimal performance. Additionally, its integration with Qlik Sense apps allows users to incorporate predictive analytics into existing reports and dashboards, enhancing their analytical capabilities.

Qlik AutoML adds significant value to reports by providing predictive insights, explainability, and the ability to conduct what-if scenarios. It enables users to move beyond historical analysis and anticipate future trends and outcomes through model generation and predictions. The platform offers explainability data at the record level, enhancing understanding of prediction rationales and supporting informed decision-making. Users can test various scenarios in real time using Qlik's Associative Engine, evaluating the impact of potential actions on predicted outcomes. Use cases in analytics reporting include sales forecasting, marketing demand prediction, financial risk management, operational capacity allocation, HR retention analysis, and IT usage predictions. By identifying areas where predictive insights could impact decision-making and evaluating historical data for patterns, Qlik AutoML helps streamline processes and extrapolate trends for future predictions.

In the following chapter, we are going to discuss Qlik Application Automation, which provides integration capabilities between any arbitrary platform, creating powerful pipelines.

Multiple Choice Questions

1. What is the primary aim of Qlik AutoML?
    a. To visualize data
    b. To clean and preprocess data
    c. To generate machine learning models
    d. To create interactive dashboards
2. In Qlik AutoML, what does the term 'target' refer to in a machine learning project?
    a. The variable you want to predict
    b. The dataset used for training
    c. The algorithm chosen for the model
    d. The visualization of the model's results
3. What is the recommended approach for incorporating machine learning predictions into Qlik Sense analysis for non-technical users?
    a. Writing custom code to call the Qlik AutoML API
    b. Leveraging the Qlik AutoML connector within the familiar Qlik Sense environment
    c. Manually exporting predictions from Qlik AutoML and importing them into Qlik Sense
    d. Uploading the Qlik AutoML model to a separate cloud machine learning platform
    e. Migrating entirely to a different data analytics platform with built-in machine learning functionalities
4. During Qlik AutoML analysis, what can be included in the data exploration stage?
    a. Identifying patterns, outliers, and missing data
    b. Defining the target variable for prediction
    c. Selecting the machine learning algorithm
    d. Training and evaluating multiple machine learning models
    e. Deploying the chosen model for real-time use

5. Qlik AutoML offers various visualizations for model performance. Which of the following is NOT typically included?
   a. Confusion matrix (Classification models)
   b. ROC curve (Classification models)
   c. R-squared (Regression models)
   d. Lift chart (This is a visualization for uplift modeling, not a standard Qlik AutoML output)
   e. Feature importance
6. Is it possible to compare the performance of multiple machine learning models generated by Qlik AutoML?
   a. No, Qlik AutoML only selects and trains a single best model
   b. Yes, Qlik AutoML provides metrics and visualizations for comparing different models
   c. This can only be done by manually exporting and analyzing the models in a separate tool
   d. Performance comparison is limited to models of the same machine-learning algorithm type
   e. All models generated by Qlik AutoML will have identical performance

Answers

1. c
2. a
3. c
4. a
5. d
6. b

References

1. *Qlik Help*: https://help.qlik.com/
2. Research on customer churn prediction and model interpretability analysis | PLOS ONE

CHAPTER 8
Application Automation

Introduction

In today's world, where data is critical, companies aim to make their processes quicker, decision-making faster, and get the most out of their data. Qlik Cloud Application Automation makes setting up automated data workflows and analysis easy. This chapter will take you through what this powerful tool can do, covering its main ideas, features, and how it's used in real life.

Qlik Application Automation, embedded in Qlik Cloud, offers a straightforward, no-code platform that lets you quickly assemble automated analytics and data workflows. Whether it is a simple task of moving data from one app to another or a complete process from raw data to insights, automations help streamline your analytics, set up workflows based on data, and incorporate data analysis into your everyday business operations.

Setting up automations is made to be easy. With a no-code editor, you just pick and place blocks to build your workflow. These blocks can either work with data or control how the workflow moves forward. You can customize each block to fit exactly what you need, allowing you to tackle specific tasks and challenges unique to your situation.

Structure

In this chapter, we will discuss the following topics:

- Benefits and Use Cases
- Technical Foundations
- Working with Automations

Benefits and Use Cases

Overcoming the challenges of manual data tasks and information silos, Qlik Application Automation enhances efficiency and insight depth by automating routines. This enables a no-code approach, allowing users to easily create automations that integrate disparate data for a cohesive overview. The following list highlights some of the benefits of the Qlik Application Automation usage:

- **Increased Efficiency:** Automate repetitive tasks such as data refreshes, report generation, and data transformations, freeing up time for valuable analysis and decision-making.
- **Reduced Errors:** Eliminate manual processes prone to human error, ensuring data accuracy and consistency in your analysis.
- **Improved Accessibility:** Democratize data analysis by enabling users with varying technical skills to build and run simple automations, fostering data-driven decision-making across the organization.
- **Faster Time to Insights:** Streamline workflows and automate data preparation, significantly reducing the time it takes to get actionable insights from your data.
- **Enhanced User Engagement:** Deliver real-time alerts and automated reports to keep stakeholders informed and engaged with data-driven insights.
- **Centralized Management:** Monitor and manage all automations from a single platform, ensuring transparency and control over your data workflows.

There are some typical use cases when the Qlik Application can be used:

- **Automated Data Refresh:** Schedule regular updates from various sources for always-fresh data and real-time insights.
- **Triggered Alerting:** Set up automated notifications based on specific data conditions, proactively alerting stakeholders to critical events or trends.
- **Automated Data Delivery:** Deliver curated data extracts or reports to different users or departments based on their specific needs.
- **Metadata Management:** Applying master items directly to new applications.
- **Qlik Cloud Tenant Administration:** automating repetitive tasks such as adding users to spaces, or checking for unused apps.
- **Integration with External Systems:** Automate data exchange with other applications and systems, streamlining data movement and fostering real-time collaboration.
- **Custom Workflow Automation:** Build complex workflows combining data transformations, analysis steps, and report generation for unique analytical needs.

These examples highlight only a fraction of the extensive capabilities of Qlik Application Automation. Its versatility enables customization to meet requirements and data-driven challenges, ultimately enhancing efficiency, accuracy, and the overall impact of data analysis efforts.

Technical Foundations

Qlik Application Automation is offered as a service within Qlik Cloud, emphasizing ease of construction and simplicity in design for automations. Utilizing the no-code automation editor, users can create automations by selecting and arranging workflow blocks in a coherent sequence.

Blocks

Automation consists of a series of blocks, each performing a specific action or serving as a trigger. Every block can reuse the result of any previously executed block and generate outputs that can be used by subsequent blocks. The process starts with a default start block, pre-positioned on the automation canvas. Constructing an automation workflow is straightforward, involving merely the dragging of new blocks onto the canvas. Upon adding a new block, the connection points on the previously placed blocks are automatically highlighted to facilitate integration.

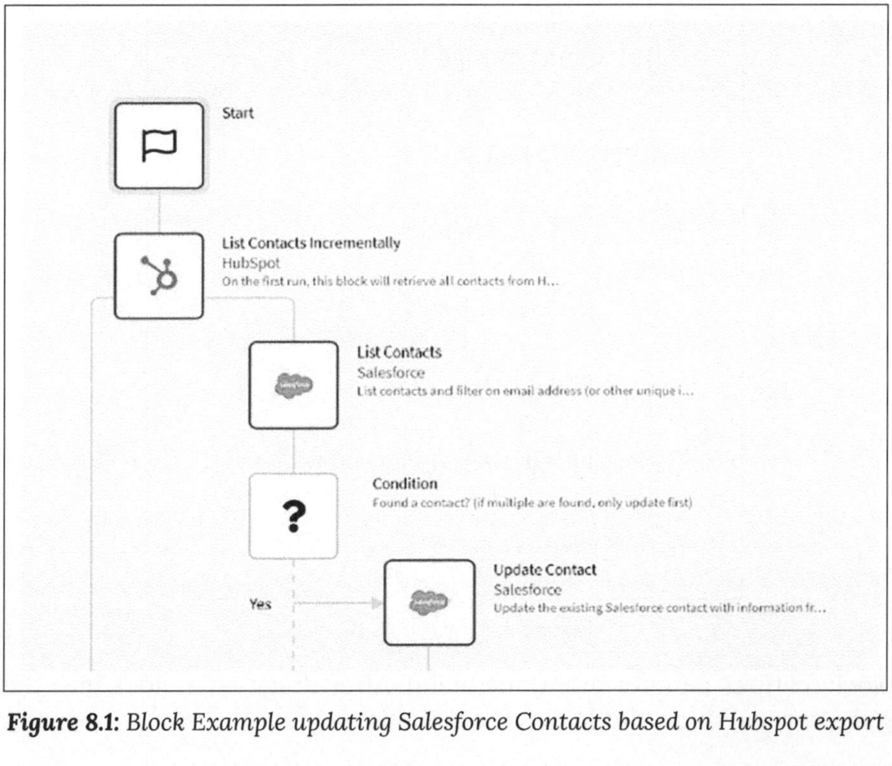

Figure 8.1: *Block Example updating Salesforce Contacts based on Hubspot export*

Blocks can be moved from the left panel to the canvas and connected to other blocks, constructing a workflow that implements the required use case.

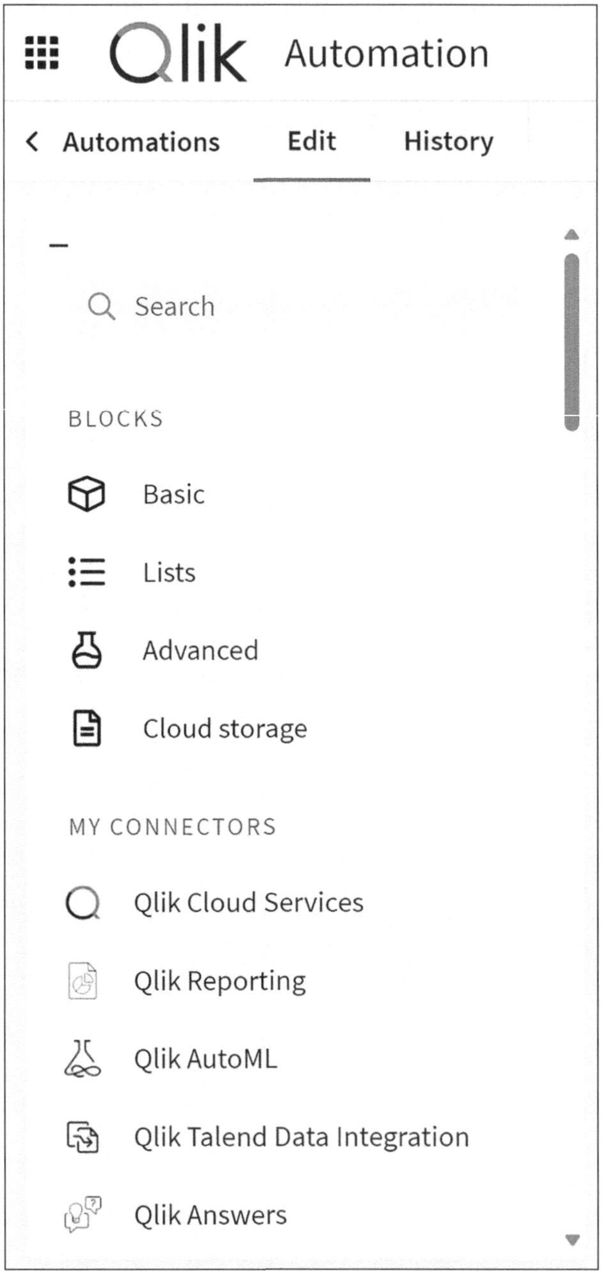

Figure 8.2: *Available Blocks*

Every block features a uniform options menu. After dragging a block into the editor, clicking the vertical three-dot icon will open this menu.

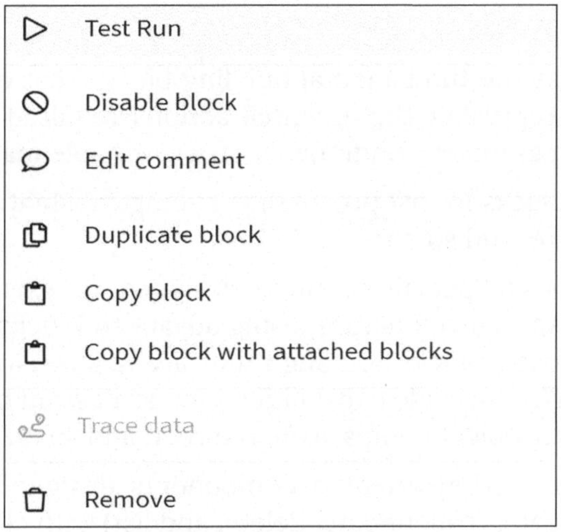

Figure 8.3: *Block common options*

The configuration for each block is accessible via the right-hand block configuration pane. While not every block shares identical options, the foundational settings remain consistent.

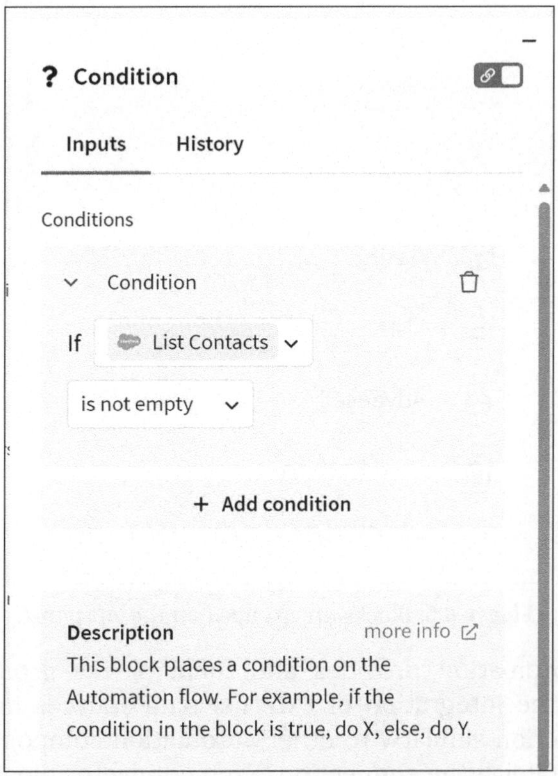

Figure 8.4: *Block Configuration*

There are some block types:

- **Basic:** Serves as the fundamental building blocks that constitute a workflow. These blocks represent the essential actions required to achieve a specific outcome, such as loops, conditionals, stops, variable management, and so on.
- **List:** Specific blocks for list processing, adding capabilities such as filter, limit, merge, compare, and so on.
- **Advanced Blocks** Specialized units designed to execute particular tasks. Despite their specialized nature, using advanced blocks is as straightforward as employing basic blocks, although they are tailored for distinct and precise applications. They provide capabilities such as custom code (using JavaScript, PHP, or Python), object comparison, redirect, and so on.
- **Cloud Storage:** Action-oriented components designed to facilitate CRUDL operations (create, read, update, delete, and list) with cloud storage services.

The blocks are grouped and available on the left side of the canvas.

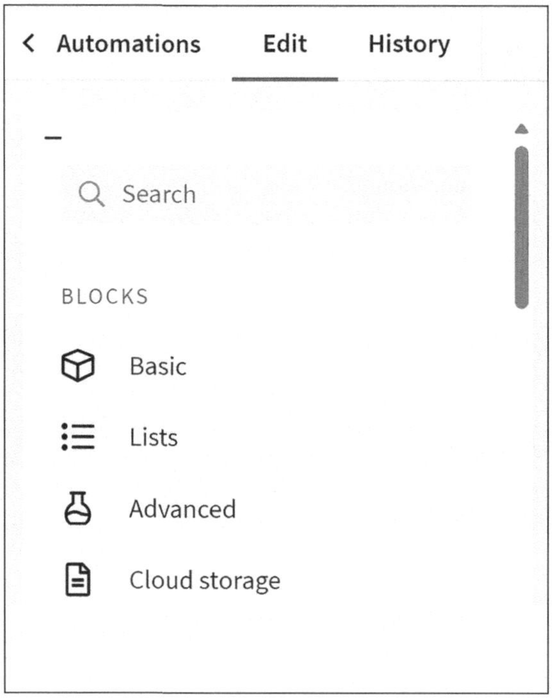

Figure 8.5: *Blocks are grouped on the left panel*

Qlik Application Automation provides additional blocks grouped in connectors. Connectors enable the integration of external data sources into your automation processes. They function similarly to other automation components but necessitate authentication to establish the connection. Each connector block executes a distinct API call to its corresponding data source connector.

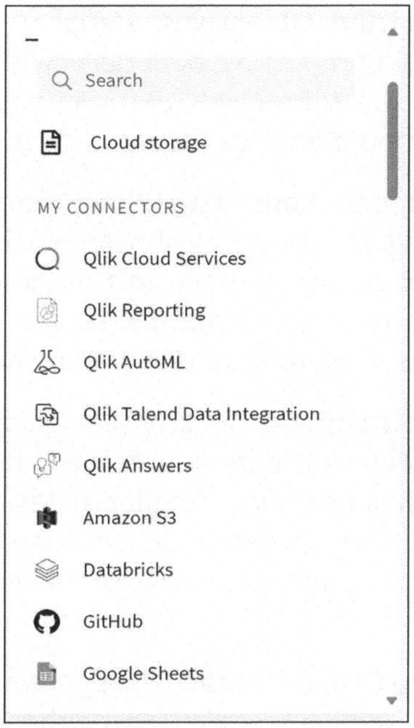

Figure 8.6: *Connector blocks*

Working with Automations

In this section, let us discuss the main concepts of how to implement a Qlik Application Automation.

Development Cycle

We recommend performing the following steps to develop your automation:

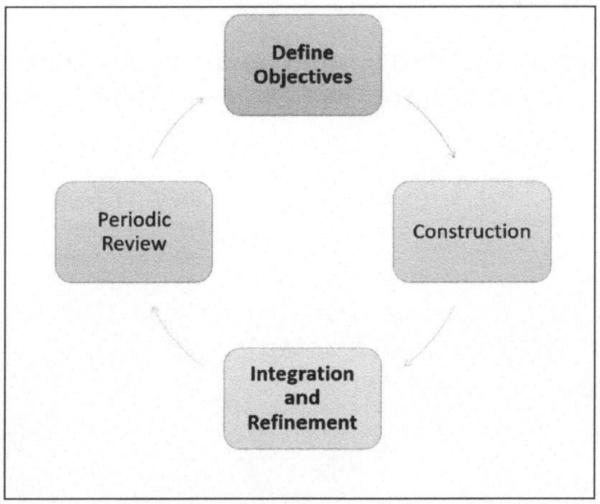

Figure 8.7: *Development Cycle*

1. **Define Your Automation Objectives:** Initiate your automation journey by meticulously identifying repetitive data tasks within your Qlik environment or another problem to solve. Precisely defining your automation goals ensures you target the right opportunities for significant improvement.
2. **Meticulously Construct Your Workflow:** Employ a strategic approach, meticulously dragging and dropping chosen blocks onto the canvas. Configure each block with specific parameters. Introduce decision-making complexity and nuance by incorporating conditional blocks, allowing your automation to react dynamically based on data values or external triggers.
3. **Integration and Refinement**: Ensure seamless operation by connecting your automation to relevant data sources and intended output destinations. Rigorously test each step using smaller datasets to validate functionality. After deployment, actively monitor the automated tasks and adjust schedules or triggers based on performance data and user feedback for continuous optimization.
4. **Embrace the Ongoing Cycle:** Embrace the dynamic nature of data, applications, and business needs. Regularly review and enhance your workflows using the previous steps, incorporating new automation features and blocks as they become available. Remember, automation is an ongoing journey, not a one-time destination. By continuously adapting and iterating, you unlock its full potential and empower your organization with a data-driven advantage.

By diligently adhering to these steps and fostering a culture of continuous improvement, you can orchestrate data excellence through Qlik automation. This empowers you to unlock remarkable efficiency, significantly reduce manual efforts, and pave the way for data-driven insights that propel your organization forward.

The Start Block

The `Start` block serves as the initial component in any automation sequence; it is automatically added to any new automation and sets the run mode as its sole required configuration.

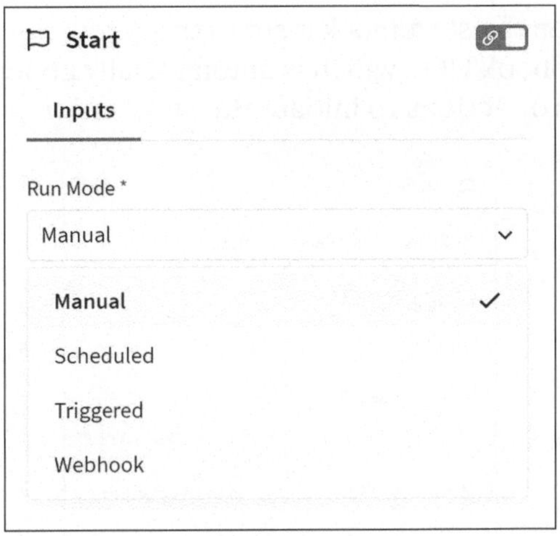

Figure 8.8: *The start block*

Based on the provided image, there are four distinct run modes:

- **Manual:** Setting the start block to manual means the automation will only activate when you initiate it by clicking **Run**. This manual run mode is commonly employed for testing purposes.
- **Scheduled:** By configuring the start block to scheduled run mode, the automation runs according to a predetermined timetable. This allows you to specify the length of the schedule, the start time, how often it occurs, and which timezone the schedule should use.

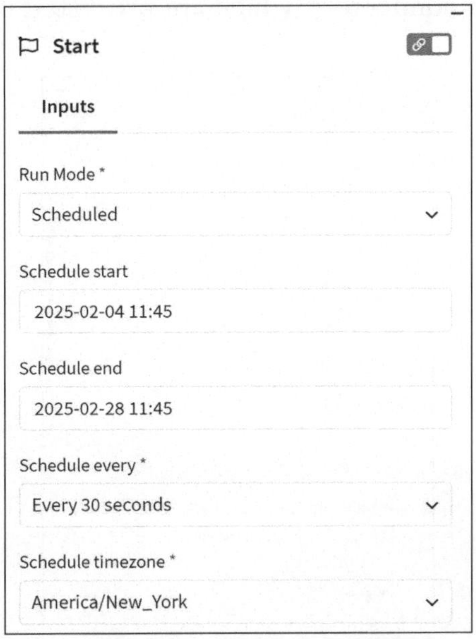

Figure 8.9: *Scheduled mode*

- **Triggered:** When the start block is set to triggered, the automation is activated through its webhook URL, which is automatically generated. This setup allows external events or actions to initiate the automation process.

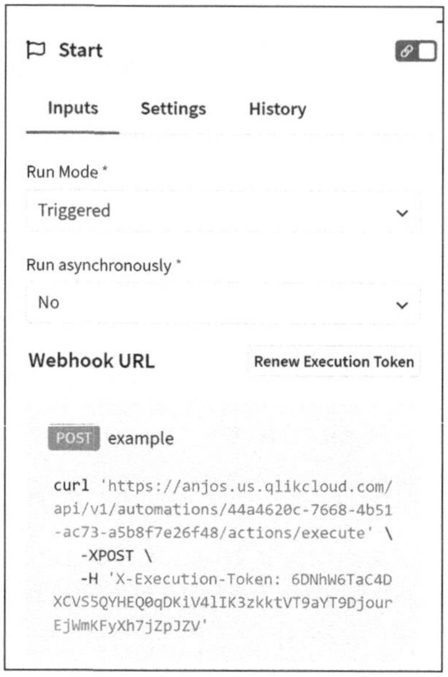

Figure 8.10: *Triggered mode*

- **Webhook:** Setting the start block to webhook mode enables the automation to be initiated by an event from a specific connector block. This functionality is limited to certain connectors, which are pre-listed in the Connector field for easy selection.

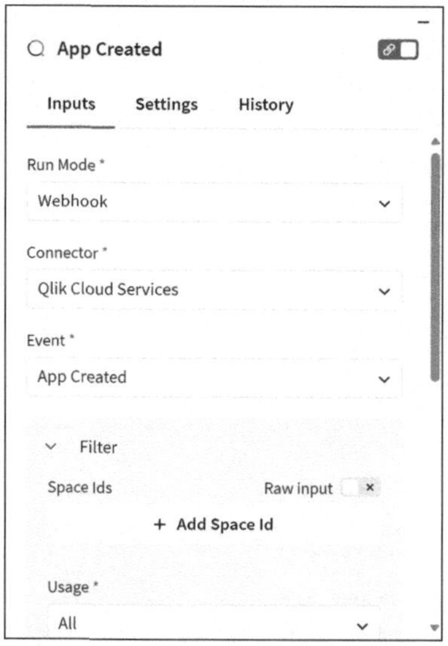

Figure 8.11: *Webhook to get called when a new app is created on Qlik Cloud*

The Input Block

The **`Inputs`** block serves as a gateway for receiving data or parameters from users or external sources, such as when the automation is triggered via its REST API endpoint.

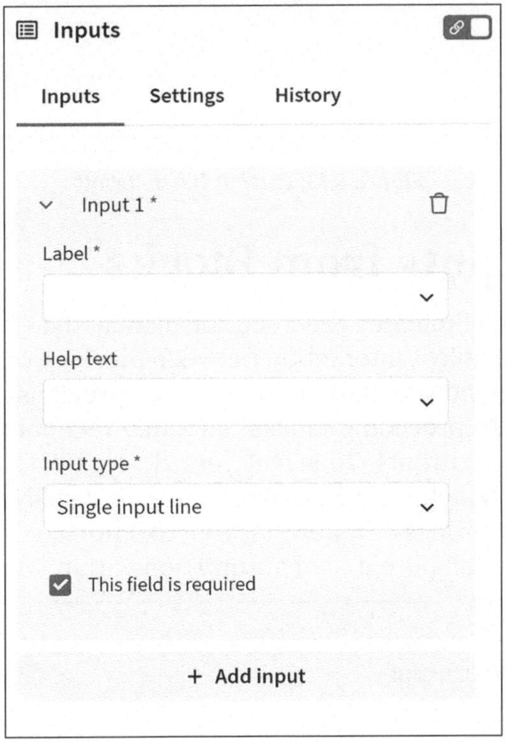

Figure 8.12: *The input block can receive values from external systems*

This block is particularly useful in scenarios such as:

- Requiring user-provided data to proceed with the automation.
- Triggering the automation through its REST API endpoint.
- Invoking the automation from another automation process.

Input blocks should not be used in automations that run on a predetermined schedule, as these cannot solicit input during their scheduled execution unless the values.

The Output Block

The **`Output`** block is a key component in automation, used to display output to users during the execution of an automation. It can show results from other blocks or user-entered data. The most common use case is where user visibility is required for the data processed by the automation. Different use cases display the inputs when the automation is called externally by one API endpoint or by another automation.

Unlike other blocks, the output block can share data beyond the scope of its execution, making it unique in its ability to communicate results externally.

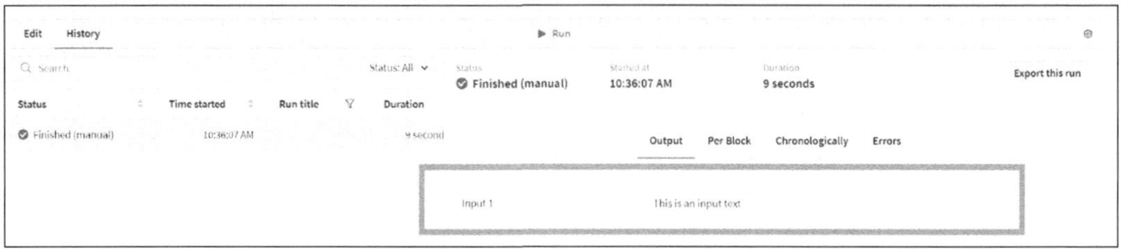

Figure 8.13: *Output Block Result*

Reusing Outputs from Blocks

Qlik Cloud Automation eliminates the need for manual data mapping when creating workflows, fostering seamless interaction between blocks. Configuring a block's input field triggers a user-friendly wizard showcasing all previously added blocks in your sequence. Each of these preceding blocks is readily recognized, and the input field understands their JSON outputs. To select your desired data point, simply click and choose from the clearly delineated available outputs displayed for each block. This intuitive and efficient process empowers you to effortlessly chain diverse blocks together, unlocking the full potential of automation within your Qlik environment.

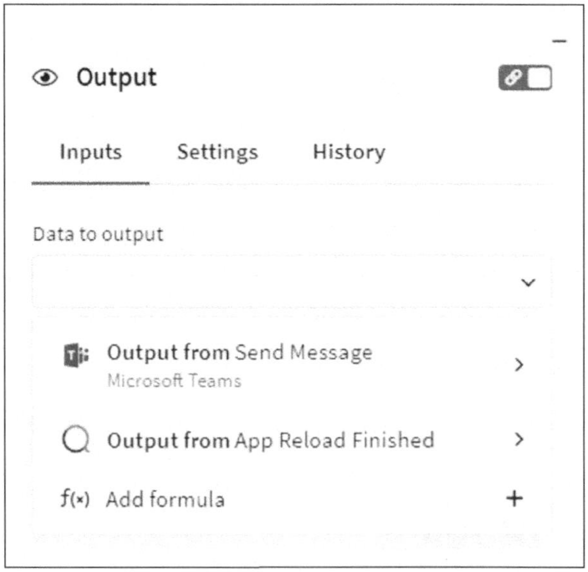

Figure 8.14: *Previous blocks outputs*

The interface simplifies navigating the complex, nested structures of any output. The wizard displays previous executions (or provides an example if there have been none) to ensure you select the precise value you need.

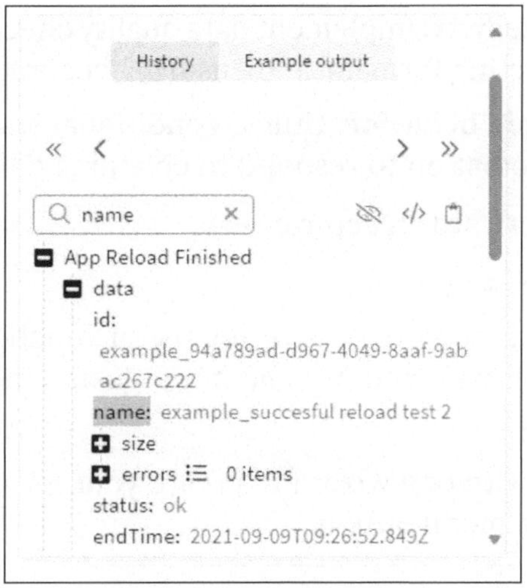

***Figure 8.15:** JSON parser*

The wizard will add a formula to extract the information you selected. For example, to access the param1 input from an Input block the formula is **`{$.inputs.param1}`**. This is called *Field mapping* and involves assigning data from one block to a field in a subsequent block. You can inspect the generated expression using the small chain icon on the block settings header.

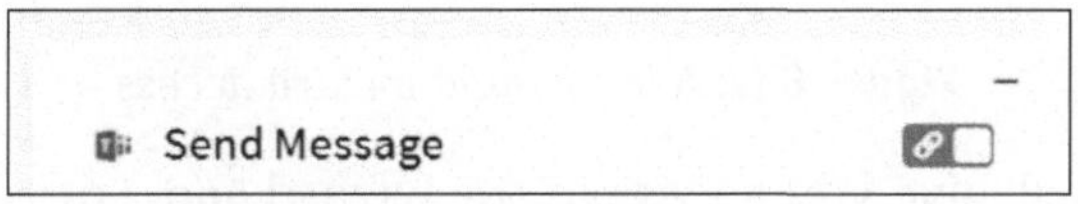

***Figure 8.16:** Send Message block*

Clicking the chain button in the aforementioned image will switch the formula parsing. Disabling formula parsing causes configuration fields to display the raw input values, showing how the fields are being mapped. With the formula parser turned off, you can manually adjust the formula.

Using Formulas

Formulas play a central role in enhancing data manipulation within the Qlik Cloud Automation workflows. They provide users with tools to:

- **Process data precisely:** Cleanse and transform incoming data by adjusting formats, extracting specific values, and ensuring proper formatting.
- **Data conversion:** You can convert data types from what is returned into an easier-to-process format. Example: convert a date input using MM/DD/YYYY format to a YYYYMMDD string to make comparisons easier.
- **Custom calculations:** Address unique data manipulation needs through formulas tailor-made for specific scenarios, going beyond pre-built blocks.

- **Maintain data integrity:** Implement data quality checks by removing unwanted characters, correcting formats, and ensuring accuracy.
- **Introduce dynamic behavior:** Utilize conditional statements within formulas to enable the automation to respond to changing data or conditions.

Formulas use a straightforward structure:

```
{FunctionName : Argument}
```

Where *FunctionName* is a comprehensive library of functions, each dedicated to a distinct data manipulation task, and *Argument* represents the data point or value that the function operates on.

Qlik Cloud provides you with one wizard to create your formula that can be accessed through the **`Add formula`** menu option.

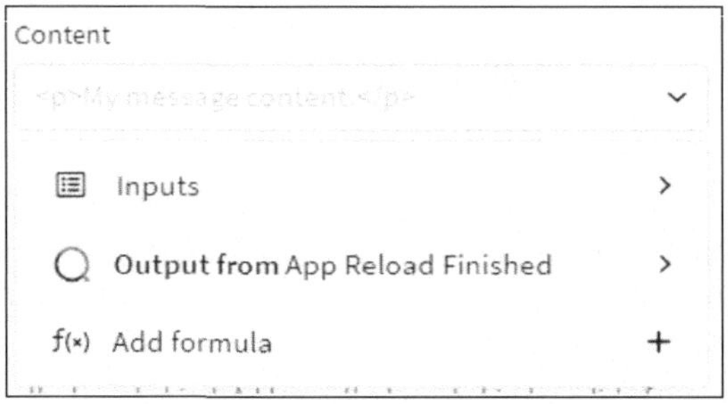

Figure 8.17: *Add formula wizard access*

Pressing that option will give you access to the wizard **`Add Formula`**, which guides you to create formulas using an intuitive interface.

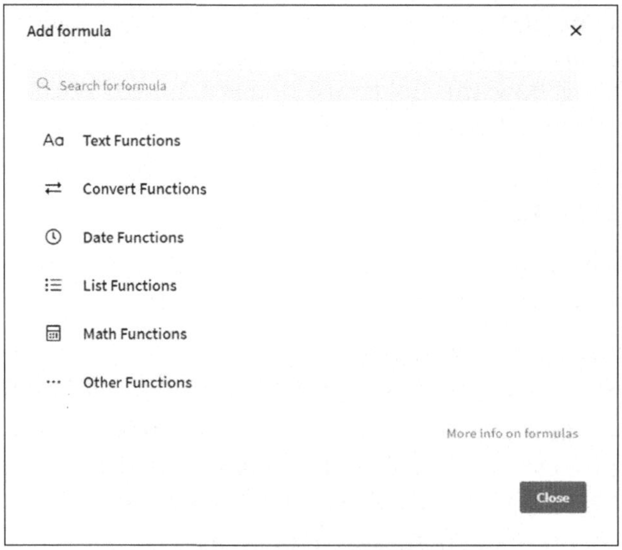

Figure 8.18: *Add formula wizard*

Formula Examples:

- **String uppercase**:

  `{uppercase: {$.inputs.param1}}`
- **String concatenation**: (adding slash as separator)

  `{$.inputs.param1}/{$.inputs.param2}`
- **Checking if one string is a valid email**:

  `{isemail: {$.AppReloadFinished.extensions.userId}}`

For a more in-depth exploration of formulas and the extensive function library, refer to the provided "*Working with formulas*" resource. By familiarizing yourself with these fundamentals, you unlock the potential to wield formulas effectively and manipulate data with precision within your Qlik Cloud Automation endeavors.

Creating an Automation

Creating automations in Qlik Cloud involves several steps, focusing on the design and execution of a workflow to automate tasks within your Qlik application. Following is a step-by-step guide outlining the process and the options you have at each step:

1. Access the Automation Interface using the **`Automations`** option from the left menu.

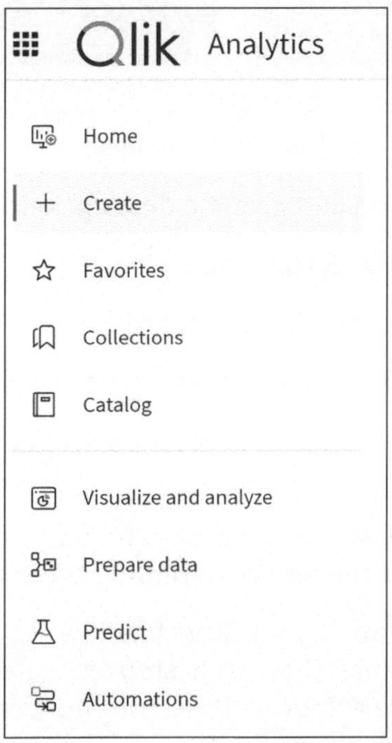

Figure 8.19: *Accessing the Automations portal*

2. Create a New Automation by clicking **`Create new automation`**.

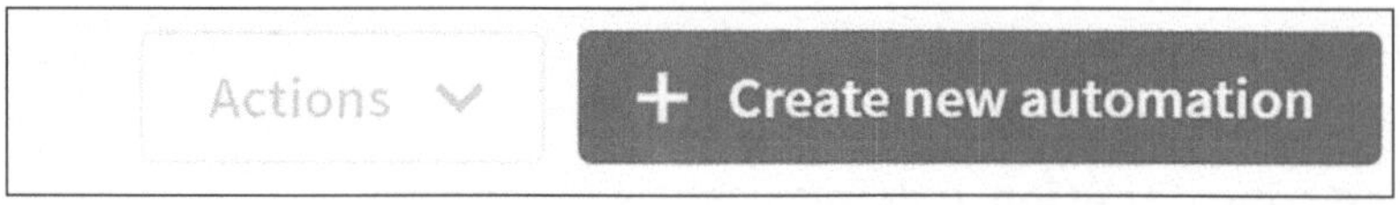

Figure 8.20: *Create new automation button*

3. Select a template to have the initial logic pre-populated or use the **`Create without template`** button.

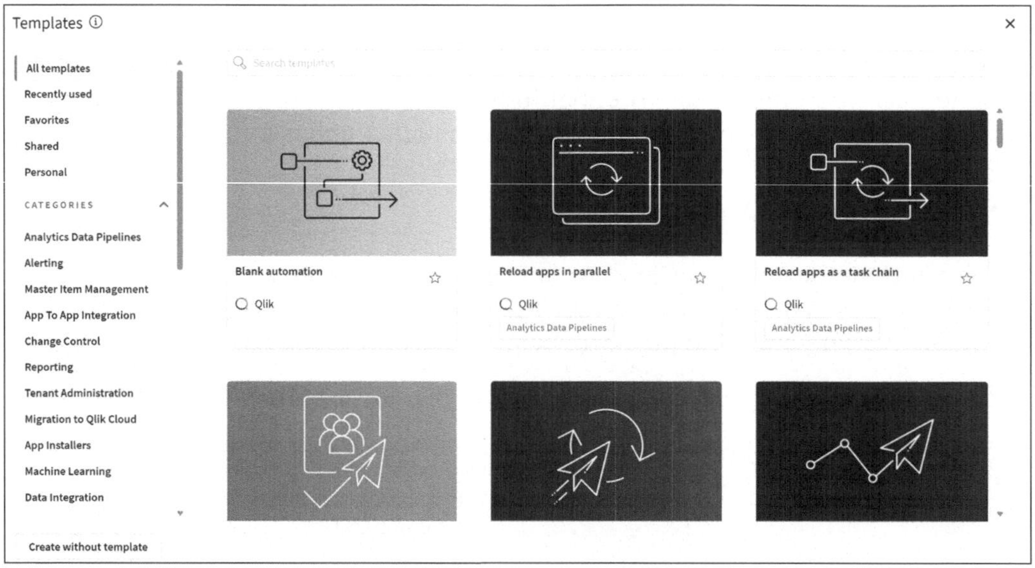

Figure 8.21: *Templates*

4. Name your automation and give it a description.
5. Configure the Start Block run mode.
6. Add an input block to the flow if needed.
7. Add blocks by dragging and dropping them as needed into your workflow.
8. Configure Connector Blocks. You might need to authenticate the block connections.
9. Define Logic and Flow positioning your blocks to define the flow of your automation. Connect the blocks to outline the sequence of actions.
10. **Testing and Validation**: If your Start block is set to Manual, click "**`Run`**" to test the automation. Ensure that each step executes as expected and that the desired outcomes are achieved. Based on the test results, make any necessary adjustments to the blocks or flow.

11. **Deployment**: If you are using a Scheduled or Triggered start mode, configure the necessary schedules or triggers.
12. **Monitor Performance**: Use the Automations dashboard to monitor the execution and performance of your automation.

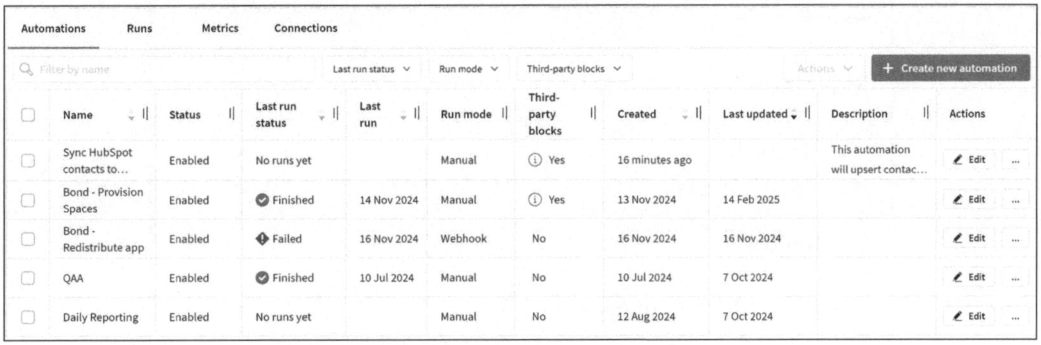

Figure 8.22: *Automations Dashboard*

This guide provides a general overview. Always refer to the latest Qlik documentation for the most accurate and detailed instructions.

Use Cases Examples

Let us give some examples of tasks that can be automatized using Qlik Application Automation.

Notify a Teams channel when reload fails:

- **Problem**: A reload failure may lead to errors in analysis using outdated data.
- **Solution**: Notify a Teams Channel for errors on app reloads.

Step by step:

1. Configure the **`Start`** Block to be triggered by the **`Qlik Cloud Services`** connector and the event **`App Reload Finished`**.

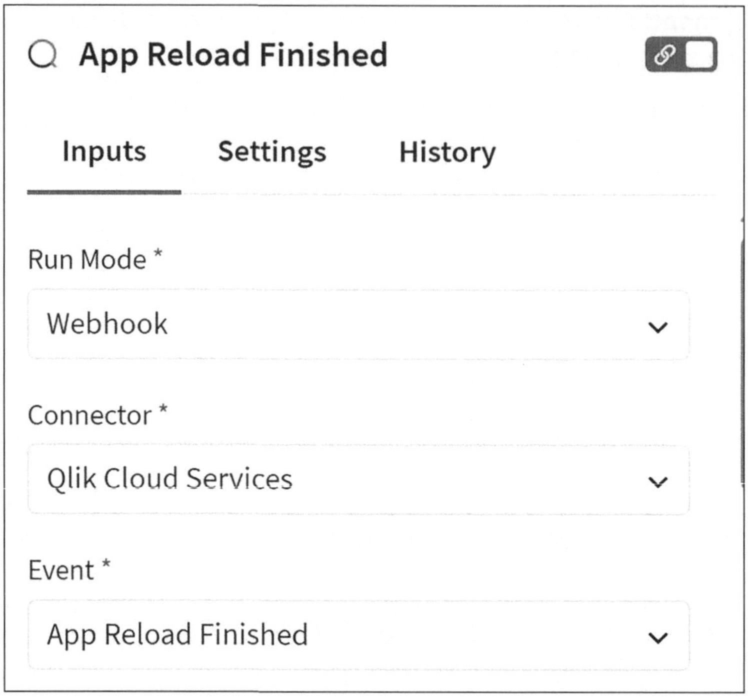

Figure 8.23: *Configuring the Start button to be triggered by a reload*

2. Using the **`do lookup`** option from the **`Filter`** session top, search for the application(s) (you can add more than one) you want to monitor.

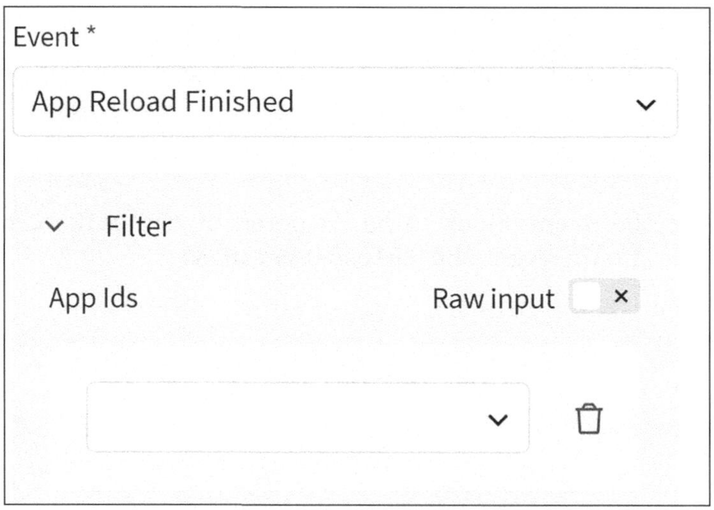

Figure 8.24: *Configuring the app ID*

3. Configure the **`Reload Status`** to be **`Failed (error)`** meaning that only reload fails will trigger the automation.

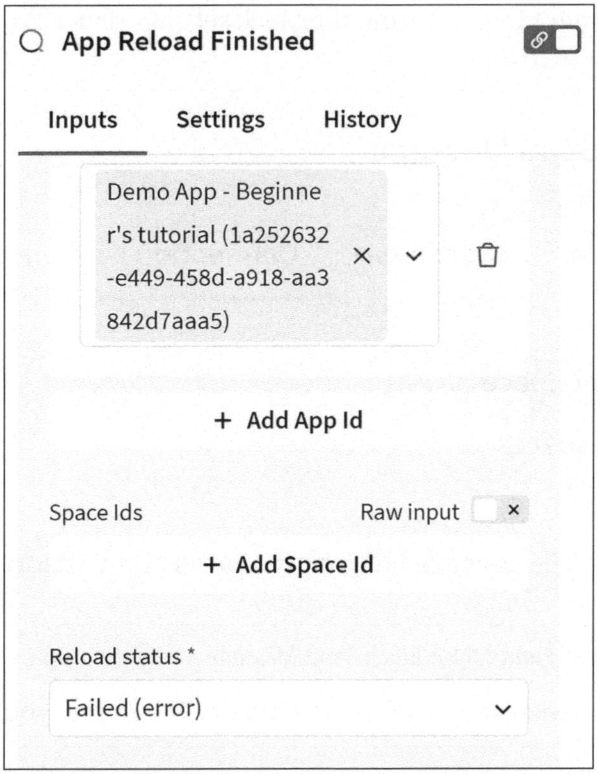

Figure 8.25: *Filtering the status*

4. Drag and drop a block of type **`Send Message`** from the **`Microsoft Teams`** connector.

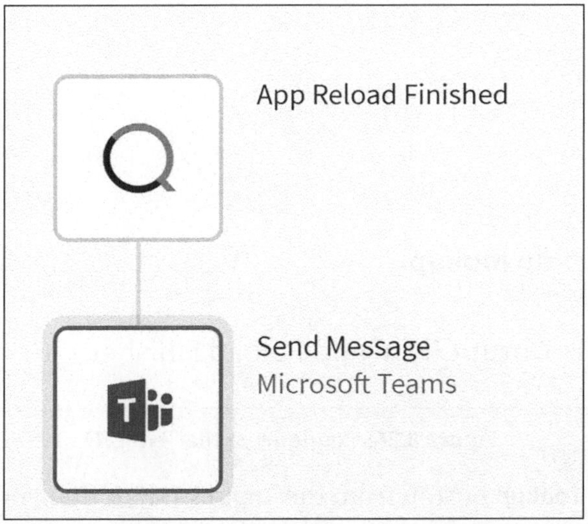

Figure 8.26: *Send Message block*

5. Use the **Connections** tab from the block settings panel to authenticate against your Teams service.

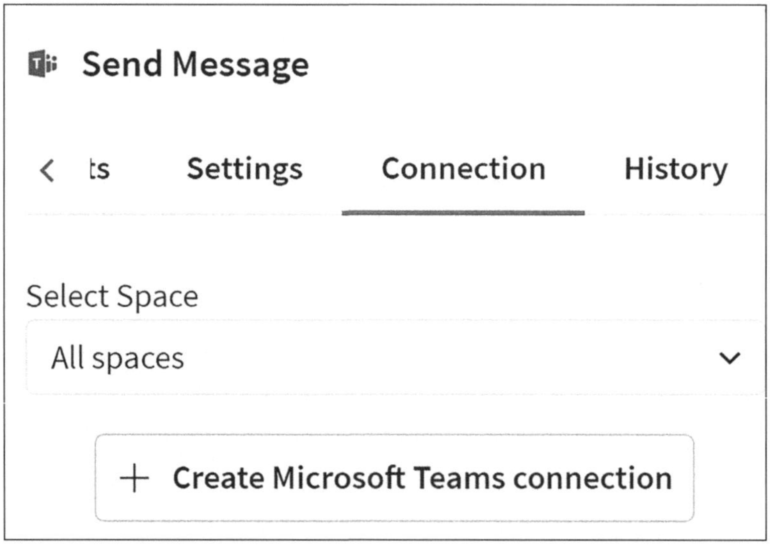

***Figure 8.27**: Block Send Message Authentication*

6. Use the **do lookup** button from the **Inputs** tab to find your **Team ID**.

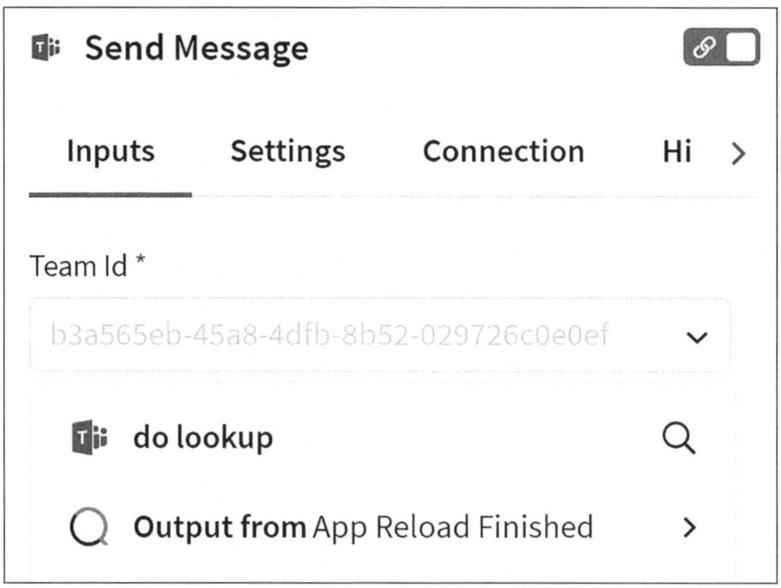

***Figure 8.28**: Configuring the Team ID*

7. Use the **do lookup** button from the **Inputs** tab to find your **Channel ID**.

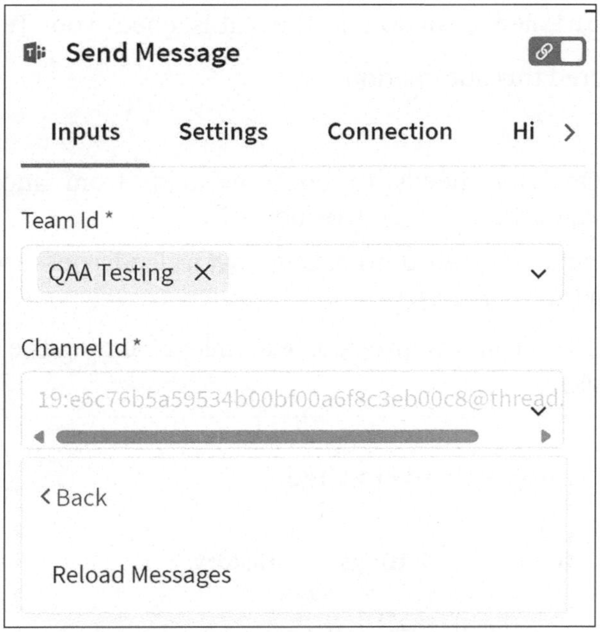

Figure 8.29: *Configuring the Channel ID*

8. Configure the message body using the **`Content`** parameter. You can use the **`Output From`** option to extract any information from the previous block.

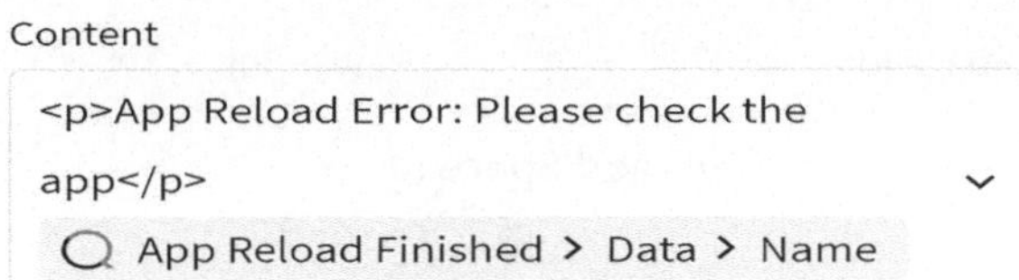

Figure 8.30: *Message Content*

9. Press the **Save** button, and then **Run.** You will be redirected to the monitoring screen, where you can see each block execution result.

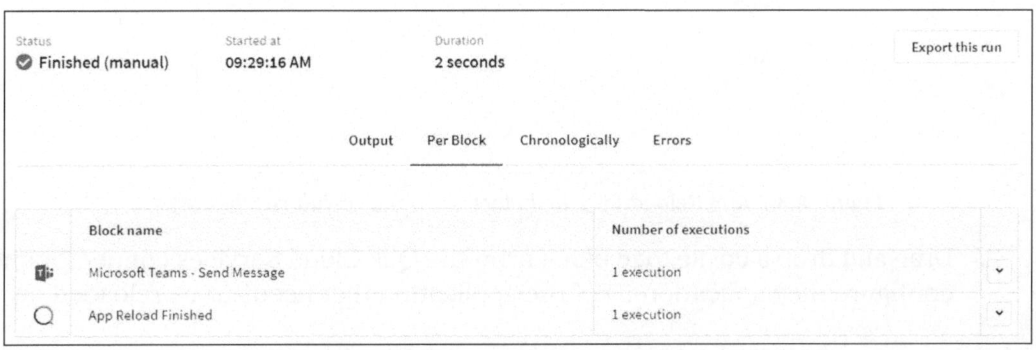

Figure 8.31: *Automation execution screen*

10. If you see **`Finished (manual)`** as the status, check your Teams for a message.
11. You completed this automation.

App task chain:

- **Problem**: One app needs to consume data from another app without concurrency, they need to run sequentially.
- **Solution**: Implement an automation that reloads one app on a successful reload from the source app.

1. Reuse steps 1-3 from the previous example, changing the **`Reload Status`** to **`Success (ok)`**.

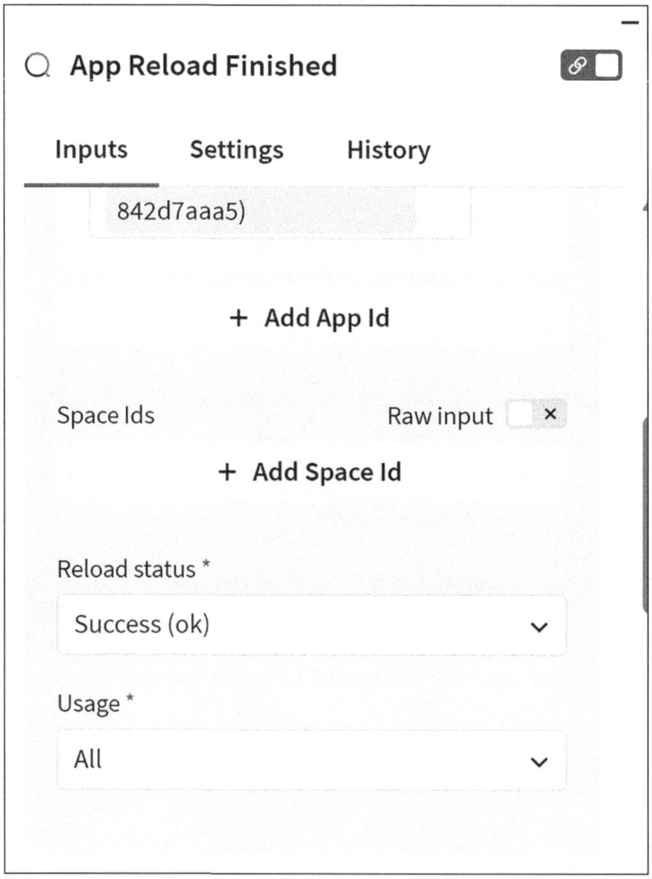

***Figure 8.32**: App Reload Finished block with Succesfull result status*

2. Drag and drop a **`Do Reload`** block from the Qlik Cloud Services connector and configure the application ID of the application that needs to be reloaded.

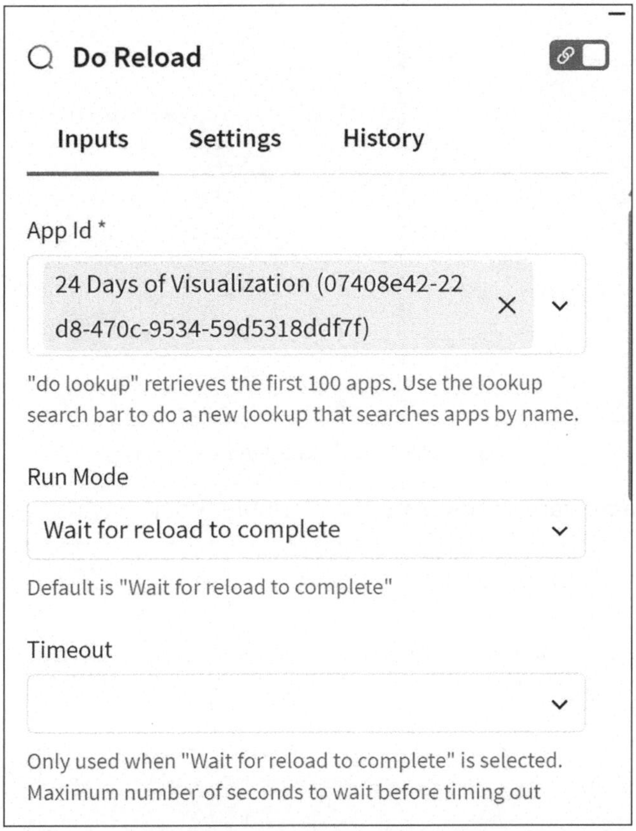

Figure 8.33: *Do Reload block settings*

3. Save and test your automation like you did on the first example.
4. You completed this automation.

Active Intelligence:

- **Problem**: A whole team needs to be notified on Teams if a certain KPI is below the expected. Currently, users need to periodically check the app and manually create a message on Teams.
- **Solution**: Set up an automation that monitors a KPI in a Qlik application and sends a message via Teams if the KPI falls below a predefined threshold (defined as a variable). Given that KPI values update only upon app reload, initiate this automation in response to a successful app reload event.

1. Reuse steps 1-3 from previous examples, configuring the **`Reload Status`** to be **`Success (ok)`**.
2. Drag and drop a **`Variable`** block from the Basic object set.

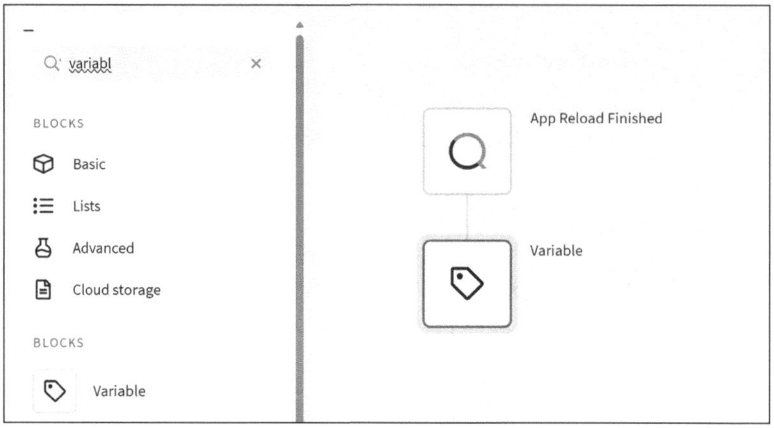

***Figure 8.34:** Adding a Variable block*

3. Click **`Manage variables`** from the Variable block settings panel.

***Figure 8.35**: Variable block settings*

4. Add a variable using the **`Number`** type, press the **`Add new variable`** button, and then press the **`Save`** button.

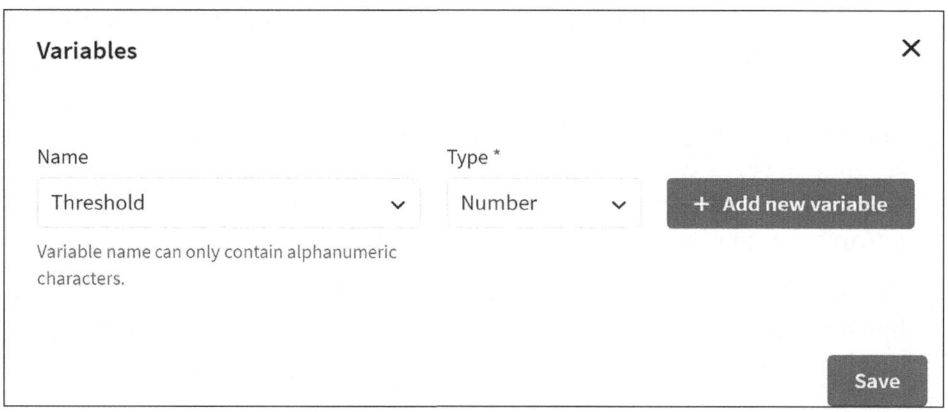

***Figure 8.36**: Adding a variable*

5. Add one **Set value** operation and configure it to value (100, for example).

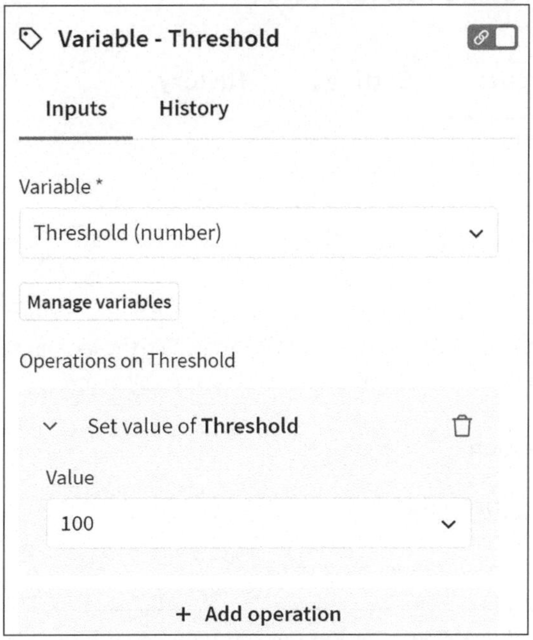

***Figure 8.37**: Setting variable value*

6. Drag and drop a **Get expression value** from the **Qlik Cloud Services** connector.

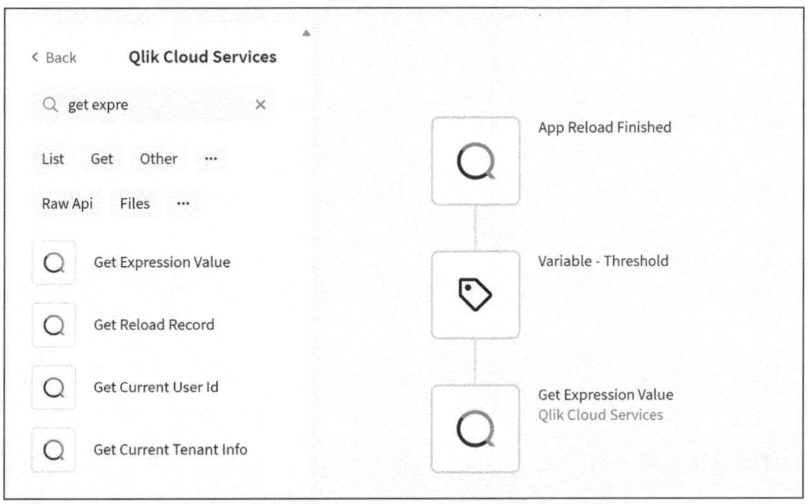

***Figure 8.38**: Get Expression Value block*

7. Using the block settings panel, configure the application you are referring to and the expression that you want to evaluate. This needs to use Qlik expression syntax (please refer to previous chapters about Qlik expressions).

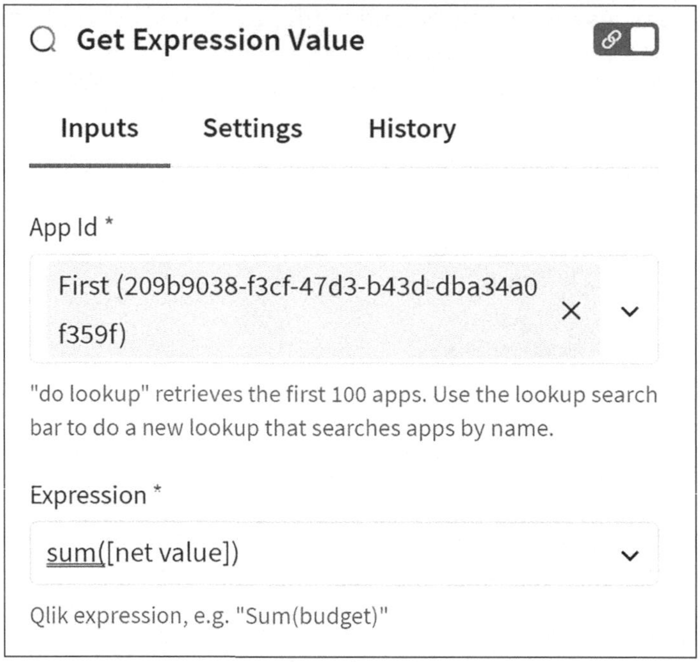

***Figure 8.39**: Get Expression Value configuration*

8. Add a **`Condition`** block from the **`Basic`** set to your workflow.

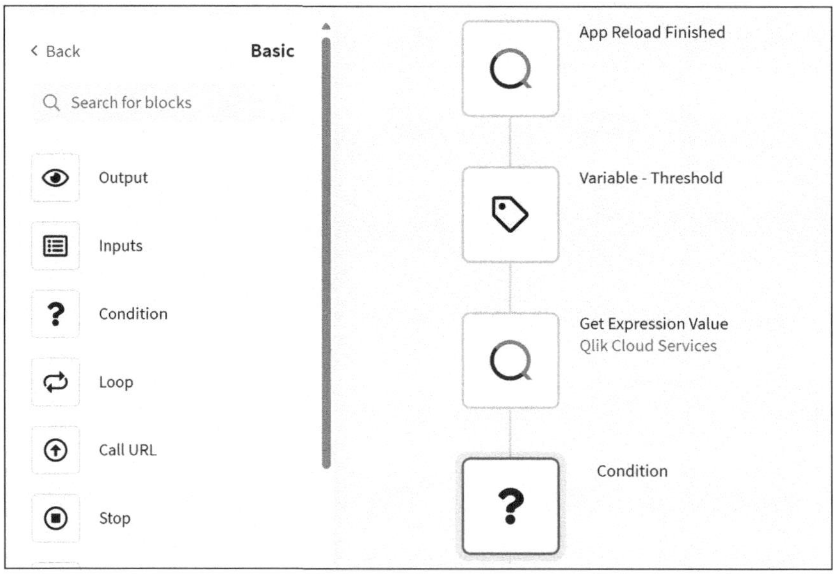

***Figure 8.40**: Adding a Condition Block*

9. Using the block settings, configure the condition to use the result from the **`Get expression value`** and compare it with the variable value.

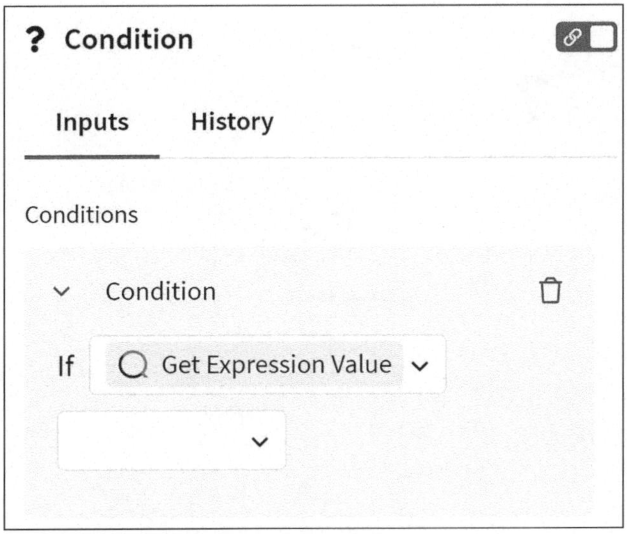

Figure 8.41: *Configuring the condition*

10. Your condition should be similar to *Figure* 8.42.

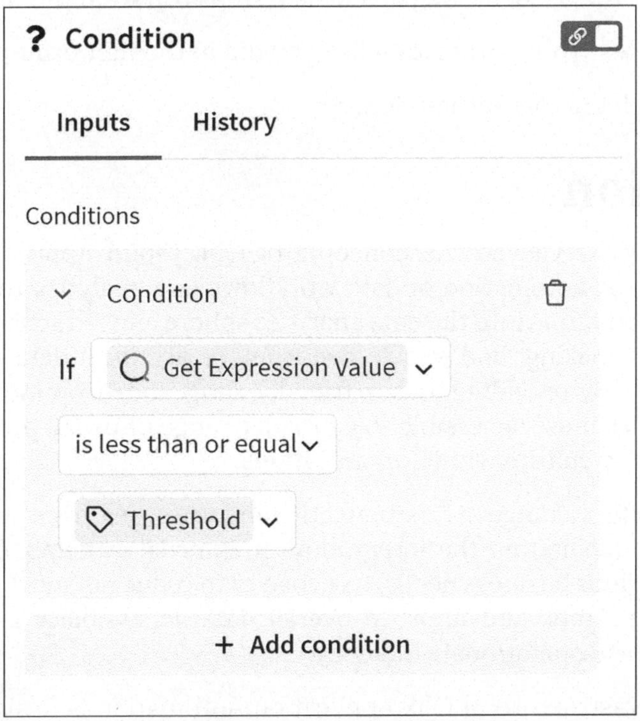

Figure 8.42: *Condition block settings*

11. Drag and drop a Teams **`Send Message`** block to your workflow, linking it to the **`Yes`** of the Condition Block, as in *Figure* 8.43.

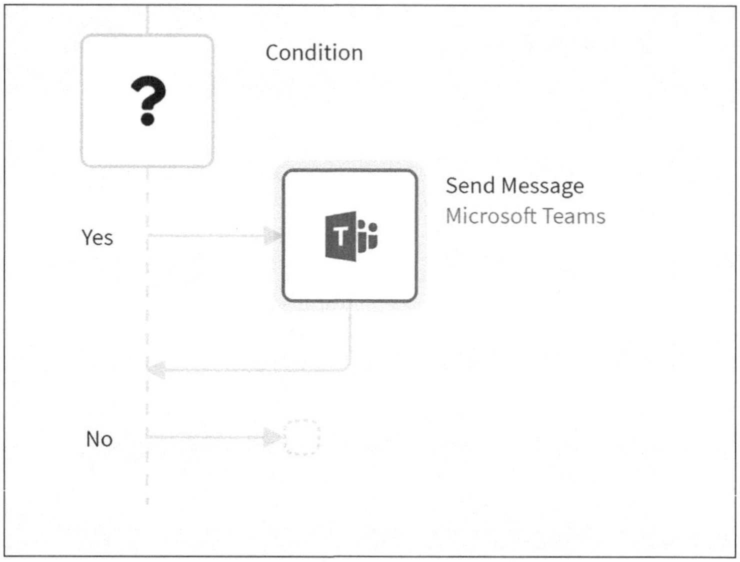

***Figure 8.43**: Setting the Send Message to be executed on the Yes condition*

12. Configure the **`Send Message`** block like steps 6-8 from the first example.
13. Save and test your automation like you did in the first example.
14. You completed this automation.

Conclusion

In this chapter, we reviewed the concepts of Qlik Cloud Application Automation, which facilitates the automation of data workflows and analytics through a no-code approach. Its introduction into the data analytics sphere aims to streamline operations, enhance decision-making, and enable faster, more accurate data utilization across various industries. By providing a user-friendly, drag-and-drop interface, it seeks to make data analytics more accessible to a broader range of users, potentially fostering a more data-centric culture within organizations.

The application offers a range of functionalities and use cases, from automating routine data refreshes to facilitating the integration of external systems, demonstrating its adaptability to various business needs. Its capacity to reduce manual errors, accelerate the delivery of insights, and improve overall data accessibility is indicative of its potential to increase operational efficiency.

The technical infrastructure of Qlik Application Automation is designed to provide a variety of blocks for different tasks and a straightforward interface that supports the construction of customized workflows. The development cycle, which includes stages such as definition, construction, integration, and refinement, suggests a structured approach to creating and optimizing automations.

In the next chapter, we will delve into the realm of Insight Advisor. The Qlik Insight Advisor is designed to assist in constructing visualizations and scrutinizing data. It will enable natural language interaction with your data, simplifying the process of posing questions and uncovering insights.

Multiple Choice Questions

1. What is the primary purpose of Qlik Application Automation?
    a. To create interactive dashboards within Qlik applications
    b. To automate repetitive data tasks and workflows in Qlik applications
    c. To analyze large datasets using advanced statistical techniques
    d. To collaborate on data insights with team members
2. Which of the following is NOT a core use case of Qlik Application Automation?
    a. Scheduling data refreshes at specific intervals
    b. Customizing dashboards based on real-time data
    c. Writing complex scripts for advanced automations
    d. Manually manipulating data within the application
3. Which of the following is NOT a way to create automations in Qlik Application Automation?
    a. Utilizing pre-built blocks within the Automation module
    b. Writing custom scripts using Qlik Scripting language
    c. Integrating with external tools and services through APIs
    d. Manually triggering actions within the Qlik application automation interface

Answers

1. b
2. b
3. b

Additional Resources

The following links complement this chapter, bringing more resources to the reader with more examples and details. Please be aware that as Qlik introduces new product versions, the documentation might be found under a different link.

- **Getting Started with Qlik Application Automation:** (https://help.qlik.com/en-US/cloud-services/Subsystems/Hub/Content/Sense_QlikAutomation/introduction/getting-started.htm)
- **Blocks:** (https://help.qlik.com/en-US/cloud-services/Subsystems/Hub/Content/Sense_QlikAutomation/introduction/blocks-intro.htm)
- **Working with Formulas:** (https://help.qlik.com/en-US/cloud-services/Subsystems/Hub/Content/Sense_QlikAutomation/working-with-automations/working-with-formulas.htm)
- **Tutorials:** (https://help.qlik.com/en-US/cloud-services/Subsystems/Hub/Content/Sense_QlikAutomation/tutorials/tutorials.htm)

Chapter 9

Insight Advisor

Introduction

Navigating the complexity of data to extract valuable insights can be challenging, with traditional methods often requiring specialized knowledge and complex query languages, limiting accessibility for many. Qlik Insight Advisor introduces a solution by enabling natural language data exploration within Qlik, simplifying the process for a wider audience.

This chapter examines the key features of Qlik Insight Advisor, which allows users to interact with data using natural language queries, thereby broadening data exploration accessibility. It highlights the tool's capacity to facilitate natural language queries, provide deeper insights, and reveal new patterns to support decision-making based on data.

Natural Language Generation (NLG) is a branch of artificial intelligence that transforms structured data into human-like text or viceversa. It is used for automated report generation, personalized content creation, and making complex data more understandable, enhancing communication and insight derivation.

Structure

In this chapter, we will discuss the following topics:

- Capabilities and Functionality
- Advanced Features
- Integration with Other Tools

Capabilities and Functionality

Qlik Insight Advisor expands the realm of data exploration within Qlik applications by empowering users to not only interact with existing visualizations but also generate custom visualizations and analyses tailored to their specific questions and needs.

Navigating pre-built app visualizations can be a limiting experience, especially when users have specific inquiries or prefer a particular type of analysis but are not familiar with the technical steps to achieve them. This can happen when users know the questions they want to answer or the types of insights they seek but lack the knowledge of how to translate them into actionable data exploration steps.

Qlik Insight Advisor addresses this challenge by facilitating the dynamic creation of visualizations directly aligned with user queries. Users can specify the desired type of analysis and select the relevant data points, and Insight Advisor will automatically generate charts and visualizations that meet their specific requirements.

Furthermore, it offers a search-based interface that allows users to articulate their questions using natural language. Insight Advisor then interprets these questions and presents visualizations that directly address the user's inquiries.

This capability significantly enhances the data exploration experience within Qlik, offering a more interactive and user-centric approach. By automating the visualization creation process, Insight Advisor not only simplifies the exploration of complex data sets but also accelerates the discovery of actionable insights. This makes it an invaluable tool for users at all levels of data literacy, enabling them to leverage data more effectively in their decision-making processes.

Insight Advisor is available from the sheet view of an app. Click the **`Insight Advisor`** tab to open it.

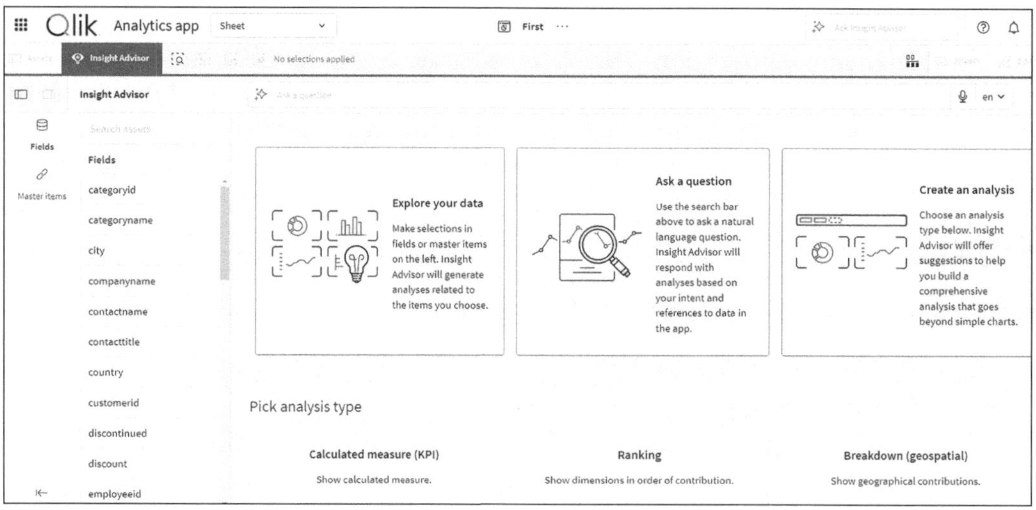

Figure 9.1: *Insight Advisor main screen*

Insight Advisor is also available at the hub, using the **`Ask Insight Advisor`** button on the top menu.

Figure 9.2: *Accessing Insight Advisor at the hub*

When you access the Insight Advisor from the hub, the experience becomes like a chatbot answering questions.

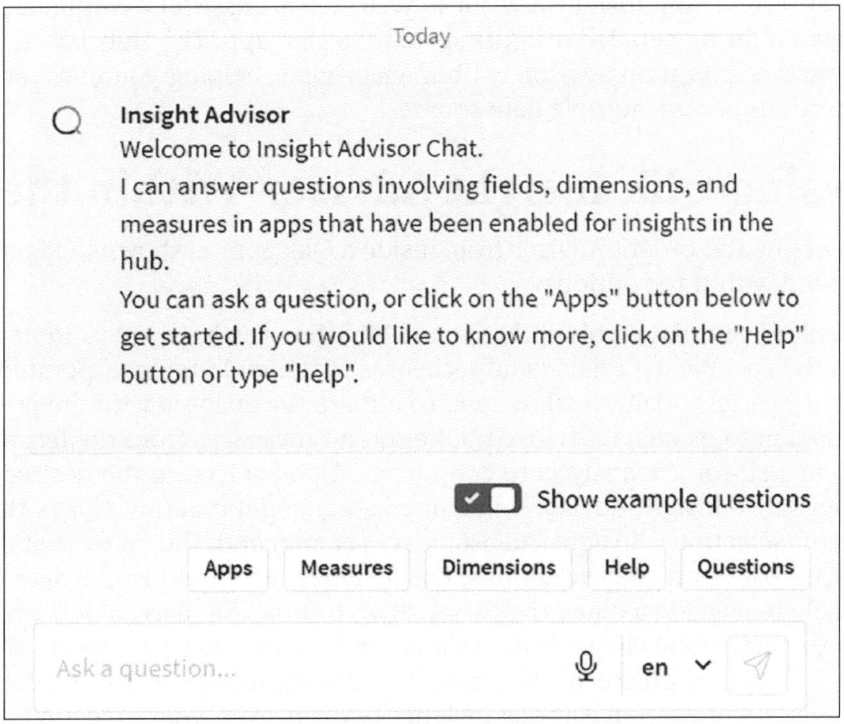

Figure 9.3: *Insight Advisor accessed from the hub*

Here is a breakdown of the differences between accessing Qlik Insight Advisor in the app or the hub, highlighting the nuances and unique advantages of each approach:

- **Accessing Qlik Insight Advisor within the App:** Closely integrated with a specific Qlik application, it analyzes the data and visualizations within that app. It provides insights and suggestions tailored to the app's data model, ensuring the relevance of its recommendations. This feature supports seamless interaction with existing visualizations, offering contextual analysis, and proposing enhancements or alternative explorations. Furthermore, it enables direct manipulation, allowing users to interact with visualizations by clicking on them and asking questions about the displayed data, facilitating an interactive user experience.

- **Accessing Qlik Insight Advisor in the Hub:** Broad search scope, extending across multiple Qlik apps accessible to the user, thereby enabling comparative analyses and exploration of data spanning different applications. This capability facilitates the exploration of global questions that transcend single data sources or applications, supporting users in uncovering new relationships and trends across multiple datasets. The focus on discovery encourages users to delve into and analyze the interconnectedness of data from various sources, enhancing the comprehensiveness of the insights derived.

In summary, the In-App Insight Advisor is your "*expert assistant*" within a particular data domain, offering detailed insights specific to that app. The Hub-based version is like your "data exploration advisor" with a wider view, helping you uncover patterns and connections across multiple data sources.

Accessing Qlik Insight Advisor Within the App

When accessing the Insight Advisor from inside a Qlik app, as shown in *Figure* 9.1, you are presented with three options:

- **Explore your data:** This option is suitable when you have a clear understanding of the specific data fields and measures that should be incorporated into the analysis. Essentially, it allows you to initiate the analysis with the precise data you aim to examine. Choose the fields and measures from the left panel, and then wait for the analysis to commence. Upon selecting the desired fields or measures, Insight Advisor will immediately begin creating charts that match your selections. Insight Advisor can recommend the most suitable chart types based on your selections. For instance, when utilizing a date field, it is likely to suggest a chart that is sensitive to time. Similarly, if you are working with categorical values (such as customer or category) alongside a measure, it will opt to create a bar chart. On the right side of the screen, Insight Advisor will present various insights derived from your selection, including key performance indicators (KPIs) such as grand total, top contributors, and Pareto Analysis. Alternatively, it will generate other charts and tables grouped in **`Additional results`**, and you can decide what best describes what you want to see.

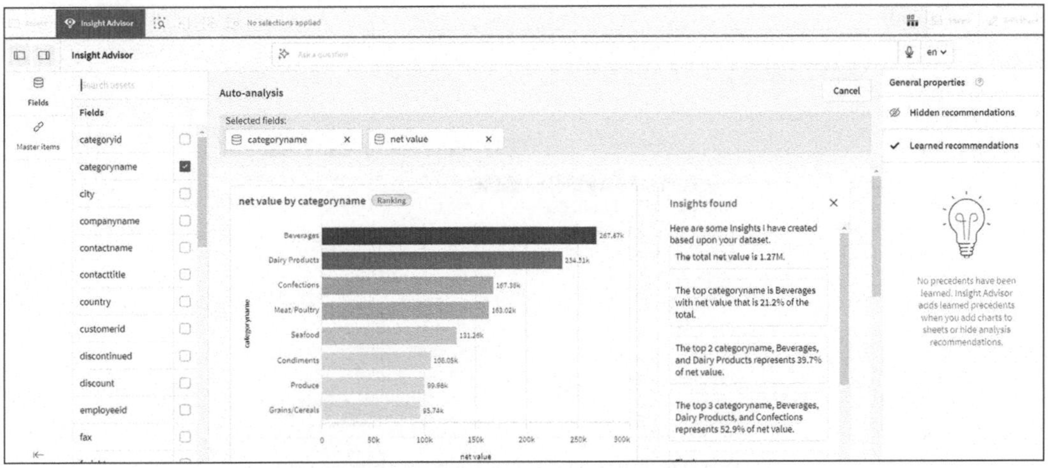

***Figure 9.4**: Explore your data example*

- **Ask a question:** Using this approach, you can ask a question in natural language, and the Insight Advisor will generate the answer based on your prompt. To effectively use natural language for questions and searches, it is essential to use field names or synonyms from the app's data model. Further along in this chapter, instructions on adding synonyms or refining the responses from Insight Advisor will be provided. Inputs should be made at the top of the Insight Advisor, utilizing either a keyboard or microphone, in a supported language. In the following example, we ask Insight Advisor to generate an analysis based on a prompt referring to two fields.

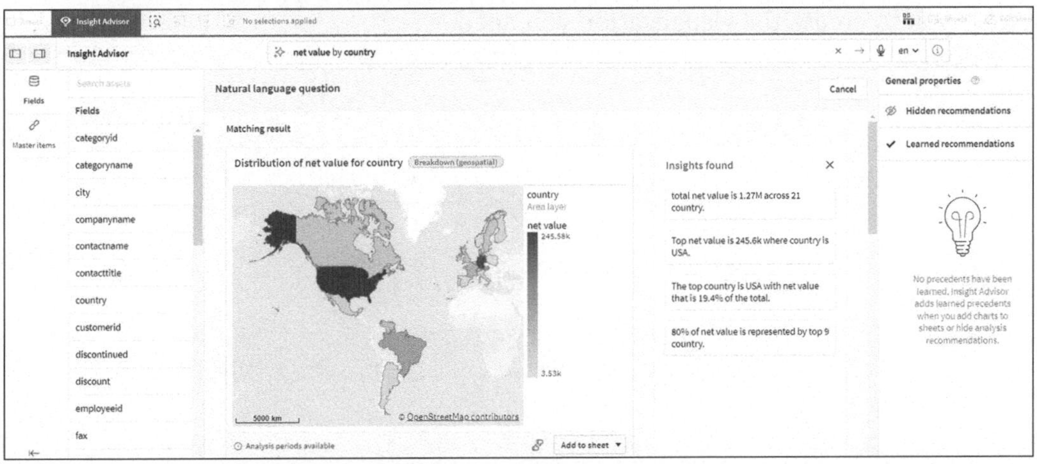

***Figure 9.5**: Auto-generated chart based on field selection*

The user can refer to data points as well; in this scenario, the Insight Advisor will automatically filter the dataset based on the prompt. In the following example, we are asking a question focusing on one specific country.

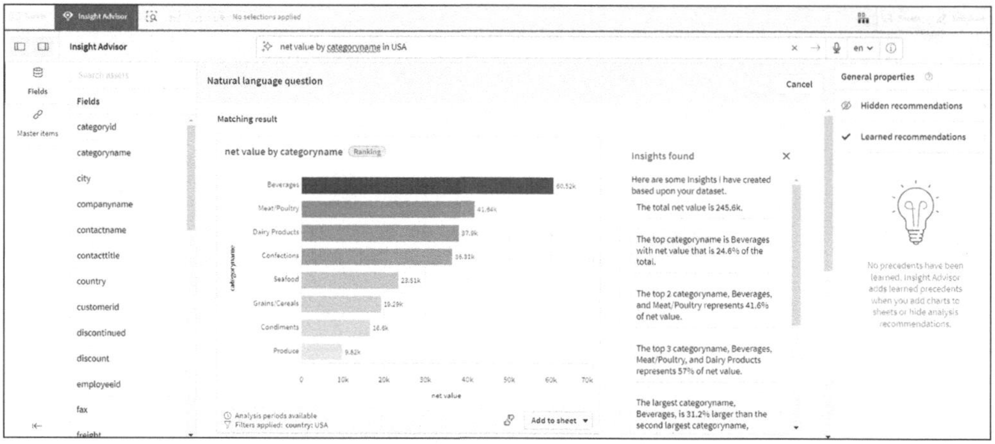

Figure 9.6: *Filtered chart based on the prompt*

- **Create an analysis:** For users who have a clear understanding of the desired analysis type and the relevant data they want to explore, Qlik Insight Advisor offers a guided approach. This method involves selecting the preferred visualization type, such as a bar chart or pie chart, and triggering a wizard that provides instructions for selecting the appropriate data. Users then specify the specific data fields or master items they wish to include, and Insight Advisor automatically generates the corresponding visualization based on their choices. This streamlined process empowers users who are confident in their analysis goals but might require assistance with the technical execution of creating the visualization. When you select this option, a wizard will guide you to create the visualization you need.

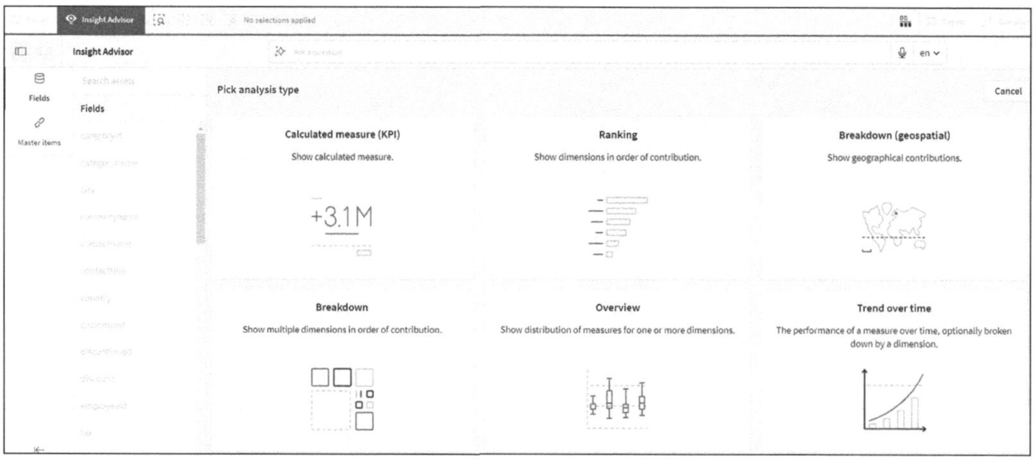

Figure 9.7: *Analysis types available*

For example, if you select the option **`Trend over time`**, you will be guided by how many dimensions and measures are needed to build that visualization.

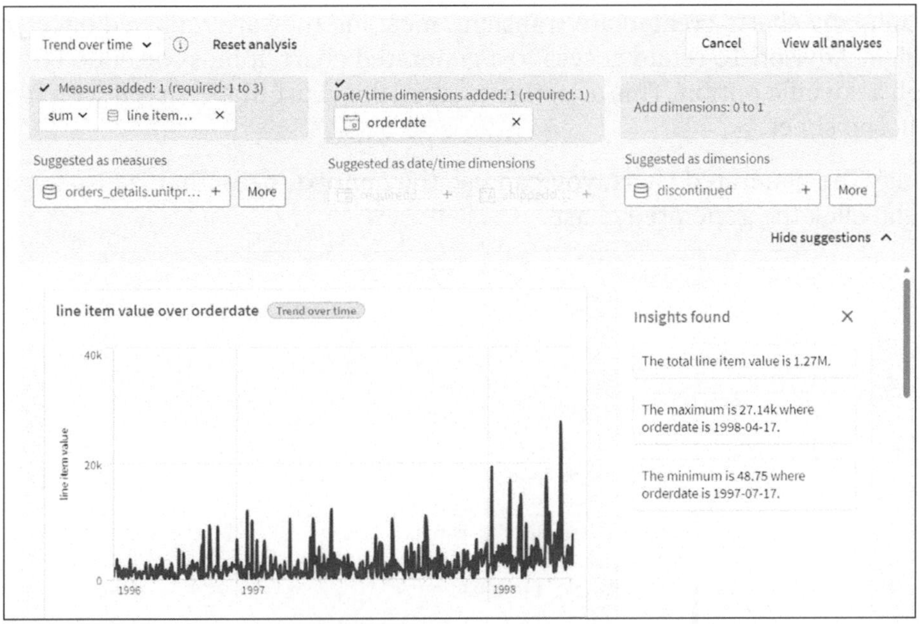

Figure 9.8: *Generated chart*

No matter what option you used to generate the charts, some options are available to you to use or modify the output from the Insight Advisor. Let us start with the **`Add to sheet`** button available at the bottom of the generated charts.

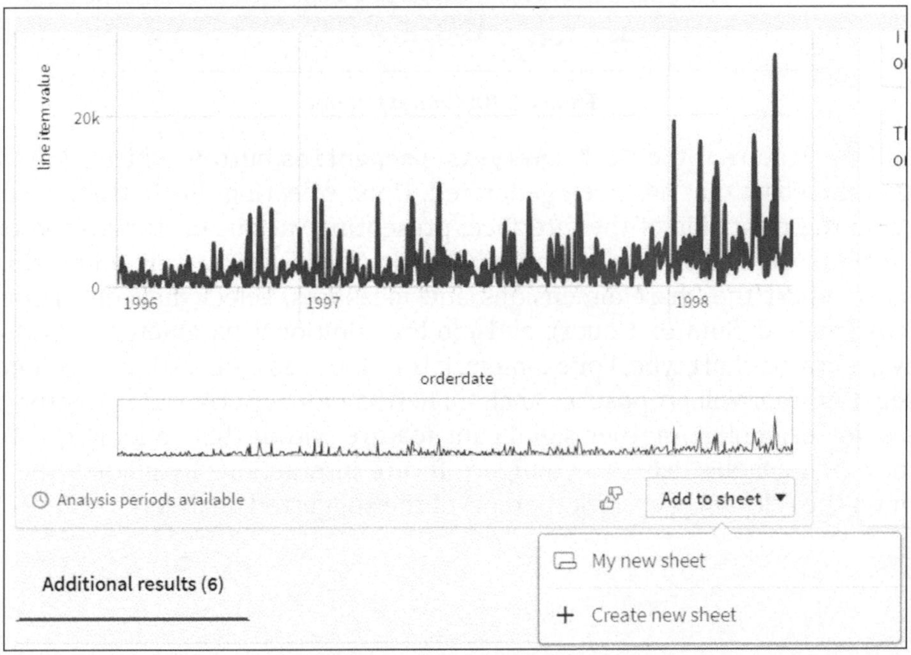

Figure 9.9: *Adding the chart to a sheet*

By default, any charts created are transient, meaning they are removed once you exit the Insight Advisor. To retain access to a generated chart, it must be added to a sheet through a specific option. This action preserves the chart in its current configuration on a chosen sheet.

To modify the generated chart, you can use the context menu that is displayed when you right-click the generated chart.

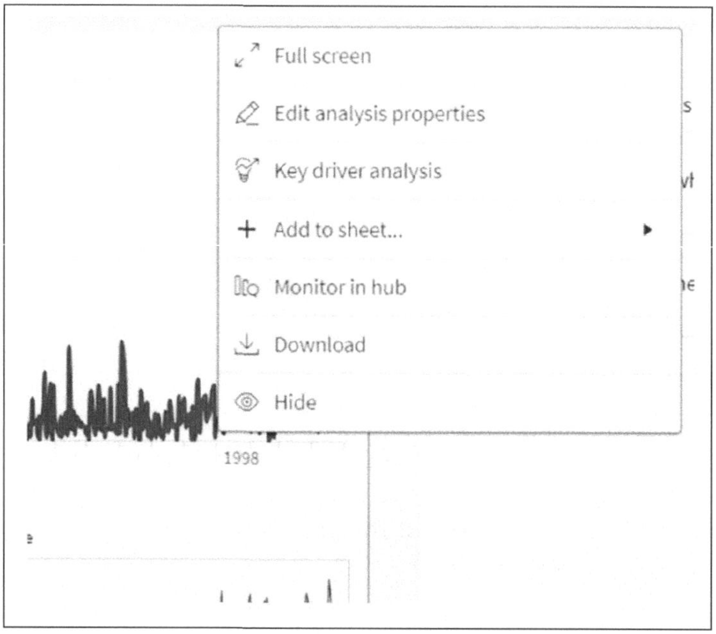

Figure 9.10: *Context menu*

One available feature is the **`Edit analysis properties`** button, which allows for the editing of the chart that has been generated. Upon selecting this button, a panel will emerge on the right side of the interface, presenting various customization options. These include the ability to alter the chart type (for example, from a line chart to a bar chart), adjust the chart dimensions and measures, select different aggregation functions (such as Sum or Count), and modify additional parameters based on the initially generated chart type. For example, if the chart has date or time as a dimension, the Insight Advisor will propose an Analysis Period more appropriate (months instead of dates, for example). Another significant feature within this panel is the **`Details`** section, which enables users to configure future interactions by guiding the Insight Advisor on the relevance (or lack thereof) of the suggested analysis.

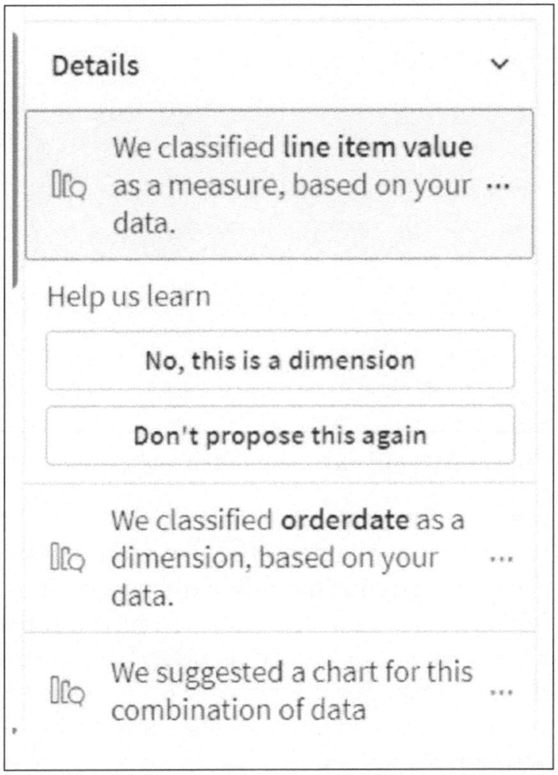

Figure 9.11: *Feedback on the generated insights*

Providing feedback to the Insight Advisor is crucial, as it informs the system of the relative importance the user assigns to specific analyses and data fields. Through appropriate training, the Insight Advisor will enhance its efficiency progressively.

Within the context menu, users also have the option to add the generated chart directly to the hub. This feature allows for the inspection of the analysis within the hub itself, eliminating the need to open the application and navigate to a specific chart.

Accessing Qlik Insight Advisor in the Hub

Another method of engaging with the Insight Advisor occurs within the hub, through the `Ask Insight Advisor` option available in the top menu, as shown in *Figure* 9.2. This feature facilitates a purely conversational user experience. Users can input any query, which is then evaluated across all enabled applications (refer to the documentation for enabling instructions), yielding relevant responses. In this interactive mode, the Insight Advisor retains the context of the conversation, eliminating the need for users to repeatedly specify the context they are referring to.

In our example, a question such as "*line item value by city in Germany*" will return the following answer with the desired result:

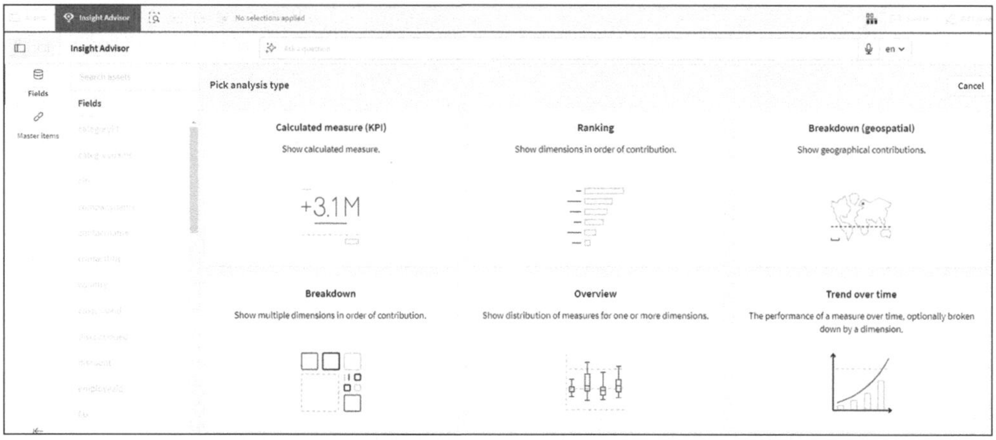

Figure 9.12: *Interaction with the Insight Advisor*

Responding to a single user prompt, the Insight Advisor generated a bar chart showcasing the contribution of each city within Germany, as specified by a selection filter. Additionally, it provided insights, including the grand total of the measure under consideration, and highlighted the contributions from the top-performing cities. At the bottom, a link to the source application is added if the user wants to continue with the analysis. Additional prompts will be answered in the same way, keeping the conversational experience, like the following figure answering the question *line item by* **`categoryname`** in Germany.

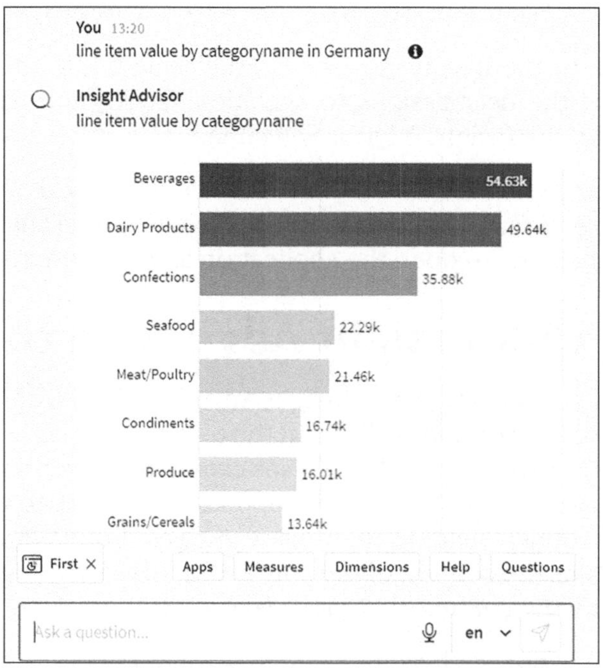

Figure 9.13: *Another question being answered*

To verify whether the Insight Advisor is utilizing the correct fields to provide an answer, the user can click the button adjacent to the prompt. This action reveals how the Insight Advisor interpreted the user's query.

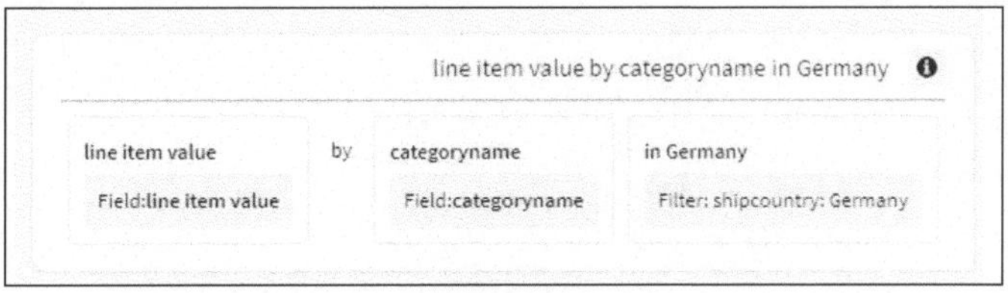

***Figure 9.14**: How the prompt is being evaluated*

Advanced Features

Advanced customization and other options are available for users who wish to tailor the Insight Advisor's responses and analyses. These options enable users to customize the experience or use the generated insights to evaluate key driver analyses.

Vocabulary

One way to customize the Insight Advisor is by creating Synonyms, Custom analysis, or Example questions. The application owner can add vocabulary to the app, improving the user experience.

In the drop down list from the top under Business logic, you can enhance natural language query success by creating vocabularies in the Vocabulary section.

***Figure 9.15**: Accessing the Vocabulary*

A vocabulary allows you to define alternative names or terms for fields or master items, such as using "**`Sales`**" and "**`Revenue`**" as synonyms for the "**`line item value`**" field.

***Figure 9.16**: Adding vocabulary terms*

After a term is established, the Insight Advisor utilizes the field associated with the vocabulary term to respond to user prompts. In the subsequent figure, it is demonstrated that the **`"Sales"`** expression was accurately mapped to the corresponding field, thanks to a term that establishes this connection.

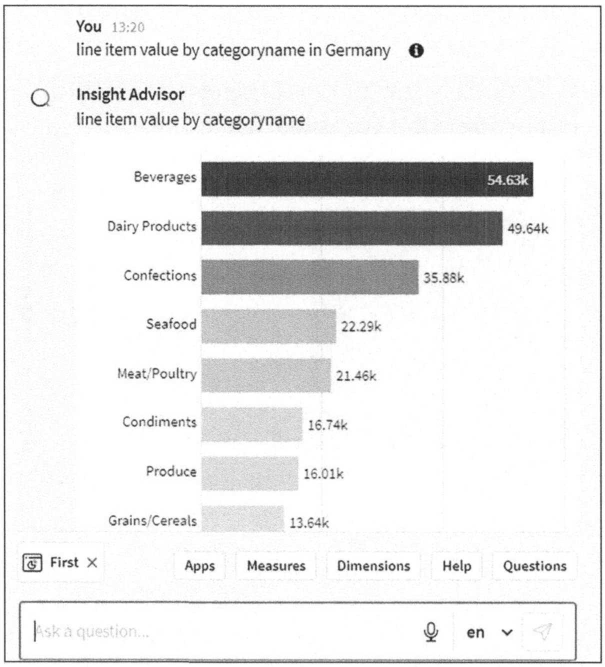

***Figure 9.17**: Term being used to refer to a field*

Another application involves creating logical groups of data values to enhance the user experience. For instance, by creating a term "**`Americas`**" that encompasses all countries within that region, when a user enters a prompt concerning "**Americas**," the appropriate values are automatically selected, ensuring accurate and region-specific responses.

***Figure 9.18**: Term grouping data values*

The following chart shows how the Insight Advisor answered a prompt with a term grouping data values and another term referring to a field name.

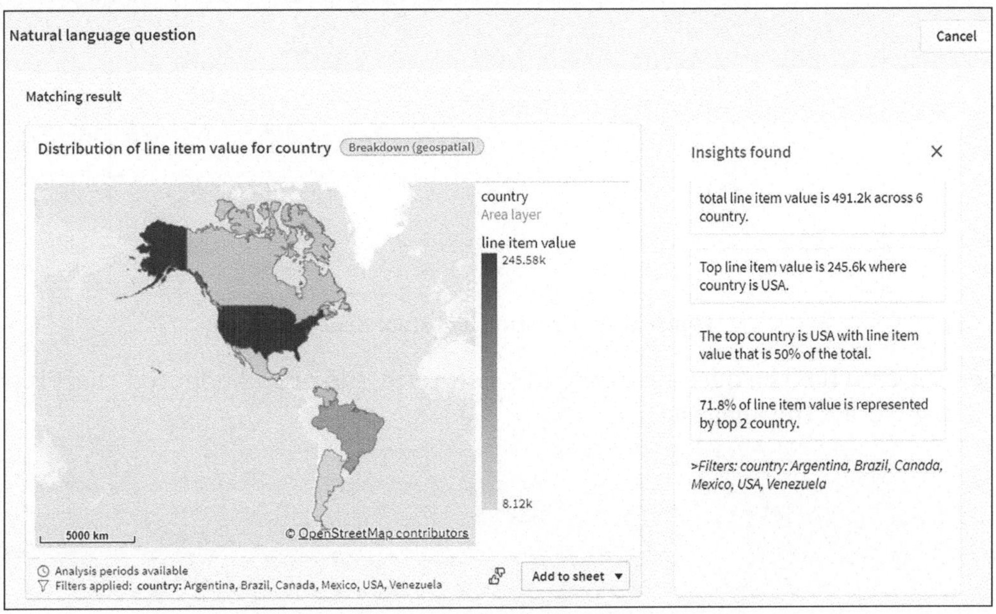

***Figure 9.19**: Grouping results based on a term*

Modifying the behavior of the Insight Advisor can also be achieved through the creation of custom analyses. This allows for the specification of preferences based on a term, such as prioritizing a certain chart type or automatically filtering a subset of the data. By defining these custom analyses, users can tailor the Insight Advisor's responses to better suit their specific requirements or analytical goals. In the following example, we are creating a term called GeoSales that refers to a geo breakdown `Country` >> `City`.

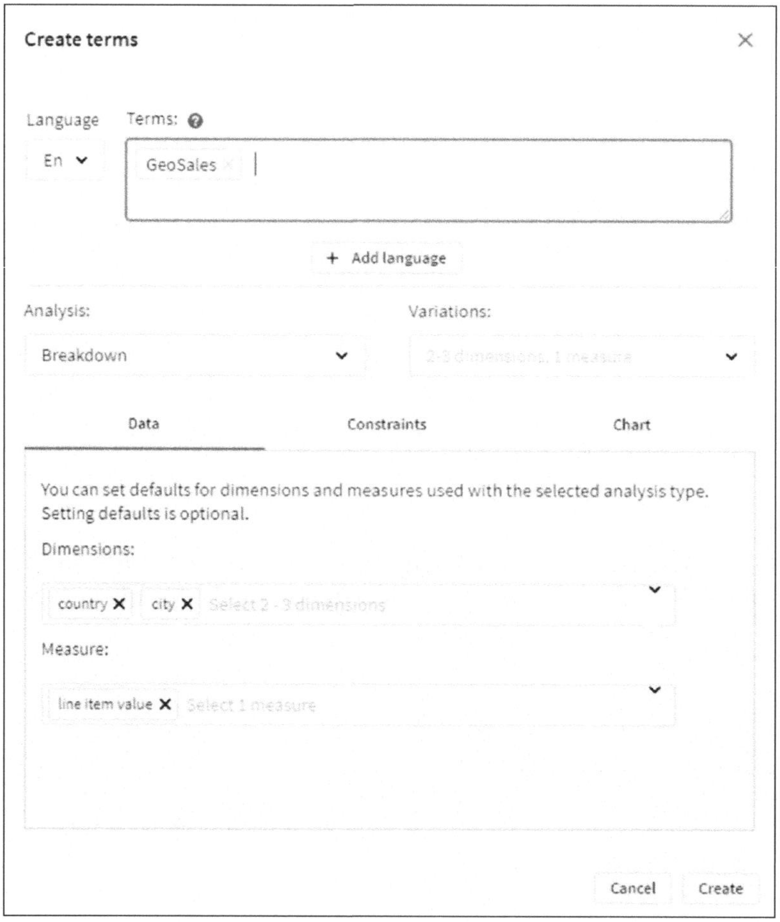

***Figure 9.20**: Creating a custom analysis*

When a user submits a question using this new term, the pre-configured chart type is used to generate the analysis.

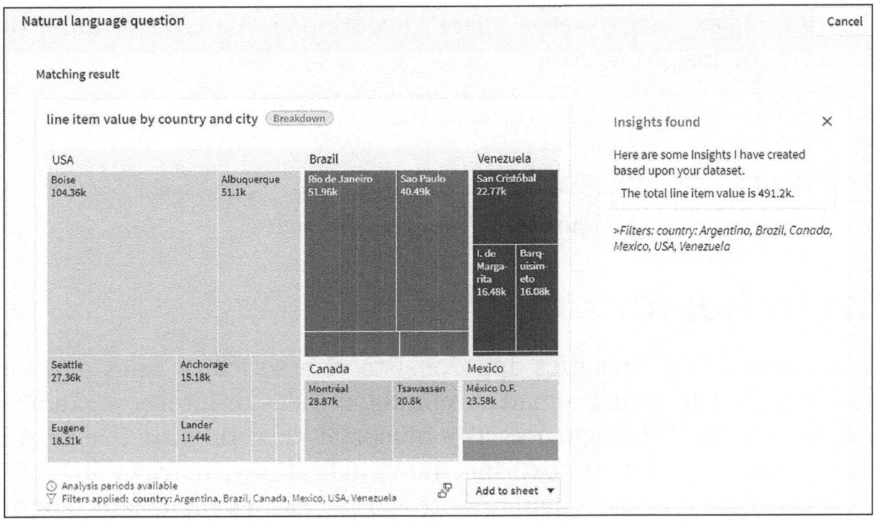

***Figure 9.21:** Custom Analysis being used*

The final method to enhance the vocabulary involves adding example questions that are displayed when users access the Insight Advisor. By providing pre-canned questions, users gain familiarity with the system, becoming more comfortable using the Insight Advisor and adapting their prompts to achieve desired outcomes. This approach not only guides users in formulating effective queries but also helps in showcasing the capabilities of the Insight Advisor, encouraging exploration and efficient use.

***Figure 9.22:** Adding an example question*

In the following image, you can see the user's experience where the example questions are displayed in the Insight Advisor:

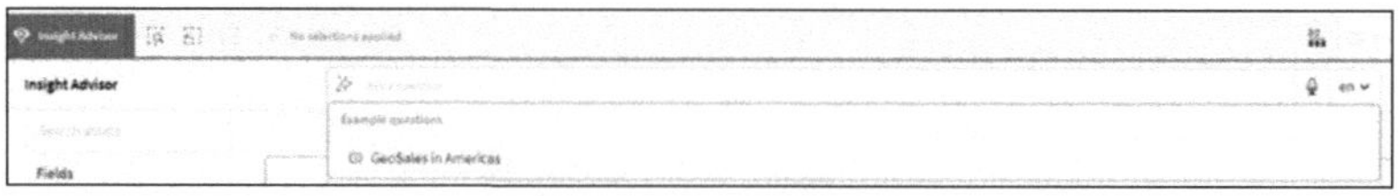

***Figure 9.23**: Example Questions*

Business Logic

Business Logic in a Qlik Analytics app consists of a series of rules and guidelines applied to the app's data model, aimed at refining how data is interpreted and analyzed by the Insight Advisor. This logic acts as a blueprint, directing the Insight Advisor to produce more accurate and context-specific visualizations, analyses, and answers to natural language queries. Upon data import, Qlik examines the interrelations among fields to create a foundational logical model, crucial for guiding the Insight Advisor's data conceptualization and interpretation. This model enables the Insight Advisor to navigate through data associations and hierarchies effectively, thus enhancing its capacity to deliver pertinent and insightful outcomes. The entire process is automated to provide a structured analytical environment, though the default model can be adjusted for more precise control over the Insight Advisor's operations. Please refer to the documentation for more details on the Business logic custom models. When you access the option **`Logical Model`** from the **`Prepare`** menu, you are prompted if you want to customize the default model. You can revert to the default model if the custom model does not perform as you expected.

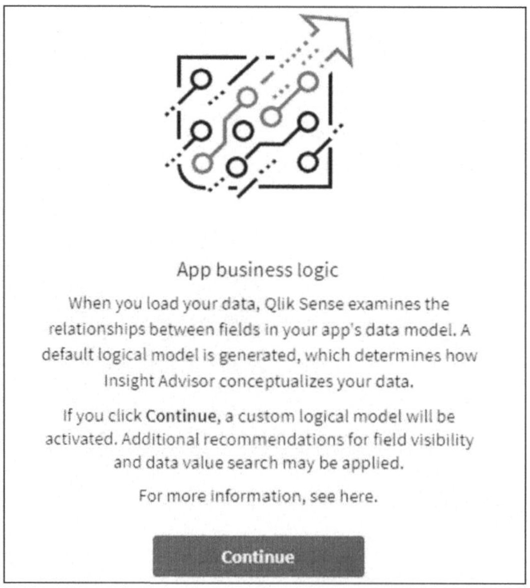

***Figure 9.24**: Customizing the logical model*

A custom model looks like the following image:

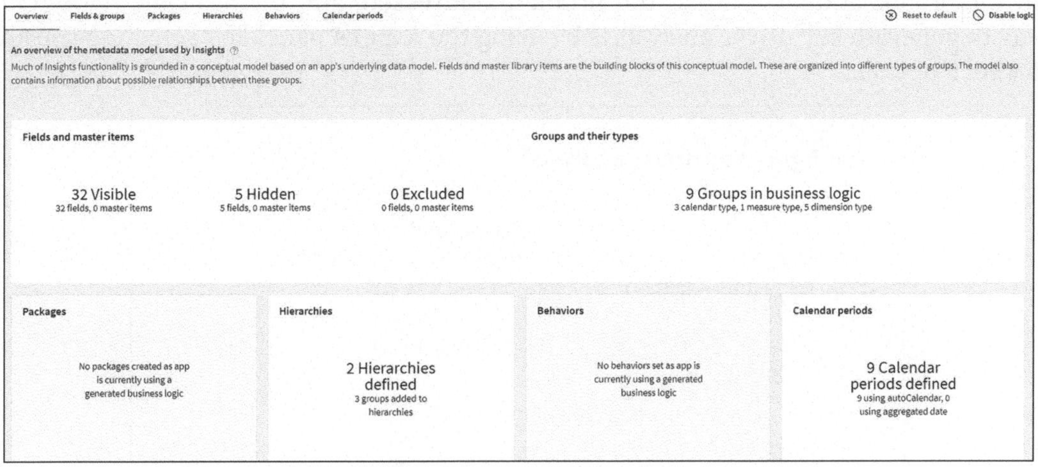

Figure 9.25: *Custom Model*

The core components of Business Logic include:

- **Fields and Groups:** This feature allows for the specification of logical groups within the model, categorizing fields and master items accordingly.
- **Packages:** Assemble related groups, ensuring unrelated groups are not combined.
- **Hierarchies:** Facilitate the establishment of drill-down relationships among groups, enabling more detailed data exploration.
- **Behaviors:** Define preferences or restrictions for field relationships and can mandate specific selections.
- **Calendar Periods:** Default analysis periods for the Insight Advisor, streamlining the process of temporal data analysis.

By incorporating Business Logic, Qlik Sense apps can provide users with a more intuitive and effective data exploration experience, allowing for easier discovery of insights and a more natural interaction with the Insight Advisor. It tailors the app's analytical capabilities to better match the specific business context and user expectations.

Key Driver Analysis

Qlik Cloud Analytics enables users across all roles to utilize the platform for conducting key driver analysis. This concept is a statistical method for identifying how various factors influence a specific outcome metric, applicable to both quantitative and qualitative data. Its goal is to uncover the causes behind data trends, enabling focused actions or improved organizational insight. In Analytics, it often targets metrics such as Sales, Customer Satisfaction, and Margin, with key drivers including

Product, Location, and Manager. The selection of metrics and drivers varies based on the organizational context, the problem addressed, and the available data. One way to generate key driver analysis is by using the **`Assets`** panel and selecting the **`Key drivers`** option.

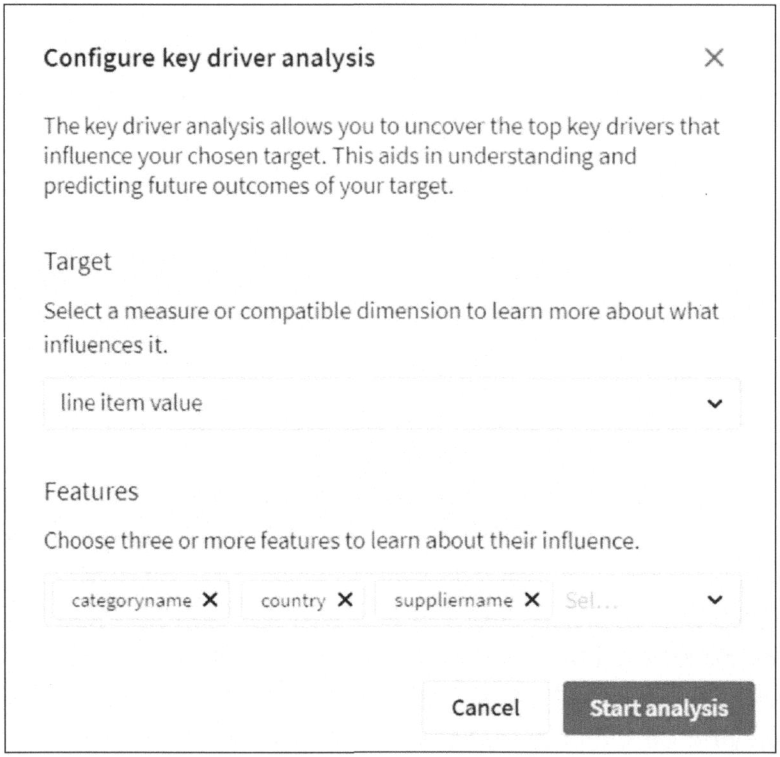

***Figure 9.26**: Key driver analysis configuration*

In the preceding image, the wizard automatically chose the measure, offering the option to switch the analysis to other fields. To initiate the analysis, the user must specify three or more additional fields. This process assesses the impact that those fields have on the target measure. Following this setup, the user must click the **`Start analysis`** button. Shortly thereafter, the key driver analysis will be accessible from the **`Assets`** panel, which can be reached via the top menu.

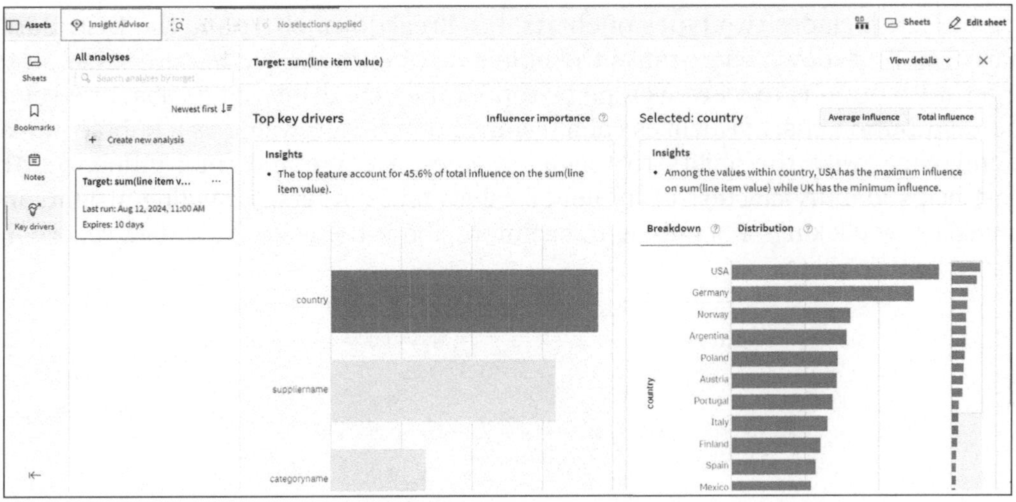

Figure 9.27: Key driver analysis

To view detailed information about your analysis, select **`View details`** located in the top right corner of the results page. This provides key insights, including the creation date, the last run, and the expiration date of the analysis. Additionally, it outlines the target and manual features selected for the analysis configuration, as well as any selections applied within the app at the time of setting up the analysis.

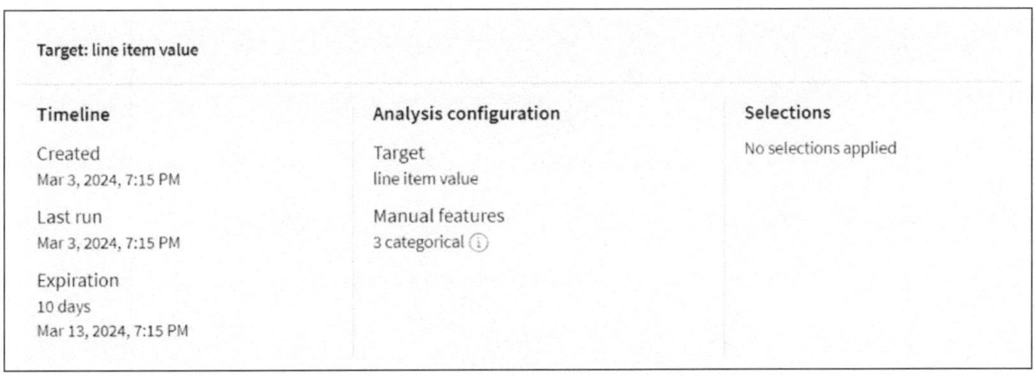

Figure 9.28: Key driver analysis details

The **`Top key drivers`** section displays each feature's influence on the target through a bar chart and insights, ranking them from most to least influential. Influence values are absolute, meaning a feature with a strong negative impact could appear highly influential. The most significant key driver is highlighted and further analyzed in the adjacent section, allowing for a detailed exploration of its specific impact. On the right side, the interface provides a detailed view of the selected key driver, offering insights into how its unique values impact the target. Changing your selection in the chart updates this detailed view, allowing for a deeper understanding of each feature's influence.

The analysis includes two types of charts: the Breakdown chart and the Distribution chart. The Breakdown chart ranks the influence of each unique feature value on the target, with options to view average or total influence, displayed as absolute values. The Distribution chart visualizes each instance of a feature value as a bubble, ranked by influence, with the ability to toggle between average and total influence. This chart helps identify clusters of influence values and outliers, providing insights into anomalies by clicking on a bubble to see more about the associated data record and related feature values.

Figure 9.29: *Key driver analysis detailed view*

Key components of this analysis include:

- **The Target:** The specific field under analysis, such as the *sales line item*, which determines the type of problem (example, regression or binary classification) the analysis will address.
- **Features:** Key drivers influencing the target, which can be dimensions such as **`categoryname`**, **`country`**, or **`suppliername`**.

Key driver analysis calculation involves a subset of data selected by the user, including the defined target and multiple features. A specific dataset is created from the user's data model based on these selections for analysis.

The influence of features on the target is quantified using SHapley Additive exPlanations (SHAP) values, derived from a model trained by Qlik AutoML, typically utilizing the random forest algorithm. SHAP values measure the impact of a feature's data value on the target, considering the configuration of the key driver analysis.

For regression analyses, the target involves numerous unique numeric values. Binary classification analyses occur when the target comprises two unique values, categorizing the analysis into a binary classification problem.

Overall, key driver analysis in Qlik Sense enables users to identify and quantify the influence of various factors on a targeted field, utilizing a specific subset of data for focused analysis.

Integration with Other Tools

The integration of the Qlik Insight Advisor with third-party tools via Application Programming Interfaces (APIs) extends the platform's analytical capabilities into external applications, aligning with the principles outlined in *Chapter 5, Embedding and Extending*. This approach offers the same use cases and advantages, bridging Qlik's powerful analytics with other business tools and environments.

Qlik Cloud offers a comprehensive suite of RESTful APIs designed to facilitate seamless interaction between the Insight Advisor and external applications. These APIs support a wide range of operations, including data retrieval, in-depth analysis, and the processing of natural language queries. Through this integration, it is possible to embed the sophisticated analytics and insights generated by the Insight Advisor directly into third-party applications, websites, or portals. Consequently, users can access and leverage Qlik's actionable insights within the familiar interfaces of their existing business tools, enhancing decision-making processes and operational efficiency. This integration not only democratizes data across platforms but also enriches user experiences by embedding intelligent, context-aware analytics into the workflow of other software solutions. In the following figure, we are using Postman (refer to the *Additional Resources* for explanations) to connect to the Natural Language API and sending a prompt, **`"Sales in Americas by country"`**.

Figure 9.30: API call

The prompt is populated in the **`text`** parameter, and we can indicate the app we are referring to using the parameter **`app.id.`** The API will return the answer in the **`conversationalResponse.responses[].narrative`** exactly like the Insight Advisor at the hub would answer. A link to the generated chart is returned in **`conversationalResponse.responses[].imageUrl`** that can be used to display the generated chart. Additionally, a link to a detailed analysis is provided in the field **`conversationalResponse.drillDownURI.`**

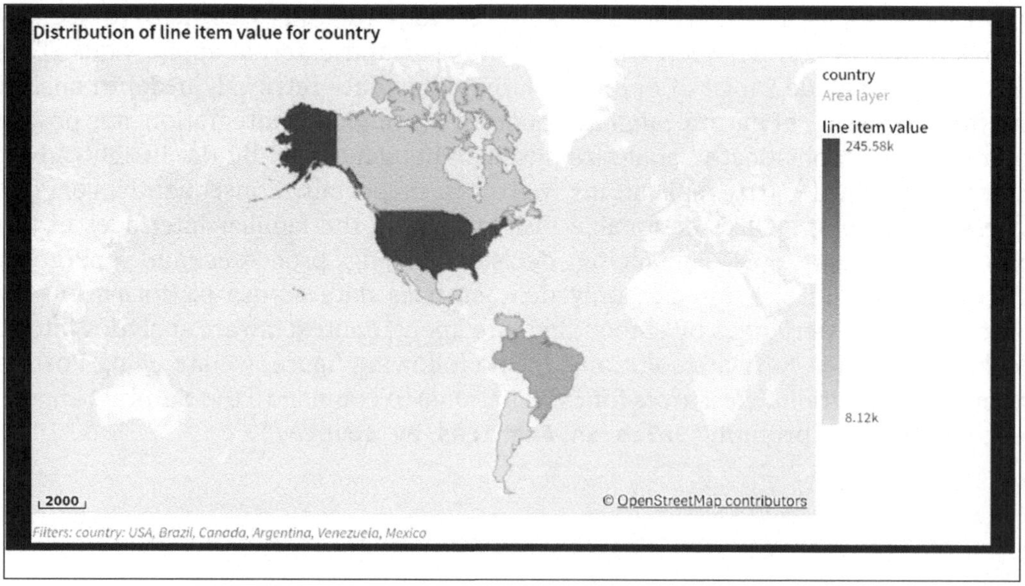

Figure 9.31: *Insight Advisor API link returned by the API call*

The API documentation link is available in the Additional Resources section, as is a link to how to implement a chatbot using the APIs.

Conclusion

In this chapter on Qlik Cloud Insight Advisor, we have explored an array of functionalities that highlight its significance in the realm of conversational data analytics. The Insight Advisor offers users a seamless and intuitive interface for data analysis. Through its sophisticated use of AI and natural language processing, the Insight Advisor empowers users to generate visualizations, perform analyses, and interact with their data in conversational language. This capability not only simplifies the data analysis process but also makes it more accessible to users across different skill levels, from beginners to advanced analysts.

Moreover, the Insight Advisor's ability to integrate with third-party tools via APIs extends its utility beyond the confines of the Qlik Cloud environment. This integration facilitates a cohesive workflow, allowing users to embed Qlik's powerful analytics within other software solutions. Whether it is through enhancing decision-making processes or providing actionable insights within familiar business applications, the Insight Advisor enriches user experiences and democratizes data access.

In the following chapter, we will discuss the Reporting capabilities of Qlik Cloud leveraging the distribution of reports to audiences in a simple way.

Multiple Choice Questions

1. What is the primary function of the Qlik Cloud Insight Advisor?
   a. To manage user permissions and security settings
   b. To provide data storage solutions
   c. To generate visualizations and insights through natural language processing
   d. To facilitate cloud-based file sharing
2. How does the Qlik Cloud Insight Advisor integrate with third-party tools?
   a. Through manual data entry
   b. Using direct database connections only
   c. Via Application Programming Interfaces (APIs)
   d. Through email notifications

3. Which of the following features is directly supported by the Qlik Cloud Insight Advisor?
    a. Automatic generation of RESTful APIs
    b. Customizable user interfaces for data presentation
    c. Analysis and visualization generation from natural language queries
    d. Physical data storage devices management
4. In the context of Qlik Cloud Insight Advisor, what is Business Logic used for?
    a. To define the physical structure of databases
    b. To set up email servers for automated report distribution
    c. To enhance data interpretation and analysis through predefined rules and structures
    d. To manage cloud storage costs and billing
5. What does the integration of Qlik Cloud Insight Advisor with external applications enable?
    a. The ability to increase the physical memory of the cloud servers
    b. The capability to embed Qlik's insights into third-party applications, websites, or portals
    c. Direct modification of the source code of the Qlik platform
    d. Reduction in the need for data analysis and visualization

Answers

1. c
2. c
3. c
4. c
5. b

Additional Resources

The following links complement this chapter, bringing more resources to the reader with more examples and details. Please be aware that as Qlik introduces new product versions, the documentation might be found under a different link.

- Exploring analyses with Insight Advisor: https://help.qlik.com/en-US/cloud-services/Subsystems/Hub/Content/Sense_Hub/Insights/insight-advisor-exploring-analyses.htm
- Exploring apps with conversational analytics: https://help.qlik.com/en-US/cloud-services/Subsystems/Hub/Content/Sense_Hub/Insights/insights-chat.htm
- Qlik AutoML: https://help.qlik.com/en-US/cloud-services/Subsystems/Hub/Content/Sense_Hub/AutoML/home-automl.htm
- Customizing logical models for Insight Advisor: https://help.qlik.com/en-US/cloud-services/Subsystems/Hub/Content/Sense_Hub/BusinessLogic/business_logic.htm
- Natural Language REST: https://qlik.dev/apis/rest/questions
- Generate analysis with AI: https://qlik.dev/embed/gen-ai/share-insight-advisor-feedback/#insight-advisor-feedback-api-endpoint

CHAPTER 10
Reporting Service

Introduction

Qlik Cloud offers a suite of data visualization and analysis tools, including the Qlik Reporting Service. This chapter explores the functionalities and considerations surrounding the Qlik Reporting Service, enabling users to leverage its capabilities for automated report generation and distribution.

Structure

In this chapter, we will discuss the following topics:

- Reporting Options
- Subscriptions
- Qlik Application Automation Integration
- Reporting Service Technical Foundations

Reporting Options

Qlik Cloud offers several options for generating and distributing reports, catering to diverse needs and technical expertise.

- **Subscription:** Business users can subscribe to pre-built content (sheets or visualizations) and receive automated reports delivered directly to their email inbox. This self-service experience eliminates the need for additional development efforts.
- **Tabular Reporting:** Application and report developers can use the Qlik add-in for Microsoft Excel to create report templates, which are then utilized in report tasks managed within Qlik Cloud applications. These tasks allow for the configuration of distribution lists and report filters to facilitate large-scale report distribution. Reports can be emailed or sent to Microsoft SharePoint-connected folders and can be personalized through task-level or user-specific filtering to enable burst report delivery. The reports are available in .xlsx or

PDF formats and can be sent to users within the same Qlik Cloud tenant or external recipients.

- **Integration with Qlik Application Automation:** Application and report developers can leverage the Qlik Reporting Service and Qlik Application Automation to distribute customized automated reports. These reports, which can be based on Qlik Sense sheets, are delivered as PDF or PowerPoint files. They can be sent to both Qlik Cloud users within the system and external recipients. Developers have the option to generate multi-page reports using automation templates or to craft entirely bespoke report definitions.
- **Custom Reporting using the APIs:** Qlik Cloud exposes APIs (listed in the section Additional Resources) to allow developers to achieve any reporting requirement not covered by previous options. It allows fine-grain control over the results, allowing integration with third-party solutions.

Choosing the Right Option

The selection of an appropriate reporting tool within Qlik Cloud Analytics depends on several factors, including:

- **Basic reporting needs**: Use the built-in tabular reporting within Qlik Sense apps.
- **Automated report generation and distribution with basic functionalities**: Utilize Qlik Reporting Service (QRS).
- **For complex report automation workflows with advanced features**: Explore Qlik Application Automation, especially if combining information for multiple apps is a requirement.
- **Self-service experience and simple reports**: Use the subscribing feature.

Additional Considerations

- **Subscription level:** Qlik Reporting Service is only available in Qlik Sense Enterprise SaaS subscriptions, not the free trial or Qlik Sense Business plans.
- **Limits:** Qlik Reporting Service has limitations on the number of reports and recipients.

By understanding these options and considerations, you can choose the most suitable approach for your reporting needs within Qlik Cloud.

Subscriptions

Qlik Cloud Analytics offers subscription reports, a functionality that allows users to schedule automated email deliveries of specific data visualizations. These reports can include sheets or charts from Qlik Sense apps.

Subscriptions enable users to define the content they receive by applying filters to focus on relevant data points. This ensures users receive the information they need, delivered directly to their inboxes.

For example, users can schedule daily emails containing the latest sales data for a specific region. This eliminates the need for manual updates, saving time and improving efficiency and flexibility. Users can modify them at any time to adjust the content, filters, or delivery schedule as their requirements change.

Subscription reports within Qlik Cloud Analytics function similarly to access controls for apps, data, and spaces. Ownership and recipient designations are determined by section access, permission levels, and user entitlements (specifically, Professional and Analyzer roles). This ensures recipients only receive data they are authorized to view.

The content of a subscription report email typically includes:

- **Attachment:** A file containing the subscribed visualization(s) or sheets. This file can be in either PDF or PowerPoint format, with an image resolution of 300 DPI. (Note: The format depends on the type of content subscribed to.)
- **Visualization Image (Optional):** An image of the subscribed visualization is included if applicable. This element is omitted for subscriptions solely containing sheets.
- **App Link:** A link directing the recipient to the original app where the analysis originated. If the subscription encompasses multiple sheets, the link opens the first sheet on the list.

The following screenshot shows a message received by a user who has subscribed to a chart within an application showing the attachment, the image, and the link.

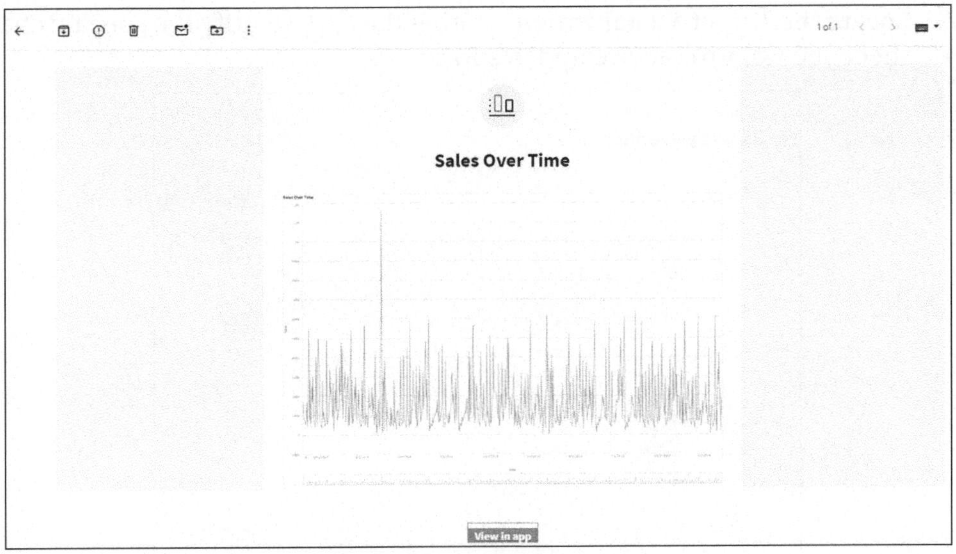

Figure 10.1: *Chart subscription*

This section outlines the steps a user can follow to subscribe to charts or sheets within an application:

1. **Access the Desired App**: Navigate to the Qlik Cloud Hub and locate the application containing the charts or sheets you wish to subscribe to. Open the app to proceed.

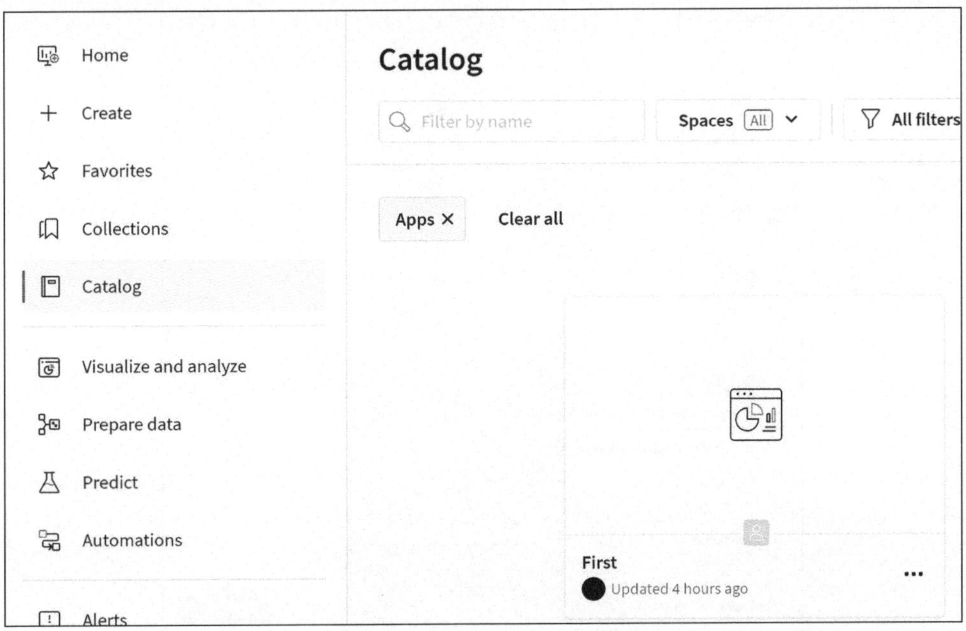

Figure 10.2: *Opening on app*

2. **Locate the Target Visualization:** Within the app, identify the specific chart or sheet you want to receive updates for.

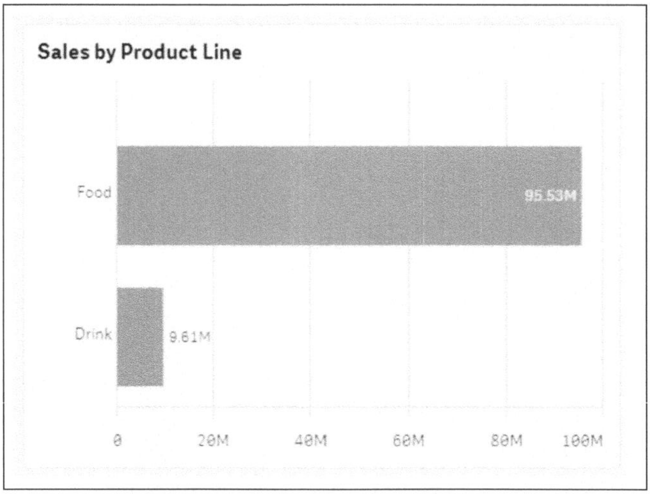

Figure 10.3: *Visualization to be subscribed*

3. **Access the Subscription Menu:** Depending on the visualization type (chart or sheet), the method for accessing the subscription menu may differ slightly. In general, locate an ellipsis (...) or similar menu icon associated with the chosen chart or sheet. Click this icon to reveal the available options.

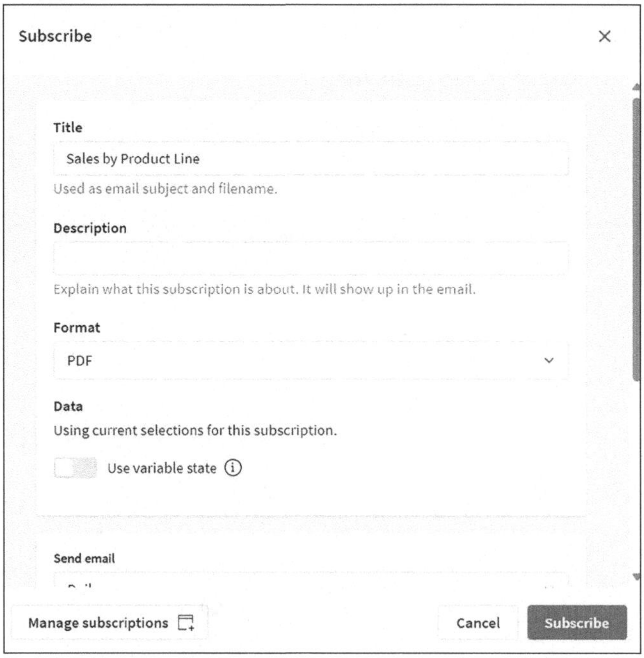

Figure 10.4: *Context menu*

4. **Select "`Subscribe`" Option:** Within the menu displayed in step 3, the user needs to identify and select the option **`Subscribe`**.

5. **Customize Subscription Settings:** Upon selecting the subscription option, a dedicated menu will appear for configuring your subscription preferences. Here, the user can typically define the following:

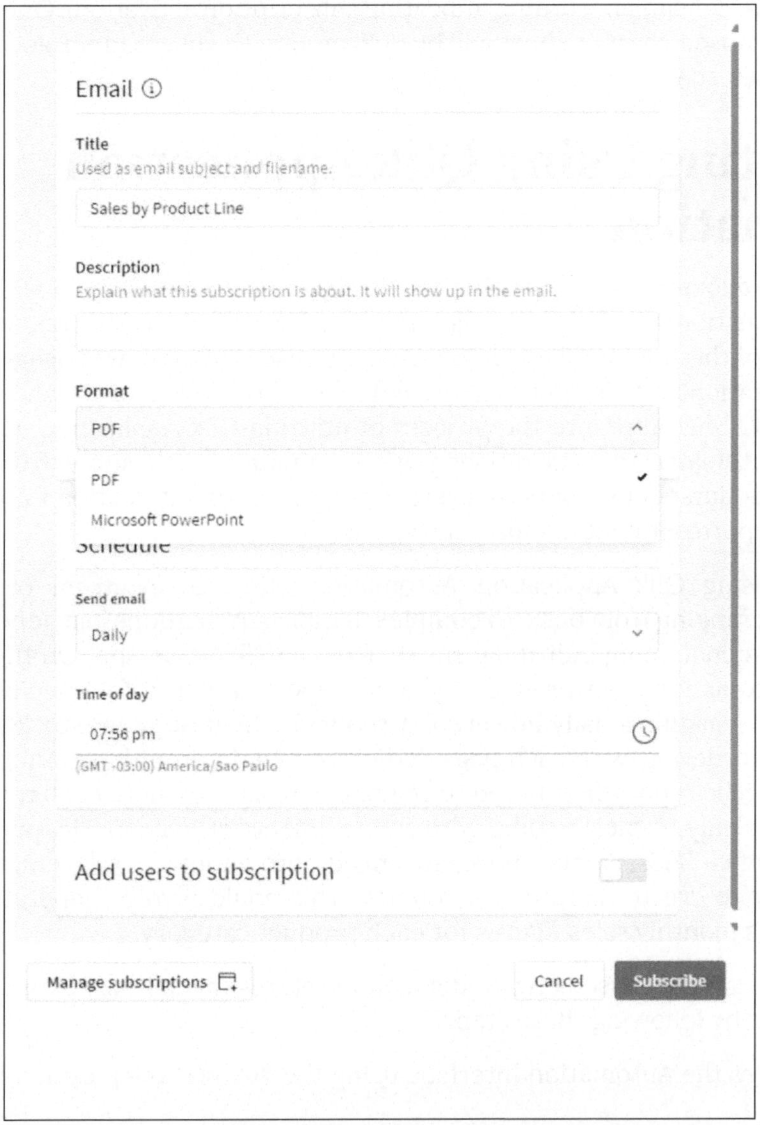

***Figure 10.5**: Subscribing options*

   a. **Delivery Format:** The user can choose the desired format for the email attachment containing the subscribed content. Options may include PDF or PowerPoint.

   b. **Schedule:** The user can define the desired frequency of email delivery by selecting from available scheduling options. These options typically include daily, weekly, or monthly intervals.

6. **Finalize Subscription:** Upon defining preferences within the subscription menu, the user should confirm their selections by pressing the **`Subscribe`** button (or similar wording indicating subscription activation). Once confirmed, the chosen chart or sheet will be delivered to the user's inbox according to the chosen schedule.

Reporting Using Qlik Application Automation

This section explores the integration of Qlik Application Automation with Qlik Cloud reporting functionalities. Qlik Application was described in *Chapter 8: Application Automation* of this book, and one important use case is to empower users to automate report generation and distribution, streamlining workflows, and enhancing reporting efficiency. We will delve into the process of utilizing Qlik Application Automation to construct automated reports, drawing upon data and visualizations from Qlik Sense apps. This section equips users to leverage the power of automation for creating and delivering reports without manual intervention.

Reporting using Qlik Application Automation offers a spectrum of automation possibilities, ranging from basic to complex. Simple automations can generate reports such as PDFs containing individual sheets from a Qlik Sense app. On the other side, complex automations can produce dynamic reports tailored for specific audiences. For instance, imagine a daily PowerPoint report highlighting low-stock supply items requiring re-ordering, with each page dedicated to a different item. Another example might be a cyclic report distributed to regional managers, where each recipient views data relevant only to their region, with the recipient list dynamically populated from Microsoft Office 365. Furthermore, advanced automations can leverage Qlik's level functionality to create hierarchical reports. This could involve generating a report that presents monthly sales figures for each product category.

Let us create a report based on two demo applications that already exist on every Qlik Cloud tenant by following these steps:

1. Access the Automation Interface using the **`Automations`** option from the left menu.

Figure 10.6: *My Automations*

2. Create a New Automation by clicking on the **`Create new automation`** button.

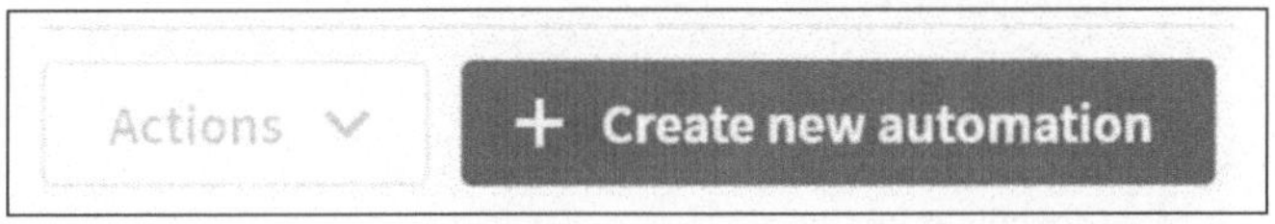

Figure 10.7: *Press this button to create the automation*

3. Press the **`Create without template`** button.

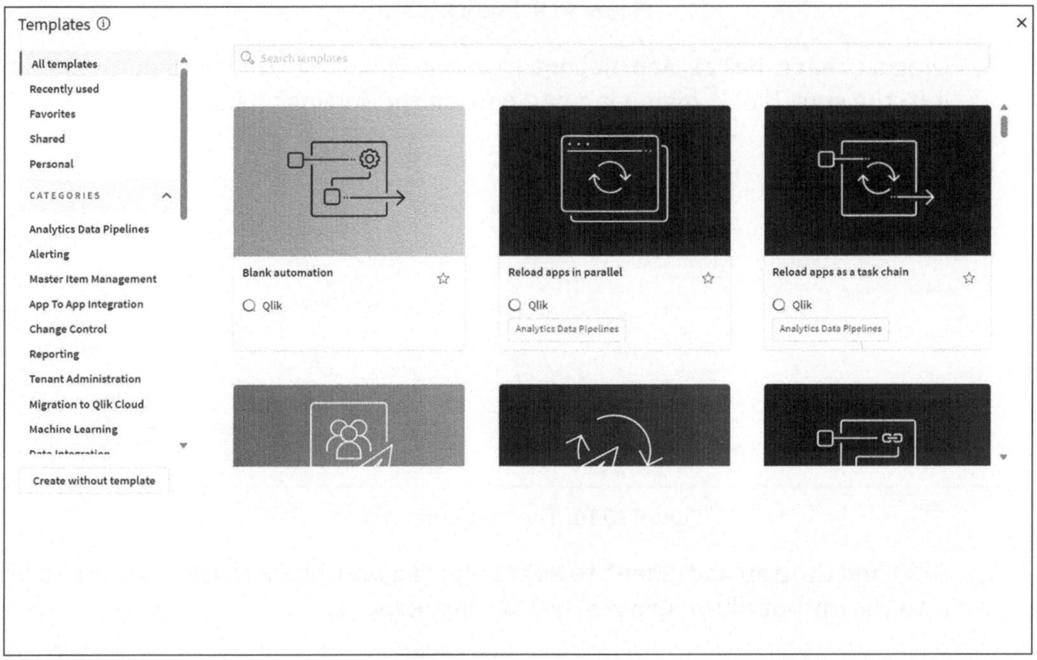

Figure 10.8: *Templates*

4. Name your automation and give it a description.
5. Configure the **`Start`** Block run mode to be scheduled once a day using the settings panel.

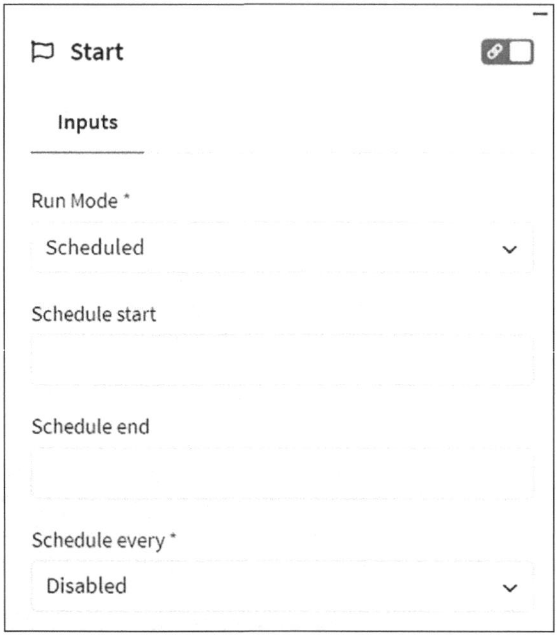

Figure 10.9: *Daily Report*

6. Drag a **`Create Multi App Report`** from the Qlik Reporting connector and link it to the start block, giving it a name using the settings panel.

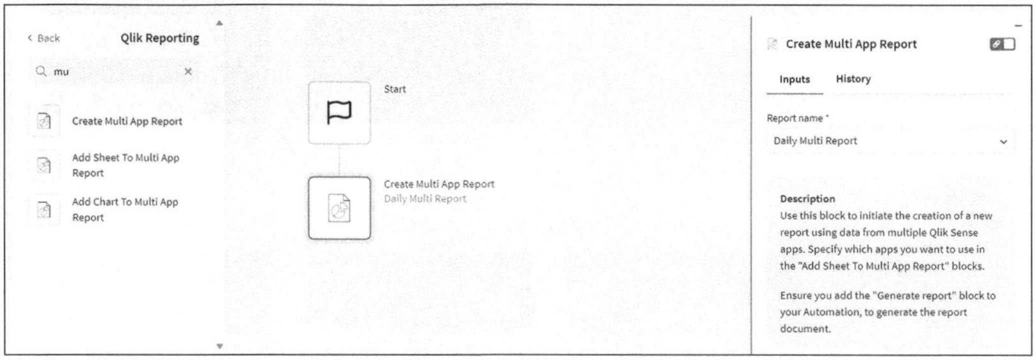

Figure 10.10: *The Multi app report*

7. Drag and drop an **`Add Sheet`** to **`Multi App Report`** block to the canvas and link it to the output of the **`Create Multi App Report`**.

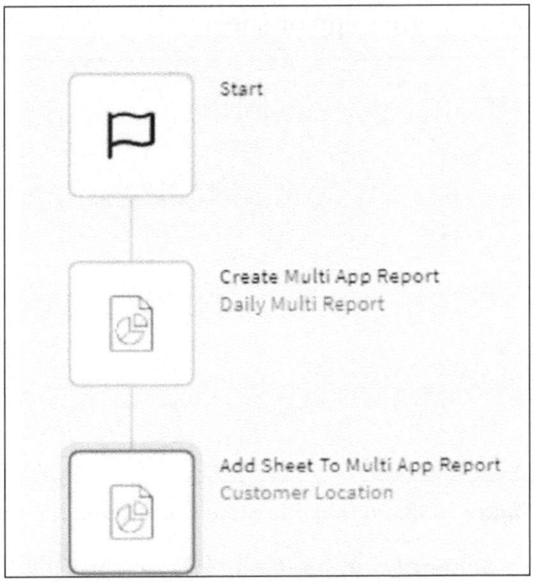

Figure 10.11: *Add Sheet block*

8. Configure the block using the Settings panel. Configure the report to be the same report you created on step 6, and using the **`do lookup`**, select one of the **`Demo App`** apps. Then select a sheet from the app.

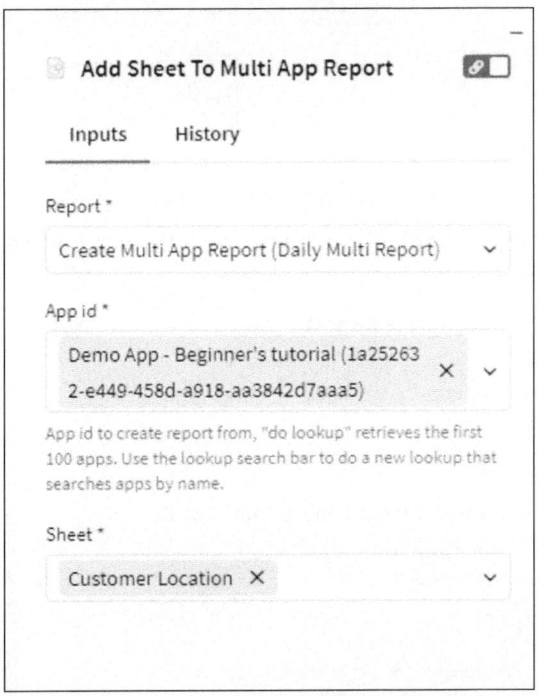

Figure 10.12: *Add sheet block settings*

9. Repeat step 8 with another app or sheet.

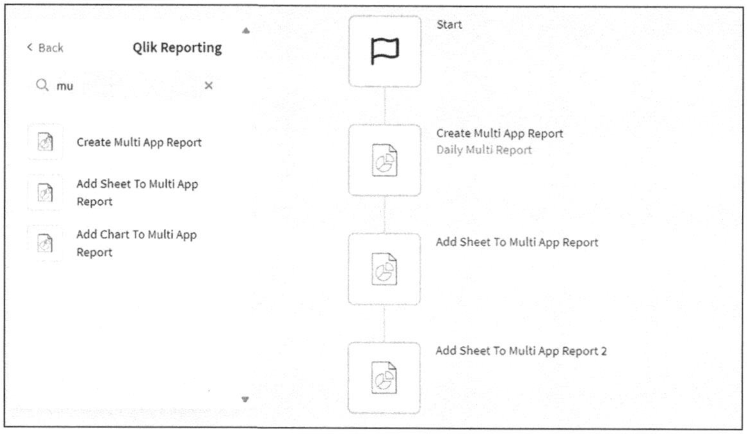

***Figure 10.13**: Adding one more sheet to the report*

10. Drag and drop a **`Generate Report`** block from the Qlik Reporting connector.

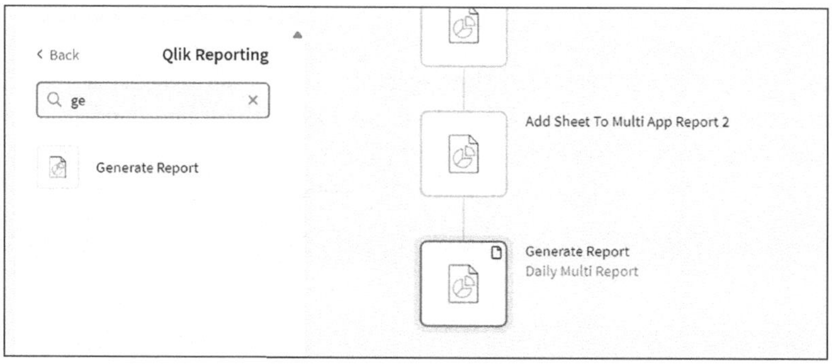

***Figure 10.14**: Generate Report*

11. Using the Settings panel, choose **`PDF`** or **`PPT`** as the **`Format mode`**.

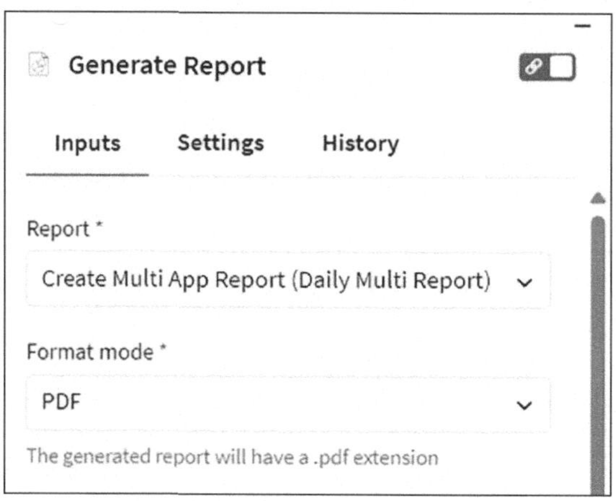

***Figure 10.15**: Select the format mode*

12. Drag and drop a **`Send Mail`** block to the canvas and link it to the flow.

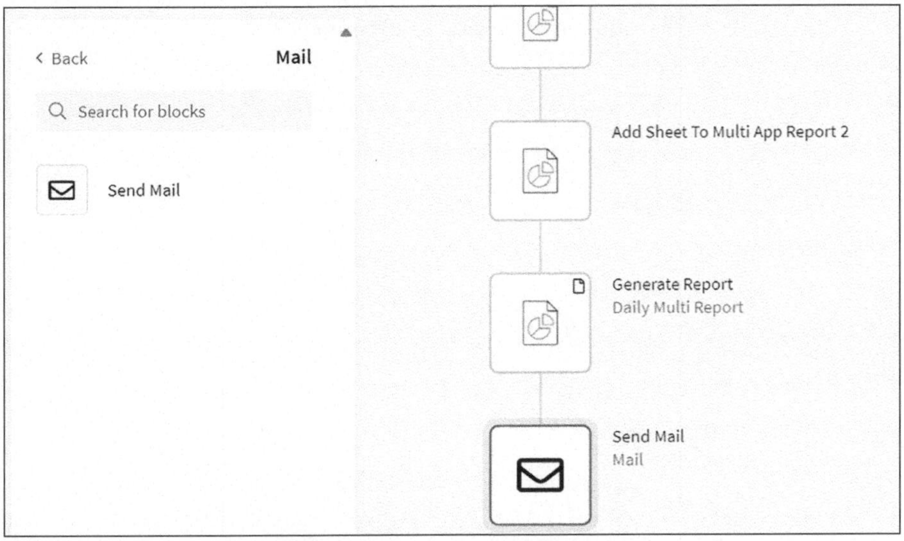

***Figure 10.16**: The Send Mail block*

13. Configure the SMTP using the **`Connection`** tab on the block Settings.

***Figure 10.17:** Mail connection*

14. Configure the **`To`**, **`Cc`**, **`Bcc`**, **`Subject`**, and **`Body`**.

***Figure 10.18**: Send Mail settings*

15. Configure the **`Attachment`** using the output of the **`Generate Report`** block.

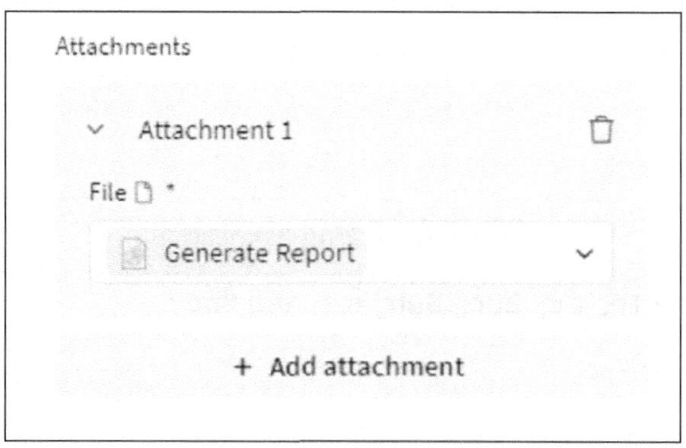

***Figure 10.19**: Attachment*

16. Save and test your automation.

    Exercise: Make selections on sheets before adding them to the report using the **`Add Selection to Sheet`.**

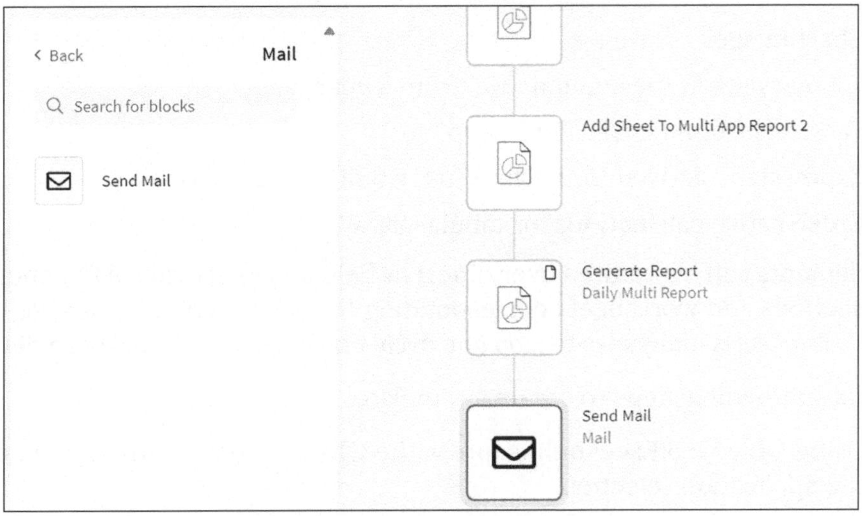

Figure 10.20: *Add Selection Block*

Tabular Reporting

Tabular reports present data in a structured format, aiding in data analysis. We explore creating and customizing these reports using the Qlik add-in for Microsoft Excel alongside Qlik Sense apps. This approach leverages Excel's familiarity with Qlik's data analysis power. Qlik Cloud supports delivery options such as email and Microsoft SharePoint integration in XLSX and PDF formats.

This option requires integration with Office365 and administrative rights. Before starting to develop your report, it is mandatory to deploy the Qlik add-in for Microsoft Excel as described in the documentation (Additional Resources link).

Once the add-in is deployed to your organization, report developers can add the add-in to their Excel (local or browser) and configure the report.

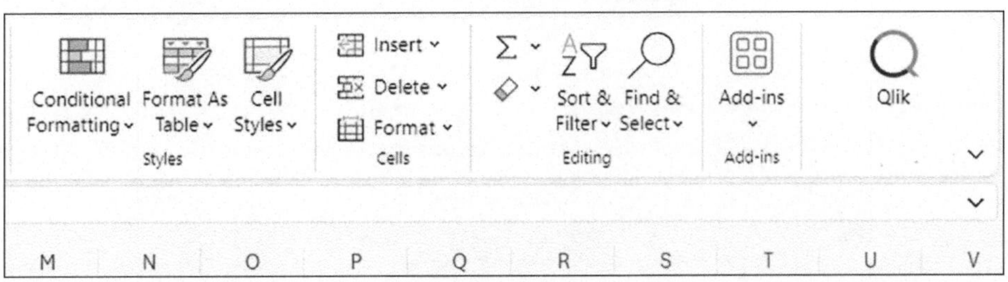

Figure 10.21: *Add-in*

Once this is done, a report template can be created. A report template establishes the report's structure and the included data. It is linked to a single Qlik Sense application, utilizing tags and image placeholders to depict app data. The template allows for various data incorporation methods, such as:

- Chart images
- Tabular data at the column level from a chart
- Variables from the Qlik Sense app
- Expressions derived from Qlik Sense's built-in calculations
- Excel-native calculations for tabular data

Report elements can be iterated over different field and chart values to generate new filtered sections and worksheets corresponding to these specific values. Refer to the section "*Using levels and pages to loop and cycle report elements*" for more details.

Follow the succeeding steps to create a template:

1. Using Office365 Excel online, press the Qlik Icon on the top ribbon, exposing the application selection.

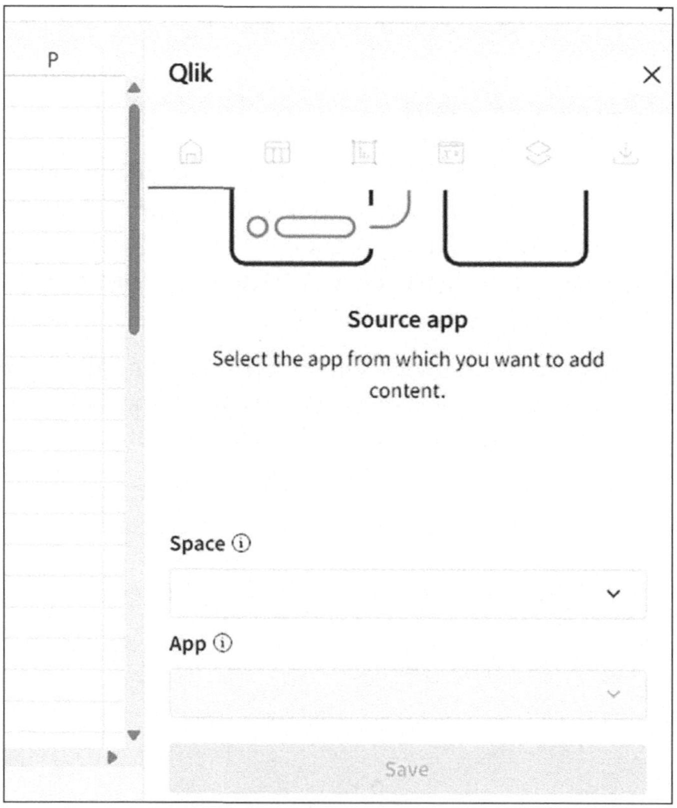

Figure 10.22: *Application Selection*

2. Choose which type of object you want to embed using the top list.

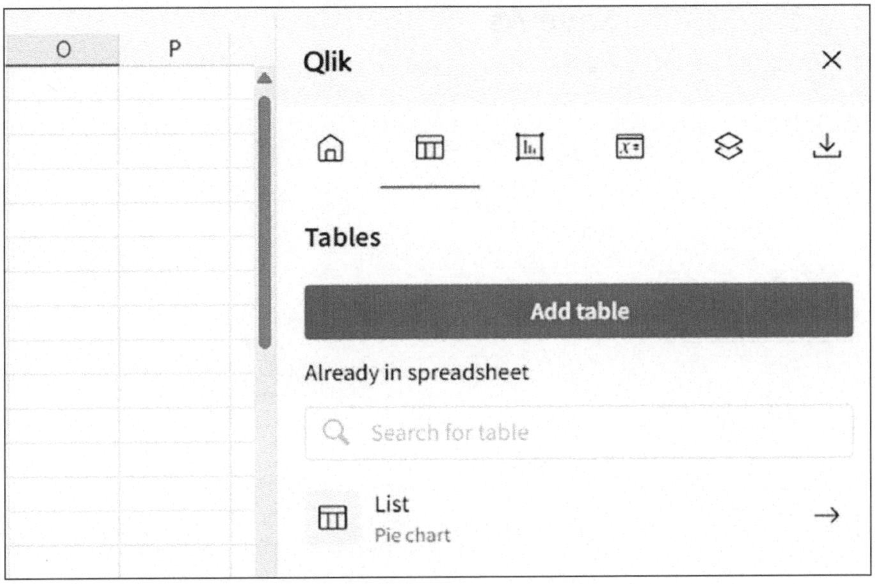

Figure 10.23: *Object Selection*

3. Add the object to the Excel, resizing, or adding more sheets if needed.

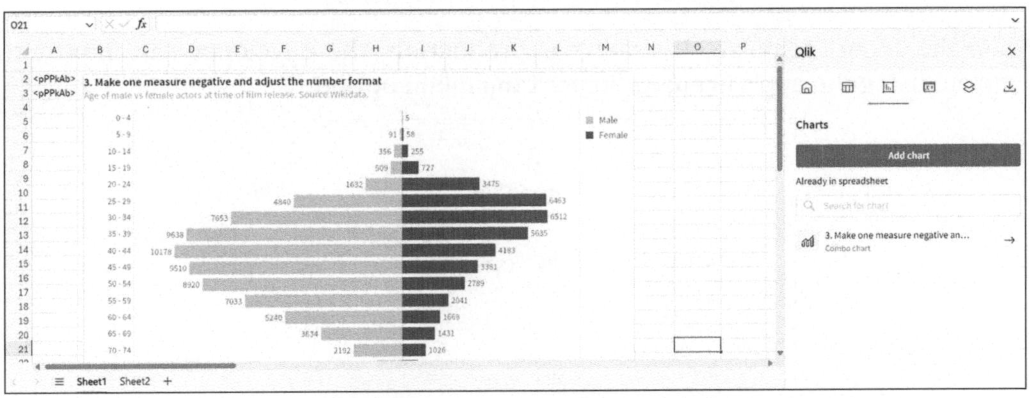

Figure 10.24: *Chart added to the template*

4. Download a copy of your template using the `File/Save As` option.

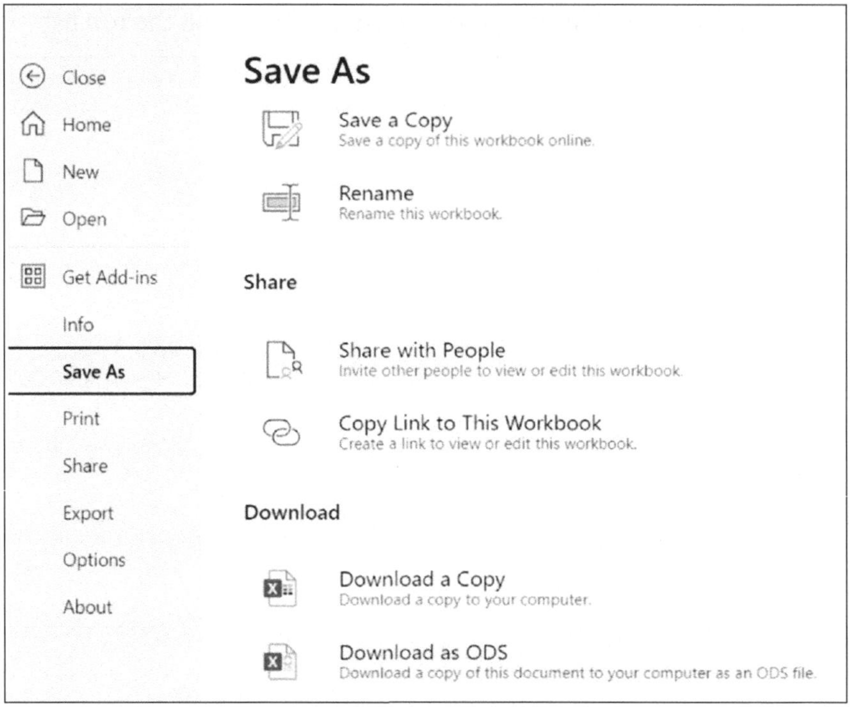

Figure 10.25: *Downloading the Template*

When the report template is ready for production, the developer can import the template using the app's **`Prepare/Reporting`** menu option.

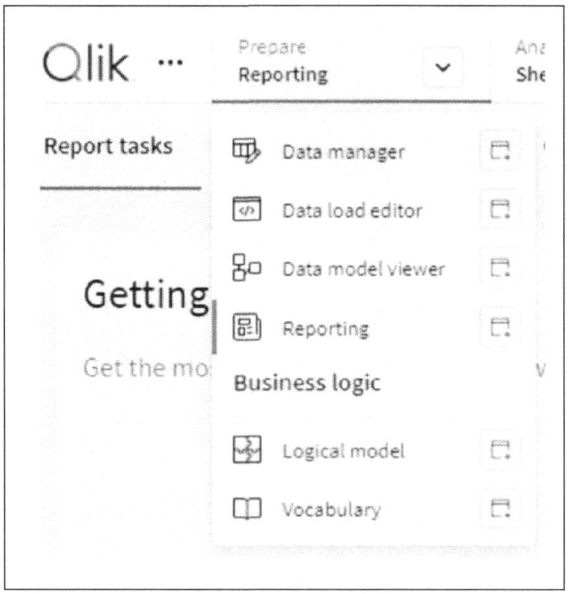

Figure 10.26: *Menu option to configure the report*

After the template is uploaded, the developer can configure the recipients, filters, and other parameters to achieve the desired result.

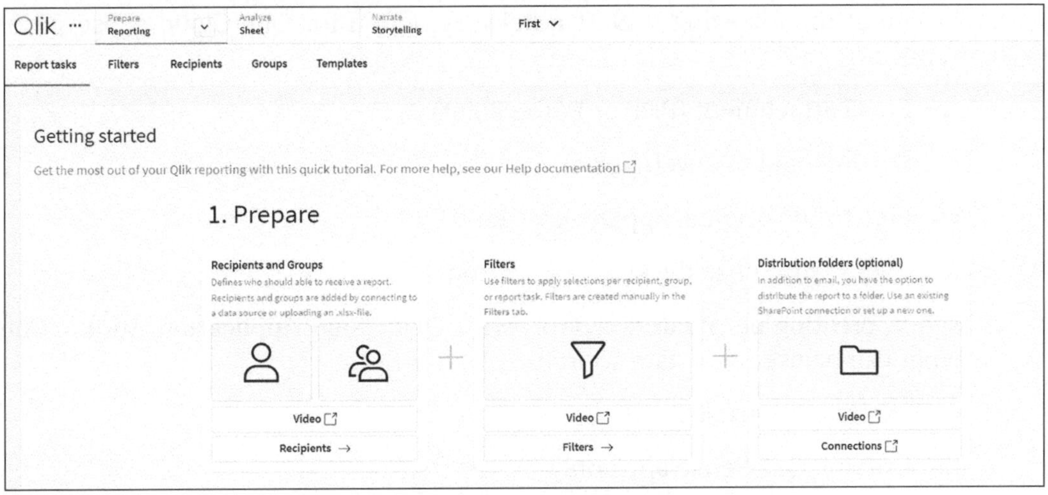

***Figure 10.27**: Tabular reporting configuration*

Conclusion

This chapter has explored the reporting functionalities within Qlik Cloud Analytics. We examined the creation and customization of tabular reports within Qlik Sense apps. Additionally, the chapter addressed the use of Qlik Application Automation for streamlining report generation and distribution workflows. Subscription reports were also discussed, highlighting their role in delivering automated data updates via email.

The diverse reporting features within Qlik Cloud empower users to transform data into clear and informative reports. Tabular reports present data in a structured format, facilitating analysis and communication. Automated reports enhance efficiency by eliminating manual generation, saving time and resources. Subscription reports ensure users stay informed with the latest data delivered directly to their inboxes.

In conclusion, Qlik Cloud offers a comprehensive suite of reporting tools for data analysis and communication. The knowledge gained from this chapter equips users to leverage these capabilities and effectively present data insights within their organizations.

In the next chapter, we will discuss the options organizations can rely on to bring local resources (databases, files, and more) to be consumed in Qlik Cloud using the Direct Access Gateway.

Multiple Choice Questions

1. Which of the following is NOT a delivery option for Qlik Cloud subscription reports?
   a. Email attachment (PDF or PowerPoint)
   b. Secure login to a web portal
   c. Link to the original app in Qlik Cloud
   d. User's Qlik Sense desktop application
2. When creating automated reports with Qlik Cloud Application Automation, what can be used as a data source?
   a. External databases only
   b. Existing Qlik Sense apps only
   c. Both external databases and existing Qlik Sense apps
   d. User-uploaded spreadsheets only
3. What factors should be considered when choosing between Qlik Cloud's built-in tabular reporting and Qlik Reporting Service (QRS)?
   a. User's technical expertise
   b. Report complexity and formatting needs
   c. Desired level of automation for report generation
   d. All of the above

Answers

1. d
2. b
3. d

Additional Resources

The following links complement this book, bringing more resources to the reader with more examples and details. Please be aware that as Qlik introduces new product versions, the documentation might be found under a different link.

- **Deploying and installing the Qlik add-in for Microsoft Excel**: (https://help.qlik.com/en-US/cloud-services/Subsystems/Hub/Content/Sense_Hub/Reporting/excel-add-in-install.htm)
- **Building report templates with the Qlik add-in for Microsoft Excel**: (https://help.qlik.com/en-US/cloud-services/Subsystems/Hub/Content/Sense_Hub/Reporting/excel-add-in-overview.htm)

CHAPTER 11
Direct Access Gateway

Introduction

This chapter is all about introducing you to the Direct Access Gateway in Qlik Cloud. We will start from the basics, such as what the gateway is and how you can get it. Then, we will walk you through the steps to install it on your system. Along the way, we will talk about the different parts that make up the gateway. Our goal here is to give you a good understanding of how the gateway works and how you can use it in your work. So, let us dive in and explore the world of the Direct Access Gateway together.

Structure

In this chapter, we will cover the following topics:

- Working of the Gateway
- How to Install the Gateway and the Prerequisite
- The Best Practices of Using the Gateway

Getting Started

The Direct Access Gateway within Qlik Cloud serves to establish a secure and encrypted connection between Qlik Cloud and an organization's data sources, eliminating the necessity to open inbound firewall ports.

Pros of using Gateway:

- **Enhanced Security**: Positioned behind the organization's firewall, it enables Qlik Sense SaaS applications to securely access data residing behind the firewall.
- **Streamlined Connectivity**: Data flows directly from the data source to Qlik Cloud via a Web Socket Secure (WSS) connection, ensuring that data remains in transit and does not reside on the Direct Access Gateway server.

- **Simplified Accessibility**: Overcoming challenges posed by stringent firewall policies that restrict external access to data sources facilitates cloud analytics while upholding security standards.

Utilizing the Direct Access Gateway is advisable when seeking a secure and real-time data link to Qlik Cloud for analytical purposes, particularly in scenarios where organizational security protocols prohibit direct access to data sources from the cloud. Many businesses often implement stringent firewall policies to prevent external access to their data sources. This poses a significant challenge when accessing data from the cloud for analytical purposes. However, the Qlik Data Gateway - Direct Access addresses this challenge by **eliminating the necessity to open inbound firewall ports**. Positioned behind the organization's firewall, the Direct Access Gateway enables Qlik Sense SaaS applications to securely access data residing behind the firewall. This access is facilitated through a strictly outbound, encrypted, and mutually authenticated connection.

Working of the Gateway

The Qlik Direct Access Gateway is designed for deployment on a Windows Server machine positioned behind our firewall.

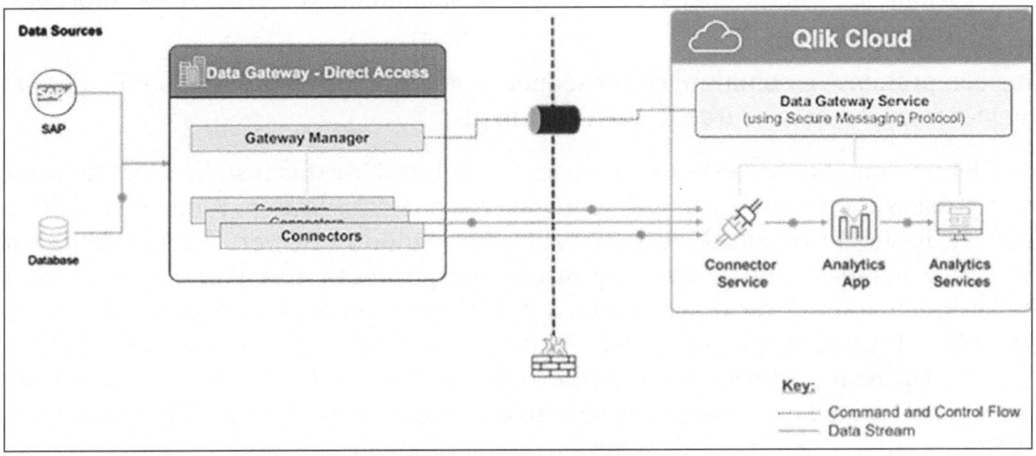

Figure 11.1: *Direct Access Gateway Architecture*

Let us start with understanding the key architecture components:

- **Initiation of Connection**: We begin with the Direct Access Gateway, which serves as a secure intermediary between Qlik Cloud and your data source, initiating a connection to Qlik Cloud. This connection undergoes mutual authentication, wherein both parties verify each other's identities, and encryption via Hypertext Transfer Protocol Secure (HTTPS), ensures that transmitted data remains coded to prevent unauthorized access.

- **Dispatch of Query**: Upon establishing the connection, Qlik Cloud sends a load statement–a query or request for specific data–to the Direct Access Gateway.
- **Forwarding of Query**: Subsequently, the Direct Access Gateway forwards this query to the pertinent data source, which typically comprises the database or system housing the requested data.
- **Data Transmission**: The requested data is then transmitted directly from the data source to the Qlik Cloud. This transmission occurs through WebSocket Secure (WSS), a protocol facilitating secure real-time data transfer via a single TCP connection.
- **Data in Transit**: It is imperative to note that throughout this process, the data remains in transit, continuously moving from the data source to the Qlik Cloud. At no point does it physically reside or get stored on the Direct Access Gateway server.
- **Key-Pair for Security**: To bolster security, a unique key-pair is established for each Direct Access Gateway server connected to the Qlik Cloud tenant. This key pair serves the dual purpose of authentication–validating the identities of communication participants–and end-to-end data encryption, ensuring data security from its departure from the data source to its arrival at Qlik Cloud. This additional security layer complements the HTTPS transport-level encryption.

This comprehensive communication sequence guarantees a secure and efficient data transfer from the data source to the Qlik Cloud.

Now, let us examine the server specifications required for this installation. The server must possess the capability to efficiently access our data source. When installing the gateway, it should be allocated to a dedicated Windows Server, distinct from both the actual database server and any other Qlik products. Compatibility extends to the latest versions of Windows, with additional requirements such as .NET, ASP, and Visual C++. Hardware specifications recommend a minimum of 8 cores and 32 GB of memory. **Optimal performance is achieved by installing the Direct Access Gateway on a server located as close as possible to our data source.** This strategic placement minimizes latency and maximizes system stability, ensuring smooth operations.

Let us break down the process of setting up the **Qlik Data Gateway - Direct Access** into easy-to-understand stages:

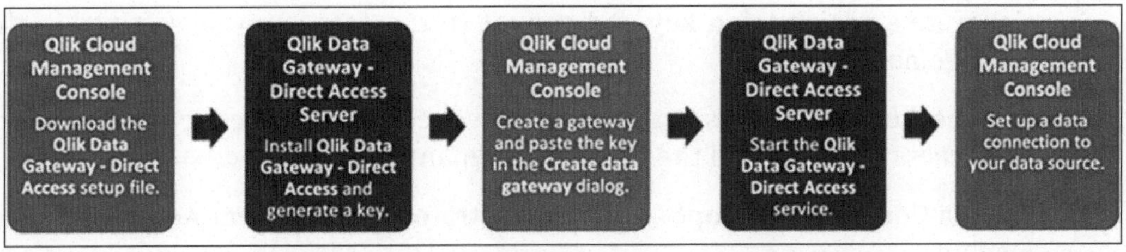

Figure 11.2: *Set up of Direct Access Gateway*

Stage One: Download Qlik Data Gateway - Direct Access

1. In the **`Management Console`**, navigate to **`Data Gateways`**.
2. Existing data gateways are listed in a table with basic information about each gateway.
3. Click the **`Deploy`** toolbar button.
4. The **`Deploy data gateway`** dialog opens.
5. Select **`Data Gateway - Direct Access`**, accept the **`Qlik Customer Agreement`**, and click **`Download`**. This will download the **`Direct Access Gateway setup file`** (`qlik-data-gateway-direct-access.exe`) to your machine.

Stage Two: Install the Direct Access Gateway

This stage involves installing the Direct Access Gateway on a server behind the firewall protecting your data sources. You can choose to install it interactively or silently.

1. After downloading, copy the setup file to a **Windows Server machine** behind the firewall.
2. Ensure that the machine can communicate with your data sources.
3. Open the file to launch the **`Setup Wizard`** and follow the prompts until setup is complete.
4. Note: Direct Access Gateway requires **Microsoft .NET 6. x**. If an earlier version is detected, you will be prompted to install the required version. After the .NET installation, restart the data gateway server and run the Direct Access Gateway setup again.
5. Setup may also prompt you to install **Microsoft Visual C++ 2015-2022 Redistributable (x64)** if it is not already installed.

Stage Three: Setting Up Direct Access Gateway

1. Set your **Qlik Cloud tenant URL**.
2. Optionally, configure a **proxy server**.

3. Generate a **registration key** and copy it to the data gateway settings in the Management Console.
    a. The key establishes an authenticated connection between the Direct Access Gateway and the Qlik Cloud tenant.
4. Open a **Command Prompt** as an administrator on the Direct Access Gateway machine.
5. Change the working directory to the ConnectorAgent subfolder (usually **`C:\Program Files\Qlik\ConnectorAgent\ConnectorAgent`**).
6. Set the Qlik Cloud tenant using the following command (without a proxy server):

    `connector agent qcs set_config --tenant_url <your-qlik-cloud-tenant-URL>`

Stage Four: Register the Data Gateway

1. Return to the **`Management Console`** and select **`Data Gateways`**.
2. Click the **`Create`** Toolbar button.
3. In the **`Create data gateway`** dialog:
    a. Specify a name for the data gateway.
    b. Optionally, provide a description.
    c. Select **`Direct Access`** from the data gateway type drop-down.
    d. Paste the registration key.

Stage Five: Start the Qlik Data Gateway - Direct Access Service

1. Windows Services Console Method:
    a. Open the **`Windows Services`** console.
    b. Look for the **`Qlik Data Gateway - Direct Access service`** in the list.
    c. Start the service.
2. Command Prompt Method:
    a. Open a **Command Prompt** as an administrator.
    b. Change the working directory to the ConnectorAgentsubfolder (usually located at **`C:\Program Files\Qlik\ConnectorAgent\ConnectorAgent`** with a default installation).
    c. Run the command: **`connector agent service start`**

d. You will receive a confirmation message if the service starts successfully.

Stage Six: Add a Connection to Your Data Source

1. Locate Your Gateway:
   a. Check the **`Data gateways list`**.
   b. Verify that your gateway's **`Status`** is **`"Connected"`** (you might need to refresh your browser to see the status).
2. Add a Connection:
   a. Once your gateway is connected, proceed to add a connection to your desired data source.

To obtain the gateway executable, we navigate to the Qlik Management Console (QMC). From there, we select the **`"Deploy"`** option to access and download the executable file.

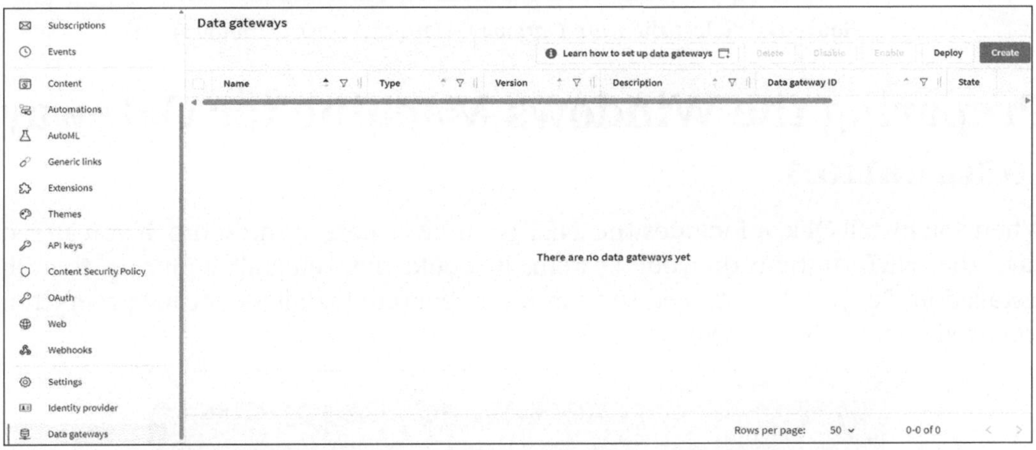

Figure 11.3: *Downloading the Direct access gateway executable file from the QMC*

In this chapter, we will work on the direct access Gateway, so we will select this in the option.

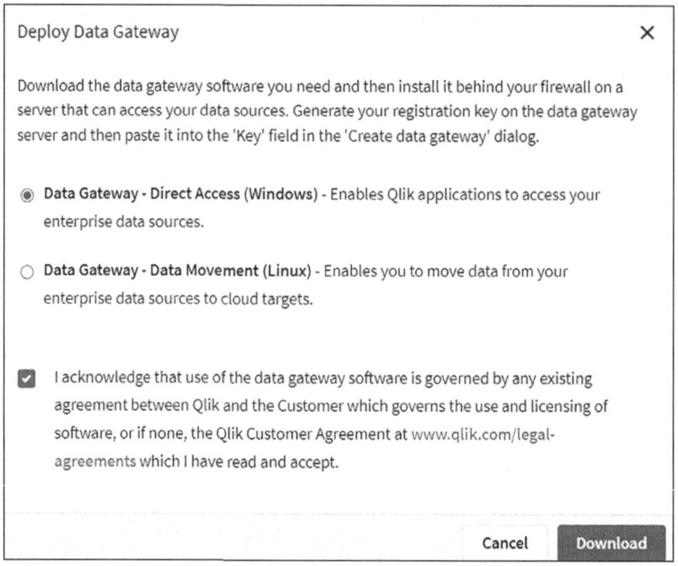

Figure 11.4: *Select the Data Gateway – Direct Access (Windows)*

Preparing the Windows Machine for Gateway Installation

When you install Qlik, it includes the .NET runtime as part of the setup. If you already have the .NET runtime on your system, it would not reinstall it during the Qlik installation. So, you do not need to search for separate installers because everything you need comes with the Qlik setup file.

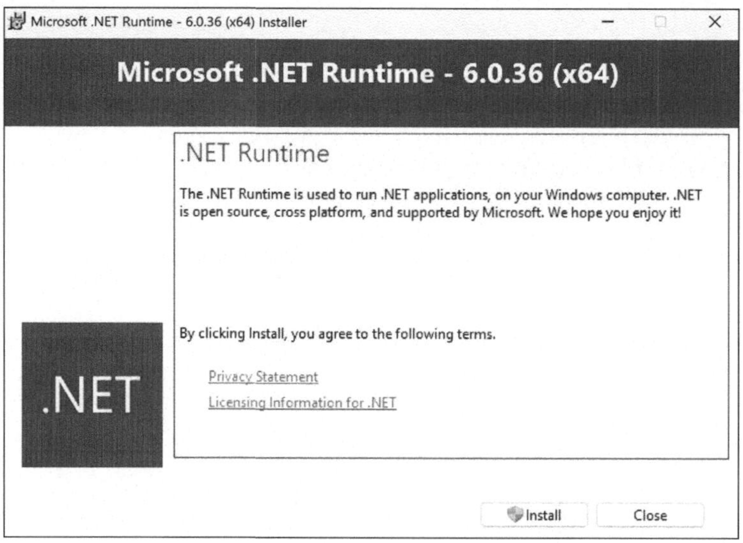

Figure 11.5: *.NET Runtime installation*

The .NET runtime stands as a pivotal element within the .NET framework, furnishing the essential environment for executing applications developed with .NET. It encompasses critical services such as memory management, garbage collection, exception handling, and security, all of which contribute to the robustness and reliability of applications.

In the case of the Qlik Direct Access Gateway, its reliance on the .NET runtime is imperative due to several reasons:

- **Execution Environment**: The .NET runtime presents a managed execution environment, ensuring applications operate in a controlled and isolated manner, thereby heightening security and stability.
- **Compatibility:** It guarantees compatibility between the Direct Access Gateway and the .NET libraries and components with which it was constructed.
- **Performance**: Optimized for performance across diverse operating systems and architectures, the .NET runtime is particularly vital for the data-intensive operations undertaken by the Direct Access Gateway.

In essence, the presence of the .NET runtime is indispensable for the operation of the Qlik Direct Access Gateway, furnishing a secure and efficient platform for its functionality.

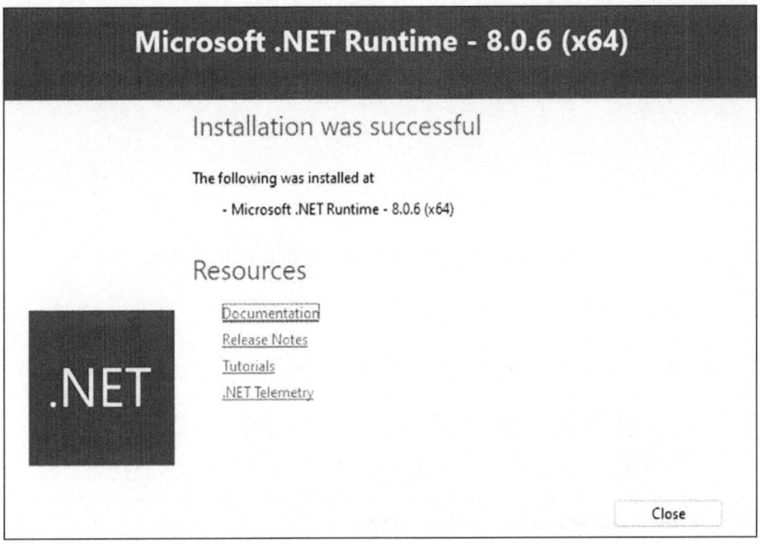

***Figure 11.6**: .NET successfully installed*

Essentially, the ASP.NET Core Shared Framework comprises a collection of libraries built atop the .NET runtime, aimed at furnishing a sturdy foundation for web applications. This framework serves as the operational backbone for the Qlik Direct Access Gateway, facilitating its functionality.

Next, we proceed to install ASP.NET Core. This component is included as part of the installation process within the data gateway installable package.

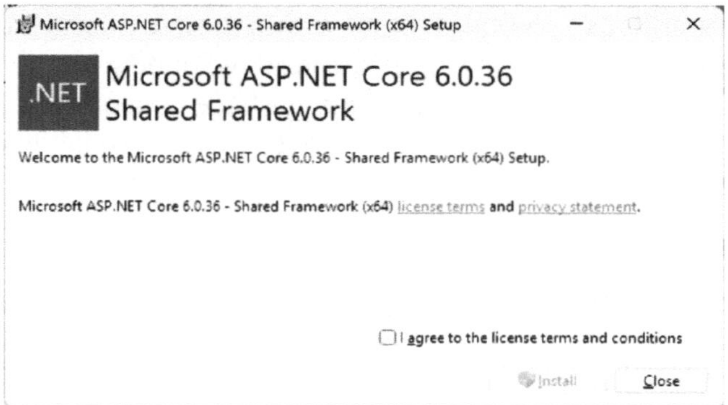

***Figure 11.7**: Installing the ASP.NET framework*

Upon successful completion of this installation, we receive a message confirming successful completion, as shown here:

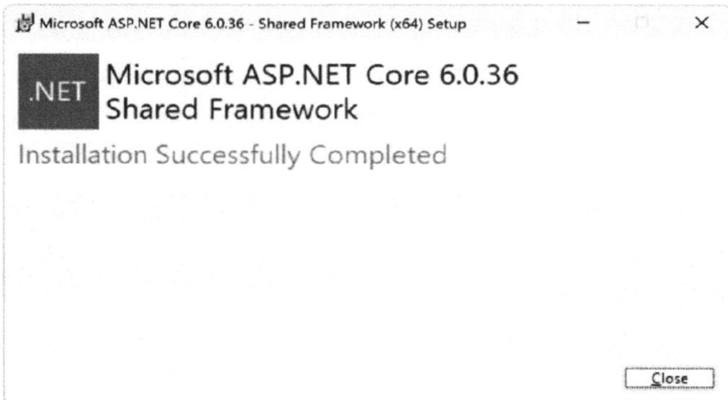

***Figure 11.8**: ASP.NET framework completed*

Next, we proceed with the installation of Visual C++.

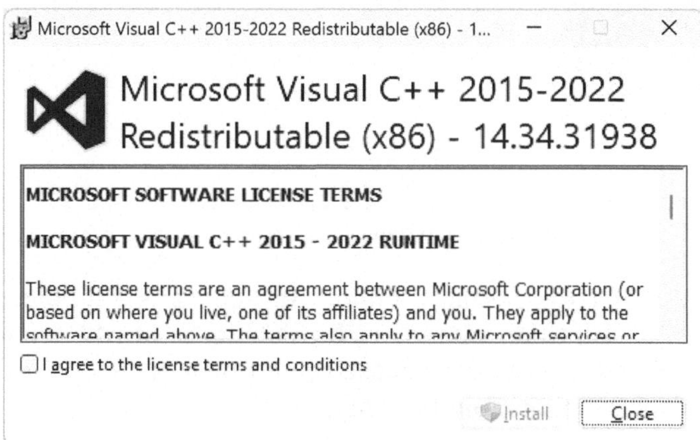

***Figure 11.9**: Visual C++Installation*

The Qlik Direct Access Gateway necessitates these components due to its reliance on underlying technologies. Specifically, the .NET versions are essential for executing the gateway application, while the Microsoft Visual C++ Redistributable furnishes necessary runtime components for C++ applications developed using Visual Studio, including the Qlik Direct Access Gateway. These components collectively ensure seamless operation of the gateway, facilitating its interaction with vital system resources and services provided by the .NET framework and the C++ runtime libraries.

Next, we proceed with the installation of the .NET Framework.

1. Click on the **`Install`** button, as shown in *Figure 11.10*.

Figure 11.10: *Installing the .NET framework*

2. Click on the **`Finish`** button

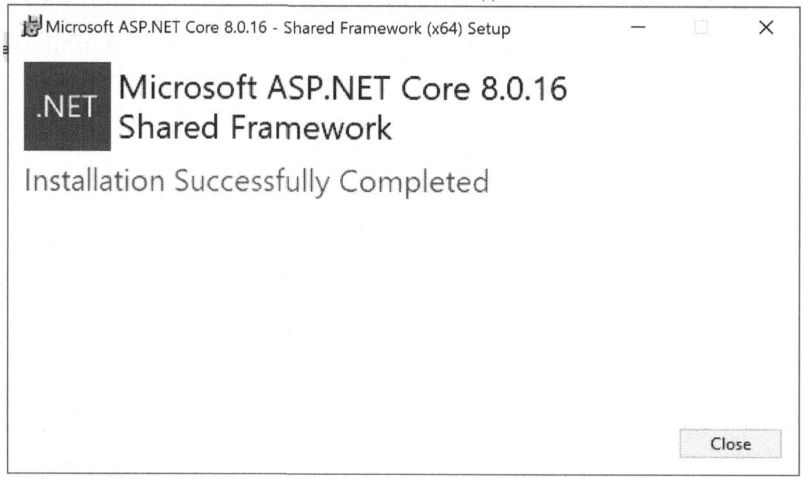

Figure 11.11: *Click on Finish*

3. Restart the computer to complete the installation

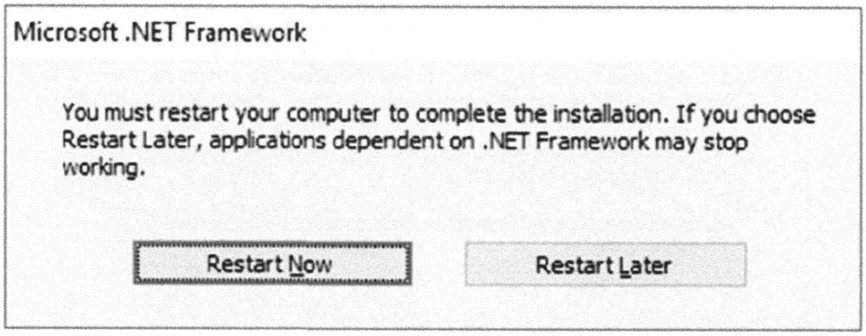

Figure 11.12: *Complete the installation*

Installing the Gateway

Finally, we installed all the prerequisite packages and restarted the machine. Now, the executable file can initiate the installation process for the Direct Access Gateway directly.

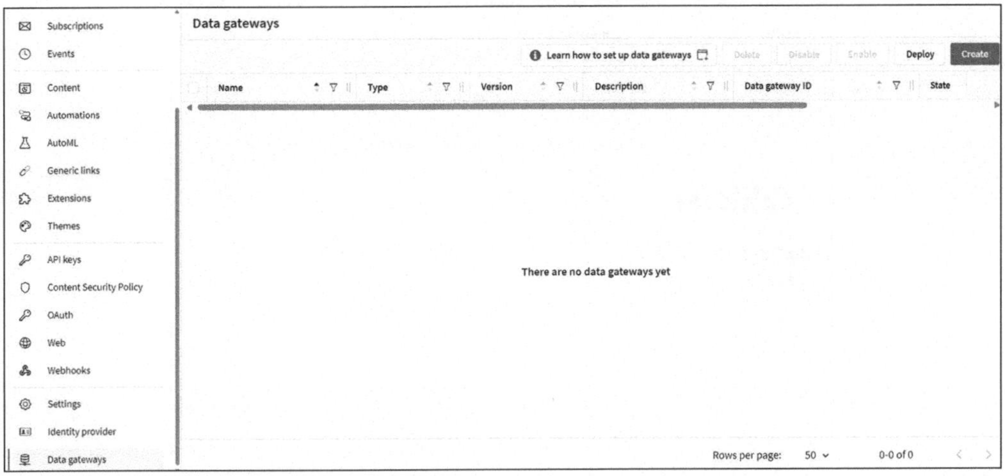

Figure 11.13: *Installation of the Qlik Direct Access Gateway*

Once the gateway installation commences, we proceed by selecting **"Next"** to initiate the installation process from the main screen.

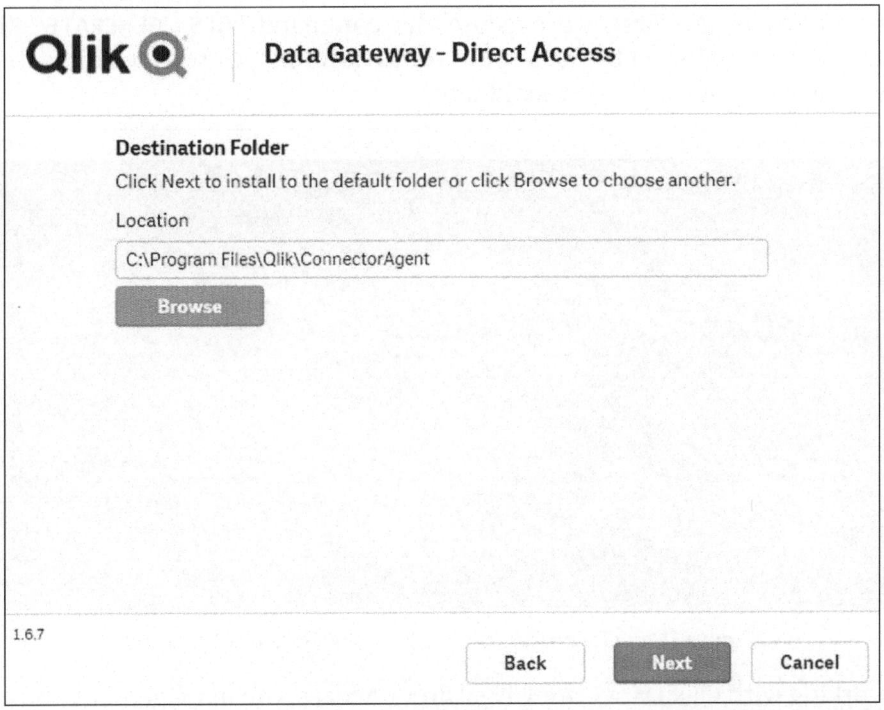

Figure 11.14: *Installation of the connector Agent folder location*

Next, we will proceed to select the destination folder location. Typically, the default path is on the C drive.

***Figure 11.15**: Successful completion of the Gateway installation*

Now that the gateway is installed, we proceed to connect to the tenant and perform the key pair exchange. First, we execute the command **"QCS GENERATE KEYS"** to generate the keys, followed by **"QCS GET_REGISTRATION"** to retrieve the actual keys. These keys will be copied to the tenant later.

***Figure 11.16**: Generating the Keys in the Gateway machine*

When working with Qlik Data Gateway - Direct Access, the management and creation of gateways occur within designated data spaces:

Gateway Spaces:

- **Shared Spaces**: Within a shared space, individuals possessing connection user permissions in the gateway space can utilize gateway connections from any other space. This fosters collaboration and facilitates data access across various domains.

- **Managed Spaces**: In a managed space, users holding connection creation permissions within the gateway space can establish new gateway connections within any space. Managed spaces offer enhanced control over data connections.

Roles and Permissions:

To establish a data connection in one space utilizing a data gateway from another space, the user must hold the "Can consume data" role within the data gateway space.

To create a data gateway itself, the user must either be a space owner or possess the "Can manage" role.

Setting Up Gateway in the SaaS Tenant

Now that the gateway is set up, we proceed to the SaaS tenant. Here, we create a new gateway and link it to a designated space. Subsequently, we copy the keys generated in this process for configuration purposes.

Figure 11.17: *Creating a gateway*

Once the gateway is created, we will start it by using the Command Line Interface (CLI). The command to use is "**`connector agent service start`**".

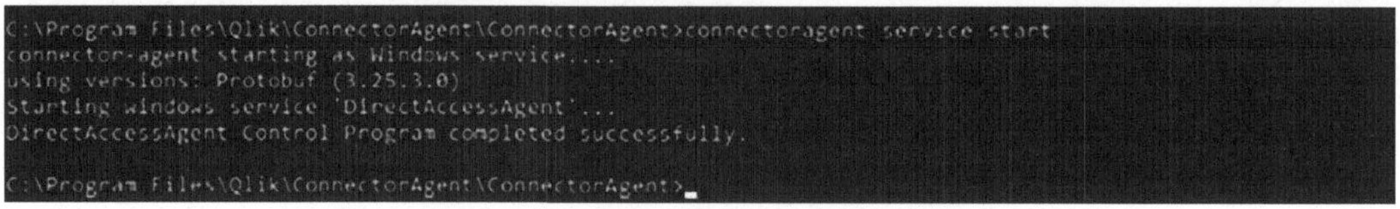

***Figure 11.18**: Starting the gateway service*

The gateway in the QMC now changes to "**`Connected State`**".

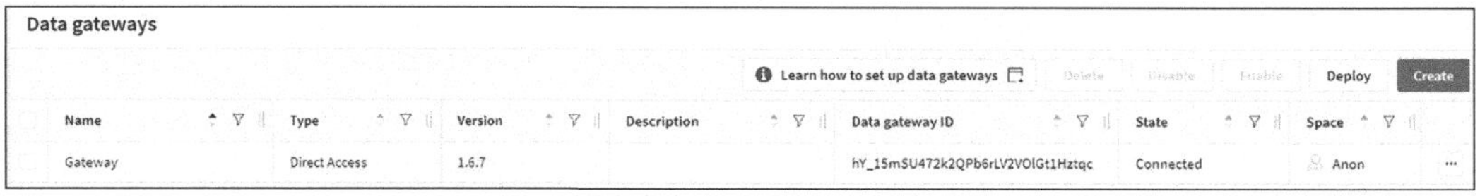

***Figure 11.19**: Monitoring the gateway service*

In the QMC, we always see details about the gateways, including the following:

- **Name**: This is the name given when the data gateway was first created.
    - **Type**: This is always "Direct Access." It is the kind of connection the data gateway uses.
    - **Description**: This is a short explanation given when the data gateway was made.
    - **Data gateway ID:** This is a unique code for each data gateway. It is like a special code that helps identify the data gateway, especially when solving problems.
    - **Status**: This shows what is happening with the data gateway. It can be:
- **Connected**: The Direct Access Gateway service has connected to Qlik Cloud.
- **Disconnected**: The Direct Access Gateway service is not connected to Qlik Cloud. If you see this, you need to start the service again.
- **Disabled**: The data gateway has been turned off in the Management Console.
- **Establishing session**: This means the data gateway is setting up a connection to the data source.
    - **Space**: This is the specific area in Qlik Cloud that the data gateway is linked to.
    - **Date created:** This is when the data gateway was first created.

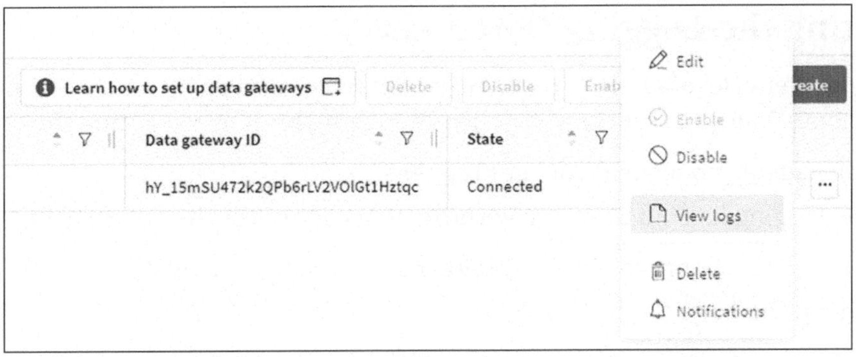

Figure 11.20: *Viewing the logs of the gateway service*

Understanding the Logs and Troubleshooting

The initial troubleshooting step involves accessing the logs. Within the Qlik Management Console, navigate to the Data Gateways section and locate your Direct Access Gateway. By clicking on the three dots at the end of the row and selecting **"View logs"**, you can open the Log Viewer window. Here, you have the option to choose the type of log you wish to view or download, such as Direct Access Gateway logs, DCaaS logs, or various connector logs. You can navigate through the log file using the provided navigation buttons and even download the log file for offline analysis.

Furthermore, you can directly access the logs from the Direct Access Gateway machine. By default, these logs are located in:

`C:\\Program Files\\Qlik\\ConnectorAgent\\data\\logs.`

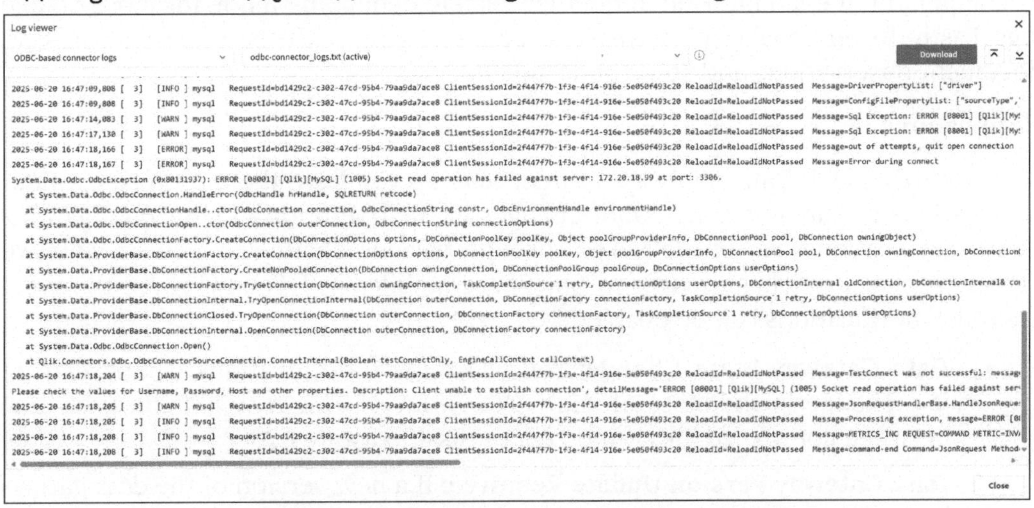

Figure 11.21: *Detailed logs of the gateway service*

Adjusting the Logging Detail Level

The logging detail level of the Direct Access Gateway logs can be tailored to meet your requirements. You can ascertain the current logging level by executing the command.

```
connector agent configuration getloggers
```

To set the logging level to Trace or Verbose, you can utilize the commands.

```
connectoragent configuration setloggers -l Root -v DEBUG
```

Interpreting the Logs

Interpreting the logs entails comprehending the various log levels, such as INFO, DEBUG, WARN, and ERROR. Each log entry contains a timestamp, aiding in tracing the sequence of actions. Log entries may encompass details regarding initialization, requests, responses, errors, connections, authentication, and performance metrics.

Logs often furnish contextual information, including the Request ID, User, Endpoint, and Data Source. In the event of errors, scrutinize stack traces, which delineate the call stack and facilitate issue pinpointing.

Utilizing the Logs

When utilizing the logs, incorporate keywords pertinent to the problem under investigation. This might entail error codes, component names, or data source names. Additionally, it is crucial to correlate logs across different components and ascertain if events in one log are related to events in another. In instances where logs are extensive, contemplate filtering by relevant criteria, such as date, severity, or component. If encountering difficulties, enable debugging mode for more detailed logs. Lastly, foster collaboration with colleagues, engage with community forums, and document observations and steps undertaken.

Notifications

When utilizing Qlik Data Gateway - Direct Access, you have the option to configure notifications to stay informed about changes in the operation of your data gateway. These notifications can be delivered through various channels, such as your web browser, email, or push messages to Qlik Sense Mobile SaaS. Following are the events for which notifications can be enabled:

- **Data Gateway State Change**: You will receive notifications whenever there is a change in the state of your data gateway. This may include transitions between connected, disconnected, or disabled states.
- **Data Gateway Version Update Required**: If a new version of the data gateway becomes available, you will receive a notification. Keeping your gateway up-to-date ensures optimal performance and security.

Figure 11.22: *Notifications in the gateway*

Creating a Connection Using the Gateway

When establishing a connection, the process closely resembles what we would typically do in an on-premises setup. However, instead of choosing a conventional connection, we opt for the one specifically designed for a direct access Gateway, adhering to the connection type required.

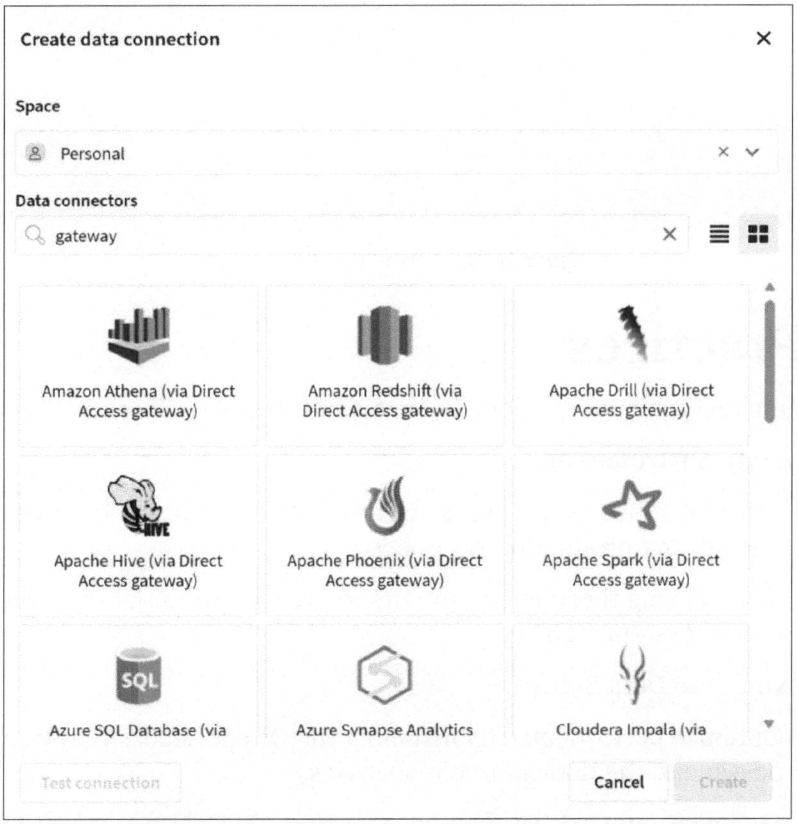

Figure 11.23: *Creating a connection via the Direct Access Gateway*

Like the process followed when installing software on-premises, when working with the Direct Access Gateway, we have the option to input the server's name as **"localhost"**.

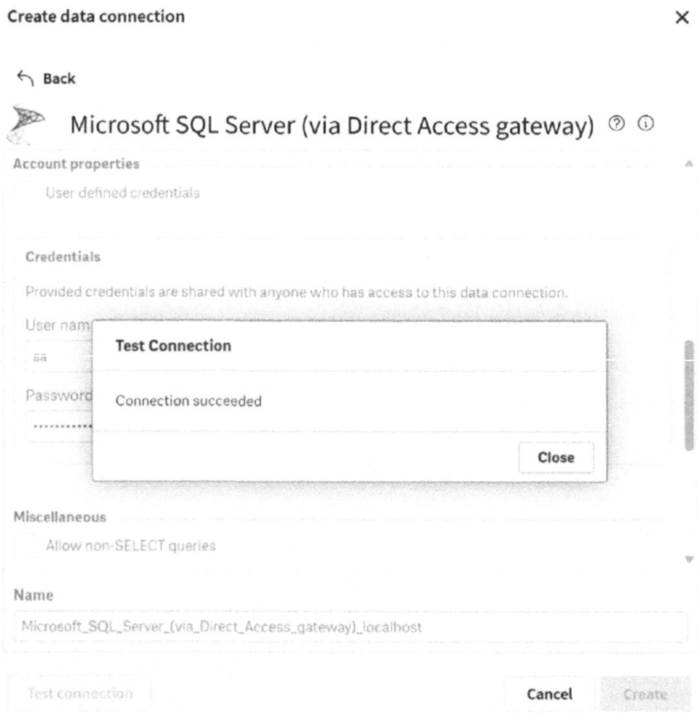

Figure 11.24: *Testing the connection*

Best Practices

Here are some recommended practices for maintaining the Direct Access Gateway:

1. **Separate Environments**:
    a. Utilize distinct Direct Access Gateways for development, user acceptance testing, and production purposes.
    b. Avoid mixing these environments to prevent potential resource strain and ensure system stability.
2. **Proximity to Data Source**:
    a. Optimize performance by installing the Direct Access Gateway as close as possible to the data source it accesses.
    b. Minimize network latency by ensuring physical proximity between the gateway and the data it interacts with.

3. **Dedicated Windows Server**:
    a. Enhance system reliability by installing the Direct Access Gateway on a dedicated Windows Server.
    b. Avoid co-locating it on the primary database server or alongside other Qlik products to mitigate potential conflicts and performance issues.

Conclusion

In this chapter, we examined the Qlik Direct Access Gateway. This is a solution designed to facilitate secure access for Qlik Sense SaaS applications to data located behind your organization's firewall. It operates behind the firewall, establishing a mutually authenticated and encrypted connection to Qlik Cloud via HTTPS. The gateway functions as an intermediary, relaying queries from Qlik Cloud to the pertinent data source, and subsequently streaming the data directly from the source to Qlik Cloud.

In exploring the enhanced benefits of the Qlik Direct Access Gateway, we find several advantages. Firstly, it enhances security by providing a secure method for accessing and analyzing data located behind your organization's firewall, thereby ensuring the integrity of network security. Additionally, it simplifies port management by eliminating the need to open inbound firewall ports. Lastly, it enables outbound connectivity with encryption and mutual authentication, ensuring a strictly secure connection.

In the upcoming chapter, we will dive into the exciting realm of data integration. Qlik Cloud Data Integration emerges as a robust solution for data engineers, empowering them to deliver, transform, and unify enterprise data in real-time. It boasts support for automated, governed, and reusable data pipelines, facilitating seamless data movement from both on-premises and cloud sources into Qlik Cloud and other prominent cloud data platforms.

Multiple Choice Questions

1. What is the primary purpose of Qlik Data Gateway - Direct Access?
    a. To manage user access permissions
    b. To securely access behind-the-firewall data for analytics
    c. To create visualizations in Qlik Sense
    d. To schedule data reloads
2. Which type of connection does the Direct Access gateway establish with Qlik Cloud?
    a. Inbound, unencrypted

    b. Outbound, encrypted
    c. Bidirectional, unauthenticated
    d. Peer-to-peer, unsecured

3. Where should you ideally install the Direct Access gateway?
    a. On a public cloud server
    b. On a workstation
    c. Close to the data source
    d. Anywhere within the organization's network
4. Which Windows Server editions are supported for the gateway installation?
    a. Windows Server 2008
    b. Windows Server 2016, 2019, 2022
    c. Windows Server 2012
    d. Windows Server 2003
5. Which port is used for communication between the Direct Access gateway and Qlik Cloud?
    a. TCP-80
    b. TCP-443 (HTTPS)
    c. UDP-53
    d. TCP-25

Answers

1. b
2. b
3. c
4. b
5. b

References

1. *Qlik Help*: https://help.qlik.com/

CHAPTER 12

Getting to Know Qlik Talend Data Integration

Introduction

This chapter provides a comprehensive overview of Qlik Talend Data Integration. This platform is a robust data integration framework that enables data engineers to deliver, transform, and consolidate enterprise data in real-time through automated, governed, and reusable data pipelines.

Structure

In this chapter, we will discuss the following topics:

- Data Movement Gateway
- Data Pipeline
- Automated Pipeline

Understanding Qlik Talend Data Integration

In previous chapters, we've examined the features Qlik offers for an analytics solution. Now, let's delve into data integration, where the modern data stack is the talk of the town. The modern data stack encompasses a suite of technologies, tools, and processes collaboratively employed to acquire, process, store, manage, and analyze raw data, ultimately transforming it into actionable insights for an organization. However, the modern data stack is fragile and faces certain deep challenges, including but not limited to:

Complexity and Fragmentation:

The modern data stack comprises numerous components, each with its unique interface, configuration, and maintenance requirements. This complexity and fragmentation make it difficult to integrate, monitor, and troubleshoot data pipelines.

Data Quality and Governance:

In the modern data stack, data is often transferred and transformed across multiple platforms and environments, introducing the potential for errors, inconsistencies, and delays. This compromises the quality and reliability of the data and raises concerns about data governance, including issues of security, privacy, and compliance.

Data Accessibility and Usability:

While the modern data stack aims to improve data accessibility and usability for diverse stakeholders, such as analysts, data scientists, and business users, it simultaneously introduces barriers and bottlenecks. These challenges may manifest as the need for specialized skills, tools, and permissions to access and utilize the data effectively.

In the next chapters, we will explore the data integration part of the Qlik platform which can address the challenges of the modern data stack.

Qlik Talend Data Integration is a powerful data integration fabric that helps data engineers deliver, transform, and unify enterprise data in real time via automated, governed, and reusable data pipelines.

This is a cloud-hosted and managed Integration Platform as a Service (iPaaS) that empowers data engineers to streamline real-time data delivery, transformation, and unification across diverse enterprise data sources. It enables organizations to replicate data from on-premises or cloud environments into Qlik Cloud or other cloud-based BI platforms in near real-time, ensuring seamless data accessibility and analysis.

Through Qlik Talend Data Integration, organizations can create comprehensive data pipelines that automate incremental data movement, leveraging real-time, log-based change data capture (CDC). This automated process ensures that data is updated continuously, providing a dynamic and up-to-date data landscape. Additionally, Qlik Talend Data Integration facilitates data transformation, enabling organizations to refine and prepare data for specific analytical needs. It transforms data into a format that is optimized for analysis and insights, eliminating the need for manual data manipulation.

Qlik Talend Data Integration further empowers organizations by automating the creation of data marts, which are focused data repositories tailored to specific business needs. It automatically generates data marts with the appropriate facts and dimensions, ensuring that data is organized and easily accessible for analysis. Additionally, it enables organizations to generate historical data stores, preserving a record of past data for comparative analysis and trend identification.

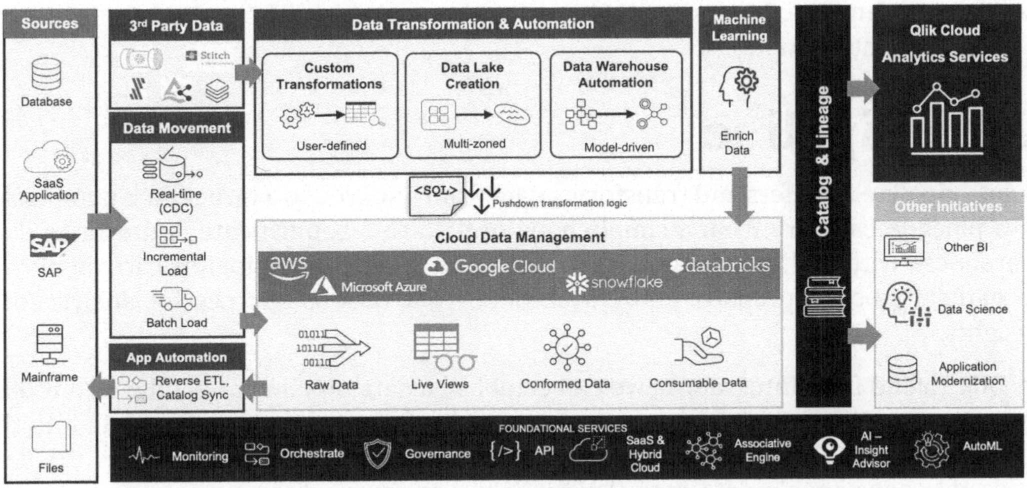

Figure 12.1: *High Level Feature Overview of Qlik Talend Data Integration*

Using Qlik Talend Data Integration, we have the capability to:

- Transfer data from on-premises or cloud origins to Qlik Cloud and various prominent cloud data platforms, such as Snowflake, Azure Synapse, Google Big Query, Databricks, Redshift, or On-Prem Targets.
- Transform raw data into consumption-ready data using a no-code interface or custom SQL. We can apply filters, joins, aggregations, calculations, and more to prepare the data for analytics, machine learning, or digital transformation projects.
- Streamline workflows and procedures that encompass top-tier SaaS applications, triggering alerts or initiating subsequent actions.
- Catalog and monitor the lifecycle of data regardless of source or end-user analytics environment. We can track data lineage, quality, usage, and governance, and ensure your data is always accurate, consistent, and secure.

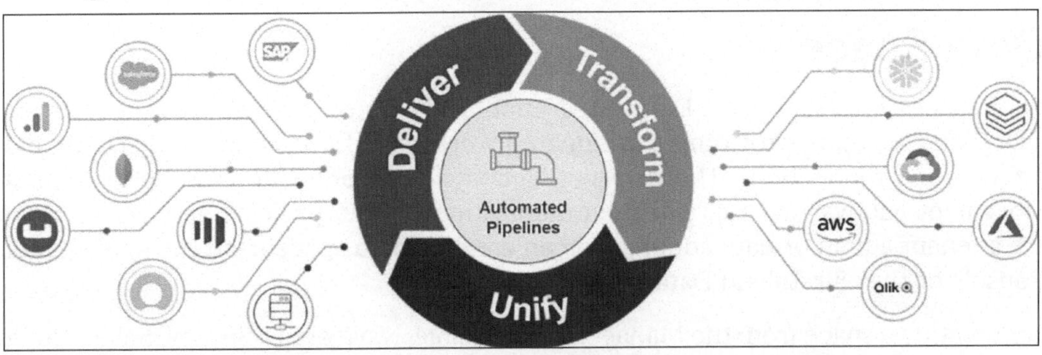

Figure 12.2: *Feature Overview Qlik Talend Data Integration*

Let us now familiarize ourselves with a few key terms and how they apply to Qlik Talend Data Integration:

Data Pipeline

A data pipeline transfers and transforms data from a source to a target. The complexity of a pipeline can vary from a simple copy of data to a sophisticated enterprise data warehouse with multiple data marts for different needs. Data pipelines are employed to gather, process, prepare, and enrich data from various sources for analysis and insights.

In Qlik Talend Data Integration, we can establish a data pipeline to handle all our data integration within a data project using data tasks. Onboarding transfers data into the project from data sources that are on-premises or in the cloud and stores the data in readily consumable data sets. Additionally, we can perform transformations and create data marts to capitalize on our generated and transformed data sets. The data pipeline can be straightforward and linear, or it can be a complex pipeline consuming several data sources and generating numerous outputs.

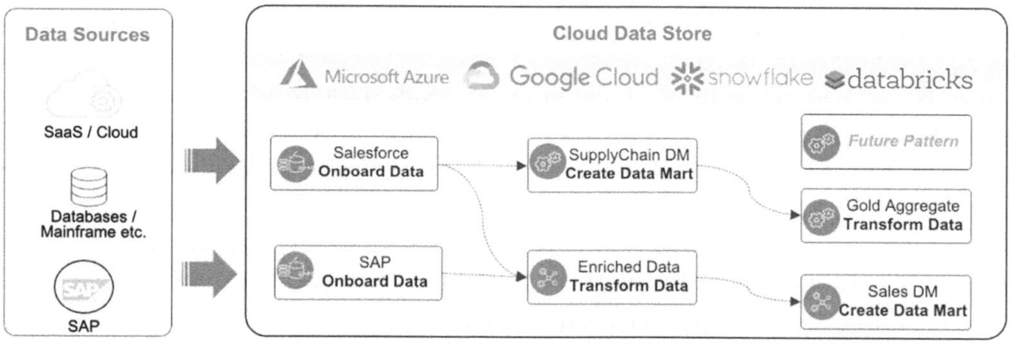

Figure 12.3: *Overview of a data pipeline*

Data Space

Data spaces in Qlik Talend Data Integration serve as controlled areas within your Qlik Cloud account, providing a designated workspace for creating and storing data projects and connections. These spaces facilitate data connection management, Data Movement gateway access, and the organization of data projects and assets. If you are a tenant admin or data admin, you can create a data space from the Management Console or the Qlik Talend Data Integration home.

For creating a space from the Management Console, Navigate to Spaces, Select Create New, then Select Type as Data. Then, add a suitable Name and Description to the Data Space.

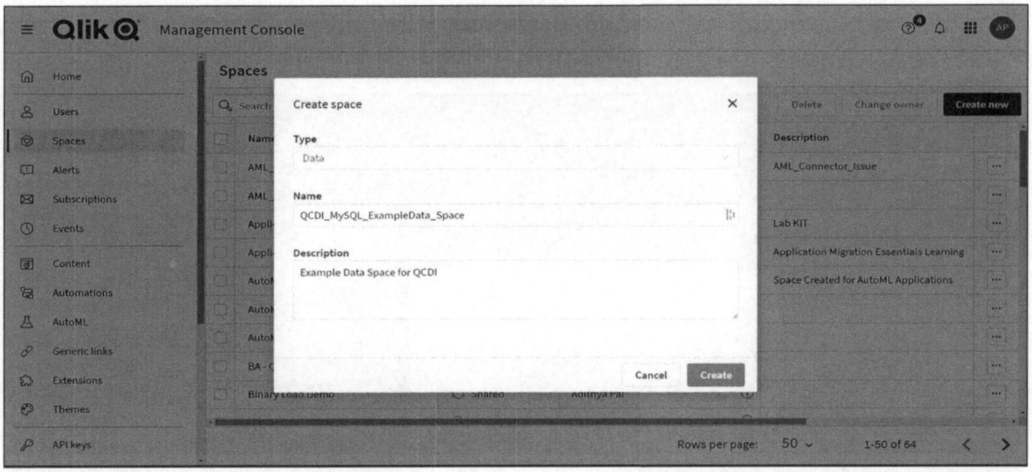

Figure 12.4: *Creating a space from the QMC*

Once the space has been created successfully, you will receive a notification saying: **`New Space Successfully Created`**

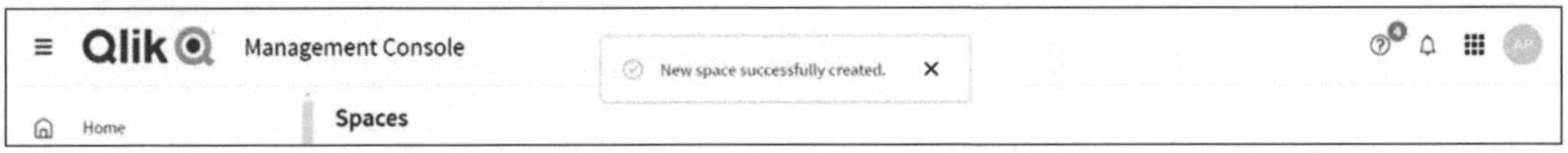

Figure 12.5: *Success message on space creation*

You can utilize data spaces to enforce data governance and management practices. Additionally, you can control who accesses the space and their corresponding permissions within it.

To add members to the space, we need to go to the data integration tab and choose the space we created. Then, we click on **`Space Details`** to see the options for the space. To add new members, we go to the members' section.

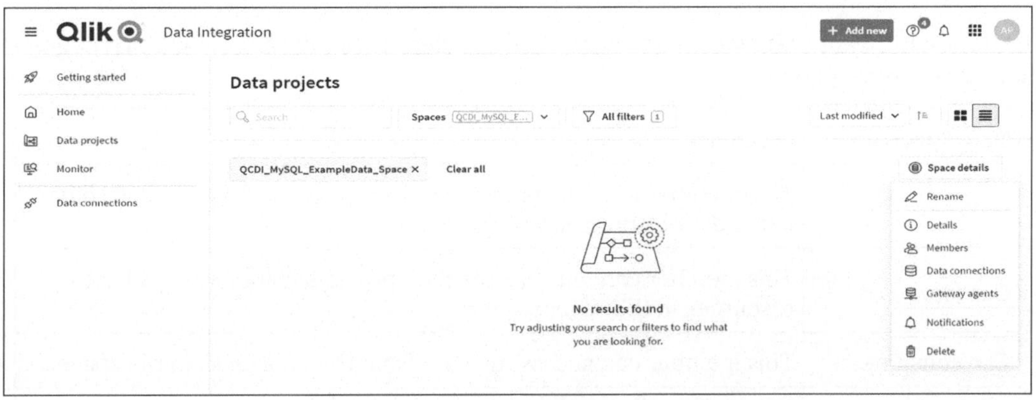

Figure 12.6: *Adding members to a space*

To add members, we click on the **`Add Members`** option and choose the users from the tenant. Then, we assign the permissions they need.

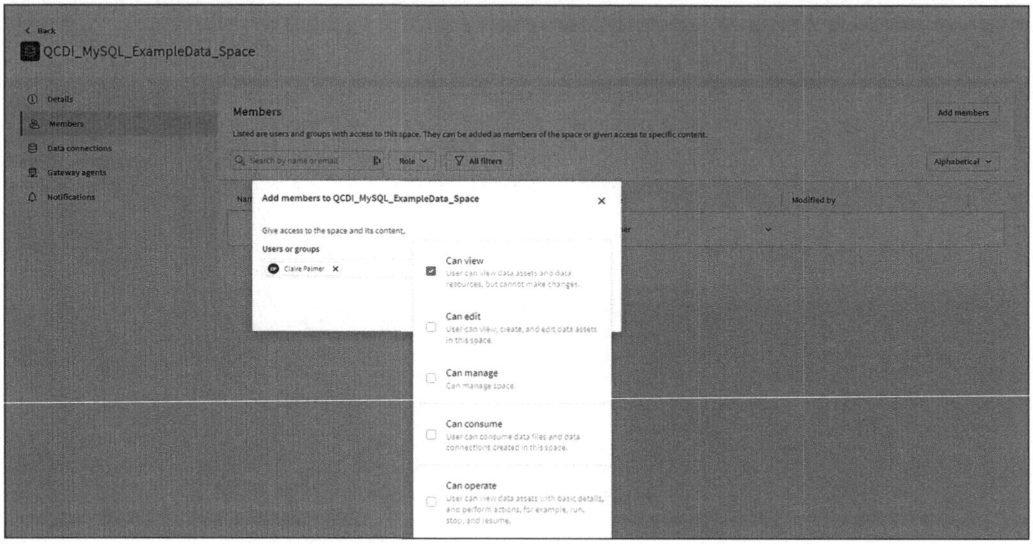

Figure 12.7: *Configuring roles for space members*

To access a data space, we need to meet two conditions. First, we need to be members of the data space that we want to access. Second, we need to have the appropriate roles assigned to us by the owner or manager of the data space.

The roles that we have in a data space determine what actions we can perform with the data projects and assets that are inside the data space. For example, some roles allow us to create, manage, or monitor data assets and resources, while others only allow us to view them. Additionally, we can use the data assets from a data space when we are building apps in other types of spaces, such as personal, shared, and managed spaces.

The following table shows a summary of the roles available and what privileges do each of these roles provide:

Data Space Role	**Summary**
Is owner	This member has full control over the space, its data projects, data tasks, data resources, and members.
Can view	This member can only see the data projects, data tasks, and data resources in the space.
Can consume	This member can access the data from the data tasks in the space.
Can manage	This member can change the space settings and members.

Data Space Role	Summary
Can operate	This member can view the data projects and data tasks, and perform actions like run, stop, and resume.
Can edit	This member can view, edit, and create data projects and data tasks in the space.

Table 12.1: *Table containing the summary of different default roles available and the privilege that the role would provide*

Data Project

The first step to creating a data pipeline in Qlik Talend Data Integration is to create a project.

A data project serves as a container that holds all the components required for a data pipeline. Within this container, you can create, manage, and orchestrate your data pipeline. The data project is associated with a data platform, which acts as the target destination for all data processed within the pipeline. You can construct either a straightforward linear pipeline or a complex pipeline that ingests data from multiple sources and generates various outputs.

Data Tasks

Data tasks are the fundamental building blocks of data pipelines within Qlik Talend Data Integration. These tasks facilitate the orchestration of data movement, transformation, and storage across diverse sources and destinations.

Qlik Talend Data Integration provides five primary types of data tasks:

The initial focus of a data project is onboarding the data. This involves transferring the data continuously from the on-premises or cloud data source and generating datasets in read-optimized format. Onboarding involves two steps: landing and storing.

1. **Landing**: The first step of transferring data when onboarding is landing the data. We can extract data from one or more sources, such as on-premises databases or cloud-based data sources, and subsequently replicate it to a designated landing area. This landing area serves as a temporary repository where the data is stored before undergoing further processing or being integrated into downstream systems.

    a. **Registered Data**: We can streamline the utilization of data that has already been onboarding into the data platform using tools other than Qlik Talend Data Integration, such as Qlik Replicate or Stitch. By registering this pre-existing data, we can seamlessly integrate it into our data pipelines without the need for additional data movement.

2. **Storage**: The storage data task draws upon data that has been ingested into the cloud landing area by the landing data task. It produces consumable datasets in a cloud data warehouse or Qlik Cloud, utilizing the data replicated by the landing data task. These datasets can be maintained in alignment with the landing data without manual intervention.

Once the data is Onboarded, we can transform the data and build data marts on top of the data.

1. **Transform**: Enabling efficient data transformation for cloud-based data warehouses and data lakes, Qlik Talend Data Integration's transformation service empowers users to create reusable and rule-driven transformations within their data pipelines. These transformations can be incorporated during data onboarding or utilized as reusable data tasks, facilitating row-level manipulations and the generation of materialized tables or on-the-fly transformation-enabled views.
2. **Data Mart**: Once we have integrated our data, we can create data marts using the information from either Storage or Transform tasks. We can establish as many data marts as our business requirements demand. Ideally, our data marts should serve as repositories of aggregated data compiled for analysis within specific business units or sections such as the Finance department. The process for building a data mart remains consistent regardless of whether it originates from a Storage or Transform task. We construct data marts to accumulate and condense data extracted from various sources. We organize and aggregate data from multiple datasets to provide a holistic overview of specific business aspects or areas of interest.

In the next chapters, we'll embark on a comprehensive exploration of each of these assets, diving deep into their intricacies.

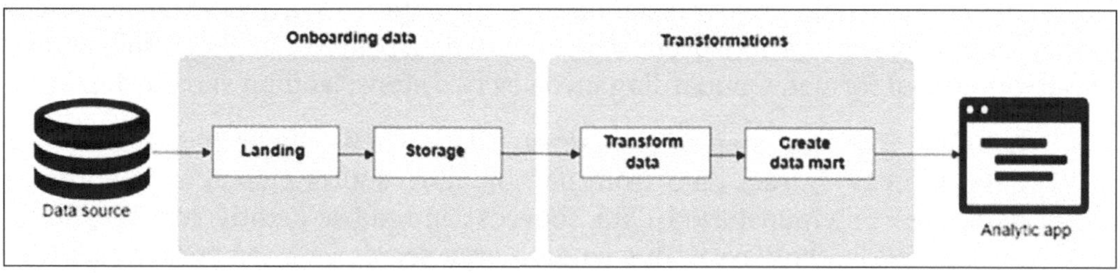

***Figure 12.8**: Asset flow diagram for a data pipleine*

Data Movement Gateway

Our first focus is the Data Movement gateway; it is a tool that helps businesses securely transfer data between their on-premises data sources and the cloud. It acts as a middleman, ensuring that the data is protected and encrypted throughout the transfer process. The Data Movement gateway is a pivotal component enabling seamless data transfer between enterprise and SaaS applications to supported targets.

Qlik Data Gateway - Data Movement is a component controlled from Qlik Cloud, but physically located near to your data. Data Movement is a secure solution for accessing on-premises and private cloud data sources without exposing them to the public internet. It manages connections to source and target systems, orchestrating full loads and change data capture (CDC). The gateway onboards source data directly into the target cloud platform, preserving data security. It establishes an outbound connection to Qlik Cloud for command and control, while Qlik Cloud initiates a reverse tunnel for secure communication.

To facilitate near-real-time data capture from on-premises targets without compromising security, the Data Movement gateway employs a robust, secure connection that eliminates the need for open inbound firewall ports. This mechanism safeguards enterprise data from unauthorized access while maintaining seamless data flow.

End-to-end data protection is ensured by employing a unique key pair for authentication and encryption on each Data Movement gateway server. This secure communication, initiated solely via outbound connections, eliminates the need for inbound ports on your corporate network, enhancing overall security posture.

The Data Movement Gateway establishes an outbound connection to Qlik Cloud when it is started. Qlik Cloud then creates a reverse tunnel to the gateway for management and control.

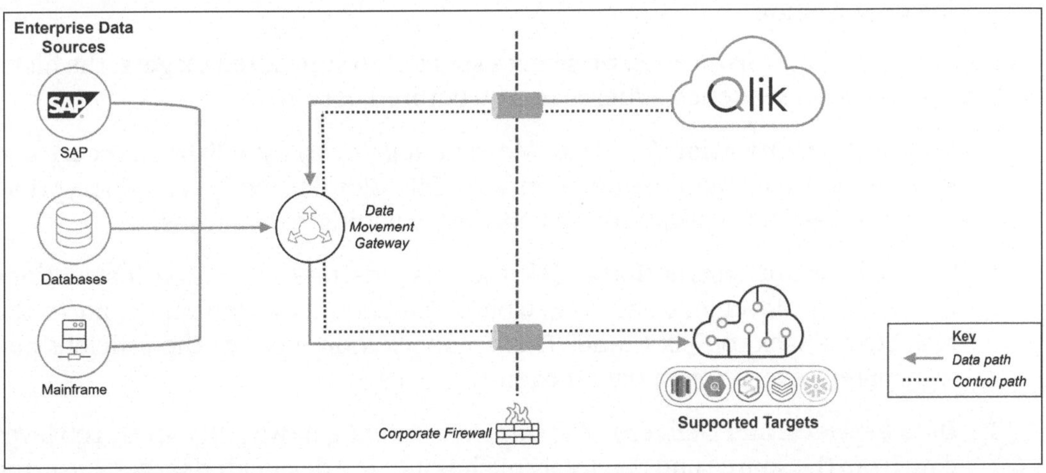

Figure 12.9: *General architecture of the Data Movement Gateway*

The deployment of Data Movement gateways is tailored to specific environments and use cases. If your data sources and targets are relatively close and Qlik Cloud can directly access your target, a single gateway is often adequate. However, in situations where data sources are geographically dispersed, involve large data volumes from multiple sources, or require movement to targets inaccessible from Qlik Cloud, deploying multiple gateways is considered best practice.

For instance, when ingesting data from disparate sources spread across multiple locations, leveraging multiple gateways can optimize data movement efficiency and reduce latency. Similarly, handling large data volumes simultaneously from multiple sources necessitates a distributed approach, with gateways placed closer to each source to minimize network overhead. Finally, for targets that reside in virtual private clouds (VPCs) or other restricted environments, where direct access from Qlik Cloud is limited, setting up gateways near the targets ensures seamless data transfer.

Let's explore the common architectures used for three common scenarios:

- **Moving data from enterprise data sources to supported targets**: This involves extracting data from various enterprise systems, such as CRM, ERP, and data warehouses, and integrating it with supported data destination cloud data platforms.
- **Moving data from SaaS applications to supported targets**: This involves extracting and transforming data from cloud-based applications such as Salesforce and consolidating it with other data sources for analysis and reporting.
- **Moving data from SaaS applications and enterprise data sources to supported targets:** This combines the processes of moving data from both enterprise and SaaS systems, enabling comprehensive data integration and analysis across the organization.

To efficiently move data **from enterprise data sources to supported targets**, the high-level communication sequence adheres to a structured pattern:

1. **Mutual Authentication**: The Data Movement gateway establishes a secure and mutually authenticated connection with Qlik Cloud using HTTPS encryption. This ensures that only authorized entities can initiate data transfer.
2. **Task Execution Instructions**: Qlik Cloud sends task execution instructions to the Data Movement gateway, which diligently monitors and reports the task status back to Qlik Cloud. This feedback loop ensures the efficient and transparent execution of data movement tasks.
3. **Data Retrieval and Delivery**: The Data Movement gateway efficiently retrieves data from the source and flawlessly pushes it to the designated target, ensuring seamless data transfer without compromising data integrity or security.

This standardized communication sequence enables the gateway to move data securely and efficiently from their on-premises systems to cloud-based targets, facilitating data-driven insights and decision-making.

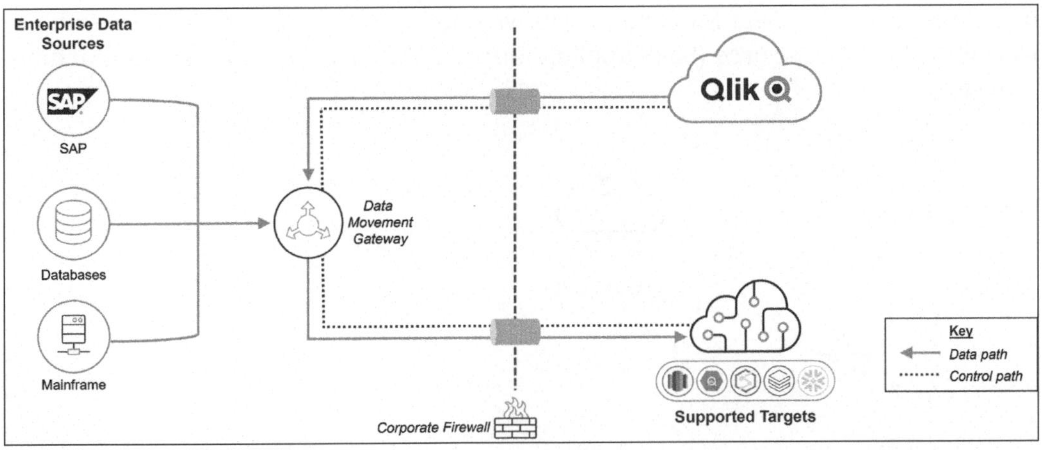

Figure 12.10: *Gateway architecture when moving from enterprise data sources to cloud targets*

The architecture diagram depicts a gateway installed within the corporate firewall that can access change logs from various enterprise sources and deliver the updated data to supported targets beyond the firewall. The Qlik Cloud serves as a control center, allowing for the management of data movement and the setting of various data loading parameters. The Qlik Cloud provides a centralized platform for managing the data movement process. It allows users to monitor the data flow, schedule data transfers, and configure data loading parameters.

In the next chapter, we will dive into the specific data loading parameters that can be set using the Qlik Cloud. These parameters control how data is extracted.

Efficiently transferring data from **SaaS applications to supported targets** involves a secure and streamlined communication sequence:

1. **Authentication and Connection**: The Data Movement gateway initiates a secure HTTPS connection with Qlik Cloud, verifying their identities and establishing a trusted channel.
2. **Task Execution Instructions**: Qlik Cloud conveys the execution instructions for the data landing task to the Data Movement gateway, which diligently monitors and reports the task's progress back to Qlik Cloud for real-time visibility.
3. **Data Retrieval**: When the landing task commences, Qlik Cloud retrieves the desired data from the corresponding SaaS application, ensuring data integrity and accuracy. The data is then securely stored in Qlik Cloud's designated repository.
4. **Data Delivery**: The Data Movement gateway fetches the extracted data from Qlik Cloud's secure storage and seamlessly pushes it to the specified target destination, enabling its integration and analysis.

In this scenario, the Data Movement gateway does not require installation behind a firewall, as both the source (SaaS application) and the target are not located behind a firewall.

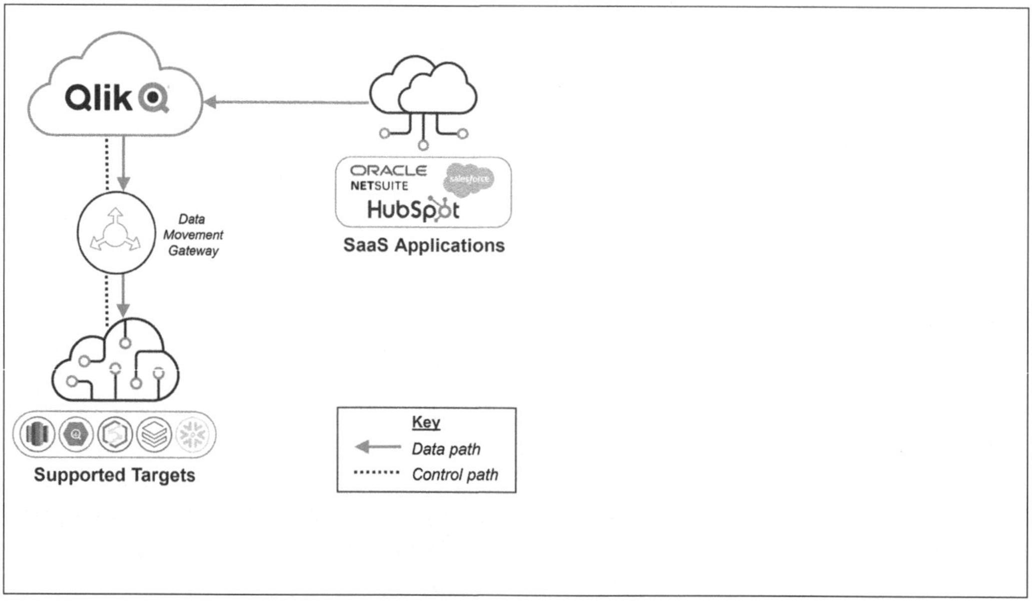

Figure 12.11: *Gateway architecture when moving from SaaS Applications to supported targets*

In this case, the Data Movement gateway does not need to be installed behind the firewall because both the source (SaaS application) and the target are not located behind a firewall. This simplifies the deployment process, if both the source and the target are not located behind a firewall, then the Data Movement gateway can be installed in a more accessible location. In this example, the Data Movement gateway is installed on a public cloud server. This allows it to access both the SaaS application, which is also hosted on a public cloud, and the target. The Data Movement gateway can then transfer data between the source and the target without having to go through any firewalls.

In the scenario where we are moving data from both **SaaS applications and enterprise data sources** to supported targets, two distinct Data Movement gateways are deployed on separate machines–one dedicated to the enterprise data source and the other managing the SaaS application. The Data Movement gateway overseeing the SaaS application doesn't need installation behind a firewall, given the absence of a firewall-protected environment for either the source (SaaS application) or the target.

The overall communication sequence seamlessly integrates elements from both the enterprise data sources to supported targets and SaaS applications to supported targets' use cases.

The Data Movement gateway responsible for the SaaS application establishes a secure and mutually authenticated connection with Qlik Cloud using HTTPS. Once initiated, Qlik Cloud dispatches landing task execution instructions to the Data Movement gateway, which promptly relays task status updates back to Qlik Cloud. Subsequently, the Data Movement gateway retrieves the SaaS application data from Qlik Cloud and delivers it to the designated target. This process ensures efficient data movement and consolidation, empowering users to derive valuable insights from a centralized repository.

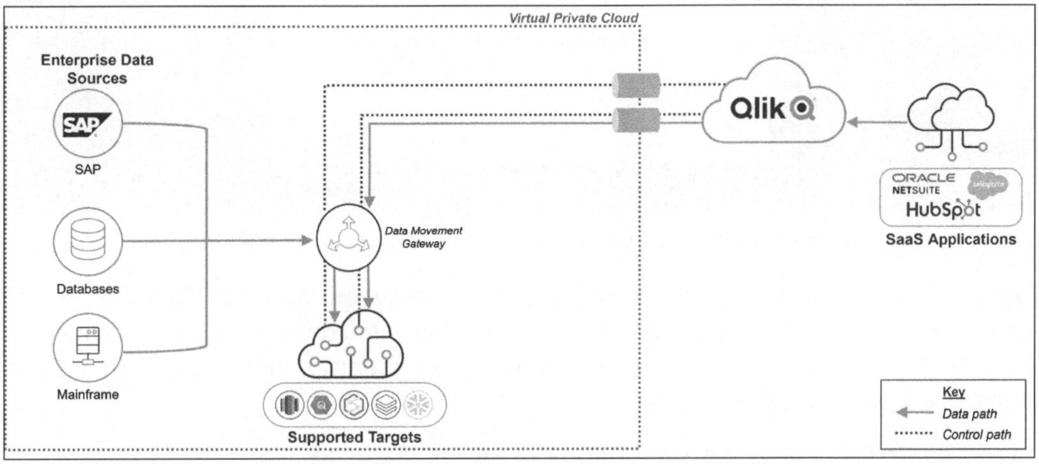

Figure 12.12: *Gateway architecture when moving from enterprise data sources and SaaS Applications to supported targets*

Gateway Installation

Navigate to the **`Data Gateways`** tab in the Management Console to gain insights into the data gateways managed within your Qlik Cloud environment. This tab provides comprehensive information about each gateway, including its name, type, description, data gateway ID, status, space, and date created.

The installation of the data movement gateway is a straightforward process, consisting of five stages that can swiftly have us up and running with the gateway installed and ready. The following are the stages:

Stage One: Download the Data Movement Gateway

In the Management Console, select Data Gateways. Click the **`Deploy`** toolbar button. The Deploy data gateway dialog opens. Select the **`Data Gateway - Data Movement`** option, accept the Qlik Customer Agreement, and click **`Download`**. The Data Movement gateway RPM will be downloaded to your machine.

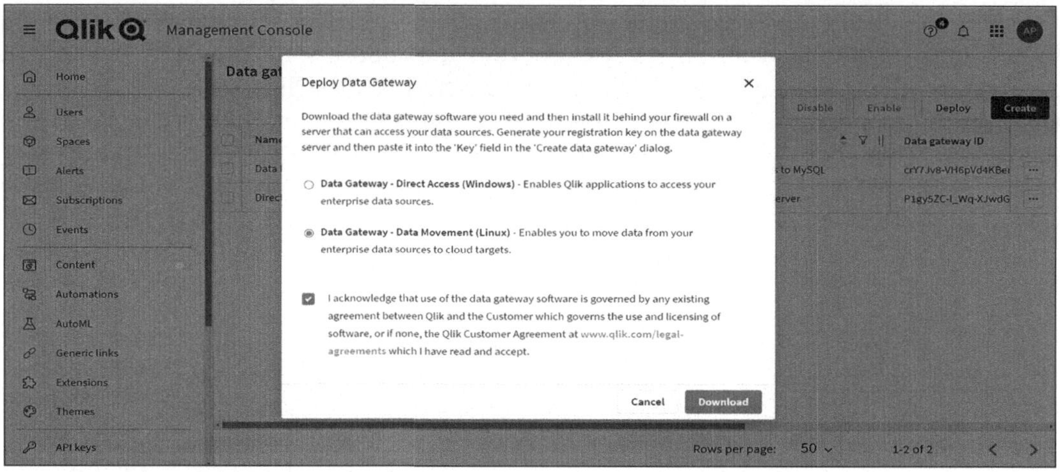

Figure 12.13: *Downloading the gateway RPM file from the QMC*

Note: *This section of the book explains the data movement gateway, which is not the same as the direct access gateway. The direct access gateway is discussed in the earlier chapters. You can learn more about the direct access gateway, its uses, deployment, and use cases on page 248 of this book.*

Stage Two: Install and Set up the Data Movement Gateway

In this stage, the installation of the Data Movement gateway involves setting the Qlik Cloud URL and generating a registration key. This key is crucial for establishing an authenticated connection between the Data Movement gateway and the Qlik Cloud tenant. After downloading the RPM file, it needs to be copied to a designated Linux machine, ensuring it is behind the firewall and can communicate with both data sources and Qlik Cloud.

To install the gateway, use the following command:

```
sudo QLIK_CUSTOMER_AGREEMENT_ACCEPT=yes rpm -i qlik-data-gate-
way-data-movement.rpm
```

After the installation is complete, navigate to the bin folder:

```
cd /opt/qlik/gateway/movement/bin
```

In the bin folder, enter the name of your tenant:

```
./agentctl qcs set_config --tenant_url yourtenant.qlikcloud.com
```

If the configuration is successful, you will see this message:

ReplicateAgent Control Program completed Successfully.

To get the registration keys, use this command:

```
./agentctl qcs get_registration
```

Stage Three: Return to the Management Console and Register the Data Movement Gateway

In this stage, navigate to the **`Management Console`**, specifically the **`Data Gateways`** section. Click **`"Create"`**, and proceed to input the necessary details for generating a Data Movement gateway. Paste the registration key, click **`"Create"`**, and seamlessly integrate the gateway into the Data Gateways list for efficient Qlik environment management.

Figure 12.14: *Registering the Data Gateway*

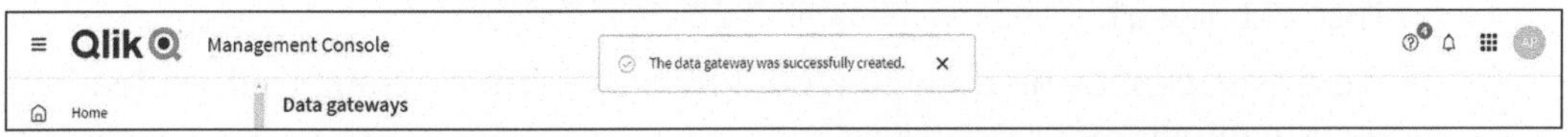

Figure 12.15: *Success message on Data Gateway Creation*

Stage Four: Start the Data Movement Gateway Service on the Server

Now that the setup is finalized, proceed to initiate the gateway and verify its status to ensure it is running smoothly. Upon starting the gateway service, remember to refresh your browser to observe the updated data gateway status (Connected) in the Management Console.

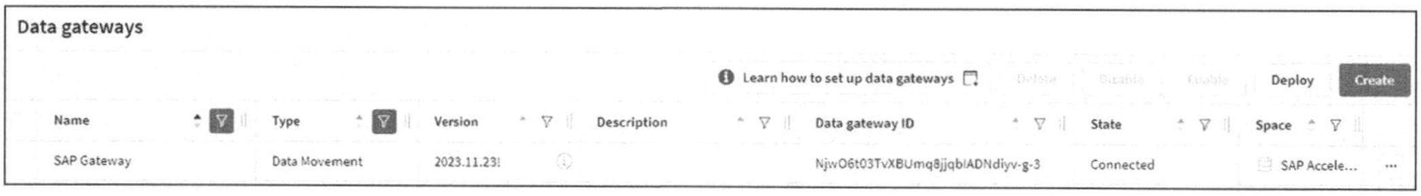

Figure 12.16: *Gateway with the status "Connected" in the Management Console*

Stage Five: Utilize Data Movement Gateway Data Sources in your Data Projects

Ensure the Data Gateways list in the Management Console is current by refreshing your browser. Confirm in the Data Gateways list that your gateway is marked as **`"Connected"`**. Once this status is verified, you can proceed to utilize the Data Movement gateway to access your data sources and supported targets.

With the completion of the installation process, the next crucial step involves installing the drivers essential for your data source and target platform. A database driver, acting as an intermediary between an application and a specific database management system (DBMS), serves as a translator, converting application requests into commands the database understands. This standardized interface enables applications to connect and interact with various databases, irrespective of the specific DBMS in use.

The selection of drivers depends on your data source and target platform. In certain cases, installing these drivers on a strategically deployed Data Movement gateway near your source or target is necessary. To simplify the installation process, it is recommended to use the driver installation utility, which automates downloading, installing, and configuring the required driver, eliminating the need for manual steps. The utility also provides scripts for easy updating and uninstalling of the driver as needed.

For example: To install the MySQL driver, follow these steps:

1. Change the working directory to

   `opt/qlik/gateway/movement/drivers/bin`

2. Run

   `./install mysql`

3. If the driver cannot be downloaded, follow the instructions to download and copy it manually

4. Accept or reject the EULA by typing **`"y"`** or **`"n"`**

   The driver will be installed

This straightforward process ensures seamless driver installation, enabling you to connect to your chosen data source and leverage the Data Movement gateway effectively.

Monitoring the Gateway

To stay informed about critical changes in the data gateway's operation, you can configure notifications to receive timely alerts via browser notifications, email, or push messages to Qlik Sense Mobile SaaS.

To set up these notifications, select the **"Notifications"** option for the desired data gateway and choose which events trigger alerts, such as changes in the data gateway state, version requirements, or forced deactivation by Qlik. By leveraging these notifications effectively, we can enhance the overall performance, reliability, and compliance of your data integration initiatives.

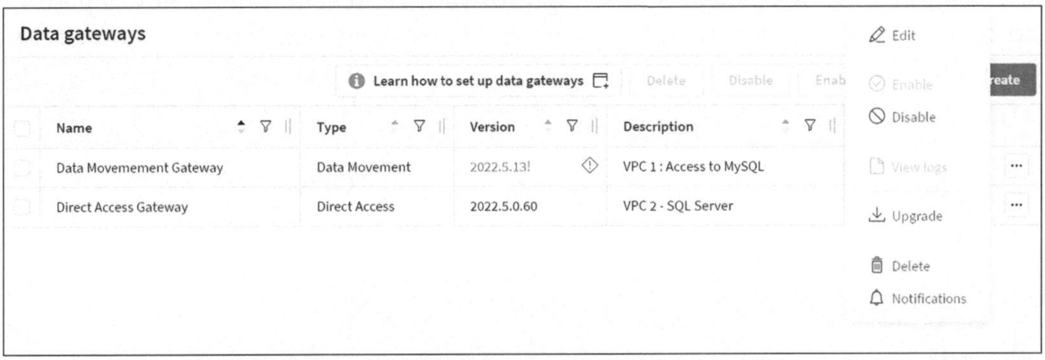

***Figure 12.17:** Setting up notification for a gateway*

***Figure 12.18:** Managing notification for a gateway*

Now that we have seen what a gateway is, what it does, and where to get it - in the next chapters, let us go through in detail each of the components.

Sample Data Pipeline

In the sample image illustrating a pipeline, you can observe various onboarding assets along with their statuses. For example, the status of the onboarding gateway asset is currently marked as **"stopped"**, indicating that the gateway has been disconnected. This disconnection implies that data onboarding and change data capture cannot proceed.

The pipeline view also includes the landing asset, where you can monitor its status, and the storage asset, where you can see the frequency of its operations. Additionally, the pipeline contains a transformation asset and a data mart asset. It is important to note that multiple transformation and data mart assets can be present within a pipeline.

This example provides a clear and straightforward representation of how a gateway and other assets function within a pipeline, showcasing their current statuses and operational details.

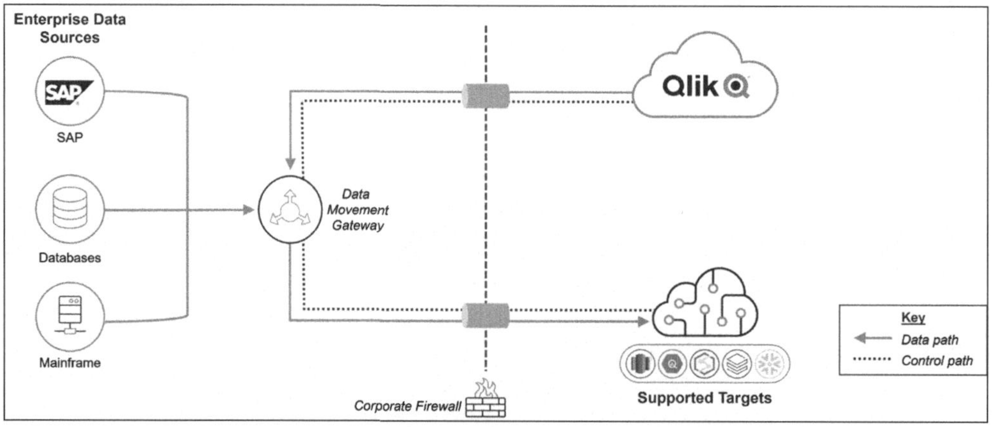

Figure 12.19: *Sample Data Pipeline*

Conclusion

We have learned about the Qlik Talend Data Integration solution, which is a powerful tool that enables you to connect, transform, and stream data from various sources to the cloud. This solution helps you solve the problem of data silos and data quality issues, by providing a unified and reliable data platform. By using this solution, you can benefit from faster data delivery, lower costs, higher scalability, and better security.

In the next chapters, we will dive into each of the asset types – landing, staging, transformation, and data mart and understand in detail the working of these assets.

Points to Remember

- Qlik Talend Data Integration is a data integration fabric that delivers, transforms, and unifies enterprise data in real time via automated, governed, and reusable data pipelines.
- Qlik Talend Data Integration supports real-time data movement from on-premises or cloud sources to Qlik Cloud and other leading cloud data platforms, using CDC (Change Data Capture) or batch technologies.
- Qlik Talend Data Integration enables data transformation with a no-code interface that creates consumption-ready data sets based on rules and custom SQL.
- The data movement gateway is part of the data integration offering, while the direct access gateway is part of the data analytics offering.
- The data movement gateway is used to move data from on-premises or cloud sources to cloud data warehouses or data lakes, while the direct access gateway is used to fetch data from on-premises sources and load it into a Qlik Sense app.
- The data movement gateway can replicate data in real-time and catalog data sets without manual scripting, while the direct access gateway can connect directly to data sources and load data from there.
- The data movement gateway requires a subscription to the data integration product, while the direct access gateway is included in the Qlik Cloud Services subscription.

Multiple Choice Questions

1. Which of the following statements is true about the data movement gateway and the direct access gateway?
   a. The data movement gateway is used to fetch data from on-premises sources and load it into a Qlik Sense app, while the direct access gateway is used to move data from on-premises or cloud sources to cloud data warehouses or data lakes.
   b. The data movement gateway enables data transformation with a no-code interface that creates consumption-ready data sets based on rules and custom SQL, while the direct access gateway does not support data transformation.
   c. The data movement gateway is part of the data analytics offering, while the direct access gateway is part of the data integration offering.

    d. The data movement gateway requires a subscription to the data integration product, while the direct access gateway is included in the Qlik Cloud Services subscription.

2. What is the main benefit of using the Data Movement gateway for accessing on-premises and private cloud data sources?
    a. It makes the data sources faster and more reliable
    b. It transforms the data sources into different formats
    c. It protects the data sources from unauthorized access
    d. It connects the data sources to different cloud platforms
3. What is one scenario where multiple Data Movement gateways are recommended?
    a. Moving data from data sources that are close to each other
    b. Moving data to a target that is directly accessible from Qlik Cloud
    c. Moving data to a target that is inaccessible from Qlik Cloud
    d. Moving data from data sources that are updated frequently
4. What are data spaces used for in Qlik Talend Data Integration?
    a. To create and store data projects and data connections
    b. To define the data platform and the output format
    c. To perform data transformations and create data marts
    d. To schedule data tasks and monitor data pipelines

Answers

1. d
2. c
3. c
4. a

References

1. *Qlik Help*: https://help.qlik.com/

CHAPTER 13

CDC and Landing Data in Real Time

Introduction

This chapter delves into the intricacies of Change Data Capture (CDC), shedding light on its ability to expedite data transfer from on-premises environments while minimizing the strain on the underlying database. We'll delve into the diverse application scenarios for Qlik pipelines and comprehensive data pipelines.

Structure

In this chapter, we will discuss the following topics:

- Change Data Capture
- History of Change Data Capture
- CDC in Qlik Talend Cloud
- Landing Asset
- Storage Asset
- Scheduling the Storage Asset
- Live View
- History View

Change Data Capture

Before we embark on understanding Qlik Talend Data Integration change data capture (CDC) mechanism, let's delve into the fundamentals of CDC, its purpose, and why we don't resort to straightforward select statements or even enhanced select statements with timestamps, to replicate data.

- **Inefficiency and Resource Consumption:**

  Continuously querying source tables to extract updated data for replication is an inefficient approach, especially for large tables or complex queries. It involves significant data fetches and index exploration, placing a strain on database resources. This can lead to performance bottlenecks, increased latency, and higher operational costs.

- **Data Inconsistency and Lag:**

  Relying on select statements for replication can result in data inconsistencies and lag due to the reliance on transaction isolation levels and commit frequencies. These factors determine when changes are visible to other applications, potentially leading to discrepancies between source and target tables. Additionally, the frequency of select statements can introduce delays in capturing the latest data changes, compromising data freshness.

- **Locking and Contention Issues:**

  Constantly polling source tables for updates can introduce locking and contention issues, affecting the performance and availability of other applications. This can hinder data processing and overall application responsiveness.

- **Missing or Duplicate Data:**

  The absence or inaccuracy of timestamps in the source table can lead to data loss or duplication. Without timestamps, it becomes challenging to identify and capture the most recent changes, potentially resulting in the replication of outdated or duplicate data.

- **Inadequate Timestamp Coverage:**

  Timestamp columns may not capture all the changes such as deletes or updates on the same row within a short time frame. This can lead to inconsistencies in the replicated data, as the absence of timestamps may not reflect the complete history of changes.

These limitations make continuous select statements an inadequate approach for efficient and reliable data replication. To overcome these challenges, CDC techniques are employed to capture and replicate only the changes made to the source data, ensuring data consistency, freshness, and minimal resource consumption.

To consider an alternative perspective, let's examine the key features that a CDC solution offers:

- **Reduced Network Load and Source System Impact:**

  CDC eliminates the need for full table scans or index exploration, minimizing network traffic and minimizing the load on the source system. It only transfers the actual changes made to the data, significantly reducing the data volume and network bandwidth utilization.

- **Real-time or Near-real-time Data Synchronization:**

  CDC enables efficient data synchronization between source and target systems in real-time or near-real-time, ensuring data consistency and freshness. This facilitates real-time analytics and data-driven decision-making across disparate data systems.

- **Support for Modern Data Architectures and Platforms:**

  CDC seamlessly integrates with modern cloud-based data architectures, including data lakes, data warehouses, and data lake houses. It provides efficient and scalable ingestion and movement of data across these platforms, enabling large-scale data processing and analysis.

These advantages make CDC a superior approach for data replication compared to continuous select statements. It ensures efficient data transfer, real-time data availability, and seamless integration with modern data architectures, enabling organizations to harness the power of data for meaningful insights and actionable decisions.

History of CDC

The concept of data replication has its roots in the early days of database systems, where data was primarily stored in flat files or hierarchical databases. Synchronizing data between these disparate systems was a laborious task that often involved custom programming to compare source and target data, manually applying any discrepancies. This manual approach was error-prone, time-consuming, and inefficient, causing significant downtime and network strain.

The advent of relational database systems in the 1970s and 1980s revolutionized data synchronization with the introduction of transaction logs. These logs meticulously tracked all data changes sequentially, enabling CDC (Change Data Capture) solutions to extract and deliver only the specific changes to target systems. This approach significantly reduced network traffic and minimized the impact on source systems, facilitating near-real-time data synchronization.

As data warehousing and business intelligence gained prominence in the 1990s and 2000s, CDC solutions evolved to become more sophisticated and customizable. Users could now filter, transform, and enrich the change data to suit their specific business needs. CDC expanded its support for diverse data formats, including XML, JSON, cloud platforms, and big data ecosystems. These enhanced capabilities enabled real-time analytics and data science, providing fresh and accurate data for business insights and decision-making.

Today, CDC has matured into a widely adopted and indispensable technology for modern data architectures and applications. CDC seamlessly integrates with other technologies, such as streaming platforms, data pipelines, and data lake houses, to facilitate efficient and scalable data ingestion and movement. This integration has made CDC a cornerstone of data-driven organizations, empowering them to harness their data assets and gain a competitive edge.

Change Data Capture in Qlik Talend Data Integration

In the previous chapter, we completed the installation and setup of the Qlik Sense Gateway, including downloading, installing, configuring, and exchanging key pairs. We also created a data space and installed the appropriate driver. Now, we are ready to initiate the data movement process. For our first example, we will move data from an on-premises MySQL source to a target platform - Snowflake, in this case. However, Qlik Sense's multi-platform capabilities enable data movement to various target destinations.

Let us first start with creating a database which will be our target database; to do this, we navigate to our target platform (snowflake) and create a database using the command:

```
CREATE DATABASE QCDI_MySQL_Sales;
```

Creating the Data Project

Once the database is created, we have our destination ready, and we can get started by creating a project in the data space.

We will select the space that was created in the previous chapter and navigate to the **+Add New** Icon.

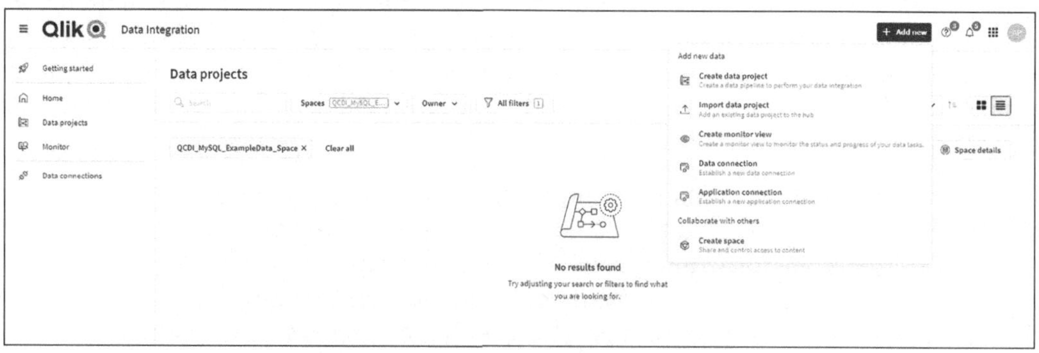

Figure 13.1: *Creating a new data project*

Next, we'll proceed to configure the project details, including its name, description, and the chosen data platform – in this case, Snowflake. It's crucial to note that the selected data platform cannot be altered after the project is created. While we can transfer a project from a development Qlik SaaS Tenant to a production SaaS Tenant and modify connection names, migrating a project initially built on Snowflake to another platform, such as Redshift, is not possible. For such scenarios, a new project would need to be constructed from scratch in the target data platform.

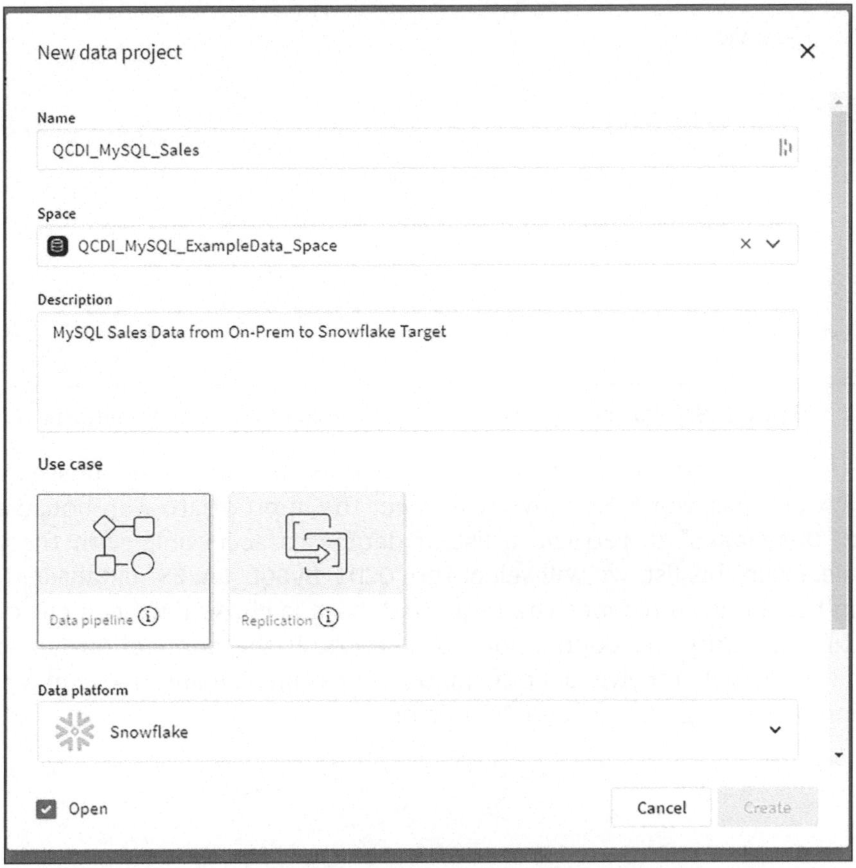

Figure 13.2: *Creating a new data project*

Use Case:

Data Pipeline

In this use case, we build data pipelines around a single platform, using this we can perform all our data integration within a data project using data task. This involves on-boarding, transforming, creating, and managing the data marts.

Replication

In this use case, we build point-to-point replication tasks. Data replication automates the movement of data between sources and targets, ensuring data availability, improving performance, and enhancing consistency. Two main use cases include replicating data to any supported system and landing data in a data lake for analysis.

We will now need to create a connection to our target platform; we will select the option **`Create new`**.

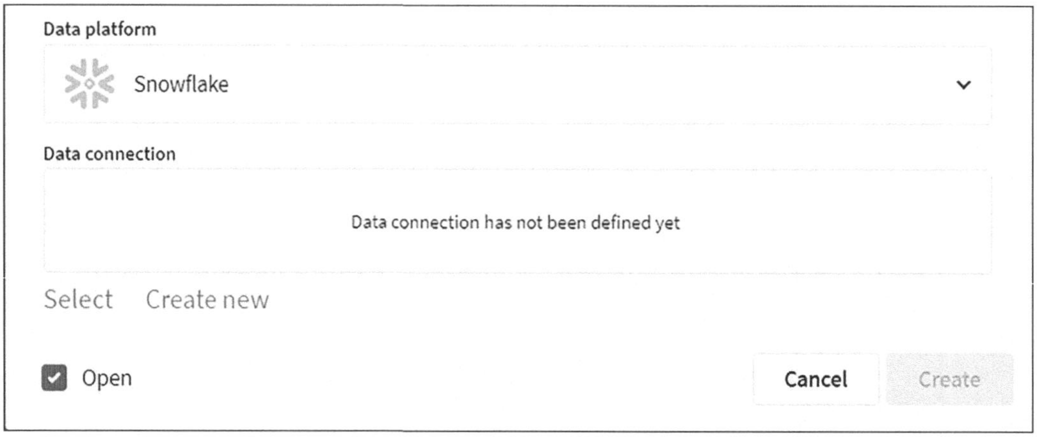

***Figure 13.3**: Creating a new database connection to the target platform*

We will then proceed to enter the server details, including the hostname, login credentials, and password. Next, we will select the appropriate warehouse and click on "**`Load Databases`**" to retrieve a list of databases accessible with the provided credentials. From this list, we will select the "**`QCDI_MySQL_SALES`**" database, which we created in the initial step. Once the target database is chosen, we can click on "**`Test Connection`**" to verify the connection parameters. If the connection is established successfully, we will receive a confirmation message. Finally, we can create the connection by clicking on the "**`CREATE`**" button.

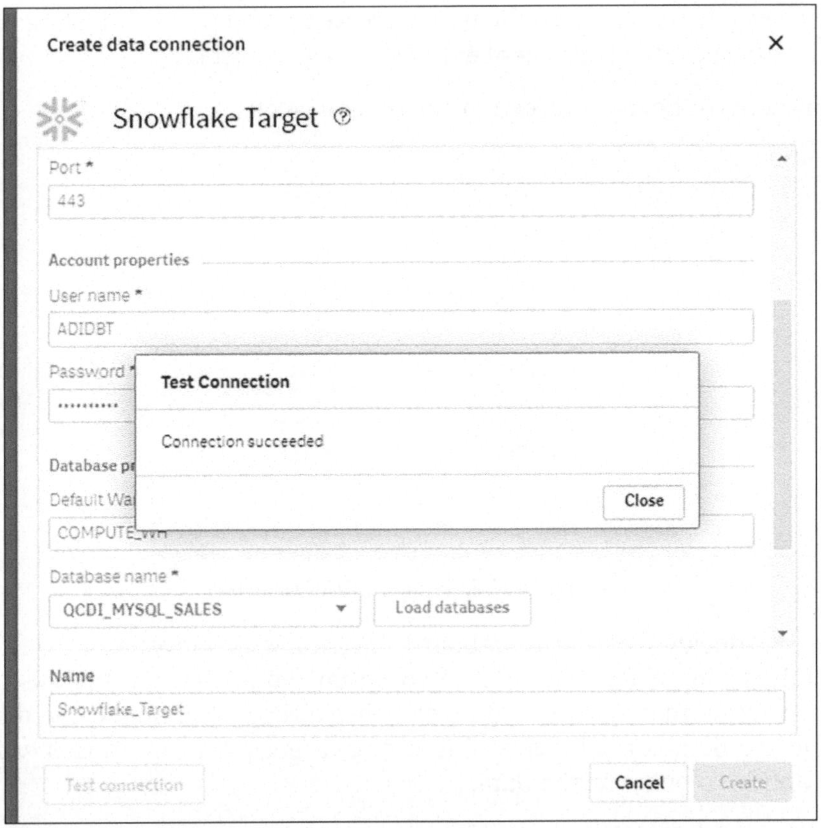

Figure 13.4: *Testing the connection parameters and creating the connection*

Once the connection has been created, we can see the connection details in the main project window under data connection.

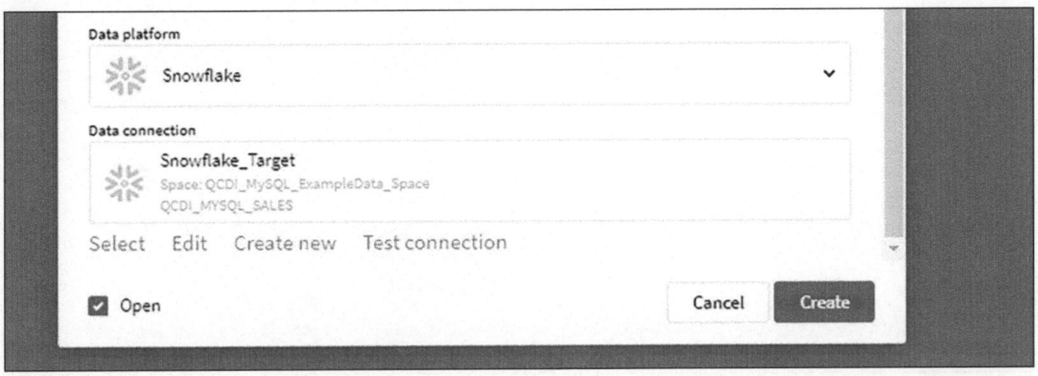

Figure 13.5: *Target data connection created*

Now that we've completed the initial project configuration, we can proceed to finalize the creation process by clicking on the "**Create**" button. The "**Open**" checkbox situated on the left side determines whether we remain on the same screen after project creation or navigate directly into the newly created project. In this instance, let's keep the checkbox ticked and click "**Create**" to set up the project.

We are now sent to the main screen of the data project:

Figure 13.6: *Project initial screen*

In this step, we decide whether to onboard the data, which involves retrieving it from an on-premises source and storing it in an optimized format for analysis or register the data, indicating that another data loader has already completed the data landing process and the data is readily available in the target platform. In this case, we will select the option to onboard the data.

Pick a suitable name and description for the on-boarding asset.

Figure 13.7: *Initial screen of creating an onboarding asset*

To establish a connection to the on-premises data source, we'll utilize the gateway.

Note that we must choose the same data space where the gateway was initially installed.

Figure 13.8: *Create a connection to the on-prem data source*

As illustrated in the following diagram, there is an extensive and impressive array of connectors available. These connectors, widely used by enterprises globally, can be integrated effortlessly by default.

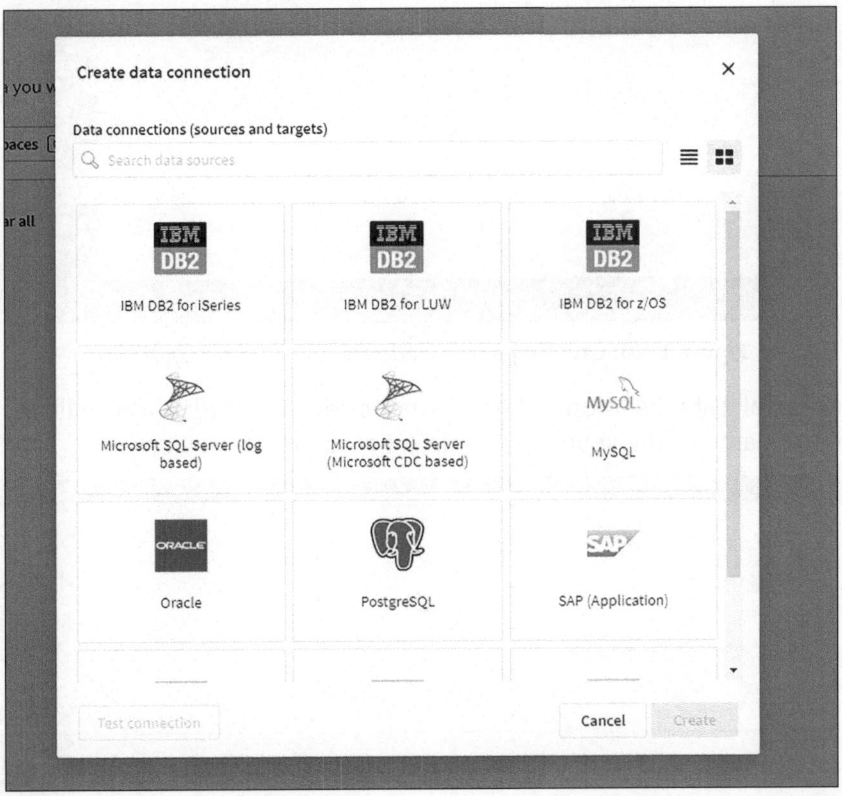

Figure 13.9: *Select the data source (in this case we select the MySQL Data Source). As we scroll down, we can see the list of available sources*

We will choose the data movement gateway with access to the MySQL data source, providing additional details, such as the username and password. After entering all the necessary information, we will initiate a test connection, akin to the process used for validating the connection to the target platform. Upon successful validation, we will proceed to select the **`'Create'`** option.

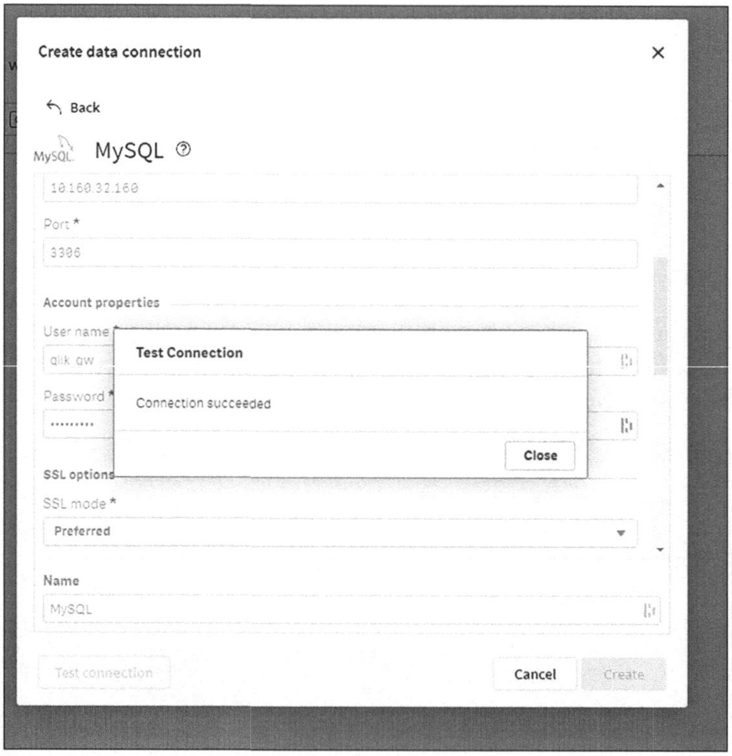

Figure 13.10: *Creating a connection to the on-prem gateway*

Upon successful establishment of the connection, a notification will be received, indicating the name of the space in which the connection was created.

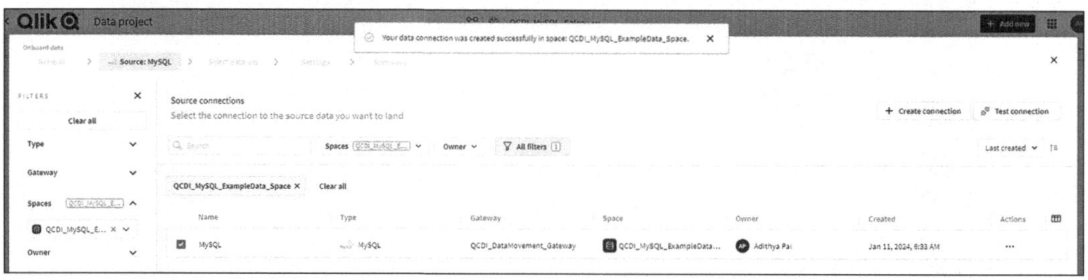

Figure 13.11: *Success message on creation*

Having successfully established connections to both the source and target, the subsequent step involves specifying the exact data from the source that needs to be loaded. We will proceed to select the source tables, schemas, and views that are intended for loading.

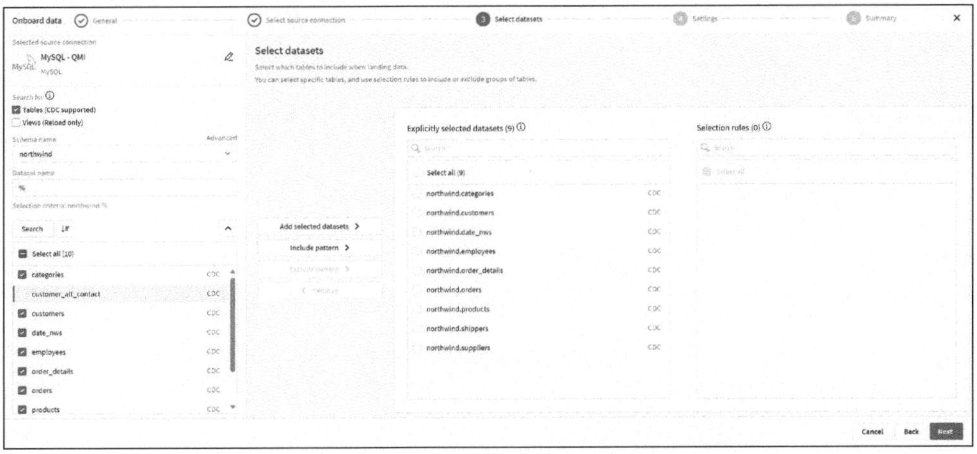

Figure 13.12: *Selection of the schemas to be loaded*

In this scenario, our selection will include all the tables within the Sales schema. Nonetheless, there exists the flexibility to selectively include all tables/views from the Sales schema while excluding one or more specified tables/views. Alternatively, exclusions can be made at the schema level, allowing for the replication of the entire endpoint with exceptions for specific tables/views. The utilization of the "_" wildcard character is also an option, facilitating the matching of a single character as needed.

Once we have selected the desired tables, we select the **`Next`.**

In the **`Settings`** section, the update method can be determined. The onboarding process commences with a full load, and there are two options available to define the post-full load behavior:

- **CDC Mode**: Utilizing Change Data Capture (CDC) technology, this mode ensures that the landed data remains synchronized with the source data after the initial full load. While notably faster and more efficient, it's important to note that CDC mode may not be supported by all data sources.
- **Reload and Compare Mode**: In this mode, a complete reload of the source data is performed each time the data task runs. Although slower and more resource-intensive, this mode is compatible with any data source.

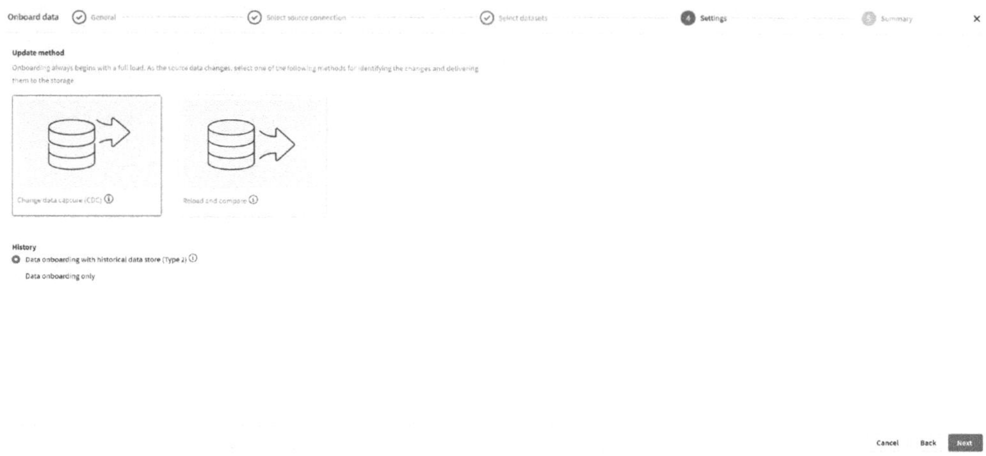

***Figure 13.13**: Configuring the settings of the Project*

Within the Settings section, there is also an option to select the history mode:

- **History Type 2**

This mode involves replicating data while preserving the historical changes in the source data. It introduces two additional columns to the target table: a start date and an end date. These columns indicate the validity period of each record. When a record is updated or deleted in the source, a new record is inserted in the target with the current date as the start date, while the previous record is updated with the current date as the end date. This method ensures that the target table maintains a comprehensive history of all changes in the source data.

Following are some use cases when we might want to consider having type 2 history enabled:

- We want to preserve the history of changes in the source data, such as customer information, product prices, or inventory levels.
- We want to perform trend analysis or time-based analysis on the historical data, such as sales performance, customer behavior, or product demand.
- We want to audit the data quality or integrity of the source data, such as detecting data anomalies, errors, or inconsistencies.
- We want to create a full historical data store (HDS) that can be used to create analytic data marts or applications.

Data Replication Only

In this mode, data replication occurs without preserving the historical changes in the source data. It simply copies the current state of the source data to the target, without introducing any additional columns. Any updates or deletions made to a record in the source are mirrored in the target, allowing the target table to reflect the latest state of the source data.

On the settings summary screen, we have the option to modify the names and descriptions of the landing and storage assets. Additionally, we can choose the action to take once the pipeline is created; by default, it's set to `'do nothing'` but we can opt to have it open the landing and storage asset directly. We maintain the default 'do nothing' option, click on `'create'` and Qlik Talend Data Integration will generate the pipeline with the landing and storage assets accordingly.

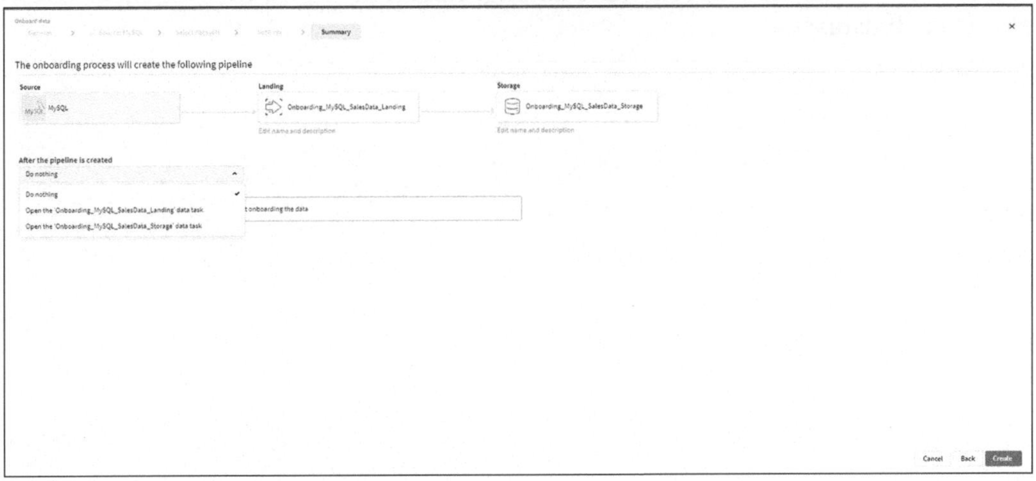

***Figure 13.14:** Summary view of the project creation*

Setting up the Onboarding Assets in the Data Project

After completing the project setup, we transition to a screen displaying the landing and storage assets ready for configuration and preparation. At this stage, these assets are preliminary and only exist within Qlik. Subsequently, we will delve into each asset, comprehend its structure, and proceed to set up and prepare them. When preparing a data asset in Qlik, the system will automatically generate the corresponding assets in the target platform, including the necessary tables and views.

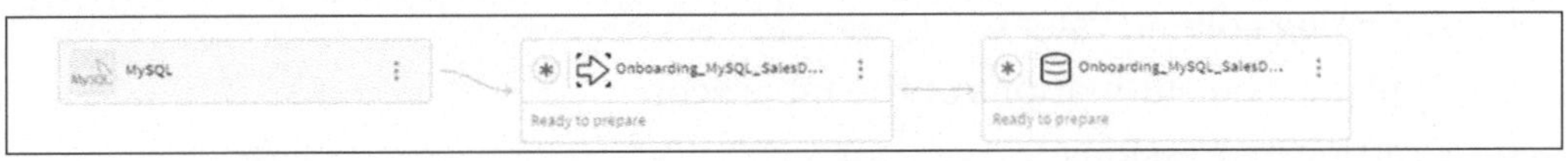

***Figure 13.15:** Landing and storage assets upon project creation*

Landing Asset

The first step in bringing in data during onboarding is the landing process. This means consistently moving data from the on-premises source to a designated landing area.

We have the flexibility to land data from various sources by utilizing source connections. The landing area is determined when setting up the data project.

For Qlik Cloud (via Amazon S3), landing data allows us to create QVD tables that are prepped for analysis in Qlik Cloud.

If we land data in a cloud data warehouse like Snowflake or Azure Synapse Analytics, you can store tables directly in the same cloud data warehouse.

Once the project is set up, we create the landing and storage assets based on our earlier choices. Now, let's set up the landing asset. Just click on the three dots icon, choose "**open**", and you'll be taken to the landing asset configuration screen. Here, on the left, you'll see all the datasets we're adding, and on the right, you can check out the fields in each dataset.

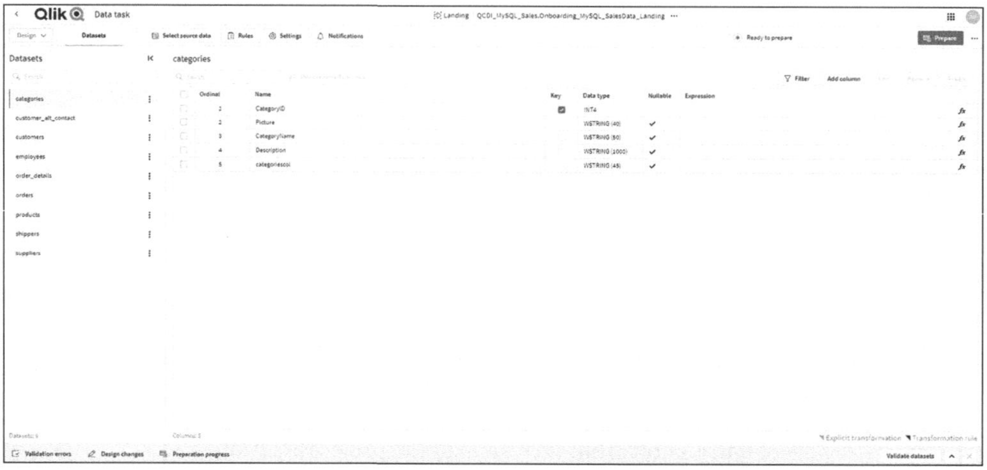

Figure 13.16: *Design view of the landing data asset*

We have the flexibility to perform various actions on fields, such as making selections, adding or removing columns, and implementing straightforward transformations. While more intricate transformations requiring custom SQL will be covered in the next chapter with the introduction of the transformation asset, it's worth noting that even in our current assets, we can execute simpler transformations. These include:

Row-level transformations:

- Adjusting column values
- Applying transformations at the table scope
- Crafting expressions

Moreover, we can also carry out metadata transformations involving:

- Dataset names
- Dataset keys
- Column names
- Column data types
- Column nullability

In the data set we have, we do not need a specific column – we navigate to the employee's data set and select the column we do not need – in this case, it is the Notes column. We will then navigate to the top right where we will select the option **Remove** which will exclude the column.

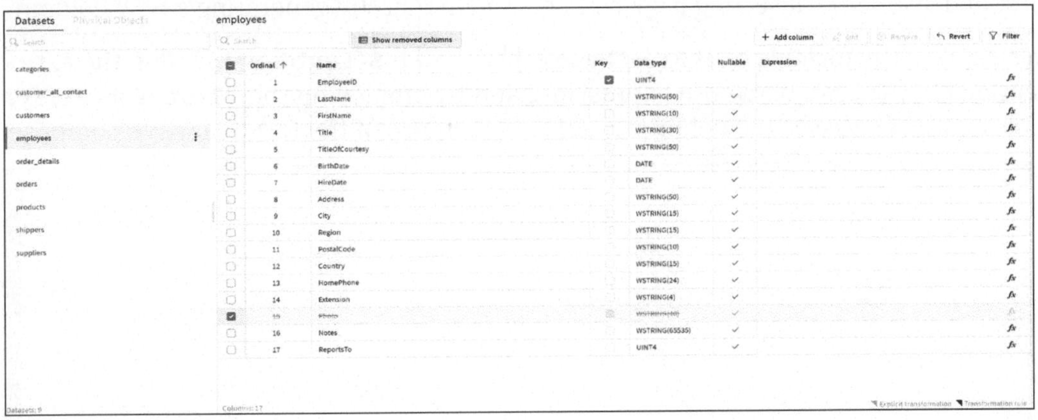

***Figure 13.17**: Removing an unwanted column from the landing asset using the Remove option*

Likewise, we can display the columns that were removed, make edits to existing columns, and revert any changes made to a column. Now, let's delve into the process of adding a new column and incorporating basic SQL logic to populate data into this freshly created column.

To add a new column, we choose the "**Add Column**" option. In the pop-up window, we specify the name of the new column, select the desired data type, and set the length, in this case defined as 50. Once these parameters for the new column are configured, we click "**OK**" resulting in the successful creation of the new column. Subsequently, we proceed to introduce the logic that will populate data into this freshly added column.

***Figure 13.18**: Adding a new column*

Next, we click on the "**Fx**" option, which navigates us to a screen where we can articulate the formulas for the column. In this instance, we'll simply concatenate the first and last name, inserting a space in between, thereby generating a new column.

We express the formula as **`${FirstName} || ' ' || ${LastName}.`** Using the extract parameters, we can parse the expression, and by employing the "**`Test Expression`**" option, we can assess the coherence and correctness of the formula we've composed.

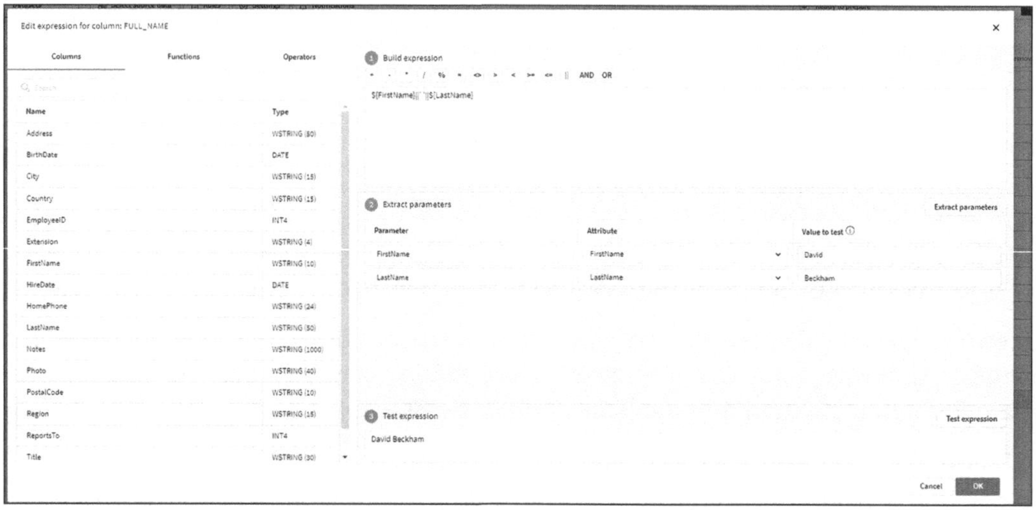

Figure 13.19: *Creating a new field*

Furthermore, there is an option to explore various functions and operators. These functions fall into five distinct categories. By opening each category, we can gain insights into the specific functionalities that each set of functions offers.

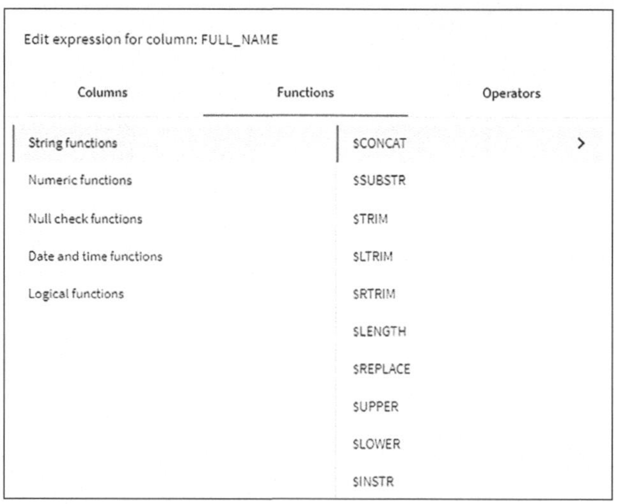

Figure 13.20: *Function categories and list of functions available in Qlik Talend Data Integration landing asset*

Similarly, we can investigate the diverse mathematical and logical operators available. These operations represent the supported mathematical and logical functionalities within the landing asset.

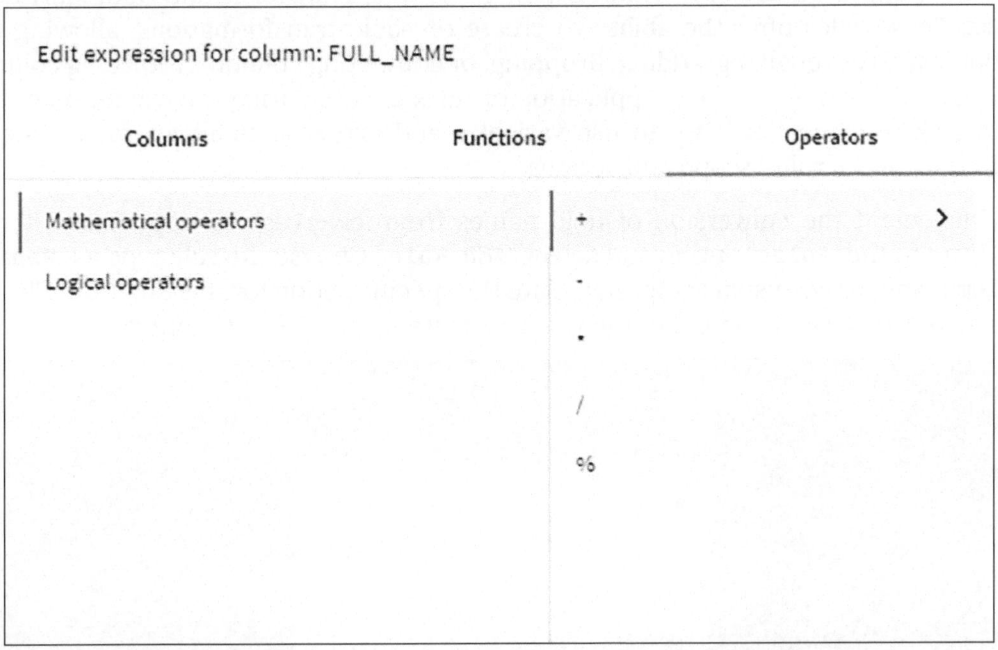

Figure 13.21: *Operators available in the Qlik Talend Data Integration landing asset*

After successfully creating the column, defining its logic, testing it, and saving the changes, we can observe the logic associated with the newly created column displayed on the main screen. On this interface, the expression we formulated for the **"FULL_NAME"** column is visible and can be modified if necessary. This provides a user-friendly way to review and adjust the logic as needed.

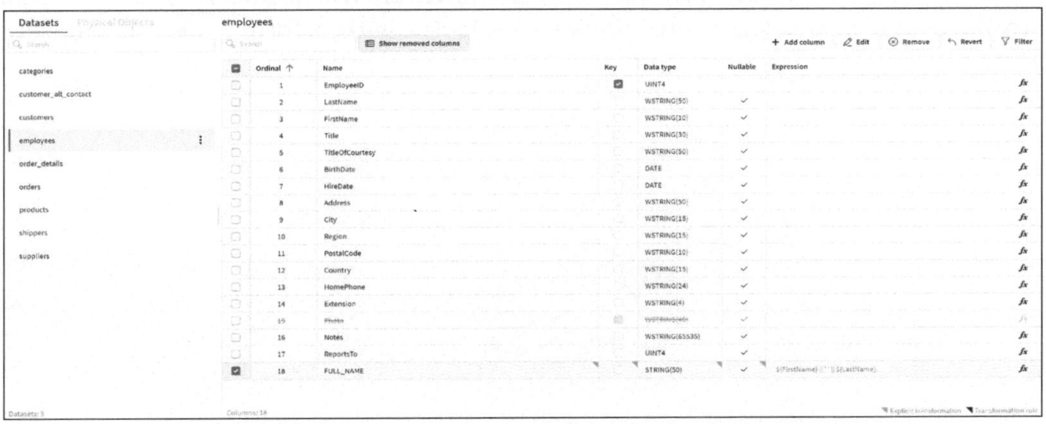

Figure 13.22: *Summary of the transformations in the landing asset*

Global Transformation Rules

In Qlik Talend Data Integration, rules serve as a mechanism for implementing universal transformations on datasets within Landing, Storage, Transform, and Data Mart data tasks. These rules offer the ability to create reusable transformations, allowing for actions, such as renaming, adding, dropping, or converting columns, replacing column values, and filtering data. The application of rules occurs during the execution of the data task, and the flexibility to use variables and expressions allows for a precise definition of the rules' scope and actions.

To implement the conversion of field names from lowercase to uppercase letters, navigate to the "`Rules`" option and select "`Add Rule`." Choose the rule type as "`Rename Column`," and in the ensuing step, articulate the specific action for this function. Clearly define the scope and context of the rule to ensure its precise application.

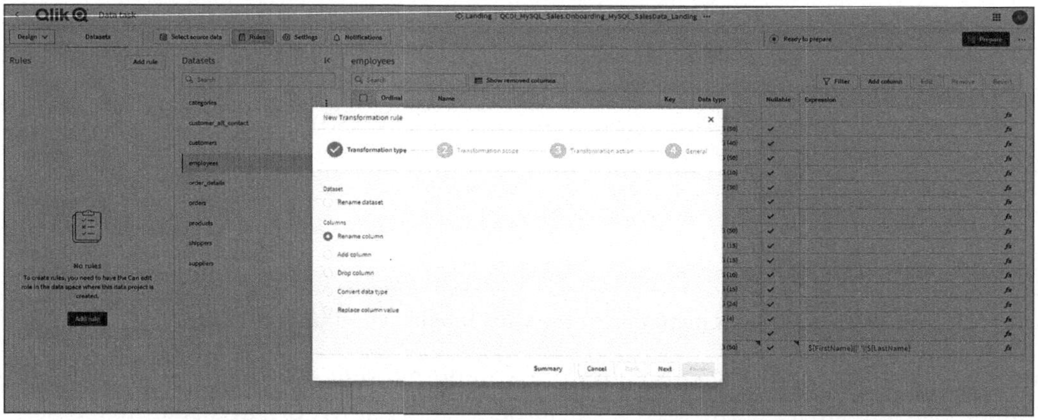

Figure 13.23: *Selecting the Rule Type as "Rename Column"*

For universal applicability across all datasets in the pipeline, we will maintain the default selections without any alterations. However, it's noteworthy that we can introduce logic at this stage, enabling us to selectively transform a specific dataset if needed.

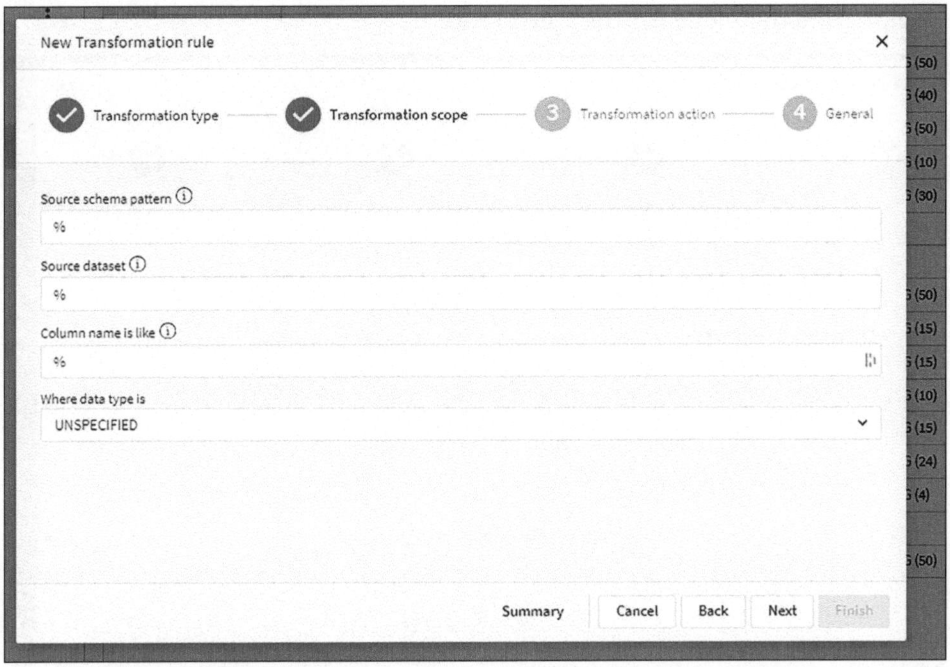

Figure 13.24: *Applying the scope of the Rule to include all Rules*

We will specify the case of the column names to be **"upper case"**.

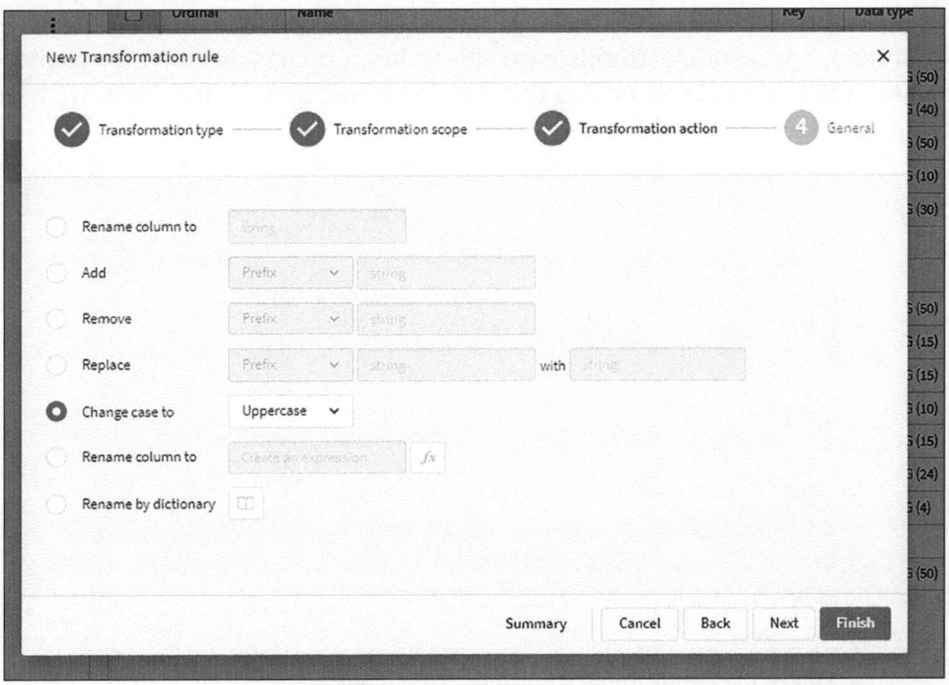

Figure 13.25: *Select the case in uppercase*

Next, we provide the name for the rule created.

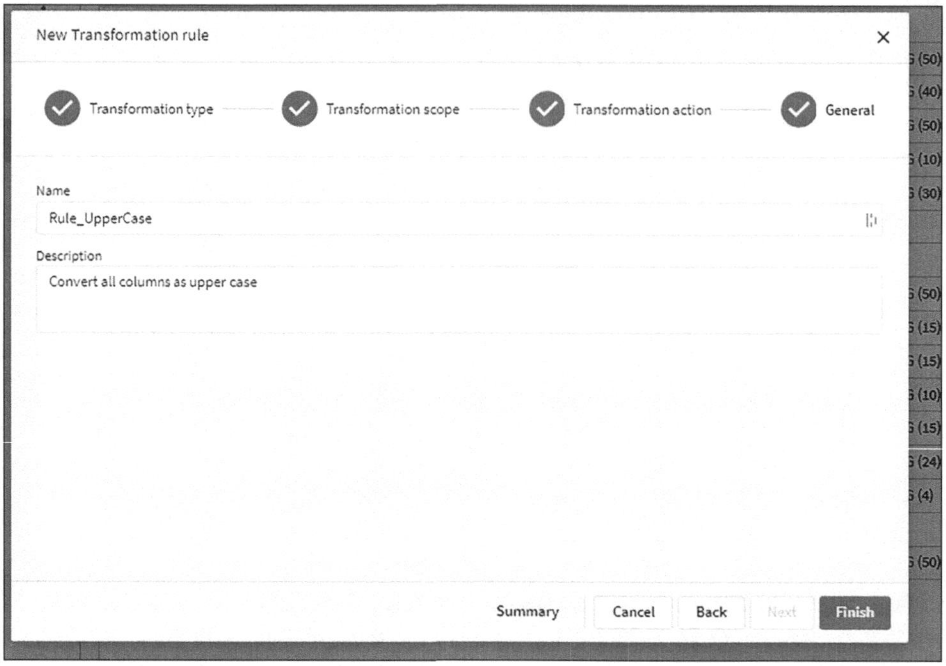

Figure 13.26: *Provide Rule name*

Upon creating the rule, a notable advantage is the immediate visualization of results on the screen. For instance, in this case, the column names are directly displayed in uppercase. Additionally, by choosing the individual rule in the left corner, we have the option to disable or delete the rule as needed.

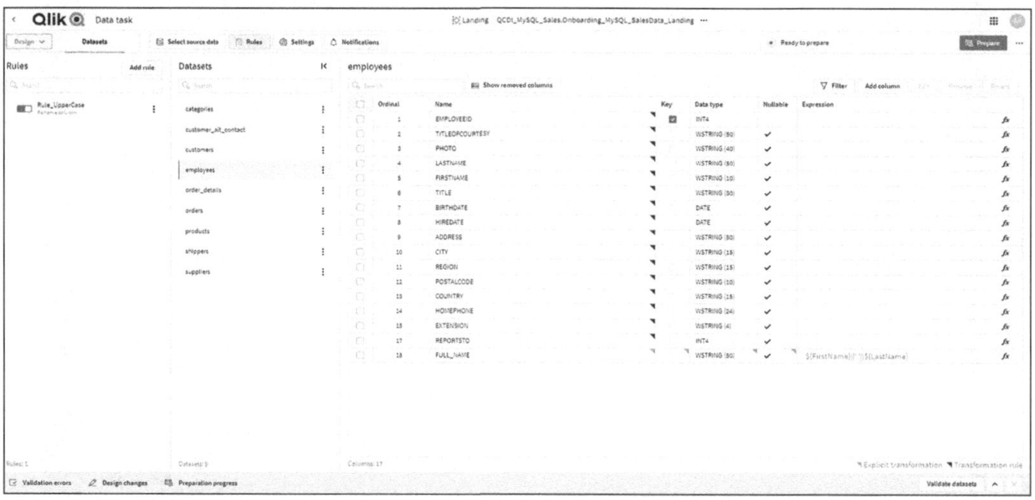

Figure 13.27: *Rule applied for upper case conversion in design view*

Landing Task Settings in Data Pipeline

Let us now explore the settings available for the landing task in a data pipeline. We have the **"General"** tab where it is possible to change the Database, Schema, prefix, and update methods - whether we want to use CDC or Reload and Compare. These settings were the same when we built the project, and they are shown as default selected options.

We also have the option of using a proxy server when employing the data gateway.

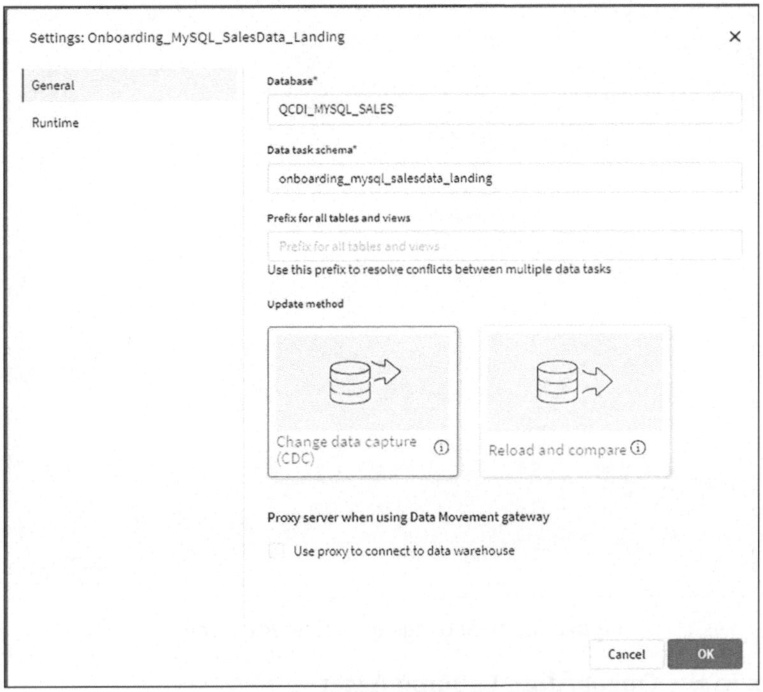

***Figure 13.28**: Settings overview general tab*

In the `Runtime` tab, we can select the options with LOB and Full Loads, where we have the option to include LOB columns and specify the maximum LOB size. Any LOBs exceeding the specified maximum size will be truncated. Qlik provides options to customize the handling of LOBs, including replicating LOB columns, permitting unlimited LOB size, and imposing limits on LOB size.

LOB stands for Large Object, which is a data type capable of storing up to 2GB of binary or character data in a database. LOB columns undergo distinct handling compared to other data types within both the database and the replication process. Depending on the source and target endpoints, LOB columns may necessitate a lookup from the source table to retrieve the value, potentially impacting performance.

In the Full load's settings, we can configure the maximum number of data connections for full loads to a value ranging from 1 to 5. The impact of having 1 parallel execution vs. 20 parallel executions depends on several factors, including the source and target endpoints, the size and structure of the table, and network bandwidth. Generally, increasing the number of parallel segments can enhance the performance of the full-load task by enabling more concurrent data transfers. However, there are potential drawbacks such as increased resource consumption on the source and target servers, which may impact other tasks or processes.

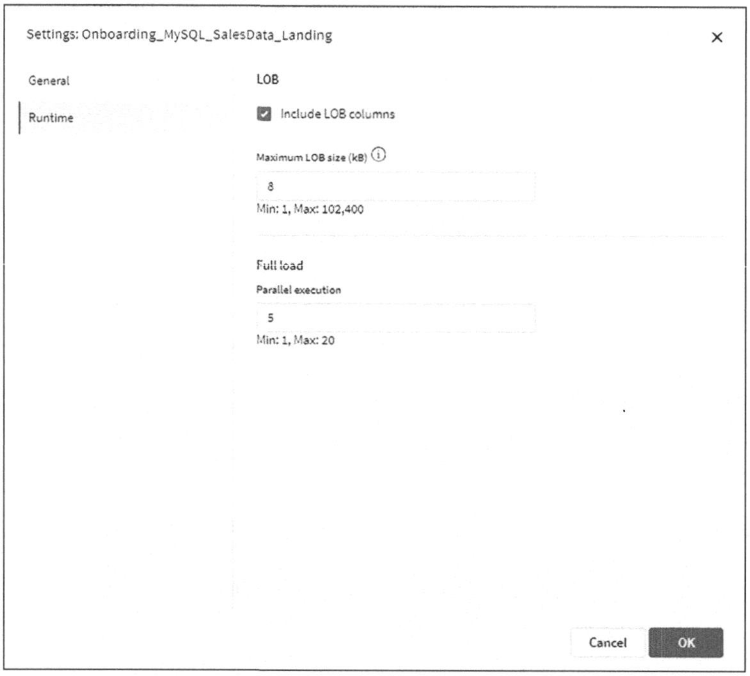

***Figure 13.29**: Settings overview Runtime Tab*

Notifications in the Onboarding Landing Asset

We can easily tailor notifications to keep us informed of operational changes within our data pipeline. Notifications can seamlessly reach us through the browser, email, or as a push message via Qlik Sense Mobile SaaS. It's essential to note that these configured settings will supersede the default notification preferences.

These notifications are designed to provide updates on key events within the onboarding asset, including:

Status Changes: Receive notifications whenever the task status transitions from start to stop or vice versa.

Table Suspension with Errors: Stay alerted when a table is suspended due to errors.

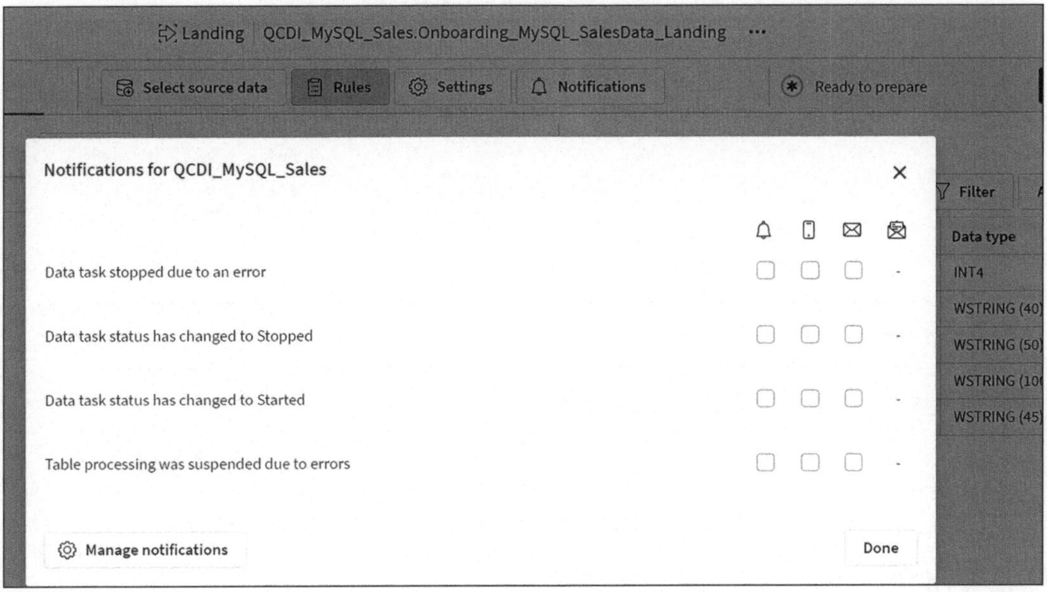

***Figure 13.30**: Notifications for onboarding assets*

Validating the Dataset

Now that we've applied all the rules, explored the settings, and configured notifications, our next step before preparing the dataset involves validation to ensure its integrity.

The validation option is located at the bottom of the screen, encompassing checks for the presence of a primary key for all tables, the absence of missing attributes, and the absence of duplicate table or column names.

Furthermore, a list of design changes compared to the source will be provided, including added tables and columns, dropped tables and columns, renamed tables and columns, and changes in primary keys and data types.

For a comprehensive view of validation errors and design changes, we can expand the Validate and Adjust section. Corrections will be made for any validation errors, followed by a revalidation of the datasets. While most design changes can be automatically adjusted, changes in primary keys or data types require dataset synchronization.

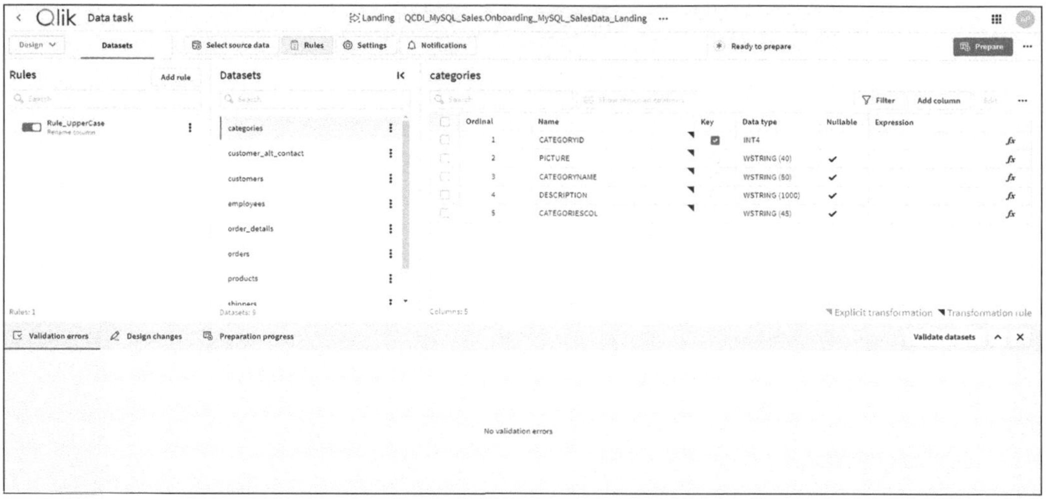

Figure 13.31: *Validation tab for onboarding landing asset*

Preparing the Data

With the dataset now configured to meet our specified rules, the next crucial step is to prepare the dataset.

Located in the top right corner, an icon named "**`Prepare`**" initiates a task for execution, encompassing multiple essential processes. This involves the validation of the design's integrity, the creation or modification of physical tables and views to align with the designated design, the generation of SQL code for the data task, and the creation or modification of catalog entries for the task's output datasets.

To monitor the progress seamlessly, we can track the Preparation progress in the lower part of the screen:

Upon selecting the "**`Prepare`**" option, the status message transitions from "**`Ready to Prepare`**" to "**`Creating Artifacts.`**" The specific artifacts being generated during this phase are visible in the Preparation Progress section at the bottom of the screen. A detailed log view provides comprehensive insights into the ongoing processes, and this log view can be further exported as a CSV file for thorough documentation and analysis. This feature allows for a transparent and detailed understanding of the creation of artifacts during the preparation phase.

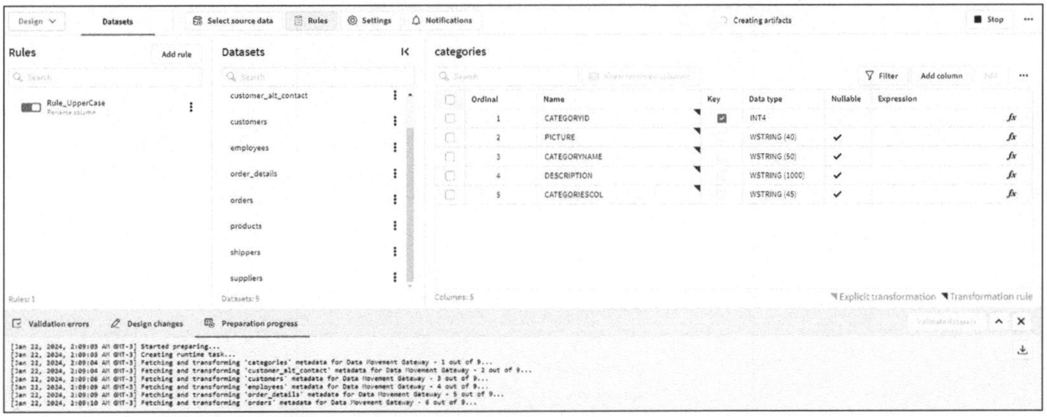

Figure 13.32: *Creating the artifacts in the target*

Once the artifacts have been successfully created, the system prompts a message stating **"`Finished Preparing Successfully`"**. Subsequently, the datasets that have been published in the target platform become visible.

At this point, the status undergoes a transition from **"`Preparing Artifacts`"** to **"`Ready to Run`"**. This shift indicates that the preparation phase has been completed successfully, and the datasets are now prepared and ready for execution.

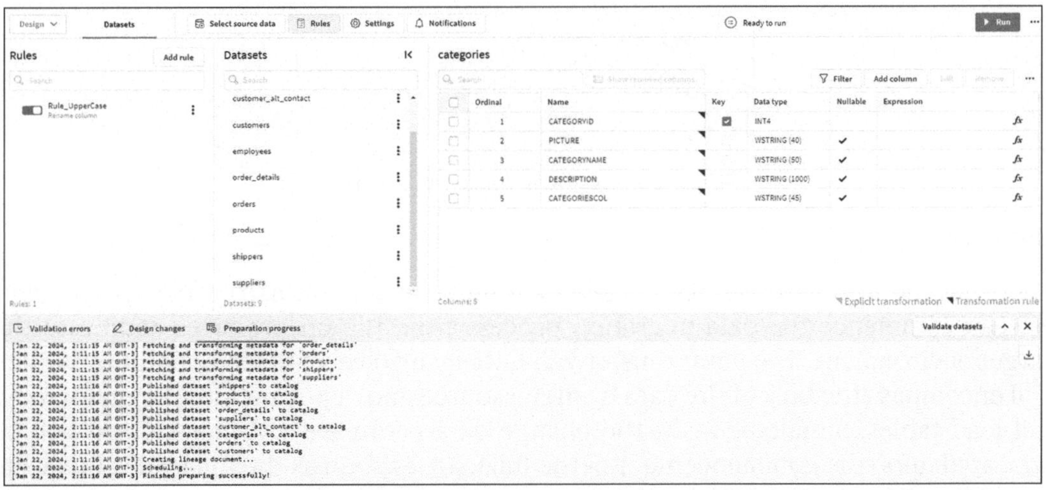

Figure 13.33: *Artifacts successfully created*

We will now navigate to the target platform and observe the structure that has been created for onboarding (landing) the data in Snowflake. Notably, we can confirm the presence of the **"`FULL_NAME`"** column we previously created, which is now established as a separate column in the target table. Furthermore, the uppercase rule is applied, and the column names are automatically formatted in uppercase. The entire process is fully automated, and Qlik's platform takes care of generating the complex SQL CREATE statements on our behalf.

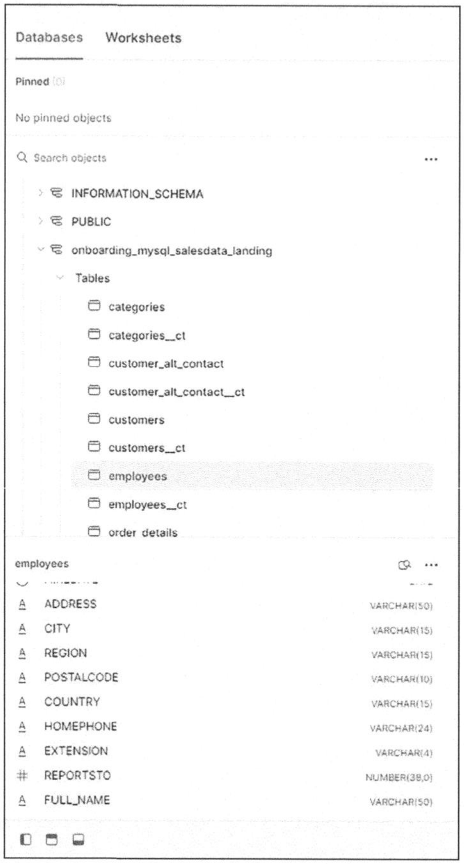

***Figure 13.34**: Target Schema created*

Data Load

Now that the necessary source, target, data pipeline, and infrastructure are in place, we can commence the data migration process from the on-premises source to the target environment. The data transfer will initially involve a full load operation, which will encompass the bulk of the data from the source and deposit it into the onboarding full load tables. Simultaneously, the change data capture (CDC) mechanism will be activated upon the commencement of the full load. As soon as the full load is finalized, the CDC will begin transmitting the data modifications to the change table using only insert operations. It is crucial to emphasize that the full load tables remain static and always reflect the data state at the time of the full load execution. The changes are conveyed as insert-only operations and stored in the change table. Upon consolidation within the storage asset, we obtain the resulting net new views at the storage level.

Upon selecting the Run option, the data load starts, and we are taken from the design view to the monitor view. Qlik Talend Data Integration offers two essential perspectives for managing data integration tasks: the monitor view and the design view. The monitor view provides real-time insights into task performance, displaying crucial information, such as task status, completion percentage, execution time, and error messages. It also allows users to interact with tasks by starting or stopping them, viewing detailed task information, and rerunning tasks if necessary. On the other hand, the design view is where we create and modify data integration tasks. In this view, users can connect to various data sources, define transformations (such as filtering and sorting), and specify data destinations. Once a task is created in the design view, it can be saved and executed in the monitor view, ensuring a seamless transition from task creation to execution and monitoring.

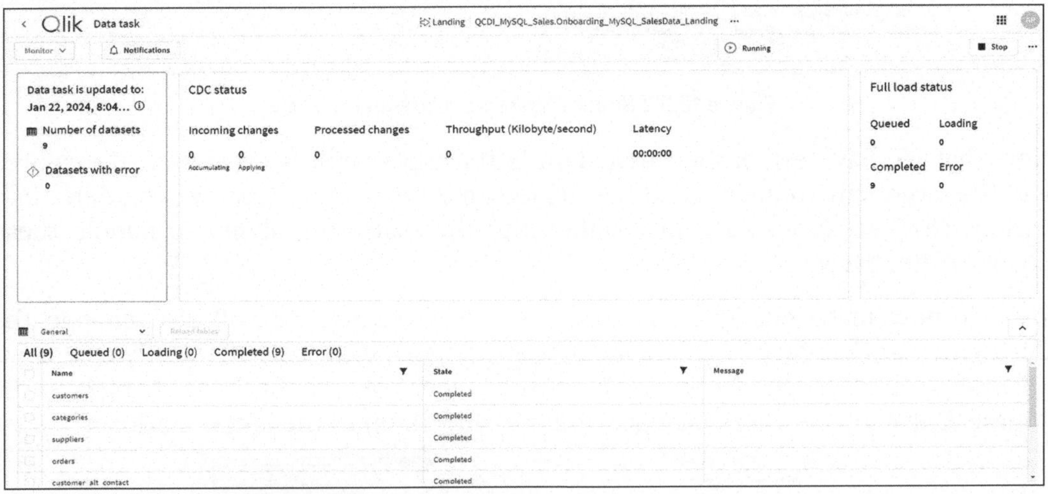

Figure 13.35: *Monitor view showing the data load*

Upon the successful execution of the full load, we can access the target environment and conduct selective queries against the tables to verify their accuracy and completeness. By comparing the target tables with the source tables, we can confirm that the entire dataset has been successfully migrated from the source to the target.

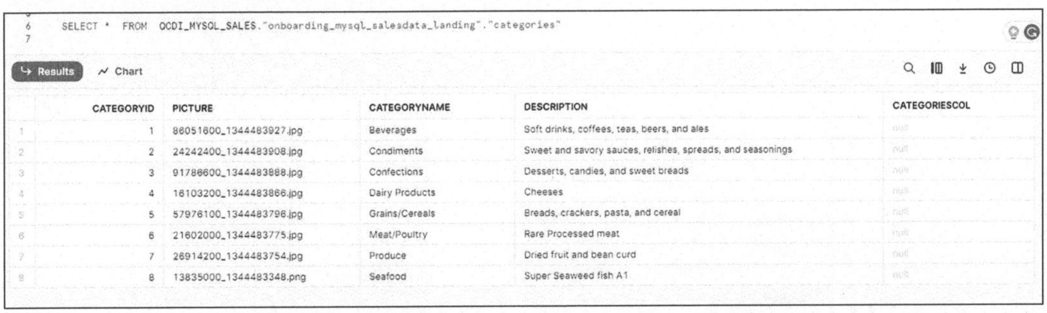

Figure 13.36: *Target System – Categories table*

In the following figure, the data in the source system's SQL server is depicted. It is crucial to review the data in the source before making any changes. After implementing the changes, we can then examine the data in the target system.

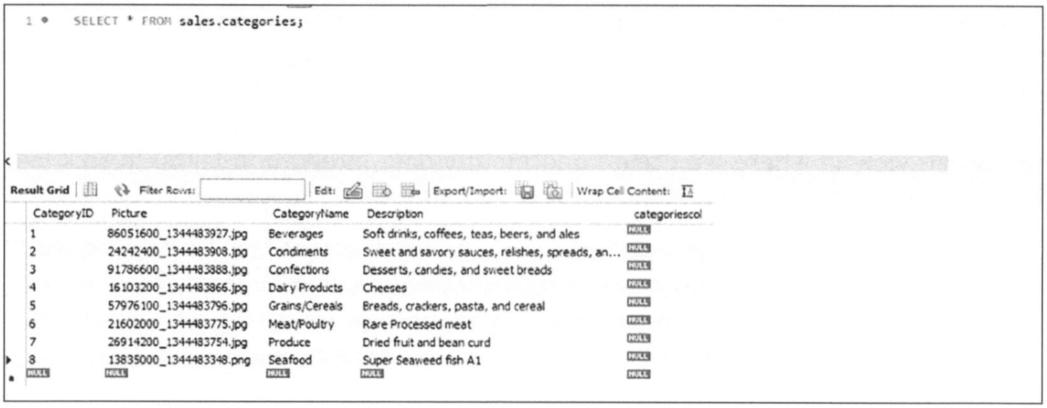

Figure 13.37: *Source System – Categories Table*

Now that we have established that data is flowing seamlessly between the source and the target environments and the full load has been completed, we can delve into various CDC scenarios to gain insights into the platform's ability to handle these changes effectively.

We will now make changes and insert a new category, we will also change the description of Category ID 8 and add a new Category ID 9. This effectively means we performed an insert and an update operation. Once we commit these changes to the source, Qlik captures these changes and migrates them to the target platform.

Figure 13.38: *Update, Insert Operations on the source system*

We will now proceed to apply the change. Once this change is implemented, it will be reflected in the database system.

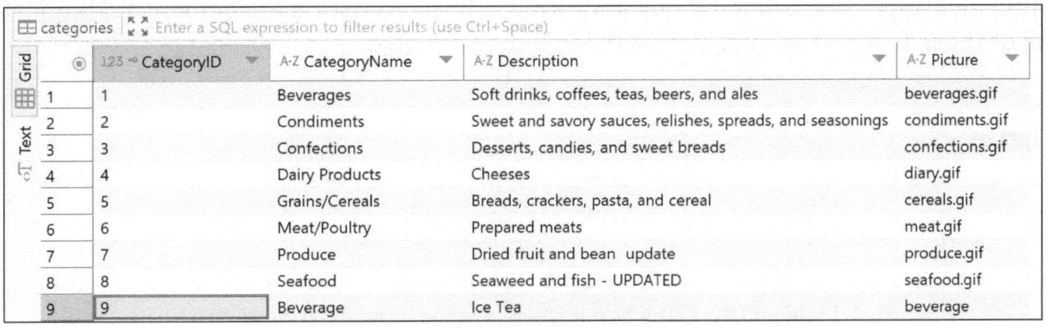

Figure 13.39: *Updated Source*

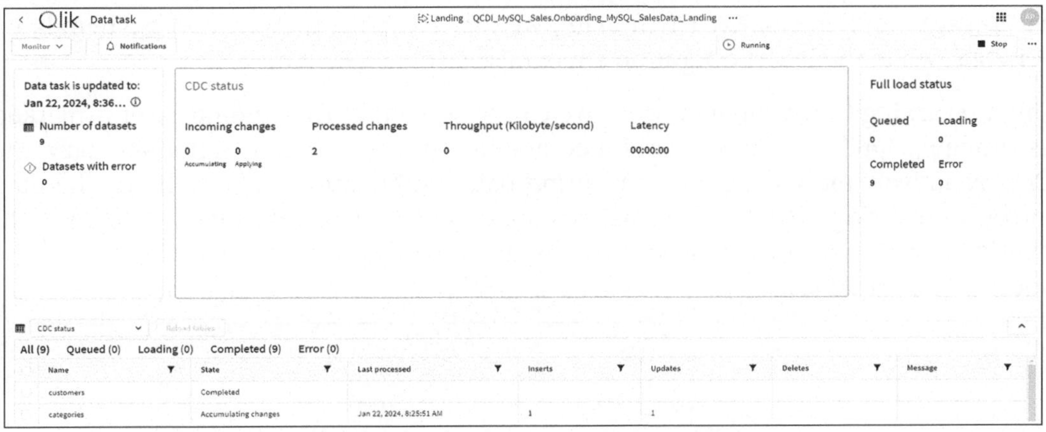

Figure 13.40: *The monitor view indicates two distinct updates – one insertion and one modification*

Now, navigate back to the target system. Run a **SELECT** statement, and you will see that the data has been transferred there in near real-time.

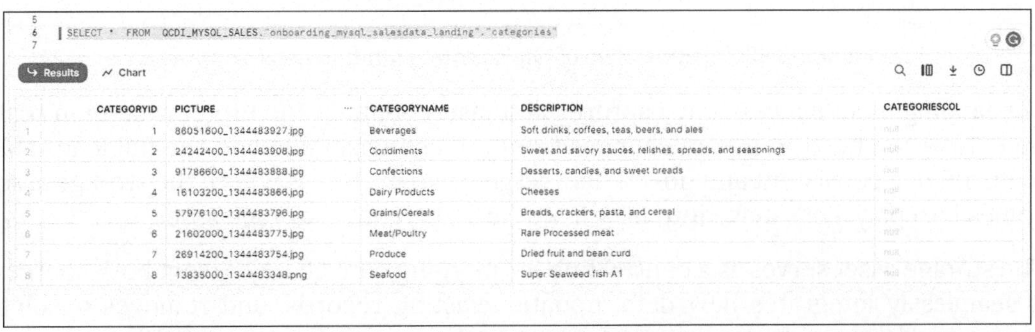

Figure 13.41: *The full load target landing table, there are no changes here*

It's not just about moving the changes. We can also track what has changed and when it has changed. This capability is incredibly beneficial for various reasons, such as implementing Type 2 dimensions and other advanced data management techniques. All of these features are readily available out of the box.

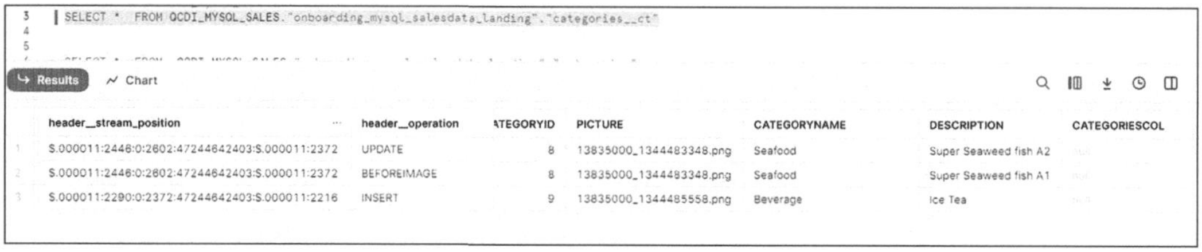

Figure 13.42: CT (Change Table) *Onboarding asset landing*

As depicted in *Figure* 13.42, the change table presents the insert and update operations as **"Insert"**-only rows. For the update, we observe both the pre-and post-updated versions, while the insert operation appears as a sole insertion.

Upon returning to the pipeline view, we can observe that the landing asset is marked as running, signifying the successful completion of the full load. Simultaneously, the CDC is actively monitoring and capturing data modifications in real-time. The data introduced during the full load remains immutable in the full load table, while the CDC continuously tracks and incorporates any updates or deletions occurring within the specified set of tables.

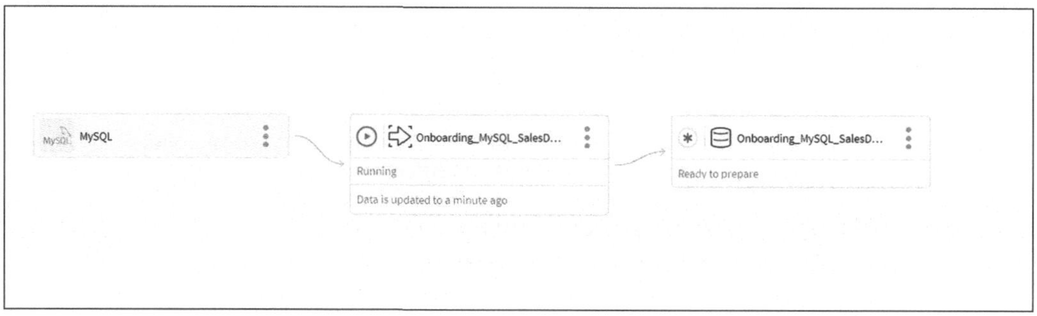

Figure 13.43: *Pipeline view of On-boarding landing asset running*

The landing asset successfully captures and inserts data in the target system in real-time. Now, we need to merge changes from the changes table and the full load table to maintain a consistent and up-to-date target system. This is where the storage asset comes into play. Let's delve into how it works and create a storage asset.

The storage asset serves as a central hub for merging data changes from both sources. It seamlessly integrates new data, updates existing records, and removes obsolete rows, ensuring that the target system mirrors the source data accurately.

Storage Asset

Datasets can be stored using a storage data task, which takes in data previously landed in the cloud landing area by a landing data task. These stored datasets can then be utilized in analytics applications, such as tables in an analytics app.

To design a storage data task, the status of the landing data task must be at least **`"Ready to prepare"`.** Subsequently, the storage data task can be prepared when the landing data task status reaches "Ready to run". It's noteworthy that the storage data task aligns its mode of operation (whether Full load or Full load and CDC) with the consumed landing data task. Configurations and monitoring options differ between these modes. In the case of a cloud target landing data task employing Full load only, the storage data task will generate views of the landing tables rather than creating physical tables. This mechanism ensures flexibility and adaptability in managing and utilizing datasets within the cloud environment.

The storage asset mirrors the structure of the landing data asset, providing similar functionalities. We can implement global transformation rules, configure notifications, add new columns, and tailor the dataset to our specific needs. Additionally, it offers scheduling and modeling options, further enhanced by the comprehensive settings view. The model will be explored in the next chapter.

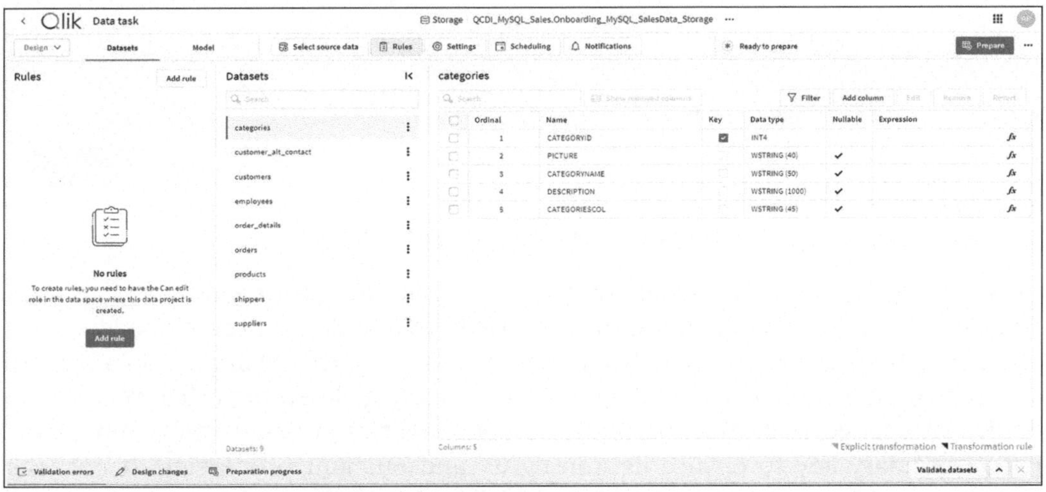

Figure 13.44: *Storage Task design view*

Storage Asset – Settings

In the general view, we have that settings allow us to customize the storage task schema, internal schema, and prefix for tables and views created within the task. The database specifies the data source to connect to.

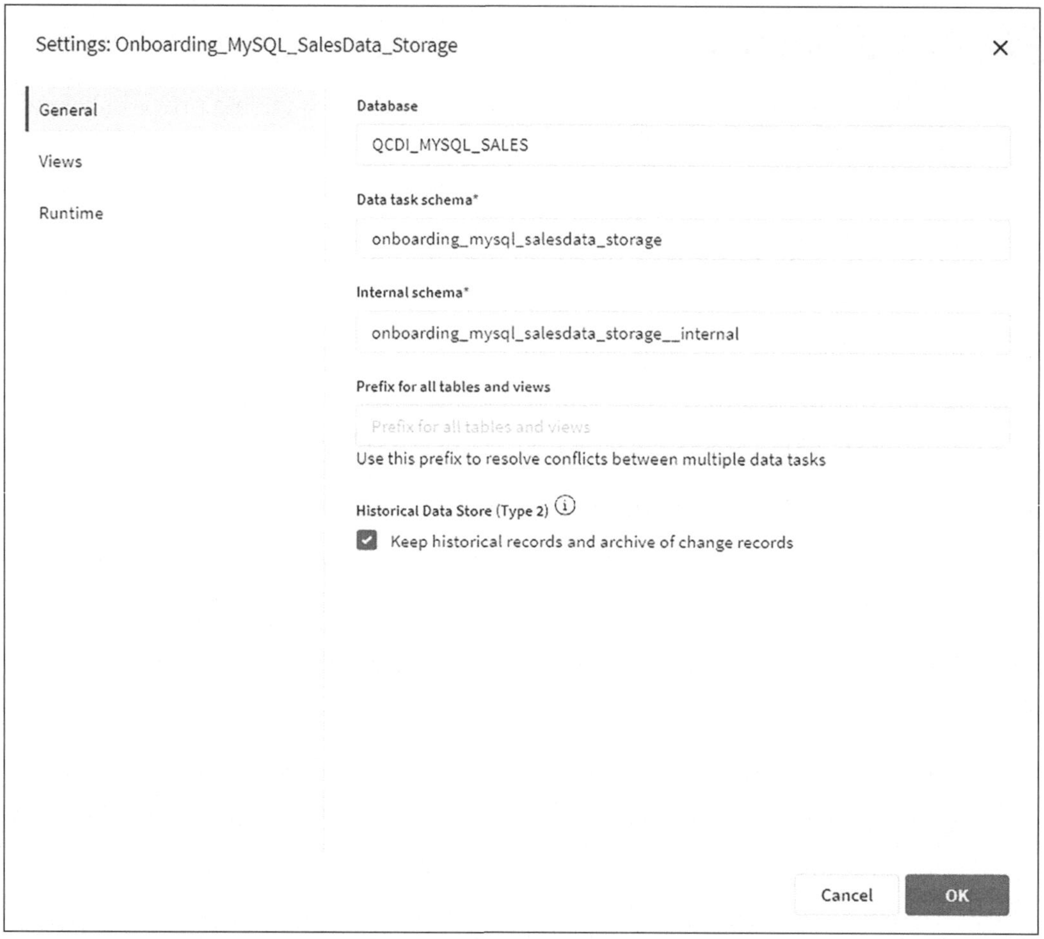

***Figure 13.45**: General Settings in Storage*

We also have the option to decide on the Historical Data Store where we can retain historical change data to facilitate the reconstruction of data states at specific points in time. Utilize history views and live history views to explore historical data patterns and trends. Enable historical change data by selecting "Keep historical records and archive of change records". Storage data tasks necessitate the establishment of a defined primary key to ensure data integrity and efficient processing. If not, each landing data reload will trigger an initial load for the Storage data task, potentially impacting performance.

In the settings tab, we can enable the live view:

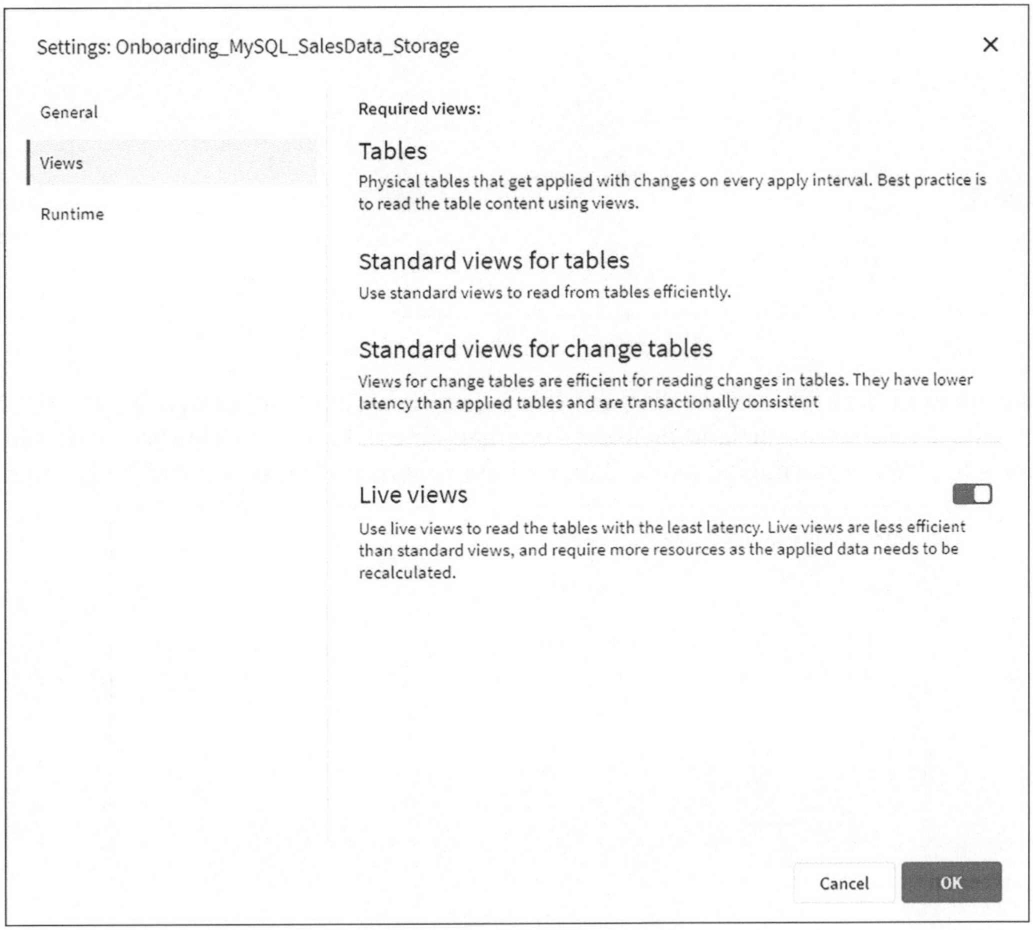

Figure 13.46: *View Settings*

Live views in Qlik Talend Data Integration enable real-time access to the latest data from our data sources, eliminating the need to wait for data processing and storage in the cloud data warehouse. They dynamically generate views for each selected source table by merging the table with the changes captured from the change table, which utilizes change data capture (CDC) technology to track real-time modifications in the source systems. This approach provides low-latency data access and reduces the computational overhead associated with frequent processing of landed data. Live views are automatically generated when creating a data pipeline, ensuring that they are readily available for immediate use.

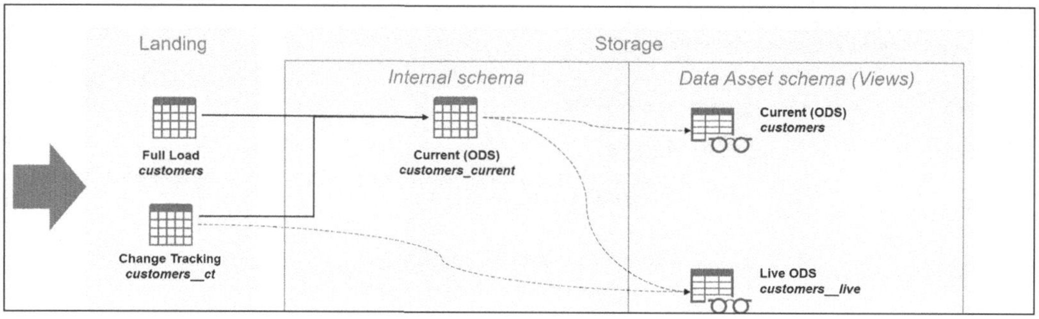

Figure 13.47: *Live view architecture*

As evident in the architecture diagram, live views draw data from both the operational data store (ODS) and the landing asset's change table (CT). This integration allows live views to provide the most current data without relying on the scheduled merge task.

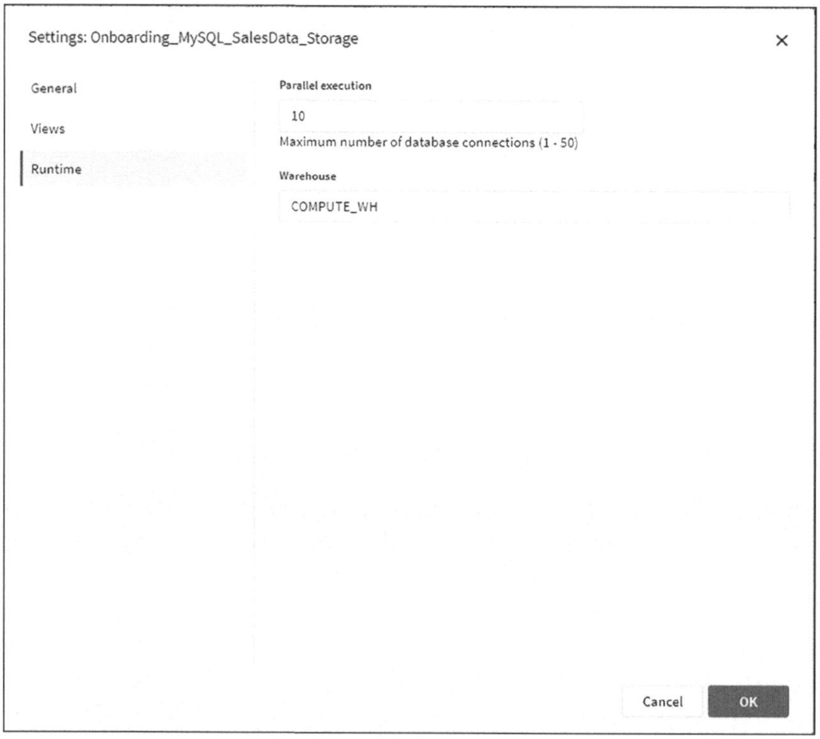

Figure 13.48: *Runtime settings option in storage asset*

The parallel execution setting in the storage settings of Qlik Talend Data Integration enables the simultaneous execution of multiple storage tasks within a data pipeline. This feature can significantly enhance the performance and efficiency of the data pipeline by minimizing the wait time and resource consumption associated with each storage task. A storage task involves the transfer of data from a source to a destination such as a cloud data warehouse or a file storage service. Storage settings for each task can be configured in the data pipeline editor, including the source and destination data connections, target table name, load mode, and parallel execution option. The optimal value for the parallel execution setting depends on various factors, such as data size and complexity, network bandwidth and latency, source and destination load and availability, and the number and frequency of storage tasks.

In general, a higher degree of parallelism can boost the throughput and speed of the data pipeline, but it may also raise the likelihood of errors, timeouts, or throttling, especially when the source or destination has limited resources or imposes rate limits on the number of requests or connections. Therefore, it is crucial to test and monitor the data pipeline's performance to ensure optimal parallel execution settings.

The warehouse option allows for the selection of a specific warehouse to execute the storage task. By default, the same warehouse as the storage asset is used. However, it is possible to employ separate warehouses for the storage and landing assets. This setting is particularly relevant for Snowflake deployments. The name field is only applicable to Snowflake and specifies the target warehouse name.

Running the Storage Asset

Having successfully established and thoroughly configured the storage asset, we shall proceed to prepare the asset. Upon completion of this preparation phase, we will load the data and observe its structure across various underlying tables and views. As with preparing the asset in the landing zone, we will select the **"Prepare"** option. Once the assets are created, we will initiate the data load when the asset indicates **"Ready to Run"** and similarly to previous steps, we will transition from the design view to the monitor view to monitor the data loading process.

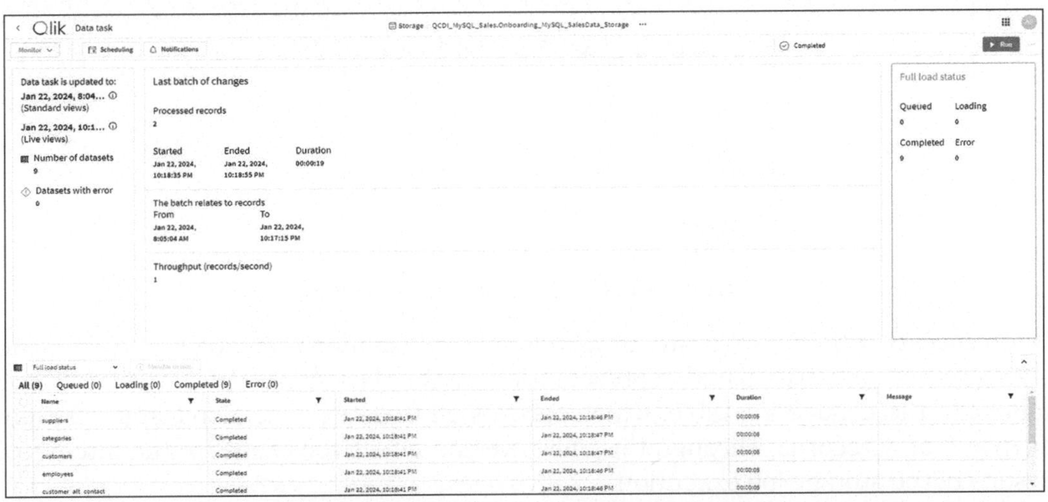

Figure 13.49: *Storage Asset monitoring view*

Now, let's navigate to the Target and examine the schemas that have been generated and loaded with data. Within the storage asset, we can observe that schemas have been generated specifically for storage. These schemas reside within the actual storage schema, encompassing views such as the categories view, changes view, history view, and live view.

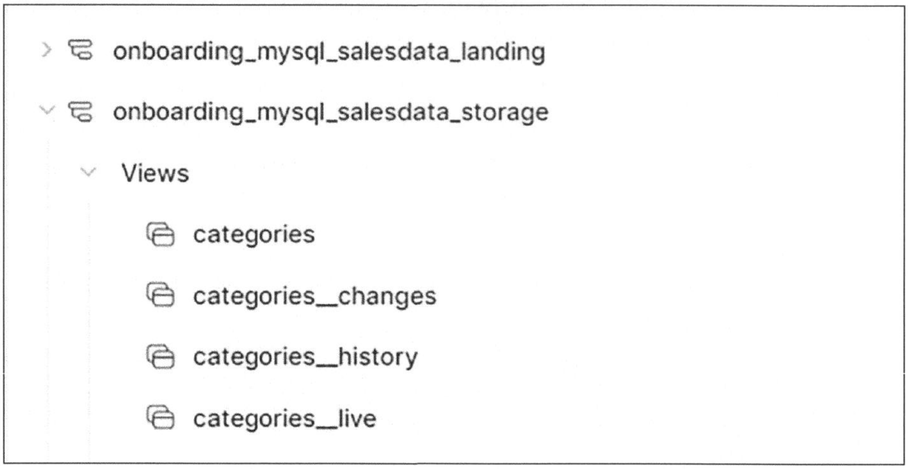

Figure 13.50: *Storage asset views*

Figure 13.51: *Storage asset internal tables*

Upon accessing the target system, we will initially examine the categories view. This view presents a consolidated representation of the data merged from the full load table and the change log table, which records all updates, insertions, and deletions as insert-only records. Through this view, we can effectively visualize the integrated results of the storage job execution.

As we can observe in this view, the newly added category ID is available, and the updated record with Category ID 8 is also visible. Upon completion of the storage job, this view serves as the primary source for accessing the most up-to-date data.

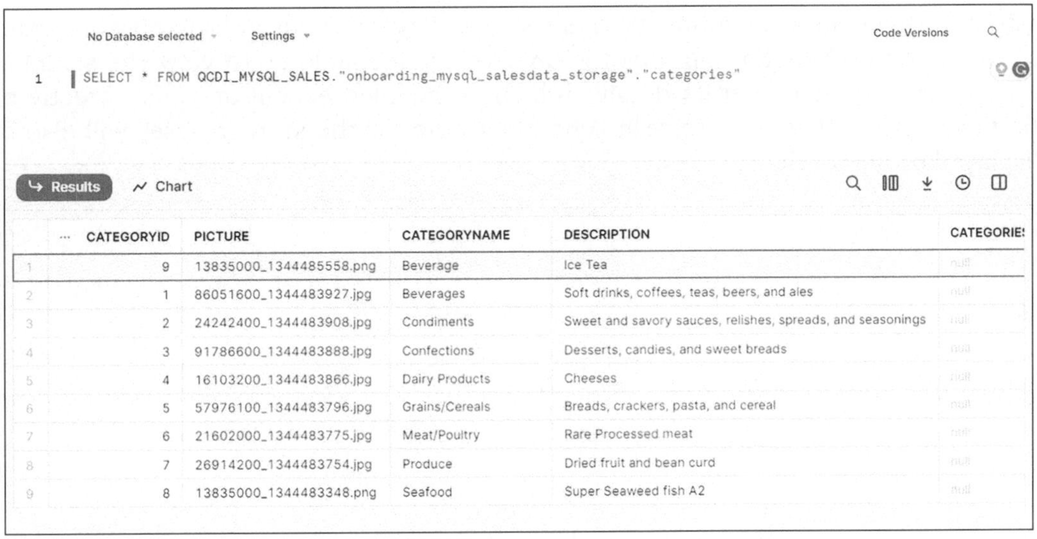

Figure 13.52: *Target View*

Scheduling the Storage Asset

To automatically execute the merge statement at a predefined time, we'll establish a schedule for the storage asset. To initiate this process, click the **"..."** icon adjacent to the desired data task and select **"Scheduling."** This action will enable you to create a schedule for the task. The default scheduling configuration is inherited from the data project's settings. However, to activate the schedule, we must explicitly set the "**Scheduling**" option to **"On."**

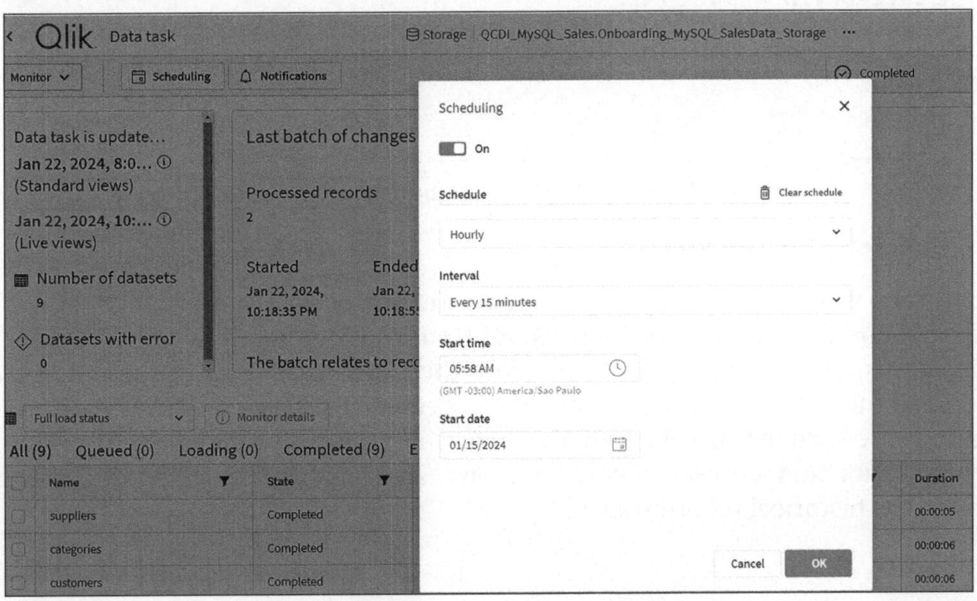

Figure 13.53: *Scheduling view of Storage Task*

Within the main project window, navigate to the **"Layers"** icon and set the status, data freshness, and scheduling options to **"On"**. This will enable us to view the schedule we just created, including its details and the scheduled execution time, directly on the main screen. The next refresh scheduled time for the storage asset will also be displayed prominently.

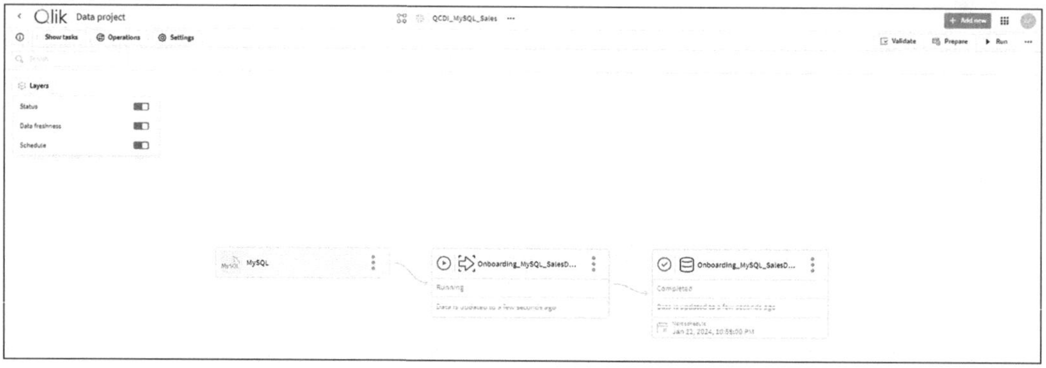

***Figure 13.54**: Pipeline view of Project after initial run of storage task*

Storage Asset – Changes view

As the name implies, the storage asset's changes view provides a detailed record of data alterations. It displays the current values of the modified records and the type of operation that triggered the change. In this instance, we can observe that the update operation is denoted by an **"U"** in the **"hdr_operation"** field for the **CategoryID = 8** record, while the insert operation is identified by an **"I"** in the **"hdr_operation"** field for the **CategoryID = 9** record.

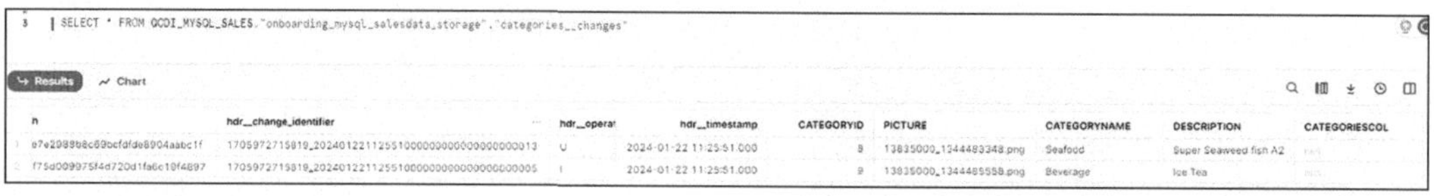

***Figure 13.55**: Data View of Storage asset, changes table*

Storage Asset – History View

The history view provides a comprehensive record of data modifications, enabling us to examine the evolution of each record from its inception to its current state. By utilizing this view, we can gain insights into the historical values of each record and determine the duration for which each value persisted. This capability is essential for creating type 2 dimensions in your data mart. The **"HDR__Store"** field distinguishes between prior and current record versions, allowing you to effectively navigate through the historical record trail.

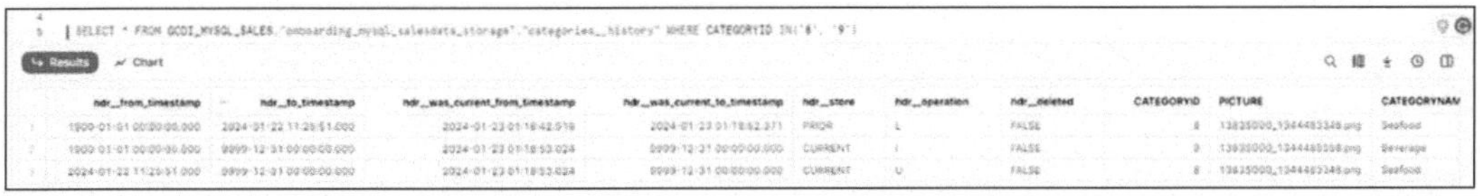

Figure 13.56: *Data View of History asset*

Storage Asset – Live View

The live view, as the name suggests, provides real-time access to the most up-to-date data. It consolidates information from both the landing asset change table and the merged data from the storage asset. The **"HDR__Store"** field indicates the data source, allowing you to distinguish between current and prior versions. In this case, since the job has already merged the data, all changes are reflected in the live view, and the **"HDR__Store"** value is **"CURRENT"** for all records.

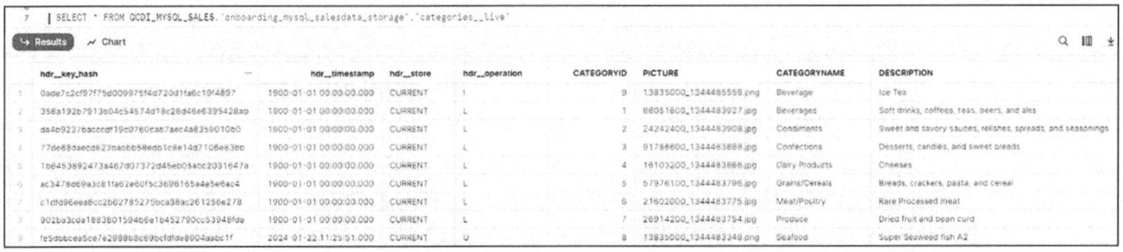

Figure 13.57: *Live view with no pending apply merges as per storage schedule*

To illustrate the live view's real-time capabilities, let's make an update to the source data. We will navigate to the source and modify the description for **Category ID = 8**. This update will be instantly transmitted to the target database, where it will be added as an insert-only record in the landing zone change table. Our live view will promptly capture this change and display the most up-to-date data. Here, we can observe that the **"HDR__Store"** field indicates the source as **"CT"** (Change Table). Once the scheduled storage job executes, the value of the **"HDR__Store"** field will transition to "CURRENT," ensuring that the Live view always reflects the most recent data.

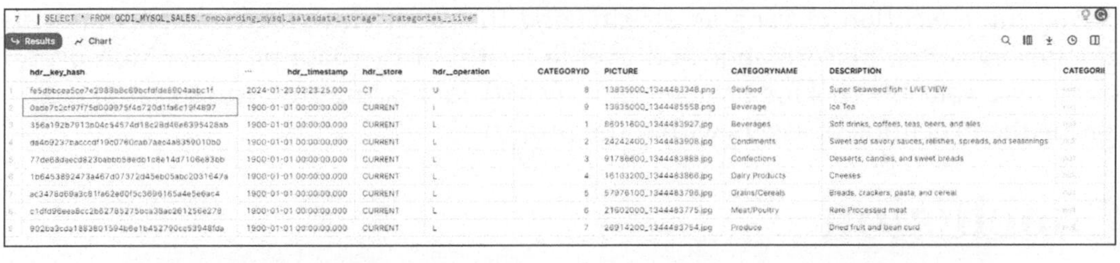

Figure 13.58: *Live view with pending apply merges as per storage schedule*

Additionally, we can confirm that the data has not yet been updated, as per the scheduled merge job, and the category view still displays the older data without the merge having been executed.

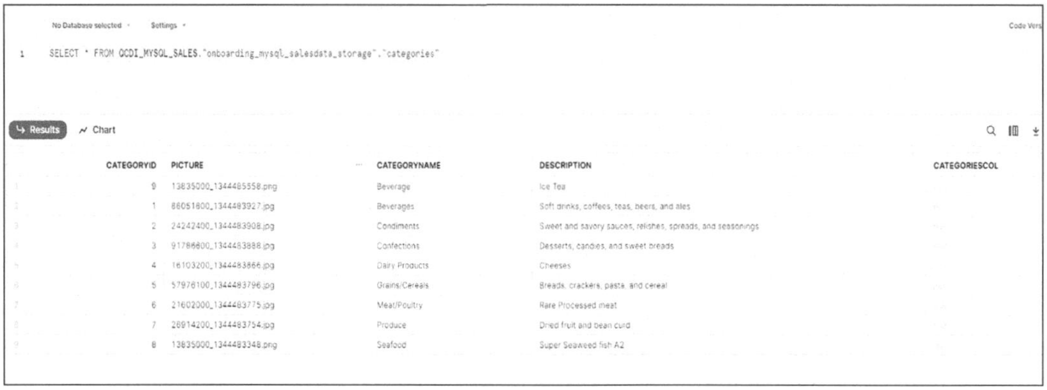

Figure 13.59: *Pending changes to be applied*

Live History View

The live history view is an invaluable feature that grants real-time access to the most recent historical data from your data sources, eliminating the need to apply the changes to the target platform's tables or views. This approach effectively reduces the latency and computational burden associated with data integration processes. The live history view achieves this by seamlessly integrating data from the change tables generated during the landing task. It serves as a crucial tool for data consumption and analysis, providing users with a comprehensive perspective of both the most current and historical data available. Essentially, it embodies a live version of the historical view we explored earlier.

Asset State Table

An asset state table is a dedicated table within a Qlik Talend Data Integration data project that maintains the current state of each asset. These assets can encompass various components, such as data sources, data tasks, connections, or gateways. The asset state table serves as a comprehensive record, tracking key information, including the status, start time, end time, duration, and any encountered errors or warnings during the execution of each asset. Utilizing the asset state table enables effective monitoring of the performance and overall health of the data pipeline. Moreover, it serves as a valuable tool for troubleshooting and addressing any issues that may arise during the execution of assets within the project.

Conclusion

In Qlik Talend Data Integration, landing assets and storage assets are pivotal components with distinct roles in the data pipeline process. A landing asset serves as a staging area for data, acting as a temporary repository for raw data extracted from various sources. Conversely, a storage asset represents a destination for transformed and cleansed data.

We have explored how simple data transformations can be conducted during the landing or storage phases. Additionally, we delved into various views, including the live view, history view, and changes view, understanding the unique functionalities of each.

In summary, landing assets act as a holding area for raw data, while storage assets provide a repository for prepared data suitable for analytics and reporting. Together, they form integral components of Qlik Talend Data Integration's robust data pipeline architecture.

Multiple Choice Questions

1. Which of the following is a special type of view that provides real-time access to data changes as they occur?
    a. Live view
    b. External view
    c. Historical data store (HDS)
    d. Master data service (MDS)
2. Which of the following is the ASSET_STATE table in Qlik Talend Data Integration?
    a. A table that stores any errors that have occurred during the refresh process
    b. A table that stores the current refresh status of a storage asset
    c. A system table that stores information about the state of storage assets
    d. A table that stores the last refresh date and time of a storage asset
3. Which of the following is the purpose of the scheduling option on a storage asset?
    a. To define how and when the data in the landing asset should be refreshed
    b. To define how and when the data in the storage asset should be refreshed
    c. To improve the performance of the refresh process
    d. To automatically retry failed refreshes

Answers

1. a
2. c
3. b

References

1. *Qlik Help*: https://help.qlik.com/

Chapter 14
Transforming Data

Introduction

This chapter delves into the transformation of data. In the previous chapter, we explored the process of extracting data from an on-premises source in near real-time and inserting it into our target data platform. While we could apply certain transformations in the landing assets, the focus now shifts to the necessity of composing intricate transformations. To accomplish this, we rely on the transformation asset. This asset simplifies the process of crafting custom SQL code, enabling the application of complex business logic with ease.

Structure

In this chapter, we will discuss the following topics:

- Transformation Asset
- Materialization
- Incremental Load
- Macros
- SQL Execution

Getting Started

Qlik Talend Data Integration is a service designed to facilitate the delivery, transformation, and unification of enterprise data in real time, supporting analytics, machine learning, and digital transformation initiatives.

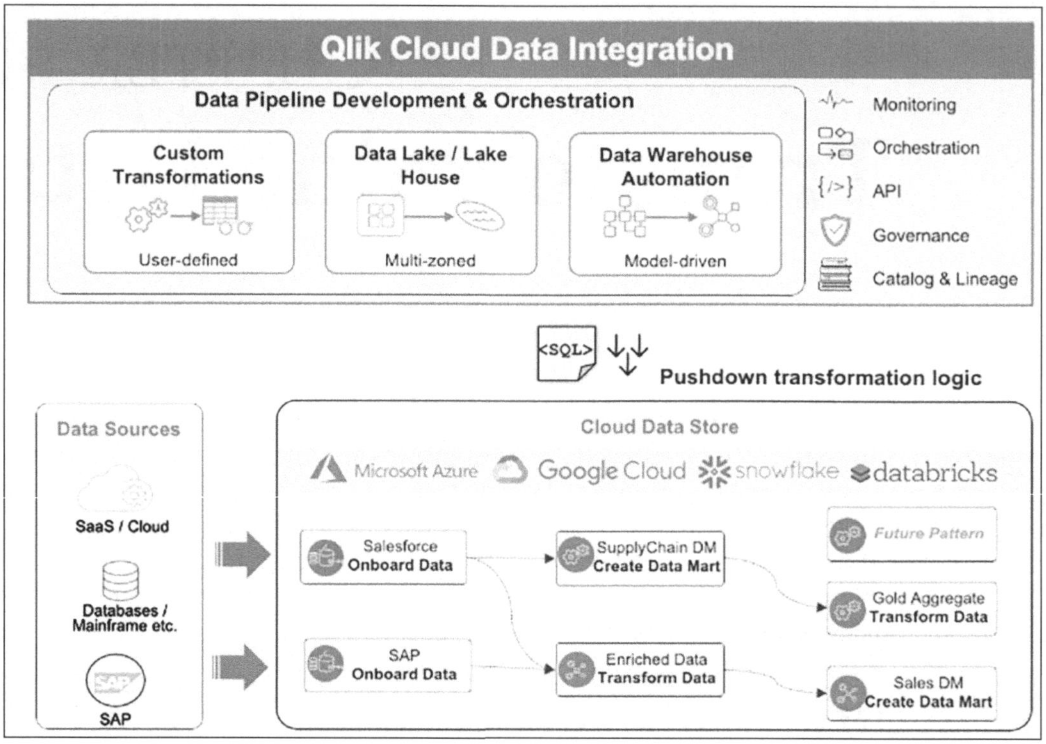

Figure 14.1: *Qlik Talend Data Integration Overview transformations*

A transformation asset within this framework serves as a reusable and rule-based data task, empowering users to execute row-level transformations on source data. These transformations encompass actions, such as filtering, renaming, standardizing, or aggregating columns.

Key functionalities of Qlik Talend Data Integration - Transformation Asset include:

- **No-Code Interface:**

  Utilize a user-friendly, no-code interface to effortlessly incorporate table-based transformation rules or generate star schema data marts within your target data warehouse.

- **Customization Options:**

  Leverage custom SQL or third-party data transformation tools for executing advanced transformations, providing flexibility and adaptability to diverse data processing needs.

- **Time and Cost Efficiency:**

  Realize time and cost savings as well as risk reduction by ensuring that data across various cloud environments is readily available for use and action throughout the entire business.

In the preceding chapter, we successfully onboarded and stored the data. In the current phase, our focus shifts to the application of business rules through the composition of custom SQL within the transformation asset. This pivotal asset serves as the gateway to achieving a high level of customization for our datasets.

To initiate this process, follow these steps:

1. Click on the onboarding asset icon
2. From the ensuing drop-down menu, select the "**`Transform Data`**" option

This simple yet crucial sequence will set the stage for the subsequent application of business rules, allowing us to harness the power of custom SQL within the transformation asset for a tailored and nuanced approach to data customization.

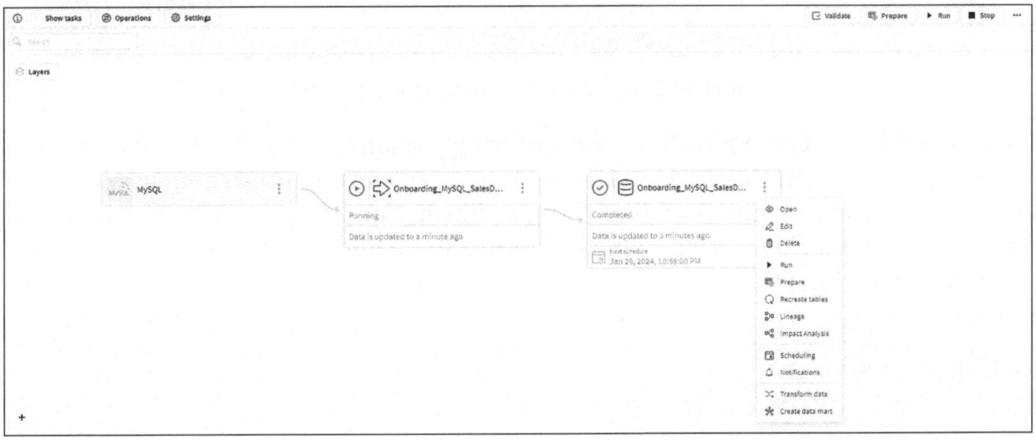

Figure 14.2: *Creating a transformation asset*

Next, we proceed to assign a name and a fitting description to the transformation asset. The name provided at this stage will serve as both the identifier for the data task schema and the internal schema. By default, the internal schema will append "**`__internal`**" to the provided name. It is noteworthy that this default naming convention can be modified in the settings to better align for specific requirements.

Figure 14.3: *Naming the Transformation asset*

Upon clicking the **`Create`** button and entering a name, the interface directs us to the design screen. On this screen, all the sources from the onboarding asset become visible. It's crucial to emphasize that the transformation asset grants the capability to join multiple onboarding assets. This functionality enables the formulation of logic or data transformations that extend across tables originating from diverse schemas and sources.

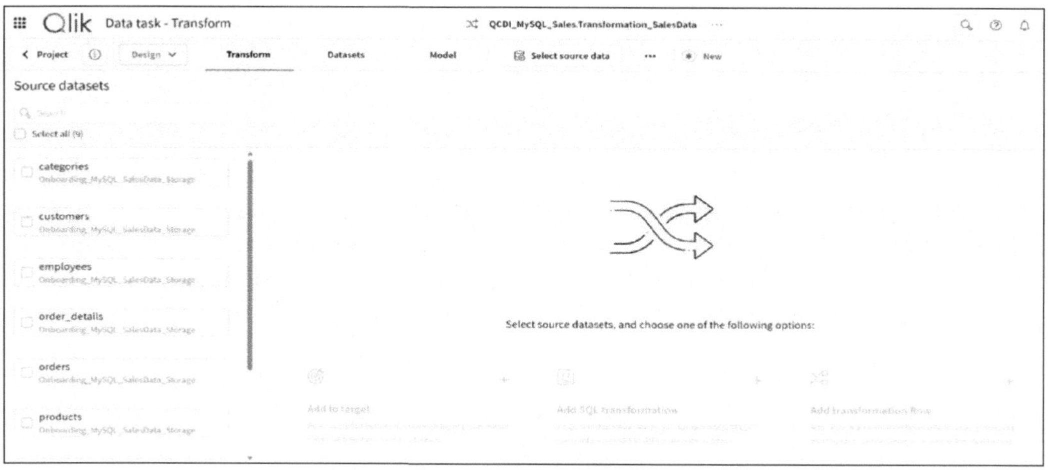

Figure 14.4: *Design view of Transformation asset*

In the **`Design`** view, we can see a list of onboarding datasets. Now, we'll pick a few datasets and use SQL statements to change the data in them. We'll make things more interesting by adding different levels of complexity to how we handle the data. We'll try out situations where we add functions to combine information in a single table and make a new dataset by putting together data from two tables.

We'll choose the Storage task from Customers and then click on **"Add SQL Based Dataset"**.

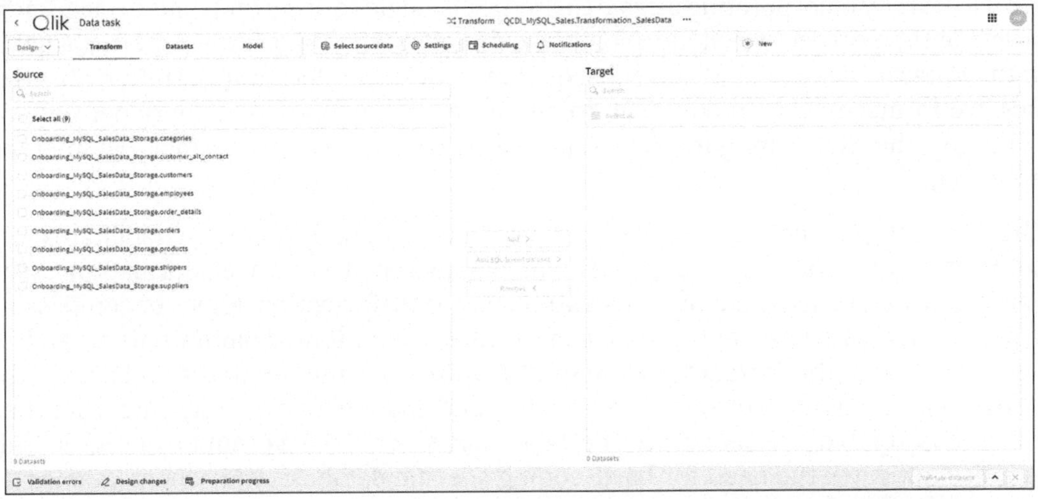

Figure 14.5: *Selecting the Customer Data Set and selecting Add SQL Based data set*

Now, we need to configure the settings for the SQL-based dataset. By default, this dataset adopts settings from the project level. However, we have the flexibility to customize these settings. In this section, we can choose whether we want the data to be materialized. If we opt for materialization, then we can further decide if the dataset should undergo incremental loading; we will select the default option and select **Next**.

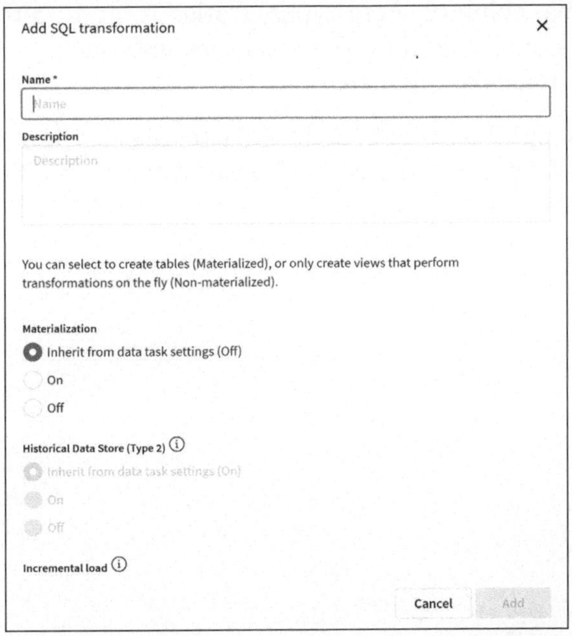

Figure 14.6: *Materialization settings, incremental load options*

Writing a SQL-Based Transformation

We will start by incorporating a basic Custom SQL Logic to ascertain unique customers based on their respective cities. Initially, we designate the Data Set by entering a name in the Dataset Name field (1) and subsequently provide a relevant description (2). After this, we formulate the custom SQL to aggregate the distinct customers per city (3). Following the SQL configuration, we proceed to choose the "extract parameters" option (4).

The "extract parameters" feature in Qlik Talend Data Integration facilitates the automatic generation and assignment of parameters to the transformation asset. Parameters serve as variables for customizing transformation logic, encompassing aspects, such as source and target names, filter conditions, column names, and so forth. The use of the **"extract parameters"** features streamlines and standardizes the transformation asset, enhancing reusability and maintenance. When incorporating a SQL-based table, we substitute the table names with the **`${TABLE}`** notation. This practice mitigates the need for hard-coding specific database and schema names, as these may change when transitioning between different environments, such as from development to production.

In this scenario, we opt not to modify the parameters and select the **`"describe table"`** option (5).

The **`"describe table"`** option in Qlik Talend Data Integration enables the inspection of table metadata within the data platform. This feature permits an examination of the table's schema, columns, data types, statistics, and a preview of the data. It proves valuable for comprehending the structure and quality of data, aiding in the identification of any issues or anomalies.

In this case, an anomaly is identified: **`"This Dataset has no key columns assigned"`**. This anomaly arises from the absence of identification for the field that will serve as the key column for this table.

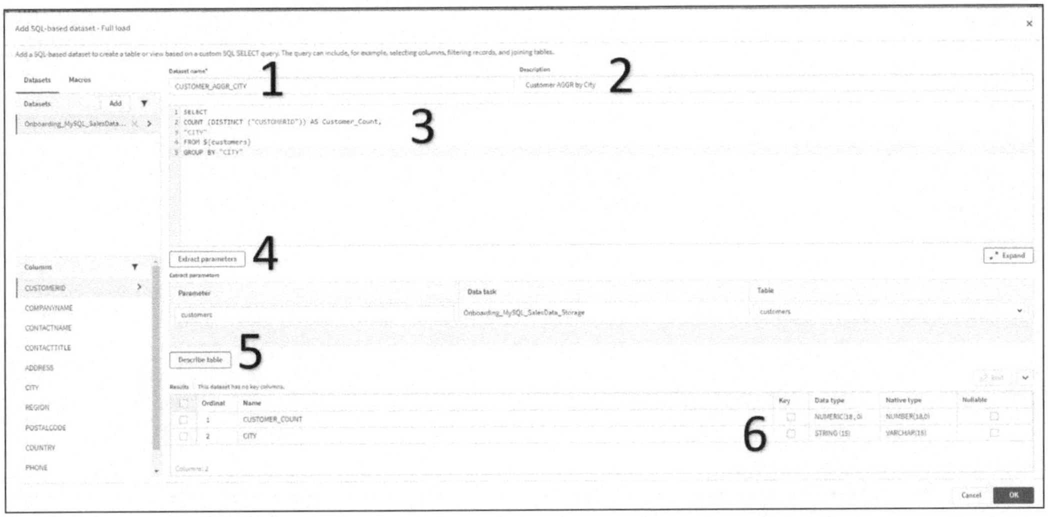

Figure 14.7: *Adding an SQL-based full load data set: customer*

To address this issue, we simply need to specify the column that should be recognized as the key for the dataset. This can be achieved by selecting the checkbox (6) corresponding to the Key Column.

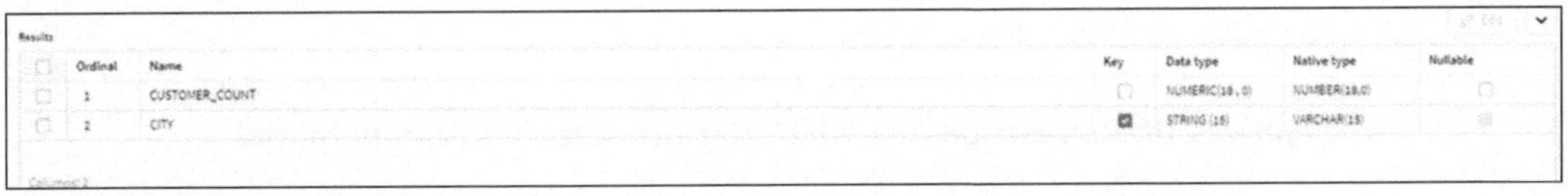

Figure 14.8: *Selecting the key column for the SQL dataset*

Upon selecting **"OK"**, we are redirected to the Transformation Design View. Successfully, we have established our first Non-Materialized Custom SQL Transformation using Qlik Cloud. This process is streamlined and facilitated by Qlik, sparing us from intricate tasks. Instead, we concentrate on articulating the precise business logic without delving into the intricacies of crafting complex SQL CREATE table statements, as all such processes are automated by Qlik. This approach allows us to focus our efforts on formulating the actual business logic.

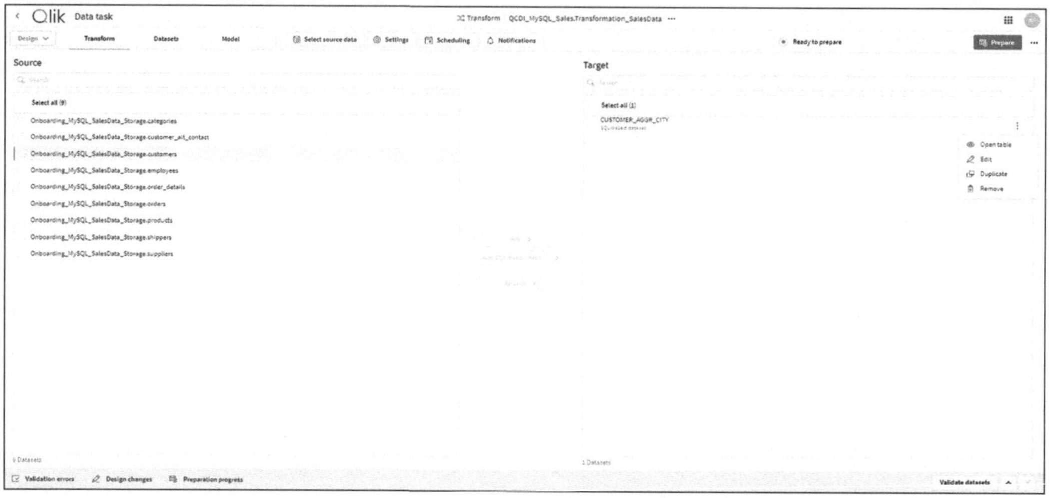

Figure 14.9: *Transformation design view with the first Custom SQL Table created*

Now, we will prepare the dataset using the "**prepare**" option, conduct a data load, and then examine the underlying structures that have been created. We will observe the transformed and newly generated data.

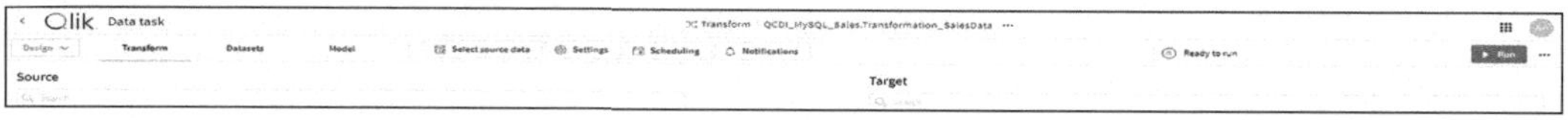

Figure 14.10: *Run Button available after the asset has been prepared*

As we choose the "**run**" option, we notice that we are not in the monitoring view. In this view, we can observe the status of the full load, much like the landing and storage assets. Like the design view, now we can monitor the data loads of the transformation asset via the monitoring view.

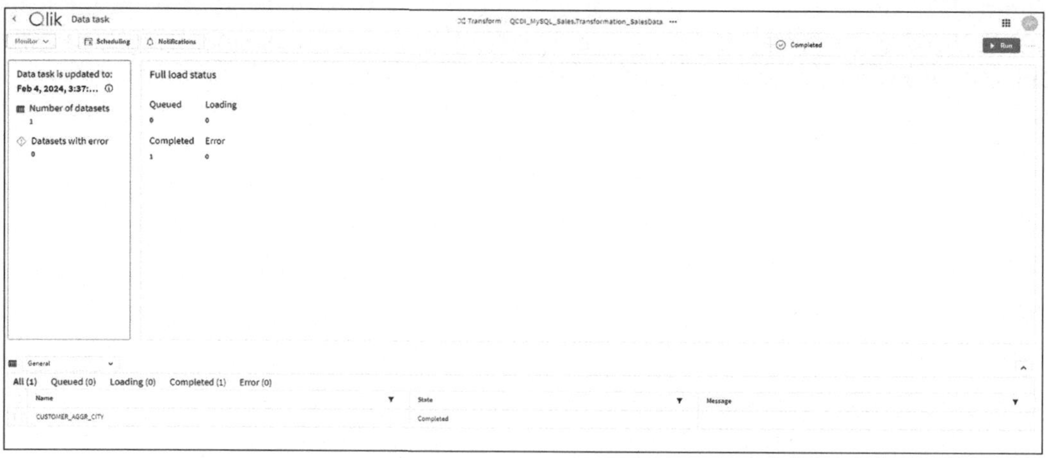

Figure 14.11: *Monitoring view of Transformation asset*

Let us now navigate to the target platform and check the assets that have been created.

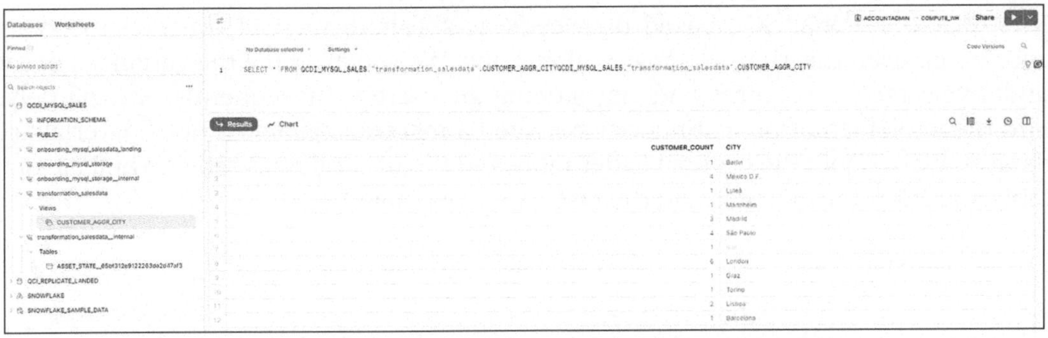

Figure 14.12: *SQL-based dataset – non-materialized created*

We observe that the **CUSTOMER_AGGR_CITY** view has been successfully created in the target platform. However, it's important to note that we do not possess the capability to track changes or the history of the SQL-based dataset. Examining the **transformation_salesdata_internal** schema reveals that no new table for **CUSTOMER_AGGR_CITY** has been generated.

If no new table has been created, the source of data for this view needs to be understood. The logic behind this view is straightforward; it is derived from the storage asset. In essence, the data for the **CUSTOMER_AGGR_CITY** view is sourced directly from the storage asset, incorporating the logic defined in the transformation process.

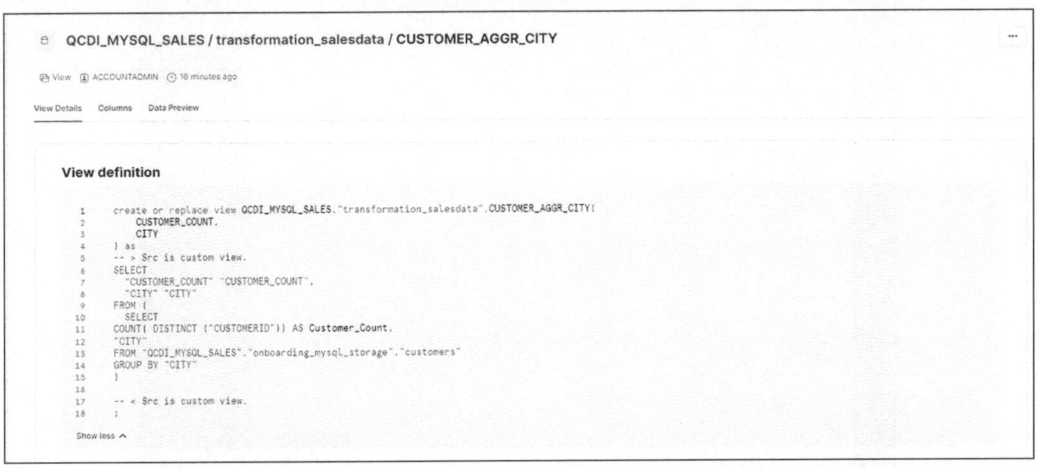

Figure 14.13: *View definition for non-materialized transformation*

Executing the query, we can validate that the results align with the logic we implemented. Specifically, we have the count of unique customers organized by city.

When the logic is straightforward, a non-materialized view suffices. For more intricate transformations and scenarios where historical views and change tracking are necessary, we opt for a materialized view. Let's explore this in the next step.

Creating a SQL SQL-based data set that is materialized

Now that our initial SQL-based dataset is established, we will proceed to create another dataset, this time as a materialized one. We will examine the variances in the underlying table structures and views being generated. Subsequently, we will delve into the implementation distinctions between a materialized and a non-materialized dataset. We will join the orders header table and the order details table to build a joint table and track the changes and the history of this table.

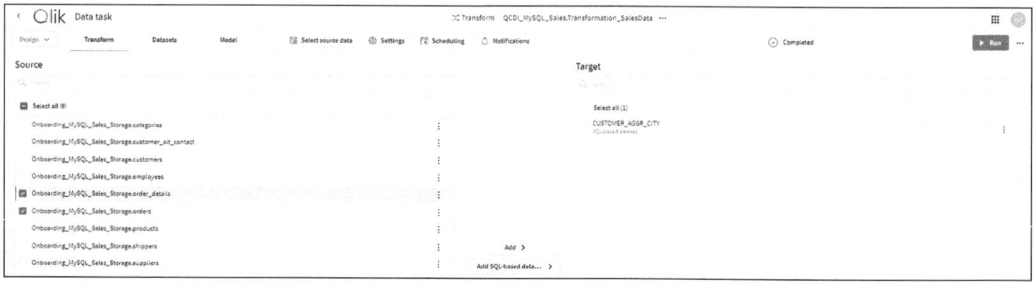

Figure 14.14: *Order header and order details selected and Add SQL Based Data set selected*

In this transformation scenario, we opt not to adhere strictly to the materialization rules set at a task level. Instead, we choose to materialize the data as part of this process.

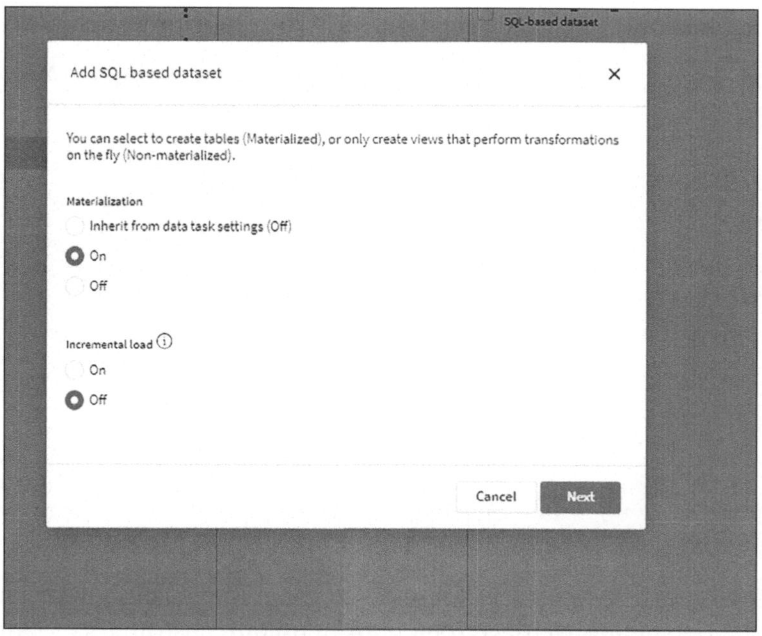

Figure 14.15: *Select the materialization option when creating the SQL-based dataset*

We will formulate a logic to calculate the gross price by multiplying the unit price and quantity. Additionally, we will determine the net price by multiplying the unit price and quantity and then subtracting the discount. The next step involves joining the order details and order header tables to generate the resulting dataset.

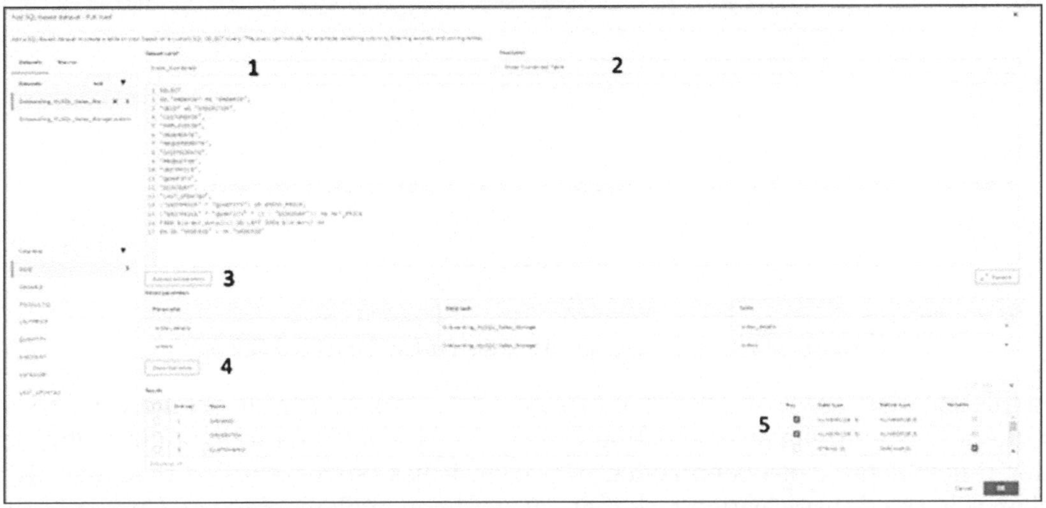

***Figure 14.16**: Creating a dataset with Orders and Order Details and applying business logic*

As we did for the previous SQL-based dataset asset, we will begin by specifying the dataset name (1) and providing a relevant description (2). Following that, we will craft the SQL script encompassing the necessary business logic, including calculations for GROSS_PRICE and **`NET_PRICE`**, along with the extraction and examination of Parameters (3). Subsequently, utilizing the **`"describe table"`** option, we will verify the correct definition of the table. Finally, considering the granularity requirements - in this case, the key being a combination of **`ORDERED`** and **`ORDER ITEM`** (5) - we will select OK to finalize the dataset definition.

We move back to the design view and here we will select the option to **`validate the dataset`**. This option in Qlik Talend Data Integration serves as a tool for assessing the quality and consistency of datasets prior to their storage in a cloud data warehouse or Qlik Cloud. This feature assists in identifying and rectifying errors or design changes that may impact the data pipeline.

Whenever alterations occur in the dataset, such as the addition, removal, or renaming of tables and columns, changes in primary keys, or modifications to data types, the "validate dataset" option presents a comprehensive list of validation errors and design changes when compared to the source. Users can then choose to automatically adjust the design changes or synchronize the datasets manually, depending on the impact of the changes. Certain changes, such as modifications to primary keys or data types, may necessitate table recreation from the source to avoid data loss.

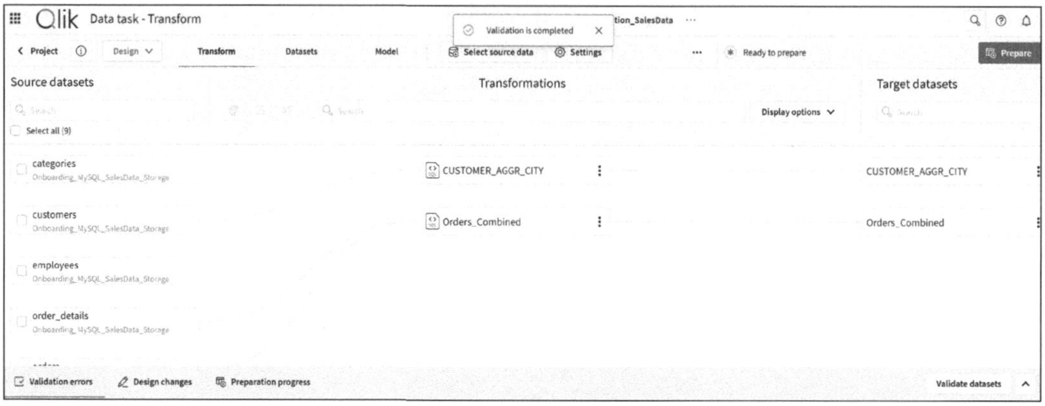

Figure 14.17: *Validation results of the Order Combined Dataset*

In this situation, as we are introducing a new dataset and have successfully defined it without encountering any validation errors, Qlik Talend Data Integration highlights that a new dataset has been added. However, it has been identified that there is a change in the transformation task that has not been implemented yet. Currently, the new dataset only exists in Qlik, and the underlying tables for this dataset have not been created in the target platform, with no data loaded.

Following a similar approach to when we created the Customer Aggregated Count asset, we will now proceed to update the transformation asset in the target system to incorporate this newly defined dataset.

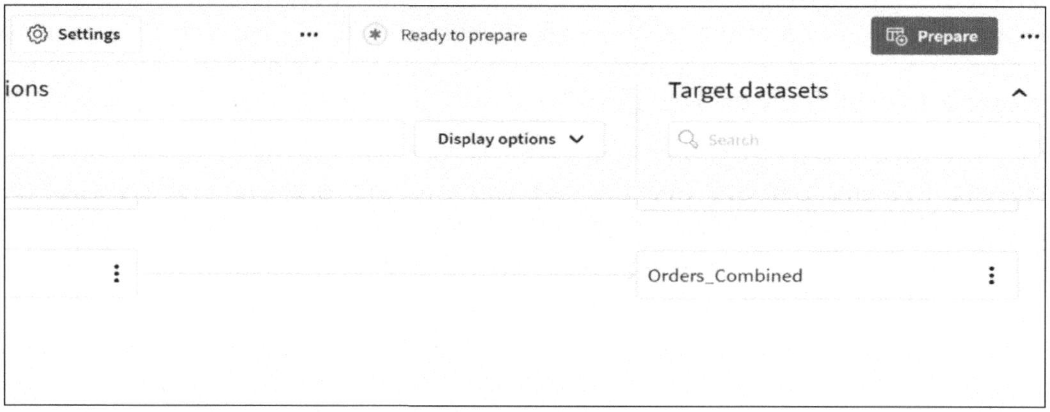

Figure 14.18: *Prepare newly defined dataset*

To initiate the creation of the Orders Combined dataset in the target system, we navigate to the top right of the design view, select the ellipsis icon, and then choose the **"prepare"** option. This action will commence the process of preparing the dataset, resulting in the creation of the new dataset in the target system.

After the process is completed, the design changes that were initially flagged in the validated dataset are no longer present, indicating that they have been successfully applied, and there are no pending changes. Additionally, the status now transitions to **"ready to run"**.

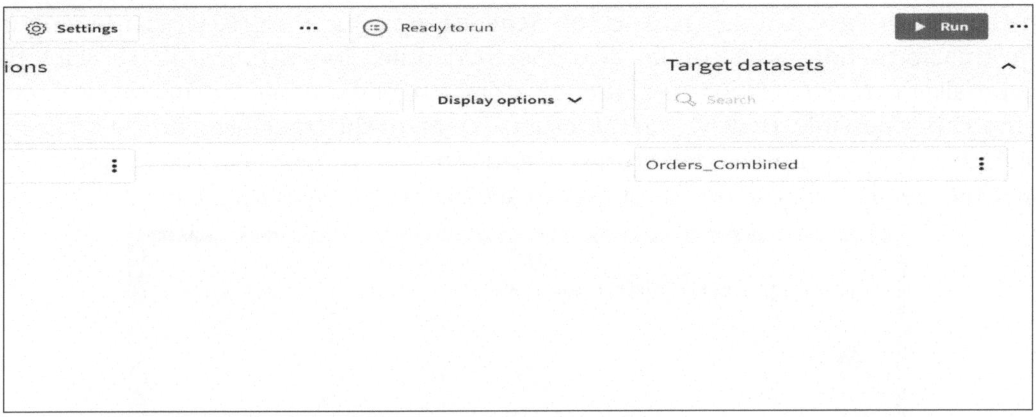

Figure 14.19: *New Data set added and transformation is ready to Run*

Upon navigating to our target system, we observe that the new SQL-based dataset added for **Orders_Combined** differs from the previous Customer count dataset. This dataset now encompasses multiple views, specifically the changes view and the history view. In the internal table, in contrast to the Customer count dataset where no new materialized table was created, we now have the **__CT** table, the **__Current** table, and the **__Prior** table generated for the **Orders_Combined** dataset.

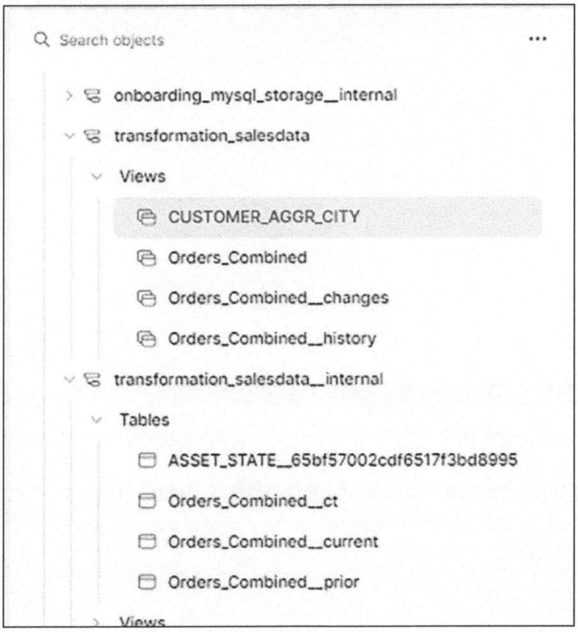

Figure 14.20: *Views and internal datasets created for the Orders_Combined dataset*

To comprehend the functionality of each of these tables and views, let's return to our source system, make changes in the data, and observe how they are processed in each view. Initially, let's schedule the transformation asset to run at a predefined time.

In the design view, we navigate to the **`Scheduling`** option. Here, we can configure the transformation asset to run at a specified time. For instance, if we want the materialized transformation to run once a day and the storage to run every 15 or 5 minutes, it's possible. However, in this case, we aim for the transformation asset to run each time there is a processed storage event. Therefore, we select the option **`"on a specific event"`**, choose the input task to act as a trigger, and then click **`OK`**.

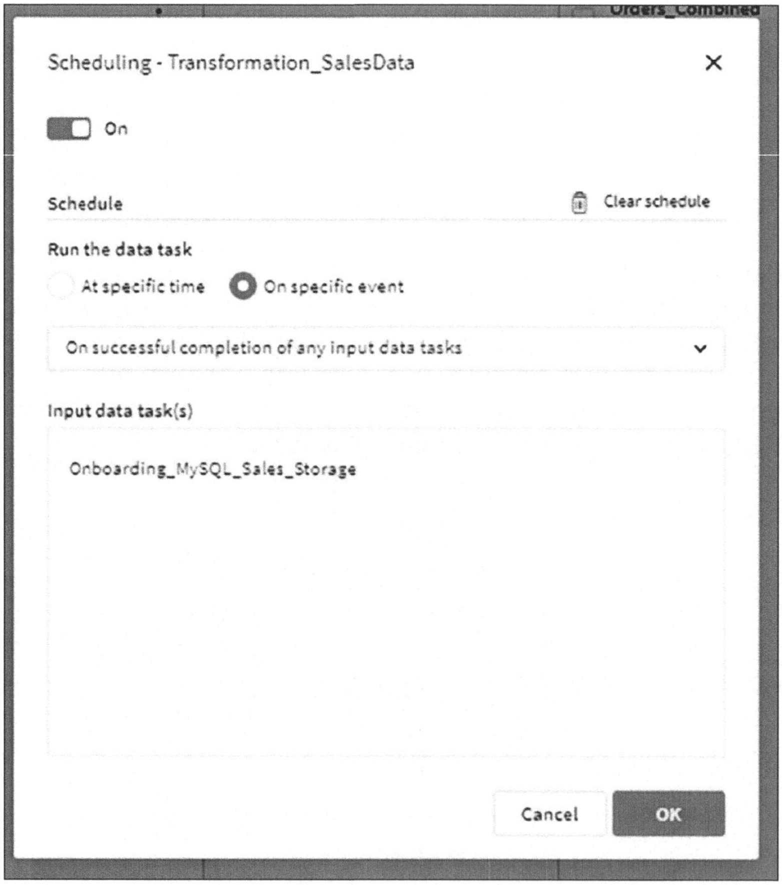

Figure 14.21: *Scheduling the transformation asset*

Detailed scheduling options are available in the Scheduling pop up.

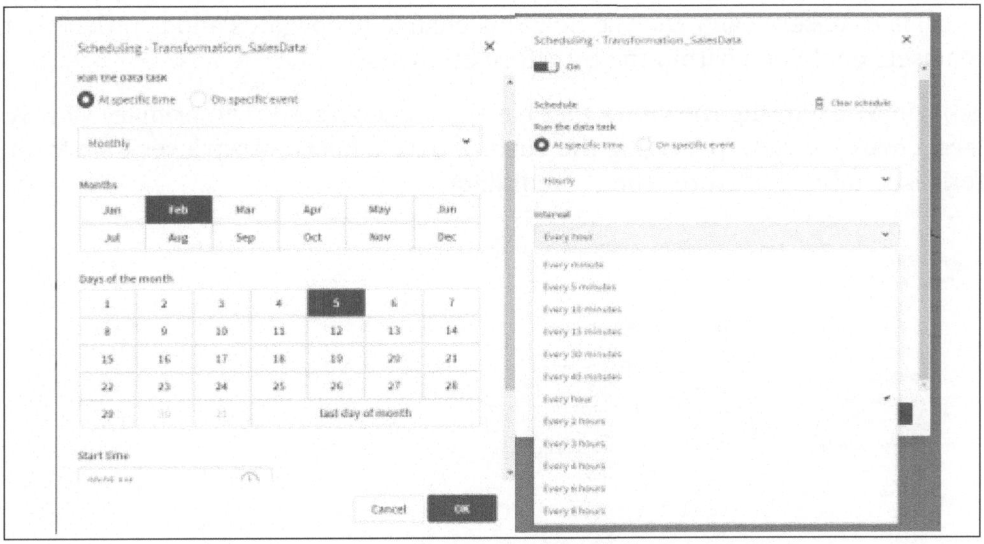

Figure 14.22: *Scheduling the transformation asset*

Once selecting **OK**, we can see that the schedule has been successfully saved.

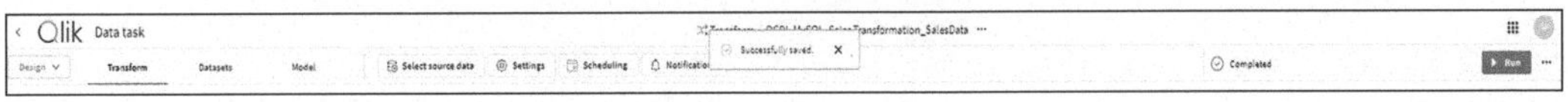

Figure 14.23: *Scheduling saved for the transformation asset*

If we return to the project, we can observe the entire sequence of tasks. First, the landing task, which operates to obtain data in near-real-time. Following that, the storage task is scheduled to run according to our specified requirements. Finally, the transformation task is configured to execute each time there is an execution in the storage task. This scheduling detail can be viewed in the "**`next schedule`**" tab.

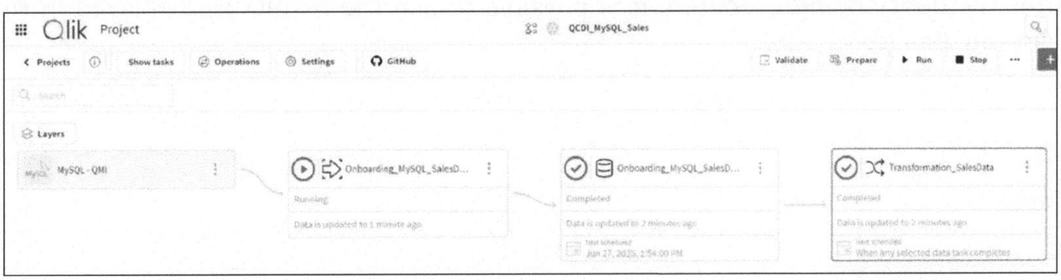

Figure 14.24: *Schedule for the Landing, Storage, and Transformation assets*

In the source system, we access the MYSQL database, specifically targeting the relevant dataset. Subsequently, we update the discount for one record, intentionally increasing the discount. Following this update, we await the predetermined time, aligned with the schedule we have configured for both the storage and transformation assets. After the scheduled time has elapsed, we proceed to examine the outcomes within the transformation asset.

The goal is to observe and analyze how this change propagates and is reflected in all the datasets contained within the transformation asset.

Let's begin by exploring the views that have been generated. The primary view is the **Orders_Combined** view, providing the current data. This view retrieves data from the materialized table that stores the current data.

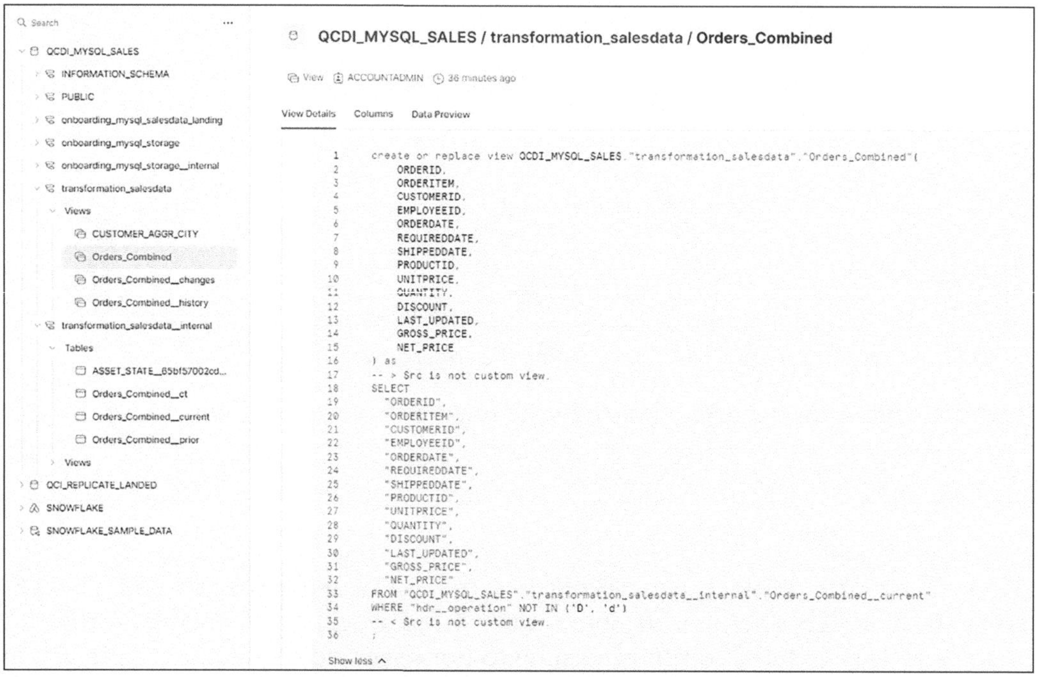

Figure 14.25: *Current Data view (behind the scenes)*

After the query being executed, it is possible to see the results as displayed in the following image:

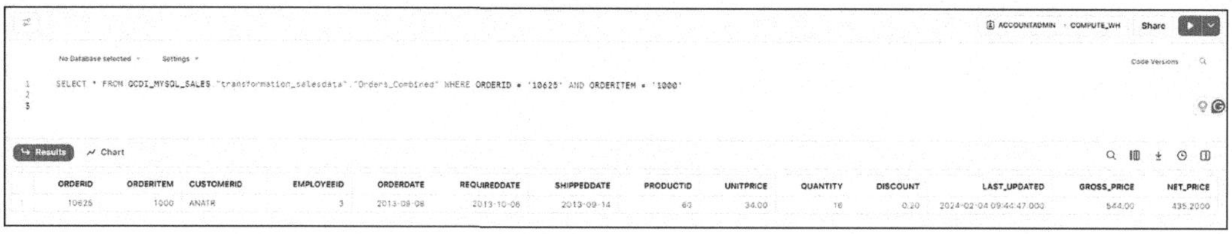

Figure 14.26: *Updated Discount*

The discount update for this record, transitioning from 16 to 20, is indeed reflected in the Combined view.

What distinguishes Qlik is its transparency in providing detailed insights into the data loading process. It avoids being a black box where operations are opaque. To delve into the intricacies of the data loading process, we navigate to the monitoring view and select the last batch of changes. Here, we can explicitly see that one record was updated, along with the time it took for the update to be processed.

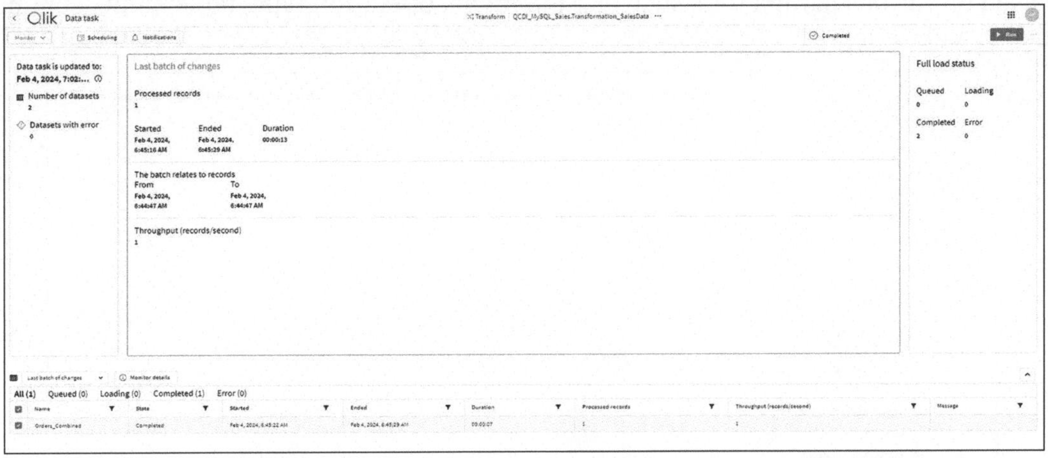

***Figure 14.27**: Updated records in the monitoring view*

When opting for the **"monitor details"** option, a pop-up screen emerges, providing a comprehensive breakdown. Although code modification is not permitted in this interface, it offers a step-by-step elucidation of each operation. Moreover, it affords a closer look at the underlying code, specifically showcasing the SQL queries running in the background.

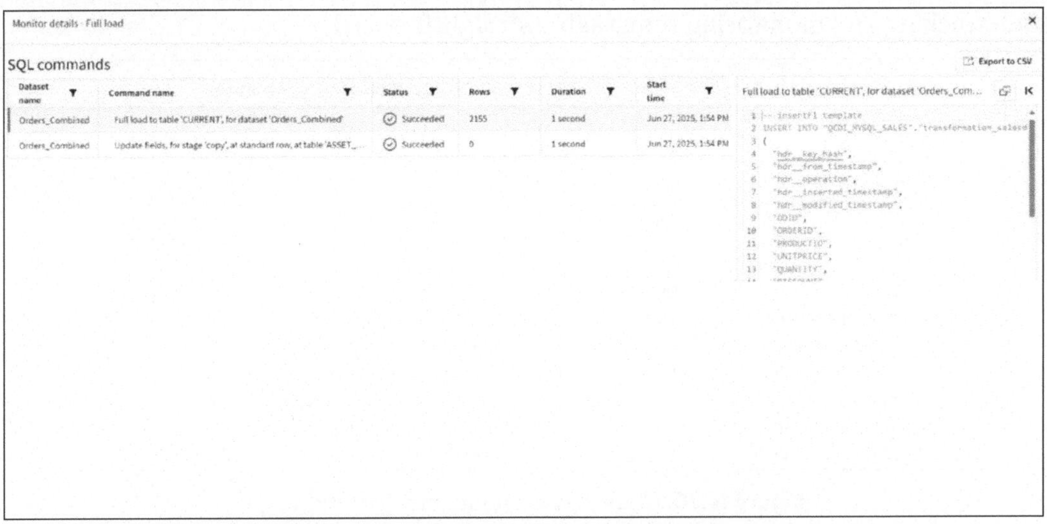

***Figure 14.28**: Monitoring of Data Load process*

SQL-Based Data Set – Changes Table

The changes' view, deriving its data from the `__CT` table, is a notable advantage of materialization. This view serves as a tool to observe alterations in your data sources over time. It facilitates monitoring data quality, identifying anomalies, and troubleshooting issues within our data pipeline. Additionally, we can filter the changes based on various parameters, such as time range, operation type, table name, column name, and value.

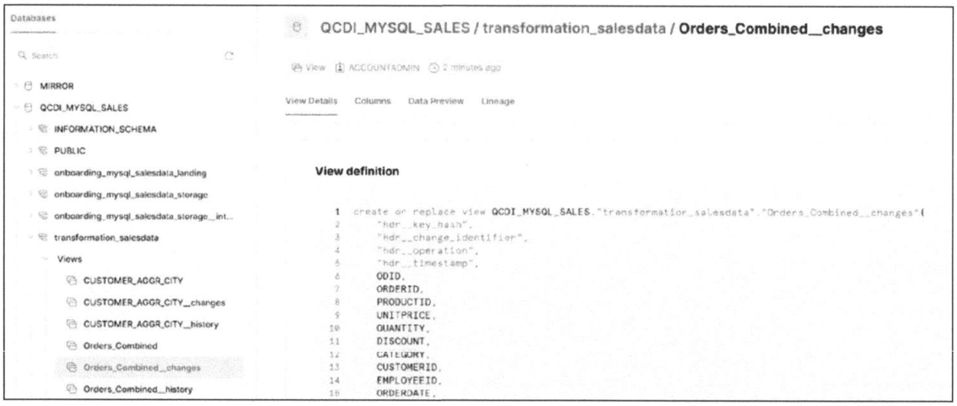

Figure 14.29: *Changes Data View (Behind the Scenes)*

For our specific record, the changes' view captures the type of operation that brought about the change. In this instance, the field **`"hdr__operation"`** has been populated with the value **`"u"`**, clearly indicating that it was an update. Furthermore, the **`"hdr__timestamp"`** field precisely informs us about when this update occurred. Qlik automates this tracking process with the simple action of selecting a button, making such tracking and monitoring remarkably straightforward.

Figure 14.30: *Change timestamp and operation type*

In addition to the **`"hdr__operation"`** and **`"hdr__timestamp"`** fields, there are other metadata fields included in the changes view. The **`"hdr__change_identifier"`** and **`"hdr__key_hash"`** fields are part of the metadata columns integrated by Qlik Talend Data Integration into the storage tables in the cloud data warehouse. These fields play a crucial role in tracking changes and maintaining the history of data records.

The **"hdr__change_identifier"** field serves as a unique identifier for each change record. It is constructed from the source name, table name, change sequence number, and operation type (insert, update, or delete).

On the other hand, the **"hdr__key_hash"** field is a hash derived from all the primary keys of the record. It aids in identifying the record across different tables and views.

These fields prove valuable for querying the changes and historical views, enabling the examination of how the data has evolved and facilitated the recreation of data as it appeared at a specific point in time.

SQL-Based Data Set – History View

Let's move on to the third view within our transformation dataset – the historical view. This feature allows us to examine the historical data that has been captured and stored in your cloud data warehouse. The historical view proves instrumental in analyzing how our data has evolved, and it facilitates the recreation of data as it appeared at a specific point in time.

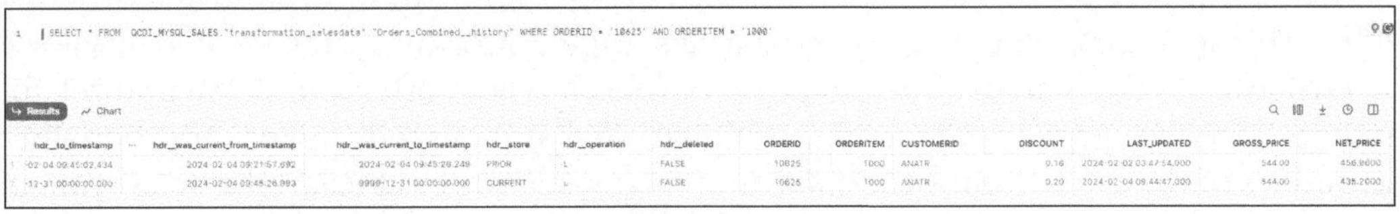

***Figure 14.31**: Historical View*

Executing a query on the historical view reveals some remarkable insights. For this SQL-based dataset we've created, meticulous tracking of changes is now achievable. For the initial record, we observe a value of 0.16 for the discount, representing the initial value. Interestingly, the **"hdr_was_current_from_timestamp"** indicates the time the data load was initially performed, and **"hdr_was_current_to_timestamp"** represents the time until when the record maintained the discount value of 0.16 until the subsequent load updated the value.

The comprehensive historical view serves as a potent tool for generating Type 2 dimensions. It leverages the principles of the Type 2 slowly changing dimension method, meticulously tracking changes in data records over time. This methodology involves creating new records for each change while preserving the integrity of the old records. The historical view, rooted in the Type 2-dimension approach, enables a thorough and insightful analysis of changes in our data over time.

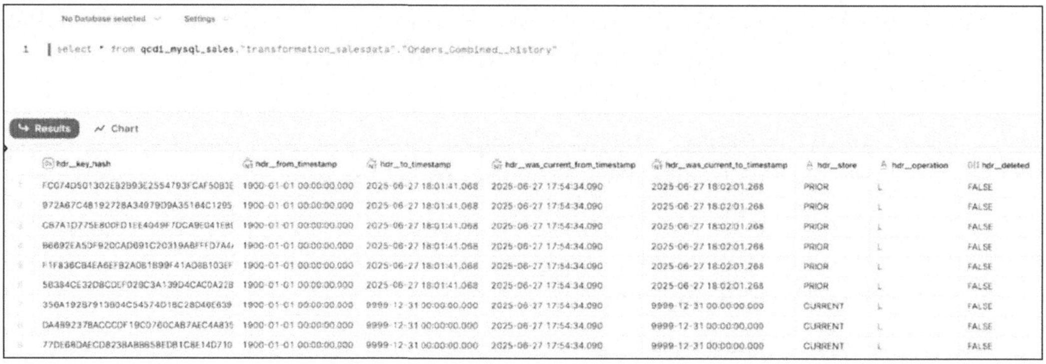

hdr__key_hash	hdr__from_timestamp	hdr__to_timestamp	hdr__was_current_from_timestamp	hdr__was_current_to_timestamp	hdr__store	hdr__operation	hdr__deleted
FC074D501302EB2B93E2554793FCAF50B3E	1900-01-01 00:00:00.000	2025-06-27 18:01:41.068	2025-06-27 17:54:34.090	2025-06-27 18:02:01.268	PRIOR	L	FALSE
972A67C48192728A34979D9A35184C1295	1900-01-01 00:00:00.000	2025-06-27 18:01:41.068	2025-06-27 17:54:34.090	2025-06-27 18:02:01.268	PRIOR	L	FALSE
C87A1D775E800FD1EE4049F7DCA9E041EBI	1900-01-01 00:00:00.000	2025-06-27 18:01:41.068	2025-06-27 17:54:34.090	2025-06-27 18:02:01.268	PRIOR	L	FALSE
B6692EA5DF920CAD691C20319A8FFFD7A4	1900-01-01 00:00:00.000	2025-06-27 18:01:41.068	2025-06-27 17:54:34.090	2025-06-27 18:02:01.268	PRIOR	L	FALSE
F1F836CB4EA6EFB2A0B1B99F41A08B103EF	1900-01-01 00:00:00.000	2025-06-27 18:01:41.068	2025-06-27 17:54:34.090	2025-06-27 18:02:01.268	PRIOR	L	FALSE
58384CE32D8CDEF028C3A139D4CAC0A228	1900-01-01 00:00:00.000	2025-06-27 18:01:41.068	2025-06-27 17:54:34.090	2025-06-27 18:02:01.268	PRIOR	L	FALSE
356A19287913804C54574D18C28D40E639	1900-01-01 00:00:00.000	9999-12-31 00:00:00.000	2025-06-27 17:54:34.090	9999-12-31 00:00:00.000	CURRENT	L	FALSE
DA489237BACCCDF19C0760CAB7AEC4A835	1900-01-01 00:00:00.000	9999-12-31 00:00:00.000	2025-06-27 17:54:34.090	9999-12-31 00:00:00.000	CURRENT	L	FALSE
77DE68DAECD823BABB658ED81C8E14D710	1900-01-01 00:00:00.000	9999-12-31 00:00:00.000	2025-06-27 17:54:34.090	9999-12-31 00:00:00.000	CURRENT	L	FALSE

Figure 14.32: *Additional record changes in historical view*

Making another change, this time increasing the discount to 0.25, reflects in the historical view as a new record being added with the corresponding timestamp fields updated.

The historical perspective is formed by extracting data from internal transformation tables. The accompanying image serves as a sample, offering a high-level overview of the structure of this perspective. Its primary function is to offer a uniform and reliable method to retrieve order data from both historical and current tables. Additionally, it introduces metadata columns to monitor changes and order status. Qlik automatically generates this code in the background, ensuring the selection of the correct data from the appropriate table in the backend, depending on whether the value is current or historical.

```
CREATE OR REPLACE VIEW "QCDI_MYSQL_SALES"."transformation_salesdata"."Orders_Combined__history" AS

-- Start definitions of Common Table Expressions (CTEs).
WITH

-- Define Common Table Expression (CTE) - 'hds_data'.
"hds_data" AS (
SELECT
  'PRIOR' "hdr__store",
  "hdr__key_hash",
  "hdr__from_timestamp",
  "hdr__to_timestamp",
  "hdr__operation",
  "hdr__was_current_from_timestamp",
  "hdr__was_current_to_timestamp",
  "ODID",
  "ORDERID",
  "PRODUCTID",
  "UNITPRICE",
  "QUANTITY",
  "DISCOUNT",
  "CATEGORY",
  "CUSTOMERID",
  "EMPLOYEEID",
  "ORDERDATE",
  "REQUIREDDATE",
  "SHIPPEDDATE",
  "SHIPVIA",
  "FREIGHT",
  "SHIPNAME",
  "SHIPADDRESS",
  "SHIPCITY",
  "SHIPREGION",
  "SHIPPOSTALCODE",
  "SHIPCOUNTRY"
```

Figure 14.33: *Historical View (behind the scenes)*

Materialization versus non-Materialization

After reviewing both settings, it is crucial to distinguish when to opt for materialization versus a pass-through transformation.

Materializing data for a transformation in a view involves creating a physical table to store the transformed data, as opposed to generating a view that performs the transformation on the fly. In the context of Qlik Talend Data Integration, here are some pros and cons associated with this approach:

Pros:

- **Improved Query Performance:** Materialized tables can enhance query performance by avoiding the overhead of running the transformation logic every time the data is accessed.
- **Support for Incremental Data Loading:** Materialized tables support incremental data loading, allowing tracking of changes in the source data and applying them to the target table.
- **Enable Data Lineage and Governance:** Materialized tables facilitate data lineage and governance by providing metadata and audit information about the data transformation process.

Cons:

- **Increased Storage Consumption:** Materialized tables may consume more storage space as they duplicate the data from the source tables.
- **Introduction of Data Latency:** Materialized tables can introduce data latency since they need periodic refreshes to reflect the latest changes in the source data.

If we are using a pass-through, we should consider using non-materialized views. Materialization isn't necessary as these are typically straightforward selections from the source. The data becomes available in those views once storage processes or prior tasks process it.

For custom SQL, we weigh the importance of history. If history isn't a concern and the SQL isn't overly complex, non-materialization is feasible. However, as the SQL complexity increases, it adds more workload for users downstream, whether in cloud data integration or utilizing direct queries in Qlik Sense in the cloud.

The recommendation leans towards materialization, especially if historical support is vital. In such cases, materializing the dataset is advised.

	Non-Materialized	Materialized	Recommendation
Passthrough	• Views • CDC supported • History Supported	• Tables & Views • CDC supported • History supported	Non-Materialized
Custom SQL	• Views • NO CDC • NO History	• Tables & Views • Compare & apply (full SQL executed) • CDC calculated • History supported	Materialized

Figure 14.34: *Materialization versus Non-Materialized Data*

If all datasets in the task are non-materialized, there's nothing to run since the transformation occurs on the fly with views. Despite this, you can establish a schedule for a non-materialized transformation to execute when the schedule condition is met. The task will conclude promptly, potentially triggering a downstream task, such as a data mart. This enables the creation of an event-based pipeline schedule incorporating non-materialized transformations without disrupting the pipeline flow.

Applying Design Changes

We have previously discussed the adjustments made to the app with the addition of the new sales order data. Now, let us delve further into this topic, recognizing that changes are inevitable throughout the project's lifecycle. Managing these changes in the data pipeline is essential, and thankfully, Qlik simplifies this process. To implement these adjustments, we will revisit our operational transformation asset, which is already up and running. We will add additional tables into our pipeline, observing how Qlik streamlines this integration.

In the transformation asset, we choose all the foundational datasets. This time, there won't be extensive SQL transformations or custom SQL additions. Instead, we'll directly include them by opting for the `'Add to Target'` feature.

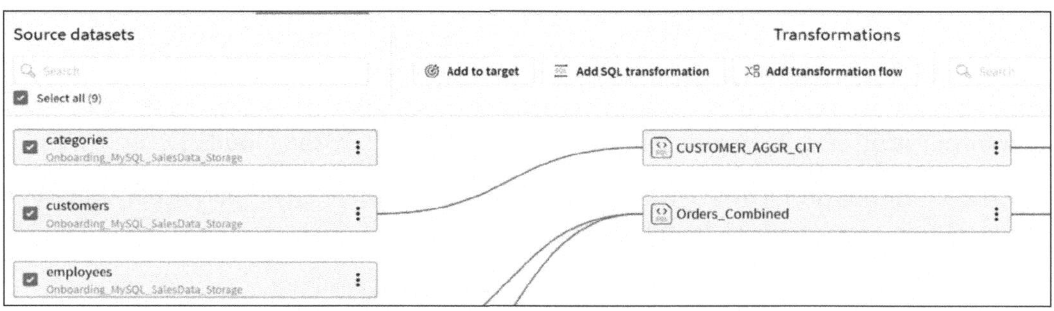

Figure 14.35: *Adding Non-SQL-based Data Sets*

After adding the datasets, we move to the Datasets tab. Here, we will find a list of all datasets along with their keys, akin to the storage and design asset. This is where we can perform straightforward transformations, define rules, and add columns. Anything that doesn't require manual SQL-based coding can be handled here in a more straightforward manner.

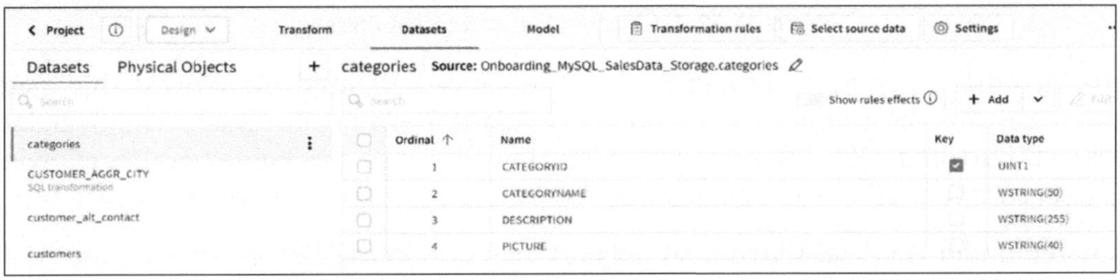

Figure 14.36: *Data Set View in Transformation Asset*

We will now comprehend the nature of validation errors, their implications, and how to identify them. Although this dataset currently lacks inherent errors, our focus shifts to the category's dataset. In this instance, we intentionally uncheck the KEY option and manually remove the defined keys. Our objective is to observe how the validation error manifests when we manually eliminate a designated primary key from the dataset.

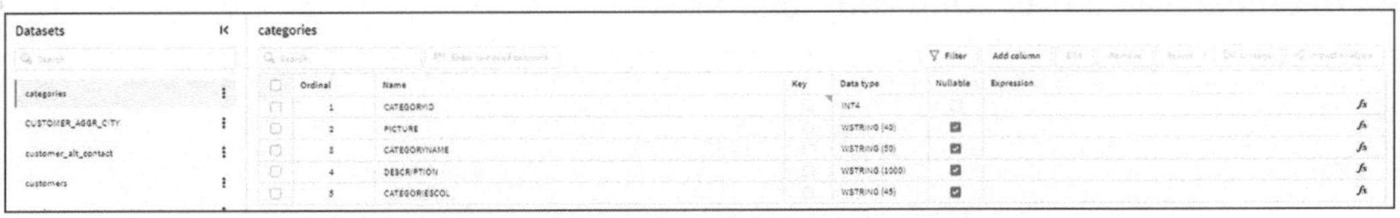

Figure 14.37: *Removing the defined primary key from a dataset*

Once the key is removed, we select the "**`Validate Dataset`**" button located at the bottom right of the screen. Immediately, a popup message informs us that the validation has failed, and Qlik has identified a problem. To delve into the specifics of the issue, we can refer to the description provided.

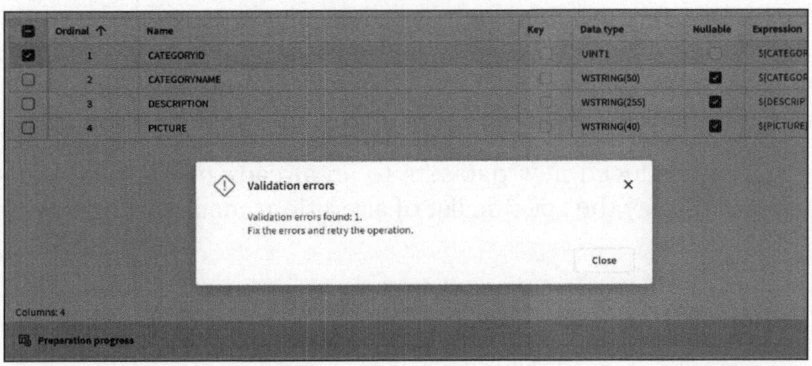

Figure 14.38: *Validation errors*

We can identify more details in the validation error tab.

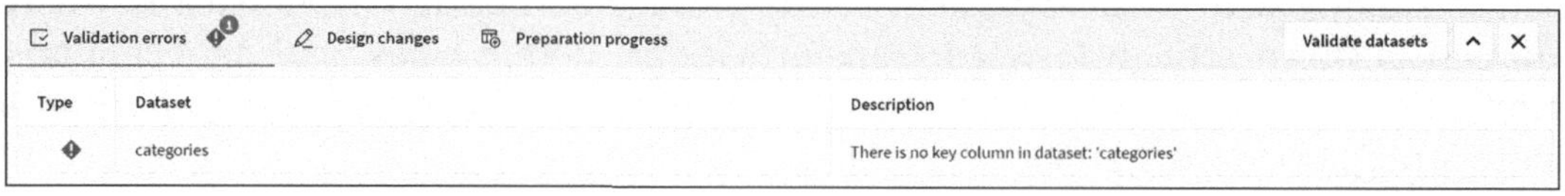

Figure 14.39: *Validation error detailed message*

Qlik identifies the missing key, indicating the dataset affected. To address this issue, simply restore the removed key, and the validation error will vanish. The "Validate Dataset" button in Qlik Talend Data Integration serves as a valuable feature, allowing us to ensure the validity and consistency of your datasets before executing data tasks.

Situated under the **`"Validate and adjust"`** section in the Design view of your data task, this button performs several checks when clicked:

- Ensuring all tables have a primary key.
- Verifying the absence of missing or duplicate columns.
- Confirming compatibility in data types and formats.
- Checking for circular dependencies or conflicts between datasets.

A successful validation prompts a message stating **`"No Validation Errors"`** allowing you to proceed with executing your data task.

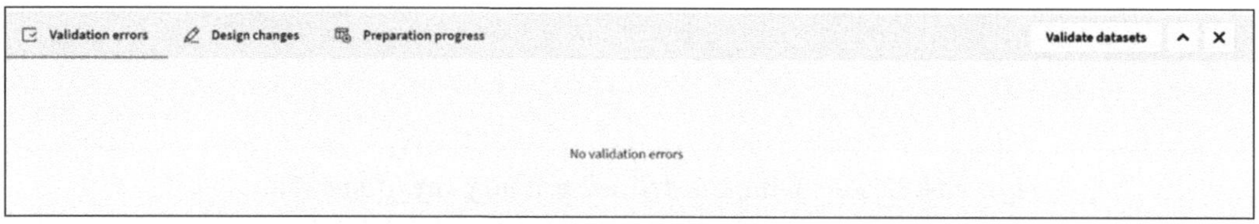

Figure 14.40: *No Validation errors in the Dataset*

Design Changes

The **`Design Changes`** tab in Qlik Talend Data Integration is a valuable feature that enables you to monitor and manage alterations made to your data project. Upon selecting the Design Changes tab, we will encounter a detailed list outlining the changes made to your data project. These changes encompass additions, deletions, or modifications of data tasks, datasets, connections, or transformation rules.

Now, as we have introduced new datasets to an already operational transformation asset, this tab will display the specific list of alterations made during this process.

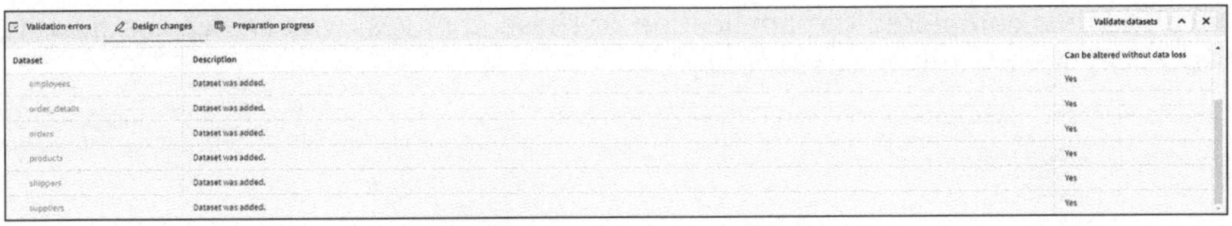

Figure 14.41: *Design Changes*

To implement these changes, navigate to the ellipsis icon, select it, and proceed by clicking the **`"Prepare"`** button.

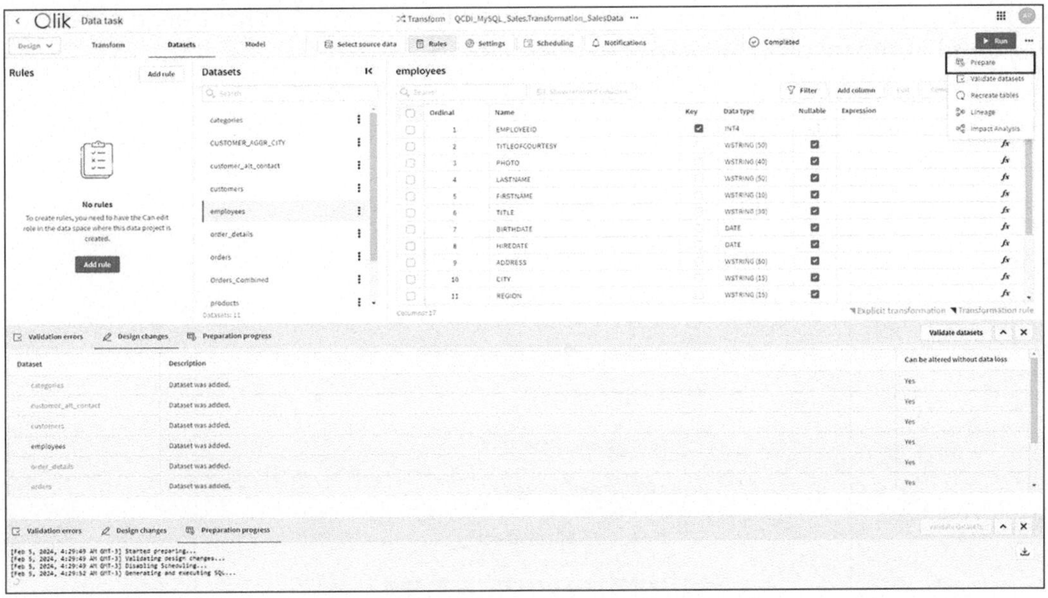

Figure 14.42: *Applying the design changes*

By leveraging the preparation progress bar, we can gain insights into the progression of changes. This detailed view provides an understanding of the specific tasks Qlik is undertaking, encompassing the generation of SQL scripts for applications and updates to catalogs. The logs, downloadable in CSV format, delineate the process. This involves validating design changes, disabling scheduling, generating and executing SQL statements, updating the catalog for various tables, creating a lineage document, deploying and scheduling the task.

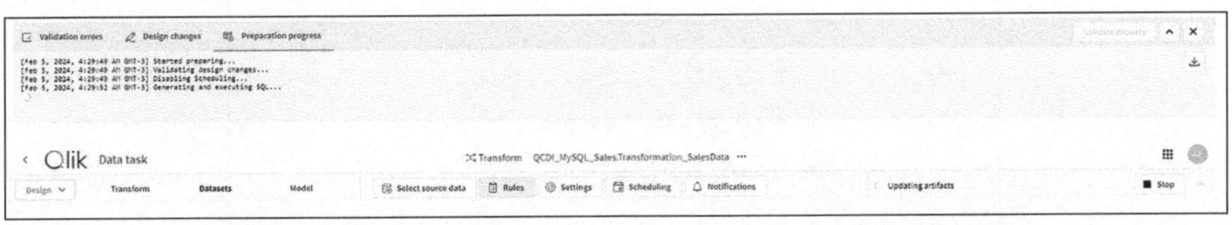

Figure 14.43: *Monitoring the application of the design changes*

Once Qlik has completed the application of these changes, we can see the message **"Finished Preparing successfully"**.

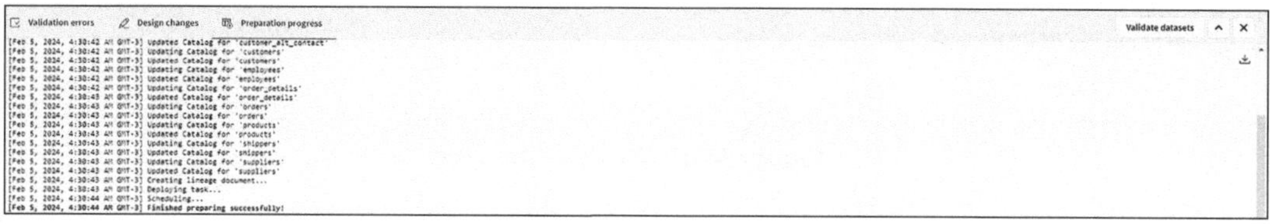

Figure 14.44: *Successful application of the design changes*

Inspecting the Snowflake console, we can see all the objects that have been created, as displayed in the following image.

Figure 14.45: *Target Platform after application of the design changes*

We can also navigate to the Target platform, and it now shows that a structure has been created to accommodate all the newly added and created datasets in the transformation.

Settings of Transformation Asset

Now, let's delve into the settings within the transformation asset, understanding their meanings and functionalities. The settings encompass two tabs: general and runtime settings.

In the general settings, we configure the database for our data source. This involves selecting the specific database, naming the schema for storing data task information (default is **"store"**, but customizable), and specifying a schema for internal storage (default is **"store__internal"**, but can be renamed). To enhance organization, it's advisable to set a prefix for all tables and views generated by this task, ensuring uniqueness, especially if used across multiple tasks.

We are faced with the decision of creating physical data tables (**"Materialized")** or opting for on-the-fly transformation views (**"Non-Materialized").** Finally, we can choose the retention of historical change data. This facilitates the recreation of past states, accessible through history and live history views.

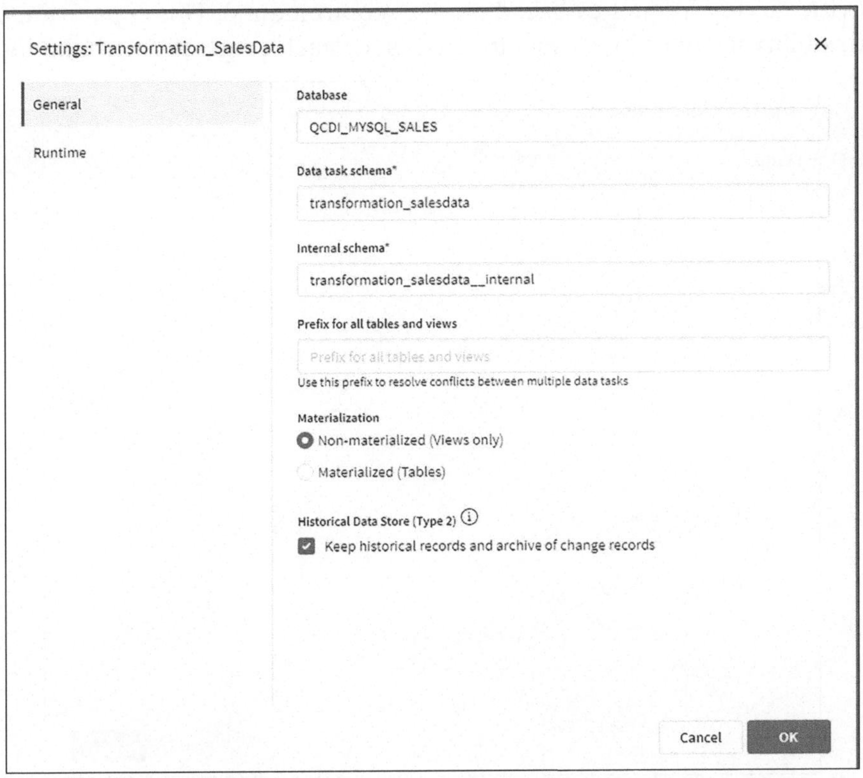

Figure 14.46: *Settings of Transformation Asset (General)*

In the runtime settings, we can configure the following options:

1. **Parallel Execution**: We can set the maximum number of data connections for full loads, choosing a number from 1 to 5. The impact of adjusting parallel executions in Qlik Talend Data Integration depends on various factors, including the number and complexity of datasets, available resources, and the performance of source and target data platforms.

   Generally, increasing parallel executions can improve data processing speed and reduce task execution time. However, this may consume more resources and increase the risk of errors or conflicts. On the other hand, decreasing parallel executions conserves resources, ensuring data quality and consistency, but it might slow down data processing and extend overall task execution time. There's no fixed rule for the optimal number; we need to experiment with different values and monitor the results to find the right balance between performance and efficiency.

2. **Warehouse**:

   We specify the name of the cloud data warehouse. We can potentially have distinct warehouses for the landing (constantly active) and the transformation (with varying frequency based on our requirements). This separation allows us flexibility in adapting to specific needs for each stage of data handling.

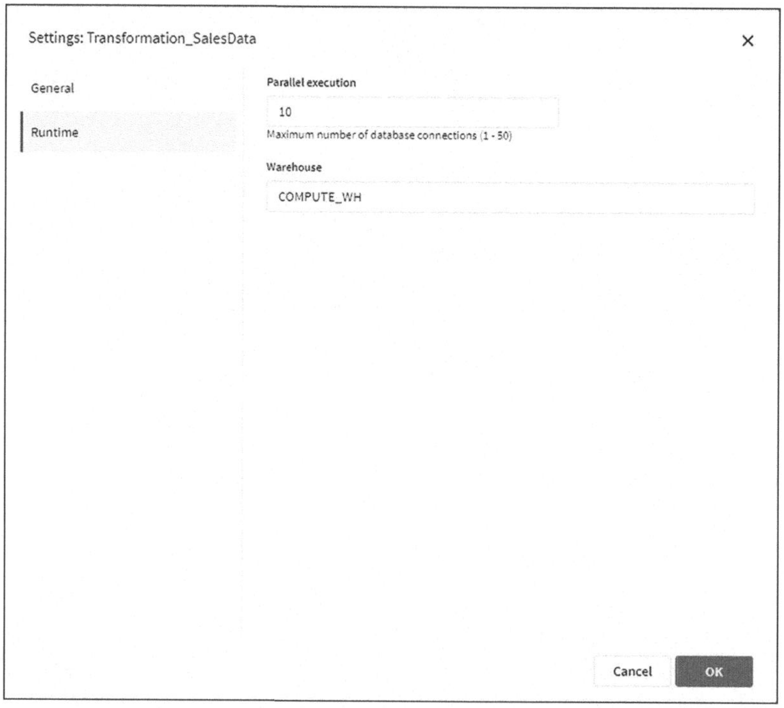

Figure 14.47: *Runtime tab of Transformation Asset Settings*

Complex Transformation Pipelines and Third-Party Transformation

In Qlik Cloud, the pipelines generated are not confined to a single transformation asset; we can incorporate as many transformation assets as dictated by the business logic. This flexibility aids in segregating, maintaining, and dividing complex business logic into step-by-step transformations, where each transformation manages a specific scenario.

Key features of these pipelines include:

- **Multiple Source Data Assets**: Transform tasks can seamlessly read from multiple source data assets, enhancing the versatility of data processing.
- **Complex Transformation Pipelines**: Users can construct intricate transformation pipelines as direct acyclic graphs (DAGs), allowing for a comprehensive representation of business logic.
- **Mix, Match, and Chain Tasks**: Pipelines can include a mix of pass-throughs and custom SQL tasks, offering a wide range of options for implementing and customizing transformations.
- **Logic Encapsulation and Re-use**: The system supports logic encapsulation and reuse, promoting efficient management of transformation processes.

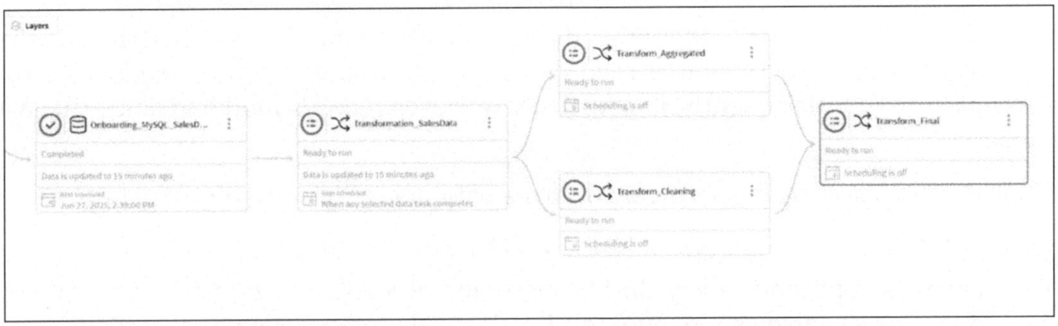

Figure 14.48: *Multiple Transformations in a pipeline*

Qlik Talend Data Integration also seamlessly integrates with third-party data transformation tools like Qlik Replicate and Talend, allowing us to register and incorporate existing data landed in our chosen cloud platform directly into our data pipelines. This eliminates the need to duplicate existing processes and consume data twice, empowering us to create transformation tasks, cleanse data, and automate data warehouse operations effortlessly. By embracing third-party transformation, we adhere to Qlik's core principles of leaving the data where it is, registering it, understanding its structure, enhancing its quality, and delivering it promptly. Whether we're migrating from legacy tools, leveraging an existing cloud data warehouse for new projects, or collaborating with proprietary solutions, third-party transformation provides a versatile and efficient solution.

Incremental Loading SQL Data Set

For SQL Based Data, we can optimize the dataset loading process by adopting an incremental approach. This entails appending only new or modified records from the source to the target, rather than reloading the entire dataset on each iteration. This strategy not only enhances performance but also minimizes network traffic and conserves storage space by circumventing unnecessary data duplication.

For successful implementation of incremental loading, the source data must incorporate a distinguishing field, such as a timestamp, a sequence number, or a flag, capable of identifying new or altered records. Furthermore, the target data necessitates a primary key to facilitate the seamless merging of records. Upon activating incremental loading, macros become instrumental in customizing the query based on whether it constitutes an initial or incremental load. Macros, denoted by special keywords enclosed in curly braces, like {initial} or {incremental}, enable the insertion of conditions, filters, or parameters into the query.

Illustratively, the subsequent macro serves to filter the source data based on the modification time.

```
field:{incremental: WHERE ModificationTime >= {last_execution_time} AND
ModificationTime < {current_execution_time}}
```

This macro exclusively operates during incremental loads, comparing the ModificationTime field of source records with the last and current execution times of the data task. Consequently, it selectively retrieves records modified since the last execution.

Similarly, the following macro incorporates a parameter linked to the target object:

```
{incremental: AND PrimaryKey NOT IN ({target:PrimaryKey})}
```

This macro is applicable solely during incremental loads, utilizing the primary key field of the target table as a parameter. It selectively fetches source records that do not exist in the target table. Multiple macros can be seamlessly integrated into a single query, provided they are separated by spaces.

For instance, consider the following query encompassing the two macros:

```
SELECT FIELD(S) FROM SourceTable {incremental: WHERE ModificationTime >=
{last_execution_time} AND ModificationTime < {current_execution_time} AND
PrimaryKey NOT IN ({target:PrimaryKey})}
```

Post-query input, alongside the macros, clicking `'Parse'` facilitates the parsing of parameters within the **`SELECT`** query. These parameters can be mapped to either source or target objects, associating with History type 2 structures (**`_history`**), Current structures, or Target objects. Notably, mapping to target objects is restricted to scenarios where a parameter is defined within an incremental macro.

Moreover, the option to replace a parameter with a reference is available, enhancing query readability. Simply modify the value in the Parameter, and the reference in the SELECT query will adjust accordingly.

Conclusion

In this chapter, the Transformation Asset in Qlik Talend Data Integration is explored, showcasing its capabilities in enhancing agility, efficiency, and automation in data management. It leverages SQL-powered cloud-native transformation to facilitate the design, deployment, and orchestration of data pipelines on leading cloud platforms, such as Snowflake, Azure Synapse, Google Big Query, and Microsoft SQL Server. A template-driven approach ensures efficiency by allowing users to define reusable transformations and policies, while built-in automation adheres to DataOps best practices, ensuring reliability and efficiency at scale. Integration with data movement services enables near-real-time transformation and delivery of analytics-ready data, while granular rule-based control ensures precision in data processing.

Additionally, users can derive intelligence from data through various methods, define logical relationships between datasets for deeper insights, and choose between materialization and virtualization options based on specific technical requirements. Low-latency data movement with Change Data Capture (CDC) supports incremental updates while harnessing native cloud data warehouse power optimizes technical performance by tapping into the processing capabilities of chosen cloud data warehouses. Overall, the Transformation Asset in Qlik Talend Data Integration empowers users with a comprehensive suite of technical features to streamline and optimize their data journey.

In the upcoming chapter, we will delve into the role of Data marts within Qlik Talend Data Integration, which function as repositories for summarized data collected for analysis within specific sections or units of an organization.

Multiple Choice Questions

1. What is the benefit of choosing materialized tables over virtual views in the Transformation Asset?

    a. Improved performance for frequent data access

    b. Reduced storage footprint for rarely accessed data

    c. Easier integration with external data sources

    d. Increased flexibility for data manipulation

2. How does the Transformation Asset leverage cloud data warehouse capabilities?
    a. By providing pre-built connectors for specific platforms
    b. Through template-driven configuration for each platform
    c. Using push-down processing to utilize native platform power
    d. By offering a separate processing engine within the asset
3. What is one of the benefits of using third-party data transformation with Qlik Talend Data Integration?
    a. It allows us to duplicate existing processes and consume data twice
    b. It allows us to create transformation tasks, cleanse data, and automate data warehouse operations
    c. It allows us to migrate data from cloud platforms to legacy tools
    d. It allows us to disregard Qlik's core principles of data management

Answers

1. a
2. c
3. b

References

1. *Qlik Help*: https://help.qlik.com/

Chapter 15
Data Marts

Introduction

In this chapter, we will explore the advanced capabilities of Qlik Talend Data Integration to construct data marts, associate facts with dimensions, and manage type 2 dimensions, all while ensuring minimal coding requirements.

Structure

In this chapter, we will discuss the following topics:

- Data Models
- Data Marts
- Type 2 Dimensions

Data Marts

Data marts, subsets within data warehouses tailored to specific business functions or subject areas, stand as essential components in the modern data landscape, enhancing analytical efficiency and accessibility for targeted user groups. Despite often being overlooked amidst the vastness of data warehouses, their distinct history and ongoing relevance underscore their unique value.

Data marts, foundational subsets of data warehouses, began evolving in the late 1980s and early 1990s as part of the broader data warehousing movement pioneered by experts like Bill Inmon and Ralph Kimball. While the term "data mart" gained prominence later, the concept of targeted data storage for analytical purposes has its roots in the data management practices of the 1980s.

Over time, data marts have transcended basic reporting, evolving to handle complex analyses and ad-hoc queries, propelled further by the democratization brought by self-service BI and cloud computing. This evolution has led to diversification, with data marts now tailored to meet the specific needs of departments, hybrids, and operational functions within organizations. Looking ahead, data marts are poised for further innovation, expected to embrace agility, real-time capabilities, and integration with cutting-edge technologies, such as AI and machine learning, all while continuing to empower users through self-service analytics and intuitive interfaces, thereby shaping the future of data-driven decision-making.

Data Marts in Qlik Talend Data Integration

In the preceding chapters, we explored the capabilities of QCDI, demonstrating its utility in performing change data capture from RDBMS sources and extracting data according to predefined schedules for SaaS applications. We also delved into the transformation process facilitated by transformation assets, enabling the addition of business logic to prepare data for consumption. Now, armed with this understanding, we shift our focus to constructing data models, data marts, and data lakes, preparing them for utilization by analytics tools such as Qlik Sense. Within this framework, we have the flexibility to create data marts using storage data tasks or transform data tasks, tailoring them to meet our specific business requirements. The ideal scenario involves crafting data marts as repositories of summarized data, meticulously collected and organized for analysis within designated sections or units of an organization. This approach ensures that our data resources are optimally structured and readily accessible for insightful analytics, thereby empowering informed decision-making across the organization.

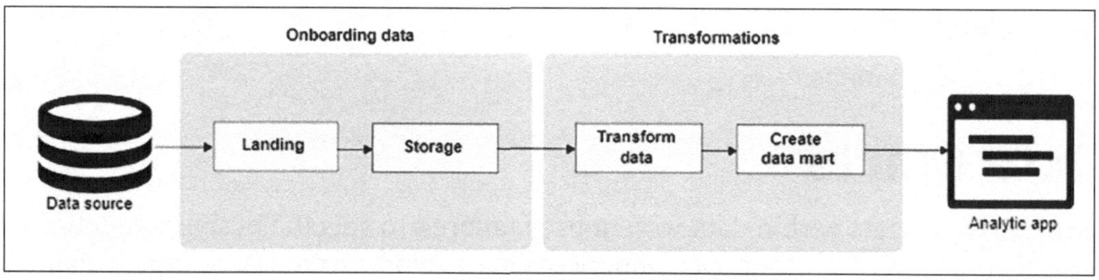

Figure 15.1: *Data Flow*

Data Model

Before constructing a data mart, it's crucial to establish the relationships between the tables using a data model. Building a data model in Qlik Talend Data Integration entails establishing relationships between the datasets incorporated in a Storage or Transform data task. This data model can subsequently be leveraged by a data mart to automate code generation for the denormalization of dimensions and fact tables.

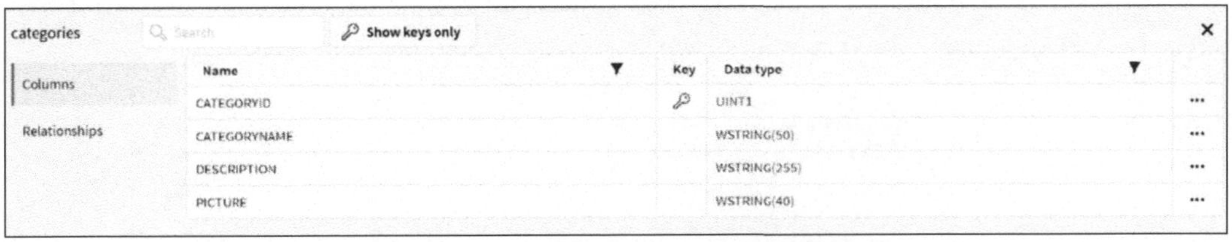

***Figure 15.2**: Data Model in a storage asset*

We observe that there is an opportunity to view the data model in both the storage asset and the transformation asset.

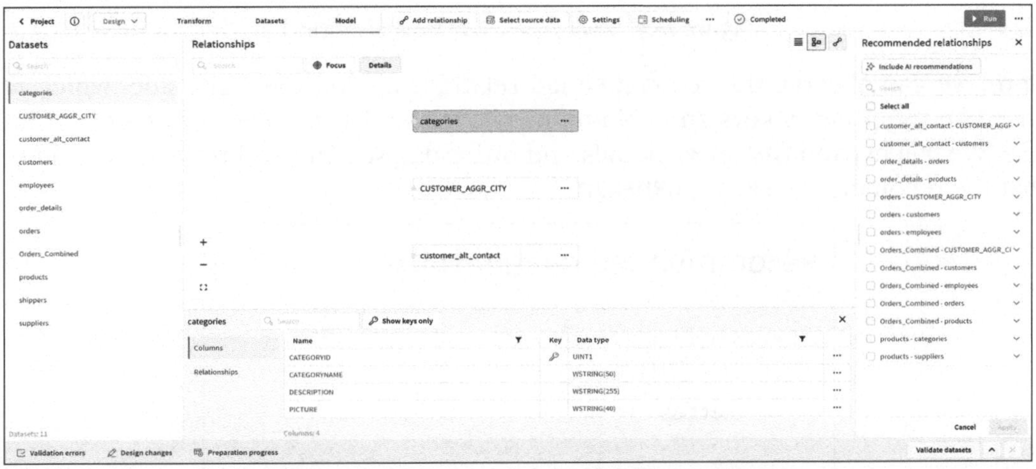

***Figure 15.3**: Data Model in a transformation asset*

As we can see in the preceding two images, this can be accomplished either within a storage asset or a transform asset. Technically, you can have a landing-storage setup alongside a data mart. However, it is recommended to consistently incorporate a transform asset. This ensures the asset's future resilience. Transformation facilitates the merging and extraction of data from multiple datasets. Even if minimal activity occurs within the transformation asset initially, it's prudent to have a pass-through transformation asset. This guarantees that any future updates can be implemented with minimal disruption.

Building a Data Model

We will navigate to the transformation asset and then, access the model view within it.

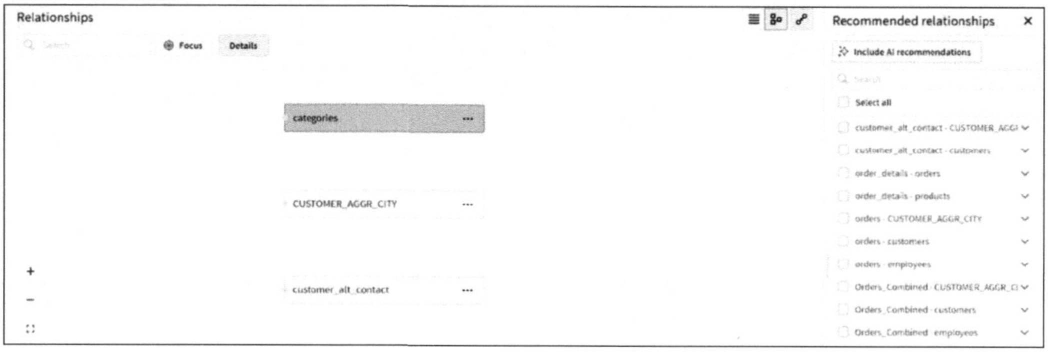

Figure 15.4: *Model View in Transformation*

Here, we can observe the recommended relationships on the right side, which are based on the primary keys and column names in the dataset. Let's delve deeper into this. We will expand the order details and order dataset. In this instance, we can see that the recommended key is **ORDERID**.

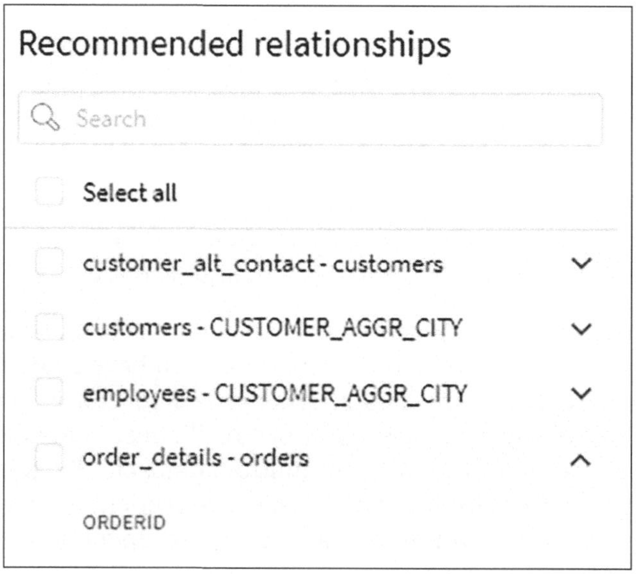

Figure 15.5: *Expanding recommended relationship*

Upon selecting the checkbox, we can observe that the **order_details** and **orders** are now connected via a green dotted line. This illustrates the proposed relationship. It's crucial to note that at this stage, the relationship is merely a proposal.

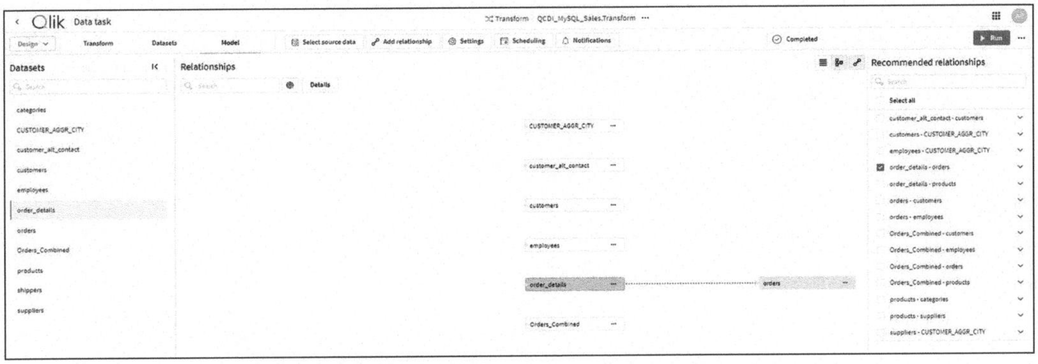

***Figure 15.6**: Order Details and Order Relationship*

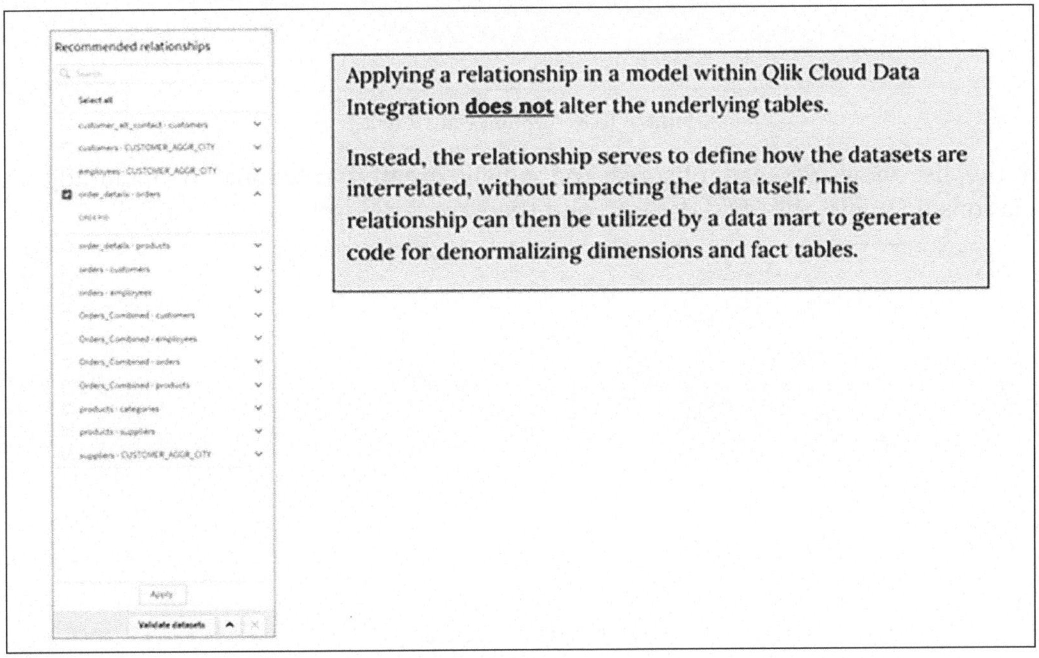

***Figure 15.7**: Applying the relationship*

After selecting the apply button, you'll notice that there is no "**`prepare`**" action occurring in the base tables, unlike when we added new datasets earlier. This is because the relationship is virtual. Upon application, the green dotted line transforms into a solid gray line, indicating the transition from a "**proposed**" relationship to an **applied** one.

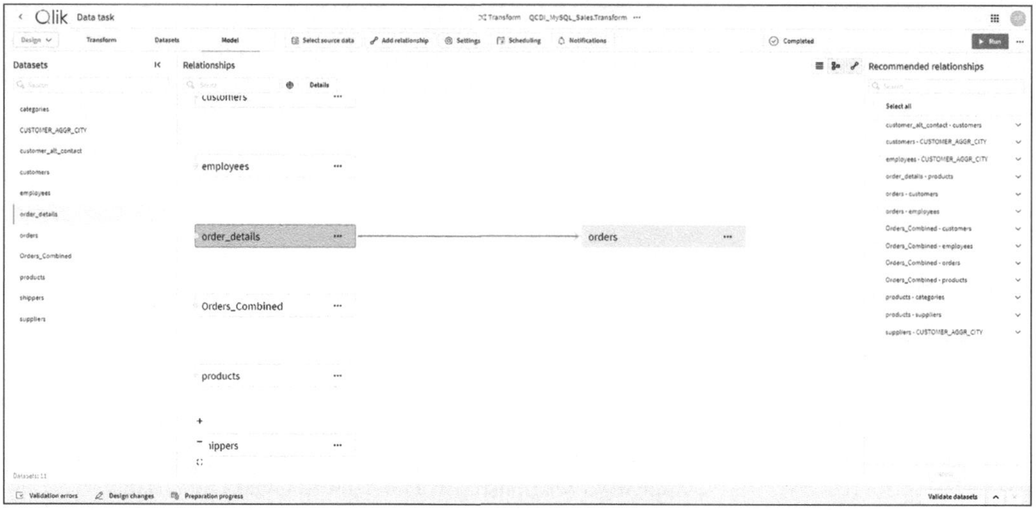

Figure 15.8: *Applied relationship*

In the list view, we can observe the newly created relationship, including the relationship name, the child dataset, and the parent dataset.

Figure 15.9: *List view*

A child dataset maintains a relationship with another dataset, known as the parent dataset. This relationship depends on matching columns in the two datasets such as primary keys or foreign keys. Typically, a child dataset is associated with only one parent dataset, while a parent dataset may have multiple child datasets. This relationship between a child and a parent dataset serves as the foundation for constructing a data model, which can then be utilized by a data mart to automate code generation for denormalizing dimensions and fact tables.

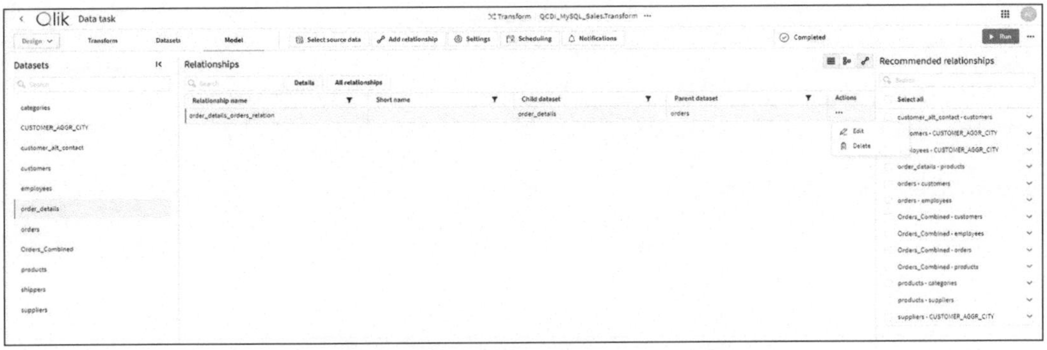

Figure 15.10: *Edit the existing relationship*

We can also navigate to the ellipsis icon in the list view. Here, we have the option to edit the relationship. We can modify the name and description of the relationship. Additionally, we have the flexibility to adjust the key used for linking the two datasets. If we recognize that the dataset should be joined via a different key, we can select the desired key from the dropdown menu. Let's proceed by changing the relationship name and short name.

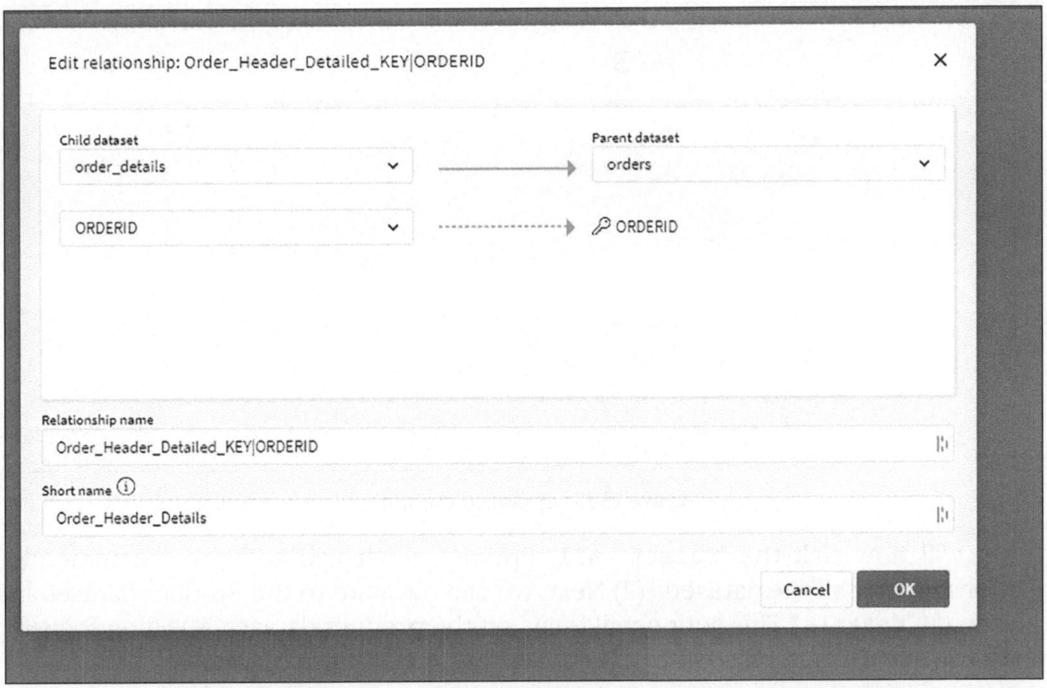

Figure 15.11: *Editing the relationship between tables in a data model*

The updated relationship, as previously observed, is also visible in the list view, as demonstrated here.

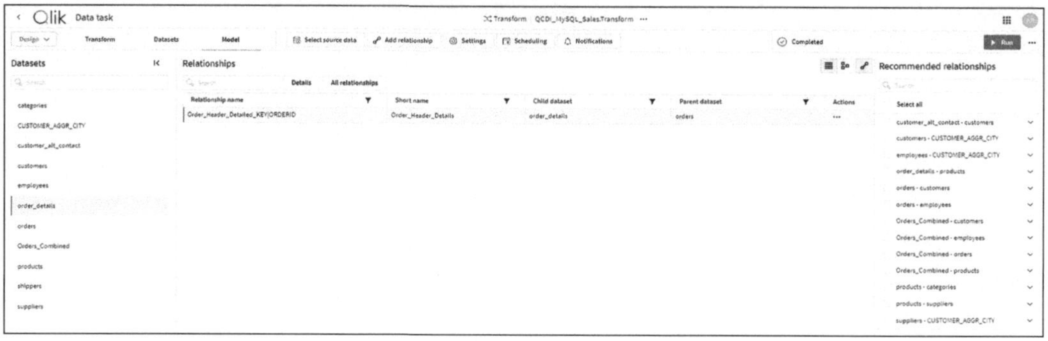

Figure 15.12: *Updated Relationship between order header and item*

Now that we've applied the relationship between the two tables, our next step is to apply this across the entire data model. However, it's crucial to remember that we must validate each suggestion provided by Qlik. While Qlik offers recommended relations based on the primary key of the table and the field name, it's essential to validate them manually. This validation is necessary because sometimes, due to inconsistencies in database design.

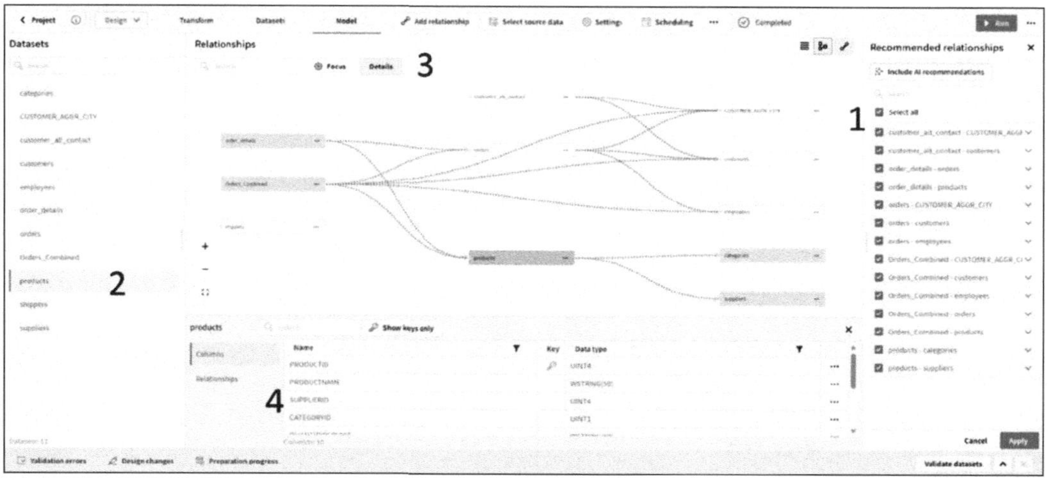

Figure 15.13: *Applying the model*

(1) We will now tick the **"`select all`"** option, which will add the recommended relationships for all the datasets. (2) Next, we can navigate to the Product dataset and click on (3) **"`details`."** This action will focus on the product dataset. (4) Upon focusing in, we can see the columns - the column names for the selected dataset.

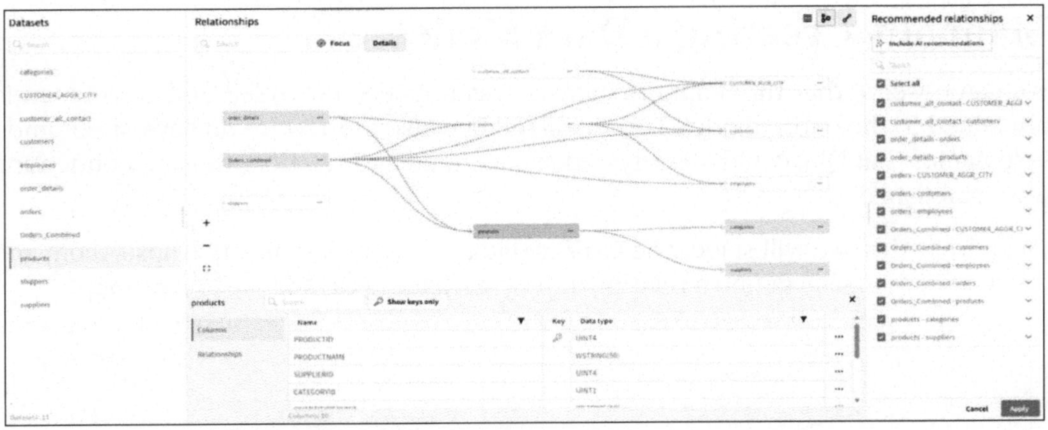

Figure 15.14: *Applying all the recommended relationships*

Once all the recommended relationships are applied, we'll notice that no more recommended relationships appear in the recommended relationships section on the right.

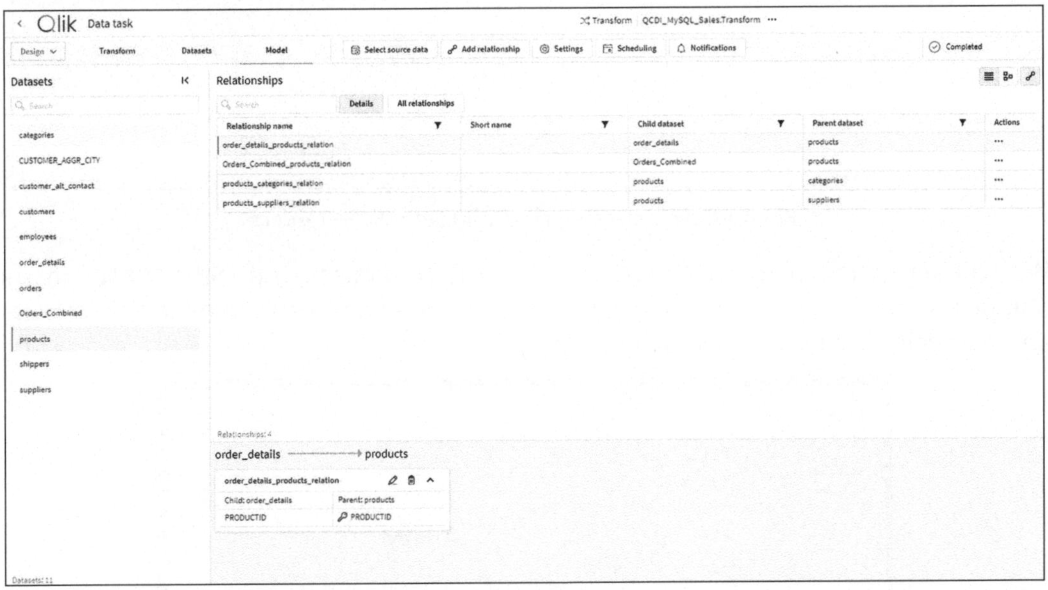

Figure 15.15: *Relationships in products dataset*

In the relationship dataset, we can observe all the relationships to which the Product dataset has been linked. Like how we edited the earlier Order Header and Detailed datasets, for each of the relationships we see here, we can edit and change the keys and descriptions as needed.

Manually Creating a Data Model

We can observe that the Shippers dataset was not recommended and consequently not added to the entire model. This occurred because there were no keys or common field names that Qlik could identify and recommend as a relation, thus no connection was established.

To address this, we will select the Orders dataset, then click on the ellipsis icon, and proceed to manually define a relationship by navigating to **"`Add Relationship`."**

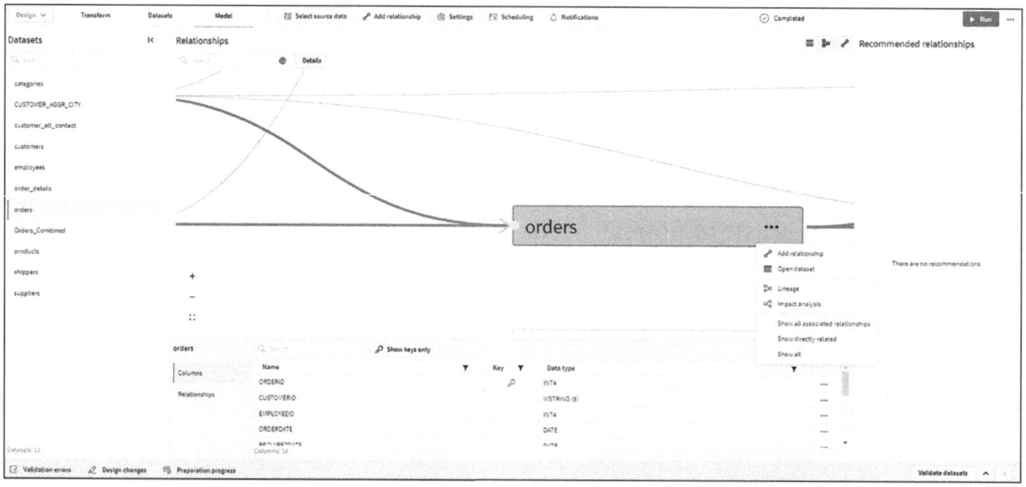

***Figure 15.16**: Selecting the Child Data Set – Orders*

We will select the field **"`SHIPVIA`"** in the Orders dataset and **"`SHIPPERID`"** in the Shippers dataset. It's evident why Qlik didn't recommend or recognize this relation automatically, but we will manually set it up.

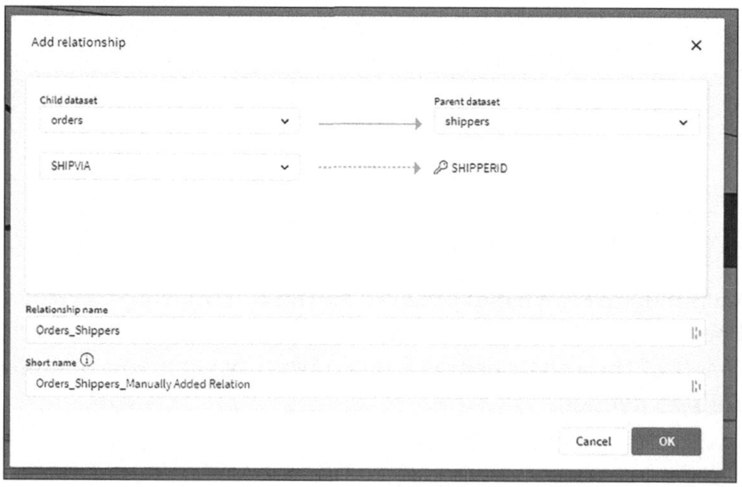

***Figure 15.17**: Defining the relationship between the child and the parent*

Once we click "**`OK`**," the relationship is added. With multiple datasets in the model, we can then choose the dataset "**`Orders`**" and select "**`Show Directly Related`**." In the data model, this action will display only the relationships that directly link to the parent or child tables of the orders table.

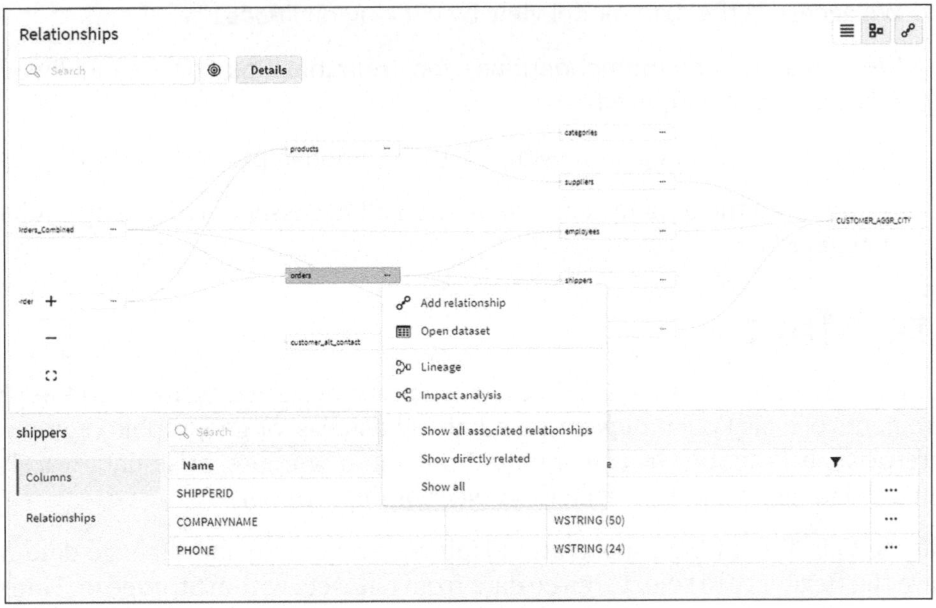

Figure 15.18: *Using Show Directly Related*

In *Figure* 15.19, Only Directly related relations are shown.

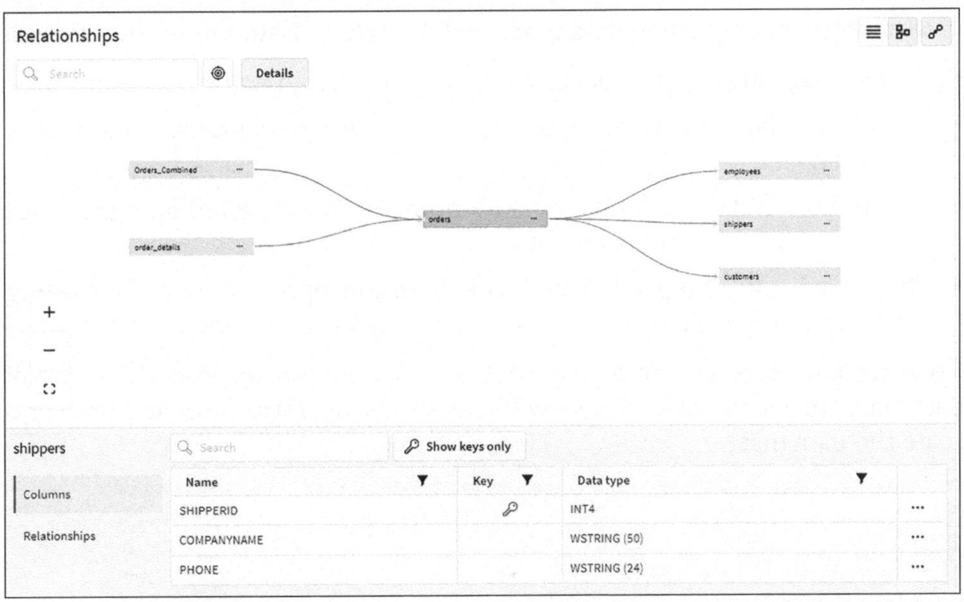

Figure 15.19: *Only Directly related relations for the Orders Data Set*

We have developed a data model that enables a data mart to automate code generation for the denormalization of dimensions and fact tables.

To summarize our actions:

1. We accessed the data model view by clicking on "**`Model`**".
2. We obtained recommendations for relationships or manually added relationships as required.
3. We applied the changes to establish the relationships.
4. We initiated the data task and generated all necessary artifacts by clicking on "**`Prepare`**".

Data Mart

A data mart serves as a structured data repository designed to meet the analytical requirements of a particular department, line of business, or geographic region within an enterprise. It functions as a segmented portion of an enterprise data warehouse, containing data pertinent to a specific subject or department.

Within the Qlik Talend Data Integration Hub, we can create and manage data marts. We have the flexibility to select source data from datasets within Storage or Transform data tasks, and then incorporate dimensions and a fact into our data mart. Additionally, we can construct a star schema to denormalize our data, optimizing it for analysis purposes.

Some advantages of employing data marts in Qlik Talend Data Integration include:

- Expedited and simplified access to data, tailored to specific needs and interests.
- Enhanced data quality and governance, ensuring accuracy, consistency, and security.
- Reduction in data redundancy and storage costs by eliminating the need to store and process duplicate data.
- Improved data integration and collaboration opportunities, facilitating the sharing and combination of data from various sources and departments.

Now that we have created the data model, our next step is to proceed with building the data mart. To accomplish this, we will select the transform asset and then proceed to create the data mart.

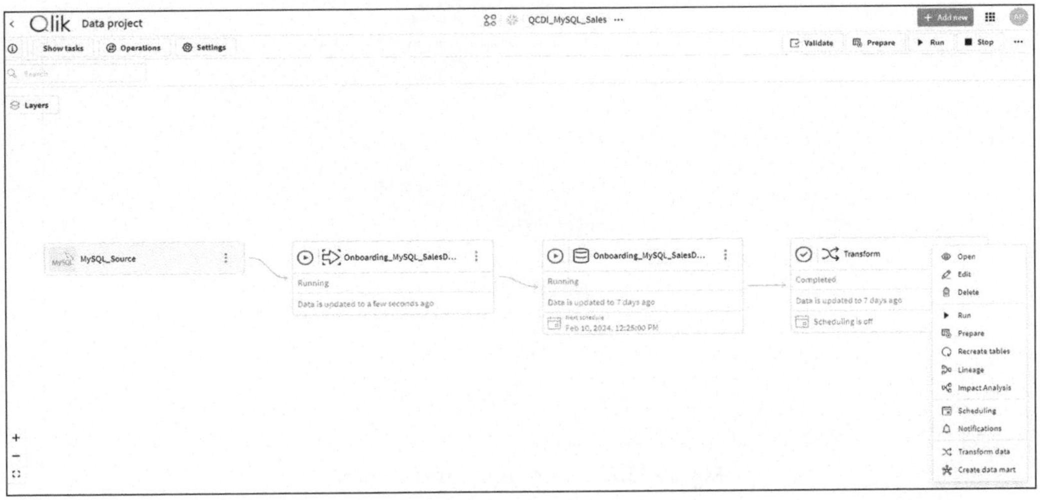

Figure 15.20: *Creating a data mart*

Here, we will furnish an effective name and description for the data mart that requires creation.

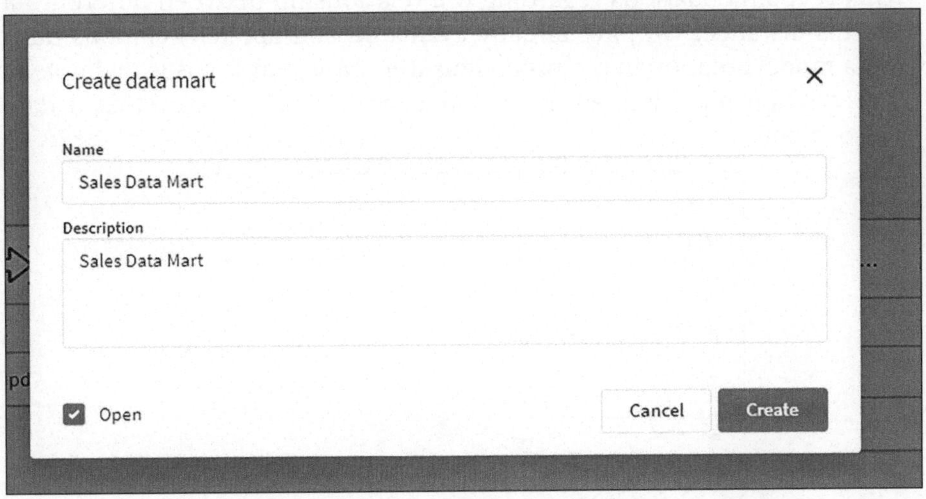

Figure 15.21: *Provide name and description of the data mart*

1. We are currently in the data mart asset. Here, we can begin by adding the FACT and dimensions to our data mart.

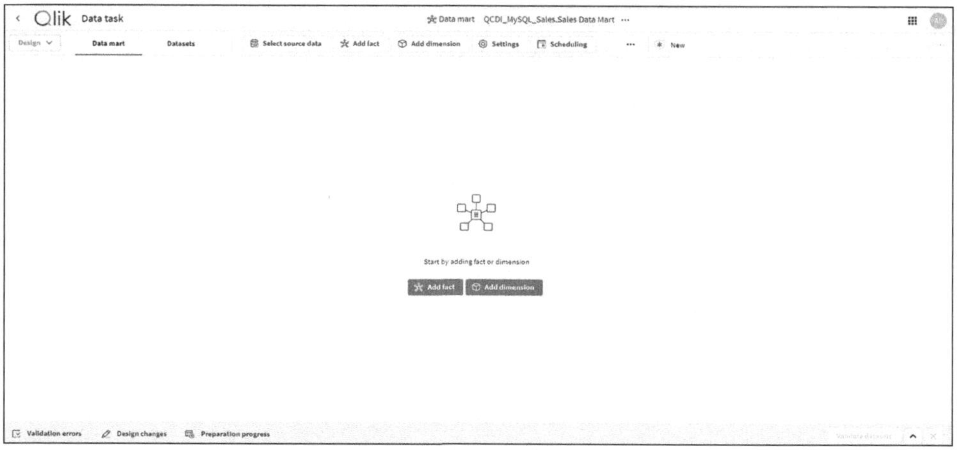

Figure 15.22: *Data Mart Initial screen*

2. We will proceed by selecting "**`Add Fact`**." Initially, we will add the facts and then include the dimensions. Subsequently, we will create a relationship between the facts and the dimensions. It's crucial to emphasize that we are not seeking Qlik recommendations regarding the relationship between different datasets in this instance. We have already evaluated and applied relations during the data model creation in the preceding step. Now, our focus is on implementing the relationships defined in the data model and constructing a data mart accordingly.

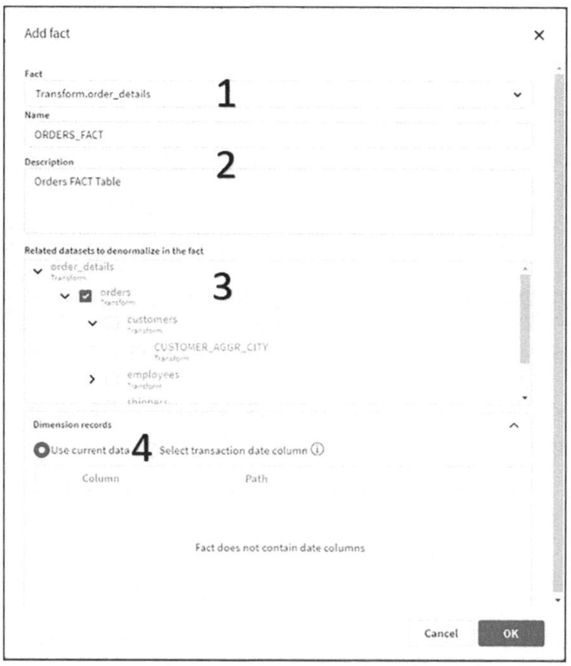

Figure 15.23: *Configuring a Data Mart*

3. We are now tasked with configuring the fact table. Firstly, we will designate the most granular dataset for inclusion in the **FACT** table, which is the **order_details** table. Subsequently, we will assign a suitable name to this dataset; in this instance, we shall refer to it as **FACT_ORDERS**. Following this, we will proceed to select the datasets we intend to denormalize alongside the order details table. Under option (3), we can explore the available choices. We have the option to denormalize solely with the order header. If necessary, we may include any other dataset linked via the data model we have constructed. For this scenario, we will exclusively select the order header table (orders).

   Denormalization is a way to make databases work faster by putting some extra information in tables. This makes it so we don't have to do as many complicated joins when we ask the database questions. It's usually done after we've organized the data neatly in a process called normalization.

   In Qlik Cloud Data Integration, denormalization means bringing together data from different places into one table using the relationships we've set up in the data model. These combined tables, called data marts, are helpful for looking at and reporting on data in a simpler way. Qlik Cloud Data Integration makes this easier by automatically writing the code to combine these tables based on the data model and the type of data mart we choose.

4. In the fourth step, we will retain the **"Use Current Date"** option. Nevertheless, there is also an alternative to select the transaction date column. By opting for this choice, we can then designate a specific date column. This feature proves beneficial in scenarios where our star schema incorporates type 2 dimensions, enabling us to pinpoint the accurate data for a particular transaction.

For instance, if a customer possesses multiple addresses, this option facilitates locating the correct address based on the order date. Consider a scenario where a retailer aims to establish a data mart for scrutinizing the correlation between orders and customers. The data mart should possess the capability to address inquiries such as: **"Which city had the highest count of delivery in June 2024?"**

Creating Fact Data Set

Now that we have completed the initial configuration setup, where we determined the base table and the tables with which it will be denormalized, we can examine the model and its relationship to the entire schema of the data model. This can be achieved by navigating to the **FACT** Model tab within the fact table. Here, we can comprehensively view the model and identify the tables that have been denormalized to form our fact table.

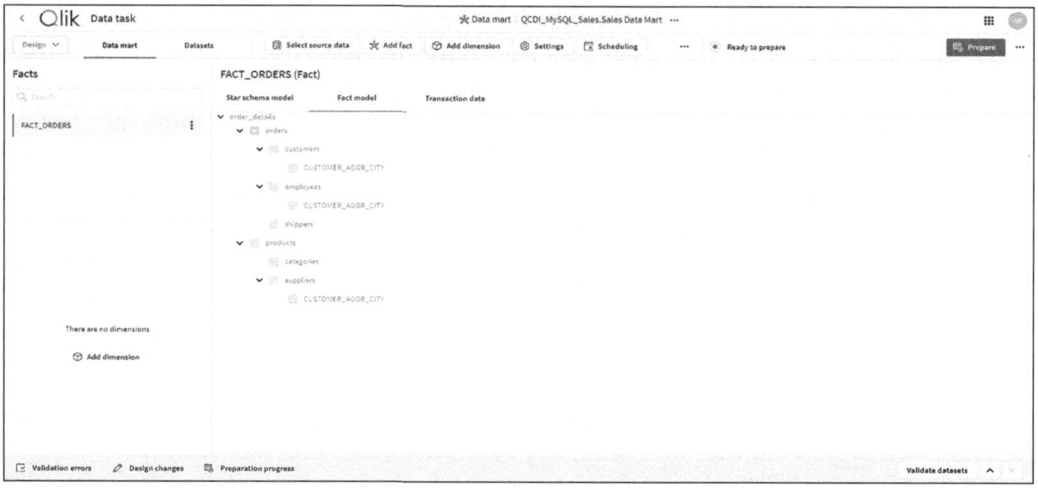

Figure 15.24: *Fact Model*

Similar to previous assets, we will opt for the "**`prepare`**" option, prompting Qlik to automatically generate the data mart - -fact table within the target system. Upon completion of the preparation process, the status will transition from "**`Ready to prepare`**" to "**`Ready to run`**."

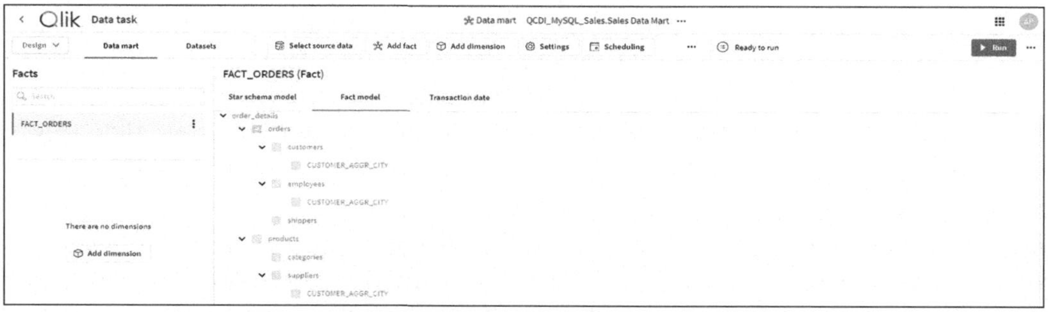

Figure 15.25: *Data Asset Prepared*

Upon creation of the asset, we will proceed by selecting the "**`Run`**" option, directing us to the monitoring view. Here, we gain access to real-time updates on the status of the data load process.

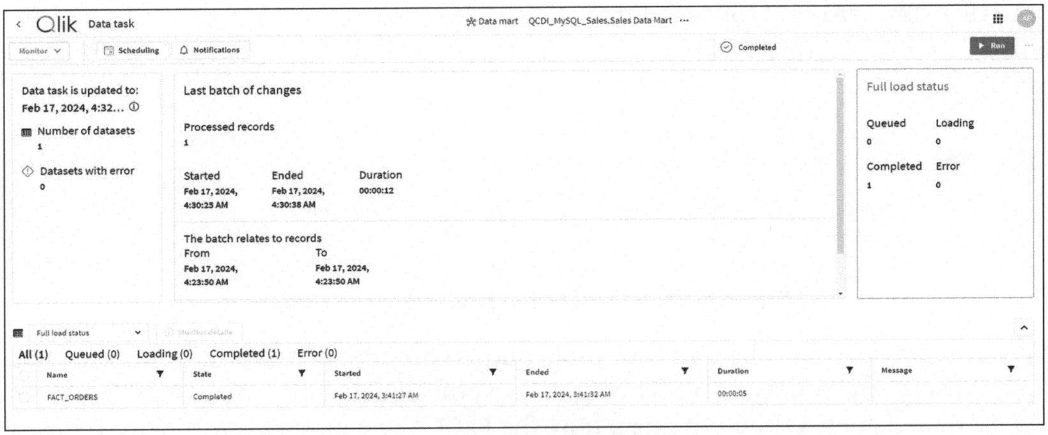

Figure 15.26: *Monitoring view of the Data Mart Fact Table*

Upon navigating to the designated target, we observe the structures that have been established. We notice the integration and denormalization of the order item table and the order header table, with Qlik managing the joins. Any modifications made to either the order header or order item table will seamlessly propagate to this data mart.

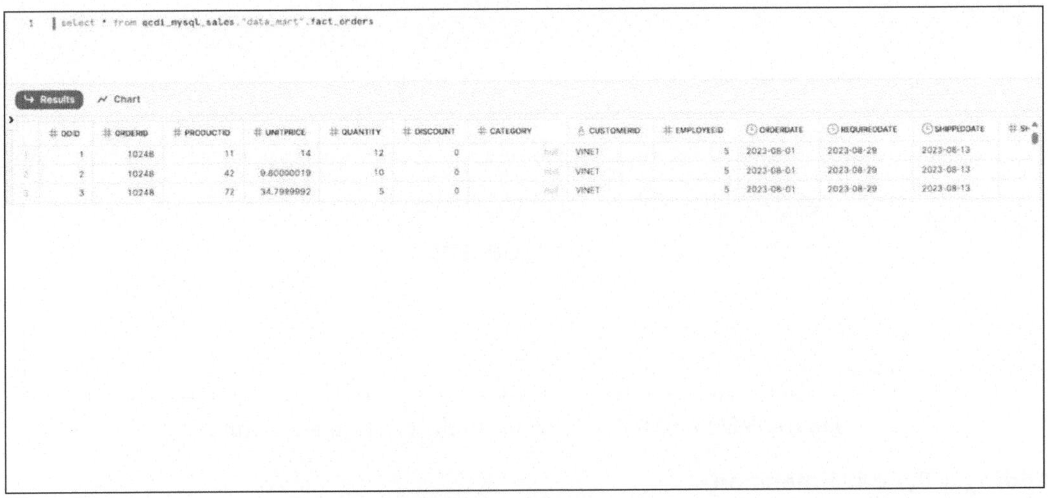

Figure 15.27: *Seeing the data in the target system*

Now, a question arises: What occurs when a record is deleted? Do we require custom code to manage deletion scenarios?

No, Qlik automates this process for us. To observe this automatic maintenance, we utilize the **"hdr_deleted"** field, which indicates whether a record was deleted from the fact table. Upon executing a delete statement in the source, we observe that after a pre-configured time, the **"hdr_deleted"** field transitions from **false** to **true**, reflecting the deletion event.

```
DELETE FROM `sales`.`order_details` WHERE (`odID` = '3');
```

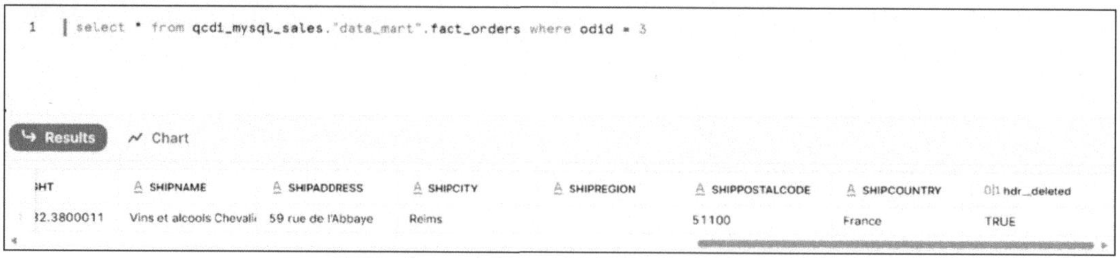

Figure 15.28: ***hdr_deleted*** *field changes to* **TRUE**

Now that we've established a **FACT** table and comprehended the deletion scenario's functionality, we proceed to incorporate several dimensions, including Type 1 and Type 2 dimensions. We aim to grasp how the **FACT** table interacts with both types. To initiate this process, we navigate to the **"Add Dimension"** button, located either in the left-hand panel or on the top menu.

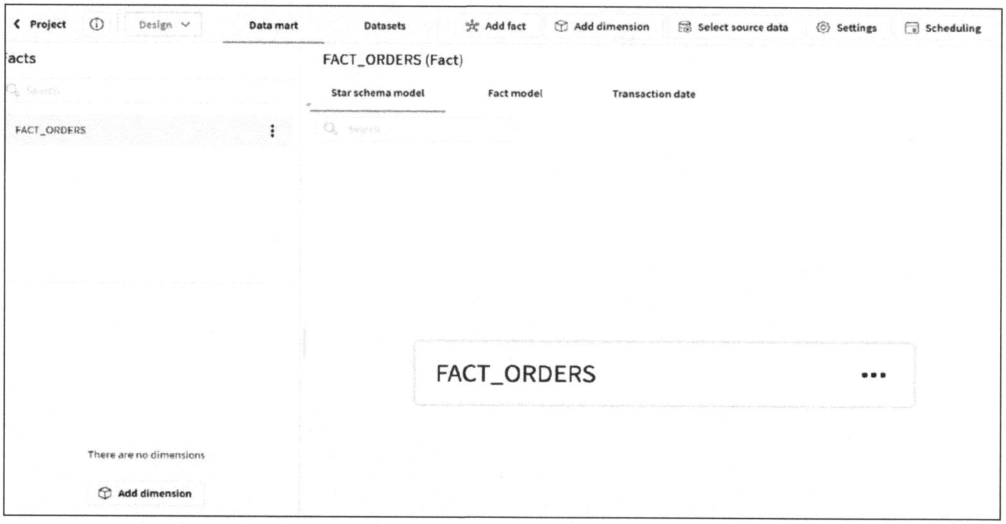

Figure 15.29: *Adding dimensions to the existing FACT table*

Adding a Type 1 Dimension

Within the Add Dimension screen, we begin by selecting the most granular dataset, which, in this instance, is the customer dataset. Subsequently, we assign it an appropriate name, such as **DIM_CUSTOMER**, along with a relevant description. For this dataset, we maintain the history type as **Type 1**. Select **OK**.

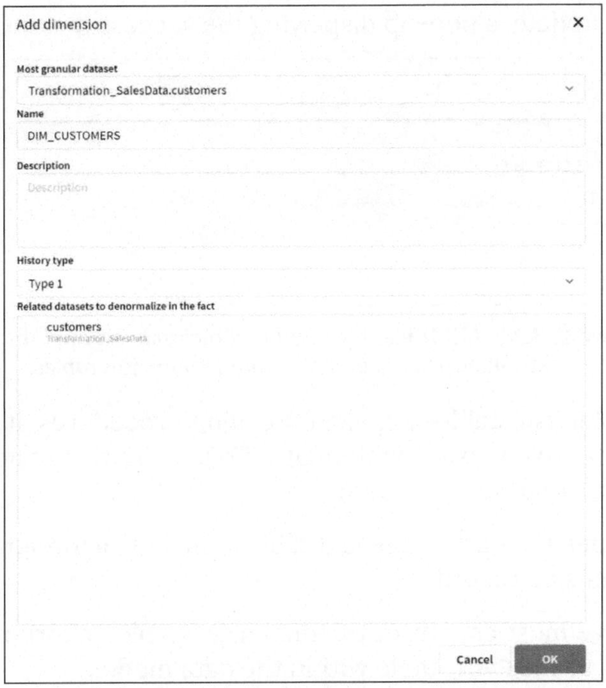

***Figure 15.30:** Configuration of the Type 1 Dimension*

Once we have determined the configuration of the dimensions, our next step is to establish their connection with the existing **FACT** table. In a manner akin to the transformation process we conducted in the asset, and drawing from the model we previously defined, Qlik will propose potential relationships between the fact and dimension datasets via green dotted lines. We can then opt to **apply** these suggested relationships.

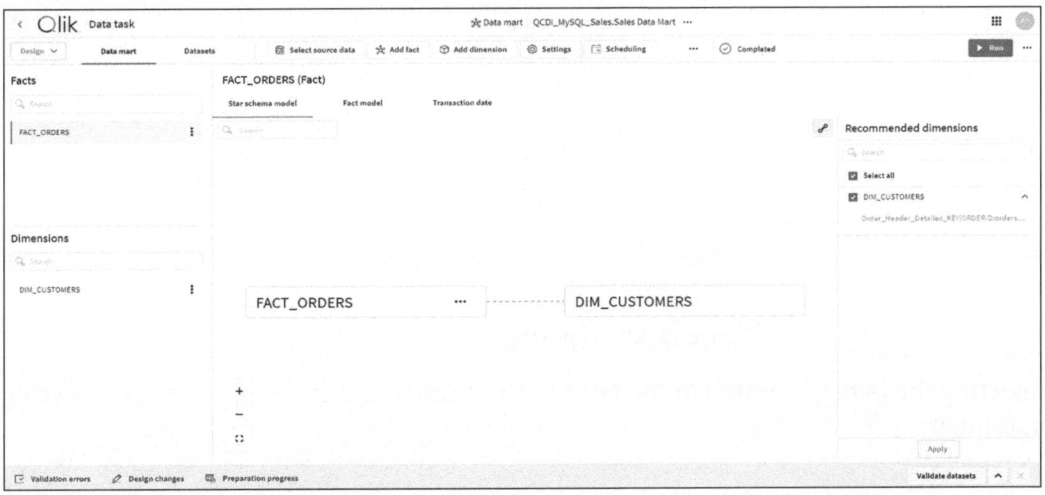

***Figure 15.31:** Applying the relationship between **FACT** and **Dimension** tables*

Upon applying the update, a pop-up displaying the success message will appear.

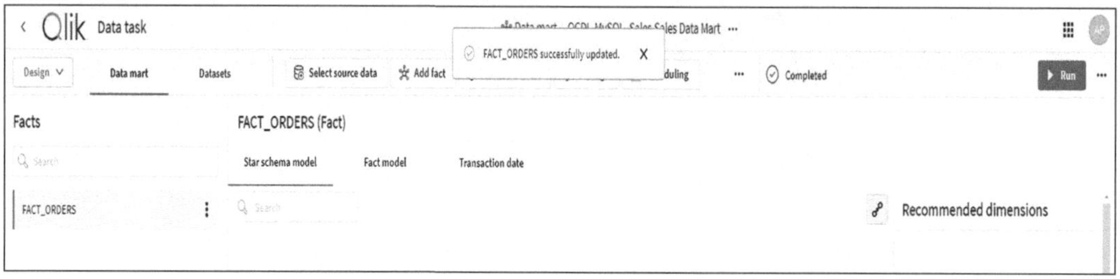

***Figure 15.32**: FACT Table is an updated message on applying the relationship between FACT and Dimension tables*

Once the relationship is established, like preceding procedures, it's essential to note that this relationship solely exists within Qlik. To solidify this relationship within the model, two essential steps are required:

1. Firstly, we need to update the fact table to include a foreign key indicating the linked dimension record.
2. Secondly, we must construct the dimension table, incorporating the key that connects it to the **FACT** table within the data model.

Once these data model artifacts are generated and the fact table artifact is updated with the new foreign key, data loading can proceed.

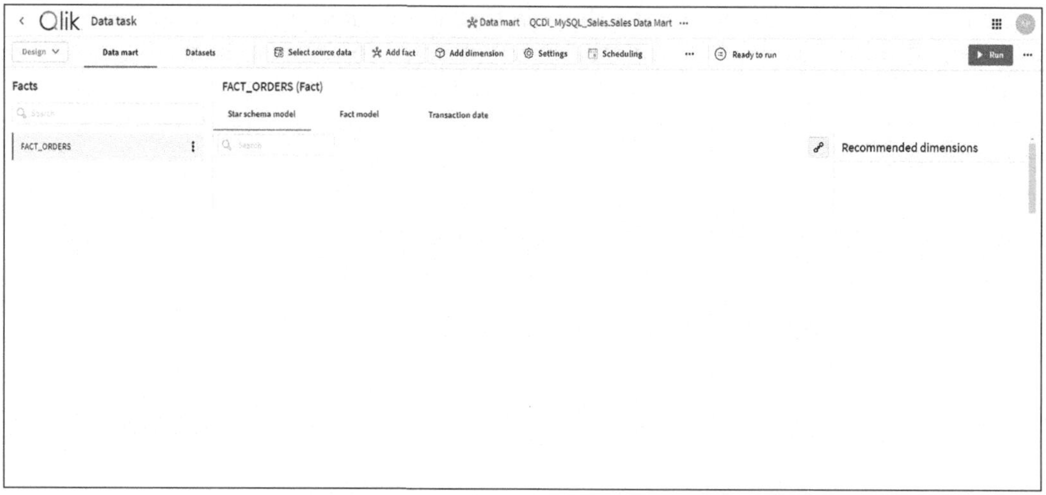

***Figure 15.33**: Preparing the new dimension*

Selecting the data generated in the **FACT** table at the target system, we execute a select statement.

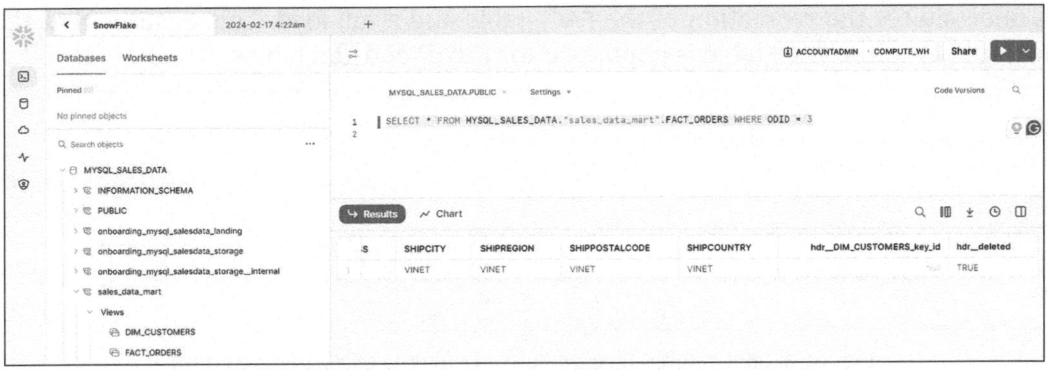

Figure 15.34: *The existing FACT dataset has a new column added* – HDR_DIM_CUSTOMERS_KEY_ID

The newly added field in the **FACT** table consistently follows the format "**hdr_{dimension-name}_key_id**," serving as an integer reference to both Type 1 and Type 2 dimensions. Each dimension is represented by a distinct column in the fact view.

It is important to note that we have just added a new column to the **FACT** table without starting over with the data. So, what does this mean? It means the **DIM_key** in the fact table will not be filled in for data that has already been loaded.

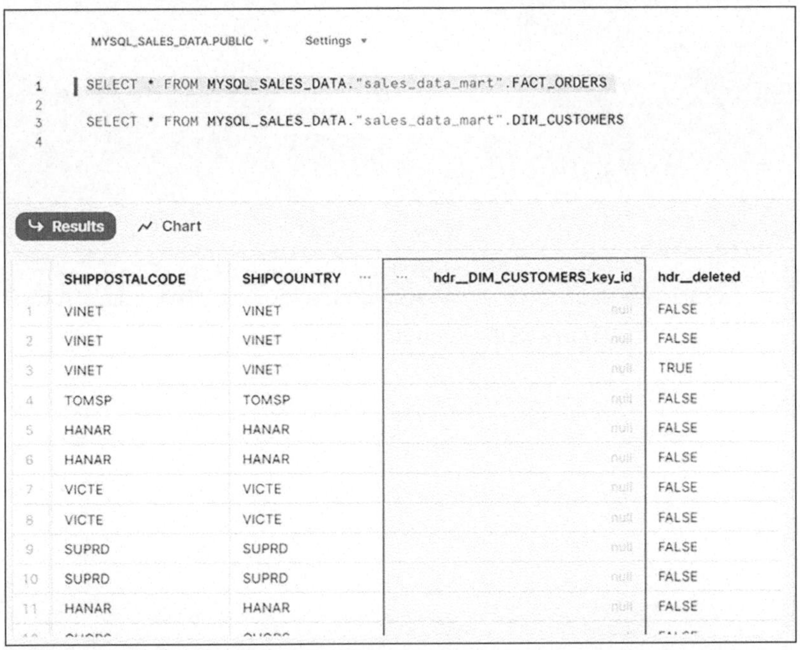

Figure 15.35: *The newly added field by default does not have reference values populated*

Since the dimension records are updated through change data capture, their loading prompts updates in the corresponding fact table. Whenever a dimension is added, it necessitates the recreation of the **FACT** table and a full load. This ensures that the foreign key in the **FACT** table is populated for the dimension tables.

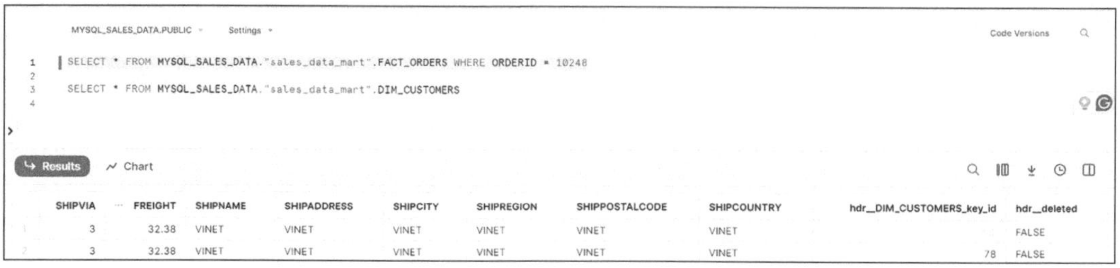

Figure 15.36: *Updated foreign key only for the CDC-updated data*

We will re-create all the tables by navigating to the design view and selecting the appropriate icon. Then, we'll press **"Recreate Tables"**. This action will drop the **FACT** table, recreate it, and then proceed with a reload.

Figure 15.37: *Recreating the FACT table*

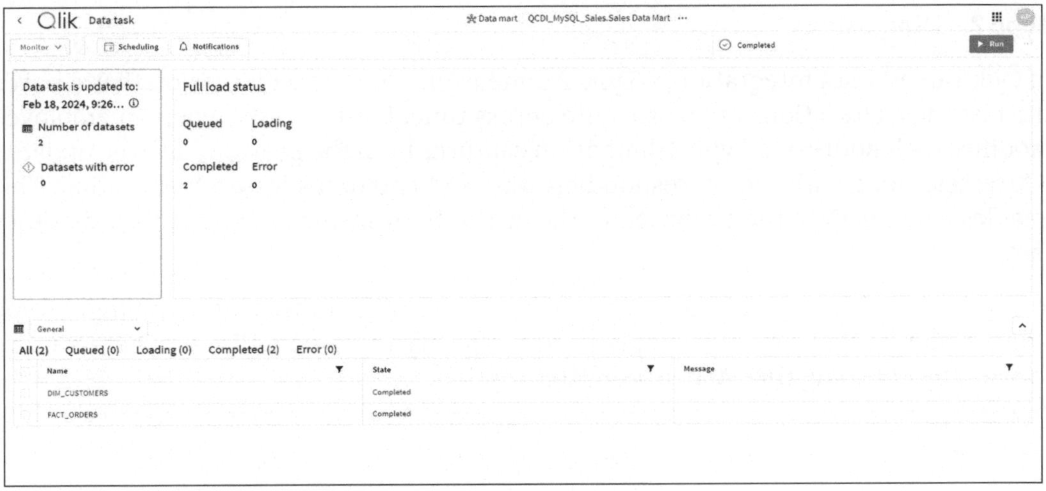

Figure 15.38: *Reloading the FACT and Dimension tables*

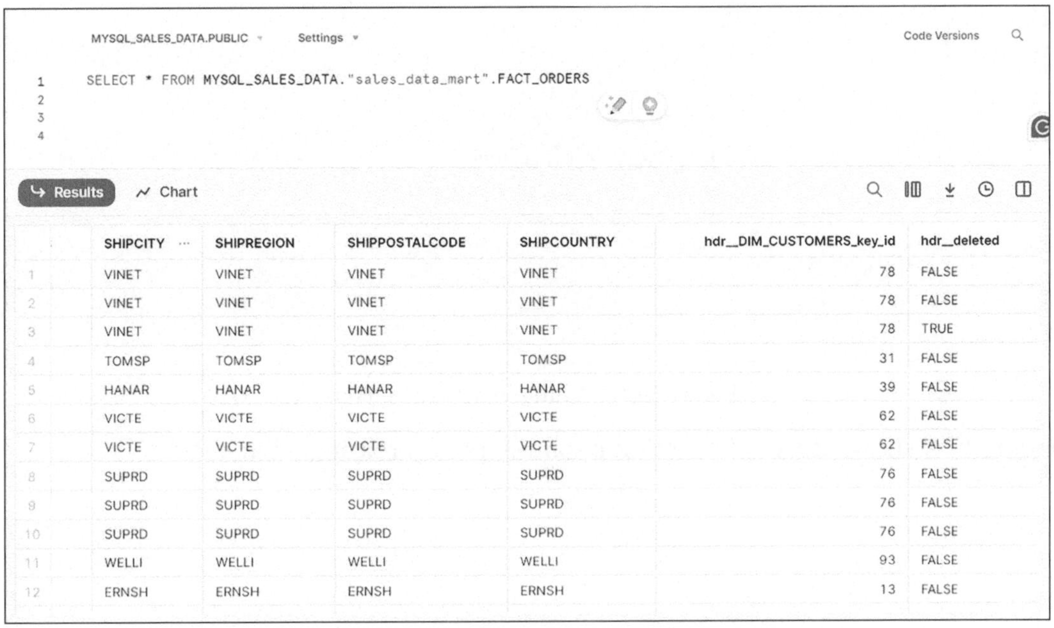

	SHIPCITY	SHIPREGION	SHIPPOSTALCODE	SHIPCOUNTRY	hdr__DIM_CUSTOMERS_key_id	hdr__deleted
1	VINET	VINET	VINET	VINET	78	FALSE
2	VINET	VINET	VINET	VINET	78	FALSE
3	VINET	VINET	VINET	VINET	78	TRUE
4	TOMSP	TOMSP	TOMSP	TOMSP	31	FALSE
5	HANAR	HANAR	HANAR	HANAR	39	FALSE
6	VICTE	VICTE	VICTE	VICTE	62	FALSE
7	VICTE	VICTE	VICTE	VICTE	62	FALSE
8	SUPRD	SUPRD	SUPRD	SUPRD	76	FALSE
9	SUPRD	SUPRD	SUPRD	SUPRD	76	FALSE
10	SUPRD	SUPRD	SUPRD	SUPRD	76	FALSE
11	WELLI	WELLI	WELLI	WELLI	93	FALSE
12	ERNSH	ERNSH	ERNSH	ERNSH	13	FALSE

Figure 15.39: *Foreign key population after reload*

We began by creating a fact table and comprehending the functionality of the deletion flag for a record within it. Subsequently, we advanced our understanding by incorporating a dimension table, observing how Qlik automatically establishes the foreign key relation between the **FACT** and dimension tables. We witnessed the population of FK fields during the initial load and whenever a new dimension was added. Additionally, we explored the process of recreating the fact table and then associating historical records with the key to the dimension table's foreign key. Now, let's delve deeper and grasp the mechanics of a Type 2 dimension.

Type 2 - Dimensions

In Qlik Talend Data Integration, a Type 2 dimension refers to a dimension that records the historical alterations of an attribute across time. For instance, when an employee modifies their address, a Type 2 dimension captures both the previous and the updated addresses, along with the corresponding start and end dates for each alteration. This enables us to analyze the evolution of the attribute over time and its impact on other metrics.

The process of incorporating a Type 2-dimension mirrors that of including a Type 1 dimension. In this case, we simply need to specify the type as Type 2. Let us move forward by choosing the "`Add Dimension`" option.

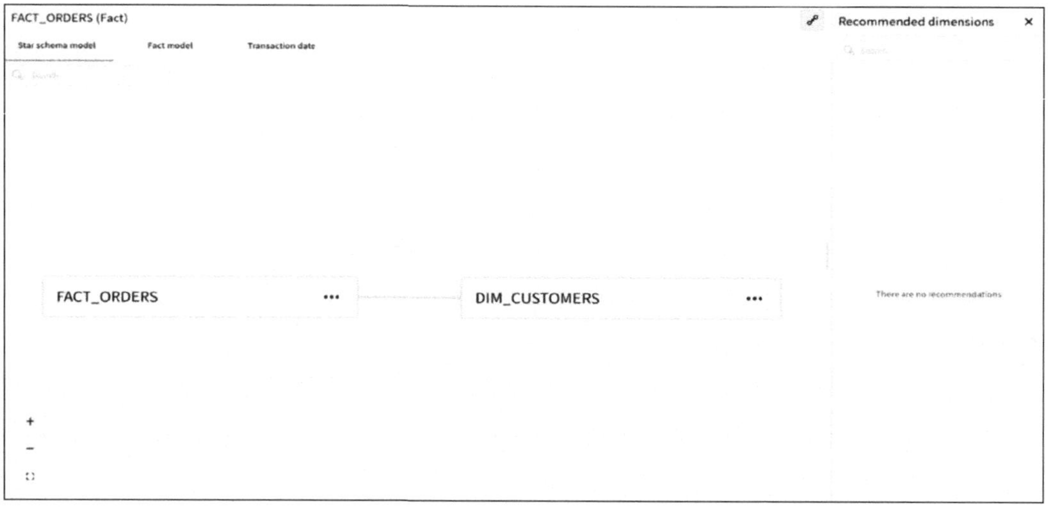

Figure 15.40: *Adding a new dimension*

Figure 15.41 shows the configuration parameters for creating a dimension:

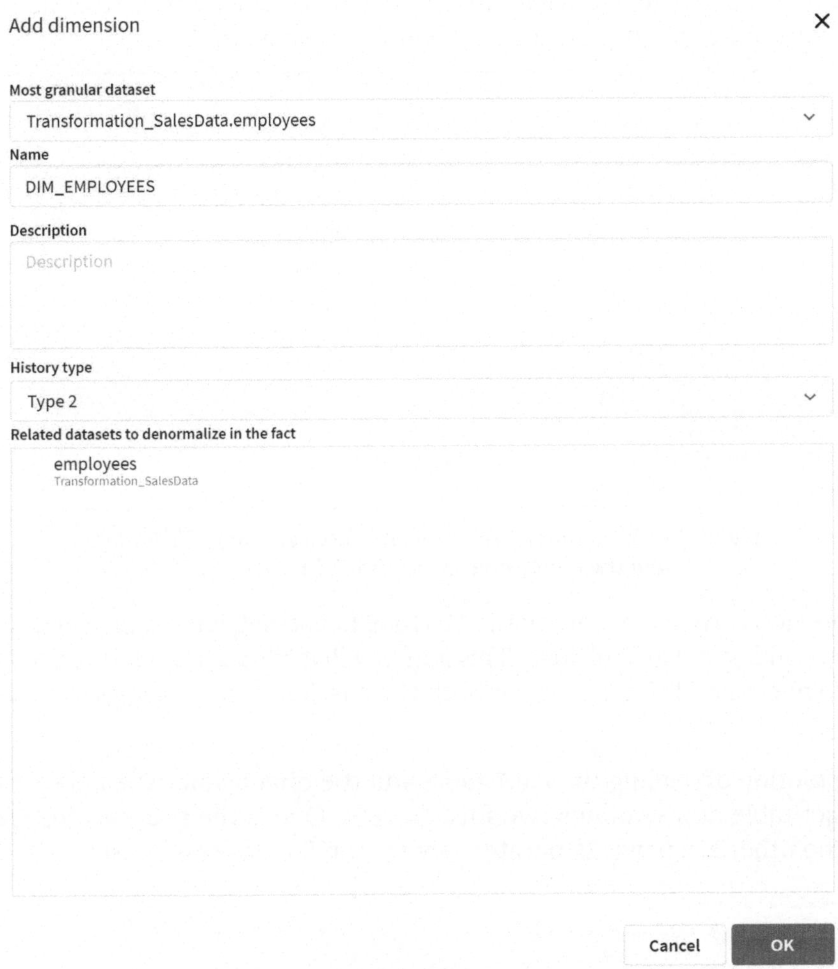

Figure 15.41: *Employees Dimension being configured as Type 2*

When deciding between Type 1 and Type 2 dimensions, consider:

- Does the attribute's history need to be retained for analytical purposes?
- How frequently does the attribute undergo changes, and are those changes significant for analysis?
- What are the storage implications of maintaining historical records versus updating the current state?

Once the dataset has been configured, we observe in the design changes that a new dataset is accessible. Now, we will choose the **FACT_ORDERS** dataset and establish the relationship between the existing **FACT_ORDERS** dataset and the customer dimension. Additionally, we will link the **FACT_ORDERS** dataset to the employee dataset. We can select the relationship through the recommended dimension option and proceed to click **"Apply"**. This action will create the dimension on the target and update the **FACT** table to incorporate the foreign key for this new dimension.

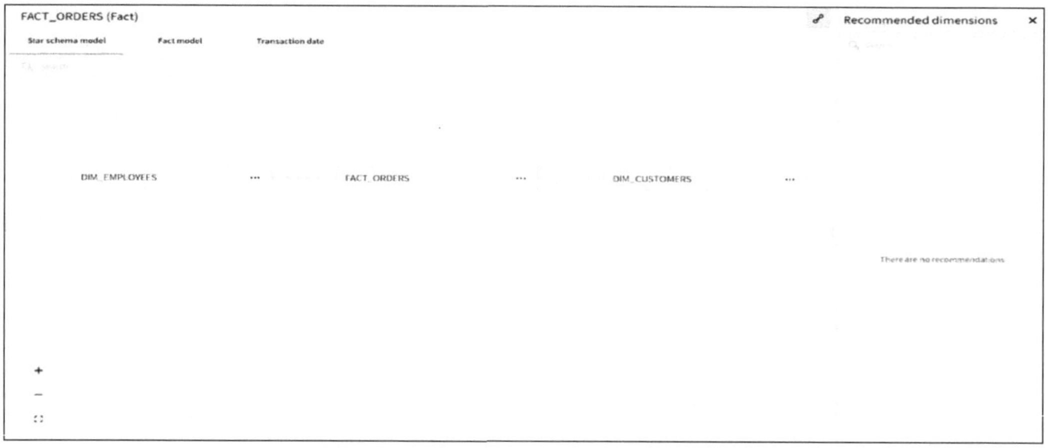

Figure 15.42: *Define the relationship between the FACT Orders and the newly created EMPLOYEE DATA SET*

Like our previous process of adding the **CUSTOMERS** dataset, we will proceed to recreate the datasets and perform a full load. This action will facilitate populating the **FACT** table with all the necessary foreign keys for both the customers and the newly incorporated employee dimension.

Upon completion of loading the **FACT** table and the dimension tables, we can observe that the fact table now contains two foreign keys. One is the pre-existing Customers **KEY**, and the other is a newly generated key for the Employees dataset.

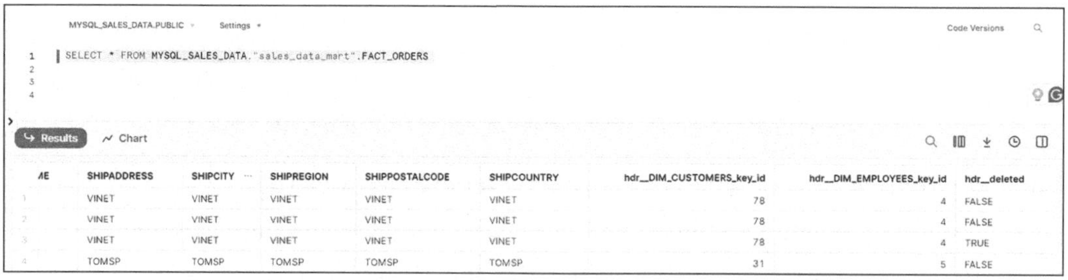

Figure 15.43: *Updated FACT table concerning 2 dimensions*

Let us witness the Type 2 dimensions in action by navigating to the source system and accessing the employee tables. Here, we will modify it to a record–for instance, changing the designation of Employee 1 from Sales Representative to Sales Manager.

In the source system, only the current version of the record is retained without any historical data. However, within our dimension model, it is imperative to track the employment history, understanding the various roles individuals have held and the respective periods. The advantage lies in the fact that we do not need to delve into writing intricate SQL code to enable this tracking; Qlik has facilitated this for us by selecting the employee dimension to be Type 2.

```
UPDATE `sales`.` employees` SET `Title` = 'Sales Manager' WHERE
(`EmployeeID` = '1');
```

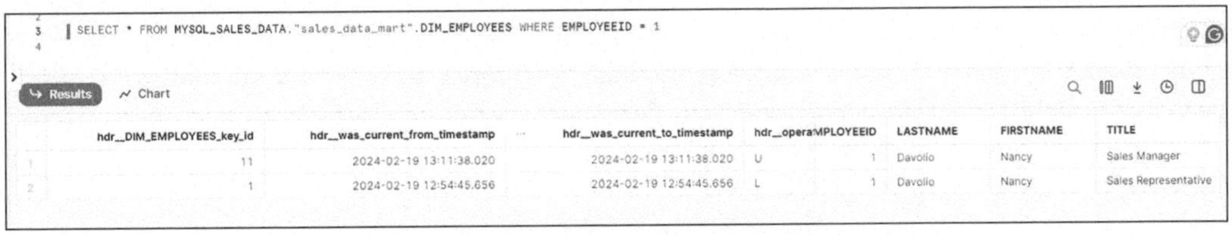

Figure 15.44: *Type 2 Dimensions for Employees*

In this case, we can see that when we query the Target system – the record updated has been created (tagged as "U"), and we can see that a timestamp is maintained that tells from when to when –the record value was.

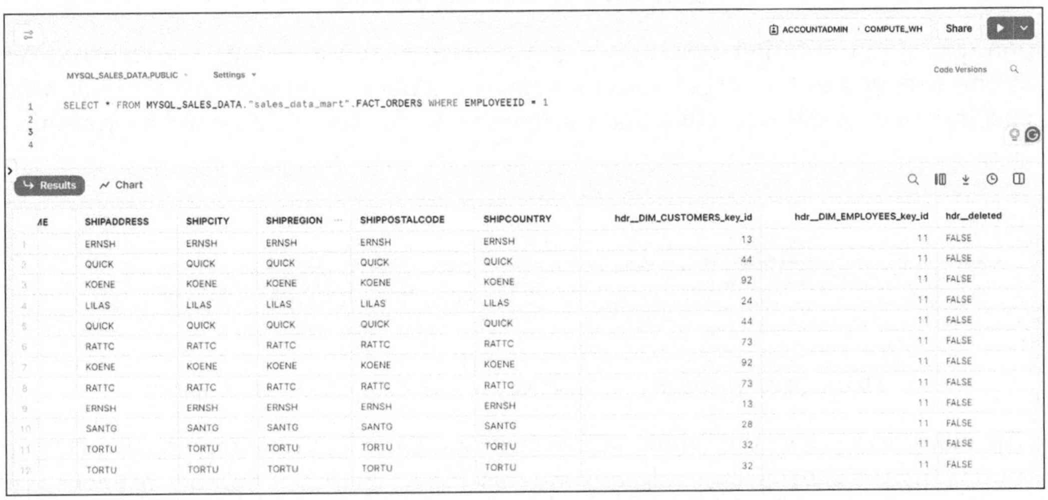

Figure 15.45: *The FACT TABLE is updated with the latest record foreign key*

The current version of the employee is identified with the **`Foreign Key = 11`**. Now, we can proceed to make further changes—we will update this record to reflect the designation as a **`Senior Sales Manager.`** This action will generate a new record in the dimension table. Subsequently, it will automatically update the FACT table to reference the latest foreign key, reflecting the most updated value of the record.

```
UPDATE `sales`.` employees` SET `Title` = 'Senior Sales Manager' WHERE
(`EmployeeID` = '1');
```

The FACT table has been successfully updated. All records corresponding to **`EmployeeID = 1,`** previously linked to the **`Foreign key 11`**, are now associated with **`Foreign key 14`**, which corresponds to the updated record in the dimension table.

Qlik has automatically generated this update, ensuring that the old records in the **FACT** table now reflect the most recent foreign key values.

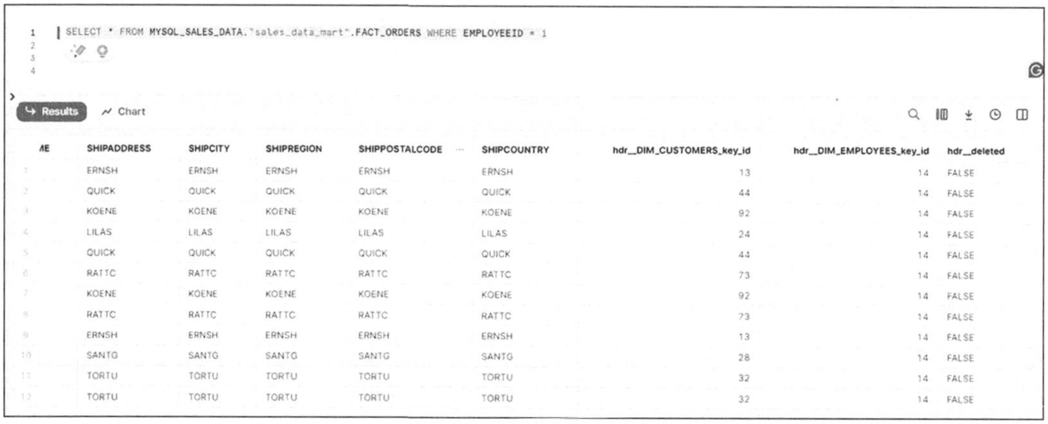

```
SELECT * FROM MYSQL_SALES_DATA."sales_data_mart".FACT_ORDERS WHERE EMPLOYEEID = 1
```

	ME	SHIPADDRESS	SHIPCITY	SHIPREGION	SHIPPOSTALCODE	···	SHIPCOUNTRY	hdr__DIM_CUSTOMERS_key_id	hdr__DIM_EMPLOYEES_key_id	hdr__deleted
1		ERNSH	ERNSH	ERNSH	ERNSH		ERNSH	13	14	FALSE
2		QUICK	QUICK	QUICK	QUICK		QUICK	44	14	FALSE
3		KOENE	KOENE	KOENE	KOENE		KOENE	92	14	FALSE
4		LILAS	LILAS	LILAS	LILAS		LILAS	24	14	FALSE
5		QUICK	QUICK	QUICK	QUICK		QUICK	44	14	FALSE
6		RATTC	RATTC	RATTC	RATTC		RATTC	73	14	FALSE
7		KOENE	KOENE	KOENE	KOENE		KOENE	92	14	FALSE
8		RATTC	RATTC	RATTC	RATTC		RATTC	73	14	FALSE
9		ERNSH	ERNSH	ERNSH	ERNSH		ERNSH	13	14	FALSE
10		SANTG	SANTG	SANTG	SANTG		SANTG	28	14	FALSE
11		TORTU	TORTU	TORTU	TORTU		TORTU	32	14	FALSE
12		TORTU	TORTU	TORTU	TORTU		TORTU	32	14	FALSE

Figure 15.46: *Updated Employee Key*

Upon querying the target system, we can precisely identify what has occurred. We will now proceed to the target system, compose a query, and examine in detail what transpired during this operation and the specific actions performed by the system.

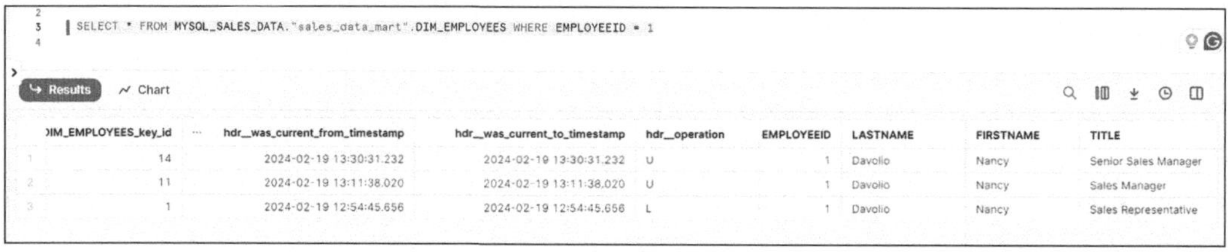

```
SELECT * FROM MYSQL_SALES_DATA."sales_data_mart".DIM_EMPLOYEES WHERE EMPLOYEEID = 1
```

	DIM_EMPLOYEES_key_id	···	hdr__was_current_from_timestamp	hdr__was_current_to_timestamp	hdr__operation	EMPLOYEEID	LASTNAME	FIRSTNAME	TITLE
1	14		2024-02-19 13:30:31.232	2024-02-19 13:30:31.232	U	1	Davolio	Nancy	Senior Sales Manager
2	11		2024-02-19 13:11:38.020	2024-02-19 13:11:38.020	U	1	Davolio	Nancy	Sales Manager
3	1		2024-02-19 12:54:45.656	2024-02-19 12:54:45.656	L	1	Davolio	Nancy	Sales Representative

Figure 15.47: *Updated Employee Key in the EMPLOYEE_DIM table*

In the monitoring view, the number of records indicates the ongoing activity. Despite not updating the **ORDERS** table directly, we observe a significant number of **Processed records** in **FACT_ORDERS**. This activity signifies Qlik's process of updating the **FACT_ORDERS** table to reflect the latest foreign key values.

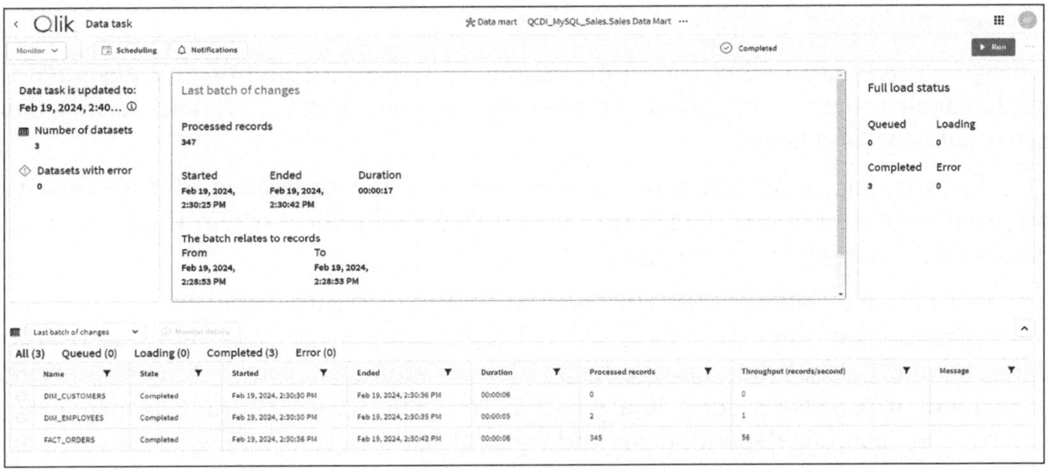

Figure 15.48: *Monitor view during CDC and update involving type 2 dimensions*

In summary, we have established a comprehensive understanding of our observations. We initiated the process by constructing a fact table and delved into Qlik's approach to managing deletions, specifically addressing the utilization of deletion flags. Subsequently, we explored the creation of type 1 dimensions, highlighting the automatic generation and updating of foreign keys. Following this, we proceeded to develop a type 2 dimension, recognizing its capacity to preserve historical perspectives and facilitate retrospective analysis of record values over time. Furthermore, we examined Qlik's automated mechanism for updating foreign keys in both fact and dimension tables.

Figure 15.49: *Start Schema Data Mart created*

Lineage and Impact Analysis

Lineage within Qlik Talend Data Integration represents a functionality designed to meticulously trace the inception and alteration of your data throughout various data tasks, datasets, and fields.

This feature empowers users to visually map out the trajectory of data flow via graphical representations, facilitating interactive exploration of both upstream and downstream dependencies for any given data component.

Lineage in Qlik Talend Data Integration offers insights into the origins and transformations of data, providing a visual representation of data flow across tasks, datasets, and fields. While lineage helps identify inefficiencies, such as bottlenecks or redundant processes, its primary role is to ensure data accuracy, transparency, and trust by mapping dependencies and transformations. Here's how we can leverage lineage:

1. Identify and address time-consuming data tasks by scrutinizing their execution durations and investigating potential causes and remedies.
2. Assess the repercussions of alterations or removals of data tasks, datasets, or fields on downstream elements to prevent disruptions or decelerations in the data flow.
3. Streamline resource allocation by eliminating superfluous or redundant data tasks, datasets, or fields that remain unused or unutilized by any other component, thereby freeing up resources and storage space.

Lineage is accessible for each component within our system. For this instance, let's initiate by selecting the **DIM_CUSTOMERS** component, followed by clicking on the lineage icon. We will see a lineage graph that shows the inputs and outputs of the selected element, as well as the details of each node and edge in the graph.

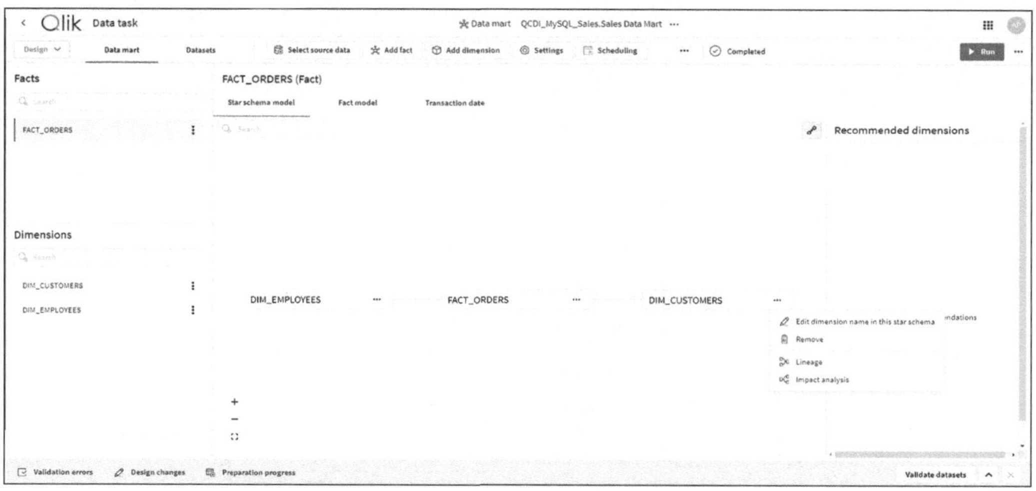

Figure 15.50: *Lineage of QCDI Data Mart*

We can view lineage in the new tab and customize its details as needed. We can drill down and explore everything.

Figure 15.51: *Data Set Level Lineage*

Dataset-level lineage provides a comprehensive visualization of the data flow across data tasks, datasets, and applications, represented in a graphical chart. It offers insights into the inputs and outputs of each data element, along with detailed information about every node and edge within the graph. By utilizing dataset-level lineage, users can gain a clear understanding of the derivation of their data, the involved sources, and transformations, as well as anticipate the potential impact of data modifications on other interconnected elements.

On the other hand, field-level lineage offers a focused view, highlighting the specific data sources and transformations associated with individual fields. This feature enables users to discern how individual fields are calculated and trace their origins across various transformations and applications. Field-level lineage enhances data trust and comprehension, facilitating the identification of efficiencies within the data pipeline.

To access field-level lineage, we begin by navigating to the dataset of interest. Within this dataset, we identify and select the specific field we wish to examine—in this case, the **FULL_NAME** field, which we previously crafted through manual transformations in earlier chapters. Once the **FULL_NAME** field is selected, we proceed by clicking on the ellipsis icon (...) and subsequently choose the Lineage option. This action enables us to delve into the lineage of the selected field, providing insights into its sources, transformations, and dependencies within the data ecosystem.

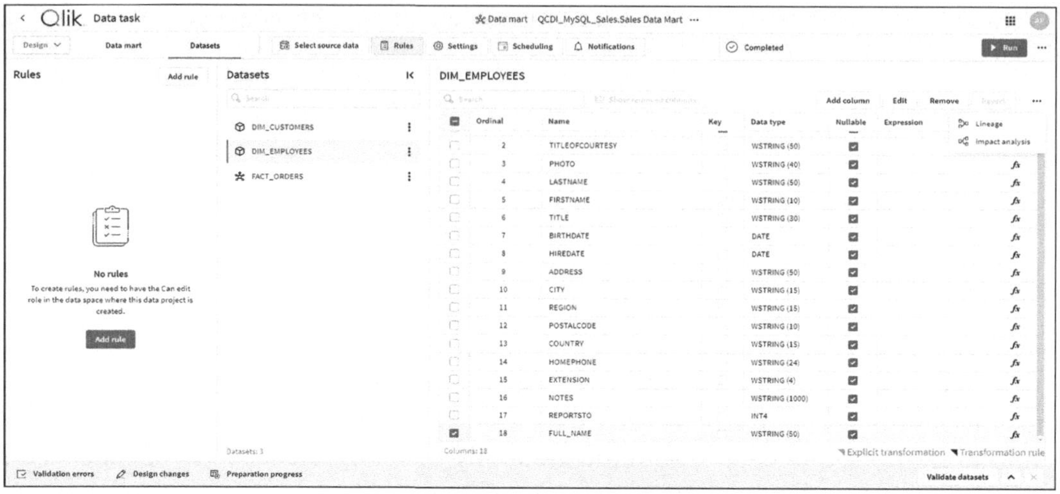

Figure 15.52: *Field-level lineage*

As we trace the lineage, it becomes evident that the field **`FULL_NAME`** does not originate directly from the data model within the source. Rather, it is a derived field created through transformations. By following the lineage, we can discern the specific data asset responsible for generating this field.

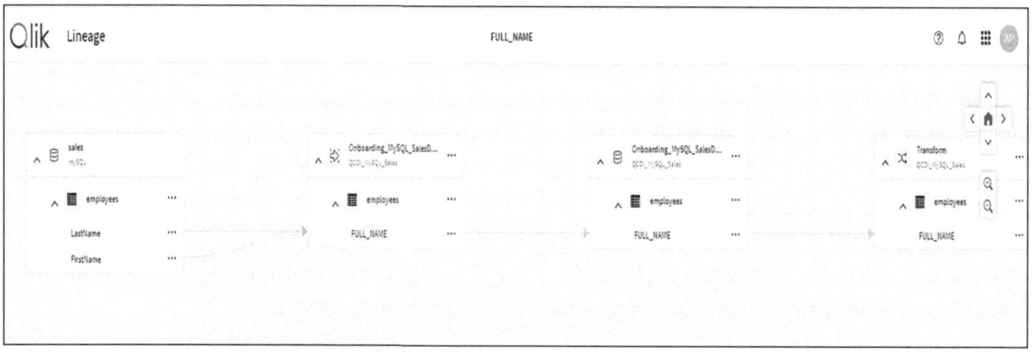

Figure 15.53: *Tracking the logic written for* FULL_NAME

The lines connecting the nodes in the lineage graph are termed edges. These edges signify the relationships between nodes, illustrating associations such as datasets landed by landing tasks or data produced by transformations. The combination of nodes and edges constitutes the lineage graph.

Nodes can collapse or expand, allowing for the revelation of hierarchy levels. This hierarchy progresses from a coarse level to finer granularity, starting with higher-level objects and extending down to the most detailed level, which encompasses field-level attributes.

Additionally, we can navigate directly to the underlying data asset from the lineage view to verify the logic. By selecting the ellipsis icon (...) and choosing the option to open the data task of interest, we can seamlessly transition to the associated data asset. This streamlined process allows us to validate the logic behind the transformations directly within the context of the underlying asset.

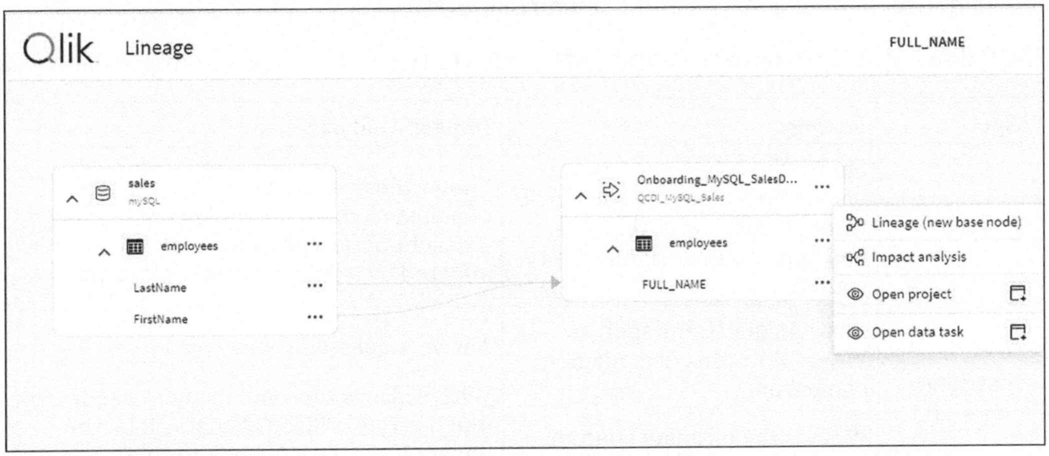

***Figure 15.54**: The Lineage option is displayed when you click on the ellipsis*

In the preceding image, it is shown that lineage enables us to track the data flow from the source to the onboarding asset and beyond. Access to lineage is contingent upon permissions. Users must possess appropriate authorization to view tasks within the data space of the data project to access lineage information. This necessitates having one of the following roles:

- Owner
- Can view
- Can operate
- Can edit

If users can observe the lineage graph for a base node, they possess the capacity to view basic details regarding the upstream lineage objects.

Impact Analysis

Impact analysis in Qlik Talend Data Integration offers a forward-looking perspective on the downstream dependencies of data tasks, datasets, or fields. It provides insights into how changes to data can affect various elements in the data pipeline, including datasets, data tasks, apps, and fields. This feature enables users to assess the implications of modifying or removing a data task, dataset, or field, thereby preventing disruptions or slowdowns in data flow.

Additionally, users can identify the types of objects affected by changes to a field and analyze both direct and indirect dependencies. Qlik Cloud also offers an aggregated summary of downstream impacts, allowing users to interactively explore dependencies and drill down to specific impacted fields. Furthermore, impact analysis facilitates communication with owners of affected items and supports comparison of impact analyses across different data tasks, datasets, or fields, promoting efficient reuse and consolidation of data sources and transformations.

The following table summarizes the differences between Lineage and Impact analysis:

Aspect	**Lineage**	**Impact Analysis**
Overview	Shows the origin and history of a data element, tracing back through data tasks, datasets, and apps, to the original data source.	Shows the downstream dependencies of a data element, including data tasks, datasets, apps, and fields that would be affected by a change to that element.
Questions Answered	Answers questions such as: Where does this data element come from? What is the ultimate source? How was it calculated?	Answers questions such as: Where else is this data element used? How much is this utilized? What will be the impact if I make a change to this?
Use Cases	Understand how your data is derived, what sources and transformations are involved, troubleshoot errors, and ensure data quality and governance.	Assess the impact of changing or deleting a data element, avoid breaking or slowing down the data flow, communicate with the owners of the impacted items, and reuse or consolidate common data sources and transformations.

Table 15.1: *Lineage versus Impact Analysis*

To gain deeper insights into impact analysis, we initiate by navigating to the landing asset. Within this asset, we specifically select the categories dataset. Subsequently, we click on the ellipsis icon (...) and proceed to choose the option for impact analysis. This action allows us to explore and evaluate the downstream dependencies of the categories dataset, providing valuable information on how changes to this dataset might affect other elements within the data ecosystem.

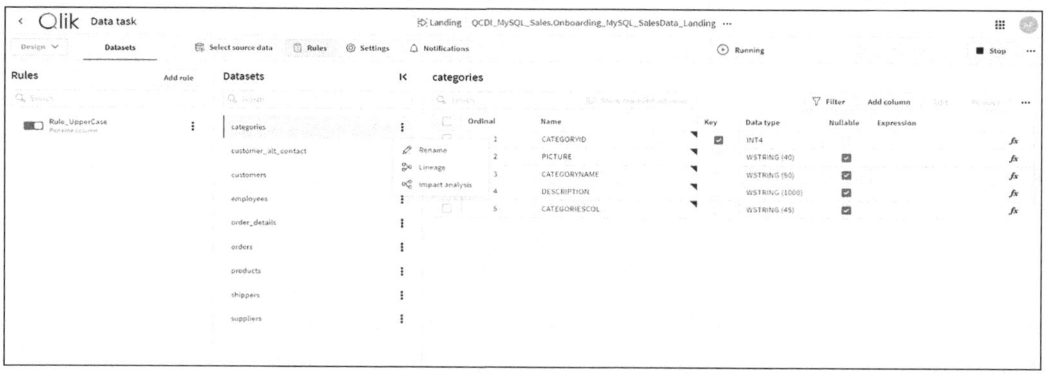

Figure 15.55: *Impact Analysis of Landing Asset*

Figure 15.56 shows Summary of Impact analysis:

Here, we have the opportunity to observe all the activities and interactions taking place. From this onboarding asset, we can identify which other assets are utilizing specific fields and determine the exact fields being used by each asset. Essentially, we have comprehensive visibility into the entire process. This is the key point we wish to emphasize.

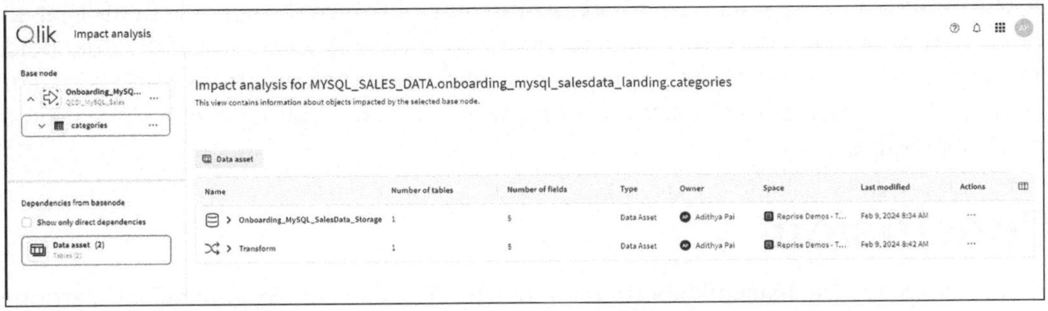

Figure 15.56: *Impact analysis of Categories Data Set – Summary view*

Figure 15.57 shows the Drill down of Impact analysis:

From this same view, we can drill down to a field level, which is very important. If we encounter a scenario where a specific field needs to be removed, we need to understand where this field is located and identify all the assets that are using it. Additionally, we can assess the upstream utilization of this field.

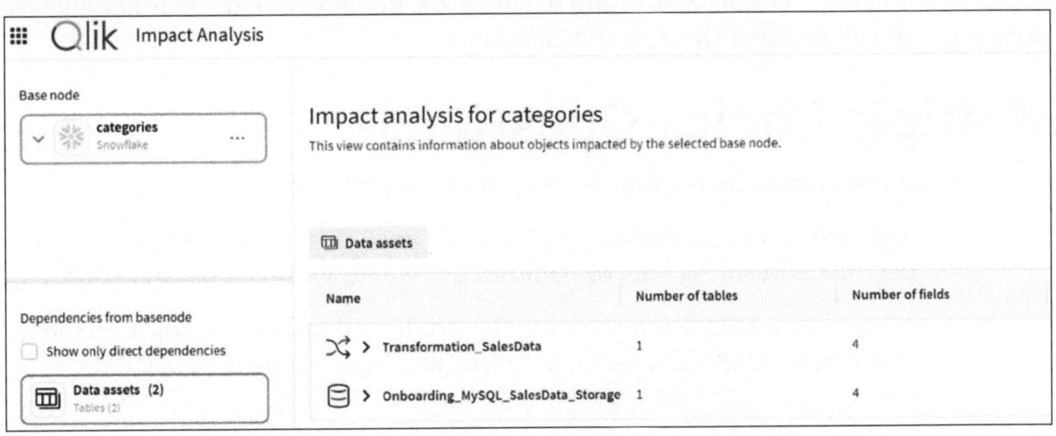

Figure 15.57: *Impact Analysis of Categories Data Set – Drill down*

In Qlik Talend Data Integration, Impact Analysis Summary View and Field Level View serve as two distinct methods for visualizing the downstream dependencies of a data element. They play a crucial role in comprehending the potential effects of data modifications on other elements within the data pipeline, such as data tasks, datasets, apps, and fields.

The Impact Analysis `Summary View` provides an aggregated summary of both direct and indirect dependencies of a data element categorized by type, such as databases, file storage, apps, and links. This view also includes information about the owners of the impacted items and the number of dependencies per type. By leveraging the Impact Analysis Summary View, users can effectively assess the impact of altering or deleting a data element and engage with stakeholders as necessary.

On the other hand, the `Field Level View` offers insights into the specific fields that are sourced from or dependent on a data element. Users can discern how individual fields are calculated and trace their origins across various transformations and apps. This detailed view enhances data trust and comprehension, facilitating the optimization of the data pipeline.

Conclusion

In this chapter, we learned about data marts. They're like organized storerooms for data that are customized to fit the needs of specific parts of a company, such as departments or regions. You can set up a data mart in two main ways, either to store data or to change it to fit certain needs. Usually, they're structured like a star, with different pieces of information about things (like products or locations) called dimensions, and numbers (like sales or profits) called facts. To fill up a data mart with information, you can use either SQL scripts or special tools called Qlik Lineage Connectors. Once it's all setup, you can analyze the data using tools such as Qlik Sense or QlikView to create visual reports and dashboards. And if you're using other analysis tools, you can still connect them to the data mart.

Multiple Choice Questions

1. What does a data mart entail in Qlik Talend Data Integration?
   a. A structured data repository serves the analytical needs of a specific department, business line, or geographic region within an organization.
   b. A visual representation showing the origin and history of a data element, tracking through data tasks, datasets, and apps, to the original data source.
   c. A graphical view depicting the downstream dependencies of a data element, including data tasks, datasets, apps, and fields affected by changes to that element.
   d. A customized SQL script or Qlik Lineage Connector allows the addition of extra data sources or transformations to your data mart.

2. What distinguishes dataset-level lineage from field-level lineage in Qlik Talend Data Integration?

    a. Dataset-level lineage illustrates the data progression through data tasks, datasets, and apps, whereas field-level lineage highlights the data sources and transformations associated with a specific field.

    b. Dataset-level lineage reveals the data sources and transformations linked to a specific field, whereas field-level lineage demonstrates the flow of data through data tasks, datasets, and apps.

    c. Dataset-level lineage showcases the downstream dependencies of a data element, while field-level lineage indicates the upstream dependencies of a data element.

    d. Dataset-level lineage represents the upstream dependencies of a data element, while field-level lineage represents the downstream dependencies of a data element.

3. How does lineage differ from impact analysis in Qlik Talend Data Integration?

    a. Lineage portrays the origin of a data element, while impact analysis depicts the history of a data element.

    b. Lineage illustrates the history of a data element, while impact analysis showcases the origin of a data element.

    c. Lineage indicates the upstream dependencies of a data element, while impact analysis reveals the downstream dependencies of a data element.

    d. Lineage highlights the downstream dependencies of a data element, while impact analysis elucidates the upstream dependencies of a data element.

4. How do you access lineage and impact analysis in Qlik Talend Data Integration?

    a. By selecting a data task, dataset, or field from the catalog, and then clicking on the lineage or impact analysis icon.

    b. By selecting a data mart, app, or script from the catalog, and then clicking on the lineage or impact analysis icon.

    c. By selecting a data task, dataset, or field from the data pipeline view, and then clicking on the lineage or impact analysis icon.

    d. All of the above.

5. How can you create a data mart from a data task in Qlik Talend Data Integration?

    a. Selecting a data task from the catalog, and then clicking on the Create Data Mart icon.

    b. By selecting a data task from the data pipeline view, and then clicking on the create data mart icon.

    c. Select a data task from the catalog, and then click on the Create dataset icon.

    d. None of the above.

Answers

1. a
2. a
3. c
4. d
5. b

References

1. *Qlik Help*: https://help.qlik.com/

Index

Symbols

A

B

C

D

E

F

I

J

K

L

M

P

R

S